PELICAN BOOKS

A HUNDRED YEARS OF PHILOSOPHY

John Passmore was born in Manly, Sydney, in 1914 and graduated from Sydney University with first-class honours in both English literature and philosophy. He trained to be a secondary school teacher, but accepted a position as assistant lecturer in philosophy at the University of Sydney in 1934 and continued to teach there until 1949. He first ventured abroad in 1948 to study at London University and to write in the British Museum. From 1950, for five years, he was professor of philosophy at Otago University in New Zealand. He spent 1955 in Oxford on a Carnegie grant, returning to Australia to take up a post at the Institute of Advanced Studies in the Australian National University. Since then he has travelled a good deal; he was Ziskind visiting professor at Brandeis University in the United States in 1960, and has given lectures in England, the United States, Mexico, Japan, and a number of European countries.

A Hundred Years of Philosophy has been translated into Hindi; translations into other languages are in course of preparation. His other books include *Ralph Cudworth* (1951), *Hume's Intentions* (1952), *Philosophical Reasoning* (1961) and *Joseph Priestley* (1965). He has also written many articles for encyclopedias and philosophical periodicals.

John Passmore retains a strong interest in the theatre, literature, music and the fine arts, and is a director of the Elizabethan Theatre Trust. He is also very interested in history and science, and he enjoys travel – particularly wandering around in large cities. He is married and has two daughters.

A HUNDRED YEARS
OF PHILOSOPHY

John Passmore

PENGUIN BOOKS

Penguin Books Ltd, Harmondsworth, Middlesex, England
Penguin Books Inc., 7110 Ambassador Road, Baltimore, Maryland 21207, U.S.A.
Penguin Books Australia Ltd, Ringwood, Victoria, Australia

—

First published by Duckworth 1957
Second Edition 1966
Published in Penguin Books 1968
Reprinted 1970

—

Copyright © John Passmore, 1957, 1966

—

Made and printed in Great Britain by
C. Nicholls & Company Ltd
Set in Monotype Times

Contents

Preface

THE title *A Hundred Years of Philosophy* promises more than it offers, in two ways: this book in fact restricts itself to epistemology, logic and metaphysics; and it is written from an English point of view, so far at least as that is possible for an Australian. On the first point, I intend no insult to such branches of philosophy as aesthetics, ethics, philosophy of religion, social philosophy, philosophy of law. Economy was the deciding factor; what the reader has in front of him, even now, is a reduced version of a considerably larger original. I chose themes which weave together into a reasonably coherent pattern; but the general effect of the book, it must be confessed, is somewhat narrow and professional, just because I have had so little to say about those branches of philosophy which most nearly touch upon the interests of non-philosophers.

On the second point, I have deliberately chosen to be insular, exhibiting, however, that kind of insularity which does not rule out an occasional Continental tour or a slightly more extended stay in the United States – without in either case 'going native'. Quite a little is said about American and Continental philosophers, but the story as it is told here is not the story as an American or a Frenchman would tell it. My criterion was: to what extent have the ideas of this writer entered into the public domain of philosophical discussion in England? Would the reader of *Mind* or *The Proceedings of the Aristotelian Society* be likely to encounter his name?

A similar criterion has helped me to decide what writers to treat at length, and which ones to mention only in passing. The space I have allocated to writers by no means corresponds to my own judgement of their individual merits; I have tried, I do not know with what success, fairly to represent the part they have played in the philosophical controversies of their time. Similarly, rather than attempt to summarize their books, it has been my object to pick out those aspects of their work the world has so far found most interesting. I have tried to write a history of philosophical controversy rather than to compile an annotated catalogue. I do not profess to be speaking for eternity; it is a salutary reflection that had I written this book in 1800 I should probably have dismissed Berkeley and Hume in a few lines, in order to concentrate my attention on Dugald Stewart – and that in 1850 the centre of my interest would have shifted to Sir William Hamilton.

This book contains a large number of errors: errors of omission, faults of judgement, simple slips and plain mistakes. So much I know *a priori*, but not, of course, what they are. I should be glad to have my attention drawn to errors and omissions, in case there should ever be an opportunity to correct them.

The philosophers of three different countries – New Zealand, England, Australia – have had to suffer the effects of my attempts to compose this book; many of them have helped me in one way or another. But no one has seen the completed book, and it would be kinder, therefore, not to mention any names. I shall content myself with thanking Mr R. G. Durrant, Mr R. Bradley, Mrs F. Dadd, and – above all – my wife, who have assisted me so considerably with the more tedious aspects of book production. The bibliography owes a great deal to the work of Miss Dagmar Carboch. Finally, I should like to take this opportunity of expressing my gratitude to the Carnegie Corporation of New York who made it possible for me to spend a year in Oxford – a year which, although it was an interlude in the composition of this book, has greatly facilitated its completion – and to the President and Fellows of Corpus Christi College for doing so much to make that year a memorable one for me.

Dunedin – Oxford – Canberra.   JOHN PASSMORE

Preface to Second Impression

I have taken the opportunity, in this second impression, to correct a number of errors to which correspondents and reviewers were good enough to draw my attention. As well, I have slightly amended the text at a few points, where that could easily be done, in order to refer to events which have occurred since the appearance of the first impression. Fundamentally, however, the text is unchanged.   J. P.

Preface to Second Edition

THE major changes in the second edition consist of considerable additions to my account of Ayer, Popper, Wittgenstein and Sartre, completely rewritten and much enlarged sections on Austin, Jaspers and Heidegger, a new section on Merleau-Ponty and an additional chapter on some recent developments in philosophy. As well, there are a good many minor corrections and bibliographical changes throughout, although, for technical reasons, the text in the first three-quarters of the book is largely unchanged.

Over the last nine years a great deal of extremely competent philosophy has been published. I have preferred to make the final chapter turn around a single controversy rather than attempt the task of compiling an encyclopedic survey of very recent philosophy, which would have swollen to vast proportions. I am only too aware that, as a consequence of this decision, justice has not been done to many individual philosophers. I hope, however, that I have somewhere in the new edition drawn attention, even if, often enough, in a ridiculously cursory fashion, to a reasonable proportion of the most important work in 'pure philosophy' which has been published since 1957 – always with the provisoes mentioned in the preface to the first edition. It has become more and more difficult to observe those provisoes, and, in particular, not to 'spill over' into ethics and the philosophy of history. But I have tried to do so, even if on no better ground than that this book is already long, and life, in contrast, is only too short.

Thanks are due for useful suggestions, to Professor A. N. Prior, Dr C. Rollins and Dr R. Brown, to many correspondents and to my graduate students. I should also like to thank Mrs J. di Fronzo, Mrs F. Dadd, Miss J. Coward and, above all, my wife for their degree of success in coping with my deplorable illegibility, inaccuracy and general cussedness.

J. P.

Abbreviations

Actualités	Actualités Scientifiques et Industrielles
AJP	Australasian Journal of Philosophy (until 1947, Australasian Journal of Psychology and Philosophy)
APQ	American Philosophical Quarterly
BJPS	British Journal for the Philosophy of Science
BPM	British Philosophy in the Mid-Century (1957), ed. C. A. Mace
CAP I and II	Contemporary American Philosophy, Vols. I and II (1930), ed. G. P. Adams, W. P. Montague
CBP I and II	Contemporary British Philosophy, First and Second Series (1924–5), ed. J. H. Muirhead
CPB III	Contemporary British Philosophy, Third Series (1956), ed. H. D. Lewis
DNB	Dictionary of National Biography
Erk.	Erkenntnis
JHI	Journal of the History of Ideas
JP	Journal of Philosophy
JSL	Journal of Symbolic Logic
LL I and II	Logic and Language, Vol. I (1951), Vol. II (1953), ed. A. G. N. Flew
PAS	Proceedings of the Aristotelian Society
PASS	Proceedings of the Aristotelian Society, Supplementary Volume
PBA	Proceedings of the British Academy
Phil.	Philosophy
PPR	Philosophy and Phenomenological Research
PQ	The Philosophical Quarterly
PR	The Philosophical Review
PS	Philosophical Studies
PSC	Philosophy of Science
RIP	Revue internationale de philosophie
RM	Review of Metaphysics
RMM	Revue de métaphysique et de morale
US	International Encyclopedia of Unified Science

Where a bound volume of a periodical runs over two calendar years, the date quoted in the text is the earlier of the two years, e.g. PAS, 1912 means PAS, 1912–13.

CHAPTER 1

John Stuart Mill and British Empiricism

PHILOSOPHY does not take kindly to being chopped into centuries. Like artists, philosophers constantly return to the 'Old Masters', seeking new inspiration in their inexhaustible resources. Every period has its characteristic revivals, thinks of this or that earlier philosopher, as Dante thought of Aristotle, as 'the master of those who know'. During the last century, Berkeley and Hume have come to be living forces in British philosophy, and Plato emerged, refurbished, from a period of obscurity, thanks to the devotion of a long line of classical scholars. Plato, Berkeley and Hume[1] are, indeed, among the most important philosophers of our time. Yet, obviously, this is not the occasion to explore their teachings.

It fortunately happens, however, that John Stuart Mill's *System of Logic* (1843) is a natural boundary; if on the one side it stimulated, whether in reaction or in admiration, many of the most notable developments in contemporary philosophy, on the other side it is the culmination of later eighteenth-century thought – except that Mill knew practically nothing of Hume.[2] The principal object, indeed, of Mill's remarkable education – the education he describes in his *Autobiography* (1873) – was to turn him into an eighteenth-century philosopher. For all that he came to be critical of its defects, that education fashioned Mill's life and work.

Mill's teacher was his father, James Mill, himself a distinguished philosopher, psychologist and economist, with an inexhaustible capacity for discipleship. His two particular heroes were David Hartley and Jeremy Bentham. Hartley, in his *Observations on Man* (1749), had worked out a psychological theory – associationism – which depicted the human mind and human knowledge as being built up by the operation of a few psychological laws upon the materials presented in sensation. Not at first creating any particular stir, associationism was kept alive by a few, although ardent, supporters until James Mill seized upon it and developed it in his *Analysis of the Phenomena of the Human*

13

Mind (1829), which his son was later (1869) to edit and annotate.[3]

Associationism appealed to the Mills for much the same reason that the theory of the 'conditioned reflex' – to which, indeed, it is closely allied – has won the support of Soviet theoreticians. It swept away, they thought, rhetoric and superstition about the soul, replacing it by scrupulous psychological analysis. More important still, by denying all innate differences it promised unlimited perfectibility. 'In psychology,' Mill wrote of his father, 'his fundamental doctrine was the formation of all human character by circumstances, through the universal Principle of association, and the consequent unlimited possibility of improving the moral and intellectual condition of mankind by education.' In one of his earliest speeches, Mill announced that he shared his father's belief in perfectibility; that same faith is no less strongly expressed in the last of Mill's writings. Innate differences he always rejected out of hand, never more passionately than in his *The Subjection of Women* (1869) in which he argued that even 'the least contestable differences' between the sexes are such that they may 'very well have been produced by circumstances without any differences of natural capacity'.

If Hartley taught Mill that perfectibility was possible, Mill learnt from Bentham that 'vested interests', supported by 'fictions' masquerading as 'sacred truths', were the great obstacle in its path. In some measure, Mill rebelled against Bentham's, as he never did against Hartley's, influence – a rebellion which rose to its highest pitch in his *Essay on Bentham* (1838). Under the influence of what he calls 'the European reaction against eighteenth-century thought', as represented in England by such writers as Coleridge and Carlyle, Mill came to feel that Bentham's radicalism was in certain respects doctrinaire, 'the empiricism of one who has had little experience'. Bentham, Mill suggests, fell into the error typical of 'a man of clear ideas', who in his zeal for clarity concludes that 'whatever is seen confusedly does not exist'; he dismissed as vague generalities what Mill calls 'the whole unanalysed experience of the human race'.[4]

Yet there could be no lasting compromise between Mill and the Coleridge school; Coleridge and his followers were beyond the pale as 'intuitionists' – Mill's favourite term of all-encompassing abuse – upholders of vested interests, that is, against the teachings of experience. Furthermore, their method, Mill thought, was a mistaken one; he remained faithful, as against the generalities of a Coleridge or a Carlyle, to what he described as Bentham's 'method of detail' – the method which consists in 'treating wholes by resolving them into their parts, abstractions by resolving them into things, classes and generalities by distinguishing them into the individuals of which they are made up; and breaking every question into pieces before attempting to solve it.'[5] He never seriously doubts that the mind is a set of feelings, society a set of individuals, a material object a set of phenomena; the philosophical problem, as he sees it, is to describe in detail the precise manner in which the world of science is constituted out of the individual and the fragmentary.

Naturally Bentham's influence was most conspicuous in Mill's moral and political writings, but Mill's Benthamism also dictated the limits, if we may so express the matter, of his logic and epistemology. Associationism, in Mill's eyes, is not merely a psychological hypothesis, to be candidly examined as such: it is the essential presumption of a radical social policy. Empiricism, similarly, is more than an epistemological analysis; not to be an empiricist is to adhere to 'the Establishment' – to be committed to the protection of 'sacred' doctrines and institutions. The notion 'that truths may be known by intuition, independently of observation and experience, is,' he wrote, 'the great intellectual support of false doctrines and bad institutions'. Notice the conjunction – 'false doctrines and bad institutions'. Thus if, at any point, Mill's philosophical reasonings threaten what he regards as the foundations of empiricism or bring into question the adequacy of associationism, his recoil is immediate, at whatever cost to consistency.

Mill's enthusiasm for French positivism, especially as it was presented by Auguste Comte[6] in his *Course in Positivist Philosophy* (1830–42), also had permanent effects on his philosophy – for all that he was to condemn Comte's *System of Positivist Polity* (1851–4) as 'the completest system of spiritual despotism which has as yet emanated from the human brain'. At first, he did not recognize the totalitarian implications of Comte's social philosophy; he saw in him, simply, a philosopher who conjoined Bentham's scientific attitude to society – so conspicuously lacking, he thought, in Coleridge and Carlyle – with the feeling for history in which Bentham, as Coleridge and Carlyle had taught him, was deficient.

Comte's 'positivism', his thesis that all knowledge consists in a description of the coexistence and succession of phenomena, was already familiar to Mill, as his father's teaching; the novelty lay in Comte's historical hypothesis that positivism is the last stage in the development of inquiry, preceded first by theology and then by metaphysics. In the theological stage, Comte argued, men explain phenomena by referring them to the arbitrary acts of spiritual beings; in the metaphysical stage, they substitute 'powers' or 'faculties' or 'essences' for spirits; only in the third, positive, stage do they come to see that to 'explain' is simply to describe the relations holding between phenomena.

Some forms of inquiry, according to Comte, reach the positive stage more rapidly than others. The sciences fall into a logical order – one science depends upon another for certain of its laws – and this is also the historical order in which they developed. First came mathematics, as the general theory of number, followed in turn by physics, chemistry and biology. The social sciences had to wait upon the development of physics and biology; now it was their turn: in his own work, Comte thought, science is for the first time applied to society.

This conclusion depended in part upon Comte's rejection, as unscientific, of economics and psychology: economics on the ground that it abstracts 'wealth' from its social context and is thereby debarred from understanding the nature and development of economic activity, psychology on the ground that it is impossible for anyone to observe his own mental processes without in that very act altering them. These were arguments which Mill, the loyal son of a psychologist-economist, was much concerned to dispute. He agreed with Comte, nevertheless, that the social sciences were backward, and that this backwardness derived from the fact that society had not so far been studied in a properly scientific way – as opposed to the 'intuitionist' view that society is not the sort of thing which lends itself to scientific investigation.

Furthermore, Comte's work suggested to Mill that a somewhat novel method – still, of course, scientific but differing in important respects from the methods used in physics or in chemistry – might need to be employed in the study of society. With this clue, he could hope to complete his *System of Logic*, on which he had already been working for some time; it is a principal object of that book to formulate what Mill calls 'the logic of the moral sciences' – in the language of our own day, 'the methodology of the social sciences'. But first the ground had to be cleared; a general logic had to be worked out before a special logic of the moral sciences could be systematically developed. Here Comte was of very little use to him: in Mill's judgement, he was admirable in describing methods of inquiry but supplied no criterion of proof. He did not even seem to admit the possibility of distinguishing between valid and fallacious inferences. Comte, indeed, was content to *describe* the methods of science; Mill wished to *justify* them.

By 'logic' Mill means 'the science of proof or evidence'. All proof, he says, rests on 'original data', but logic leaves to metaphysics the elucidation of their nature, concerning itself only with the way in which data are organized for scientific purposes.* Of such methods of organization, the most fundamental, he considers, is the operation of naming; that is why, Mill explains, his *Logic* opens with an 'analysis of language'.

For Mill, it will be observed, an analysis of language consists in a description of the process of naming. This is one of the points on which he was later to be most severely criticized; some recent philosophers, indeed, see in the identification of language-use and naming the root of all philosophical evils. Mill divides words into two classes: those, like 'Socrates', which can stand by themselves as names and those, like 'of', which have meaning only in a context, as part of such a naming-phrase as 'the father *of* Socrates'. Of words like 'or', 'if', 'and', he says that they are abbreviations, 'if' in, for example, 'if p, q' conveying that q is a legitimate inference from p.

All nouns and all adjectives, Mill presumes, are context-free names, so that whenever we meet a word of this sort it is sensible to ask, 'what does it name?' Abstract nouns like 'whiteness',

---

*The word 'metaphysics' is troublesome. Mill means by it something like what would now commonly be called 'the theory of knowledge', Comte, and most later positivists, any theory which professes to give us information about what lies beyond experience.

according to Mill, name a quality or attribute; the adjective 'white' names the various things which are describable as 'being white'; 'John', 'the sea', 'the father of Socrates', name individual things. 'Whiteness' and 'John', he goes on to argue, differ in a crucial respect from 'white'; they are 'non-connotative'. Mill defines a 'connotative term' as one which 'denotes a subject and implies an attribute'. The word 'white', he argues, as well as signifying – 'denoting' – the various things we call 'white', also conveys the attribute of 'whiteness' which these things have in common. Similarly 'man', according to Mill, denotes Socrates, Plato, etc., and connotes such attributes as rationality and animality. 'Socrates', in contrast, denotes a particular person without telling us anything about his properties; proper names, therefore, unlike such phrases as 'the husband of Xantippe', have no connotation.

Every proposition, on Mill's analysis of the proposition, conjoins names. 'All men are mortal', for example, conjoins two connotative names, 'men' and 'mortal'. What does such a proposition tell us? Remembering Mill's empiricist antecedents, we might expect him to answer that it relates classes, informs us that the particular things we call 'men' are included among the particular things we call 'mortal'. But in fact Mill rejects that view: the notion of an attribute is, he says, prior to that of a class, since a class can only be defined as the set of things which possess a certain attribute in common. The primary import of 'all men are mortal', according to Mill, is that the 'attributes of man are always accompanied by the attribute mortality'. Since, however, every attribute is 'grounded' in phenomena, the ultimate, metaphysical, significance of a proposition, he considers, is that certain phenomena – certain 'experiences' – are regularly associated one with another. On the other side, the *scientific function* of a proposition, as distinct from its metaphysical analysis, is, Mill says, to tell us what to expect in certain circumstances; from this point of view, the 'import' of 'all men are mortal' is that the presence of manhood is 'evidence for', a 'mark of', the presence of mortality. These three interpretations of the proposition, according to Mill, are equivalent; he therefore feels himself free to make use of whichever one of them best suits his particular purposes at a given point in his argument.

By means of his theory of connotation, Mill hopes to give a satisfactory account of 'necessary truths' or 'analytic propositions' without departing from empirical principles. Such propositions – he instances 'every man is rational' – are, he says, merely 'verbal'. As soon as we understand the word 'man', he argues, we know that men are rational; that is just what is meant by saying that rationality forms part of the connotation of man. 'All men are rational', then, makes explicit a connotation, reminds us how we use a word, but tells us nothing about men. Mill contrasts it with 'all men are mortal'. Since mortality does not form part of the connotation of 'man', this proposition, he says, gives us 'real' information – but by the same token it is not a necessary proposition: further experience could lead us to reject it as false. Only verbal propositions, then, are strictly necessary.

What of the propositions of mathematics? Surely they are both 'real' and necessary? Mill does not maintain, as some of his successors were to do, that mathematical propositions are necessary only because they are verbal. Not that this possibility does not occur to him: Dugald Stewart had already suggested that mathematics consists wholly in working out the implications of definitions; and definitions, according to Mill, are, as statements of connotation, verbal. But Mill does not follow Stewart on this point: he argues, against Stewart, that mathematical axioms cannot be reduced to definitions. So the only alternative left to him is to deny that mathematical propositions are 'necessary truths' in the strict, logical, sense of that phrase. As 'real' propositions, he argues, they must be generalizations from experience – subject to correction, therefore, in the light of subsequent experience.

In thus disputing the claim of mathematical propositions to be necessary truths, Mill found himself at odds with one of the most interesting of his contemporaries, William Whewell.[7] Whewell's existence saved Mill the trouble of inventing him. He was 'the intuitionist' in person; at once a champion of 'the Establishment' – of Church, State and unreformed universities – and an upholder of the doctrine of necessary truths. 'Necessary truths,' he wrote in his *History of Scientific Ideas*, 'are those in which we not only learn that the proposition is true, but see that it *must* be true; in which the negation of the truth is not only false but impossible;

in which we cannot even by an effort of the imagination, or in a supposition, conceive the reverse of that which is asserted.' To which Mill replies that Whewell is confusing logical and psychological necessity. The falsity of a proposition comes to be 'inconceivable', he argues, as a result of the association of ideas; since all our experience impresses upon our mind that two and two make four, we reach a point at which we cannot conceive that they should make five. But many propositions which men once could not 'conceive' to be false have, in the end, been universally rejected: inconceivability is not, therefore, a proof of necessity. Mill persists, then, in his assertion that no 'real' proposition can be logically necessary.*

As for the objection that the entities with which mathematics concerns itself (positions without magnitude, lines without breadth and so on) are never met with in our experience, Mill replies that we can pay attention to certain features of our experience while ignoring other aspects of it: to define a 'line' as having length but no breadth is to announce that we intend to ignore the breadth of lines in our geometrical reasonings. Thus we reach conclusions, he thinks, which we can apply in practice by making the necessary corrections – by taking account of the breadth of the particular line we happen to be considering.[8]

What now of inference? In this case, too, Mill thinks that we need to distinguish between 'real' inferences and 'merely verbal' transformations. Such a transition as that from 'some sovereigns are tyrants' to 'some tyrants are sovereigns' is, he thinks, obviously verbal: both propositions say precisely the same thing, viz. that in some cases certain attributes 'go together'. On the other hand, inference from experience to general propositions is, Mill considers, obviously a 'real' inference: in this instance, there

---

*At the same time he had second thoughts on this matter (for which see Anschutz, *op. cit.*). Note also Mill's review of Grote's *Aristotle* (1873), in which he criticizes Grote's assertion – which accords with his own *System of Logic* – that even the law of contradiction is a generalization from experience. As soon as we understand the words 'is', 'is not', 'true', 'false', Mill argues, we see that the affirmation and denial of a proposition cannot both be true. This suggests that logical truths are 'strictly necessary' or verbal. But when philosophers talk about 'Mill's theory of logic and mathematics' they mean the view that mathematical and logical propositions are generalizations from experience, the position adopted in his *System of Logic*.

is that movement from the known to the previously unknown which Mill takes to be the sign of a genuinely inferential process. Granted, then, that immediate inference is 'verbal', and that induction is 'real', inference, the controversial question, he thinks, is whether syllogism is in this respect like induction or like immediate inference.

Mill's attitude to syllogism is often misunderstood; he is read as being, like Locke, an unsparing critic of the traditional logic.[9] This is not at all the case; indeed, he is always ready to defend formal logic against those empiricists who condemn it out of hand as 'mediaeval rigmarole'. Mill's father had not been one of them, and Mill had been brought up on a regimen of formal logic. Meanwhile, however, Richard Whately in his *Elements of Logic* (1826) had revived the study of formal logic in England, after two centuries of neglect. In the process, he had advanced considerable claims for the traditional syllogism; it is, he says, 'a method of analysing that mental process which must *invariably* take place in all correct reasoning'. Now, although Mill so far departed from the teachings of his empiricist predecessors as to admit that the syllogism has its usefulness, he agreed with them, as against Whately, that it is not the type of scientific inference, that, indeed, considered as a form of inference it is circular, not a 'real' inference. He had to make this point firmly, and that explains why he is so often regarded as a hostile critic of syllogism.

Take the traditional example: 'all men are mortal, Socrates is a man, and therefore Socrates is mortal'. Then, says Mill, the premise 'all men are mortal' already contains the conclusion that 'Socrates is mortal'. Even if we have never heard of Socrates when we assert that 'all men are mortal', we are nevertheless asserting his mortality when we put forward the universal proposition about 'all men'. Thus to prove that 'Socrates is mortal' by deducing it from the proposition that 'all men are mortal' is to assume from the very beginning, Mill thinks, what we profess to be proving.

If, then, we accept the traditional interpretation of the syllogism as an inference from a universal law to a particular case we are bound to class it as a verbal transformation, the mere picking out of one ingredient from a conjoint assertion. But in fact, Mill tries to show, there is a real inference which underlies syllogism, an inference which the form of the syllogism tends to conceal: the real inference is *from the evidence on which our assertion about all men is based* to our conclusion about Socrates. This evidence, according to Mill, must consist of particular observations: Smith is mortal, Brown is mortal . . . From our experience in these cases we conclude that other men, Socrates for example, will also die. The inference, therefore, is from particular cases – not, as the traditional logic supposed, from a universal proposition – to another particular case. But the same evidence, Mill argues, allows us to assert, if we choose, the general proposition: 'all men are mortal'. If our inference from 'Smith, Brown, etc. are mortal' to 'Socrates is mortal' is a valid one, its validity will be unaffected if we substitute any other man for Socrates. This fact can be set out thus: 'there is a rule of inference that we can validly argue from the presence of humanity to the presence of mortality'. In other words, 'man' is evidence for, a mark of, 'mortality'. And this, as we have already seen, is the practical – the scientific – import of 'all men are mortal'.

'All men are mortal', then, is not a premise from which we conclude that 'Socrates is mortal'; it is a formula reminding us of the manner in which we have in the past inferred, and are in the future entitled to infer, from particular cases to particular cases. Reasoning can quite well proceed without such a formula, and in ordinary life, Mill thinks, it generally does: we argue directly from 'this and that fire burnt me' to 'this other fire will burn me' without pausing to assert that 'all fires burn'. Scientists, on the other hand, prefer to make the formulae of their inferences explicit; so that they argue first from particular cases to a general rule, and then from the rule to some other particular case. In adopting this roundabout method, Mill is ready to admit, they are proceeding sensibly, because they are more likely to detect weaknesses in their rules if they make them explicit. But the only part of this procedure, according to Mill, which can properly be described as inference is the transition from particular cases to a general law – or what amounts to the same thing, from particular cases to a particular case; the so-called 'inference' from general law to particular case is simply an interpretation of a formula, not a passage to anything previously unknown. The 'rules of syllogism' are a set of precautions to ensure that our interpretations are consistent with our formulae; they are valuable because consistency is valuable. 'What is called Formal Logic', he writes, 'is the logic of consistency.'[10]

This analysis of the syllogism admirably accords with Mill's general defence of experience against intuition. Experience, he had learnt from Hartley and from Bentham, is always of particular phenomena; we do not directly experience general connexions. If, then, universal propositions assert general connexions, and if, furthermore, such propositions – as Whately had maintained – form the point of departure in all scientific thinking, it would seem to follow that science is not wholly empirical. This argument, indeed, was the great standby of intuitionists in their battle against empiricism. If, on the other hand, all reasoning is from particulars to particulars, if universal propositions are convenient devices, forming no essential part of scientific inference, then, Mill thought, empiricism has a complete answer to its critics.

By reducing what is strictly inferential in syllogism to argument from particulars to particulars, Mill thinks he has shown that all real inference is inductive in character. ('Induction' is ordinarily defined as inference from particular cases to general laws; but this inference, Mill has argued, is *identical with* inference from particular cases to particular cases.) 'What induction is,' he therefore concludes, 'and what conditions render it legitimate, cannot but be deemed the main question of the science of logic.' That question Mill now sets out to answer.

Conventionally, two sorts of induction had been distinguished: perfect and imperfect. Sometimes, it had been said, we wish to consider whether a certain property is possessed by all of a limited set of entities – say, the apostles; then by examining each member of the set in turn we can conclude by a perfect induction that the property in question belongs to the whole group. Sometimes, on the other hand, we are only in a position to examine certain members of the group, and then our induction is 'imperfect'. Perfect induction, on this view, is set up as the ideal to which all induction aspires. True to his general principles, however, Mill dismisses perfect induction as a merely verbal transformation: there is, he says, no real inference from 'Peter, Paul, John and every other apostle was a Jew' to 'all the apostles were

Jews' – the second proposition is simply an 'abridged notation' for the facts conveyed in the first proposition. He is not even prepared to describe 'all the apostles were Jews' as a 'general proposition'; the whole point of a truly general proposition, he argues, lies in its reference to cases which we have not actually experienced.

It would seem, then, that we are driven back upon 'imperfect' induction, as not merely the second-best but the only sort of inductive inference. Everything Mill has so far said would lead us to suppose that this, for him, is the paradigm of real inference. But now there comes a sudden twist to his argument. In some cases, he admits, imperfect induction – or, as he prefers to call it, 'induction by simple enumeration' – is wholly adequate. The truths of mathematics are derived in this way, and so are those very general principles – of which the most important is the law of causation – Mill collectively describes as 'the principle of the uniformity of Nature'. These cases, however, are peculiar, quite untypical, because all our experience, in other respects immensely diversified, imprints them upon the mind. We could scarcely have failed to notice an exception to them, he says, did one exist. They are not 'necessary truths' in a strict sense – it would be rash, Mill says, to presume that the law of causation applies to distant parts of the stellar regions – but this is only to say that they are not verbal. They have all the necessity we can expect experience to supply us with.

When, however, we set out to show – as we do, according to Mill, in the physical sciences – that a specific phenomenon *A* is the cause of a specific phenomenon *B*, the situation is entirely different. For we are well aware that a phenomenon can have antecedents and consequents on a variety of occasions and yet may exist without them on other occasions; when, then, we are in search of a 'cause' – defined as an '*invariable* and *unconditional* antecedent' – we cannot rest content with a general superficial survey of those cases we happen to have noticed.

In an *Edinburgh Review* (1829) castigation of James Mill's *Essay on Government* Lord Macaulay had taken his stand on 'the teachings of experience' against James Mill's attempt to work out a deductive science of political action. Mill agreed with Macaulay against his father that political science cannot be derived from axioms in the manner of geometry. At the same time Macaulay's appeal to experience – to 'the teachings of history' – was, Mill thought, an attack upon the scientific attitude, in the name of unsystematic commonsense. Thus he found himself with a war on two fronts; he had to defend experience against Whewell, and indicate its limitations against Macaulay. That is why 'empiricism', in Mill's mouth, is so often a term of abuse; he uses it in such phrases as 'bad generalization or empiricism', 'direct induction usually no better than empiricism'. He himself, he always insists, is an 'experimentalist', not an 'empiricist' – he left empiricism to Macaulay. But how are we to proceed if not by generalizations from experience? What other grounds have we, except our observation of regularities in our experience, for believing that we are entitled to proceed from a particular A to a particular B, or, what is the same thing, to assert the rule of inference that the appearance of A is 'a mark' that B is to come? Mill's answer is most succinctly stated in his *Auguste Comte and Positivism* (1865): 'A general proposition inductively observed,' he there writes, 'is only proved to be true when the instances upon which it rests are such that if they have been correctly observed, the falsity of the generalization would be inconsistent with the constancy of causation; with the universality of the fact that the phenomena of nature take place according to invariable laws of succession.' Now we see in what direction Mill is driven by his rejection of 'empiricism'. When we read his criticism of the traditional analysis of the syllogism, we had in our minds all the time the ideal of a 'logic of inquiry' which would somehow be superior to the 'logic of consistency' – or formal logic. But now it turns out that 'inductive proof' is itself part of the 'logic of consistency'; the proof that 'A causes B' is just that it would be inconsistent with the law of causality to assert that it does not.

Mill himself suggests, indeed, in his discussion of 'the evidence of uniform causation' that the relation between the causal principle and specific causal assertions is identical with that which holds between 'all men are mortal' and 'Lord Palmerston is mortal'. Obviously, this will not do as it stands: if 'every event has a cause' is parallel to 'all men are mortal', then 'this event has *some* cause' is the analogue to 'Lord Palmerston is mortal' – not 'this event has B as its cause'. And it is propositions of this latter specific form which Mill hopes to establish by showing that their contradictory is inconsistent with the law of causation.

There is a gap here – the gap between saying that an event is caused and saying that it has such-and-such a specific cause; if Mill does not, at this point, notice it, this is because he thinks he has already filled the gap by means of his 'experimental methods' – the methods of agreement, difference, residues, and concomitant variation.[11] The general pattern of these methods can be illustrated from the best known of them, the method of difference. Suppose we are trying to discover the cause of rust in iron. Then we shall need to consider some situation in which iron rusts, and analyse it into the various factors it contains. We might discover that moisture, oxygen, hydrogen and nitrogen are all present. After the removal of the hydrogen and the nitrogen, we find, the rust continues to form; on removing the moisture and the oxygen the rusting process ceases. Then since the rust, according to the Principle of Causation, must have an *invariable* antecedent, we can only conclude that this is the moist oxygen, which is present when the rust is present, and absent when it is absent.

Set out briefly, then, the argument runs thus: 'all events have a cause, the only possible cause in the present case is the moist oxygen, therefore moist oxygen is the cause.' Let us presume that the 'real inference' in this case can be set out as an argument from particulars to particulars. Then we can still ask: in what does the validity of this inference consist? On Mill's general principle that the validity of the inference is established by the same method as the truth of the universal premise, we shall have to answer: 'it is justified by simple enumeration.' Now Mill has told us that 'the business of inductive logic is to provide rules and models (such as the syllogism and its rules are for ratiocination) to which if inductive arguments conform those arguments are conclusive and not otherwise'. In fact, however, the only 'rules' which have been brought to our attention are not analogues to the rules of syllogism, but those very rules themselves; for the rest, we are forced to rely upon simple enumeration. Thus, some of Mill's successors concluded, either there is no special logic of induction whatever, or else Mill is wrong in thinking that the certainty derived from enumerative induction is of a purely psychological character, founded on the laws of association. The 'problem of induction', then, was converted into the problem of finding a *formal* justification for imperfect induction – with the help, say, of the theory of probability – something Mill had not so much as attempted.

In another important respect, Mill's attempt to substitute experimentalism for empiricism led him into difficulties. It is essential to his 'inductive proof' that we can analyse a situation into just so many characteristics. Thus, in our rust example, we had to presume that nothing is present except hydrogen, nitrogen, oxygen and moisture; then we argued thus – by another purely formal proof: 'the cause is either hydrogen, oxygen, nitrogen or moisture, since these are the only antecedent conditions; but it cannot be hydrogen or nitrogen because they are not invariable antecedents; therefore it must be the only invariable antecedents, moisture and oxygen.' Obviously, such an argument raises a serious problem: how do we know that there are not some other antecedent conditions which we have overlooked?

Mill's methods rest on the presumption that a particular situation comes before us as a bundle of general properties, out of which it is our task to select the cause. This involves a radical departure from the traditional empiricist doctrine, to which he officially subscribes, that experience presents us with 'pure particulars' out of which generality has somehow to be built up. Induction, it now appears, is not an inference from particulars to other particulars, but rather a method of choosing between a set of *prima facie* general connexions – a method of deciding whether A, or B, or C is the 'true cause'. And once again, the only 'logic' this method employs is formal logic.

If there were a special 'logic of induction' it would take the form, presumably, of rules telling us how to decide which general connexions form the set from which we have to select. Such a logic Mill never attempts to construct. As Whewell commented: 'Upon these methods, the obvious thing to remark is that they take for granted the very thing which it is most difficult to discover. . . . Where are we to look for our *A*, *B*, *C*? Nature does not present to us the cases in this form; and how are we to reduce them to this form?' Here, again, was a point of departure for certain of Mill's successors; they sought to work out a logic of elimination which should not be subject to Whewell's strictures.

Mill saw for himself a great many of the difficulties to which his critics have drawn attention; he admitted, for example, that it is impossible to be sure that we have not overlooked a crucial factor in the situation we are considering. He made matters still more difficult for himself by admitting a 'plurality of causes'. In spite of the fact that he had defined a cause as an *invariable* antecedent, he grants that the same effect can be produced on different occasions by a variety of different causes – which would bring to ruin the argument essential to his methods, that if the effect is still present when a certain factor is removed, that factor is not its cause. But all of these, he thinks, are practical difficulties; to draw attention to them is merely to say that scientific investigation is not easy. The fact remains, he thinks, that the four methods are both the only way of arriving at conclusions by experiment and observation and, more important still, the only way of *proving* an inductive conclusion. He admits, however, that the practical difficulties are enormous; the physicist, and even more the social scientist, find it necessary, therefore, to employ supplementary procedures.

The physicist, according to Mill, begins by establishing, with the help of the four methods, a number of laws, each of them describing a general tendency. This is as far as the experimental method, by itself, can carry him. From no such law taken by itself, however, can the physicist predict the behaviour of a particular physical object; the laws have therefore to be compounded. To predict the path of a falling body, for example, the physicist compounds the laws of gravitation and the laws of friction – as he can do because the joint effect of these laws is mathematically calculable. Next, the physicist checks his calculations by observing the actual behaviour of a falling body; if there is a discrepancy between its behaviour and his predictions, he concludes that he has overlooked some factor in the situation; he seeks out some further law to account for the discrepancy. This method – the conjunction of experimentally derived laws to reach conclusions which can be checked by observation – is, in Mill's opinion, the one 'to which the human mind is indebted for its most conspicuous triumphs in the investigation of Nature'. Clearly Mill is here moving towards a more realistic appraisal of the situation in which the scientist actually finds himself; we have no longer to suppose that he sets out from a completely analysed situation.

The emphasis now is on prediction and testing: this way of looking at the matter, too, supplied texts for Mill's successors.

In his description of the methods of the social sciences, Mill works even further away from his original conception of scientific method. In those sciences the scientist makes use, Mill says, of the 'inverse deductive' method. It is quite unrealistic for the social scientist to imitate the methods of geometry, as Mill's father had attempted to do, because what happens in society is always affected by the precise historical situation at a given time; nor is the model of physics a satisfactory one, for there is no way of estimating the joint effect of social tendencies. We have to begin, in Macaulay's manner, by examining society directly and constructing generalizations, based on the evidence of history, about its manner of development. However, we cannot rest at that point: 'the vulgar notion that the safe methods on political subjects are those of Baconian induction,' he wrote, 'will one day be quoted amongst the most unequivocal marks of a low state of the speculative faculties in any age in which it is accredited.' The social scientist must go on, as Macaulay did not, to show that these historical generalizations are precisely what our knowledge of psychology – Comte would have said, of biology – leads us to expect or, at least, that they are not inconsistent with such laws. Thus instead of trying to deduce social laws from an experimental science of human nature, the social scientist first constructs generalizations by historical observation and then proceeds to show that these laws *could* have been deduced from the experimental laws. Mill's detailed analysis of scientific procedure, then, is much more subtle and complex than the broad outlines of his theory of induction would lead us to expect.

It would carry us too far from our central topics to pursue this matter further; we must rather proceed in the opposite direction – to examine, not the applications of Mill's logic, but its metaphysical foundations. What is the nature of 'experience', of those 'primitive data' from which, so Mill argues, inference takes its departure? That question Mill sets out to answer, although in a polemical framework, in his *Examination of Sir William Hamilton's Philosophy* (1865). Hamilton[12] was a philosopher with an enormous, not to say fantastic, reputation. He inherited the tradition of 'Scottish philosophy' initiated by Thomas Reid in his

Inquiry into the Human Mind on the Principles of Common Sense (1764), a work which Hamilton edited with copious annotation. But, as well, he brought to philosophy an awe-inspiring erudition – not always, indeed, of the most accurate sort, but there were few fit to dispute his scholarship. In particular, he wrote as an expert on Continental philosophy, which he set out to conjoin, at certain points, with the Scottish tradition. The greater part of Mill's *Examination* is devoted to showing that this combination is an unstable one, that Hamilton's philosophy, indeed, is a tissue of inconsistencies and ambiguities. So effectively did he undertake this thankless task that the 'Scottish school' never really recovered from the blow, although it lingered on for some time in Scotland and in the United States, where it became a sort of 'official philosophy' in the less adventurous Colleges.[13]

Mill particularly objected to Hamilton's attack on 'experience' in the name of 'what consciousness tells us'. The appeal to 'consciousness', Mill thought, is a species of obscurantism. Certainly, if consciousness means self-consciousness, awareness of our own feelings, then Mill was willing to agree that consciousness is infallible: we cannot doubt, he thought, that we experience such-and-such feelings. Thus interpreted, however, 'consciousness' cannot tell us that anything exists except feelings, whereas Hamilton supposes it to be a direct deliverance of consciousness that, for example, we have free-will. Consciousness, Mill argued, can never tell us what it is *possible* for us to do; this we can only learn from experience. 'If our so-called consciousness of what we are able to do,' he writes, 'is not borne out by experience, it is a delusion. It has no title to credence but as an interpretation of experience, and if it is a false interpretation, it must give way.'

This is the general pattern of Mill's argument: what Hamilton ascribes to the intuitions of consciousness, or Reid to 'Natural Belief', are actually inferences from experience. Mill's attempt to show that this is true of our belief in an 'external world' – i.e. our belief in the existence of things which exist whether we are perceiving them or not – brings him close to Berkeley.

In his essay on 'Berkeley's Life and Writings' (1871), Mill ascribes two great discoveries to Berkeley. The first is his theory of vision. We ordinarily believe that we immediately experience things as being at a distance from us, but in fact, according to Berkeley, this belief arises as an inference from our experience of muscular and visual sensations, which we learn to interpret as signs of distance. This doctrine Mill describes as 'the earliest great triumph of analytic psychology over first appearances (dignified in some systems by the name of Natural Beliefs) ... the power of the law of association in giving to artificial combinations the appearance of ultimate facts was then for the first time made manifest'.

Berkeley's second great discovery was that, as Mill expresses the matter, 'the externality we attribute to the objects of our senses' consists simply in the fact that 'our sensations occur in groups, held together by a permanent law'. But the defect in Berkeley's view, Mill thought, is that he does not apply in this case the psychological methods of *The Theory of Vision*; instead of arguing that our belief in permanence arises out of the operations of association, he ascribes to ideas a real permanence in the mind of God. Mill sets out so to modify Berkeley's view as to give an account of our belief in the independence and persistence of material objects without having recourse to God.

We need, he says, two general suppositions. The first is that our mind contains expectations, i.e. that it can form the idea of possible sensations, sensations which we are not now feeling but could feel under different circumstances – as when we say to ourselves 'I should be cold if the fire were to go out'. The second supposition is that the mind works associatively: if two sensations have been experienced together they tend to be thought of as regularly going together, and if that association has been frequent and invariable we are eventually unable to separate, even in imagination, the sensations concerned.

Just because we have expectations, Mill argues, we are able to construct for ourselves a world which consists only to a slight degree of the sensations we are at the moment experiencing. Suppose we go out of a room; we think of its contents as existing even although we can no longer see them, because we should expect to experience certain sensations were we to re-enter the room. 'The permanent existence of the room' is constituted by the fact that it is permanently possible for us to have certain sensations; our expectations of 'possible sensations', as a result of psychological processes which Mill describes in detail, give rise to our belief in what we call 'substance' or 'matter' and imagine as existing within an 'external world'. Matter, indeed, Mill defines as 'the permanent possibility of sensation', the 'external world' as 'the world of possible sensations succeeding one another according to laws'. Far from being, as the Scottish school argued, a 'direct deliverance of consciousness', our belief in the existence of an external world is built up gradually by associative processes.

Can a parallel account be given of our belief in the continuous existence of our own mind? Mill thinks not, because mind includes not only sensations but also memories and expectations; and these already incorporate within themselves the belief that *I* once had, or that *I* am to have, certain experiences. 'If, therefore, we speak of the Mind as a series of feelings,' he wrote, 'we are obliged to complete the statement by calling it a series of feelings which is aware of itself as past or future; and we are reduced to the alternative of believing that the Mind or Ego is something different from any series of feelings, or possibilities of them, or of accepting the paradox that something which *ex hypothesi* is but a series of feelings can be aware of itself.' In this statement of the case, some of Mill's successors thought they could see the breakdown of his phenomenalism; to others it was a challenge to restate phenomenalism in a more satisfactory way.

Hamilton was not merely the champion of Natural Beliefs; he was famous as an exponent of 'the philosophy of the unconditioned' or 'the relativity of knowledge'. Roughly speaking – Mill has no difficulty in showing how variously Hamilton uses his key-phrases – this doctrine consists in asserting that although we are directly conscious of independently existing qualities of mind and matter, we have no direct acquaintance with mind-in-itself or matter-in-itself; we know things only as they are related to our experience of them, not as they exist in an 'unconditioned' form. Hamilton's best-known disciple, Henry Mansel, dissented from this doctrine in so far as it applied to our knowledge of our self, but applied it to the knowledge of God in his *The Limits of Religious Thought* (1858). It is impossible, Mansel argued, to know God as he is in himself: the descriptive epithets we apply to him must be taken analogically, not literally. To take them literally is to be led into immediate contradictions.[14] Thus if we say that God is good, this goodness, according to Mansel, must differ from human goodness not merely in degree but in kind. 'The infliction of physical suffering, the permission of moral evil, the adversity of the good, the prosperity of the wicked,' Mansel wrote, 'these are facts which no doubt are reconcilable, we know not how, with the Infinite Goodness of God, but which certainly are not to be explained on the supposition that its sole and sufficient type is to be found in the finite goodness of man.'

This attack on natural theology aroused the full fervour of Mill's moral indignation. 'I will call no being good,' he wrote, 'who is not what I mean when I apply that epithet to my fellow-creatures; and if such a being can sentence me to hell for not so calling him, to hell I will go.' Mill's own theology is most fully formulated in his posthumously published *Three Essays on Religion* (1874).[15] His father had condemned Christianity not merely as 'a mere delusion' but as 'a great moral evil' – indeed as 'the greatest enemy of morality'. Mill was inclined to express himself more moderately: 'Experience,' he wrote, 'has abated the ardent hopes once entertained of the regeneration of the human race by merely negative doctrine – by the destruction of superstition.' But he could not accept the conventional doctrine of a Creator who is at once omnipotent and benevolent: the most we are entitled to say, he thought, is that there is some, although by no means decisive, evidence in favour of the supposition that the world was created by an 'intelligent Mind, whose power over his materials was not absolute, whose love for his creatures was not his sole actuating inducement, but who nevertheless desired their good'. This evidence, however, consists in the presence of design in nature; there are adaptations in nature of a kind which men would create had they the power, and which it is therefore reasonable to suppose were created by a more powerful – although not an omnipotent – mind. If Mansel were right, Mill concludes, in supposing that the divine mind is entirely different in kind from the human mind, the sole argument for the existence of God would collapse.

For the rest, we can if we like, Mill thought, believe in immortality: there is no decisive argument against it. The rational attitude to adopt in religious matters is neither belief nor atheism but scepticism. It is not irrational, however, to indulge our hopes. Our fundamental duty, Mill thought, is to fight for good and against evil: the belief that in this conflict we are 'cooperating with the unseen being to whom we owe all that is enjoyable in life' has value for Mill, in so far as it helps to sustain us in this struggle. The Religion of Humanity, the Religion of Duty, which Comte envisaged cannot but be lent support, Mill wrote, by 'supernatural hopes in the degree and kind to which what I have called rational scepticism does not refuse to sanction them.'[16] It cannot be said that this modified rapture provoked any considerable enthusiasm, whether amongst theologians or amongst the unregenerate materialists who were by this time taking the centre of the stage.

CHAPTER 2

Materialism, Naturalism and Agnosticism

THE phrase 'nineteenth-century materialism' is now a familiar one; often enough it is so used as to suggest that materialism is a purely nineteenth-century product, a philosophical expression of the horrors of industrialism, the money-grabbing of the 'new rich', and the 'hard facts' of Mr Gradgrind. In fact, however, nineteenth-century materialism is, for the most part, a refurbishing of eighteenth-century materialism, and that derives, not very remotely, from Ancient Greece. Materialism, indeed, is almost as old as philosophy: its nineteenth-century exponents restated it in the language of contemporary science – that is one reason why their writings now 'date' – but they had little to say that was philosophically original. Most of them, in fact, were not philosophers at all, in any but the most extended sense of that accommodating word; they were scientists, usually physiologists or biologists, and their materialism, so they alleged, was a direct deduction from the discoveries of natural science, not the product of philosophical speculation.

This is particularly true of the German materialists of the eighteen-fifties, men like L. Büchner,[1] whose *Force and Matter* (1855) quickly established itself as 'the Bible of the materialists'. In Germany, one must always remember, with its State-controlled universities, there was an 'official' philosophy – at this time a watered-down version of Hegelianism, dedicated to the defence of 'the spiritual life' against the inroads of natural science, and of the State against radical reform. Naturally enough, its official position brought philosophy into disrepute wherever in Germany new forces were abroad, a disrepute accentuated by the complete failure of German idealism to comprehend the empirical spirit of natural science, its attempt to lay down *a priori* – by means of 'natural philosophy' – just what, in detail, the world must be like. Natural science, men like Büchner were driven to reply, has no need of philosophy; from its own resources it can produce a general picture of the world, firmly based upon empirical inquiry and not in the least dependent upon philosophical speculation.

This 'world-view' was materialistic. 'Science,' according to Büchner, 'gradually establishes the fact that macrocosmic and microcosmic existence obeys, in its origin, life and decay, mechanical laws inherent in the things themselves, discarding every kind of supernaturalism and idealism in the explanation of natural events.' To the objection that 'inert matter' could never give rise to the active life of the spirit, Büchner replied that matter is *not* inert; there is no matter without force. Equally, he argued, there is no force without matter; every agent is material.

Büchner's formula – 'no force without matter; no matter without force' – was particularly directed against supernaturalism; as such it supplied a 'philosophy' for the vigorous Continental radical movement, which was as critical of the Church as it was of the State.[2] Often enough, the German materialists deliberately set out to shock, as in Karl Vogt's pronouncement in his *Physiological Epistles* (1847) that 'the brain secretes thought, just as the liver secretes bile'; this was part of their campaign against the respectabilities of Idealism.

In England, the social and intellectual situation was quite different. Mill was certainly not 'a lackey of the State' – the charge ordinarily directed by scientific radicals against Continental philosophy – nor did he try, in the words of Büchner's criticism of German Idealism, 'to construct nature by thought rather than to observe it'. And there was nothing revolutionary in England, as there had been in Germany, in Büchner's proclamation that 'it lies in the nature of philosophy to be common property – expositions which cannot be grasped by every educated person are scarcely worth the paper they are written on'. Yet when German materialism came to England, its impact – for all that, in the characteristic English manner, its violence was mitigated, its radicalism deprecated, its outspokenness muted – was none the less sensational.

In his *Essay on Liberty* Mill had remarked: 'With us, heretical opinions ... never blaze out far and wide, but continue to smoulder in the narrow circles of thinking and studious persons among whom they originate ... and thus is kept up a state of things very satisfactory to some minds, because, without the unpleasant process of fining or imprisoning anybody, it maintains all prevailing opinions outwardly undisturbed, while it does not absolutely interdict the exercise of reason by dissentients afflicted by the malady of thought.' This convenient social arrangement was disrupted by the new scientific publicists, men like J. Tyndall, T. H. Huxley, W. K. Clifford[3] – in descending order of respectability – who, for the first time, took science to the working-man, and, with science, those heretical ideas about God and the soul which had previously been confined to a closed circle of 'intellectuals'.

Their arguments were more effective, from a purely polemical point of view, than the reasonings of philosophers, which generally have about them a superfine air, more than a suspicion of logic-chopping and word-play, to an audience unfamiliar with the philosophical tradition. Science was gaining ground rapidly, pulled along, we might say, by the locomotive, which for the first time made tangible the advantages of scientific progress. And the scientist had new and fascinating facts at his disposal, facts which seemed to make it more and more difficult to believe in God, freedom and immortality – at least in their popular acceptation.

These new discoveries came from a variety of sources. First, there was physiology. The discovery that a frog could perform apparently purposeful actions even when its brain and with it, presumably, its consciousness, had been cut off from the source of stimulation suggested that *all* apparently purposeful actions might be automatic or 'reflex' reactions to stimuli – 'a frog with half a brain having destroyed more theology than all the doctors of the Church with their whole brains could build up again.'[4] E. Du Bois-Reymond's work on *Animal Electricity* (1848), similarly, did much to diminish the mysteriousness of physiological processes by assimilating them to familiar physical laws. And these are only examples.

In physics the theory of 'conservation of energy', which H. Helmholtz (1847) had applied to organic as to inorganic life, told against the view that men can influence the course of events by the exercise of a personal force (free-will) which forms no part of the general energy-system: in chemistry the synthesis of urea (1828) destroyed the supposition that there is an impassable gap between the chemistry of the living organism and the chemistry of the laboratory. Meanwhile, L. A. Quételet, as a result of his study of 'moral statistics', disclosed in his *Sur l'homme* (1835) that 'in everything which concerns crime, the same numbers recur with a constancy which cannot be mistaken; and this is the case even with those crimes which seem to be quite independent of human foresight, such, for instance, as murders'. How could this constancy be reconciled, men asked, with the traditional doctrine of free-will? In a different sphere, the application of 'Higher Criticism' to the Bible, testing its authenticity by the ordinary canons of scholarship, considerably diminished the force of any appeal *against* science to the infallibility of scripture doctrine.

Then there was Darwin.[5] The 'religion of science', as 'the Monsignore' described it in Disraeli's *Lothair* (1870), has two ingredients: 'Instead of Adam, our ancestry is traced to the most grotesque of creatures; thought is phosphorus, the soul complex nerves, and our moral sense a secretion of sugar.' The English ingredient in this 'religion' – the Darwinian theory of evolution – was no less potent than German medical-materialism. Darwin himself did not at first (*The Origin of Species*, 1859) explicitly apply the evolutionary theory to Man. 'You ask me whether I shall discuss man,' he wrote in 1857, 'I think I shall avoid the whole subject, as so surrounded by prejudice.' But others – Huxley, for example, in his *Man's Place in Nature* (1863) – were quick to make the application, as did Darwin himself in *The Descent of Man* (1871).

The theory of evolution as such, the view that the animal species which now surround us have gradually developed their present characteristics over a long period of time, was by no means first promulgated by Darwin, and even his special hypothesis of 'natural selection' had its forerunners.[6] But at Darwin's hands evolution matured into a well-developed scientific theory, and took a form which admirably accorded with prevailing tendencies in biological and social theory. No 'vital urge', no anthropomorphically conceived 'desire to better themselves', had now to be ascribed to evolving species; those variations established themselves firmly which could cope with the unceasing struggle for resources, a struggle the economist Malthus had already detected (1798) in human history.

The effect of Darwin's work was still further to undermine the view that Man stands over and against Nature as a potentially supernatural being. Furthermore, it seemed to destroy that argument from design on which, so Mill had argued, a natural theology must depend. For if the 'fitness' of the human organism for the environment in which it finds itself arises from an interplay between chance variations and fluctuating circumstances, 'fitness' can no longer be regarded as evidence of a special divine dispensation.

Altogether, the prospects for religion were alarming, to say the least of it. A wave of materialism, atheism and determinism could quite reasonably be expected. And these were the doctrines which their opponents thought they detected in the writings of Huxley and his fellow-publicists.

Huxley, however, denied with some heat that he was either a materialist or an atheist. Certainly he believed that human beings are conscious automata but he was not, he explained, a materialist; even if he rejected every argument for the existence of God, he told his readers, he was not an atheist – indeed, if God be defined as 'the infinite and absolute', Huxley was prepared to subscribe himself a theist, for 'energy', he thought, was both infinite and absolute. He admitted to being a determinist but that, he said, was a perfectly respectable view, orthodox Calvinism in fact.[7]

Huxley's attitude to materialism most effectively illustrates the peculiarities of his philosophy. For the true materialist – he refers to Büchner – whatever exists is a modification of matter and force. But consciousness, Huxley argues, is not such a modification, although it is 'intimately connected' with a material organism. The nature of this 'intimate connexion' is more closely defined in Huxley's 'epiphenomenalism', as presented in his 'Of the Hypothesis that Animals are Automata'. 'The consciousness of brutes,' he said, 'would appear to be related to the mechanism of their body simply as a collateral product of its working, and to be as completely without any power of modifying that working as the steam-whistle which accompanies the work of a locomotive engine is without influence upon its machinery.' (This very metaphor, by the way, comes straight from Büchner.) What is true of brutes is true also of men. 'Consciousness' does not, and cannot, *act* since it has no energy of its own; it is merely 'given off' by the workings of the brain – the ineffectual ghost of an entity.

So far, this is German materialism in English clothing. But

now comes a sudden twist to the argument. 'The arguments used by Descartes,' Huxley announces, 'to show that our certain knowledge does not extend beyond our states of consciousness ... appear to be irrefragable.' Mind is only an 'aura' of matter: all the same, he argues, 'our one certainty is the existence of the mental world'.

This philosophical impasse delighted Huxley, who in his book on *Hume* (1879), warmly recommended Hume's 'mitigated scepticism'. It gave him all the more reason for being an 'agnostic' – a word of his own coinage.[8] 'The problem of the ultimate cause of existence is one which seems to be absolutely out of reach of my poor powers' – that is Huxley's regular reply to those who accuse him of atheism and materialism. Huxley and his fellow-publicists were, indeed, the most exasperating of controversialists. They could always elude their critics with cries of 'Of course, we don't *really* claim to know'. The Bishops might agree with Lenin that 'in Huxley, agnosticism serves as a fig-leaf for materialism'; but Huxley was content to reply that 'If I were forced to choose between Materialism and Idealism, I should elect for the latter'. What more was there to be said?

So convenient a doctrine naturally did not lack supporters. Darwin himself came to describe his attitude to religion as 'agnostic'; Leslie Stephen's *An Agnostic's Apology* (1893, first published as an essay in 1876) lent to agnosticism the weight of his authority as an historian of ideas; in Germany E. Du Bois-Reymond created a considerable stir with an address on *The Limitations of Natural Knowledge* which was at once anti-religious and agnostic, in the best English manner.[9] But it was left to Herbert Spencer to develop an agnostic-evolutionary philosophy which swept the world.[10] To a large degree, of course, his *System of Synthetic Philosophy* (1862–93) attracted attention as biology, psychology, sociology, rather than as philosophy; his *Education* (1861) did a great deal to spread his reputation; and his vigorous defence of private enterprise in *The Man versus the State* (1884) won him fame in quarters where philosophy seldom penetrates. But the philosophical doctrines he set out in his *First Principles*, the opening volume of his *Synthetic Philosophy*, were, in themselves, sufficient to arouse the enthusiasm of his contemporaries.

He is trying to do two things: first, to reconcile science and religion, and secondly, to find a place for philosophy in a world which seemed to be partitioned between the special sciences. On the first point, he quotes at length from Hamilton and Mansel to show that 'ultimate scientific ideas are all representative of realities which cannot be comprehended'. The scientist, he concludes, 'more than any other, truly knows that in its ultimate nature nothing can be known'. Even if physics resolves all material objects into manifestations of force in Space and Time, the nature of matter, Spencer assures us, is still as mysterious as ever, since force, Space and Time 'pass all understanding'; even if all mental actions can be reduced to collections of sensations, mind is still an enigma, for the scientist 'can give no account of sensations themselves or of that which is conscious of sensations'. Thus Science, as Spencer interprets it, leads us to the Unknowable.

Furthermore, this Unknowable is apprehended as a Power, although an Incomprehensible One (the capital letters are Spencer's). Hamilton was right, Spencer argues, in asserting that we have no definite consciousness of anything but the Relative, but wrong in concluding that we can know nothing of the non-relative; we have, in fact, 'an indefinite consciousness which cannot be formulated' of the Absolute. Had we no consciousness whatever of the Absolute, Spencer argues, it would not even make sense to say that our ordinary consciousness is of the *Relative*, for we could not answer the question 'Relative to what?' To give any account of the world we meet in experience, he concludes, we must think of the appearances with which experience presents us as manifestations of an Actuality beyond. 'And this consciousness of an Incomprehensible Power,' according to Spencer, 'is just that consciousness on which religion dwells.'[11]

Religion thus given its rights as an indefinite consciousness, which cannot be formulated, of an Incomprehensible Power, Spencer had still to allocate to philosophy its proper task. He defines it as 'completely-unified knowledge', in contrast with the 'partly-unified knowledge' of science. The philosopher, as Spencer envisages his duties, unifies the sciences by discovering principles of 'the highest degree of generality', which he can then exhibit at work in the various special sciences. Thus, like many another nineteenth-century philosopher – G. H. Lewes, for example[12] –

Spencer thinks of philosophy as an empirical inquiry, scientific in spirit, but distinct from the special sciences in virtue of its greater generality.

Spencer then sets to work to discover these general principles; of the many he formulates the best known is his law of evolution and dissolution. Spencer was an evolutionist before Darwin. Darwin's biology is in his eyes merely a special illustration of a general principle; evolution is a cosmic law, not confined in its operations to biological species. (Darwin remarked in a letter to Fiske, 1874, that 'with the exception of special points I do not even understand H. Spencer's general doctrine'.) 'Evolution,' Spencer pronounces, 'is an integration of matter and concomitant dissipation of motion; during which the matter passes from an indefinite, incoherent homogeneity to a definite coherent heterogeneity; and during which the retained motion undergoes a parallel transformation.'[13] His *Synthetic Philosophy* is an application of this principle to biology, psychology and sociology: the inorganic sciences being omitted as not being of such 'immediate importance' – although his critics were swift to allege more substantial reasons for his not venturing into this field. The very circumstances which won for the *Synthetic Philosophy* such contemporary renown – the fact that it was a systematic guide to the rapidly developing biological and social sciences – now 'date' it badly. As Mill wrote: 'Spencer throws himself with a certain deliberate impetuosity into the last new theory that chimes with his general way of thinking.' His contributions to moral and political philosophy still have a certain interest but we shall look in vain to Spencer for any rigorous discussion of philosophical issues. He is the nineteenth-century publicist *par excellence*.

Of course, there were other evolutionary 'philosophers'. One of them, Ernst Haeckel, in his *The Riddle of the Universe* (1899) wrote a text-book of post-Darwinian naturalism which is still widely read. He had none of Darwin's qualms or uncertainties: 'Natural selection,' he wrote, 'is a mathematical necessity of nature that needs no further proof.' Nor would he have subscribed himself an agnostic: 'Evolution is henceforth the magic word by which we shall solve all the riddles that surround us, or at least be set on the road to their solution.' Agnosticism, to Haeckel, was simply a form of obscurantism, an accusation he particularly directs against Du Bois-Reymond in his *Freedom in Science and Teaching* (1878). But his polemics in that volume have as their main target a fellow biologist, R. Virchow, who had recently proposed a compromise with Religion. Science, Virchow thought, should concern itself with 'facts' only, leaving all 'speculation about consciousness' to the Churches or even to the State, which has the right to lay it down that disturbing speculations should not be promulgated.

Haeckel would have none of this. He denied, in the first place, that 'facts' and 'speculation', science and philosophy, can be sharply separated. 'All true science,' he wrote, 'is natural philosophy' – a startling statement at a time when 'natural philosophy' was generally identified with the wilder speculations of the post-Hegelian School. Such a philosophy, he argued, must take the form of 'Monism', defined as the view that 'a vast, uniform, uninterrupted and eternal process of development obtains throughout all nature; and that all natural phenomena without exception, from the motions of the heavenly bodies and the fall of a rolling stone to the growth of plants and the consciousness of men, obey one and the same great law of causation; that all may be ultimately referred to the mechanics of atoms'. It should be added that each of these atoms, according to Haeckel, has a soul;[14] but this view that souls are everywhere and that, as he expresses the matter in *Last Words on Evolution* (1905), 'God is the all-embracing essence of the world, and is one ... with space-filling matter' did nothing to soothe the feelings of theologians. This was 'the religion of science' in a form far more disreputable than Huxley's agnosticism, and against it the critics of nineteenth-century materialism have particularly inveighed.

Yet other versions of evolutionary philosophy emerged in America.[15] There the great publicist was John Fiske in his *Outlines of Cosmic Philosophy* (1874) and *The Idea of God as Affected by Modern Knowledge* (1886). Fiske enthusiastically adopted Spencer's resolution of 'the apparent antagonism between Science and Religion'. But the Unknowable, in Fiske's philosophy, assumes a distinctly more Christian form: 'The infinite and eternal Power that is manifested in every pulsation of the universe is none other than the living God.' At first the great stronghold of

Naturalism, evolution was soon adapted, as we shall see later, to the purposes of Idealism.[16] Scientific discoveries have not uncommonly been thus amenable to the diverse intentions of philosophers.

Of all the varieties of nineteenth-century materialism the most influential, if influence can be assessed by counting the number of professed disciples, has been the 'dialectical materialism' of the Marxists. But this influence is a result of what can only be described, from the standpoint of a history of philosophy, as 'an accident of history'. Like scholasticism, which also can count its adherents in thousands, it is a philosophy which is intimately associated with a particular set of social institutions – in this case, with the Soviet Union and the Communist Party – exerting very little influence except on philosophers who are committed to those institutions, but claiming their unconditional allegiance.

It is not at all easy to give a clear account of 'dialectical materialism'.[17] Not uncommonly, its critics identify Marxian materialism with the 'medical materialism' of Büchner and his associates. Büchner probably did something to prepare the intellectual atmosphere for Marxism; the fact remains that Frederick Engels in his *Ludwig Feuerbach and the Outcome of Classical German Philosophy* (1888) dismisses the medical materialists as 'vulgarising pedlars' and 'hedge-preachers'. Neither Marx nor Engels had any sympathy with Büchner's attack on 'speculative' philosophy, in the name of science. They admit only two masters – Hegel and Feuerbach.

What is now best-known in Feuerbach's teaching[18] is medical materialism with a vengeance – his dictum that 'man is what he eats' – but this doctrine belonged to his later days. The Feuerbach who aroused the enthusiasm of Marx and Engels was the Feuerbach who in his *Critique of the Hegelian Philosophy* (1839) argued that Hegelian metaphysics is simply theology in disguise – 'the last refuge, the last rational support of theology' – and in his *Essence of Christianity* (1841) that theology itself is a confused, fantastic, way of depicting social relationships. Man makes God, he said, in his own image: 'Religion is the dream of the human mind.' Yet a dream, he argued, is not quite devoid of reality: 'we see real things, but in the entrancing splendour of imagination and caprice instead of in the simple daylight of reality and

44

necessity.' Feuerbach's object was to 'open the eyes' of theology; like Comte, he hoped to substitute a 'Religion of Humanity', based on love, for what he regarded as the 'fantasies' of super-naturalism.

Feuerbach, the Marxists thought, had destroyed metaphysics and religion in a single blow, leaving only 'nature', as something to be studied by observation, not deduced by 'thought'. But in reacting against Hegel, Marx argued, Feuerbach had failed to appreciate Hegel's great contribution to philosophy – his dialectical method. What was this dialectic? Engels summarizes its three main laws in his *Dialectics of Nature* (written 1872–86; first published 1925): the law of the transformation of quantity into quality, the law of the interpenetration of opposites, the law of the negation of negation. The first can be illustrated by the fact that when the temperature of water is lowered – a change in quantity – it turns into ice, i.e. changes in quality; the second by the presence of contradictions in nature; the third by the way these contradictions are resolved into a higher unity.

The main controversy turned around these last two laws. E. Dühring[19] in his *Course of Philosophy* (1875) was sharply critical: 'There are no contradictions in things,' he wrote, 'or, to put it in another way, contradiction applied to reality itself is the apex of absurdity.' To which Engels replies (*Anti-Dühring*, 1878) that this is true only when we consider things as static. 'Motion itself,' he argued, 'is a contradiction: even simple material change can come about only through a body being in one place and in another place, being in one place and also not in it.' Engels goes on to give other examples, which bring out the unusual, not to say peculiar, manner in which he uses the word 'contradiction': as when he talks of 'the contradiction between the innumerable masses of germs which nature produces in such prodigality and the slight number which can come to maturity' or of 'the glaring contradiction' between capitalistic modes of production and capitalistic forces of production.

The 'negation of negation' Dühring had also rejected as 'Hegelian word-juggling'. But, Engels replies, negations of negations are perfectly familiar both in science and in everyday life. Consider the algebraic magnitude 'a'. Negated, this becomes '$-a$'; negate that negation, and the result is 'a^2', the original positive magnitude 'a' raised to a higher power. Again, he argues, a barley-plant negates the seed from which it arises; this negation produces a crop of seed, which is thus the negation of a negation – seed at a higher level.

It will be sufficiently obvious that 'negation', like 'contradiction', has to be understood in a peculiar and undefined sense, in which to multiply by '—1', to multiply by '—a', and to develop from seed into plant are all 'negations'. Is 'matter' more strictly defined? At this point, Marx and Engels keep close to Feuerbach. 'I do not generate,' wrote Feuerbach, 'the object from the thought, but the thought from the object; and I hold that alone to be an object which has an existence beyond one's own brain.' This doctrine, which Feuerbach describes, indifferently, either as 'realism' or as 'materialism' is the essence of Marxian materialism. By 'materialism', indeed, the Marxists usually mean what it is more customary to call representationalism – the view that 'the concepts in our heads' are 'images of real things'. Thus in V. Lenin's *Materialism and Empirio-Criticism* (1908) matter is defined as 'that which, acting upon our sense-organs produces sensation; matter is the objective reality given us in sensation'.

Then Berkeley's criticism has to be answered, that if matter is not itself a sensation but only 'that which gives rise to sensation', we can have no evidence that there is such a thing. Berkeley, Engels admits, is 'hard to beat by mere argumentation'. 'But,' he goes on, 'before there was argumentation, there was action. In the beginning was the deed.' In our practical dealings with things, he argues, we learn to distinguish between those ideas which do, and those which do not, 'copy material things'.[20] This was the doctrine Marx had already sketched in his *Theses on Feuerbach* (1845): 'The question whether objective truth can be attributed to human thinking is not a question of theory but is a practical question.' This side of Marxism leads it into close relations with pragmatism.[21]

Thus, to summarize, dialectical materialism is the theory that things exist independently of us and are 'reflected' in our minds as ideas. These objective existences, as well as our ideas of them, are in a constant state of flux, the flux which Engels describes as the overcoming of contradictions, the negation of negations.

Thus Marx rejects what, in *Capital* (1867), he calls 'the abstract materialism of natural science, a materialism that excludes history and its process', the materialism that is, which thinks of natural objects simply as arrangements of unchanging atoms. This Hegelian emphasis on flux has helped dialectical materialism to win the allegiance of more than one scientist, in a period when science, too, has turned against the more primitive forms of atomism.[22] The very vagueness of dialectical materialism, in contrast with those forms of nineteenth-century materialism which depend upon the definitions of 'matter' and 'force' which were then current, has made of it a flexible polemical weapon.

CHAPTER 3

Towards the Absolute

NONE of the nineteenth-century scientific publicists is of any great importance as a philosopher. Yet their work had a considerable impact upon the development of philosophy, just as the existence of an underworld affects the lives of respectable citizens who never venture into it. Materialism and atheism could no longer be dismissed as the secret vices of a few eccentric individuals. There was much philosophical shutting of windows and closing of doors; in some quarters, philosophy was henceforth pursued mainly as a defence of religion and traditional morality against the inroads of the mechanical world-view.[1] Furthermore, the security of philosophy itself was threatened. Rough voices accused it of barrenness, emptiness, futility.

In Germany, the advance of the physical sciences – assisted by internal dissensions within Hegelianism – brought to ruins with astonishing rapidity the whole structure of post-Kantian Idealism. Everywhere the cry arose: 'Back to Kant!'[2] The new Kantians, however, were by no means of one mind about the tendency of Kant's teaching. Some restricted their attention to Kant's *Critique of Pure Reason*, with its critical analysis of the foundations of human knowledge; such an analysis, they argued, is the only proper task for philosophy in a scientific age. Others sought inspiration in his *Critique of Practical Reason*, which they interpreted as subordinating science to morality and religion, or in his *Critique of Judgment*, which they took to assert that ends, purposes, values, are the clue to the understanding of art, science and religion alike.

For all these divergences, German neo-Kantianism had one general effect: in imitation of science, philosophers began to specialize, devoting their attention to the theory of knowledge, or to the theory of value, or to the philosophy of religion, instead of embarking upon the construction of philosophical systems. In particular, there was an enthusiasm, new to Germany, for the theory of knowledge; and with it a revival of interest in British empirical philosophy, which had always been epistemological in its emphasis.[3] For a short time, indeed, traditional roles were curiously reversed: philosophizing of the British type was at its most powerful in Germany just at the time when philosophizing of the German type was exerting its greatest influence in Britain. And then later it was with weapons forged in Britain but sharpened in Germany that twentieth-century British empiricism won its victories over Anglo-German Idealism.

Not all German philosophers, however, were prepared utterly to abandon metaphysics for epistemology. Of the dissentients perhaps the most influential, in England especially, was R. H. Lotze.[4] 'The constant whetting of the knife is tedious,' he wrote in his *Metaphysic* (1879), 'if it is not proposed to cut anything with it.' The thing to do, according to Lotze, is to tackle philosophical problems directly, to seek knowledge itself, rather than anxiously to inquire whether, and how, knowledge is to be obtained.

Yet in some measure Lotze shared the neo-Kantian hostility to system. Materialists and Hegelians, in his judgement, both made the same mistake: they tried, and necessarily tried in vain, to deduce the rich diversity of experience from some single principle, whether it was mechanical action, as in the case of the materialists, or the necessities of thought, as in the case of the Hegelians. To proceed thus, he argued, is to misunderstand the nature and the limitations of metaphysics. Metaphysics is 'an inquiry into the universal conditions, which everything that is to be counted as existing or happening at all, must be expected to fulfil'; to learn what does *in fact* happen, we must turn to experience, not to metaphysics.

Lotze's philosophy[5] is what came to be called an 'Ideal-Realism' – understanding by 'Realism' the view that the way things happen is determined by mechanical conditions, and by 'Idealism' the view that things happen in accordance with a plan, or in order to fulfil an Ideal purpose.* His earlier medical

---

*British philosophy, preoccupied with the theory of perception, tends to classify philosophical theories by their attitude to the perception of material things: 'realism', for it, is the view that material things exist even when they are not being perceived, and 'idealism' is, most commonly, the view that they exist only as objects of perception. (See, for example, A. C. Ewing: *Idealism: a Critical Survey*, 1934, and R. F. Hoernlé: *Idealism as a Philosophical Doctrine*, 1924). Thus Huxley called himself an 'Idealist' because he said that matter is no more than a set of sensations. But many of the

writings – he was trained as a doctor – such as his *General Physiology of Bodily Life* (1851) pressed 'realism' so far, by their resolute adoption of mechanical analyses of physiological processes, that they did much to assist the diffusion of materialistic ideas in Germany. But his own intention, so he explained in his *Microcosmus*, was to show '*how absolutely universal is the extent* but at the same time, *how completely subordinate the significance*, of the mission which mechanism has to fulfil in the world'. For 'all the laws of this mechanism', so Lotze argues, 'are but the very will of the universal soul'; they are 'nothing else than the condition for the realization of Good'. This conclusion, he honestly admits, is one that he cannot demonstrate. To human reason there is an unbridged gap between 'the world of values' and 'the world of mechanism', between the world in which things are as they are because this is how it is best for them to be and the world in which they are as they are because this is what the pressure of mechanical forces compels them to be. 'With the firmest conviction of the unity of the two,' he admitted, 'we combine the most distinctly conscious belief in the impossibility of this unity being known.' So those who lacked Lotze's 'firm convictions' had no difficulty in developing this or that partial aspect of his metaphysics to suit their own purposes. Often enough, he is regarded as the spokesman of those who distinguish sharply between facts and values, positive and normative inquiries, even although it was a main part of his object to destroy that antithesis.

It is, indeed, the common judgement on Lotze, and a just one, that he was much more successful in his specific inquiries, whether in logic or ethics or aesthetics or psychology (for he was nothing if not versatile) than in bringing together these various inquiries into that 'coherent picture of the world' towards which

---

'Idealists' we shall be discussing in this chapter have no particular interest in the theory of perception and would strongly object to being classed with Berkeley, let alone with Huxley. The central core of their teaching is that to be real is to be a member of a 'rational system', a system so constructed that the nature of its members is intelligible only in so far as the system as a whole is understood. That system, however, is usually conceived as both ideal and spiritual. Thus a thing is real in so far as it participates in the Ideal – the central doctrine of Platonic Idealism – and in so far as it is either a manifestation of Spirit (Absolute Idealism) or a member of a community of spirits (Personal Idealism).

his metaphysics aspired. He craved for unity; and yet his inquiries seemed always to lead him into dualities. Few philosophers have been so pillaged – in what follows, his name will constantly recur – yet in a sense he had no disciples. The familiar verdict that 'he was only half a philosopher' is not entirely unjust. To attempt to expound his 'system' would be extremely difficult, probably impossible, and scarcely fruitful, since it was precisely his *lack* of system on which his influence depended. There was room for everybody in Lotze's Universe – but it did not do for anybody to inquire *too* curiously into his precise status in that Universe or to insist *too* rigorously on rules of precedence.

To return for the time being to Great Britain, what happened there was more than a little peculiar. William James sums it up thus: 'It is a strange thing, this resurrection of Hegel in England and here [U.S.A.] after his burial in Germany. I think his philosophy will probably have an important influence on the development of our liberal form of Christianity. It gives a quasi-metaphysical backbone which this theology has always been in need of.' In Germany, Hegelianism had completely failed to arrest the progress of materialism; the fact remains that it was introduced into Great Britain to fulfil that very purpose.[6]

The theological impulse behind the new interest in Hegel is very apparent in the work of J. H. Stirling.[7] In his *The Secret of Hegel* (1865), which – for all that its severer critics remarked that 'the secret has been well kept' – first presented Hegelianism to Great Britain in a relatively intelligible and coherent form, Stirling was perfectly frank about his apologetic intentions. 'Kant and Hegel,' he wrote, with more enthusiasm than accuracy, 'have no object but to restore Faith – Faith in God, Faith in the Immortality of the Soul and the Freedom of the Will – nay Faith in Christianity as the revealed religion'; this is the ground on which he recommended them to his readers. In the United States, that remarkable band of enthusiasts, the St Louis Hegelians, who did so much to naturalize Hegel in America, thought they descried in his philosophy 'a sword wherewith to smite the three-headed monster of anarchy in politics, traditionalism in religion and naturalism in science'.[8] These expectations were eventually to be disappointed. Neo-Hegelianism developed its own philosophical momentum which carried it far beyond the confines of even the

51

most unorthodox Christianity. But the fact that such hopes were widely entertained does much to account for the sudden popularity of Idealism in Britain in the last quarter of the nineteenth century.

Of course, this suddenness can be, and sometimes is, exaggerated. Twice before, Idealism had flourished in Great Britain; on both occasions, it is worth noting, as a defence against the advances of materialism. On the first occasion, the Cambridge Platonists, with help from Descartes and Plato, fought against the 'mechanically-atheistic' philosophies to which seventeenth-century scientific developments gave birth; on the second occasion, Berkeley was alarmed into philosophy by the materialism and the Deism which Newtonian science had unwittingly engendered. Even although there was no continuous tradition of Idealist philosophy in Great Britain, it was never quite without its advocates. 'Literary philosophers' like Coleridge and Carlyle in England, Emerson in America, helped to prepare the cultivated mind for *The Secret of Hegel* – that very title points to the feeling that was abroad, the feeling that there was 'something in' Hegel. And there were at least two Idealist thinkers, before the main wave, who deserve more than a passing mention – J. F. Ferrier and John Grote.[9]

Ferrier[10] was a scholar, with some understanding of the work of Hegel and Schelling, and an enthusiasm for Berkeley, whose work had for so long been generally ignored. In his *Institutes of Metaphysics* (1854), he is a philosopher in search of the Absolute – that which possesses 'a clear, detached, emancipated, substantial genuine or unparasitical being'. This is a philosophical ambition certainly rare – perhaps without previous precedent – in Great Britain, although common enough on the Continent. Ferrier's method of procedure was equally unorthodox: British philosophy had always prided itself on its loose, informal, even negligent, style of philosophizing, whereas Ferrier proposed nothing less than to construct 'an unbroken chain of clear demonstration' which should consist entirely of 'necessary truths', defined as truths 'the opposite of which is inconceivable, contradictory, nonsensical, impossible'.

His conclusions were perhaps less surprising. Beginning from the Cartesian doctrine, which had won wide acceptance among British philosophers, that to know anything is to know ourselves as knowing it, he set out to show, first, that the least that can be *known* is neither a pure object nor a pure subject but a-subject-knowing-an-object, and secondly, that this must also be the least that can exist, the only thing that *is* absolutely. Minds cannot be the Absolute, the independently existing, he argues, because they exist only in so far as they apprehend objects; objects cannot be the Absolute, because they exist only in so far as they are apprehended by mind. And to say that the Absolute might be something that lies outside knowledge altogether, something of which we are entirely ignorant, is to forget, according to Ferrier, that we can be ignorant only of a *possible* object of knowledge. (We can properly say that we are ignorant of the cause of cancer, only if it *has* a cause and only if we could know its cause.)

This conclusion is characteristically British in its emphasis on the knowledge-relation as providing the clue to 'Reality'; Ferrier's philosophy, however, was anything but characteristic in its attitude to 'common sense'. Of that great hero of the Scottish School, Thomas Reid, Ferrier wrote (for all that he was himself a Scottish professor): 'with vastly good intentions, and very excellent abilities for everything except philosophy, he had no speculative genius whatever – positively an anti-speculative turn of mind, which, with a mixture of shrewdness and naïveté altogether incomparable, he was pleased to term "common sense".' Ferrier's contempt for 'the submarine abysses of popular opinion' struck a new note in British philosophy; there was obviously an impatience abroad with 'hard facts', a growing unwillingness to accept the subservience of philosophical speculation to popular opinion.

John Grote was much less of a revolutionary, but his *Exploratio Philosophica I*, with the sub-title *Rough Notes on Modern Intellectual Science* (1865), is an interesting specimen of home-grown Idealism. As the title suggests, this is not at all a finished production; for the most part it consists of acute, although somewhat desultory, critical essays on Mill, Hamilton, Whewell and Ferrier. But a general position emerges, with its main feature an attempt to 'keep science in its place'. Like Lotze, Grote argues that the natural scientist should push ahead with mechanical explanations, and need have no fear of the philosophical consequences. Nevertheless, he strongly resists Mill's plea for the extension of scientific method to the moral sciences. Human feelings, as distinct from physiological processes, are not 'objects', so Grote argues, and hence they lie outside the field of science.

Science, he says, considers things in abstraction from the fact that they are known – an abstraction which is impossible in the case of feelings – whereas from the point of view of philosophy 'their knowableness is a part, and the most important part, of their reality as an essential being'. When we reflect upon objects from this point of view, according to Grote, we see that they are knowable only because they have in them 'the quality of adaptedness to reason'. They can be known, in other words, only because they are in themselves reasonable; this means, Grote concludes, that they must have mind in them – a conclusion which, he says, enables us to feel 'at home in the universe', in contrast with the 'simply phenomenalist spirit' displayed by Mill which leaves us in a state 'inexpressibly depressing and desolate'. This desire to be 'at home in the Universe', to be able to feel that the Universe is the kind of thing one might, with greater power, have created for oneself, is certainly a powerful motive in Idealist philosophy; Grote's expression of it, however, is unusually naked.

But neither Grote's acuteness* nor Ferrier's elaborate demonstrations were to found a British School of Idealism; the tide of foreign influences swept them away. At first, in the seventies, the emphasis was on translation and commentary. In Oxford, Benjamin Jowett's translation of Plato (1871) produced no less effect on a distinguished array of students than the German Idealism he also recommended to their attention. William Wallace's *The Logic of Hegel* (1874) was important both as translation and as commentary; Edward Caird produced a full-length study of Kant

---

*Grote's philosophy is in manner an early, perhaps the first, example of that Cambridge spirit – he was Professor of Moral Philosophy at the University of Cambridge – which was to reach its culmination in the work of G. E. Moore. His conversational, informal, italicized style, his acute, particularized, but not scholarly criticisms, his preference for 'the language of ordinary men' as distinct from 'the language of philosophers', are all prophetic of Moore. And certain special points of doctrine – for example, his distinction between 'knowledge by acquaintance' and 'knowledge about' – were to be prominent in later Cambridge thinking. Grote is in many ways an impressive philosopher, but his impressiveness is of the sort at which summary can do no more than hint.

(1877) – a Kant read through Hegelian spectacles – and in 1883 his brief but influential *Hegel*.[11]

Caird's *Hegel*, which is an attempt to show precisely in what the value of the Hegelian philosophy consists, illustrates very clearly the intentions and the emphasis of the Scottish Hegelians. Hegel, to Caird, is first and foremost a theologian: his speculations, according to Caird, 'were predominantly guided by the practical instincts of the higher life of man, by the desire to restore the moral and religious basis of human existence, which a revolutionary scepticism had destroyed'. And his philosophical method, the dialectic, is, as Caird sees it, a method of reconciliation. For him there are 'no antagonisms which cannot be reconciled' – there must always be a higher unity within which antagonistic tendencies will each find a place. Thus if religion and science appear to be irreconcilably opposed, this can only be an appearance; in reality they *must* form part of a higher unity.

Caird tries to show, indeed, that the conflict between conventional religion and materialistic science can be overcome, in a theology which agrees with science in maintaining that scientific laws admit of no exceptions and with religion in proclaiming the supremacy of the spiritual or the Ideal, conjoining these two superficially antagonistic principles in the doctrine that scientific law is itself spiritual. 'No longer is it possible,' writes Caird, 'as it once was, to intercalate the ideal, the divine, as it were surreptitiously, as one existence in a world otherwise secular and natural ... we can find the ideal anywhere, only by finding it everywhere.' The special spiritual interventions (miracles, for example) on which orthodox religion lays such stress must, Caird thinks, be abandoned as superstitious. There is no longer any need of them in a world that is through and through spiritual. Traditional theology sharply distinguishes between Man, God and Nature; Idealism, a truly philosophical theology, sees in all three, according to Caird, the workings of a single spiritual principle. Nor will Caird allow the familiar contrast between a 'world of facts' and a 'world of values': values, for him, are *in the facts*, or nowhere, and every fact has its value.

A second important characteristic of Caird's Hegelianism is his emphasis on development. The 'higher unity' in which antagonisms are reconciled is, he writes, 'unity as manifesting itself in an organic process of development'. Thus Caird thinks that religion, his special interest, must be studied historically, if we are to understand its true nature as a recognition of 'the spiritual principle which is constantly working in man's life'. This is the main theme in his *The Evolution of Religion* (1893) and *The Evolution of Theology in the Greek Philosophers* (1904). For him the proper question is never: 'Is that religion true or false?' but always, as he expresses the matter: 'How much truth has been brought to expression and with what inadequacies and unexplained assumptions?' Caird finds it possible to write with respect of Darwin and of Comte just because they have contributed so much to the theory of development. His width of sympathy, coupled with striking gifts of expression and an attractive personality, did much to advance the Hegelian cause both in Scotland, where he was Professor of Moral Philosophy at the University of Glasgow from 1866 until 1893, and in England, where he succeeded his old teacher Jowett as Master of Balliol.[12]

Of all the first generation Idealists, however, the most influential was certainly T. H. Green. He, more than any other man, provided, in James's phrase, a 'quasi-metaphysical backbone' for the evangelical liberalism which most strongly appealed to the earnest and public-spirited Oxford students of his time. As R. G. Collingwood says in his *Autobiography* (1939): 'The school of Green sent out into public life a stream of ex-pupils who carried with them the conviction that philosophy, and in particular the philosophy they had learnt at Oxford, was an important thing, and that their vocation was to put it into practice. This conviction was common to politicians so diverse in their creeds as Asquith and Milner, Churchmen like Gore and Scott Holland, social reformers like Arnold Toynbee.... Through this effect on the minds of its pupils, the philosophy of Green's school might be found, from about 1880 to about 1910, penetrating and fertilizing every part of the national life.'[13]

Green, indeed, like Jones and many another of the British Idealists, was predominantly a teacher, although he also participated freely in the life of a wider world as an educational and social reformer. He left behind him no fully worked-out statement of his metaphysical views; they have to be brought together, so far as they can be systematized, from his *Introduction to Hume's*

Treatise on Human Nature (1874), the introduction to his pos-thumously published *Prolegomena to Ethics* (1883) and such lecture-notes as have been printed.

One point must be stressed at the outset. It is customary to describe Green as a 'neo-Hegelian', but it was the school of Caird, not Green, who stood firmly for Hegelian principles. Green criticized the Cairdians on this very ground; they were, he thought, unduly subservient to Hegel. (Bradley wrote of him: 'Green was in my opinion no Hegelian and was in some respects anti-Hegelian even.') In a review (1880), of John Caird's *Introduction to the Philosophy of Religion* Green remarks that 'in his method, though not in his conclusion, we think he has been too much overpowered by Hegel.' He was more than ready to accept what he took to be Hegel's main conclusion: 'There is one spiritual self-conscious being, of which all that is real is the activity or expression; we are related to this spiritual being, not merely as parts of the world which is its expression, but as partakers in some inchoate measure of the self-consciousness through which it at once constitutes and distinguishes itself from the world.' At the same time, he thought that the methods by which that con-clusion had been established were insufficient – 'it must,' he wrote, 'all be done over again.'

In particular, he considered that Hegel's emphasis on 'thought' led Hegelians to write as if the spirituality of the world somehow followed from the fact that, in thinking, we are never directly aware of anything except 'our own ideas'. He was insistent, in opposi-tion to writers like Ferrier, that no true idealist could be a Berkeleian. The proper approach, he argued, is not from the individual mind to the world, but rather from the world to the universality of mind. In thus taking the world as the starting-point of his philosophy, Green, like so many of his contem-poraries, returns to Kant. His method of argument, too, is Kantian – or, often enough, Platonic, in the manner of Plato's *Theaetetus* especially – rather than Hegelian.

Green's *Introduction to Hume* is a sustained polemic, in the interests of Idealism, against that empirical tradition which J. S. Mill had recently developed and restated. Green particularly sets out to overthrow the view that to be real, or a fact, is to be a 'phenomenon' – something which is given to us in experience, as an isolated sensation. The least we can experience, he argues, is already a set of relations. Suppose it be said, for example, that we experience 'a sensation of white'. Then in calling it 'a sensation *of white*', Green says, we have already related it, whether to the object which it is supposed to depict, or – if it be denied that it is a 'picture' – to those other sensations we also describe as 'white'. Furthermore, to call it '*a* sensation' is to distinguish it from, thus relating it to, a background against which it is picked out; and to describe it as 'a *sensation*' is to think of it as related to an organism. To talk at all, Green concludes, is to relate; thus, 'to suppose that the simple datum of sense is the real ... is to make the real unmeaning, the empty, of which nothing can be said'.

The 'real', Green thinks he has shown, is either an unintelligible, unspeakable, nonentity, or is the related. But even the empiricists admitted that relations are 'the work of the mind'; if the real is the related it follows, Green feels entitled to argue, that the real is dependent for its nature on the existence of mind. Where Green parts company with the empiricists is in denying that relations are imposed upon a 'given', a set of data which contains no relations. Remove their relations, so he argues, and the objects of experience entirely vanish. The 'unrelated given' is an unintelligible fiction.

This, then, is the pattern of his argument: all reality lies in relations; only for a thinking consciousness do relations exist; therefore the real world must be through-and-through a world made by mind. Two problems immediately arise. The world as we experience it is 'objective'; it is *there* for us to experience. How can this be so, if it is made by mind? Again, we are accustomed to distinguish the real, as what is *there*, from the imaginary, as what we create for ourselves: this distinction is vital for every kind of inquiry yet it seems to vanish if the world is always of mind's making.

Green's attempt to solve these two problems carries him from the individual mind to the eternal consciousness, which he identifies with God. In knowing, he argues, we gradually, as individuals, become conscious of what has always existed as an object of the eternal consciousness. That is why what we know seems to us to be objective, independent of mind; it is independent of *our* mind, *we* do not make it. Yet even this, he maintains, is not wholly true: for in becoming conscious of what the eternal consciousness has always known we come to *be* this eternal consciousness, or at least its vehicle. 'In the growth of our experience,' so he writes in his *Prolegomena to Ethics,* 'an animal organism which has a history in time, gradually becomes the vehicle for an eternally complete consciousness.' Thus although what we know is independent of our mind *qua* an individual mind, it is constituted by our mind *qua* a participant in the eternal consciousness. Since, however, our mind is restricted by the animal organism it inhabits, it sometimes fails adequately to conceive the relations in which a thing is determined by the eternal consciousness; it relates things from a merely individual point of view. Thus there arise 'imaginary' as distinct from 'real' objects – objects which exist only as constituted by us, and not by the eternal consciousness.

The distinction between what is constituted by an eternal consciousness and what is the product, only, of an imperfect human mind accounts, Green considers, both for our experience of 'objectivity' and for our every-day distinction between the real and the imaginary, without departing from the general principle that every object of experience is mind-made. In similar fashion, he thinks, the distinction and connexion between individual and eternal consciousness allows the Idealist to admit what is true in materialism without departing from his major principles. No doubt matter is 'real', he will grant, but this is at once to say that it is the work of thought. To regard mind as a product of matter is completely to reverse the true order of dependence. Our passing mental states, the evanescent feelings which psychology studies, may be conditions of a physical organism, but these, according to Green, are not mental in the full sense, are not consciousness.[14] Mind itself, he argues, cannot possibly be a passing state, because it is not in time; if it were it could not hold together events in time, distinguishing past from future, predecessor from successor. Even Mill had admitted, Green triumphantly points out, that a fleeting mental state can never be conscious of a succession. How then can mind be fleeting? And yet those feelings which the physiologist-psychologist calls 'mind' are in a perpetual state of change.

As for evolution, the new theories, Green is happy to admit, undermine the old 'natural theology'. The fact remains, he argues in his lectures *On the Logic of the Formal Logicians*, that evolution is not only compatible with, but logically necessitates, the existence of an eternal consciousness. Otherwise, we should have to suppose that something can come from nothing, an unintelligible supposition which we can avoid only by recognizing that what from a merely human point of view 'comes to be' *always has been* to an eternal consciousness.

Green's critics were quick to point to the gaps in his metaphysics, to the fact that, to mention one of the more striking omissions, he gives no clear account of the relation between the individual and the eternal consciousness. Nevertheless, his critique of the traditional empiricism was really damaging: not a few philosophers were convinced that it had been destroyed once and for all.[15] When a group of younger philosophers published in 1883 their *Essays in Philosophical Criticism*, which first made clear the range and scope of the Idealist movement, it was appropriately dedicated to T. H. Green.*

The most rigorous metaphysician among the British Idealists, however, was certainly F. H. Bradley.[16] And if Bradley was as critical as Green or Caird of British empiricism, and far more violent in his polemical manner,[17] he no less uncompromisingly rejects Green's main thesis that the real consists in relations. And although an admirer of Hegel, he is by no means a Hegelian. His dialectic is the dialectic of Parmenides and Zeno rather than the dialectic of Hegel. It is obvious that he has learnt a great deal from Plato's *Parmenides* and *Sophist*, in which that dialectic is displayed – as indeed from Plato's dialogues in general.[18] The irony of passages like this one from his *Principles of Logic* (1883): 'I confess that I should hardly care to subject myself to all these insults; and I had rather Mr Spencer, or some other great authority

*It contains essays on logic, aesthetics, social philosophy, history, as well as metaphysics. The contributors included Andrew Seth, R. B. and J. S. Haldane, Bosanquet, Sorley, D. G. Ritchie, W. P. Ker, Henry Jones and James Bonar. Ker was to make his name as a literary scholar, R. B. (later Lord) Haldane as a statesman-philosopher, J. S. Haldane as a philosopher-scientist, Bonar as an economic historian. Thus the new Idealism was carried into a variety of fields. The Shakespearian scholar, A. C. Bradley, was closely associated with this group.

– whoever may feel himself able to bear them, or unable to understand them – should take them on himself' – could scarcely
resemble more closely the irony of Plato's Socrates.

Bradley's great critical weapon, from the very beginning, is the
accusation of self-contradiction. He has a faith in logic, a
willingness, in the Platonic phrase, to 'follow the argument where
it leads', which is rare in English philosophy. 'Criticism, if it be
criticism,' he writes in his *Presuppositions of Critical History*,
'must in the beginning and provisionally suspect the reality of
everything before it; and if there are some matters which it cannot
reaffirm without falsifying itself, these matters have themselves
to thank'. If 'facts' and principles conflict, so much the worse for
the facts; if the choice must be made between 'a great historical
fact' and a 'high abstract principle', then, says Bradley, 'the
issue I must decide in favour of the principle and the higher
truth'. This is the 'Oxford high priori road' with a vengeance!

The metaphysics to which logic leads Bradley is most fully
detailed in his *Appearance and Reality* (1893). That difficult book,
however, needs to be read in conjunction with his *Principles of
Logic*, especially perhaps the *Terminal Essays* which he added to
it in the second edition (1922), his *Essays on Truth and Reality*
(1914), and the uncompleted essay on relations which was
posthumously published in his *Collected Essays* (1935). Bradley's
Ethical Studies (1876), particularly the passionate essay it contains on *My Station and its Duties*, is also illuminating as a
revelation of the ethical impulse which gives vitality to Bradley's
metaphysical system.*

The central topic of *Appearance and Reality*, according to
Bradley himself, is the relation between thought and reality,
which *The Principles of Logic* had left in a highly unsatisfactory

---

*Bradley defined metaphysics as 'the finding of bad reasons for what we
believe upon instinct'. *My Station and its Duties* shows us what he believed
upon instinct, that there must be a place for everything and that everything
must keep to its place. For his metaphysics see also the Platonic scholar
A. E. Taylor's *Elements of Metaphysics* (1903). Taylor, later to break away
from Hegelian modes of thinking, was at that time much influenced by
Bradley, and his *Elements of Metaphysics* is in large part a careful exposition
of Bradley's philosophy. *The Faith of a Moralist* (1930), in contrast, is an
attempt to develop the moral argument for the existence of God and, indeed,
for a largely orthodox Christianity.

state. In language which is a somewhat more purple version of several passages in the works of Lotze, Bradley had rejected the Hegelian view that to be real and to be thought are the same thing. 'The notion that existence could be the same as understanding,' he writes in *The Principles of Logic*, 'strikes as cold and ghost-like as the dreariest materialism. That the glory of this world in the end is appearance leaves the world more glorious, if we feel it is a show of some fuller splendour; but the sensuous curtain is a deception and a cheat, if it hides some colourless movement of atoms, some spectral woof of impalpable abstractions, or unearthly ballet of bloodless categories .... They no more *make* that Whole which commands our devotion, than some shredded dissection of human tatters *is* that warm and breathing beauty of flesh which our hearts found delightful.'

Yet the difficulty with this conclusion was that it seemed to lead directly to agnosticism; if the real lies beyond all thought then, surely, it must be forever inaccessible to us as a mere unknowable.* Bradley's problem is to limit the pretensions of thought without cutting it off either from the resources of immediate experience on the one side or from an apprehension, however limited, of the Absolute on the other.

Bradley's metaphysic begins, then, from the conception of 'immediate experience', which he most fully describes in his essay 'On our Knowledge of Immediate Experience' (*Mind*, 1909, reprinted in *Truth and Reality*). 'We have experience,' he there writes, 'in which there is no distinction between my awareness and that of which it is aware. There is an immediate feeling, a knowing and being in one, with which knowledge begins; and though this in a manner is transcended, it nevertheless remains throughout as the present foundation of my known world.' Immediate feeling this is, pure and simple. It does not consist, Bradley argues, of *ourselves* feeling *something* – for this involves

---

*This point was immediately made by Bernard Bosanquet in his *Knowledge and Reality* (1885). He was content with Bradley's answer in *Appearance and Reality* but others were not. Compare A. E. Taylor's gibe: 'The Hegelians made merry over the Unknowable ... their own Absolute is just the Unknowable in its Sunday best' ('Philosophy' in *Recent Developments in European Thought* ed. F. S. Marvin, 1919). See also A. Cuming: 'Lotze, Bradley and Bosanquet' (*Mind*, 1917); A. Eastwood: 'Lotze's Antithesis between Thoughts and Things' (*Mind*, 1892).

the distinction between 'ourselves' and 'our objects', which is the work of thought – it is feeling as such, not somebody's feeling or a feeling of something.* It contains diversity, but a diversity which is prior to relations. Consider, he says, the experience of a red patch; this does not contain two distinct qualities, redness and extendedness, somehow linked by a relation; it is a feeling which is a unity and yet contains diversity.

As soon as we begin to talk the language of things, qualities, relations – as we must do in order to think, to judge, to lay claims to truth – we pass, according to Bradley, beyond this level of feeling. Thought, he will admit, does not entirely abandon experience, but it abstracts from it. 'Red' is picked out from the red patch as if it were an isolated quality, quite distinct from the 'this' to which we now ascribe it and yet somehow, we try to say, predicable of it. This abstraction, this attempt to separate and to connect at once, immediately leads us, so Bradley tries to show, into self-contradictions. That is the theme of the first book of *Appearance and Reality*: every ordinary judgement, everything we can possibly say about the world, is 'riddled with contradictions' and is therefore mere Appearance, not true Reality.

Consider, for example, the judgement that 'the sugar is sweet'. What is the meaning, Bradley asks, of the 'is' by which we here unite thing and quality? We do not mean that the sugar is *identical* with sweetness, because we also wish to say that sugar is hard, white and so on: it cannot be identical with each and every one of these so diverse qualities. Yet how else can it be all these qualities at once? To describe it as a mere conjunction of qualities would be to ignore its unity; yet if we try to show that it is 'something else' as well – a 'substance' for example – we find it impossible to construct an intelligible account of this 'something else'.

It might be suggested that the sugar is its various qualities together with some unifying relation between them. Then how,

*James Ward denied that there was such a thing as immediate experience in this sense. See his 'Mr Bradley's Analysis of Mind' (*Mind*, 1887) and 'Bradley's Doctrine of Experience' (*Mind*, 1925). But Bradley maintained that the general tendency of psychology was on his side and pointed especially to the psychology of William James. His doctrine of immediate experience is one of the few things which Bradley thought he had derived immediately from Hegel.

Bradley objects, does the relation unify the qualities? They cannot be predicated of one another: whiteness is not hard nor is sweetness white. Yet how else can they be related? Again, what is the force of 'is' in '*is* in relation to'? Surely we cannot mean that sweetness *is* this relation to whiteness! To replace the word 'is' by 'has', as we might be tempted to do, merely transforms the problem verbally: 'has a relation to' is no clearer than 'is in relation to'. The dilemma remains, however we may seek to evade it: either we predicate of a subject something that is different from it, so that we say that it is what it is not; or else we predicate of it what is not different, and then our judgement collapses into the mere emptiness of 'A is A'. A judgement, so Bradley summarizes his argument, must contain diversity if it is not to be a tautology; yet it must at the same time unite. And no judgement can succeed in combining unity with diversity.

This criticism of the judgement develops, in the third chapter of *Appearance and Reality*, into a general criticism of relations.[19] Of this chapter, Bradley remarks: 'The reader, who has followed and has grasped the principle of this chapter, will have little need to spend his time upon those which succeed it. He will have seen that our experience, where relational, is not true; and he will have condemned, almost without a hearing, the great mass of phenomena.' This is obviously true – if relations are defective, Space, Time, Causality, Change must all share the same defect.

Relations, Bradley begins by arguing, must link qualities; for nothing, he says, can be wholly constituted by its relations: the terms in a relation must have qualities of their own which are distinct from the relation itself. At the same time, he argues, to qualify is itself to distinguish, i.e. to relate. Thus the very same quality, it would seem, both supports and is supported by a relation; without quality there is no relation, but equally without relation there is no quality. If qualities are to play this dual role, Bradley continues, we must be able to distinguish, within any quality Q, the supporter Q_1 and the supported Q_2. Then just as it is impossible to show how a lump of sugar can be both white and sweet, so equally, according to Bradley, there is no intelligible way in which Q_1 can be linked with Q_2. Neither is the predicate of the other, and yet if they are linked by a further relation, Q_3, there will be the same difficulties in linking Q_3 with Q_1 and Q_2 as there were in linking Q_1 with Q_2. We are committed to an endless regress, Bradley concludes, which brings us no nearer the solution of our original problem.

By means of this and other comparable arguments Bradley makes his way to the conclusion that 'a relational way of thought must give appearance and not truth ... it is a makeshift, a mere practical compromise, most necessary, but in the end most indefensible'. It is 'necessary', he thinks, because the intellect cannot rest content with shifting, impermanent, immediate experience; it is a 'practical compromise' in so far as it is an attempt to retain the unity of experience while at the same time dissecting it into abstract elements; it is 'most indefensible', in so far as it leads to self-contradictions. Thought, Green was right in maintaining, is by nature relational: without relations science cannot move a step. But to say this, Bradley concludes, is to admit that thought, whether or not in the form of science, can never fully satisfy the mind.

So far, Bradley's argument might seem to be merely a complicated way of arriving at the familiar Idealist conclusion that the world with which science concerns itself is not fully real. What caused a particular stir was that Bradley applied the same line of reasoning to God and the self.[20]

The self, Bradley argues – to say nothing of its other defects, which he conscientiously explains – involves relations; it is *continuous*, i.e. its past is related to its present, and it is linked in various ways with the world around it. Philosophers who try to evade this conclusion by setting up a 'pure ego' or 'transcendental self' beyond all change and relatedness are, in Bradley's opinion, no longer talking about the self of everyday life. Nor can they link this remote 'self' with the self of everyday life without somehow ascribing change and relatedness to it. God, according to Bradley, suffers from the same defect; the God of religion is a God *related to mankind* and yet any account of the relation between man and God is inherently unintelligible. 'If you identify the Absolute with God,' he writes, 'that is not the God of religion' – because the Absolute has no personality; the only satisfactory solution is that God is 'but an aspect, and that must mean but an appearance, of the Absolute'.

This then is Bradley's first conclusion: while we use the

intellectual apparatus of things, qualities, relations, we move inevitably within the world of appearances, the world of self-contradiction and unintelligibility. But does this really matter? Have we any alternative but to accept self-contradiction with a shrug of our shoulders, if it inevitably infects *all* our thinking?

At a certain level, Bradley argues, it does not matter. To protest against a particular physical theory that it is self-contradictory, in so far as it uses relations, or against psychology that it adopts a phenomenalist approach which is not ultimately intelligible, is to employ metaphysical criticisms at a point where they are totally inapplicable.* 'The very essence of such a science everywhere,' wrote Bradley in his 'A Defence of Phenomenalism in Psychology' (*Mind*, 1900), 'is to employ half-truths, in other words to use convenient fictions and falsehoods.'

But metaphysics has higher ambitions. 'The object of metaphysics,' wrote Bradley, 'is to find a general view which will satisfy the intellect'; only what *fully* satisfies the intellect can be real or true. In practice, this comes to be identical with Lotze's definition: 'metaphysics has merely to show what the universal conditions are which must be satisfied by anything of which we can say *without contradicting ourselves* that it is or that it happens.' Nowhere short of the Absolute, according to Bradley, can this self-consistency be found, and yet nothing less can satisfy the intellect.

The Absolute cannot, of course, be thought, for all thinking is self-contradictory; at the same time it is not merely 'the Unknowable'. There are features of our experience, Bradley suggests, which enable us to realize, however dimly, what the Absolute must be like – even although, he agrees with Lotze, 'we cannot construct absolute life in its details'.

Bradley finds his first clue in immediate experience; although it is so unstable and impermanent, and therefore cannot of itself satisfy the intellect, yet it suggests to us, through the manner in

---

*A. E. Taylor tells us that Bradley taught him to take empirical psychology seriously. Bradley's own psychological work, as it is contained in his *Collected Essays*, is composed very much in the manner of British psychology of the Lockean sort. What he objected to was the attempt to think of that psychology as *philosophy*. It was his constant theme that metaphysics must be kept completely out of psychology.

which it reconciles unity and diversity, 'the general idea of a total experience where will and thought and feeling may all once more be one'. A second clue comes from the workings of thought itself; the direction in which thought finds itself compelled to move in its unavailing efforts to satisfy the intellect suggests to us, he considers, what the Absolute must be like. When we think, according to Bradley, we seek a truth of a kind which mere thought cannot give us. We try to discover *connexions*, as distinct from mere conjunctions; we want to be able to see that *A must* go with *B*, not merely that *A happens in fact* to go with *B*. Thought, however, always leaves us with 'brute' conjunctions; for even if we discover that *A* goes with *B* because it is *C*, we have only replaced the conjunction of *A* and *B* by the conjunction of both with *C*. So long as we continue to work with separate truths, which we then try to link with one another, so Bradley concludes, we cannot achieve the kind of connectedness, the inner necessity, which we are seeking. Nor, short of the Absolute, can we find the completeness, the all-encompassing view, towards which thought perpetually drives us. 'Truth is not satisfied,' he writes, 'until we have all the facts and until we understand perfectly what we have. And we do not understand perfectly the given material until we have it all together harmoniously, in such a way, that is, that we are not impelled to strive for another and a better way of holding it together.' Thought's dissatisfaction with its own products – its 'truths' – enables us to see, Bradley is arguing, what Reality must be like if it is to satisfy the intellect: it must be all-inclusive, completely systematic, entirely harmonious. And we are driven in the same direction, Bradley tries to show, if we approach the Absolute from the side of will or feeling. Only in such an Absolute, he considers, can we fully satisfy our moral impulses. In any system short of the Absolute, men are torn between the incompatible motives of self-assertion and self-sacrifice and infected by the self-contradictions of 'desire', which can satisfy itself only by utterly destroying itself.

The Absolute must be One, a Unity, Bradley naturally maintains, because plurality would involve relatedness. Yet its unity, he also wants to say, must be a unity which contains diversity: the Absolute would otherwise be empty of content. At this point, Bradley's theory of concrete universals[21] comes into its own. We are accustomed to think of things as arranged in a classificatory order: horses included among quadrupeds, quadrupeds among animals, animals among living things. As the terms in this classification increase in generality, their own content diminishes in richness – 'living things' is much more abstract, less specific, than 'horses'. If we then think of 'the Absolute' as the final point in such a classificatory system, it seems so poor in content as to vanish into nothing.

Such a classification, Bradley argues, makes use of the 'abstract' universals beloved by thought. *Horse*, the horse as such, is, he says, an abstraction from, and thus a falsification of, experience. With this abstract universal Bradley sharply contrasts the 'concrete' universal, which is not an abstraction from, but a community of, its members. It is an individual: we can understand its nature, Bradley tells us, if we consider a person or, better still, a society. A society includes the rich diversity of all its members, in all their conflicts and cooperative efforts. It is richer, not more empty, than any separate member of that society, just as a person is richer in content than any of the separate events which occur as part of his life. A person, a society, is 'universal', according to Bradley, just in so far as it brings into unity a diversity – as a class does, also – but it is individual, as a class is not. Yet its individuality, he argues, is incomplete: the completely individual can stand absolutely alone, whereas a society, or a person, always depends for part of its being upon its environment. It follows that society, as imperfectly individual, cannot be the Absolute itself. It can nevertheless show us, he thinks, how the Absolute can be at once perfectly individual, a true and all-encompassing Unity, without lacking universality, and can be universal without being devoid of content.

This much more Bradley is prepared confidently to assert: the Absolute must be 'experience'. 'An unexperienced reality,' he writes, 'is a vicious abstraction whose existence is meaningless nonsense . . . anything in no sense felt or perceived, becomes to me quite unmeaning.' At this point, Bradley falls back on the argument typical of epistemological Idealism: we cannot think of anything without thinking of it as being experienced and therefore it cannot *be* without being experienced. And yet at the same time, he does not wish to say that the Absolute is experienced – which would mean that an experiencing subject somehow lay outside of it; it is *experience*, merely.

Here then is Bradley's Absolute – 'an all-inclusive and super-relational experience'. It is not a mind, not a spirit,* any more than it is experienced *by* a Mind – either hypothesis would involve the reality of relations. 'We can form the general idea,' he writes, 'of an absolute experience in which phenomenal distinctions are merged, a whole become immediate at a higher stage without losing any richness.' This idea, realized in detail in a way which we are quite unable to understand, is the Absolute.

How is the Absolute, thus conceived, related to the multitude of its appearances? To talk of the Absolute's 'relations' is, it follows from Bradley's earlier argument, to talk improperly; and, indeed, any statement we make about the Absolute and its appearances is bound to be defective, just because it must use the language of thought, of 'truths'. But every appearance, in virtue of the fact that the Absolute is all-inclusive, must somehow find a place for itself in the Absolute.[22]

How can this be, we naturally ask, since appearances are self-contradictory and the Absolute is wholly self-consistent? Bradley's answer depends upon the special theory of contradiction which he had already worked out in his chapter on 'The Negative Judgment' in *The Principles of Logic*. On the ordinary view, the contradictory of 'X' would be 'non-X', that which is intrinsically opposite to X; then no Absolute, however generously encompassing, could enfold both 'X' and 'non-X' into its unifying embraces. But, according to Bradley, 'non-X' should be interpreted as meaning 'that which is different from or other than X', as referring, however vaguely, to another positive term Y.† Thus, for example, to say that 'A is not red' is a way of asserting, if Bradley is right, that it is some other colour, green perhaps.

---

*Yet Bradley ends *Appearance and Reality* with what he calls 'the essential message of Hegel': 'Outside of spirit, there is not, and there cannot be, any reality, and the more that anything is spiritual, so much the more is it veritably real.' This is orthodox Idealism, but it is not sustained by *Appearance and Reality*.

†In technical language, Bradley identifies the contradictory and the contrary. See appendix to *Appearance and Reality*, Note A. Bradley's position is closely related to Plato's in the *Sophist*, but derives immediately, no doubt, from Hegel. See *The Logic of Hegel* (trans. Wallace), Ch. VIII.

Now, it is no doubt impossible, Bradley will admit, for 'the same point' to be both red and green 'at the same moment of time'. But to talk thus of 'points' and 'moments' is, he says, to use the fictions of science. If we think, as we ought to do, in terms of diversified systems, there is no difficulty, Bradley maintains, in seeing how both red and green can appear within such a system. 'If one arrangement has made them opposite, a wider arrangement,' he writes, 'may perhaps unmake their opposition, and may include them all at once and harmoniously.' Certainly, we shall still find it difficult to understand how all the contradictions of everyday life could thus be resolved. But we do not need to know, Bradley says, *how* this can happen. We need only know that it is *possible* for contradictions to be overcome and that the Absolute *must* so transcend them. For – in a famous formula – 'what is possible and must be, is'.

Appearances, then, are all transcended in Bradley's Absolute. The good, the beautiful, the true – the Idealist trinity of values – are none of them there present in their familiar form. The evil, the ugly, the false must all have their rights as appearances respected; somehow, the Absolute finds a place for them. But Bradley does not draw the conclusion that all differences in value vanish. Some appearances, he thinks, stand closer to the Absolute than others; these are the most real and the most valuable. Of each appearance, he tells us, we must ask the question: with how much supplementation could this pass into the Absolute? The less the supplementation, the greater the reality of the appearance. The test of reality, for him, is coherence and comprehensiveness.

What we call 'error'[23] needs, Bradley says, supplementation of the most serious kind. He rejects the view that an error is *utterly* without reality: it is simply more false than other judgements, all of which are in some measure erroneous in so far as they fail to specify the conditions under which alone they would be true. 'The book is red', we are ordinarily content to say, but it is red, Bradley objects, not *absolutely*, as the form of our judgement falsely suggests, but only under conditions which we ought to, but never fully can, describe – never can because they involve the whole of Reality.[24] Such a judgement, if true, has for Bradley this much virtue – it is at least in some measure coherent with our other judgements about the book. If it be false, it still has a certain reality in so far as it is about *something*, but it is now inferior in coherence and, so far, in reality.

In either case, however, 'the book is red' is, by Bradley's standards, a judgement of the poorest sort, devoid of any but the slightest degree of comprehensiveness. The same is true of all those 'observable facts' in which the empiricist hopes to find reality. 'It is only the meaner realities,' he writes, 'which are able to be verified as sensible facts.' God, in contrast, has, according, to Bradley, a high degree of reality, in so far as he acts as a comprehensive object of worship, a comprehensive system of explanation.

This is Bradley's final answer to materialism. Not only are its 'facts' devoid of reality, in the fullest sense of that word, but even as appearances their degree of reality is of a lowly order. 'According to the doctrine of this work,' Bradley wrote in the Appendix to *Appearance and Reality*, 'that which is highest to us is also to the Universe most real, and there can be no question of its reality being somehow upset. In commonplace Materialism, on the other hand, that which in the end is real is certainly not what we think highest, this latter being a secondary and, for all we know, a precarious result of the former.' Of so much Bradley felt confident, although he does not attempt to undertake what he regards as the task of a completed metaphysics – the determination of the order of reality of every type of appearance. Not every Idealist, however, was satisfied with the conclusion that spirit, although not fully real, is at least more real than matter. Bradley had destroyed the antithesis between nature and spirit, fact and value, and so far he had fulfilled the task of Idealism in its struggle against 'the mechanical world-view' and its concomitant, an easy supernaturalism. But in the process, many of his critics thought, he had brought morality and religion to ruins.

CHAPTER 4

Personality and the Absolute

ANDREW SETH'S[1] *Hegelianism and Personality* appeared in 1887, six years before Bradley's *Appearance and Reality*. Only four years previously, Seth had been largely responsible for the publication of the neo-Hegelian *Essays in Philosophical Criticism*; his own contribution to that volume was unmistakably Hegelian in spirit. Yet *Hegelianism and Personality* is a protest against the whole tendency of Hegelian philosophy in the name of 'the unequivocal testimony of consciousness' – a protest which adumbrates what were to be the main lines of the 'Personal Idealist' criticism of Bradley.

Seth is, in part, reverting to the Scottish tradition, which he had explored in his *Scottish Philosophy: A Comparison of the Scottish and German Answers to Hume* (1885); philosophy, he now thinks, has somehow to justify, but must never venture to question, our 'natural belief' in God, in personal identity, in the existence of an external world. But Seth appeals also to the testimony of Lotze, whose philosophy he interprets in a sense favourable to the Scottish point of view. 'The attentive reader of Lotze,' so Bradley wrote, 'must have found it hard to discover why individual selves with him are more than phenomenal adjectives. For myself I discern plainly his resolve that somehow they have *got* to be more.' This is true also of Seth's philosophy: selves have *got* to be more than 'phenomenal adjectives', more, that is, than appearances of the Absolute.

In Hegelianism, Seth argues, all distinctness, all particularity, vanishes. The facts of nature are converted into mere exemplifications of general logical principles; human personality disappears into the Family, the Community, the Absolute. In contrast, Seth exalts the claims of the particular: 'The meanest thing that exists,' he writes, 'has a life of its own, absolutely unique and individual.' In order to consider it as an object of scientific knowledge, we must no doubt describe it in general terms. But this is only to say, Seth concludes, that knowledge

72

never grasps the thing itself – 'existence is one thing, knowledge is another.'*

This general defence of particularity Seth applies to the self. In Green's philosophy, he argues, the self is transformed into a logical device. It is merely *that which holds the world together*, and even at this level is reduced to an expression of the universal consciousness. This is not, Seth complains, the self which consciousness reveals to us, a self intensely personal – unique, he is prepared to say, even against God. 'Each Self,' he writes, 'is a unique existence, which is perfectly impervious, if I may so speak, to other selves. ... The very characteristic of a self is this exclusiveness ... I have a centre of my own, a will of my own, which no one shares with me or can share – a centre which I maintain even in my dealings with God Himself.' Selves exist, he admits, in relationship one to another – they recognize themselves as interacting with other persons and with nature – but in all such relations, according to Seth, they retain their uniqueness, their imperviousness.[2]

In Seth's philosophy, then, there is a trinity, God, Man and Nature, each having its own rights.[3] The difficulty, of course, was to show how these three distinct forms of reality were capable of interacting one with another, the very difficulty Hegelian Idealism had sought to overcome by interpreting all three as manifestations of a single Spirit. In his later writings, especially in his *The Idea of God in the Light of Recent Philosophy* (1917), Seth does much to soften the sharp edges of his original divisions. He regrets that he had ever described selves as 'impervious'; now he emphasizes the intimacy of their relation one to another and to God. He explains that although Nature does not depend for its existence on Man's knowledge of it, it still exists *for* man, as something he is to know and to enjoy. If God must be sharply distinguished from his creatures, it is nonetheless true, he now writes, that 'God and Man become bare points of mere existence – impossible abstractions – if we try to separate them from one another and from the structural elements of their common life.'

These concessions were by no means universally acceptable: Absolute Idealists thought that Seth still laid too much stress on individual selves, orthodox theologians disliked his suggestion

*Compare the existentialist doctrines described in Chapter 19 below.

that God is a mere 'abstraction' if isolated from Man, the new realists considered that he did not allow sufficient independence to Nature, the new 'panpsychists' that he distinguished too sharply between Nature and Mind. But the fact remains that Seth's philosophy had a distinct attraction for philosophers of a not too rigorous cast of mind, in search of a philosophy which would tread a comfortable *via media* between naturalism and Absolutism, science and religion, the rights of personality and the demands of the community. Thus there was generated a species of 'normal Idealism', as Metz[4] calls it, which flourished in provincial and colonial universities. Its adherents were some of them men of a wide culture, whose broad interests found satisfaction in Seth's eclecticism; but others carried their distaste for clear-cut distinctions to the point of woolly-mindedness. Philosophy at their hands was a medium for miscellaneous edification rather than a serious form of inquiry.

If Seth retreated somewhat from the individualism of his *Hegelianism and Personality*, this was because a new species of Idealism had arisen which pushed the independence of individuals to a point which Seth regarded as extreme, to such a point indeed as to threaten the very existence of God and Nature. This tendency can be observed in the work of the American Idealist, G. H. Howison.[5] Howison began his philosophical career as a leading member of the St Louis Philosophical Society: in a more uncompromising fashion than Seth, he turned against Hegel in the interests of 'personality'. Absolutism, so he argues, is an Oriental theory; Occidental man has an 'instinctive preference for personal initiative, responsibility and credit' which no monistic philosophy can ever satisfy, whether it be a naturalistic or an Idealistic monism.[6] A pluralistic Idealism, according to which Reality is an 'Eternal Republic' composed entirely of minds intimately linked one to another and to God, can make use, Howison thinks, of the Idealist arguments against naturalism without destroying individuality in the process. He will not admit that minds arise out of God: 'Not even divine agency', he writes, 'can give rise to another self-active intelligence by any productive act.' Every mind, for Howison, exists eternally in a society of spirits, with God merely a first among equals, although a first to which other spirits 'spontaneously make constant reference'.

'Personal Idealism' appeared in England, somewhat to Howison's indignation, as the title of a book (1902), edited by Henry Sturt, in which a number of the younger Oxford philosophers expressed their dissent from Bradley's Absolute Idealism. Howison obviously felt that his copyright had been infringed; and to make matters worse, many of the essayists were not 'Personal Idealists' at all, in Howison's sense of the phrase, but followers of William James, against whose philosophy much of Howison's polemical energy had been directed.[7]

Hastings Rashdall in his essay on *Personality, Human and Divine* came nearest to Howison: 'The Absolute,' wrote Rashdall, 'consists of God and the souls, including, of course, all that God and those souls know and experience.' Unlike Howison, however, Rashdall is not prepared to allow the eternity of souls. Each of them, he says, is created by God. But this concession to orthodoxy has to be counterbalanced by a heresy – God, Rashdall agrees with Mill, is finite, limited by the other selves which he creates.[8]

By now it had become sufficiently clear that the idea of Reality as a community of independent spirits could not easily be reconciled with the idea of God. Seth has no difficulty in demonstrating that Howison does not in fact limit God to the role of *primus inter pares* and that Rashdall can give no intelligible account of the relation between a finite God and the selves he creates; Rashdall and Howison can with justice reply that Seth's own account of the relation between God and individual selves is an uneasy combination of orthodox theism and unorthodox Idealism. J. E. McTaggart cut the knot. God must go: the real is a community of finite selves.

McTaggart's Personal Idealism is utterly different in tone and method from the loose-jointed pieties of Seth, Howison and Rashdall. He is, in point of ability, the Bradley of Personal Idealism; like Bradley, but unlike Howison or Seth, he has been criticized in detail by contemporary opponents of Idealism.[9]

But whereas Bradley had defined metaphysics as the finding of bad reasons for what we believe upon instinct, McTaggart is determined to find good reasons for what he believes on instinct; we are not entitled to our instinctive beliefs, so he argues, unless we can support them by metaphysical reasoning. 'No man is justified in a religious attitude,' he wrote in that instructive, semi-popular, work *Some Dogmas of Religion* (1906), 'except as a result of metaphysical study.'

The intent of *Some Dogmas of Religion* is mainly negative; McTaggart there sets out to show that popular theology cannot stand up to the probings of philosophical criticism.* In his other writings he is in search of a metaphysics which will justify a 'religious attitude' as he defines it – 'a conviction of harmony between ourselves and the universe at large'. For there to be such a harmony, he thought, the following conditions must be fulfilled: first, the universe must consist of spirit; secondly, spirit must be immortal; thirdly, spirit must be love or must contain love as a principal ingredient; fourthly, the universe must be good on the whole and must be developing towards a state of perfect goodness.

At first, he thought that he could satisfy these conditions with the help of Hegel's dialectic. Most British philosophers had dismissed the dialectic as Teutonic mystery-mongering; as McTaggart contemptuously remarked, they took over Hegel's conclusions while at the same time rejecting his proofs as worthless. In his *Studies in the Hegelian Dialectic* (1896) and his *A Commentary on Hegel's Logic* (1910) he made a genuine effort to think himself into the Hegelian method. But it is clear that he read Hegel with an eye on the conclusions he hoped to extract from him; no one has ever been convinced that the Hegel he describes exists outside McTaggart's fertile imagination. The most important of his Hegelian studies bears the somewhat un-promising and certainly misleading title *Studies in Hegelian Cosmology* (1901). This is an elaborate discussion of the ethical and religious questions which lay nearest to McTaggart's heart. He felt bound to admit that these were matters to which Hegel had paid the slightest of attention; in particular, Hegel, to Mc-Taggart's evident distress, had adopted an extremely casual attitude to immortality. Yet McTaggart was confident that the philosophical ideas which his *Studies* develop, largely by way of

*McTaggart, quite unlike the personal idealists generally, is a hostile critic of Christianity, considered either as an ethic or a theology. He wrote in a letter: 'Besides, if one was a Christian one would have to worship Christ and I don't like him very much . . . would you like a man or a girl who really imitated Christ?' See H. Rashdall: 'McTaggart's *Dogmas of Religion*' (*Mind*, 1906).

criticism of Lotze and Bradley, were Hegelian in spirit, however loosely they might be related to any Hegelian text.

These were years in which the Hegelian philosophy was being sharply attacked, especially by McTaggart's Cambridge colleagues, men like Bertrand Russell, who had turned strongly against the Hegelianism he had once admired, or G. E. Moore, who while he was not very much interested in Hegel himself, had devoted a great deal of attention to McTaggart's neo-Hegelian arguments.[10] McTaggart continued to believe that the Hegelian dialectic was of the first importance; the fact remains that when he came to write his major philosophical work – *The Nature of Existence* (2 vols 1921, 1927) – the method he employed was certainly not Hegelian.

The Nature of Existence is one of the most closely-knit works in the history of philosophy. It is almost unique in English philosophy – not unique, because this was Ferrier's method also – in attempting to work out a deductive metaphysics, which deduces its conclusions rigorously from indubitable first principles.

That something exists, McTaggart begins by arguing, is indubitable. His proof of this conclusion follows a Cartesian pattern: if we doubt whether anything exists, then this doubt, he says, must itself exist, i.e. our attempt to doubt is self-defeating. Such a 'something' must, he continues, be qualified. An unqualified something would be a bare nonentity, indistinguishable from nothing. Thus we are now in a position to conclude, he thinks, not merely that something must exist but that it really has qualities. And it follows from this, he argues, that there are qualities which it does not possess; for to say of anything that it has any specific quality is automatically to deny that it has other qualities. If, for example, it is square, it cannot be triangular. In asserting so much, however, we are, according to McTaggart, simultaneously affirming new qualities of our 'something'. For not to be triangular is to be non-triangular: more generally, in order not to have a quality a thing must have the negation of that quality. Thus whatever exists, he concludes, must possess a plurality of qualities, merely in virtue of the indubitable fact that to be anything at all it must have qualities. (McTaggart, it needs to be observed, uses the word 'quality' in its broadest possible sense: *non-white, existing, having many qualities*, to take only three cases, are all 'qualities'.)

The mere fact that it must be qualified throws light, McTaggart considers, on the nature of the existent. If it is to have qualities, there must be something for them to qualify, i.e. there must be a 'substance'. (As McTaggart uses that word, anything which can be qualitatively described – a sneeze, a group of card-players, the class consisting of all red-haired archdeacons – is a substance.) But furthermore – and McTaggart now takes his second step towards 'pluralism' – there must be more than one such substance. Once again the argument is Cartesian in form: if we try to doubt, he says, that there is more than one substance we are forced in that very act of doubting to admit the existence of at least two substances, the doubter and his doubt. Our doubt, then, would be self-defeating.

These substances, he continues, must all be similar, in so far as they all, at least, share the quality of existing; but they must also be diverse, in order to be distinguishable as 'many'. Since similarity and diversity are relations, McTaggart concludes that relations, like substances and qualities, must be real; Bradley's Absolute, devoid of relations and qualities, is thus rejected as demonstrably illogical.

Now the problem is to connect together these substances, which are so far considered as similar but isolated. For McTaggart, it will be remembered, hopes eventually to work towards the conclusion that what really exists is a *community* of selves. He makes use, at this point, of the conception of a 'derivative quality'. If *A* admires *B*, he says, *A* must possess the derivative quality of *being an admirer of B* and *B* the derivative quality of *being admired by A*. From this he infers that if any of a thing's relations alter, its nature must also change, since one of its derivative qualities will have vanished. If *B* ceases to admire *A*, for example, *A* will no longer be admired by *B* and will so far have changed its nature. An even more radical conclusion follows, he thinks: a change in any substance must involve a change in every substance. For if *B* ceases to admire *A*, every substance which was *similar to B in respect of admiring A* will lose that property, and every substance which was *dissimilar to B in respect of admiring A* will lose *that* property; and every substance must fall into one or the other of these categories. Thus, McTaggart thinks he has shown, substances must, for all their distinctness, be linked with one another in the most intimate of unities – the nature of every substance is dependent upon the nature of every other substance.

The community of substances is what McTaggart calls 'the Absolute'. It is itself a substance, he argues, because it has properties predicable of it, e.g. the property of being a system; but it is no *more* a substance than the substances which form part of it. He will not allow these ingredient substances to be condemned, in Bradley's manner, as mere appearances of the Absolute.

McTaggart's argument so far has been relatively straightforward, whatever we may think of its cogency. From this point on, the mesh is so closely-woven that only the most persevering concentration on the original text can hope to compass its interlacings. The problem McTaggart has to confront is roughly this: on his account of them, all substances are infinitely complex, for every substance – this, he says, is a self-evident and ultimate truth – has parts, and each of these parts will itself be a substance. Yet, since all substances are discriminable, it must be possible to give an account of each substance which is a 'sufficient description' of it, i.e. which will distinguish its nature from the nature of any other substance. How can a description be sufficient if, on account of the infinite complexity of the substance, it is bound always to be incomplete?

This difficulty McTaggart tries to solve by means of his 'Principle of Determining Correspondence'. 'Determining correspondence' is a relation between one set of parts of a substance and other parts of the substance such that a sufficient description of that one set of parts would act as a sufficient description of any other set of parts into which we might divide the substance – a condition which can only be fulfilled, McTaggart argues, if there are connexions of a very special kind between substances and their parts.[11] This principle is the culmination of his metaphysics, because he is going to argue in the second part of *The Nature of Existence* that, to our knowledge at least, only if substances are spirits can they be related to their parts by determining correspondence.

The first part of *The Nature of Existence* is supposed, as we saw, to be strictly demonstrative: McTaggart thinks he can prove, by using none but self-evident truths, that the Absolute is a community of substances which exhibit determining correspondence. Now he has a different problem to face. Does this metaphysics justify a religious attitude? At this point, he is prepared to admit, there must be some appeal to the empirical. For it is not possible, he considers, to demonstrate that the world *must be* the sort of world our religious attitude demands. All that metaphysics can show positively is that such a world is at least compatible with the conclusions of a demonstrative metaphysics – to which it can add the negative thesis that no other world *of those our experience enables us to envisage* would satisfy metaphysical requirements, so that the world as the materialist describes it, for example, cannot be 'real'.

Of the arguments in which this second part of his project involves him, the most discussed[12] has been his attack on the reality of time, which was first published in *Mind* as early as 1908 but now occupies its proper place within a developed metaphysical system; it will have to serve as an illustration of the general character of his argument. There are two series, he says, which we ordinarily describe as 'temporal'. In the first, the *A* series, events have a place either as past, present, or future; in the second, the *B* series, they are simply earlier or later. The *A* series, he argues, is essential to the idea of time; for when we describe events as 'temporal' we do not mean merely that they have predecessors and successors: we are making a reference, explicit or implicit, to the distinction between the present, the past and the future. This comes out, McTaggart thinks, in the fact that time is intimately related to change, which plays no part whatever in the *B* series. The fall of Rome always was and always will be earlier than the Renaissance; here there is no change. There is change only if we consider the Renaissance, for example, as a period which once was and no longer is, i.e. if we make use of the *A* series. If we destroy the *A* series, he concludes, change and time vanish with it.

Yet McTaggart thinks he can show that the *A* series cannot be real. For past, present and future, he argues, are obviously incompatible characteristics, which the *A* series nevertheless ascribes to each and every event. There is, on the face of it, an obvious reply to this accusation of contradiction – events, we would say, have these characters successively, not simultaneously. They *have been past*, *are* present, and *will be* future. But this can only mean, McTaggart objects, that there is a moment at which the event is present, a moment at which it is past, and a moment at which it is future. And each of these moments, he argues, is itself an event in time, i.e. is itself past, present and future. Thus our original difficulty breaks out all over again, and will continue to break out, according to McTaggart, in any solution we attempt to offer. In the idea of an event as past, present and future, he concludes, there lies a contradiction which no ingenuity can resolve. Time therefore – as self-contradictory – cannot be real.

But McTaggart will allow us to ask, at least, what it is that *appears* as time. Time, he tries to show, is a misperception of 'the C series'. This is an order of perceptions, each more inclusive than what we call its 'predecessor'. (From that vantage-point we call 'the present' we can perceive all that up to now has been, and from 'the next moment' can perceive as much, together with 'the present'). Thus a relation between perceptions replaces, in McTaggart's account of reality, the appearance of time.

By means of similar, but more elaborate, arguments, McTaggart sets out to show that matter, too, is unreal, that in reality nothing exists except spirits, which perceive one another, loving what they perceive with a love which is perfect passion and perfect understanding in one. Every other kind of mental life vanishes with time and matter into the limbo of appearances, as a misperception of reality. If this conclusion looks paradoxical, McTaggart will not admit that it is any the worse for that. 'No philosophy,' he writes, 'has ever been able to avoid paradox. For no philosophy, with whatever intentions it may have set out, has been able to treat the universe as being what it appears to be.' The only sort of paradox which is objectionable, according to McTaggart, is self-contradiction; in this sense of the word, it is common sense, not metaphysics, which is paradoxical. (If Cambridge should ever be unduly elated – or, what is much less probable, unduly depressed – by its common sense, let it remember McTaggart!)

James Ward[13] was also a Cambridge man, and also a rebel against the Oxford variety of Absolutism – which had indeed no

Cambridge defenders – but otherwise the two philosophers have very little in common. McTaggart either ignored or scorned science; Ward was a devoted Lotzean, whose philosophy incorporated science as one of its constituents. McTaggart had his own curious brand of religion, which was certainly not Christian; Ward was originally a clergyman, and remained a Christian theist. McTaggart was a philosopher's philosopher, if ever there has been one; Ward's work, in contrast, is of a relatively popular character, accessible to scientists or to theologians of a philosophical bent. In McTaggart's case, the difficulty is to give a summary account of a highly intricate pattern of argument; in Ward's case, to decide what he really meant to say on the issues of central philosophical importance. It is clear enough that he hoped to leave room somewhere in his philosophy for individuality and God, diversity and the Absolute; it is not at all clear how he proposed to reconcile their clamorous demands within a single system.

He first made his name as a psychologist, as a result of his famous article on psychology in the *Encyclopaedia Britannica* (1886), which dealt a mortal blow to the British tradition of associationist psychology.[14] On the associationist theory of mind, mind is a collection of ideas, and the progress of knowledge consists in the coalescence of such ideas, by means of associative mechanisms, into wider wholes. The entire process is conceived in terms of the analogy of atomic physics; ideas, like atoms, attract and repel one another. Ward, in contrast, approaches the mind as a *biologist:* mind, he says, is active, desirous; experience is not the passive reception of sensations, but the process of 'becoming expert by experiment'.

This theory of experience, and this criticism of the attempt to approach philosophical problems from the standpoint of a physicist, is carried over by Ward from his psychology to his metaphysics.[15] Descartes, he suggests, made a serious error, when he supposed that physics tells us 'what the world is really like'. Since the world the physicist describes – consisting of atoms in motion – is quite unlike the qualitatively diversified world of everyday experience, Descartes was driven into a dualism: there are for Descartes, and for the dualistic tradition which derives from his philosophy, two worlds – an external, material, mechanically operating world which is described by physics, and an internal spiritual world where qualitative diversity finds refuge along with art, religion and morality. Then an insuperable difficulty forces itself upon the philosopher's attention: how can these two, so disparate, worlds ever come into that intimate connexion which links, for example, our 'material' brain with our 'spiritual' mind? In trying to overcome this difficulty post-Cartesian philosophers have been driven to conclude either that only one of these worlds is fully real, the other being a mere 'appearance' or 'epiphenomenon'; or alternatively that neither is fully real, since both are appearances of the Absolute.

Ward attempts a different approach. Physics, he argues, is a mere set of abstractions; 'atoms' and the like are creations of the scientific mind, not concrete realities. The physicist – here Ward follows Grote – is inevitably led into abstraction, just because he tries to describe 'objects' as if they had an independent existence, out of all relation to mind. Naturalism accepts this abstraction as final; thereby, according to Ward's *Naturalism and Agnosticism* (1899), it confuses abstractions with realities – it is 'physics treated as metaphysics'.

If we want to see what reality is really like, we must turn, according to Ward, to history, not to physics. Historical inquiries take as their point of departure the active, striving, valuing individual, interacting with the world around him, seeking his own preservation and his own development. 'History offers us facts,' he wrote in his 'Mechanism and Morals' (*Hibbert Journal*, 1905), 'individuals, purpose and meaning, progress or decline, all that we miss in the world of mechanism.' There is in history, Ward thought, no falsifying abstraction of the subject from its objects; the historian takes as his theme the individual-in-his-environment, the concrete reality of everyday experience.[16]

Once we realize that this union between the individual and his environment must be our starting-point in any account of reality, we see also, Ward maintained, that there can be no sudden leap, no sharp break in continuity, between mind and matter. The materialist recognizes as much, but materialism, according to Ward, can make nothing of the striving, valuing individual: for to understand the individual, he thought, we must make use of that category of purpose which the materialist discards. But if we suppose that the environment, too, is purposive, spiritual, then, Ward tells us, all difficulties in relating man to his environment will vanish. We can understand at once, and otherwise cannot understand at all, how it happens that the mind discovers in its environment the possibility of fulfilling its ideals. This does not mean, Ward hastened to point out, that we must abandon the idea of scientific law: we come to see, however, that a law is a product of mind, of our way of dealing with the environment. A scientific law, in fact, is closely analogous to the laws which man creates in the communities to which he belongs.

So far, Ward's philosophy looks like a version of personal idealism, with biological over-tones. Reality, we expect him to say, consists of a plurality of cooperating and conflicting minds. This is how his contemporaries, for the most part, interpreted his philosophy. There is no doubt that he had been greatly influenced by Howison; Ward always insisted, nevertheless, that he was not a pluralist. Even although *The Realm of Ends* (1911) was mostly devoted to a sympathetic exposition of the case for pluralism, the outcome of it is that pluralism is not enough. 'The pluralistic whole,' he wrote, 'is a whole of experiences, but not a whole experience, a whole of lives, but not a living whole, a whole of being but without a complete and perfect being.' Only God, according to Ward, can unite this plurality into a single world. Ward admits, however, that he can offer no proof of God's existence; in those sections of his work in which he extols theism as an ideal he is so obviously the preacher rather than the philosopher that his philosophy has naturally been interpreted as a personalistic pluralism.[17]

Not content with the home-grown varieties of Personal Idealism, British philosophy imported others from the Continent. The distinctly Ward-like philosophy of Bernardino Varisco – his *I massimi problemi* (1910) was translated into English as *The Great Problem* in 1914 – had a certain vogue; and there was a more considerable enthusiasm for Rudolph Eucken, most of whose major writings were translated into English.

In Eucken's work,[18] Idealism is unashamedly transformed into a variety of spiritual revivalism. 'This work aims in the first place,' he wrote in the preface to the English edition of *The Main Currents of Modern Thought* (1912), 'at counteracting the spiritual and intellectual confusion of the present day.' This confusion, so he argued, no 'mere doctrine' could bring to order; what he sought to stimulate was 'a new sense of spiritual life' – a spiritual life defined as 'a self-contained life, itself giving rise to reality, a life which our human activity is far from penetrating, but towards which it strives as a great goal.'

There are echoes, in this pronouncement, of Hegelian Idealism. The fact remains that Eucken's 'philosophy of the spiritual life' was not philosophy at all, as men like Bradley and Hegel understood philosophy. This fact was made very clear by Bernard Bosanquet, who took upon his shoulders the task of defending the older Idealism against personalist heresies. 'There is in Eucken's immense literary output,' he wrote in the *Quarterly Review* (1914), 'no really precise and serious contribution to philosophical science. Free cognition has been submerged by moralistic rhetoric.'

Bosanquet was fighting a losing battle. Those two threads which, since Socrates, had been woven together in the philosophic tradition – the analytic thread, exemplified in such Platonic dialogues as the *Euthyphro*, and the ethico-religious thread, exemplified in the *Apology* – were no longer smoothly uniting. Socrates held them together, because his central doctrine was that knowledge is goodness: only the philosopher could know what life is really the best, and without that knowledge no one could live well. But for the new idealists 'life is more than logic' and the identification of goodness with knowledge is 'mere intellectualism'. Thus, as in Eucken's work, the exaltation of 'life' gives rise to a 'philosophy' which contains no sign of that critical method of investigation which had always been characteristic of the philosophic tradition. On the other side, the younger British philosophers were beginning to assert that philosophy is nothing but an analytic method, that the philosopher has no professional standing, is merely exercising his rights as a private citizen, when he prefers one way of life to another. The result was a cleavage within philosophy, which Bosanquet witnessed with alarm.

Bosanquet was an extremely prolific and versatile writer.[19] He is one of the few British philosophers who has taken aesthetics seriously – his *History of Aesthetic* (1892) is still a standard work;

his influence on political and social theory has been extensive; his polemical writings are almost a history of contemporary philosophy in themselves. Nothing human was alien to him – not even his fellow-philosophers. And yet this intellectual diversity did not lead him, as it had led others, into eclecticism; nor did it diminish his respect for logic. He is certainly a less rigorous thinker than Bradley – his zeal for reconciliation sometimes led him to make impossible concessions to his opponents, his enthusiasm for the good life sometimes overflowed into what is unmistakably rhetoric rather than argument – but he had no sympathy whatever with the attempt to denigrate logic in the supposed interests of a higher spiritual truth.

Amongst the earliest of his writings, indeed, was a substantial contribution to Idealist Logic – *Logic, or the Morphology of Knowledge* (1888) – and to logic he returned as late as 1920 in his *Implication and Linear Inference*. The pre-eminence of logic, furthermore, is a principal theme in his major metaphysical work, *The Principle of Individuality and Value* (1912). The Idealist opponents of logic, Bosanquet argued, did not know what logic is. For them, Ward for example, logical thinking is the process of working towards ever emptier abstractions, departing from the concreteness of everyday life into a world of general formulae which completely fail to convey the richness and diversity of our everyday experience. But to think of logic thus, Bosanquet protested, is to set up the abstract, rather than the concrete, universal as the logical ideal.[20] Logic, as Bosanquet understands it, is an attempt to grasp the whole – 'the truth is the whole'. To think logically, for him, is to move from a fragmentary experience to a system in which that experience is contained as a member, but enriched, now, by its interrelations with the system as a whole. We understand an experience for the first time, according to Bosanquet, when we see it as an ingredient in a system or, what is the same thing, see the system as ingredient in it. And this understanding logic gives us.

Logic, then, is 'the spirit of totality'; as such it is 'the clue to reality, value and freedom'. The power possessed by great ideas, a great character, great works of art, is to be measured, Bosanquet argues, by 'their logical power, their power to develop and sustain coherence with the whole'. 'Of all silly superficialities,' so he sums the matter up, 'the opposition of feeling and logic is the silliest.'

Fundamentally, Bosanquet is here accepting Bradley's metaphysics. All the same, there is a difference. Bradley's passion was directed towards the Absolute, Bosanquet's towards art, science and the community. If the metaphysical question is pushed, Bosanquet will no doubt admit that there is no true unity short of the Absolute. But whereas Bradley said 'that is only an *appearance* of the Absolute', in a depreciatory tone of voice, Bosanquet was delighted – 'that is an appearance of *the Absolute*'. 'A careful analysis,' he writes, 'of a single day's life of any fairly typical human being would establish triumphantly all that is needed in principle for the affirmation of the Absolute.' It would show us, he thought, how evils can be transmuted into higher goods – 'toil into happiness by seeing it as a pledge of devotion, and pain into love by the depth of the tenderness it evokes, and hardship into courage by its revelation of what a man is able to be.' More important still, it would show us how our personality can be submerged 'in an experience which is deeper as well as wider than our minimum self'.

These 'deeper and wider experiences' – Art, Science, Religion (defined as 'absorption in a good'), social participation – are what, on Bosanquet's view, possess real value, so far as anything short of the Absolute can be valuable. Bosanquet's emphasis on 'individuality' might momentarily deceive the careless reader into believing that for him, as for the personal idealists, value belongs to what we commonly call 'individuals' – individual persons. Nothing could be further from the truth.[21] The 'individual' in which value resides is, Bosanquet writes, 'that which is capable of standing by itself'; no separate person is such an 'individual'. 'The deepest and loftiest achievements of men do not belong to the particular human being in his repellent isolation,' he wrote in the preface to his *Philosophical Theory of the State* (1899) – and this phrase 'repellent isolation' is a recurrent theme in his philosophical writings. Human achievement, on his view, depends upon the capacity of the human being to engage in activities which carry him *outside* himself, whether in his struggles with nature or his participation in broad social movements. Apart from these struggles and that participation a 'person' collapses into nonentity.

That is the ground of his objection to pan-psychism: 'It is things, is it not?, which set the problems of life for persons; and if you turn all things into persons, the differences which make life interesting are gone.' Bosanquet welcomed 'the new Realism' inasmuch as it emphasized the fact that the objects of mind are independent of mind, resisting its endeavours and thus stirring up its latent powers; he came to dislike the name 'Idealism' because it carried with it the suggestion that Nature exists only as a product of our own mind. He felt no hostility towards physiological accounts of mind's origin; indeed, McTaggart, in his review of 'The Principle of Individuality and Value' (*Mind*, 1912), complains that 'almost every word Dr Bosanquet has written about the relations between mind and matter in this chapter [Lecture 7] might have been written by a complete materialist.'

Here is a crucial difficulty in Bosanquet's philosophy; for he is not, of course, a materialist. In the end, he is bound to affirm, Nature is mind-dependent; how can this be so if Nature is essential for the existence of mind?[22] 'Nature,' he says, 'is the world of space and time, abstracted from our momentary attitude and considered as self-existent, although at the same time held to be possessed of qualities which presuppose it to be in relation with a cognitive, sentient, purposive and emotional being.' Minds, on this view, bring to Nature a spirit of totality; without that spirit Nature would disintegrate. Yet equally, he considers, without Nature Mind is empty of all content. 'Mind has nothing of its own but the active form of totality: everything positive it draws from Nature.' What then becomes of the supremacy of mind over matter, personal idealists complained, if mind is as much dependent on Nature for its content as Nature is on mind for its form?

At every point, in fact, Bosanquet rejects the case against materialism which writers like Ward were trying to build up. Ward had tried to reinstate teleology; natural processes, so he argued, are inexplicable unless we think of them as having ends or purposes, and hence as being themselves minds or, at least, guided by minds. Bosanquet will have none of this. To talk of 'guidance', he objects, is to return to precisely that intercalation of the ideal in a natural world against which Caird had protested. It suggests, as he explained in a letter to Ward, that Mind and

Nature are two distinct entities, one of which 'guides' the workings of the other; this way of describing the relation between Mind and Nature destroys, he thought, their 'vital complementarity'.

In an address to the British Academy on *The Meaning of Teleology* (1906) Bosanquet worked out in more detail his criticism of 'the new teleology'. 'If I read the tendency aright,' he says, 'the reaction against mechanism is going near to destroy the idea of the reign of law, and to enthrone the finite subject as the guide and master of nature and history. If this is rightly read, we shall have to recall the mechanist, along with Spinoza, in the interests of the philosophy of history, and the theory of religion.' In 'the new teleology' he saw two distinct ideas: the first, that natural processes pursue ends, the second, that only such ends are valuable. Thus all values are relegated to the future, as objects of pursuit. But value, Bosanquet argues, lies here and now – 'the ideal is what we can see of the whole.' The only 'sane' sort of teleology, according to Bosanquet, consists in the recognition that every particular thing has a place in the scheme of things, i.e. in the Absolute. Within such a scheme, he was convinced, there is room for the existence of regular natural processes, working in a 'mechanical' fashion, out of which finite consciousnesses can themselves arise. 'Human ends,' he wrote, 'presuppose, accept and are founded in the actual body' – the body whose workings, however, themselves form part of a teleological scheme of things. The total scheme, on this view, not particular strivings, constitutes the Ideal. For that reason, too, it is absurd to demand immortality for the individual self; all that matters is the permanence of value, which the scheme itself guarantees.

Bosanquet's idealism attracted few disciples. In the eyes of those philosophers, a growing number, who identified philosophy with logical analysis, Bosanquet was an old-fashioned rhetorician; yet he was not sufficiently a Christian to please the theologians, nor enough of a scientist to attract the attention of idealistically-minded physicists. Of those who did follow in his footsteps, perhaps the most notable was R. F. A. Hoernlé. Hoernlé was particularly attracted by Bosanquet's broad-mindedness, which he tries to push in the direction of a 'synoptic philosophy'.

His talent was devoted rather to the skilful and sympathetic interpretation of philosophy than to the working out of fresh philosophical ideas.[23]

In America, Bosanquet's version of Idealism struck a responsive chord in men like J. E. Creighton who made use of arguments derived from Bosanquet against the rising tides of American pragmatism.[24] But America already had an Absolute Idealism of its own in the writings of Josiah Royce, who with his Harvard colleague and contemporary William James first made England conscious of American philosophy.[25] At Royce's hands, Absolute Idealism is desperately trying to maintain itself against personal idealism and, even more, the new tendencies in philosophy which the work of James exemplifies; the transformation it underwent in the process testifies to the force of the new ideas that were threatening to destroy it.

In the first place, Royce's approach to philosophy is epistemological; the theory of knowledge, not the theory of reality, is to be the road to the Absolute. 'Ontology,' so he wrote in an early article on 'Mind and Reality' (*Mind*, 1882), 'is play, the theory of knowledge is work. Ontology is the child blowing soap-bubbles, philosophical analysis is the miner digging for gold.' In this contrast can be detected the influence of 'the return to Kant', the vogue for epistemology against which Bradley and Bosanquet protested.*

Mill and Berkeley had shown, Royce thought, that all our experience is of 'phenomena' or 'ideas'; their arguments were sufficient to destroy the conception of a world that is merely natural, quite independent of mind. Yet he was dissatisfied with Mill's description of physical objects as 'permanent possibilities of sensation' on the ground that it left the status of these 'possibilities' completely obscure. 'What kind of unreal reality,' Royce asked, 'is this potential actuality?' When, in everyday life, we describe something as 'possible', we mean, Royce argued, simply this: that we can *imagine* it as happening. Such 'possibilities' are still ideas of ours. They do not lead us beyond our own ideas – as Mill's 'permanent possibilities' are supposed to

*Thus Bosanquet: 'I don't really believe in epistemology' (1914); and Bradley's ironical footnote: 'I am not competent to give any opinion as to what is to hold good within "Epistemology"' (1900).

lead us – to a world which exists even when we are not conscious of it, a world we explore, as distinct from making. There is in fact, according to Royce, only one way in which we can pass from our discontinuous and fragmentary ideas to a world which is continuous and systematic – by supposing that there is an 'absolute experience to which all facts are known and for which all facts are subject to a universal law'.

This argument, Royce admits, leads to nothing more substantial than a postulate. It does not prove that there is absolute experience; it merely asserts that there must be such an experience *if, as we cannot help believing, there is a continuous and systematic world of facts*. It still leaves open the possibility that this belief, strongly though we hold it, is actually erroneous. Royce is not content to leave the matter at such a dubious level; he looks for a demonstration that there *must be* an absolute experience.

Now comes Royce's *tour de force*. The great stumbling-block of Absolute Idealism had been error; how, its opponents asked, can error 'have a place in Reality'? But in Royce's Idealism the existence of error – itself indubitable, he argues, since to deny the existence of error would be to describe the view that error exists as 'an error' – compels us to admit an Absolute. According to traditional empiricism, error consists in having an idea which 'fails to agree with its object'. Royce raises an obvious objection: there is no error merely in having an idea which 'fails to agree', there is error only if our idea fails to agree with entities with which we *meant* it to conform. To be mistaken, he concludes, is to have a certain intention: an erroneous idea is one which fails in its purpose, which does not indicate what we intended it to indicate. There is error in the idea of a bent stick, he says, only if that idea is intended as a means of revealing the shape of a stick which is actually straight. Therefore, Royce draws the consequence, the fact that an idea of ours is erroneous can be recognized only by an intelligence which is capable of considering both our idea and what that idea, in some measure, has failed to reveal to us. 'An error,' Royce summarizes his conclusions in *The Religious Aspect of Philosophy* (1885), 'is an incomplete thought that to a higher thought is known as having failed in the purpose that it more or less clearly had, and that is fully realized in this higher thought.' We can come to be conscious of our own

errors, he thinks, in so far as we are able partially to identify ourselves with the standpoint of this higher thought, of which we are
ourselves a fragment. But the number of possible errors is infinite,
since every truth brings with it an endless number of errors[26] – the
error of supposing that it is false, the error of supposing that this
error is not an error and so on. Only an Absolute experience, he
concludes, can sustain the reality of error; no finite experience
can ever be conscious of more than a particle of the errors which
the world contains.

On Royce's view, it should be observed, error is not something
we, as human beings, fall into, something dependent for its
existence on our existence. 'Here is this stick, this brick-bat, this
snow-flake,' he writes, 'there is an infinite mass of error possible
about any one of them, and notice, not merely possible is it, but
actual. . . . You cannot in fact *make* a truth or a falsehood by
your thought. You only *find* one. From all eternity that truth was
true, that falsehood false. Very well, then, that infinite thought
must somehow have had all that in it from the beginning.'
Santayana protested that to argue thus was to found a philosophy
upon a mere 'biological accident' – the fact that human beings
make mistakes – but error, to Royce, was not a biological
accident. It was a logical necessity, an essential counterpoise to
truth. For to say that the truth has been arrived at, he thought,
was at the same time to announce the existence of certain errors
e.g. the error of supposing that the truth had *not* been reached.

So far, the Absolute is envisaged, in the traditional Idealist
manner, as 'experience'. Yet in the opening chapter to *The
Religious Aspect of Thought*, in which Royce is discussing those
religious and ethical questions which, on his view, 'deserve our
best interests and our utmost loyalty', the Absolute appears in
the guise of an Absolute Will. For Royce's ethics is Kantian:
the moral life is the identification of the human with the divine
will. Thus the Absolute to which his ethics entices him – a Divine
Will – looks very different from the Absolute which his epistemology is intended to sustain.

In *The World and the Individual*, the most influential of his
books, the will comes more prominently to the fore – the in-
influence of James coincides with the pressure of Royce's moral
outlook.[27] The emphasis is still epistemological; but an 'idea'

is now no longer a representation; it is rather – following G. F. Stout's *Analytic Psychology* – a plan, a scheme for dealing with things. An idea, he says, has an 'internal meaning', which is the purpose it fulfils. Suppose we sing a tune to ourselves; the 'internal meaning' of that tune, as Royce defines it, is the purpose that our singing satisfies. But, as well, the tune may be a copy of one we have heard on some previous occasion; we may say to ourselves: 'That is "God Save the Queen".' This reference to an original is what Royce calls the 'external meaning' of the tune.

Royce seems at first to be making a sharp contrast between the 'internal meaning' of the idea as conative, an expression of purpose, and the 'external meaning' as cognitive, as picturing an outside world. The conception of such an 'outside world', however, Royce rejects as unintelligible. No two things, he argues as McTaggart was to argue in *The Nature of Existence*, can be independent of one another; a change in either carries with it a change in the other, a loss of similarities and dissimilarities. Thus the idea of a world which is 'just there', which would be the same whether anyone knew it or not, a world which exists in utter independence of mind, Royce rejects as illogical.

There are not then, for Royce, two distinct entities, the idea and its 'external meaning'. He likes to illustrate his position by considering such a case as that in which we count, say, ten ships. Surely, it would ordinarily be said, the number of the ships is quite external to and independent of the idea which refers to them! But how does it happen, Royce asks, that we count ships instead of masts? Why do we include just these ships and exclude other ships? The answer must be, he thinks, that our own purposes, our own plans, constitute the very object which we count: it exists only as the objective of our intentions. The 'external meaning' for Royce depends upon, continues and develops, the 'internal meaning'.

An idea, Royce had already argued, is a fragment of Absolute Experience. This same conclusion he now expresses by saying that an idea is a partial and incomplete purpose, ever striving to realize itself more fully by passing beyond its own limits. In its search for a wider system in which it can be fulfilled the 'idea' is at its most cognitive; its 'external meaning' is precisely the idea's reference to something beyond itself. But this is only to say, Royce argues, that the idea now finds its place in a wider purpose, a broader plan, than any it can bring to fruition with its own resources.

At this point, Royce is once again diverted from Absolutism by the tendencies of his time and place. He is not prepared to say that the individual purpose is *totally* absorbed in the broader plan, or that its individuality is mere appearance. Each constituent element in the total scheme, on Royce's view, makes its unique contribution, and thus has a true individuality. In the Absolute, he says, each person is what he is in the eyes of those who love him – something uniquely precious, irreplaceable. 'Arise, then, freeman, stand forth in thy world. It is God's world. It is also thine.'

That, then, is Royce's conclusion, expressed with his notorious 'Californian eloquence'. To European Absolutists, Royce's concessions to the individual will were a betrayal of the Idealist tradition; to very many Americans, his Absolutism was a betrayal of American individualism. When they – men like William James – attacked Absolutism, it was Royce above all whom they had in mind. 'The radical misapprehension of English Idealism which appears to me to prevail in recent American writers,' wrote Bosanquet in his *The Meeting of Extremes in Contemporary Philosophy* (1921), 'is largely due to Royce.' On Royce's philosophy, young America sharpened its teeth, just as in England the young philosophers were sharpening their teeth on Bradley.

CHAPTER 5

Pragmatism and its European Analogues

MODERN philosophy was founded on the doctrine, uncompromisingly formulated by Descartes, that to think philosophically is to accept as true only that which recommends itself to
Reason. To be unphilosophical, in contrast, is to be seduced by
the enticements of Will, which beckons men beyond the boundaries laid down by Reason into the wilderness of error. In
England, Locke had acclimatized this Cartesian ideal. There is
'one unerring mark', he wrote, 'by which a man may know
whether he is a lover of truth for truth's sake': namely, *the not
entertaining any proposition with greater assurance than the
proofs it is built upon will warrant*. Nineteenth-century agnosticism
reaffirmed this Lockean dictum, with a striking degree of moral
fervour. The *locus classicus* is a passage in W. K. Clifford's 'The
Ethics of Belief': 'It is wrong everywhere and for anyone, to
believe anything upon insufficient evidence.'[1]

Clifford wrote these words with confidence, with the air of a
man who had progress on his side. Yet the revolt against 'intellectualism' – as its critics liked to call the Cartesian ideal – was
already well under way, in Germany especially. We have already
observed the new 'voluntarism' at work, in a somewhat at-
tenuated form, in the philosophy of Lotze, and rather more
strikingly in the writings of philosophers otherwise so different
as Eucken, Royce and Ward. But it sometimes took a still more
radical turn, most familiar to English readers through its effects
on the philosophy of William James.

Once more, the starting-point is Kant. 'I must abolish *knowledge*,' he wrote in the Preface to the Second Edition of his
Critique of Pure Reason, 'to make room for *belief*.' There is no
way of demonstrating, Kant had argued, that anything exists
except those causally conditioned phenomena which constitute
'experience'. But the obligations of morality, so he had also
maintained, compel us to think of ourselves as free agents, i.e.
as having a 'real' – or 'noumenal' – self which lies outside the

causal system. It is easy to read this doctrine as an attack on the intellect in the name of a higher morality.

Hegel, with unity as his ideal, set out to destroy Kant's distinction between phenomena and noumena; his contemporary, Schopenhauer, sought rather to reinterpret it in an anti-intellectualist spirit.[2] Schopenhauer's first step is to convert Kant's 'phenomena' into 'ideas'. British empiricism, indeed, was often to serve as an ally in the struggle against 'the pretensions of the intellect'. Berkeley was right, Schopenhauer argues, in maintaining that what is perceived exists only for the perceiver. But unlike other nineteenth-century admirers of Berkeley, Schopenhauer did not draw from Berkeley's premises the conclusion that nothing *exists* except ideas. In this conclusion, he thinks, no human being could permanently acquiesce; inevitably, we seek for a 'thing-in-itself' which underlies the ideas we perceive and gives them meaning and significance.

Where are we to find it? Certainly not, according to Schopenhauer, in the world around us; there, nothing is to be met with except our own ideas. The secret lies within, in our consciousness of ourselves as possessing a *will*. For we understand an action, he says, when we see it as a manifestation of will, in a sense in which we cannot understand a mere relation of ideas. An action has a point, a sense, as willed, which is otherwise quite lacking to it. Yet our actions, considered as a part of the world we perceive, are themselves ideas. They have a double aspect, Schopenhauer concludes. As phenomena, they are ideas; as meaningful, they are manifestations of a will.

This same duality, Schopenhauer maintains, must be characteristic of *every* idea; we know of nothing which could lend our ideas significance except will and we cannot rest in the conclusion that they have no significance. We must think of them, he concludes, as concrete exemplifications of a will. Furthermore, since ideas make up a single system of reality there must, according to Schopenhauer, be *one* thing-in-itself – *the* Will – of which the world as a whole is a manifestation. This Will, he grants, is no doubt very different from our own, in that it is not 'conscious'. But our own consciousness – and this was one of the most influential of Schopenhauer's doctrines – is itself no more than an instrument of the Will, a device which it employs in order to conserve the individual and propagate his species. Only in Art, in the disinterested contemplation of pure forms, does Schopenhauer allow that thought can manage even for a moment to free itself from the endless struggles, the frustrations and disappointment, the satiety and disgust, through which the Will inevitably manifests itself. Even the genius – whose genius, Schopenhauer suggests, lies precisely in his capacity for looking at things objectively – can achieve the level of Art only at rare moments. Mankind, so Schopenhauer draws the moral, cannot hope to find permanent release from its sufferings and misery except in that utter extinction – the *nirvana* of Eastern religions – in which the Will secures its own abolition.

Schopenhauer's pessimism has left a permanent mark on human culture, partly through its influence on von Hartmann and Freud.[3] His depiction of thought as an *instrument* more immediately concerns us: according admirably with the new Darwinian biology, it came to be – as the 'instrumentalist' analysis of human thinking – the staple teaching of influential schools of psychology. In particular, William James is at this point in the direct line of succession from Schopenhauer.[4]

Another, less spectacular, line of descent leads from Kant to James – for all that James had no patience with 'back to Kant' as a slogan – by way of such neo-Kantians as F. A. Lange. Lange's version of Kantianism,[5] as developed in the second edition of his *History of Materialism* was, like Schopenhauer's, the product of reading Kant in the spirit of British empiricism. Phenomena are transformed into sensations; and whereas Kant had tried to discover the general 'forms of thought' to which experience must conform by analysing the distinctions of traditional logic, Lange sought to derive them from psychology. It is our human nature, he argued, our character as human beings, which determines the kind of world we experience.

Again like Schopenhauer, Lange is not prepared to push the view that our experience is of sensations to the positivist conclusion that we ought to make no assertions except such as describe the relations between such sensations. He agreed with Mill that there is no possible way of *proving* that anything exists except sensations, actual or possible – but so much the worse, he thought, for proof. 'Man *needs* to supplement reality,' he wrote, 'by an ideal world of his own creation.' Considered as anything but poetry – 'the creation of a home for spirit' – metaphysics is dismissed by Lange as arrant nonsense: but to criticize it as a form of knowledge is, he says, to miss its whole point. 'Who will refute a Mass of Palestrina, or convict Raphael's Madonna of error?' A good deal more was to be heard later of this view that 'metaphysics is a kind of poetry'.

Lange's followers, especially the Kantian scholar, Vaihinger,[6] went further than their master; they set out to show that 'fictions' are no less essential to science than they are to metaphysics. Science needs the atom, Vaihinger argues, even if the idea of an atom contains internal inconsistencies; providing that 'it renders services to the science of experience', any fiction is justified. The attempt to do without fictions, he tries to show in great detail, would be ruinous to science, fatal to practical life and to philosophy. To take Clifford's dictum seriously, according to Vaihinger, would be entirely to destroy science, as well as metaphysics and religion.

Similar views were dramatically and aphoristically expressed by Friedrich Nietzsche,[7] a man of remarkable insight and brilliant literary gifts, although not at all a systematic academic philosopher. 'Philosophers all pose as if their real opinions had been discovered through the self-evolving of a cold, pure, divinely indifferent dialectic,' he wrote in *Beyond Good and Evil* (1886), 'whereas in fact a prejudiced proposition, idea or suggestion, which is generally their heart's desire abstracted and refined, is defended by them with arguments sought out after the event. They are all advocates who do not wish to be regarded as such.' (Compare Bradley's description of metaphysics as 'the finding of bad reasons for what we believe upon instinct'.)

Nor can anything else be expected, on Nietzsche's theory of the mind. There is for him no independent faculty of pure Reason, constructing its demonstrations in isolation from the life of the passions. 'Thinking', he writes, 'is a relation of impulses to one another.' Out of the struggles of the passions to achieve predominance, philosophy arises, as an instrument in that struggle. Taken literally, he concludes, every 'logic' – every general view of the nature of things – is bound to be false: it is a pattern which we impose on things, not a pattern things themselves exhibit.

But he denies that we ought therefore to do without a philosophy. 'The falsest opinions,' he writes, 'are the most indispensable to us ... the renunciation of false opinions would be a renunciation of life, a negation of life.'

What, then, is the philosopher's task, if not to deduce metaphysical truths? Certainly not, Nietzsche is quite confident, to set himself up as an epistemologist: 'Philosophy reduced to a "theory of knowledge"; that is philosophy in its last throes, an end, an agony, something that awakens pity.' British empiricism he condemned as the complete abasement of the philosophical spirit. The philosopher, he considers, has a broader task – to act as 'a physician of culture'. He is the free spirit, who transforms our attitude to life by a 'transvaluation of values'. Christianity, socialism, altruism, egalitarianism are all of them, Nietzsche thought, symbols of decadence, of an impoverished life; by denouncing the thinness and poverty of these ideals, the philosopher assists the development of a more vigorous culture. In Nietzsche's works, in fact, the conception of the philosopher as a critic of ways of life – a conception which, as we noted, has come to be widely accepted in recent continental philosophy – received its most influential statement.

In England, although less conspicuously, the same anti-intellectual ferment was at work, especially, it is worth noting, in the writings of two men who, for all their distinction in other fields, were amateurs in philosophy. The first of these is Cardinal J. H. Newman in his *An Essay in Aid of a Grammar of Assent* (1870).[8] 'Life is for action' – that is his main theme. To approach religion by means of demonstrative arguments is, he writes, 'to take chemists for our cooks and mineralogists for our masons.' Conscience, not demonstrative proof, leads us to God. Newman's book was a striking criticism, in the name of religion, of the sort of view that Clifford was to maintain – that we ought to believe only what we can prove.

The much-discussed writings of the philosopher-statesman A. J. Balfour[9] issue in a very similar conclusion. It was said of Balfour that statesmen admired him for his philosophy and philosophers for his statesmanship. But even Bradley, not given to undue reverence for mortal – or immortal – beings, took him with some seriousness and James wrote of him in his *Letters* with admiration.

In his *A Defence of Philosophic Doubt, being an Essay on the Foundations of Belief* (1879), Balfour set out to show that the naturalism of nineteenth-century science rests on principles – the principle of the Uniformity of Nature, for example – which cannot possibly be derived demonstratively. This negative conclusion is the starting-point of *The Foundations of Belief* (1895). Naturalism, Balfour argues, conflicts with our moral and aesthetic sentiments, whereas theism satisfies them. If naturalism were demonstrable, he admits, it ought for all its distastefulness to be preferred to theism; but since it is not, our feelings should carry the day. He denies that there is any impropriety in thus bowing to our feelings: our beliefs, he says, are always determined to a large extent by non-rational factors.

It is important to notice that the nature of belief is the central theme in Newman's and in Balfour's philosophy, for that was a topic on which British empirical psychology had never been at its happiest. A belief seems to be more than a vivid idea, and yet there was no room in the traditional psychology for it to be anything else. J. S. Mill commented on the unsatisfactory character of his father's theory of belief; A. Bain, equally dissatisfied, tried to work out an alternative view. He was led to define belief as 'that upon which a man is prepared to act'; to this definition, according to C. S. Peirce, 'pragmatism is scarce more than a corollary'. Thus British empiricism and German voluntarism – which itself, as we have seen, had felt the influence of British thinkers – were moving in the one direction: towards a theory in which impulse or 'preparedness to act' is the foundation of belief.

German and British speculation were amalgamated in the philosophy of Charles Renouvier.[10] The leader of the French neo-Kantians, his philosophy, like Lange's, is a British empiricist version of Kant. 'Things are phenomena in respect of knowledge,' so he writes in his *Essay in General Critique* (1854–64), 'and phenomena are things.' He does not conclude, however – in Berkeley's manner – that they depend upon *me* for their existence. What I call 'me', he says, is itself a 'synthesis of representations', with no priority over those other syntheses I call 'him', or describe as being 'outside me'.

This epistemology brings him very close to James. But James was already quite familiar with similar doctrines in the work of

Mill; empiricism was no stranger to him;[11] he could, indeed, never be happy with any philosophy which did not base itself upon experience. What interested him was that Renouvier combined his empiricism with a full-blooded defence of free will. The empiricist tradition was deterministic; but James was made miserable by the conclusion that, as he put it, 'we are wholly conditioned, not a wiggle of our will happens save as a result of physical laws', a conclusion to which both his own empirical biological studies and empirical philosophy seemed inevitably to lead him. Against that doctrine his whole nature rebelled, to the extent of driving him into an inertia which he could in no way overcome.[12]

Thus Renouvier's defence of free will in the second (1859) of his *Essays in General Criticism* came to James as a deliverance. To it he ascribed, in the preface to his posthumously published *Some Problems of Philosophy* (1911), his release from 'the monistic superstition in which I had grown up'; his gratitude to Renouvier never lessened, however little he might sympathize with the metaphysical direction of his later writings. Renouvier had convinced him that a wedge could be driven between empiricism and determinism – and to drive that wedge might fairly be described as the main motive of James's philosophy.[13]

This is the background to his essay on 'The Will to Believe' (1895); the scandal that essay created is a testimony to the general ignorance of continental philosophy in Anglo-Saxon countries. James's main thesis can be very simply stated: men cannot help going beyond the evidence. 'The absurd abstraction,' he had written in 'The Sentiment of Rationality' (1879), 'of an intellect verbally formulating all its evidence and carefully estimating the probability thereof by a vulgar fraction, by the size of whose denominator and numerator alone it is swayed, is ideally as inept as it is actually impossible.' In other words – down with Clifford! Even in deciding what – laboratory experiments or the affirmations of mystics – is to count as 'evidence', we are already, James argues, coming to a conclusion which, by the nature of the case, cannot itself wholly depend on evidence. Nor is that single decision enough; it is impossible, according to James, to say to ourselves 'I shall accept as evidence nothing except the experiments and observations of trained scientists' and proceed thereafter on that basis. For there are many matters on which we are bound to make up our minds, whether we like it or not, although the evidence is far from satisfactory.

At this point, James accepts neo-Kantian agnosticism; on the major issues of metaphysics, he is content to assume, proof is out of the question. 'The attempt to demonstrate by purely intellectual processes the truth of the deliverance of direct religious experience,' he writes in *The Varieties of Religious Experience* (1902), 'is absolutely hopeless.' But to conclude that we ought therefore not to commit ourselves to a belief in God, James argues, is to decide to act as if God *did not* exist – and this conclusion, too, goes far beyond the evidence. It is in such cases as these, where a choice *has* to be made, that James upholds the right to believe. 'Our passional nature,' he writes, 'not only lawfully may, but must, decide an option between propositions, whenever it is a genuine option that cannot by its nature be decided on intellectual grounds; for to say, under such circumstances, "Do not decide, but leave the question open" is itself a passional decision.'

The question still remains whether there is such a genuine option in the case of free will or whether the 'intellectual grounds' of determinism are decisive. For James, no universe is habitable which does not contain genuine variety and genuine novelty: he stood for 'romantic spontaneity' against the 'hurdy-gurdy monotony' of Spencer and the 'block universe' of the Absolutists. But he was prepared to admit that his personal tastes could not decide the issue; it had to be shown, at least, that the case for determinism is not unanswerable. Renouvier had suggested to him the possibility of being both an empiricist and a defender of free will. But James thought that he could borrow arguments more substantial than Renouvier's from C. S. Peirce's defence of 'novelty'.

'He is so concrete, so living; I, a mere table of contents, so abstract, a very snarl of twine' – so, in his more amiable moods, Peirce[14] contrasted his own character with James's. At other times his slender resources of patience were completely exhausted by James's 'slap-dash methods'; and these moments of irritation were not uncommonly provoked just when James innocently imagined that he was being Peirce's disciple. The fact remains that there were aspects of Peirce's philosophy which – interpreted as James interpreted them – lent themselves admirably to James's purposes.

Peirce's 'tychism' is a case in point. Peirce, like James, rejected the 'mechanical' conception of natural laws. According to the mechanical view, a law is a 'brute fact'; to ask why one law exists rather than another is to raise a question to which, by the nature of the case, there can be no conceivable answer. To Peirce, on the other hand, a law is merely a habit which certain material objects have gradually adopted. And no situation, he considers, is ever completely describable in terms of such laws: 'At any time, an element of pure chance survives and will remain until the world becomes an absolutely perfect, rational, and symmetrical system, in which mind is at last crystallized, in the infinitely distant future.'

'Tychism', here, is three things: a metaphysics, according to which the world is evolving, *à la* Spencer, from 'a chaos of un-personalized feeling' to 'a rational and symmetrical system'; a philosophy of science, according to which natural laws are statistical regularities, no more; a theory of explanation, according to which 'law is *par excellence* the thing that wants a reason', as opposed to the ordinary view that 'explaining' means 'referring to a law'. In James's philosophy, on the other hand, tychism appears as a plea for *not* demanding reasons, for accepting irregularities as inexplicable brute facts – a proposal quite as painful to Peirce as the doctrine that regularities 'just happen'. Indeed, James himself came to feel that he had at first overstated the case for contingency; it had to be redefined in a sense in which it was not absolute, there being no actual 'jumps' in Nature. Once more, he appeals to Peirce; in this case, to Peirce's 'synechism', defined in an article in Baldwin's *Dictionary of Philosophy and Psychology* (1902) as 'that tendency of philosophical thought which insists upon the idea of continuity as of prime importance in philosophy, *and in particular upon the necessity of hypotheses involving true continuity*'. Peirce's emphasis is on the words italicized; he wants to avoid the supposition that there are ultimate inexplicabilities. Every scientific proposition, on his view, describes a continuity; it refers to a situation in which there are further distinctions to be made, other matters, therefore, to be explained. To set up as a hypothesis the existence of ultimate discontinuous atoms, for example, is to sin against the spirit of science, since atoms, as discontinuous, cannot be made the subject of further scientific inquiry.

James's synechism was very different from this. 'The common objection to admitting novelties,' he wrote in his essay, 'On the nature of Reality as Changing' (Appendix to *A Pluralistic Universe*, 1909), 'is that by jumping abruptly in, *ex nihilo*, they shatter the world's rational continuity. Peirce meets this objection by combining his "tychism" with an express doctrine of "synechism" or continuity....Novelty as empirically found doesn't arrive by jumps and jolts, it leaks in insensibly.' Thus all James means by 'synechism' is that change is continuous: novelties develop out of previous situations, which do not contain them – as rationalists had wrongly supposed – but are none the less not wholly discontinuous with them.

With his devotion to 'bridge-building', James identified Peirce's synechism with Henri Bergson's *devenir réel*. Peirce was not complimented. 'The only thing I have striven to do in philosophy,' he wrote to James in 1909, 'has been to analyse sundry concepts with exactitude.... It is not very grateful to my feelings to be classed along with a Bergson who seems to be doing his prettiest to muddle all distinctions.' To Peirce, philosophy was science or it was nothing: that by itself sharply separates him from James and from Bergson. 'The Will to Believe' had shocked him; the James-Bergson type of synechism was, in his opinion, philosophy committing suicide.

James and Bergson,[15] to a degree quite astonishing, had arrived independently at identical conclusions about the nature and limits of science. Bergson's importance for James was that he gave him confidence in the battle against 'intellectualism'. James had always imagined, he tells us in *A Pluralistic Universe*, that there must be '*an intellectual* answer to the intellectualist's difficulties' – he had sought for a new logic with which to meet Bradley's attempts to demonstrate the impossibility, as anything more than 'appearances', of that variety, plurality, novelty which James thought he could see in the world around him. Bergson convinced him that his search was in vain; the truth of the matter is that logic, working as it does with general concepts, is inadequate as a tool for describing life, 'reality' in the full sense. 'When conceptualism summons life to justify itself in conceptual terms,' he writes, 'it is like a challenge addressed in a foreign language to someone who is absorbed in his own business.'

Bergson's philosophy – first outlined in his *Essai sur les données immédiates de la conscience* (1889, English translation, with revisions, as *Time and Free Will*, 1910) – begins as an analysis of time. He contrasts time as we think about it and time as we experience it. Conceptually considered, he says, time is assimilated to space, depicted as a straight line with 'moments' as its points, whereas experienced time is *duration*, not a succession of moments – it flows in an indivisible continuity. This flowing quality, according to Bergson, is characteristic of all our experience: our experience is not a set of 'conscious states', clearly demarcated. Its phases 'melt into one another and form an organic whole.'

Why do we commonly suppose otherwise? Why do we think of things as separate and distinct, of time as composed of moments, space of points? Only because, Bergson replies, our intellect, for purely practical reasons, separates this flowing unity, this 'real becoming', into sharply defined, easily manageable, conceptualized entities. No harm is done, he is prepared to admit, and much practical advantage certainly accrues, provided only that this conceptualized world is not confused with reality itself. But such a confusion can easily arise. Our language consists of distinct words with well-defined outlines; this same distinctness we are misled into ascribing to the world we symbolize in language.

So far, this is extraordinarily similar to James's account of experience in his *Principles of Psychology* (1890) as 'a stream of consciousness'. James there drew attention to what he took to be the central error of traditional empiricism – that, for it, experience consists of isolated 'impressions' or 'sensations'.[16] 'Consciousness does not appear to itself chopped up into bits,' he protested, 'it is nothing jointed, it flows.' From the beginning, according to James, our experience is of the related – a fact which escapes our notice only because for practical reasons we have so strong a tendency to seize upon the 'substantive' parts of our experience, at the expense of the 'transitive' parts. This might be Bergson talking. But Bergson went on to make that clean break with 'the logic of identity' at which James, so he tells us, had not been able to arrive by his own efforts. Bergson's argument can be illustrated by his critique of determinism.[17] According to the determinist, the same motives acting on the same person always produce the same effects. This dogma is meaningless, so Bergson argues, because motives, persons, effects, never are the same. Only in the conceptualized world are there 'identical situations'; in reality, every experience is fleeting. To attack freedom with the 'logic of identity', with its talk of 'sameness', he says, is to use as 'a weapon against life' what ought to be regarded merely as a convenient technique developed by the living organism as an instrument for dealing with experience. Life comes first: logic is no more than one of its products.

If we are really to understand 'life', Bergson maintains, we must forget the clear-cut distinctions of logic; we must follow life's contours intuitively; we must not try to compress it into the rigid compartments beloved by the intellect. James interpreted him thus: '"Dive back into the flux itself then," Bergson tells us, "if you want to *know* reality, that flux which Platonism, in its strange belief that only the immutable is excellent, has always spurned: turn your face towards sensation, that fleshbound thing which rationalism has always loaded with abuse".'

The 'radical empiricism' at which James finally arrived is an attempt to take seriously Bergson's advice to 'dive back into the flux'. In the *Principles*, he came to think, his empiricism had not been sufficiently radical – for he was still working within a dualism of 'things' and 'thoughts'. Thoughts, he had set out to show, are continuous: it still remained possible that things, the facts themselves, are as discontinuous – or as indistinguishable from one another – as the most avid intellectualist could desire. But once James had made his way to radical empiricism, this contrast between thoughts and things vanished. There was now only the one world of experience; 'things' and 'thoughts' were no more than points of emphasis within that one world. It had commonly been supposed that within knowledge we must be able to distinguish a thinker from a 'thought about'. This James now denied. 'My thesis is,' he wrote in his *Essays in Radical Empiricism* (posthumous, 1912), 'that if we start with the supposition that there is only one primal stuff or material in the world, a stuff of which everything is composed, and if we call that stuff "pure experience", then knowing can easily be explained as a particular sort of relation towards one another into which portions of pure experience may enter.' We do not need to presume either 'things' or 'consciousness', considered as entities, in order to give an account of knowledge.[18]

If we discriminate some of our experiences as existing only 'in the mind' and call others 'real' or 'objective', this, James suggests, is only because they stand in different relationships to our other experiences. 'Mental fire,' he writes, 'is what won't burn real sticks. Mental knives may be sharp, but they won't cut real wood. With "real" objects, on the contrary, consequences always accrue; and thus the real experiences get sifted from the mental ones, the things from our thoughts of them, fanciful or true, and precipitated together as the stable part of the whole experience-chaos, under the name of the physical world'.[19]

Thus freed from the encumbrances of dualism, able to argue, therefore, that what is true of experience must be true of reality, James could more confidently defend plurality – and, with it, the possibility of novelty – against Bradley's Absolute. Absolutism, he was convinced, had to be destroyed: it discouraged human efforts to make the world a better place; it created an insuperable problem of evil – for evil is explicable only if we suppose that there is a finite God working as a force for good against a plurality of oppositions; and it denied the reality of the world we actually experience. No less than materialism, it set up a 'block universe', devoid of spontaneity, novelty, variety. Thus James's 'pluralism', like his defence of the right to believe, springs from his opposition to any suggestion that the individual human being is *forced* to act, or to believe, in one way rather than another because 'the scheme of things' leaves him no option.

The fundamental point at issue, James thought, was whether relations are intelligible. Bradley, as James interpreted him,* rejected pluralism on the ground that it implied the reality of

*But cf. Bradley's *Essays on Truth and Reality*, Appendix III to Chapter V 'On Professor James's Radical Empiricism'. Bradley objects that for him 'things' are quite as unreal as 'relations', whereas James interprets him as admitting things but rejecting relations. James's argument is most fully stated in 'The Thing and its Relations' (1905), reprinted in *Essays in Radical Empiricism*.

'external relations', implied, that is, that 'the same thing' could enter into a variety of different relations without losing its identity. And this, according to Bradley, leads to contradictions, because if a thing A is related to B, it must be different, merely as *related-to-B*, from any A of which we can truly say that it is *related-to-C*, i.e. it cannot be the same A which is related-to-B and related-to-C.

No better example could be constructed, James considers, to llustrate the absurdities to which an intellectualist logic leads. The *concept* of *A-as-being-related-to-B* is certainly different, so much he freely admits, from the concept of *A-as-being-related-to-C*. But he will not grant Bradley's conclusion that A *itself* must therefore be different in the two cases. Concepts are by their nature distinct and discontinuous; if, however, we turn our attention to experience we see immediately, he thinks, that it is continuous and discontinuous at once, containing terms which are externally related, or 'strung along', one to another. 'It really seems "weird",' James wrote, 'to have to argue (as I am forced now to do) for the notion that it is one sheet of paper (with its two surfaces and all that lies between) which is both under my pen and on the table while I write – the "claim" that it is two sheets seems so brazen. Yet I sometimes suspect the absolutists of sincerity!' The world, as James sees it, is a *collection*, of which some parts are conjoined and others disjoined; it has a 'concatenated unity' as distinct from the 'through-and-through' union which the monist demands. If idealists see it differently, he argues, this is only because they are blinded by their 'vicious intellectualism' which leads them to conclude from the mere fact that conjunction and disjunction are different *concepts* that it is impossible for the same *experience* to be both conjoined and disjoined. Once this intellectualist argument is 'seen through' then it will be obvious, James thinks, that the pluralist's 'concatenated' unity is precisely the unity which experience daily reveals to us.

Yet James does not wish to maintain that *all* intellectual activity is vicious: concepts, on his view, can be misused but they can also be used; the intellect sometimes falsifies, but it may also guide. What is the *right* use of concepts? That is the question which James's pragmatism sets out to answer.

Pragmatism (1907), in which James most fully stated his pragmatic point of view, is described in its sub-title as 'a new name for some old ways of thinking' and is dedicated 'to the memory of John Stuart Mill from whom I first learnt the pragmatic openness of mind'. James here rightly insists upon the continuity of pragmatism with the tradition of British empiricism; the first point the pragmatist makes is a mere restatement of the traditional empiricist view that a useful concept must be grounded in experience.[20] As early as 1867, when James had read little philosophy except the empiricists, he wrote thus of metaphysics in a letter to his mother: 'The way these cusses slip so fluently off into the "Idea", the "Inner", etc. etc., and undertake to give a *logical* explanation of everything which is so palpably trumped up *after* the facts, and the reasoning of which is so grotesquely incapable of going an inch into the future, is both disgusting and disheartening.' Here, already, is the pragmatic criticism of traditional metaphysics, in its essence. James, however, also emphasized his indebtedness to C. S. Peirce, from whom he certainly took over the word 'pragmatism' along with what he believed to be Peirce's theory of meaning. (It is typical of the relation between the two men that Peirce at once re-named his own doctrine 'pragmaticism' – 'which is ugly enough to be safe from kidnappers'!)

In Peirce's philosophy, pragmatism is a method of determining meaning, a method first explicitly set out in an article on 'How to Make Our Ideas Clear' in the *Popular Science Monthly* (1878).[21] He then summarized the method thus: 'Consider what effects, that might conceivably have practical bearings, we conceive the object of our conception to have. Then, our conception of these effects is the whole of our conception of the object.' This is obviously a carefully thought-out definition; the fact remains that it is not easy to interpret. Peirce made many later attempts to express the pragmatic principle in a form which really satisfied him, which would exclude nonsense without at the same time being a 'barrier to inquiry'.

James, Peirce thought, had pushed the pragmatic method 'to such extremes as must tend to give us pause' – too far, that is, in the direction of admitting nonsense; there was a danger on the other side that pragmatism might rule out, as meaningless, important branches of mathematics. In an article in the *Monist* (1905) Peirce, in an attempt to avoid these dangers, restates the pragmatic dictum thus: 'The entire intellectual purpose of any symbol consists in the total of all general modes of rational conduct which, conditionally upon all the possible different circumstances and desires, would ensue upon the acceptance of the symbol.' The emphasis now, it should be noted, has shifted from concepts to the more general category of symbols – what Peirce calls 'signs' – which includes words and sentences as well as ideas and concepts. Much of Peirce's philosophy, indeed, is an attempt to work out a satisfactory theory of symbolism.

Secondly, 'practical bearings' have been transformed into 'rational conduct'. Peirce had been misunderstood, to his horror, as restricting science to the 'practically useful' in its narrowest sense. The meaning of a symbol, he now says, is the rational conduct which it stimulates. Thus we understand 'lithium' if we know what steps to take in order to pick out lithium from amongst other minerals. A sign is gibberish if, like many of the signs of traditional metaphysics, it does not lead us to some particular variety of rational conduct.

This implies, of course, that we know how to decide what conduct is rational; Peirce happily accepts the consequence that 'norms' of conduct are fundamental to inquiry. Peirce's definition has the further consequence that meaning is 'social'. The meaning of a symbol, for Peirce, does not consist, as had so often been supposed, in the 'ideas' it represents in our mind; to understand a symbol we have only to consider the conduct which it would generate in a rational man.

In James's philosophy, there is no parallel to Peirce's struggle to arrive at a satisfactory formulation of the pragmatic theory of meaning. On the contrary, when A. O. Lovejoy in his 'The Thirteen Pragmatisms' (*JP*, 1908) demonstrated that the pragmatists had failed 'to attach some single and stable meaning to the term "pragmatism"', James was enthusiastic. This was fine, this proved how 'open' pragmatism was – an attitude very different from Peirce's scrupulosities and soul-searchings.

James was interested in the pragmatic theory of meaning mainly as 'a method of settling metaphysical disputes which might otherwise be endless'; for example, the dispute between materialism and spiritualism. The pragmatic method, as he understands it, consists in interpreting each such alternative metaphysical theory 'by tracing its respective consequences'. James set out to show, in the first place, that if we examine metaphysical hypotheses as we should scientific hypotheses – by considering what difference it would make to particular occurrences if the hypothesis were true – we can find absolutely no difference between them. There is nothing of which we can say that it *could not have happened* unless the world is spirit, or is designed by God, or is inhabited by men who possess immortal souls and freedom of will; there is no way, therefore, of excluding the possibility of an alternative metaphysical theory. But we are not to conclude, with the positivists, that metaphysics is empty, futile. For, James explains, metaphysical alternatives 'so indifferent when taken retrospectively, point, when we take them prospectively, to wholly different outlooks of experience'.

He illustrates his point with a contrast between materialism and theism. Materialism, he says, with its terrible picture of a world running to a standstill, offers us no promise for the future.* It destroys that spirit of hopefulness which theism sustains. Similarly, to take the case which James felt so keenly, the theory of free will 'pragmatically means *novelties in the world*'; it tells us that improvement is at least possible, it promises us relief if we help to make the world better, and in this promise, this encouragement to action, its whole meaning consists. We are *entitled* to believe in free will – that was the lesson of *The Will to Believe;* it cannot be ruled out as logically impossible – that is the importance of 'tychism'; it is the best belief to hold – that is the pragmatic conclusion.

James was more interested in truth than in meaning, and with some encouragement from F. C. S. Schiller's 'humanism' and John Dewey's 'instrumentalism', he speedily embarked upon a pragmatic theory of truth.[22] Truth, on the ordinary view of the matter, consists in 'agreement with reality'. This definition had usually been interpreted as meaning that truth 'copies' reality. Such an interpretation, James argued in his essay on 'Humanism

---

*This is a reference to that 'nightmare of entropy' which so troubled nineteenth-century minds. The physicist Clausius introduced the word 'entropy' to refer to the fact that in all thermal changes there is a certain loss of available energy. This physical theory was picturesquely restated as 'the Universe is running down', a contingency which provoked considerable alarm in some quarters.

and Truth' (*Mind*, 1904), makes truth useless, an 'imperfect second edition', a pale and pointless replica. Occasionally, he admits, a picture of reality may be helpful to us – in order to predict the future, for example – although even in this case a symbolic formula is often more useful than a 'copy'. But when a picture is useful, its usefulness, James points out, does not consist in the mere fact that it is a copy; it just so happens that a copy, under these special circumstances, enables us to deal more adequately with experience. This is the only sort of 'agreement with reality', he thinks, which has any point in it. 'To "agree", in the widest sense, with a reality can only mean to be guided either straight up to it or into its surroundings, or to be put into such working touch with it as to handle either it or something connected with it better than if we disagreed. Better either intellectually or practically!' Thus the true idea is defined by James as the idea it is the best for us to have, best in the long run. Truth becomes a sub-species of goodness.[23]

James does not assert, as his opponents so often alleged, that every idea we happen to fancy is 'true'; the goodness – truth – of a belief, he argues, is to be tested by its fruitfulness, just as the goodness of an act – James is a utilitarian – is tested by its consequences. The idea, then, must be measured up against 'reality'. 'Reality', for James, includes sensations, our pre-existing beliefs, and those abstract relations between concepts which constitute the subject-matter of mathematics. Unless it enables us to cope with this reality more effectively, James would have us abandon our idea as false. Since 'reality' is not static, truth, James argues, is likewise 'in process' – it is that which happens to an idea when it comes to be expedient. Clearly, also, truth must be a matter of degree. Even the theory of the Absolute, James wrote, with a tolerance that did more than all his polemics to annoy his Idealist opponents, has a certain measure of truth. In so far as it teaches us that the Universe is in good hands, it permits us to take a 'moral holiday' from our perpetual striving to improve the world; and it may sometimes be expedient for us to take such a holiday.

In England, James's philosophy attracted a number of supporters, of whom the most important was F. C. S. Schiller.[24] Of his first book, *The Riddle of the Sphinx* (1891), Schiller once said that in it he had been a pragmatist quite unwittingly. And certainly, although that work is for the most part an elaborate species of evolutionary metaphysics, Schiller was already proclaiming the inability of science 'to grasp the "Becoming" of things as it really is', was describing truth as a 'value' and God as 'an eternal tendency making for righteousness, not the responsible author of evil' – all typical Jamesian doctrines.

But the fact that Schiller began as a metaphysician and James as a biologist and an empirical psychologist made a considerable difference to the structure of their philosophies. To Schiller, the crucial point was 'Humanism' – the title of his main book (1903). Truth and reality, he constantly reiterates, are man-made; Protagoras was right in proclaiming that 'Man is the measure of all things'. In that article in *Personal Idealism* (1902) on 'Axioms as Postulates' in which he first avowed himself a pragmatist, he explicitly denies that 'there is an objective world given independently of us and constraining us to recognize it'. James did not wish to go so far. Schiller accused him of exhibiting too much benevolence towards the 'new realists'; the realists rebuked him for being tainted with subjective Idealism. The fact is that James was never very happy on either side of that particular fence.[25]

Schiller's main work, however, was his lively defence of the pragmatic theory of truth. Himself an Oxford man, he was in revolt against the smugness and rigidity which, to his apprehension, Oxford encouraged and even extolled. His very style was a protest; the flippancy of his manner and the violence of his polemics induced even James to advise him to pay more attention to the academic proprieties. Bradley was a worthy opponent – Bradley of whom Schiller wrote: 'he has exercised a reign of terror based on unsparing use of epigrams and sarcastic footnotes.'

Pragmatism, so Bradley constantly maintained, is riddled with ambiguities, and on these its attractiveness wholly depends. Interpret it one way, he said, and pragmatism is a set of commonplaces; in another, it is absurd. But by bestriding both interpretations at once, the pragmatist makes it appear that he is 'preaching a new gospel which is to bring light to the world', a gospel which is at the same time that 'old teaching of common sense which few but fools have rejected'. Schiller's reply is uncompromising: 'Mr Bradley boldly begins with an avowal that he has so far failed to understand the new philosophy. This did not seem a very credible or promising premiss for a critic of Mr Bradley's calibre to set out from, but long before I had finished reading I found myself entirely in agreement with him.' ('Truth and Mr Bradley', *Mind*, 1904; reprinted in *Studies in Humanism*, 1907). Bradley, according to Schiller, looked at pragmatism through the distorting spectacles of an intellectualist: truth to him was static, fixed once for all, a mere copy of reality. Bradley, retorting, denied that his was a copy theory of truth. He had always said that there is *some* point in asserting that truth is correspondence; the fact remains that, for him, the 'truth' of a judgement is in the last resort identical with its degree of coherence.

This particular theory of truth, outlined by Bradley in *Appearance and Reality*, had meanwhile been worked out in detail by the Idealist logician, H. H. Joachim, in *The Nature of Truth* (1906). Joachim had pointed out that since, for the Idealist, there could be no absolute truth short of 'the whole', the coherence theory of truth, itself a human product, could only be partially true. In the end, then – Schiller draws the moral – even the Idealist is forced back on a 'merely human' truth. Man must be the measure; the Absolute is useless as a measuring-rod, just because it lies beyond our grasp. Bradley had admitted that we seek the truth in order to satisfy the intellect. Did he not, Schiller argued, actually use pragmatic criteria when he had to decide between 'here and now' judgements, judgements at the level of appearance, the only sort of which we are capable? 'James was always most reluctant to reply to Mr Bradley's persistent and copious strictures on himself,' wrote Schiller in his 'The New Developments of Mr Bradley's Philosophy' (*Mind*, 1915), 'because he was convinced that it was much better to leave Mr Bradley to puzzle things out for himself, as he would then in the end convert himself to something remarkably like pragmatism.'

Bradley, indeed – although he could not abide Schiller – always recognized that he had some affinity with James, not merely in his doctrine of 'immediate experience',[26] but also in his conception of 'apparent', although not of 'real', truth. That there is more than a superficial resemblance between pragmatism and absolutism is still more strongly suggested by the philosophical career of John Dewey.[27]

Dewey has described his education in 'From Absolutism to

Experimentalism' (*Contemporary American Philosophy*, Vol. II, 1930). Huxley's physiological writings first aroused his philosophical interests: they set before him 'a type or model of a view of things to which material ought to conform'. Then came Hegel – bringing with him 'an immense release or liberation'.[28] For Hegel broke down those barriers between self and world, soul and body, God and Nature, which isolated the human spirit from the rest of Nature. Dewey's philosophy reformulates this Hegelian unification in naturalistic terms. The stimulus to this reformulation came from James – more specifically from the biological tendency of *The Principles of Psychology*. To James, human beings are alive; he does not dissect them into anatomical specimens. This same living human being is the centre of Dewey's philosophy, except that he is now, before all else, a *social* animal – at this point Hegel's influence was decisive.

Dewey's new manner first became obvious in his contributions to the Chicago cooperative volume, *Studies in Logical Theory* (1903), which he later reprinted in his *Essays in Experimental Logic* (1916). His object, we might say, is to make Idealist logic concrete. With Bradley and Bosanquet, he presumes that logic is the theory of 'judgements'. But a 'judgement', to Dewey, is always *somebody judging something*; where an Idealist begins from 'thought', 'the idea', 'the judgement', Dewey considers the processes by means of which an individual investigator arrives at his conclusions – 'judgements' or 'knowledge'.

Knowledge, on Dewey's account of the matter, is a reflective or intellectual grasp of a situation, which grows out of, but is not identical with, experience. Experience he defines as a non-reflective way of meeting a situation: eating a meal – as distinct from studying the digestive system – is an 'experience', and so is admiring a picture, talking to one's friends, building a garage, or falling in love. The characteristic mistake of the philosopher, he considers, is to suppose that his *reflections* upon experience are *experience itself*. 'The sensation of blue', for example, is obviously not the kind of thing we meet with in experience. Our experience, Dewey argues, is of things in situations; 'the sensation of blue' is a product of philosophical reflection upon experience. He rejects traditional empiricism on the ground that for it immediate experience is composed of a sequence of such sensations. Thus empiricism entirely falsifies, by intellectualizing, the character of our concrete experience.

It is a no less serious error, he maintains, to imagine that concrete experience is of discrete substances. A 'thing', properly understood, is, he writes, '*res*, an affair, an occupation, a "cause", something which is similar to conducting a political campaign, or getting rid of an overstock of canned tomatoes, or going to school, or paying attention to a young woman – in short, just what is meant, in non-philosophical discourse, by "an experience"'. It is 'things' in this sense, not substances, which make up 'our experience', as Dewey describes it – experience, from the beginning, is of happenings, things going on, things being done.

Just on account of its diversity, experience contains conflicts, points of tension. Out of such a conflict – a problem – inquiry arises, as an attempt, Dewey argues, so to modify experience as to resolve the problem. The first step in inquiry, according to Dewey, is to analyse the problem and envisage means of dealing with it (hypotheses). These diagnostic procedures Dewey will not admit to be 'knowledge'; they are the means by which knowledge is pursued. We have 'knowledge' only when we have so reorganized our situation that we can overcome the difficulties it sets for us.

This is why Dewey defines knowledge as successful practice.[29] Sharply to divide theory from practice, so he constantly argues, is fatal to both. Yet he does not accept the dictum that 'thought is for the sake of action'; thought, for him, is *itself* an action, the act of experimenting, trying out. And by means of this act, he emphasizes, our experience is enriched; the situation from which we began now has a wider meaning, as containing possibilities of which we were previously unconscious. This is the point at which Dewey makes the transition from his theory of inquiry to empirical ethics and aesthetics: the peculiarly aesthetic and intellectual delights, he argues, all arise out of dealings with experience, not in the contemplation of some supra-empirical, supra-practical, world.

Dewey's theory of truth derives from this conception of knowledge as the outcome of inquiry. He is closer, in the end, to Peirce than to James. Peirce and Dewey were both dissatisfied with the simple statement that 'the true is the satisfactory' – even with the reservations and limitations James suggests at one time or another

– because it leaves the way open to fantasy and superstition. The true, on their view, must satisfy the *scientist*; it is not enough that *someone* should be satisfied by it.

This theory of truth was complicated by Peirce's 'fallibilism', which Dewey accepted. By 'fallibilism' Peirce means the scientist's recognition that he might be wrong, since those propositions which he describes as 'established truths' are 'established' merely in the sense that for the time being it would not be useful to inquire further into them. They are not 'true' in the sense of being incorrigible; included within the idea of them as a 'scientific truth' is the fact that they are in some measure erroneous. 'Truth is that concordance of an abstract statement with the ideal limit towards which endless investigations would tend to bring scientific belief,' wrote Peirce in the article on 'Truth' in Baldwin's *Dictionary*, 'which concordance the abstract statement may possess by virtue of the confession of its inaccuracy and one-sidedness, and this confession is an essential ingredient of truth.' This definition Dewey quotes with approval.

We might expect the question of truth to arise at two points in inquiry, as Dewey describes it; first when we diagnose a problem, and secondly when we solve it. But Dewey denies that our diagnostic statements – 'propositions' – can properly be designated 'true' or 'false'. Since they are merely *instruments* in our inquiry, they can be effective or ineffective, pertinent or relevant, wasteful or economical – but certainly not 'true' or 'false'. Only the 'judgements' to which propositions lead us can be 'true'; he suggests, even then, that we should replace 'true' by the less misleading phrase 'warranted assertability'. Judgements are 'true', we are 'warranted in asserting' them, when, as being derived by scientific method, they accord with that ideal limit towards which science carries us.

Dewey applies this general theory of inquiry to philosophical problems in *Experience and Nature* (1935) and *The Quest for Certainty* (1929). These works contain an attack, with a variety of historical illustrations, on what he calls 'the spectator theory of knowledge' – the view, as characteristic of modern Realists as of ancient Platonists, that knowledge is the passive contemplation of an eternal and immutable reality. Dewey denies both that there is such a permanent reality and that the knower can ever restrict himself to the role of a spectator. The things we experience are, he says, 'interrogations': they set us problems, challenge us. We are forced, in coping with them, to modify Nature, not merely to contemplate it. The 'spectator' theory, he suggests, reflects a state of society in which men were *actually* powerless and could only dream of another world – a world free of all change – in which they might achieve the security for which they long. But modern man, Dewey proudly proclaims, is no longer impotent; he has learnt to modify Nature, and in that way can arrive at a genuine, if limited, security. By the use of the experimental method he makes determinable and hence controllable what was indeterminate and uncontrollable; the doubtful and the confused, as a result of his work, are clarified, resolved, settled.

Dewey is particularly anxious to peg out a place for philosophy in this general process of settling 'the doubts in Nature'. (The 'doubtful', it should be noted, is *in Nature itself*, not merely in us.) He is not prepared to restrict philosophy to the task of analysis; nor, on the other side, to convert the philosopher into a minor prophet. The philosopher, as Dewey sees him, is *both* 'a physician of culture', in Nietzsche's phrase, *and* a logician. Philosophy he defines as 'intelligence become conscious of its own nature and methods'; just because it has achieved consciousness it can, he thinks, act as an intermediary between art, science and technology. The philosopher can help to clarify the work of the scientist, because he is more conscious than is the scientist of the methods intelligence must employ; at the same time, since his interest is in intelligence *as such*, not merely in this or that particular form of it, the philosopher can correct those narrow, specialized ideals which particular sciences, particular arts, particular social institutions, construct out of their restricted experience of intelligent action. Philosophy is a method of clarification – 'the criticism of criticisms'; and yet it is 'vision', expressing itself in 'large, generous hypotheses' which help men to see how the whole system of values is to be conserved and developed.

Many other American philosophers[30] have worked under the influence of pragmatism; and it has not been without effects on the Continent of Europe. In Italy, a group centred around G. Papini and the journal *Leonardo* (1903–7) seized upon James's philosophy as a gospel of action, and Mussolini paid James the dubious compliment of numbering him amongst his teachers.[31] In France there was a more widespread interest in pragmatism, naturally enough in view of James's close relations with French philosophy. Pragmatism provoked a considerable quantity of critical writing, and attracted the favourable attention of Georges Sorel.[32]

Sorel had already come under Bergson's influence. His *Reflections on Violence* (1908) is an attack upon 'scientism', or the conceptualist way of thinking about social action. In *The Utility of Pragmatism* (1921) Sorel welcomed James as an ally in the fight against 'scientism'. James, he thought, had been badly served by his European defenders, with the result that his philosophy was often dismissed as 'an unimportant trans-Atlantic fantasy'; Sorel's object was to demonstrate the *usefulness* of pragmatism by employing it as a weapon in controversy. Here again, as in Dewey, pragmatism spills over into social philosophy; nowadays, indeed, it is in the writings of social theorists that pragmatism is at its most vigorous.

CHAPTER 6

New Developments in Logic[1]

THE British empiricists were unanimous in their condemnation
of formal logic. Presuming that if it were of any interest whatsoever it would be as an 'art of thought', they maintained that
thought needs no art, that it works best if it is content to follow
the natural lines of its subject-matter without any reference to
formal rules. Throughout the seventeenth and eighteenth centuries, therefore, formal logic played scarcely any part in the vital
philosophical life of Great Britain, although undergraduates were
still compelled to pay it some attention in that last refuge of
medievalism, Oxford. Jowett said of logic that it was neither an
art nor a science but a dodge. That is a reasonably accurate
description of the logic taught – or, rather, learnt parrot-fashion –
at an Oxford which used as its text Aldrich's *Artis Logicae
Compendium* (1691), a hotch-potch of technical terms, carefully
disposed in mnemonic verses to assist the uninterested powers of
recollection of the undergraduate, for whom logic was, until
1831, a compulsory subject.

It is in contrast with this dreary setting that R. Whately's
Elements of Logic (1826) shone so brightly. Whately was content
to restate and defend the traditional logic. But the restatement
was sufficiently lively to be a refreshment of the spirit after the
pedantries of Aldrich. And the defence was a vigorous one: the
empiricist rejection of logic, Whately suggests, rested on a misunderstanding of its nature and purpose and, with that, an undue
respect for the powers of unaided common sense. He could justly
claim, in the later editions of his *Logic*, that his work had done
much to stimulate the notable revival of interest in logical
studies.

Sir William Hamilton lent his remarkable influence to the same
cause. A recent historian of logic refers contemptuously to Hamilton as 'a pedantic Scottish baronet'; his contemporaries saw in
him certainly the greatest scholar and probably the greatest
philosopher of his time. 'Of Sir W. Hamilton,' wrote Boole,
whom one might expect to be an unsympathetic critic, in 1847, 'it

NEW DEVELOPMENTS IN LOGIC

is impossible to speak otherwise than with that respect which is
due to genius and learning.' When Hamilton not merely extolled
the study of logic but pronounced that an age of great logical
innovations lay ahead, his listeners were duly impressed. He
exhorted them to abandon that 'passive sequacity' with which so
many logicians followed blindly in the footsteps of Aristotle; he
drew their attention to the fact that 'many valid forms of judgement and reasoning, in ordinary use, but which the ancient logic
continued to ignore, are now openly recognized as legitimate; and
many *relations*, which heretofore lay hid, now come forward into
the light'.[2] This was a far cry from Kant's pronouncement that
logic 'to all appearances has reached its completion' or Whately's
defence of the syllogism as the only form of valid reasoning.
Logic, it now appeared, might be not merely revived, but reborn.

Of the technical innovations which won for Hamilton the admiration of his contemporaries, the best known is 'the quantification of the predicate' which although it was neither original to
him[3] nor of any great permanent consequence for the later development of logic, yet interestingly foreshadowed the direction in
which logic was to move. According to the traditional logic, all
statements could be expressed in one of the 'four forms' – *all
X are Y, no X are Y, some X are Y, some X are not Y* – where the
predicate has in no case any 'sign of quantity' attached to it. In
Hamilton's logic, on the other hand, the predicate is quantified,
such forms as *all X are all Y* counting as fundamental. The effect
of this, as Hamilton says, is to reduce propositions to equations –
'a proposition being always an equation of its subject and its
predicate.' In the traditional logic, a proposition attributes a
quality to a subject; in the 'new analytic' it identifies two sets of
objects, or 'classes'. Thus for all Hamilton's notorious hostility
to algebra, the effect of his quantification of the predicate was to
make it appear that the theory of equations is the foundation of
logic. Furthermore, he associated with his equational approach
the ideal of a 'logical calculus', in the form of 'a scheme of
logical notation ... showing out in their old and new applications
the propositional and syllogistical forms, with even a mechanical
simplicity'. Hamilton's talents were not equal to his ambitions –
but the mere issuing of prospectuses can have an historic effect.

With the appearance of A. De Morgan's *Formal Logic* (1849),

121

the revolution in logic was under way.[4] De Morgan is not, now, much discussed; his innovations have been anonymously absorbed into the logical tradition. This neglect is partly a consequence of the fact that his more revolutionary contributions long lay concealed in the *Transactions of the Cambridge Philosophical Society* (1849–64), except in as far as they were briefly summarized in his *Syllabus of a Proposed System of Logic* (1860). His *Formal Logic* is not of any great interest to present-day logicians; it still moves in the Aristotelian ambit, for all that the Aristotelian logic is contemplated from a novel point of view.

Post-Cartesian philosophers had ordinarily maintained that reasoning 'relates ideas'. De Morgan revived Hobbes's heresy: logic is about 'names', i.e. words. Now Hobbes had also said that logic is a species of calculation; these two theories are naturally allied. An idea is in itself a 'meaning', whereas words can be manipulated without any reference to meaning. The analogy with algebraic calculation immediately suggests itself once logic is defined as a theory of 'names'.

But so long as it was supposed that algebraic symbols always stand for quantities, or operations – like adding – upon quantities, the analogy between logic and algebra could not be pushed very far. In the early years of the nineteenth century, however, English algebraists were extending the older conception of algebra in two important ways. They denied, in the first place, that in such an algebraic law as

$$a + b = b + a$$

a and *b* need stand for quantities. Anything whatever could be substituted for *a* and *b*, they said, provided only that it satisfied this law. And to the contention that only quantities could satisfy it, since only quantities are addible, they replied that the plus sign need not stand for addition: it could signify any relation of such a kind that when it is substituted for the plus sign this law still holds. To take De Morgan's example, the plus sign could mean 'tied to', since if *a is tied to b*, then also *b is tied to a*. Thus $a + b$ is still equal to $b + a$.

De Morgan brought this new point of view to bear on the interpretation of 'is' in the traditional logical form *S is P*. *S* and *P* had always been read as general symbols which could be replaced by any term. But 'is', it had been supposed, has a fixed meaning, for all that there might be controversy about the character of that meaning. De Morgan, in contrast, argues that 'is', too, is a general symbol, signifying any type of connexion between *S* and *P* which satisfies certain logical rules, fore xample the rule that *if S is P and P is R, then S is R* and the rule that of the two propositions *S is P* and *S is not P* only one can be true. These rules, he admits, were first suggested to logicians by a familiar sense of the word 'is', just as the rules of algebra were first suggested to algebraists by their experience of quantities. But that, he considers, is a merely historical point; for logic, the meaning of 'is' consists in the satisfaction of formal rules.

This doctrine, only briefly sketched in De Morgan's *Formal Logic*, leads directly to the theory of relations developed in his papers in the Cambridge *Transactions*. The word 'is', he now says, performs its logical functions only in virtue of the fact that it stands for a certain kind of relation, a *transitive* relation. The argument *S is P, P is Q, therefore S is Q*, on this view, does not depend for its validity on the fact that 'is' means 'is predicable of', or 'is identical with', or 'is in agreement with', but on the mere fact that 'is' stands for the kind of relation which 'runs on', in contrast, say, with the relation of loving; it is by no means true that if *A* loves *B* and *B* loves *C*, then *A* loves *C*. For the purposes of logic, according to De Morgan, we can write *S is P* in a purely symbolic form, substituting for 'is' some symbol which will simply indicate the kind of relation which the logical use of 'is' involves.

Such a discrimination of relations into types with different logical properties is now a commonplace of the text-books. But De Morgan could rightly say of his work that 'here the general notion of relation emerges, and for the first time in the history of knowledge, the notion of relation and *relation of relation* are symbolized'. Relations had in future to be taken seriously; they could no longer be condescended to as poor and inconsequential hangers-on to qualities. And the traditional supremacy of the syllogism was threatened, for it now appeared that syllogistic reasoning was a particular case of a much wider type of inference, an exemplification of the fact that some relations are transitive, not, as had been supposed, the type to which all rational thinking must conform.

One other point of special interest in De Morgan's logic is his attempt to incorporate within it the innovations which mathematicians like Laplace had introduced into the theory of probability. He objects to the restriction of logic to demonstration. 'I cannot understand,' he writes, 'why the study of the effect which *partial belief* of the premises produces with respect to the conclusion should be separated from that of the consequences of supposing the former to be *absolutely* true.' He does not mean that logic should be envisaged in Mill's manner, as a theory of discovery. Discovery, he argues – most clearly in his review of a new edition of the works of Francis Bacon, republished in *A Budget of Paradoxes* (1872) – does not depend on rules. It consists in first supposing and then testing a hypothesis; to ask where the hypothesis comes from is to ask, he considers, an unanswerable question. 'The inventor of any hypothesis, if pressed to explain his method,' he wrote, 'must answer as did Zerah Colburn, when asked for his method of instantaneous calculation. When the poor boy had been bothered for some time in this manner, he cried out in a huff, "God put it into my head, and I can't put it into yours".' But the logician can, he thinks, estimate the *probability* of a hypothesis, understood as meaning the degree of belief with which it is rational to hold to it.

We need not attempt, fortunately, to follow out in detail the consequences of De Morgan's adoption of Laplace's probability theory.[5] What is of immediate consequence is his general thesis that knowledge and belief can be 'assigned a magnitude'. At this point, there were obvious difficulties in De Morgan's account of probability, precariously balanced as it was between psychology and mathematics. Probability, he wants to say, is never 'objective' – it depends on our 'state of mind', not on any characteristics of the facts themselves, whether a belief is probable. Yet at the same time De Morgan admits that the probability of a belief cannot be identified with the degree of confidence with which we, as particular individuals, happen to regard it. The probability of a belief is the confidence we *ought* to have in it, or would have if we were purely rational – a concession which his successors took to be tantamount to the abandonment of a 'psychological' or 'subjective' theory of probability. From De Morgan's time, the attempt to work out a more satisfactory theory of probability has run parallel with the development of a 'mathematical' or 'symbolic' logic.

That logic began to assume a shape more familiar-looking to modern eyes in the work of George Boole.[6] From Boole, modern formal logic has a continuous history. Like De Morgan, Boole was a mathematician, and it was with the eyes of an algebraist that he looked at logic, particularly in his first publication – *The Mathematical Analysis of Logic, Being an Essay towards a calculus of Deductive Reasoning* (1847). Logic is there presented as a species of algebra, a non-quantitative algebra.

In the first place, it is an algebra of 'classes' – defined as 'individual things linked by a common name' – and of those processes of selecting and conjoining classes which Boole took to be the foundation of logical inference. If we examine such processes, he argues, we see immediately that certain of them can be described by familiar algebraic laws. For example, we notice that it is indifferent whether we first select from a class all the things which are X and then, from the resulting class, select all the Y or whether, having first selected the Y, we then pick out the X from them. Representing the process of selecting the X – or what will come to the same thing, the result of that selection – by the symbol x, and the process of selecting the Y by the symbol y, Boole symbolizes the fact that the order of selection is indifferent by the equation

$$xy = yx$$

The class of mammals which are quadrupeds, to take an example, is identical with the class of quadrupeds which are mammals.

Similarly, Boole points out, it is indifferent whether we pick out the X from a certain class or from each of the classes which make up that class. The class consisting of the quadrupeds in the world is identical with the class consisting of the quadrupeds in the Southern Hemisphere together with the quadrupeds in the Northern Hemisphere, a fact which Boole symbolizes as

$$x\,(m + n) = xm + xn$$

So far these are laws which hold *both* in a quantitative logic, in which x, y, m, and n stand for numbers, and in a logical algebra in

which they stand for classes. But there are other laws of Boole's
logical algebra which are not true in an ordinary quantitative
algebra. Suppose we first select all the quadrupeds from the
mammals, and then pick out the quadrupeds from the class we
have thus formed. Obviously, there still remains the same class of
quadrupeds, no larger than it was before. This fact Boole symbolizes thus

$$x \times x = x$$

and more generally,

$$x^n = x$$

Now this is certainly not a law in the sort of algebra we learn at
school. But the emergence of such a strange-looking principle did
not deter Boole from pursuing his algebraic analogies, as similar
surprises had deterred his predecessors. For this same phenomenon, of algebraic laws which hold only in a limited field of
inquiry, had already been met with in quaternion-theory, which
had recently (1843) been worked out by the Irish mathematician –
not to be confused with the Scottish philosopher – Sir William
Hamilton. Furthermore, as Boole pointed out,

$$x^n = x$$

can be quantitatively interpreted, if we lay down the rule that x
must be equal either to 1 or to 0. The 'laws of thought' – that is
how Boole described his fundamental equations – are in fact
identical with the laws of a 'dual algebra'.

The discovery of this identity was not, Boole thought, a mere
mathematical curiosity: it opened the way to a method of developing and testing the implications of everyday statements. Such
statements, however, had first to be translated into equations.
Boole, presuming that the 'four forms' of traditional logic are the
fundamental types of statement, represents them thus:

all X are Y	$x(1 - y) = 0$
no X are Y	$xy = 0$
some X are Y	$xy = v$
some X are not Y	$x(1 - y) = v$

Here 1 represents 'the Universe',* and $1 - y$ what is left when all

*Later Boole took over from De Morgan the conception of a 'universe of
discourse', considered as the area of reference to which a statement is

the y are taken out of such a Universe. The v is more difficult to interpret. Boole defines it as standing for a class with some, but an indefinite number of, members. Thus

$$xy = v$$

would mean that there is a class, with some members, containing both x's and y's. Boole finds the symbol v useful in calculations, because it can be manipulated by the same methods as x and y. He came, indeed, to use it with increasing freedom, preferring to symbolize *all X are Y* as

$$x = vy$$

(which can be read as asserting that x is identical with an indefinite part of y) rather than as the more obvious equation

$$x(1 - y) = 0$$

His successors, on the contrary, disliked v because it led to awkward, uninterpretable expressions. Making use of inequalities as well as equalities, they preferred to write *some X are not Y* as

$$x(1 - y) \neq 0$$

rather than as

$$x(1 - y) = v$$

This apparently technical point has some significance for the understanding of Boole's procedure. Boole's method was to work out the implications of a set of statements by regarding them as equations in a dual algebra, applying to them (with this restriction) ordinary algebraic processes, and then reinterpreting the result in logical terms. He was not in the least disturbed when equations appeared at various stages in this analysis of implications which could not be directly interpreted in logical terms. In other words, he worked with logic as a pure algebra, in a manner which few of his successors were prepared to imitate.

---

restricted. 'Hamlet is less respectable than Falstaff', for example, would refer, on this view, to the 'universe of fiction', whereas 'Gladstone is less respectable than Disraeli' refers to the 'real' world of history, not to the 'world of fiction'. Every statement, it is presumed, makes an implicit reference to such a universe, within which it is true or false. In his later work, therefore, Boole uses '1' to signify a 'universe of discourse', not 'the universe'.

Beginning with an algebra in which literal symbols stood for classes, Boole soon saw the possibility of offering alternative interpretations of his algebra. He first abbreviates the assertion that *if A is B, then C is D*, to *if X is true, then Y is true* where *X* and *Y* stand for propositions, not for classes; then by reinterpreting the 1 and 0 and *x* of his algebra, so that 1 stands for 'all examinable cases', *x* for 'cases when *X* is true', *y* for 'cases when *Y* is true',* he symbolizes *if X is true, Y is true* as

$$x(1 - y) = 0$$

which can now be read as *there is no case when X is true and Y is false*. In a parallel fashion, Boole thought, other statements linking propositions could be equationally expressed and algebraically developed. He was the first to see, that is, that exactly the same logical analysis could be applied both to classes and to propositions.

Boole lived to describe the publication of his first book as 'ill-advised'. Obviously he blamed himself for being, as he wrote, 'too much under the domain of mathematical ideas', a defect he sought to remedy in *An Investigation of the Laws of Thought* (1854) and, more notably, in those manuscripts and articles (1847–62) which have been brought together as *Studies in Logic and Probability* (1952). He had made it appear that logic was a branch of algebra, and yet had described it as laying down 'laws of thought', to which mathematical calculi must, by the nature of the case, be subordinate. He did not succeed in overcoming his difficulties on this point to his own full satisfaction; the metaphysical sections of Boole's *The Laws of Thought* appear as intrusions rather than as organically linked with his algebra – which is what has remained as his contribution to logic – and his subsequent reflections were unpublished and incomplete.

There was, however, one important technical development in *The Laws of Thought* and in Boole's later articles – the attempt to

*Boole came to think that there were difficulties in talking about 'cases when X is true', since, on the face of it, a proposition is either true or false: it cannot be true in some cases and false in others. He suggests that statements like *A is B*, as used in *if A is B*, always make reference to a particular time, and that therefore *x* should be read as *times when* X *is true*, and 1 as *Eternity*. Perhaps he was influenced by Hamilton's – the mathematician, not the philosopher – interpretation of algebra as a theory of temporal relations.

make use of symbolic logic in the estimation of probabilities, in particular in order to solve problems of the following form: given that the probability of an event X is p, and of an event Y is q, to find the probability of some other event Z by making use of its relation to X and Y. Boole is not suggesting that problems of this kind can be settled by pure logic, without any recourse to quantitative mathematics. But he emphasizes the importance of determining the logical relations between the events in question before embarking upon premature attempts to state the solution in quantitative terms. By disentangling the logical issues Boole drew attention to serious points of weakness in those mathematical theories of probability which Laplace had formulated and De Morgan had been content merely to apply.[7]

One other point about Boole's theory of probability is of some historical interest. The theory of probability had first been worked out as an attempt to estimate gambling odds. In that form it could readily be extended to problems of assurance, in which De Morgan was particularly interested. Boole's concern was more extensive. He had been impressed by Quételet's accumulation of social statistics, and the question which interested him was whether, by an application to such statistics of the theory of probability, the social scientist could make successful social predictions. The fact that Laplace's theory could not cope with a situation in which there are various factors at work, each of which is interacting with the other – as distinct from the typical gambling problem, in which the marbles or the cards can be considered as completely self-contained or 'independent entities' – led Boole to look for a more general theory. 'The necessity of a more general theory,' he wrote, 'is, I conceive, founded on this circumstance: that the observation, especially of social phenomena, does not in general present to us the probabilities of simple events, but of events occurring in particular connexions, whether of causation or of coincidence.' Here we see already at work one of the main motives behind the later development of a general theory of probability, in the writings of such a logician-economist as J. M. Keynes.

In England, Boole's work was the point of departure of a number of logicians, of whom the best known are W. S. Jevons[8] and J. Venn. Jevons won for himself a considerable contemporary reputation as a logician and a methodologist; his more elementary works were often reprinted and widely used as texts. He studied mathematics under De Morgan, but the cast of his mind is not mathematical. It was his object, as he wrote in his *Pure Logic* (1864), to lay bare the structure of Boole's logic by 'divesting his system of a mathematical dress, which, to say the least, is not essential to it'. Boole's system, in his opinion, is 'the shadow, the ghost, the reflected image of logic'; Jevons set out in search of the naked body.[9]

His logic, he says, has certain obvious advantages over Boole's: every process in it is self-evident, no process gives 'uninterpretable or anomalous results', and inferences can be drawn with mechanical ease. These claims are justified – if we add the proviso that, although easier in a sense, the processes of inference which he recommends are tedious and laborious in the extreme. But Jevons's ingenuity overcame this difficulty: he invented a calculating machine to carry out the necessary mechanical processes – a forerunner of the electronic 'thinking machines' of our own time.[10]

Jevons's calculus has not attracted many admirers. That side of Boole's logic which he condemned – its algebraic character – was precisely what proved fruitful, although Jevons's conception of a 'mechanical test' reappeared, if in a very different form, in the 'truth-tables' of a later logic. Certain of his innovations, however, had a permanent effect on the development of formal logic.[11] And he provided a 'Boole without tears' for the education of unmathematical philosophers; it was Jevons's logic, for the most part, which penetrated into late-nineteenth-century text-books as 'mathematical' or 'symbolic' or 'equational' logic.

Certain of the principles it involved were, indeed, commonly if wrongly supposed to be necessary ingredients of any 'mathematical logic'. This is especially true of Jevons's contention that every proposition is a species of identity – an equation. Whereas De Morgan had maintained that Hamilton's *all X are all Y* is two propositions (*all X are Y* and *all Y are X*). Jevons took it to be a *single* proposition (as meaning $X = Y$) although he was obliged somewhat wryly to admit that his calculating machine insisted on treating it as two. In his *The Substitution of Similars, the True Principle of Reasoning* (1869) he castigated the traditional 'propositional forms' in the severest possible terms. 'It is hardly too much to say,' he wrote, 'that Aristotle committed the greatest and most lamentable of all mistakes in the history of science when he took this kind of proposition (*all S are P*) as the true type of all propositions, and founded thereon his system.' The true type of proposition, for Jevons, is the equation; and the true type of inference is 'the substitution of similars', which is founded on the principle that 'in whatever relation a thing stands to a second thing, in that same relation it stands to the like or equivalent of that second thing'. This is a principle of which the syllogism is merely an exemplification – and a less clear exemplification than such arguments as that *if A is greater than B, and B is equal to C, then A is greater than C*. Such was the 'equational logic' which writers like Bradley and Bosanquet – where the name of Boole is not to be met with – took to be characteristic of a logical algebra.[12]

Another side of Jevons's work was warmly approved by the Idealists – his vigorous attack upon Mill. 'I will no longer consent to live silently,' wrote Jevons,[13] 'under the incubus of bad logic and bad philosophy which Mill's work has laid upon us.' In particular, Jevons attacked the whole conception of demonstrative inductive methods; and in his *Principles of Science* (1874) – a book which went into very many editions – he worked out an alternative theory of scientific procedure. Mill's fundamental mistakes, so Jevons argued, derived from his belief in the possibility of discovering 'causes', in the sense of necessary and sufficient conditions. Such a project, Jevons piously objects, carried us far beyond our capacity 'to penetrate into the mystery of those existences which embody the Will of the Creator'. The fact of the matter is, he tries to show, that science never passes beyond hypotheses, which have a greater or less probability.

Adapting for his own purposes a favourite example of probability theorists, Jevons compares the scientist to a person confronted by an urn containing a number of balls. On drawing balls from the urn (each ball, in this metaphor, representing a fact) the scientist notices certain regularities – that, for example, of the first ten balls drawn, three are white and seven are black. His next task is to construct as many hypotheses as he can which are compatible with this regularity. Then the scientist, as Jevons envisages his task, must compare the probability, on each of these hypotheses, of the succession taking the form it does. For example, he must compare the probability that the three white balls he has drawn are the only white balls the urn contains with the probability that the balls are half white and half black or that three-tenths of them are white and seven-tenths black. Then he should hold to the hypothesis which has the greatest probability. Obviously, as Jevons is quite willing to admit, the most probable hypothesis may turn out to be false. But it is no use, he thinks, our waiting until we can achieve 'certainty'. That never comes; either we act in accordance with probabilities or we act merely at random, and the first, Jevons argues, is the better policy.

Jevons does not take seriously Boole's criticism of Laplace; as a result his theory is infected in its details with the presumptions of Laplace's analysis of probability. In many ways, indeed, Jevons does no more than reformulate De Morgan's view that the formation of hypotheses is a matter of an imaginative leap, not of a special kind of inference, and that for the rest, 'induction' is probability-theory. It was in Jevons's formulation, however, that this analysis of scientific procedure became the standard 'alternative to Mill'.

Unlike Jevons, Venn[14] was a mathematician. His first book, *The Logic of Chance* (1866), has an important place in the history of probability-theory. He developed systematically, for the first time,[15] the 'frequency' theory of probability, the view that 'the probability' of an event's having a certain characteristic – considered as a property of the event, and as something quite distinct from an observer's feelings of confidence or of doubt – consists simply in the fact that a certain percentage of events of that kind have that characteristic. To say, for example, that the probability of a penny turning up heads is $\frac{1}{2}$ is to affirm, on this view, that in an infinite series of throws of a penny, half the throws will turn up heads.

It was not until the second decade of the present century that the 'frequency' analysis of probability came to be the favoured one – and it is now hedged with reservations and clouded with doubts. But the immediate effect, in Venn's case, was to lead him to reject the view that inductive inference consists in apportioning estimates of probability. For any such estimate, on his account of the matter, itself states a uniformity: the assertion that in sets of throws a certain percentage will turn up heads stands just as much, or just as little, in need of inductive justification as the assertion that, say, 'all men die'. Thus, probability plays a very limited part in Venn's methodology as that is expounded in his *The Principles of Empirical or Inductive Logic* (1889), which is for the most part a somewhat diffuse commentary on Mill's *System of Logic*.

The most important feature of *Empirical Logic* is Venn's argument to show that Mill's inductive methods rest on the presumption that we *already know* the possible causes of the effect into which we are inquiring. 'The claimants for that post,' he writes, 'must be supposed to be finite in number, and to have all had their names previously submitted to us, so that we have merely the task of deciding between their respective qualifications.' And there is no way of proving, Venn argues, that these are the only claimants, nor even that we have eliminated the less worthy candidates. Like Jevons, Venn insists that in these matters the risk of error is always with us; indeed he acquired the reputation of being sceptical.

Venn's *Symbolic Logic* (1881) is not a highly original contribution to formal logic, although the diagrammatic methods of representation it employs have had an honourable life as 'Venn's diagrams'. It is, rather, a thorough survey of the development of symbolic logic up to the time of its publication. For the first time, Boole's work was brought into relationship with his, largely neglected, Continental predecessors and his American and German continuators. Thus Venn initiated that tendency of symbolic logicians, in marked contrast with contemporary philosophers, to form a single international community.

In his general approach to logic, he follows Boole; and he sees what Boole would be about, as Jevons did not. 'Jevons' individual reforms in the direction of our Logic,' he writes, 'seem to me to consist mainly in excising from Boole's procedure everything which he finds an "obscure form", "anomalous", "mysterious", or "dark and symbolic". This he has certainly done most effectually, the result being to my thinking that nearly everything which is most characteristic and attractive in the system is thrown away.' Venn draws a sharp distinction between the 'petty reforms' of

Hamilton and Boole's completely fresh approach to logic: he brings out clearly what 'algebra' meant for Boole, and how little of 'quantification' there is in his theory. In fact, Boole's algebra, at Venn's hands, appears for the first time as a coherent and articulated logic. His treatment of it is devoid of Boole's mathematical complexities, and yet he preserves the spirit of Boole's approach.

One interesting novelty in Venn's logic is the appearance there of that 'conventionalism' which was later to win many supporters. Quite unlike Jevons, Venn does not fulminate against the misdeeds of Aristotle and the traditional logicians. The traditional logic, he considers, is a valuable educational instrument, not least because it keeps closer than symbolic logic to the language and the customs of everyday logic. But it cannot serve as a generalized logic; its range, he thinks, is inevitably limited. Venn's conventionalism can be illustrated by his treatment of 'existential import'. For the purposes of symbolic logic, he says, a universal proposition does not assert the existence of its subject, and a particular proposition does. Unless *all X are Y* is read as asserting only that *the class of things which are x but not y has no members* and *some X are Y* as *the class of things which are x and y has members*, the symmetry of symbolic logic, on which its power of generalization rests, is quite destroyed. He does not say that it would be wrong to read the universal proposition in any other way: he grants, indeed, that the presumption of traditional logicians that if *all X are Y* is true, there must exist at least one *X* keeps closer to ordinary usage. The question is one of convenience only, as he sees it. It follows that symbolic logic should be regarded as *a* logic, not as the only possible logic; it is a method of fulfilling certain purposes for which the traditional logic is inadequate, it is not a substitute for that logic. This is a new note in the controversies of the period.

Many other logicians were at work in America and in England during the latter years of the century.[16] At Cambridge, Venn's younger colleague J. N. Keynes, in his *Studies and Exercises in Formal Logic* (1884), attempted to incorporate the Boole-Venn innovations within the framework of a 'traditional logic'. In the process, he modified that logic so as to make it conform to Venn's analysis of existential import – his discussion and illustration of the thesis that universal propositions do not assert the existence of their subjects has been the starting-point for much subsequent controversy.

It is easy to underestimate Keynes's originality and ingenuity: his reputation as a logician was overshadowed by that of another Cambridge man, W. E. Johnson,[17] who took over Keynes's version of the traditional logic, but was a philosophical logician, as Keynes was not. Johnson's major work – his *Logic* – did not appear until 1921 and must be left for later consideration, but his earlier articles on 'The Logical Calculus' (*Mind*, 1892), are important as the first statement of that 'Cambridge philosophy' which was to be associated particularly with the names of Moore and Russell. The calculus itself need not concern us – it was another attempt, in the manner of Jevons and Venn, to develop a mechanical method of solving logical problems. But Johnson's principal concern is with the assumptions which underlie the use of a calculus of any kind. For Johnson, technical ingenuity always fell into second place.

We may easily, he thinks, underestimate the amount of intelligence that is presumed in the operation of a calculus. Jevons, for example, had supposed that a single principle – 'the Substitution of Similars' – once admitted as valid, the calculus needed no other intelligent consideration. But Jevons's calculus, Johnson argues, rests upon a complex set of presumptions: the presumptions, for example, that each symbol has an unambiguous import, that different symbols can refer to the same thing, that symbols which represent the same thing can be substituted for one another. This bringing to the surface of concealed presumptions was to be characteristic of Cambridge logical analysis.

Equally 'Cambridge' is Johnson's view that the task of logic is analysis – the breaking down of a system into its constituent basic propositions. (Contrast the doctrine of the Oxford Idealists that logic is the discovery of a system into which a 'judgement' will fit.) Every actual proposition, he admits, is complex. Nevertheless, we may set up as an ideal the conception of a 'molecular' proposition – what Russell later called an 'atomic' proposition – which cannot be analysed into further propositions but only into terms, just as a molecule can only be further broken down into atoms. Every proposition, according to Johnson, is a set of such molecular propositions linked together by what he takes to be the fundamental logical relations – the relations represented by 'and' and 'not'. 'All that formal logic can do in the way of syntheses of propositions,' he writes, 'is contained in the laws regulating the use of the little words *and* and *not*.'

Once this fact is realized, Johnson considers, we can overcome what is otherwise a serious problem: we can see how there can be facts which correspond to hypothetical and disjunctive propositions. Such propositions, it is clear, can be true – and yet nature contains nothing which corresponds to 'if' and 'or'. But provided that we are content to interpret *if p, q* as denying the truth of *p and not-q* and *p or q* as denying the truth of *not-p and not-q* these difficulties, he argues, will completely vanish – for 'and' and 'not', according to Johnson, both stand for 'factual' relations, 'not' being a way of indicating that a thing has some property other than what is being predicated of it, without actually nominating that property.

There is in Johnson's analysis a notable break with the logical tradition, for which 'if . . . then . . .' was the fundamental logical expression, inference being the normal point of departure for logic. Johnson knew that he would be criticized on the ground that our 'mental attitude' when we assert that *if p, then q* is quite different from our 'mental attitude' when we deny the truth of *p and not-q*, so that these, in the language of Oxford, are different 'judgements'. Johnson's reply is that our 'mental attitudes' have nothing to do with formal logic: logic is a theory of *propositions*, defined as 'the expression of a truth or a falsity', not of *judgements*, understood as expressing attitudes of mind. This emphasis on 'propositions' was to be typical of Cambridge logicians.

In America, meanwhile, a notably original logic was taking shape in the work of C. S. Peirce.[18] The very diversity of his logical writings, however, makes them difficult to describe. Furthermore his analyses are often compact to the point of unintelligibility. He was a mathematician and the son of a mathematician; for him nothing could be clearer than mathematical symbols. 'When a person lays it down,' he wrote to James, 'that he can't understand mathematics, that is to say, can't understand the *evident*, that blocks the road, don't you see?' He is content, often enough, to present bare results, when his readers are panting for illustrations and explanations. That is one reason, apart from the fact that much of his work was not published before its inclusion in his *Collected Papers* (1931–5), why he anticipated more than he originated; it was left to others to work out, in their slower but more intelligible way, conclusions which a flash of intuition had already suggested to Peirce. That is not to say that the symbolic logicians of his time ignored him; on the contrary, they appreciated his merits when he was otherwise scarcely known. But the full extent of his innovations escaped their notice.

The general character of his earlier logical writings can be described thus: Peirce modifies in various ways Boole's logical algebra, retaining its algebraic form, but distinguishing its purely logical ingredients from what is only interpretable in mathematical terms. And then he sets out to show that an improved version of De Morgan's logic of relations can be formulated within such a calculus. Thus he brings together, for the first time, Boole's and De Morgan's logic as a single logical structure.

But this way of putting the matter may suggest that Peirce was no more than a careful systematizer. Nothing could be further from the truth: the distinctive feature of all Peirce's work is an unmistakable originality. Sometimes crabbed and eccentric, he is never merely pedestrian. Two of his major innovations deserve special consideration, for they finally entered the main stream of philosophy – even if indirectly, through the influence of other, sometimes lesser, men.

The first is the division of predicates into three types, which he calls (*Monist*, 1897) monadic, dyadic and polyadic. A 'monadic' predicate appears in statements of the form '. . . is a man', which can be completed by the filling in of a single blank. In '. . . is a lover of . . .', there are two such blanks: 'is a lover of', therefore, is a dyadic relation. And in '. . . gives . . . to . . .' or, to take an example which Peirce particularly emphasized, in '. . . stands to . . . for . . .', there are three blanks, the relation involved being polyadic.

The admission of polyadic relations greatly enlarged the branch of logic which De Morgan, as Peirce always emphasized, had been the first to open up – the logic of relations. It made possible, he thought, the solution of a number of previously intractable philosophical problems; in particular, the recognition of polyadic relations was of crucial importance, according to Peirce, in any satisfactory analysis of meaning. As well, it must be confessed, Peirce was fascinated – in a quite Hegelian manner – by 'triads'; the distinction between 'firstness', 'secondness' and 'thirdness' is the most pervasive, if not the most lucid, of the metaphysical motifs in his philosophy, and his threefold division of predicates neatly accorded with that major metaphysical classification. He tended to argue, it is worth noting, that polyadic relations could always be expressed as a set of triadic relations.[19]

Peirce's second important innovation was of a different character: he was in search of a wider generalization, not introducing a new distinction. He abandons, as of no logical importance, the traditional distinction between terms, propositions and inferences, and the corresponding distinction between class-relations, predication and implication. On the traditional view, there is a progress in complexity from term to inference: a term is a constituent of a proposition and a proposition is a constituent of an inference. Peirce, on the other hand, maintains that the ordinary distinction has validity only as an account of the different *uses* we make of what is substantially the same logical structure with, in each case, the same principal constituents.

We are misled, he considers, by the fact that English, and indeed any modern European language, contains common nouns. In a great many English sentences these nouns, linked by verbs and conjunctions, are the most conspicuous feature. Out of this merely accidental characteristic of language, Peirce argues, the distinction between 'terms' and 'propositions' arises – terms being conceived as common nouns, and propositions as an arrangement of such nouns. But in fact, he maintains, every noun by itself 'involves a rudimentary assertion'; as comes out, he suggests, in Mill's doctrine that a term 'connotes' certain characteristics and 'denotes' what possesses these characteristics. To think, say, of a triangle is to think of *something before our mind as having certain characteristics* – in this case it is to think of a geometrical figure as having three sides. What we have before our minds in such a case is 'rudimentary', Peirce is prepared to admit, as compared with a fully quantified proposition like 'all men are mortal' but this distinction is one of degree, not of kind.

Equally, he maintains, a proposition is a 'rudimentary' inference. The difference between inference and proposition is only that in an argument we explicitly *assert*, whereas in a proposition we are content to point to a logical relation. Thus, for example, the inference 'Enoch was a man and was therefore mortal' *asserts* that Enoch was in fact mortal; the proposition 'if Enoch was a man, then he was mortal' does not assert Enoch's mortality. Nevertheless the proposition and the inference point to the same logical relationship. From the standpoint of logic, therefore – concerned as it is with modes of relationship – the inference and the proposition have the same structure. And all propositions, Peirce thought he could show, are expressible in the 'if ... then ...' form. *A is B* asserts that *anything with the character A is of the character B*, and this amounts to saying, on Peirce's analysis of it, that *if anything is A, then that same thing is B*. Thus the demonstration that propositions of the 'if ... then ...' form are rudimentary inferences amounts to a proof that *all* propositions are rudimentary inferences, including those rudimentary propositions we call terms.

The fundamental logical concept, then, is 'the illative relation', as Peirce called it, the relation expressed by 'if ... then ...' or by 'therefore'. 'I have maintained since 1867,' he wrote in 'The Regenerated Logic' (*Monist*, 1896), 'that there is one primary and fundamental logical relation, that of illation.... A proposition, for me, is but an argumentation divested of the assertoriness of its premiss and conclusion. That makes every proposition a conditional proposition at bottom. In like manner, a "term" or class-name, is for me nothing but a proposition with its indices or subjects left blank, or indefinite.... This doctrine ... gives a great unity to logic.'

The illative relation is what later came to be called 'material implication'. For *if p, q*, as Peirce interprets it, signifies no more than that *it is not the case that p is true and q is false*. Interpreted in this way, the 'if ... then ...' relation can be identified with the class-membership relation; it asserts that the cases when *p* is true are included in the cases when *q* is true. But Peirce had not the slightest desire to argue, as others did, that relations between propositions are therefore reducible to relations between classes. The tendency of his thinking is in a completely opposite direction.

'By identifying the relation expressed by the copula,' he writes, 'with that of illation, we identify the proposition with the inference and the term with the proposition.' 'Man', according to Peirce, means *there is something now before me which has the property X:* and this means *it is not the case both that there is something now before me and that this something has not the property X;* and this in turn means *if there is something now before me, it is X.* Logic is unified around 'illation' or 'material implication'.

Peirce noticed, but was not in the least disturbed by, what have come to be called 'the paradoxes of material implication' – the fact, for example, that if *p* implies *q* whenever it is not the case that *p* is true and *q* is false, then the falsity of *p* will imply the truth of any proposition we care to mention. Thus, to take Peirce's example, in 'if the Devil were elected President of the United States, this would prove highly conducive to the spiritual welfare of the people' the consequence follows in virtue of the mere fact that he will not be so elected. Far from finding such curious results alarming, Peirce made use of them in his logic – for example, in his various attempts to define negation in terms of implication by means of such formulae as *not-p=for all q, if p then q.* We need to remember, he says, that for logical purposes we must make use of a somewhat *special* sense of 'if ... then ...' This remembered, no confusion will result.

Peirce's contributions to formal logic are worked out against the background of a general theory of the nature of logic, that logic is a 'theory of signs'.[20] Of course, this definition of logic contained no novelty in itself. Locke had already defined logic as 'the doctrine of signs' – whose business it is, he says, 'to consider the nature of the signs the mind makes use of for the understanding of things, or conveying its knowledge to others'. But Peirce complains that his predecessors had not analysed signs with sufficient minuteness and laboriousness: certainly no one could make *that* complaint about Peirce's work! Without attempting to follow him through what he calls 'the labyrinth of these distinctions' we can catch a glimpse of his principal objectives.

Logic, he says, is 'the science of the necessary general laws of signs and specially of symbols'. It has three branches – once more, the love of the triad! – which are variously distinguished one from another, perhaps most clearly in a fragment he wrote about 1897. First, there is 'pure grammar', which considers what must be true of any sign – 'as used by a scientific intelligence', a condition Peirce adds in each case – if it is to have a meaning. Then there is 'logic proper' or 'critical logic' which describes the characteristics of all signs which 'hold good of objects'. And finally there is 'pure rhetoric' – or 'methodology' – which seeks to discover the laws by which 'one sign gives birth to another, and especially one thought to another'.

This threefold division rests on Peirce's definition of a sign as 'something which stands to somebody for something in some respect or capacity', i.e. as necessitating for its definition a polyadic relation.* One must remember the breadth of 'sign', as Peirce understands it. A sign need not be a word; it can be a thought, an action, or anything else which has an 'interpretant' – which, in other words, can give rise to further signs. Thus a cloud is a sign because it 'means rain', i.e. it gives rise to acts – somebody closing a window, for example – which interpret the clouds; these acts themselves can serve as signs, for they too can 'mean rain' – for example, to those who, for one reason or another, have not seen the clouds, but hear the windows close.

In all, Peirce divides signs into seventy-six types, with the aid of a number of different principles of division. Thus, to take an example, an 'icon' is a sign which resembles what it signifies, as a photograph is a 'sign' of a person; an 'index' signifies in virtue of the effects which its object produces on it, as a shadow is an 'index' of the sun's angle; a 'symbol' is associated with objects only by convention, as most words are.

What is the point of these, and other more elaborate, distinctions? Classification for classification's sake? Peirce would plead 'not guilty' to the charge of pedantry. Distinctions between signs, he argues, are important for our understanding of logical principles. Thus, for example, he makes considerable use of the distinction between 'icon', 'symbol' and 'index' in an article he contributed to Baldwin's *Dictionary* on 'Subject' – and in a way

---

*It was, indeed, Peirce's interest in 'signs' which first led him to discuss polyadic relations, which he originally named, for that reason, 'representative' relations. But it later became clear to him that they had a wider field of application.

which anticipates a good many subsequent discussions. A proposition, he there maintains, is 'a sign which separately indicates its object'. It follows that an 'icon' by itself is not a proposition, because it does not 'indicate' its object; a portrait of Nelson, for example, becomes a proposition only if it has the name 'Nelson' written underneath it: then it separately indicates 'Nelson' and tells us that this is how he looked. An index, similarly, is not, as such, a proposition, but a weathercock *tells* us from which direction the wind is blowing, because it is so constructed that it *must* point to the quarter from which the wind is blowing; it is a proposition, that is, in virtue of its general construction, and not merely because, as an index, it is on a particular occasion responding to the movement of the wind and thus acting as a 'sign' of its presence.

Thus Peirce recognizes that a proposition need not be a conventional symbol. But at the same time he points out that propositions are *usually* symbols, into which indices enter only in so far as they are deliberately intended to signify, i.e. are used as symbols. To point to a flower, for example, and say 'pretty' is to assert that this flower is pretty, *only if the pointing is intended to signify the flower* – otherwise the utterance of the word might be a mere nervous gesture, even when it is provoked by the presence of the flower and is thus an *index* of it.

Simple-minded assumptions about signs have provoked, Peirce thinks, a multitude of philosophical errors, which can be destroyed only by a really thorough analysis of the way in which signs function. Thus Locke, for example, asks what a word means and assumes that it refers to 'an idea in our mind' – as if he had only to take account of two things, the sign and its object. Once it is realized, Peirce thinks, that a sign necessarily involves an interpretant – that 'cat' is a sign only if its utterance provokes, say, 'Puss, puss' – Locke's inward and private theory of meaning, with all its attendant problems, simply collapses. In his belief that a more careful analysis of language would do much to dispel philosophical errors, Peirce is, most notably, a twentieth-century philosopher.

In spite of the mathematical character of so much of his work, Peirce did not accept the view that logic is a purely formal inquiry. 'Formal logic', he wrote, 'must not be too purely formal; it must

NEW DEVELOPMENTS IN LOGIC

represent a fact of psychology, or else it is in danger of degenerating into a mathematical recreation' – and by this reference to 'psychology', he meant that logic must take account of the nature of *inference*, considered as a form of inquiry, as distinct from *implication*, considered simply as a formal relationship. Thus his 'logic' is in large part a theory of inquiry, into which he is not ashamed to introduce psychological, social and even ethical considerations.

He distinguishes three types of inference – deduction, induction, abduction (or, 'hypothesis') – most maturely in a manuscript dated 1901.[21] There is nothing strikingly unusual about his analysis of deduction, except that, like De Morgan, he pays more attention than is customary to those deductive arguments in which the premises are 'quantitatively exact', containing precise numerical quantities. Abduction and induction, however, have unconventional features. Abduction is the process of inferring from a 'surprising fact' to an explanation of it, an explanation which fulfils the following requirement: if the explanation were true, the fact would no longer be surprising. By means of abduction the scientist arrives at an 'explanatory hypothesis'.

His hypothesis must then be tested – at this point, Peirce's methodology is pragmatic. The process of testing, as he describes it, consists in calculating what results would follow, under certain conditions, were the hypothesis true, producing these conditions by experimental means, and then seeing whether the expected results do in fact follow. If they do, he thinks, we should then extend a certain measure of confidence to the hypothesis. The whole of this procedure Peirce calls 'induction'. Its usefulness as the method of scientific inquiry rests, so he argues, on the presumption that if we take a fair sample of cases, what is true in a certain percentage of cases is likely to be true, in the same ratio, of the class as a whole. The 'typical case' of induction, as Peirce envisages it, runs something like this: our hypothesis is that Negro births contain a greater percentage of female children than do white births; we test the hypothesis by examining United States census figures; if that sample shows the anticipated tendency we affirm confidently that our hypothesis is true.

Peirce admits that this method is scarcely applicable to those cases where the hypothesis affirms that some particular thing is of a certain character (e.g. that a certain man is a Catholic priest). In such instances, he considers, our inductive argument must contain an element of guesswork, because the characteristics of a thing – of a Catholic priest, for example – are not units, and for that reason cannot be statistically sampled. He is naturally at his happiest with statistical examples, and his careful analyses of the difficulties there arising – in defining a 'good sample', for instance – anticipate most of the problems which have beset later workers in this same field.

It is obvious that Peirce's account of induction brings it into close relationship with the theory of probability. 'The theory of probabilities,' he wrote, 'is simply the science of logic quantitatively treated' – the science, that is, which determines with what probability a certain conclusion follows from given premises. The problem for Peirce is to bring this conception of probability into accord with the 'frequency' analysis of probability which he takes over from Venn. His solution runs thus: to say that a certain conclusion is 'probable' is an elliptical way of asserting that it is derived by a species of argument which leads, in a high proportion of cases, to a true conclusion. His candid examination of the difficulties which this solution brings with it is not the least valuable of his contributions to philosophy.

Peirce's modifications of the Boolean algebra were immediately recognized as important; they attracted the attention, particularly, of the German logician E. Schröder, and played a part in his classic formulation of what has come to be called 'the Boole-Schröder algebra of logic', as that is set out in his *Lectures on the Algebra of Logic* (1890–1905). But Schröder's work, for all its substantial merits, introduced no new ideas into philosophy. Ironically enough, indeed, the De Morgan theory of relations entered the main body of philosophy in the work of one who, as Peirce despondently remarks, was 'no logician' – William James.

In the famous last chapter to his *Principles of Psychology*, James disputes the view, which Mill had recently defended, that the empiricist must interpret logical and mathematical principles as 'generalizations from experience'. Like Locke and Hume before him, James argued that logic and mathematics have for their subject-matter 'relations of ideas', relations which hold independently of experience, even although the ideas themselves are products of experience. The fundamental logical and mathematical relation, according to James, is comparison; the characteristic method of proof in logic and mathematics consists in 'skipping intermediaries', as when the mathematician concludes from *A equals B* and *B equals C* that *A equals C*, by 'skipping *B*'. The mere fact that such 'skips' are not always possible (and here James refers particularly to De Morgan) – since, for example, when *A loves B* and *B loves C* it does not follow that *A loves C* – helps us to see that these relations are not of our making. It is not *our* doing that intermediaries can be skipped. This conclusion, as we shall see, was absorbed into late nineteenth-century criticisms of 'psychologism'.

That criticism had other roots, as well, in nineteenth-century logic. Once again, although in a different way, the development of mathematics was crucial for logic. Boole saw in logic an exemplification of the new kind of algebra; other mathematicians turned their attention towards symbolic logic because they were looking for help in their task of repairing the gaps which they had detected in the structure of mathematics. There was an odd exchange of international roles at this point; the Boole-De Morgan logic originated in England but was given its classical formulation by Schröder in Germany, the logic of mathematics was a Continental creation which yet achieved its classical form in Russell and Whitehead's *Principia Mathematica*.

In a variety of ways, nineteenth-century mathematicians had destroyed any obvious link between mathematics and the empirical. Algebra was no longer quantitative; Geometry generalized beyond the limits of spatial relationships; in Arithmetic, the new 'trans-finite' numbers had properties of a distinctly unfamiliar kind – it was, for example, not true of trans-finite classes that the whole is greater than the part: the infinite series of natural numbers is not a larger class than the infinite series of even numbers.[22]

As a result of these innovations, propositions of mathematics came to look more and more like propositions of logic. Mathematics, it was now argued, is a 'science of order', simply: those references to space or to quantity which apparently distinguish it from logic are irrelevant accretions to its real structure. It was only a short step from this conclusion to the attempt to demonstrate that pure mathematics is deducible from logical laws.

The new mathematics, in the opinion of its leading exponents, is an analysis of implications, not a demonstration of truths. The ordinary supposition, since Plato, had been that mathematics consists in a set of truths about 'ideal objects' – perfect circles and the like – the point of philosophical controversy being the exact relation between these ideals and the facts of everyday experience. But now it was argued that mathematics knows nothing of 'truth', in the empirical sense of that word; its object, merely, is to discover *what follows from* certain postulates. Thus, to take the most notorious instance, various 'geometries' can be set up side by side, deriving from different postulates. The question which of these geometries is true, so mathematicians were beginning to say, simply does not arise: provided they contain no contradictions, each of them has an equal right to be considered as a valid geometry, although certain geometries might turn out to have particularly useful applications.

This new conception of mathematics brought with it a demand for absolute rigour in proof. Mathematicians, of course, had always sought after rigorous and elegant proofs – but they had not supposed that this was their whole task, as they now did. They looked, therefore, for a method of setting out mathematical theories in 'logical form', in such a way that their logical structure would be immediately apparent and gaps in that structure could be readily discerned. The traditional logic could not easily symbolize mathematical reasoning; the Boolean logic looked more hopeful, even if it, too, had to be largely redesigned to suit its new purposes.

One of the important things about this development was that it provided logicians with a subject-matter. Peirce had seen the danger that logic would degenerate into a 'mathematical recreation'. Logicians like Venn might construct elaborate problems so as to demonstrate the greater facility of the new as compared with the older formal logic; but Keynes had shown that these problems were by no means insoluble in the older logic and, in any case, they were for the most part distinctly artificial problems, not likely to arise in any actual inquiry. In dealing with the arguments of everyday life, Venn was prepared to admit, the traditional logic had many advantages. What then could be accomplished with the elaborate methods Boole and his successors had invented? The analysis of mathematical reasoning – that was to be the answer.

A notable step towards the construction of a logic for mathematicians was taken by a group of Italian logicians under the leadership of G. Peano. In their *Formulaire de mathématiques* (1895–1908) Peano and his collaborators set out to demonstrate that arithmetic and algebra can be constructed on the basis of a few elementary logical ideas (such as class, class membership, class inclusion, material implication and the product of classes), three primitive mathematical ideas (zero, number, and the next number to a number) and six elementary propositions. The Cartesian ideal – a mathematics deduced from a few simple concepts – seemed at last to be nearing realization. To facilitate this deduction, Peano invented a logical symbolism which had distinct advantages over any which had been previously employed – the symbolism which, to a very large extent, Russell and Whitehead were to adopt.

In Peano's work, however, skeletons were kept to their cupboards: the broader logical issues were not investigated, and important distinctions were blurred. It is in the writings of G. Frege[23] that the fundamental problems of a logicized mathematics first clearly emerged. Frege attempts – in his *The Foundations of Arithmetic* (1884) and *Fundamental Laws of Arithmetic* (1893–1903) – to make arithmetic secure by deriving it from the laws of logic: his philosophy grows out of the problems which that attempt engenders. His problems are 'technical', therefore, in the sense in which so much recent philosophy is technical. To understand what is *troubling* him, even, is already to have made a considerable advance in philosophy, whereas anyone can understand the motives behind, say, McTaggart's philosophy, for all the difficulty there is in following his argument in detail.

Partly on account of its technical character, Frege's philosophical work was slow to attract attention. Philosophers, he complained, boggled at the symbolism, and mathematicians at the theoretical discussions. Bertrand Russell drew attention to certain features of his work in Appendix A to *The Principles of*

Mathematics, but even with this sponsorship Frege was little read until the second quarter of the present century.[24]

Frege begins from a criticism of prevailing 'philosophies of arithmetic'. He distinguishes three such philosophies: the 'pebble and biscuits' theory, psychologism and formalism. Mill thought that numbers were generalizations from our experience of the groupings of discrete objects – that is the 'pebble and biscuits' view. In a wave of enthusiasm for psychological explanations, a good many philosophers wrote as if numbers were identical with the processes by which we come to make use of them – that is 'psychologism'. Others, trying to avoid the errors of Mill and of psychologism without reinstating Platonic 'Ideas', attempted to argue that numbers are no more than signs, arithmetic being a game played with signs just as chess is played with chessmen – that is 'formalism'. None of these theories, Frege argues, can account for *all* the properties of arithmetic. Formalism can make nothing of its applicability to empirical situations, psychologism of its independence and objectivity, Mill's empiricism of its certainty and generality. (How, Frege asks, can o or $\sqrt{-1}$ refer to a group of pebbles?)

Philosophers have been forced into one or the other of these unsatisfactory theories, he thinks, because they have wrongly supposed that whatever is objective must exist in space. Thus they were compelled to choose between treating numbers as spatial (whether as groups of objects or as marks on pages) or else as subjective. But this, according to Frege, is a false antithesis: 'numbers are neither spatial nor physical nor yet subjective like ideas, but non-sensible and objective.'

We can understand how the traditional subjective-objective antithesis can be overcome, Frege argues, once we realize that numbers are applied to 'concepts' – a 'concept' understood not as an 'idea', an image in an individual mind, but as an 'object of Reason'. If we consider a physical thing, he says, we see at once that it has not in itself any *specific* number. For example, a heap of stones can be one (as a single heap) or twenty (as containing twenty stones) or five (as being made up of five layers). It has not *in itself* any of these numbers – and even more obviously, he says, it cannot be 'nought'. Frege concludes that what is being numbered is not a set of objects but a concept. 'If I say that "Venus has

0 moons",' he writes, 'there simply does not exist any moon or agglomeration of moons for nothing to be asserted of; but what happens is that a property is ascribed to the *concept* "moon of Venus", namely that of including nothing under it.'

Although Frege here affirms that numbers 'belong' to concepts, he is not maintaining that *0*, or any other number, is in itself a property of the concept. Numbers appear as *constituents* in such complex predicates as 'including nothing under it', but they do not themselves make up the whole content of such a predicate. Numbers, he thinks, are not properties, but objects. The statement 'Jupiter's moons are four', which looks as if it predicates *four* of Jupiter's moons, should be read, he thinks, as 'the number of Jupiter's moons is four', and as asserting that two objects – *the number of Jupiter's moons* and *four* – are identical. The 'is' in 'is four' is not the ordinary predicative 'is' but asserts identity, just as in 'Columbus is the discoverer of America.'

The problem for Frege, then, in giving an account of numbers, is to define this 'object', which can appear as a constituent in so many different assertions. This problem Frege restates as follows: to define the sense of the proposition 'the number which belongs to the concept *F* is the same as the number which belongs to the concept *G*'. If, without making any reference to number, we can define the expression '*X* and *Y* have the same number', then we know what number is.

Frege's solution runs as follows: the number which belongs to the concept *F* is the extension of the concept *equal to the concept F*. To assign the same number to *F* and to *G* is to affirm that the extension of the concept *equal to F* is identical with the extension of the concept *equal to G*. Thus, for example, to say that in a certain philosophy class the number of men and the number of women are identical is to say that the concept *equal to the women in the philosophy class* refers to the same class of objects (has the same extension) as the concept *equal to the men in the philosophy class*. In this way, Frege defined the concept *having the same number as* by the purely logical notions of class and extension. With this definition as his starting point, he goes on to define, in logical terms, the series of numbers. 'Nothing' is defined as the number which belongs to the concept *not identical with itself* – there being nothing which belongs to this concept – and then by a series of ingenuities Frege derives the series of numbers successive to *0* from this definition of *0*, making use only of such logical notions as identity. Thus, he maintains, the mathematician has no need of Peano's primitive mathematical ideas; arithmetic can be derived from concepts which are purely logical in character.

The philosophical problems which arise out of this account of mathematics are manifold; the most obvious is the need for providing a satisfactory account of concepts in their relation to the objects which 'fall under' them and the numbers which are 'assigned' to them. These are topics which Frege discusses in some detail in his articles 'On Function and Concept' (1891), 'On Concept and Object' (1892) and 'On Sense and Reference' (1892).[25]

What he does is to generalize the algebraic distinction between a function and an argument. In such an algebraic expression as $2x^3 + x$ the 'function', he says, is 'what is present in this expression over and above the letter x'. It can be expressed schematically as $2()^3 + ()$, where the 'argument' x could fill in the blanks. One important feature of a function, thus defined, is that it cannot stand by itself, in the sense in which x can stand by itself. A function, Frege says, is 'unsaturated', it needs to be completed by reference to an argument in order to make an expression. The question, he concludes, 'to what *entity* does a function refer?' is meaningless, since a function does not name an entity. And yet, although it does not refer to an entity, a function nevertheless has a sense, a meaning, in the context of an algebraic sentence.

In everyday statements, Frege goes on to suggest, a 'predicative expression' works like a function. The expression '. . . conquered Gaul', for example, makes sense only when a proper name is substituted for '. . .', just as '$()^2$' makes sense only when an 'argument' is placed within the brackets. 'Conquered Gaul', then, is 'unsaturated'; it expresses a function, it does not name an object. We shall be puzzled about how it can have a meaning only if we imagine that every word must have a significance which is independent of the sentences in which it occurs. Frege exhorts us to avoid this source of puzzlement by adopting the principle 'never to ask for the meaning of a word in isolation, but only in the context of a proposition'.

In the theory of meaning which he goes on to develop, predica-

NEW DEVELOPMENTS IN LOGIC

tive expressions fade out of the picture; the emphasis now is on 'proper names' – in a very wide sense in which every name of an 'argument' is a proper name – and on sentences. The main point he stresses is the importance of distinguishing, in both cases, between the 'sense' and the 'reference'.

It is obvious, he thinks, that two expressions can be 'identical in reference' – since they 'mean' the same object – while yet being different in sense. The expressions $2+2$ and 4 are a case in point. If they do not refer to the same object, it would be impossible to substitute one for the other in a mathematical equation and yet, equally, if they do not differ in sense, to affirm that $2+2=4$ would be to give no information whatsoever. Similar considerations apply to the expressions 'the evening star' and 'the morning star'. Both these expressions refer to the same object; nevertheless, it was an important astronomical discovery that the morning star is identical with the evening star. To reconcile the fact that the two expressions refer to the same object with the fact that the assertion 'the evening star is identical with the morning star' is informative – whereas 'the evening star is identical with the evening star' is not informative – we have to recognize that the two expressions differ in 'sense' even although they refer to the same 'objects'. Without the distinction between sense and reference, then, it would be impossible to indicate how we can make use of various expressions for the same object.

Similarly, he argued, we are compelled to distinguish between the sense and the reference of a sentence as a whole. Any sentence contains a 'thought' – this being what, for example, we seek to preserve when we translate a sentence from one language to another.[26] Is this 'thought', he asks, the sense or the reference of the sentence? It would be easy to presume that it is the reference, i.e. to treat the sentence as an elaborate proper name referring to the 'thought'. But, Frege argues, when we change a sentence by altering some word or phrase in it to another with the same reference but a different sense, the 'thought' alters. 'The morning star is a body illuminated by the sun' contains a different 'thought' from 'the evening star is a body illuminated by the sun'. And yet the reference of the two sentences is not altered by such a change. Thus, he concludes, the 'thought' cannot be the reference of a sentence, but must be its sense.

Are we to conclude that a sentence has no reference? If sentences appeared only as constituents in works of art, then, Frege will admit, their reference would be unimportant. 'Odysseus was set ashore at Ithaca while sound asleep' obviously has a sense and it does not matter in the least whether 'Odysseus', and hence the sentence as a whole, has a reference. But when we are interested in the truth or falsity of a sentence, the situation changes: it is then that we demand a 'reference'.

Thus we are driven, Frege argues, to the conclusion that the 'truth-value' of a sentence constitutes its reference – its reference is either the True or the False.[27] 'Every declarative sentence concerned with the reference of its words,' he writes, 'is therefore to be regarded as a proper name, and its reference, if it has one, is either the True or the False.' It will follow, of course, that all true sentences have the same reference, and so do all false sentences. Merely to know the reference of a sentence is impossible; because we never know 'the True' as such, but always a sentence which refers to the truth. But equally, we cannot merely know its sense since we 'know' only what is true.

This distinction between 'sense' and 'reference' is one of the two fundamental distinctions which run through Frege's argument: the other is that sharp contrast between 'concepts' and 'objects' on which we have already touched in sketching Frege's philosophy of arithmetic but which deserves further consideration. This is linked, as we suggested, with the traditional distinction between subject and predicate. 'The concept,' writes Frege, 'is predicative. On the other hand, the name of an object, a proper name, is quite incapable of being used as a grammatical predicate.'

There are obvious difficulties in this view, and Frege's way of treating them interestingly anticipates the trend of subsequent discussions. The difficulties derive from the fact that the subject of an assertion very often appears to name a concept, and proper names to function as grammatical predicates. All such assertions, Frege tries to show, are 'systematically misleading' – to use the language of a later day.

Suppose we make the statement, for example, that 'the morning star is Venus'. Then, certainly, this assertion *looks* as if it were parallel to 'the morning star is a planet' in which 'a planet' is certainly predicative.* But a logical, as distinct from a merely grammatical, analysis will reveal, Frege thinks, that the 'is' of the first assertion expresses identity; it is not the copulative 'is' of predication. 'The morning star is Venus', properly understood, asserts that 'the expressions "the morning star" and "Venus" refer to the same object'. Thus, despite appearances, 'Venus' is not used predicatively.

Similarly, he suggests, in 'all mammals have red blood', 'mammals' does not refer, as might be supposed, to the concept *mammal*. For this proposition merely asserts that 'whatever is a mammal is red-blooded', i.e. that certain (unnamed) objects come under both the concepts *mammal* and *red-blooded*. Thus 'mammals', in this sentence, is predicative, not, in spite of appearance, a subject.

A more serious difficulty arises out of the fact that there are, on the face of it, statements *about* concepts in which 'concepts are described in terms of second-order concepts'. It is all very well to assert that 'all mammals are red-blooded' describes not the concept *mammal* but the 'extension' of this concept, i.e. the objects which can truly be described as mammals – we can see a certain point in the assertion that it is not the concept which is red-blooded. But what of, to take a case, 'the concept *round square* is empty'? In this case, it is impossible to argue that we are really talking about a certain class of objects – those referred to by the expression 'round squares' – because it is the whole point of our remark that there are no such objects. Furthermore, Frege has argued in his theory of arithmetic that numbers are assigned to concepts, not to objects. He went to considerable trouble to prove that numbers are nevertheless objects, not concepts; the problem still remains to show how, in statements in which we assign numbers to concepts, we can avoid treating the concept as something which is named by the subject of our assertion.

Frege's argument on this point is extremely difficult to follow. He begins by denying that the expression 'the concept *horse*' is

*In *Concept and Object* Frege distinguishes between subject, copula and predicate. So he speaks of the predicate in 'the morning star is a planet' as 'a planet', not, as Peirce would have said, '*is* a planet'. But elsewhere Frege's view seems to be identical with Peirce's. A full account of Frege would have to take account of many such changes of view or, at least, of emphasis.

itself the name of a concept. In such a statement as 'the concept *horse* is a familiar one', the subject, he says, is not the name of a concept, but the name of an object – 'the concept *horse*'. That this is so comes out, Frege argues, in the fact that 'concept *horse*' is preceded by the definite article 'the', whereas true concepts are referred to by phrases containing the indefinite article 'a'. We speak of '*a* mammal' '*a* whale', '*a* man', in order to refer to a concept; of '*the* evening star', '*the* capital of Australia', in order to refer to an object. Similarly, then, '*the* concept *horse*' must be the name of an object, not of a concept.

This leads to the apparently paradoxical result that the concept *horse* is not a concept, whereas, for example, the city of Berlin is certainly a city and the volcano Vesuvius a volcano. But once again, Frege argues, the parallel is not an exact one, as comes out in the fact that we recognize the necessity of italicizing, or putting into quotation marks, the *horse* of 'the concept *horse*', whereas we feel no such necessity in regard to 'Berlin' in 'the city of Berlin'. To talk about concepts we have first to 'represent them by an object' – this is accomplished by using the phrase 'the concept X'.

The logical difference between 'the concept X' and 'X' (where 'X' refers to a concept) comes out in the fact, Frege thinks, that they work differently in sentences; a sentence which is perfectly sensible when 'X' appears as a constituent within it is quite without meaning when 'the concept X' is substituted for 'X'. Take the sentence 'there is at least one square root of 4': if we try to replace 'square root of 4' by 'the concept *square root of* 4', then, Frege argues, the resulting sentence is neither true nor false but senseless. Quite generally, according to Frege, if we try to use a proper name – the name of an 'argument' – predicatively, i.e. in the manner of functioning appropriate only for a concept, the resulting sentence will be nonsensical.

This fact may be concealed from us, however, because in our imperfect language the same phrase can stand indifferently for an object or for a concept. Anyone who wishes to think exactly, and to avoid philosophical howlers, will have to acquire the habit of so using quotation marks, or some other typographical device, as to make it perfectly clear whether he is using a concept (i.e. operating with it predicatively) or *talking about* a concept (i.e. representing it by an object). Frege's insistence on this point is one of his most conspicuous legacies to recent philosophy. Disputes about where quotation marks ought to fall have been a feature of recent controversies in *Mind;* it is safe to say that few contemporary philosophers use quotation marks without misgiving.[28]

Frege's successors have not usually been content with his mode of distinguishing between sense and reference and, in particular, with his application of that distinction to sentences. Nor have they accepted Frege's distinction between concepts and objects quite as it stands. But at least Frege raised the problems in a form in which subsequent philosophers found it fruitful to discuss them. And in arguing that it is language that leads us astray or, again, in setting up the ideal of a perfect language which would not betray us because in it every expression would have a fixed and definite sense, Frege, more than any other nineteenth-century philosopher, anticipates the preoccupations of twentieth-century positivism and its diverse progeny.[29]

CHAPTER 7

Some Critics of Formal Logic

'THE new logic' is a phrase which constantly recurs in philosophical discussions in the early years of this century. Fresh from Boole and De Morgan, one might imagine that it was their innovations, above all, which were being thus described. But that would be a serious misinterpretation; in the eyes of the 'new logicians', Boole and De Morgan merely elaborated a familiar error, the error of supposing that logic exhibits and describes formally valid patterns of inference. The 'new logic' was, indeed, an attack on the idea of *formal validity*, whether that attack took shape as Idealism or as Pragmatism, which were on this question, as on so many others, of the one mind. From its point of view *any* formal logic, traditional or mathematical, was intolerably 'abstract', and committed by that 'abstractness' to misleading trivialities. A true logic, it was argued, a logic which does not distort the processes of thought by forcing it into foreign moulds, must be 'philosophical', not formal, in its method and its emphasis.

The idea of such a philosophical logic appears as one ingredient in Mansel's eclectic *Prolegomena Logica* (1851).* As in all his other writings Mansel follows closely in Hamilton's footsteps, in this case relying upon Hamilton's description of the processes of thinking in the notes to his edition of Reid. But he went back also to the philosophers his master particularly admired, Cousin and, more particularly, Kant.

The object of the *Prolegomena* is to determine the province of logic, a logic 'neither encumbered with fictitious wealth by a spurious utilitarianism, nor unprofitably buried in the earth of an isolated and barren formalism'. To put the matter less metaphorically, Mansel is arguing against Mill that the methods to be

---

*A work, it is worth noting, which Boole greatly admired. As we saw, Boole himself was not fully satisfied by any logic which did not appear, in the end, as a description of 'laws of thought' and hence as not merely formal. Peirce, on the other hand, maintained that with Mansel's *Prolegomena to Logic* 'logic touched bottom'. 'There is no room,' he wrote, 'for it to become more degraded.'

employed in empirical scientific inquiries have nothing whatever to do with logic and against the new formalists that formal logic is 'by itself, trivial and empty'.

Mansel's *Prolegomena*, then, takes shape as an inquiry into the nature of conception, of judgement, of reasoning – an amalgam of logic, psychology and epistemology, in the manner characteristic of the British tradition. Yet the tradition is modified by Mansel's interest in Continental philosophy. In particular – and here especially he appears as a precursor of Bradley and Bosanquet – Mansel argues that the 'judgement', not simple apprehension, is the unit of thought. Thought he defines as 'the knowing and judging of things by means of concepts'; to think, in other words, is not merely to 'have an idea' but to judge something to fall under a certain concept.

Yet although Mansel has some claims to be considered as initiating the movement towards an Idealist logic in nineteenth-century England, the fact remains that Bradley and Bosanquet do not so much as refer to him, contemptuous no doubt of his allegiance to the despised Hamilton.[1] They turned direct to Germany for their inspiration, not merely to Kant and Hegel but to Herbart, Lotze, Sigwart and Ueberweg.[2] Bosanquet, indeed, did little more than acclimatize German logic in England; Bradley,[3] as usual, was distinctly more unorthodox.

Logic begins, he argues, from the judgement. Since he was breaking with the British tradition that the proper starting-point is the idea, he felt it necessary to consider in detail, as the first main issue in *The Principles of Logic* (1883), how idea and judgement are related to one another. He defines judgement as 'the act which refers an ideal content (recognized as such) to a reality beyond the act'. The starting-point of logic, then, is not the idea taken simply as something 'in my mind' – the 'ideal content' – but the idea considered as having a meaning, pointing to a reality. Confusion on this point, he thought, was the great source of weakness in British logic; it led inevitably to the muddling together of psychology and logic. Bradley came to feel, all the same, that his discussion of judgement in the *Principles* still stood too close to the Lockean tradition. For he wrote as if an idea *could* be taken as something complete in itself, even if this is not the point of departure for logic. His more mature view, presented in his *Essays on*

Truth and Reality, is that ideas never 'float', are never complete in themselves, but always appear as somehow attached to a reality which they qualify, as a characterizing ingredient in a judgement. The idea, that is, has no existence except as *meaning*; the least we can think of is a judgement, in which an idea already has a reference to Reality.

Bradley rejects, then, the traditional view that judgement consists in the application of one idea (the predicate) to another idea (the subject). In the first place, he argues, there is only the *one* 'ideal content' in a judgement – that single content which, in judging, we take to be real. On the traditional view, when we affirm that 'the wolf ate the lamb', we have first one idea – 'the wolf' – and then another idea – 'the lamb' – and then we conjoin these two ideas into a judgement which links them together. But why, Bradley asks, should we reckon the wolf as being 'one' idea? Obviously, the wolf is complex, just as the situation 'the wolf ate the lamb' is complex. If we mean by 'one' idea something which contains no complexity, then, Bradley argues, there is no such thing; and yet once we admit that ideas can be complex there is no longer any reason for denying that 'the wolf ate the lamb' is itself a single idea. 'Any content whatever,' he concludes, 'which the mind takes as a whole, however large or however small, however simple or however complex, is one idea, and its manifold relations are embraced in a unity.'

Furthermore, the view that every judgement links two ideas, subject and predicate, can make nothing, according to Bradley, of such judgements as '*B* follows from *A*', '*A* and *B* are equal', 'there is a sea-serpent', 'there is nothing here', in which it would be quite arbitrary to distinguish any particular ingredient as the subject. These examples bring out very clearly, he thinks, that the judgement is a single entity, not a set of linked 'terms' or 'ideas'. In short, Bradley is at least as critical as the 'symbolic logicians' of the traditional analysis of the proposition.

The difference is that Bradley has not the slightest intention of replacing the old propositional forms by new ones, by Jevons's equations, for example. If we take Jevons's analysis seriously, Bradley tries to show, we are forced to interpret such a proposition as 'all Negroes are men' as if it said no more than *Negro men = Negro men*. Then we have squeezed all the content out of the judgement, reduced it to an empty shell – 'the judgement has been gutted and finally vanishes'.

No doubt, Bradley admits, there is an element of truth both in the traditional and in the equational analysis of judgement. The traditional view emphasizes that every judgement holds together a diversity, the equational view that an identity underlies this diversity. But the identity of the judgement is not, so Bradley tries to show, a relation between its 'terms'; it consists in the fact that the judgement ascribes an ideal content to the single system of Reality. 'All Negroes are men', for example, asserts that *Reality is such that Negroes are human:* it unifies by ascribing a predicate to a single Reality, although this predicate is itself a diversified one. No other interpretation of the judgement, Bradley argues, can reconcile its unity with its diversity. Formal distinctions between propositions, it immediately follows, are superficial, insignificant: all propositions, ultimately, have the same form – they assert an ideal content of Reality.

There is an obvious objection to this view, one which Herbart had already emphasized in his *Introduction to Philosophy* (1813); many of our judgements, he said, are not about realities but about possibilities, or even impossibilities. Such a judgement as 'a four-cornered circle is an impossibility' is clearly, Herbart pointed out, not about a *real* four-cornered circle. This judgement, Bradley replies, has been wrongly expressed: we are being misled by the verbal formula we have chosen to employ. Reframe it as *the nature of space excludes the connexion of round and square* and the apparent reference to unreal entities completely vanishes – yet we have said all that the original assertion could possibly intend. Thus, Bradley, like Frege, emphasizes that the grammatical form of a statement can be quite misleading as a guide to its logical form.

Other points which Herbart raises are, in Bradley's opinion, more serious. Bradley has somehow to destroy Herbart's arguments which profess to show that the apparently categorical character of judgements, the appearance they present of being about Reality, is in every case an illusion, a judgement being by its nature hypothetical. Ideas, Herbart had contended, are by nature general; to judge, to relate ideas, is therefore to link two general, or universal, entities. To assert that 'all whales are mammals', for example, is to judge that *anything of the whale-kind is of the mammal-kind*. This judgement makes no reference whatever, except hypothetically, to *specific* mammals or *specific* whales. Facts, on the other hand, are particular. Hence, Herbart concluded, there is a gap between judgement and reality. The judgement, presuming it is true, makes the merely hypothetical assertion that if anything is supposed to be of the whale-kind it must also be supposed to be of the mammal-kind; a fact, on the contrary, is an actual, not a merely hypothetical, connexion between particular existences.

Herbart's argument begins from the presumption that a judgement relates ideas; this granted, Bradley considers, it is unanswerable. No doubt, he admits, the empiricist would attempt an answer; he would say, as Mill sometimes did, that although a *universal* judgement has only an indirect relation to reality, this is not true of the *singular* judgement: that 'I have a toothache', for example, is a direct record of a specific fact, even if 'all whales are mammals' only asserts a connexion between universals. Bradley rejects this contrast between singular and general propositions; both 'I' and 'toothache', he argues, must refer to general ideas. The singular judgement 'I have a toothache', for example, means that *anything supposed to be the sort of being I am must be supposed to be suffering from toothache*. Nor can this generality be avoided, Bradley argues, by substituting a proper name like 'Jones' for 'I'. He rejects Mill's view that proper names 'have no connotation': 'Jones' in a sentence like 'Jones has toothache' must have a meaning which goes beyond this specific event, he argues, if we are to avoid Lotze's conclusion that such statements merely assert the identity *toothaching Jones is toothaching Jones*. 'Jones' refers to something with persistent attributes, something identifiable over a period of time, and these persistent attributes are the connotation of 'Jones'. Similarly – here following Plato's *Sophist* – Bradley asserts that 'here' and 'now' are meaningless unless they have a general significance.

Thus, if the universal proposition suffers from the defect of unreality, the singular proposition must share this defect. Furthermore, according to Bradley, the singular judgement, in however elementary a form, mutilates; it is never, as the empiricist supposes, an accurate record of a situation. We say, for example, 'there is a wolf'. Such a judgement is a 'poor abstraction' compared with what we actually observe; when we describe what we see as 'a wolf' rather than as 'an animal baring its teeth' we have quite arbitrarily selected one aspect of the total reality which confronts us. To regard such an assertion as 'the whole truth' is, Bradley argues, to falsify reality. We can 'save' such propositions as these, he thinks, only if we regard them as asserting a general connexion between such-and-such features of the environment and *being a wolf*. Then we are no longer abstracting; we place the wolf in the concrete system in which we perceive it. We cannot, then, 'save' the reality of our judgements, in the empiricist manner, by arguing that even although universal judgements have only an indirect relation to reality the singular judgement simply records the facts. If Herbart's objections are to be met, more radical steps are needed. The 'reality' of our judgements can be maintained, Bradley once more argues, only by rejecting the traditional theory of judgements in two respects – denying that a judgement relates ideas and denying that its *apparent* subject is its real subject. If *all X are Y* were really about *X*, he freely admits, it could assert only the hypothetical *if anything is X, then it is Y*, and Herbart's argument is unanswerable. But if, as Bradley has argued, it asserts that a Reality of which *X* is predicable also has *Y* predicable of it, if its true subject is a Reality which is not explicitly mentioned but is nevertheless the ultimate ground of our assertion, then the categorical nature of the judgement is saved.

Bradley has still to meet an objection from a quite different quarter: that although such a judgement as *all X are Y* hypothetically asserts *Y* of *X*, it categorically denies that *X* is *non-Y*, so that it can be interpreted as having a categorical meaning simply as it stands, as a statement about *X*, without having recourse to an underlying 'Reality'. Venn, for example, had suggested in his *Symbolic Logic* that 'in respect of what such a proposition [a universal affirmative proposition] affirms it can only be taken as conditional, but in respect of what it denies it may be regarded as absolute'. Bradley, on the other hand, tries to show that the negative judgement is *never* absolute, that it always rests on unstated conditions. To assert that *X is not Y*, on his account of the matter, is to take *X* as having some property which prevents it from being *Y*, even if we do not (usually) know what this property is. On this showing, we know what we are *denying* when we say that X *is not Y* – because its contradictory X *is Y* is a definite assertion – but we do not clearly know what property we are positively asserting X to have. Affirmation, to Bradley, is primary, negation is parasitic – this is an important point of contrast between Idealist and Boolean logic.

From the judgement, Bradley turns to consider inference. Once more, he is severely critical of the traditional logic. He begins by listing a set of what he thinks are indisputably 'inferences', of which every theory of inference must take account. These include a number of relational inferences and others of a kind which the traditional logic had tended to neglect. On the basis of these examples, Bradley rejects as an 'effete superstition' the classical doctrine that every inference depends on a universal major premise. 'Begotten by an old metaphysical blunder,' he writes, 'nourished by a senseless choice of examples, fostered by the stupid conservatism of logicians, and protected by the impotence of younger rivals this chimaera has had a good deal more than its day.' And once this 'chimaera' is recognized for what it is, the supremacy of syllogism over all other forms of inference can no longer, he thinks, be sustained. Syllogism is a type, but only *one* type, of inference.

What, then, is inference? It consists, Bradley at first suggests, in the discovery of a relation – this is one of the many points at which James and Bradley came together.[4] We consider the relation of A to B and of B to C; we then construct an 'ideal group' which unites A, B, C on the basis of some single principle. We note, for example, that $A = B$ and $B = C$; we then combine A, B, C into a whole, united by quantitative identity. In so doing we perceive the relation between A and C. There are no rules governing this process, according to Bradley, and no models to imitate. 'It is the man who perceives the points of union within his premises,' he writes, 'who is able to reason. And for the process of inspection one wants a good eye, for there are no rules which can tell you what to perceive.' At best, the logician can draw attention to excessively general principles, to the fact, for example, that if A stands in a temporal relation to B and B to C, there must be some temporal relation linking A with C. But to find out *what* that relation is, we must use our powers of synthesis.

This preliminary account of inference, as 'an ideal synthesis, which unites around a centre of inference not less than two terms into one construction', is critically re-examined in the second volume of *The Principles of Logic*. On the face of it, Bradley points out, there are inferences which this formula does not cover, inferences in which there is no 'centre', no interposing term to link the extremes. Immediate inference is a case in point; so are addition and subtraction. But it might be disputed whether these are inferences. Bradley, therefore, is led to face once more the general question: in what does inference consist?

To infer, he says, is to reason. And we reason whenever we come to see that Reality *must be* what a judgement asserts it to be, instead of merely affirming that as a matter of fact this is how things are. Reasoning, he considers, always takes the form of an operation on a *datum* – 'an ideal experiment upon something which is given' – by means of which the reasoner arrives at a result which he then ascribes to his original datum. He may begin, for example, with a reality qualified by the pair of relations *A's being to the right of B* and *B's being to the right of C;* operating upon this datum he arrives at a synthesis – an 'ideal whole' – in which these relations appear as elements, and then, finally, he returns to ascribe to Reality the relation *C–B–A*. The essence of reasoning, then, lies in the discovery of a systematic interconnexion between the predicates of Reality, not in the linking of two terms by means of a third.

To describe inference as an 'ideal experiment', however, makes it appear that inference is wholly of our making, that our conclusion is the result of some operation which we deliberately choose to employ. Here we have lost sight, Bradley thinks, of the necessity which properly attaches to inference. To do justice to this necessity, he suggests, we need to emphasize that in such an 'ideal experiment' the *datum* must, in a way, be left to develop in its own manner; any step in the inference which is peculiarly 'ours', an expression of a merely personal interest, is a departure from reasoning. And thus Bradley is led to redefine inference, particularly in the first *Terminal Essay*, as 'the ideal self-development of an object'; the crucial thing is what an 'object' actually implies, not what *we* infer from it. This self-development, according to Bradley, is never complete; at this point Bradley's logic leads directly to the 'negative metaphysics' of *Appearance and Reality*. In some measure we, as finite human beings, are inevitably condemned to abstraction and falsification. But this metaphysical limitation need not disturb the logician. Like a special scientist, he is entitled to take his subject-matter for what it is worth, without raising the question whether it can *ultimately* satisfy.

It will be obvioius that Bradley's logic is very different indeed from any kind of formal logic, traditional or 'mathematical'; against the possiblity of such a logic, a logic in which implication is described as a conformity to general patterns, Bradley's *Principles* is a continual protest. At the same time, Mill's 'psychological' logic is denounced in no less uncompromising terms. The traditional logic at least had the virtue, in Bradley's eyes, of admitting the reality of universals, in contrast with what he takes to be Mill's doctrine that reasoning proceeds merely by the association of ideas, each of them particular. The facts on which associationism relies for its plausibility can be summarized, Bradley suggests, in 'the law of redintegration' – a name he took over from Hamilton, 'having found nothing else we could well take'. This law he summarizes thus: 'any element tends to reproduce those elements with which it has formed one state of mind.' Thus, for Bradley, association consists in the reinstatement, by a psychical element, of the system in which it is a part. (A picture of the Tower Bridge recalls London to us, because London is a system in which the Tower Bridge is a constituent.) 'To talk of an association between psychical particulars,' he writes, 'is to utter mere nonsense. These particulars in the first place have got no permanence; their life endures for a fleeting moment. . . . There is no Hades where they wait in disconsolate exile, till association announces resurrection and recall. . . . These touching beliefs of a pious legend may babble in the tradition of a senile psychology, or contort themselves in the metaphysics of some frantic dogma, but philosophy must register them and sigh and pass on.'

The association of ideas, as Mill envisaged it, once rejected, the whole fabric of Mill's logic, Bradley thinks, will collapse. Mill, Bradley will allow, deserves some credit for noticing the defectiveness of a syllogistic logic; but he wrongly supposed that the alternative to syllogism is inference from particulars. Observing that

we may come to a particular conclusion after experience of particular cases, Mill mistakenly concluded, according to Bradley,
that the inference is from the particular cases. To argue, as Mill
suggests that we should, from 'this burnt' and 'that burnt' to
'this other thing will burn' is to commit an obvious fallacy; to
conclude instead that 'this *resembling* thing will burn' is to introduce in the notion of resembling, so Bradley objects, the universal
which Mill had promised to do without.

Bradley's lively criticism of Mill's 'inductive methods' follows
similar lines. These methods presume, he argues, that our experience from the beginning is of general connexions between
universals, not at all, as Mill imagines, of 'purely particular'
facts. To say, as Mill does, that we encounter situations which
differ in only one circumstance is to imply, Bradley thinks, that
these situations have just so many general properties, i.e. that
they are not purely particular. And then the so-called methods
consist merely in excluding one or the other of these properties
from being the cause we are seeking. We are dealing all the time,
then, with universals, not making deductions from particulars.
Inductive logic, he concludes, is a fiasco.

Bradley's *Logic* is a product of his Lotzean period; he was at
that stage prepared to draw a contrast, more or less sharp, between thought – the province of logic – and 'ultimate reality',
the province of metaphysics. Thus his logic, particularly the first
volume of the *Principles*, has a measure of independence from his
Absolutist metaphysics; it has excited the admiration of, and has
even influenced, a good many philosophers who are bored or
irritated by *Appearance and Reality*. In his *Knowledge and Reality*,
we have already seen, Bernard Bosanquet, speaking for the
Hegelian tradition, rebuked Bradley for thus divorcing thought
from reality. There is a penitent tone in a good many of Bradley's
additions to the second edition of the *Principles;* he refers his
readers more than once to Bosanquet's *Logic* for 'the true view'.
For a strictly Idealist logic, devoid of Bradley's penetrating eccen-
tricities, we must turn, indeed, to Bosanquet.

His *Logic* (1888) bears the subtitle *The Morphology of Knowledge*. That summarizes its contents. The *Logic* is an attempt, in
the manner of Hegel and of Lotze – even although in opposition
to Lotze's metaphysics – to depict the stages through which

thought passes from the simplest form of judgement ('this is red') to that complex disjunctive in which is exhibited the concrete universal, the universal which is a systematic interrelation of its constituent parts. It is interesting to observe that, quite unlike Bradley, Bosanquet refers to Mill with warm admiration. There is more in this than an exemplification of Bosanquet's general tendency to see the good in people (the Reality to which they point) as contrasted with Bradley's tendency to see the bad (the superficial Appearance with which they are content). Bosanquet had his dislikes, for all that they were not usually expressed with Bradley's acerbity – and formal logic was not the least of them. 'The reform of logic *in this country*,' writes Bosanquet, 'dates from the work of Stuart Mill, whose genius placed him, in spite of all philosophical shortcomings, on the right side as against the degenerate representatives of Aristotle.' The great point in Mill's favour is that for him logic is primarily a theory of inquiry. But whereas Mill distinguished syllogistic logic as the logic of consistency from inductive logic as the logic of truth, to Bosanquet all logic is the logic of truth – even if truth is resolved into a species of systematic consistency, or coherence. 'The degenerate representatives of Aristotle' are not to be allowed any cubby-hole of 'consistency' in which they can hide from Bosanquet's wrath.

To follow through the details of Bosanquet's logic – he published a shorter version of it in *The Essentials of Logic* (1895), a much reprinted work – would be unprofitable: in large part, it is a restatement of the familiar metaphysics of Idealism, and much also derives directly from Lotze or from Bradley. But there were certain views of a semi-formal character of which Bosanquet came to stand as the representative.[5]

Thus Bosanquet particularly stresses the categorical foundation of hypothetical judgements, in opposition to that interpretation of '*if ... then ...*' which Peirce had sketched and Russell was more fully to work out. 'Hypothetical affirmation', Bosanquet goes so far as to say, 'is a contradiction in terms, and so is hypothetical inference. The whole process apart from any categorical meaning it may make explicit ... is a mere make-believe'. He illustrates his thesis by means of the following example: 'if a donkey is Plato, it is a great philosopher.' This is not a statement at all, he argues, because it 'scatters underlying reality to the winds'. A *Reality such that a donkey is Plato* would be, in Bosan-quet's eyes, an utterly incoherent system, and hence no reality at all. Any intelligible hypothetical is an assertion, he considers, about a connexion which *actually* or *categorically* holds within the system of reality. 'If the heart stops, the body dies', for exam-ple, asserts a connexion within organic structures between two 'adjectives' – a stopping heart and a dying body.

Bosanquet's attitude to the hypothetical illustrates the character of his opposition to formal logic. A genuinely philosophical logic, he argues, concerns itself with 'the conditions of logical stability'. It tries to discover, he agrees with Lotze, the ideal judgement, the elements of which are apprehended as necessarily connected in a system. Formal logic, in contrast, makes use of 'terms' and 'pro-positions' as if they were distinct entities which can be related just as the logician pleases. Thus Bosanquet criticizes the syllogism, for example, on the ground that it links premises and conclusion, major, middle and minor term, in a merely external way; for Bosanquet the question is not, in the classical example, how Socrates is related to mortality, but whether a certain complex, *the Socratic-human sort of mortality*, can properly be ascribed to Reality. That question the syllogism, with its emphasis on distinction, is incapable, he thinks, of either raising or sett-ling.

Particularly notorious in Bosanquet's logic was his insistence upon reciprocity.[6] This appears most clearly in his analysis of hypotheticals. The typical hypothetical, for him, is the assertion that *if A is B, A is C*. Now, he argues, if *A's being B* really necessi-tates its being *C*, this is simply to say that there is some system in which *A, B, C*, cohere. Since coherence is symmetrical it will follow that *A's being C* must also necessitate *A's being B*. This conclusion, of course, cuts directly across the traditional view that hypo-thetical assertions are irreversible. But it is naturally connected both with the coherence theory of truth and with the Lotzean presumption that every proposition expresses an identity. Bosan-quet admits that 'if he is drowned, he is dead', for example, does not seem to affirm reciprocal connexions. And he does not want to read this assertion merely as 'if he is dead, he is dead' – although it is worth noting that he is tempted by this interpreta-tion. He thinks that he can maintain diversity within such an assertion while pointing to the identity which underlies that diversity by reading it as 'if he is drowned, he is dead through suffocation by water'. Only by means of such an interpretation, he argues, can we satisfy logic's demand for coherence. All 'giving of grounds', in fact, is reciprocal – 'it is only because the "grounds" alleged in everyday life are burdened with irrelevant matter or confused with causation in time,' Bosanquet writes, 'that we consider the hypothetical judgement to be in its nature not reversible.'[7]

In this point of view Bosanquet persisted. His last logical writing was his *Implication and Linear Inference* (1920) in which he argued that deductive and inductive logicians fall into the same error: they both presume that inference is 'linear', a matter of making our way from a set of propositions to some other proposition. This error which they share is more important, he considers, than the points which divide them. Properly understood, according to Bosanquet, inference consists in coming to see the necessity of a judgement – seeing that it is *this or nothing* – and such an apprehension of it is possible only if we recognize it as having a place in a system. To infer, for Bosanquet, is to see the implications of a judgement, not in the sense, merely, of noting that this or that other judgement follows from it but in a more radical sense: to infer, we need to be confident that if this judgement were not true the system of thought to which it belongs, the Reality to which it points, would be destroyed. This way of looking at inference carries with it the consequence, in sharp contrast to what writers like Russell had been maintaining, that every method of inquiry forms part of the subject-matter of logic. Every way of coming to see that a judgement is true, however informal, is a logical process, a method of achieving stability of thought.

Not all Idealists, it is worth noting, agreed that a philosophical logic must be anti-formal: on this point, with his strong mathematical interests, Royce stood quite apart from Bosanquet and Bradley.[8] That does not mean that he ceased to be an Idealist. His logic might be described as a synthesis between Idealist philosophy and the logic of the mathematicians, as that had been developed by Peirce – whose influence on Royce was considerable – and by Russell.[9] In the brief 'Logic' he wrote for the *Encyclopedia of the Philosophical Sciences* (Eng. trans., 1913), in which he develops the line of inquiry he had already embarked upon in his paper on 'The Relation of the Principles of Logic to the Foundations of Geometry' (*Trans. Am. Math. Soc.*, 1905), Royce defines logic as 'a science of order'. Such an order can either be described in formal terms or interpreted philosophically as a necessity of thought; to consider it from the first point of view is to follow Peirce and Russell, to consider it from the second point of view is to follow Bradley and Bosanquet. And Royce saw no reason why he should not do both. Thus although the general pattern of Royce's logic is Idealist, he was also one of the principal media through which mathematical logic was transmitted to younger American logicians.

Meanwhile there were logicians who fought with equal vigour against both parties of this alliance – the 'instrumentalists'. In England, an unorthodox attitude to logic had been perseveringly sustained by Alfred Sidgwick, in a series of books which began with his *Fallacies: a view of Logic from the Practical Side* (1883). Logic, according to Sidgwick, is primarily 'the science of avoiding fallacy'. The logician, he argues, ought to inquire into the ways of going wrong, a subject he usually discusses only scantily and apologetically. The ordinary 'logical rules' are not, as Mill had thought, an effective barrier against fallacy, because they take no account of ambiguity. There is no formal way of determining, for example, whether in the syllogism 'All models are well-poised, this is a model, therefore this is well-poised', we mean the same by 'model' in both premises. In general, Sidgwick complained, logicians write as if their starting-point were unambiguous 'propositions' or 'judgements', whereas in fact they begin from statements, the interpretation of which always involves ambiguities, uncertainties and hesitancies. Any logic which has the least utility, any logic which is more than a game, must abandon, Sidgwick concludes, the attempt to work out 'formally valid' relations between propositions; it must settle down to the detailed task of finding out what people are *actually* saying or *actually* arguing in this or that particular case.

Sidgwick's line of argument was taken over and further developed by F. C. S. Schiller. In a long series of books and articles he waged a vigorous campaign against the very possibility of a formal logic, and he tried to work out a 'voluntarist' alternative in his *Logic for Use* (1929). Like the Idealists, Schiller begins from the judgement. But, following Dewey, he denounces Bradley on the ground that he has 'degraded the judgement into a proposition'; in other words, he has discussed the judgement as if it were something quite impersonal, with an existence independent of the interests and hopes of the judger. Judgement, Schiller argues, is always a judging, a personal act, with a specific intention which constitutes its meaning; the meaning of a judgement is the way it is used in a context. What we mean, he concludes, can never be deduced merely from the words we use or the signs we make; account must be taken of what we are intending to do with those words and signs. Thus, for example, if we were to assert that 'the square is round' the formal logician would condemn our assertion as self-contradictory. No doubt it is, Schiller admits, *if we intend these words to describe a geometrical figure*. The fact remains, he says, that if we are describing a London square our assertion may be true; in other contexts it might be a joke, or a way of saying that someone had drawn a square badly. To determine what we are saying the logician has to study the context in which the sentence is being used; formal rules are unavailing.

Equally, Schiller continues, no formal rules can tell us what a judgement implies or does not imply. If the logician is to analyse the structure of actual inferences he will need to abandon the whole conception of 'validity' or 'logical truth'. At this point, Schiller goes further than Sidgwick; he rejects fallacy along with validity. The logician ought, he thinks, to concentrate his attention upon the distinction between truth and error; formal logic merely distracts him in the search for truth by setting up the ideal of a purely formal 'validity' or 'fallacy'. Properly understood – notice the extent to which Schiller and Bosanquet are in accord – logic will be a theory of inquiry, inquiry considered as a concrete human task. It will help men to understand how they come to fall into error, and it will evaluate the different procedures they employ in the search for truth. It will not, however, make inquiry 'safe'; Schiller has no intention of abandoning syllogism merely in order to fall back upon a Cartesian 'direct intuition' or Millian inductive methods. 'No care in observation,' he writes, 'no skill in experimentation can guard scientific evidence against unforeseen objections, new conditions and unknown possibilities or error.' The best we can do, according to Schiller, is gradually to work towards a situation in which the balance of probabilities in favour of our hypothesis is overwhelming.

This conception of logic as the theory of inquiry had, of course, already been suggested by John Dewey[10] in his *Essays on Experimental Logic* (1916) and was later to be worked out in detail in his *Logic, the Theory of Enquiry* (1938). Dewey sets out to show that formal distinctions arise within 'the matrix of inquiry', and have no significance except as ingredients in that matrix. Logical principles, on his view, are not eternal truths, which have been laid down once and for all as supplying a pattern to which all inquiry must conform; on the contrary, they are principles which science, at a certain stage in its development, has found to be involved in its own successes. When science develops new methods of inquiry, he therefore maintains, logic ought to be modified accordingly.

Traditional logic, Dewey argues, is associated with the Platonic conception of science, which sees in it a mode of apprehending relations between essences. The syllogism represents that process of inquiry in which species are brought under genera. Modern science, however, relates quantities, not essences; and the relations to which it points cannot be analysed, Dewey thinks, within the formal pattern which was suitable for species-genus classifications. Contemporary formal logic, he concedes, had shown itself to be partially conscious of that defect in the traditional logic; it had added relational propositions and inferences to the familiar schedules of subject-predicate propositions and syllogistic inferences. But it had thereby confused, Dewey argues, rather than clarified; it had added new forms where it should have radically reconsidered the older forms. Modern logicians abstracted logical patterns from the context of inquiry, describing them as 'merely formal'; what is really needed, according to Dewey, is a new logic of inquiry, in which the sharp distinction between formal and material will be as out of place as it is in Greek logic. Aristotelian logic was a satisfactory analysis of what the Greeks meant by 'knowledge'; the new logic should be an equally satisfactory analysis of what modern science means when it claims to 'know'.

We can illustrate Dewey's analysis of formal relationships from a simple case – the traditional 'logical relations' of contrariety, sub-contrariety, and contradiction. Contrariety, exemplified in the relation between *All X are Y* and *no X are Y*, arises, Dewey thinks, in the course of setting 'limits' to inquiry. In themselves, contrary propositions are 'logically defective' – as comes out in the fact that *both* contraries may be 'invalid' – but they help us to circumscribe the field within which a solution to our problem must be found, somewhere within the area delimited by *X being invariably Y* and its *never being Y*. The placing of any possible solution within that area is the whole point, the only conceivable significance of contrariety. Sub-contrary propositions – *some X are Y* and *some X are not Y* – lead us further towards our solution, Dewey thinks, in that they set us a definite problem: the problem of determining what it is that 'makes the difference' between those *X* which are, and those which are not, *Y*. Not the 'merely formal' fact that these two propositions cannot both be false, but the 'material' fact that they set a problem for us, constitutes the logical significance of sub-contrariety.

The crucial case, in Dewey's opinion, is contradiction. Formal logic is content with the bare assertion that, say, *all X are Y* and *some X are not Y* contradict one another. But to stop at this point, according to Dewey, is quite to misunderstand the nature of contradiction. The scientist never merely shrugs his shoulders at a contradiction, as a mere 'formal relationship'. For him, contradiction is a spur to inquiry, initiating a new investigation in which the original generalization that *all X are Y* is so modified as to take account of the contradicting case – the *this X is not Y* which, according to Dewey, is the true contradictory of *all X are Y*.

The link between Dewey's 'instrumental' logic and the logic of Hegel will be obvious. And if we look more closely into the details of Dewey's critique of formal logic, we are constantly struck by his affinities with such post-Hegelian logicians as Bradley and Bosanquet. Thus, for example, he argues that a 'truly' universal judgement must point to a necessary connexion and that the hypothetical judgement is 'logically satisfactory' only if it is reversible. And his whole theory of inquiry is a protest against the view that propositions can have any truth except as phases in a system. What is striking in his *Logic*, however, is that he replaces the conception of a static Reality by the idea of systematic inquiry, being more sympathetic, indeed, to Hegel's 'Spirit' than to Bradley's 'Absolute'. His criticism of formal logic contains few novelties for those who approach it through a study of Hegel and post-Hegelian Idealism; what is of importance is that positive theory of inquiry which has already (in Chapter 5) attracted our attention.

For the replacement of formal logic by a theory of inquiry is characteristic of the whole movement of thought from Lotze to Dewey. Of course, this point of view is not novel; indeed, it is Cartesian, and was taken over from Descartes by Locke. But it had to be restated when formal logic experienced its nineteenth-century renaissance. The fundamental question, as has already been suggested, is whether logic is concerned with inference or with implication – with the human activity of inferring or the formal relationship of implying. If we say that inference is its theme, then we are bound to conclude that the study of formal relationships has at most a subordinate role to play; if implication, then we shall reject as 'psychologism' all reference to the processes of inquiry. And with the contrast between inferring and implication goes another, between judgement, understood as a momentary concentration on some particular aspect of the field we are investigating, and the 'proposition', understood as a self-contained entity which *implies* in a manner independent of any context. Are there propositions? and is there formal implication? – those were the points at issue.

CHAPTER 8

The Movement towards Objectivity

THE main tendency of nineteenth-century thought was towards the conclusion that both 'things' and facts about things are dependent for their existence and their nature upon the operations of a mind. Mill set out to show how they are built up by associative mechanisms, fed by sensations; Green that they are constructed by thought; Bradley that they are a finite being's distortion of Reality; James and Bergson that they are tools built by the mind to cope more effectively with the endless stream of experience. They all agreed that if there were no mind there would be no facts; they disputed, only, about what there *would* be – the Absolute, sensation, or a stream of experience.

But we have already detected signs of uneasiness on this point. Mill's 'permanent possibilities' had a substantial look about them. James wavered: facts are made by us and yet facts resist our operations. In Bosanquet's Idealism Nature achieves a striking degree of independence; in Mach's phenomenalism 'sensations' are replaced by 'elements', so as not to presume that the constituents of facts are mind-made. And Avenarius, developing suggestions made by Herbart, caused something of a stir with his analysis of 'introjection',[1] understood as the psychological mechanism which misleads us into believing that what we directly apprehend is always an 'image' or a 'representation' and never an independently existing object.

Yet none of these writers – however near they came to this point – was prepared explicitly and consistently to assert that facts are merely *recognized* by a mind, not *made* by it. And in this refusal they were seconded by the genetic sciences – biology, psychology, anthropology – which flourished in the nineteenth century as never before.

The rise of these sciences is, indeed, the most striking of nineteenth-century cultural developments. With the new enthusiasm for genetic inquiry there naturally came a different way of looking at questions, deriving in the end, perhaps, from Hegel, but without Hegel's metaphysics. Confronted with, say, our belief in God,

174

or our belief in the external world, or our acceptance of certain mathematical or logical principles as axiomatic, philosophers had been accustomed to ask themselves: 'Is this belief true?' Post-Kantian agnosticism, however, had undermined the presumption that this is an intelligible question, one that can be answered in principle, even if only with difficulty in practice. The genetic sciences rushed into the vacuum thus set up. The *proper* question, it was now argued, is the historical one: 'How did such beliefs as these arise?' To ask whether they are true, the suggestion was, is scholastic, reactionary, metaphysical; to ask how they arose, on the contrary, is to set a problem – a genuine, soluble, problem – in empirical science, to be tackled by the new genetic methods.

This point of view was sufficiently common within philosophy itself. Mill, to take a case, worked out a 'psychological theory' to account for our belief in an external world, our belief in matter, our habit of distinguishing between primary and secondary qualities, having ruled out *ab initio* any attempt to *prove* that there is an external world or that things in it have such-and-such properties. 'I do not believe,' he says, 'that the real externality to us of any-thing, except other minds, is capable of proof.' Similarly, Spencer developed an elaborate theory, based on evolutionary principles, to account for the origin of our belief that certain mathematical and logical propositions are necessary; their 'necessity', that is, was to be 'explained' by reference to their origin, not justified by an analysis of their nature.[2]

Naturally enough, the genetic scientists themselves were still more enthusiastic in their claims for the genetic method. Anxious to assert their independence of philosophy, they were heartened by a doctrine which allowed them not merely independence but actual supremacy. There was some dispute, acrimonious at times, as to whether psychology, or biology, or anthropology, should be proclaimed 'The Queen of the Sciences'; but any metaphysics which laid claim to the title was at once howled down as the Old Pretender.

Yet, oddly enough, a new movement which was to be marked by its insistence that every issue is objective, that the primary ques-tion is always: 'Is this true or false?' had already stirred to life within the writings of a psychologist, a psychologist, furthermore, who was an admirer of the British psychologizing tendency in philosophy, of Mill in particular, and a warm advocate of the view that psychology is the fundamental science. But Franz Brentano was an Aristotelian, a scholastic-trained priest, as well as the continuator of Hume's *Treatise;* and his *Psychology from an empirical Standpoint*[3] (1874) reinstated the objectivity characteristic of Aristotle[4] and certain medieval philosophers.

The title of Brentano's book may mislead the modern reader, for, as a result of the alliance between genetic scientists and anti-metaphysical philosophers in the nineteenth century, 'empirical' psychology has come to mean 'genetic' psychology, which traces the origin of mental states, usually by referring them to physiological processes. Brentano was writing at a time when the publication of G. T. Fechner's *Elements of Psycho-physics* (1860) had considerably stimulated such psycho-physical investigations. Brentano took a considerable interest in this work; but was not prepared to admit that it exhausted the field of psychology. Thus he was led to distinguish 'descriptive' psychology – a 'pure' non-physiological psychology – from 'genetic' psychology, with its physiological ingredients.[5] He came to feel, indeed, that in his *Psychology* he had not made this distinction with sufficient sharpness. Perhaps that is why he never completed his *Psychology*, preferring to revise and republish, as *On the Classification of Psychical Phenomena* (1911), only that segment of his book in which he approximated most closely to the ideal of a 'descriptive psychology'. In his doctoral thesis (1866) he had followed Mill in maintaining that 'the methods of psychology are the methods of the natural sciences', but although he continued to insist that his psychology is empirical, it came less and less to resemble an ordinary natural science.

A major point of difference is that Brentano's 'empirical psychology' does not rest primarily on observation. Following Comte, Brentano denied the possibility of introspection, considered as the observation of our mental processes; the attempt to observe, say, our anger – to concentrate our attention upon it – at once, he says, destroys it. Comte had concluded that psychology is impossible and ought to be replaced by sociology. Brentano does not accept this consequence: the psychologist, he says, has other methods of observation at his disposal – he can *remember* his mental processes, he can observe the insane, or simpler forms of life, or the behaviour of other people. But he admits that such observation by itself would not carry the psychologist very far, and in *On the Classification of Psychical Phenomena* these techniques fade into the background.

The foundation of psychology, for Brentano, is the fact that we can *perceive* our own mental acts, even although we cannot *observe* them. To understand this distinction, we must begin from a Cartesian presumption which Brentano accepts as indisputable – the presumption that in being aware of a 'representation' we are simultaneously aware of the act of representing it to ourselves. Thus, for example, we cannot hear a sound, Brentano argues, without being conscious not only of the sound itself but also of the act of hearing it. These are not two distinct acts of awareness, he considers; there is only the one act with two different objects – the sound ('first object') and the act ('second object' – which is thus a kind of reflexive object). If there were in any such case two acts, then the Cartesian presumption, he points out, would lead to an endless multiplication of mental acts. It would mean that to be aware of a sound was to be aware of being aware of a sound, and then, equally, to be aware of being aware of a sound would involve being aware of *that* awareness, and so in indefinitely. The only way out of an incredible multiplication, he considers, is to deny that the act of being aware of our awareness of a sound is a different act from the act of being aware of a sound. To attempt to *observe* a mental act, however, is to attempt to make it the 'first object' of *another* act – when we talk of observation we presume a distinction between observer and observed – and this, Brentano is quite prepared to agree with Comte, is impossible.

Here, then, is an important difference between psychology and any other empirical inquiry: in psychology we 'perceive', in Brentano's special sense of that word, whereas in the other sciences we 'observe'. The advantage, it might seem, lies with the other sciences; but this Brentano categorically denies. The natural scientist, Brentano agrees with Locke, has no direct access to those natural objects which he attempts to describe; anything he says about their 'real nature' can only be a conjecture, based upon his experience of their 'appearances'. He can 'observe' sounds, colours and the like but he can never 'perceive' the physical object itself, i.e. he can never be directly and immediately aware of it. In complete contrast, the psychologist, according to Brentano, has an immediate and direct apprehension of the realities which constitute his subject matter; each mental act perceives itself directly as its 'second object' – not as an 'appearance', not as something from which the real character of the mental act has to be inferred, but precisely as that mental act actually is. That is why, to Brentano as to Hume, psychology stands first amongst the sciences; both accept the Cartesian doctrine that our knowledge of the mental is peculiarly direct and certain as compared with our knowledge of anything else.

But Brentano separated himself from the Descartes–Locke tradition and made his impact upon the movement towards objectivity by redefining the 'psychical' or 'mental'. The characteristic mental phenomenon, Locke had supposed, is the 'idea', and to such 'ideas', he had also argued, our experience is inevitably limited. Thus if, as stricter empiricists were to maintain, there is no knowledge except through experience, it seemed to follow that whatever we can know is bound to be 'mental'. The distinction between mental and non-mental, which Brentano was particularly anxious to maintain because of its connexions with immortality, must be wholly rejected, so it appeared, by any thorough-going adherent of 'the empirical standpoint'.

Brentano hoped to cut through this chain of reasoning by rejecting the preliminary assumption that to be mental is to be an idea. The characteristic feature of a 'psychical phenomenon', he argues, is that it *'points towards an object'* or *'relates to a content'* – these phrases he takes to be synonymous. The mental, then, is an 'act'; the non-mental, in contrast, is quite incapable of 'pointing' or 'having a content'. Brentano's emphasis on the 'act' provoked misunderstandings, as did his description of the objects of acts as possessing, in the scholastic phrase, 'intentional inexistence'. His choice of the words 'act' and 'intentional' led to his being grouped with the followers of Schopenhauer as a 'hormic' psychologist, for whom 'objects' are purposes, or ends, and 'acts' are the impulses which strive towards those ends. To avoid such misinterpretations, Brentano later abandoned the language of 'intentions'. A 'mental act', he explains, is merely the manner in which a mind is related to an object; an 'object' is that which the mind has before it as the content of its act.[6]

The simplest mental act, according to Brentano, is what he calls 'representation' – the bare *having* of an object before the mind. On 'representation' all other mental acts are founded, in the sense that it supplies them with their object, to which, however, they take up an attitude of their own. Obviously, 'representation' has affiliations with Locke's 'experience'. But in Locke's philosophy, although experience supplies judgement with its raw materials, in the form of 'simple ideas', the actual object of a judgement is something quite different from the object of experience. It is not an idea, but a set of ideas bound together by relations of agreement and disagreement. Brentano, on the other hand – again like Hume – denies that the object of a judgement is at all different from the object of a representation.

He takes Hume's example. An 'existential' judgement – a judgement of the form *x exists* – contains, he says, only the single idea *x*, not two ideas *x* and *existence* linked together by a relation. So far, this only shows that a judgement can *sometimes* have a single idea as its object, so that the multiplicity of its objects cannot be the defining characteristic of a judgement. But Brentano goes further than Hume did. *Every* simple judgement, he says, can be reduced to the existential form. 'Some trees are green' does no more than affirm, and 'no trees are green' merely denies, that *green trees exist*. The content of these judgements, he concludes, is that very same 'green trees' which we can represent to ourselves as an idea. The difference between judgement and representation lies not at all in the object but entirely in the manner in which we conceive it: to judge is to affirm or deny the object, to represent is merely to have an object before us.

This theory obviously has its difficulties; not the least important is that of giving a satisfactory account of the status of 'objects' and their relation to 'mental acts'. The object, it is supposed, is in some way the 'content' of an act – it is that which differentiates one act of judgement, say, from another. But take the case where we deny the existence of an object: suppose, for example, we deny that round squares exist. Our act of denial is real enough; but how can it have 'round squares' as its content, when the very purpose of the act is to deny that there are round squares? How, in short, can a real act have an *unreal* content? The traditional theory saw no difficulty on this point. For it there is simply, in such cases, 'the idea of a round square'; this is real *qua* idea, although it may fail to represent anything beyond itself – it has what Descartes called 'objective', even if no 'formal', reality. But once make that idea the 'content' of an act which has 'formal' reality and those problems immediately arise which the more critical of Brentano's admirers set out to answer.

In particular, this is the point of departure for Meinong's 'theory of objects'. Meinong worked under Brentano at Vienna and began his philosophical career, therefore, as a psychologist. But it is significant that his first major publication consisted of two volumes of *Hume Studies* (1877–82), in which, furthermore, he paid special attention to Hume's theory of abstract ideas and his analysis of relations. He was a 'psychologist', that is, only in the sense that Hume was. He accepted the British empiricist view that relations and universals are 'the work of the mind'; it seemed to follow that the theory of relations, of meaning, of truth, of judgement must all fall within the province of psychology.[8]

His method was Brentano's – that painstaking analysis of specific problems which was to be characteristic of twentieth-century British philosophy and contrasts so strikingly with the philosophical habits traditional in the German countries, although much less powerful in Austria than in Germany itself. To Brentano and his disciples, philosophy is science or it is nothing. They had no patience with Lange's view that philosophy is a kind of poetry, a large-scale imaginative construction. The philosopher, they thought, should choose a clearly-defined problem and grapple with it to the best of his ability. In many ways, indeed, their approach is reminiscent of the elaborate analyses of the scholastics. Philosophers since Descartes had been mainly intent upon destroying scholastic distinctions; Meinong creates new distinctions, pointing to differences where his predecessors had insisted upon similarities.

By 1904, when he wrote *Investigations into the Theory of Objects and Psychology*, it had become clear to Meinong that although psychology might be relevant to the work he was undertaking, his work was not itself 'psychological', even on the loosest possible interpretation of that not unduly restrictive word. To suppose otherwise was to confuse, as Brentano had done, 'content' and 'object'. Meinong came to distinguish sharply between content and object with the help of the Polish philosopher, K. Twardowski, who in his *Towards a Theory of the Content and Object of Presentations* (1894) had distinguished three distinct elements in a 'psychical phenomenon' – the mental act, its content, and its object.[9] The effect of identifying content and object, Meinong considers, is to make it appear that what is *before* the mind (the object) is somehow a part (the content) of the apprehension of it. But this, he argues, is a quite untenable view. For what is before the mind is most often a physical thing, extended and solid; such an object cannot possibly be a constituent of a mental act. Furthermore, even when we are thinking of a non-existent object,* the mental act of thinking actually exists. Whatever is part of its *content*, therefore, must also exist – it follows that a round square, for example, cannot be a content, although it can clearly be an object.

At the same time, Meinong considers, there must be *something* in the act which corresponds to the fact that it is directed towards one object rather than another. This 'something' is its content. The content is not – unlike Locke's 'ideas' – a picture, perfect or imperfect, of the object. Nor is it some kind of 'sensation'. For such a picture, or such a sensation, would merely be another object. We should still need to explain, according to Meinong, why the mental act is directed towards one 'picture' or one 'sensation' rather than towards some other. The 'content', indeed, cannot be more specifically defined than as that quality of a mental act which enables it to point to such-and-such an object. Meinong admits that it is not easy to pick out such a 'content'. But he thinks that it can be done: if we find it difficult, this is partly because our attention is usually directed towards the object rather than towards the mental act, and partly because we go in search of some particular *thing* – 'the content' – instead of recognizing that the content is simply an *attribute* of the mental act.

The importance, for Meinong, of this distinction between content and object is that it opened the way towards 'a completely

---

*An 'object' is defined as that towards which a mental act can be directed. Thus an 'object' need not be a 'thing'; mermaids, unicorns and the square root of two are all objects, presuming only that we can think of them.

new philosophical discipline' – the theory of objects – which is not reducible, so he argues, to any of the familiar natural sciences and yet which is none the less empirical, not metaphysical. Attempts to found a new discipline – theory of objects, phenomenology, analysis, logical syntax, semantics – were to be a feature of twentieth-century philosophy. The reason is not difficult to discover. The rise of the social sciences to an independent status had the consequence that philosophers could no longer devote their attention to psychology or political theory or sociology and call the result 'philosophy'. On the other side, very few philosophers – with striking exceptions like McTaggart – were prepared to affirm that it was their task to construct a supra-empirical metaphysics. It looked very much as if philosophy might disappear: if, as more and more philosophers believed, all knowledge is empirical, did it not follow that the whole field of knowledge should be divided between the various natural sciences? Thus the problem arose of discovering a field for the exercise of philosophical talents which was empirical – and therefore acceptable to non-metaphysicians – and yet which employed the reflective techniques proper to philosophy rather than the laboratory techniques of the natural sciences. The 'theory of objects' was an attempt to satisfy this new demand. Philosophy was not after all the descriptive branch of psychology; it had a field of its own to conquer – the 'theory of objects'.

Some objects, but only some, Meinong describes as 'existing'. Thus, for example, *a green leaf* exists. Other objects are said to be 'real', without existing. *The difference between red and green*, for example, is a 'real' difference, but it does not 'exist' in the sense in which a red book and a red leaf both 'exist'. Indeed, no 'objects of a higher order' – objects which contain a relationship between existences – can, Meinong thinks, properly be said to exist. Nor does *the number two* exist, although it is none the less 'real'. All such 'real non-existents' Meinong describes as 'subsisting'.

The possibilities, so Meinong argues, are still not exhausted by this division of objects into the existent and the subsistent. For some objects – *a round square* for example – neither exist nor subsist; they lie 'outside of being'.[10] But they are still 'objects'. It is our 'prejudice in favour of the actual', Meinong suggests, which leads us wrongly to suppose that all objects must be actual, in the sense in which green leaves are actual. Once we abandon this prejudice as unworthy of a philosopher, a vast new field of inquiry – the character of and distinction between objects as such – spreads like a Promised Land before our eyes.

Of distinctions between 'objects', one is particularly important: the distinction between those objects which are, and those which are not, 'objectives'. (For convenience, I shall call those objects which are not objectives 'mere objects'.) A mere object – *a golden mountain*, for example – can exist, or not exist; but it would be nonsense to say that it is, or is not, 'a fact' or 'the case'. In contrast, an objective – *the existence of golden mountains*, for example – cannot be sensibly said to exist (although as an 'object of a higher order' it does 'subsist') but it either is or is not a fact.

The nature of an objective, Meinong considers, can most easily be seen if we think of it as the meaning of a sentence – not what a sentence expresses, the mental act out of which it arises, but what it is about. Now, if we ask: 'What is the sentence "a golden mountain does not exist" about?' we shall most likely get the answer 'a golden mountain'. And that answer, Meinong admits, is a quite intelligible one. Just because it is intelligible, we are liable to conclude that there are only 'mere objects'; that these are what sentences, as well as separate words, refer to. But then we have not brought out the difference, Meinong says, between the phrase 'golden mountains' and the sentence 'golden mountains do not exist'; to understand that difference, we are compelled to recognize that our sentence is about *the non-existence of golden mountains* – not about *golden mountains* simply – compelled, then, to recognize 'objectives' as distinct from 'mere objects'.

The same point might be put differently, by saying that objectives are the objects of our judgements. But this, Meinong points out, would not be quite accurate. For we can concern ourselves with an objective without actually judging – we can 'suppose' an objective, think of it *as* existing, without actually affirming or denying it, as we must in order to judge. I can 'suppose' that Hitler is still alive, think of him as being alive, without either affirming or denying that he is *in fact* alive. The objective *the existence of a living Hitler* is the same as it would be if I judged

Hitler to be alive, but the mental act is a 'supposal' not a 'judgement'. A 'supposal' (*On Supposals*, 1902) lies between apprehension and judgement: like a representation it does not involve affirmation or denial, like a judgement it is directed towards an objective.

About an objective, thus described, we can go on to ask a variety of questions. The main question, Meinong thinks, is whether it is 'a fact' – what we want to know above all is whether it is a *fact* that Hitler is alive – but we can also ask whether it is necessary, probable, possible and so on. These are properties of the objective, on Meinong's view, not of the act of mind which is directed towards it. To say that *the existence of a living Hitler* is a possibility is to point to a property of that objective; it is not merely to say, for example, that we 'feel doubtful' whether he died. It is objectives, too, which are 'true' or 'false'.

Truth, however, Meinong makes secondary to 'factuality'. Truth involves, on his analysis, a double reference, first, to the factuality of the objective, secondly, to the fact that someone has actually *affirmed* the objective to be factual. An objective is factual or non-factual whoever affirms or fails to affirm its factuality, but it is *true* only when it has been affirmed. It is or is not a fact that Hitler is still alive, independently of the question whether anyone has ever judged that he is, but to say 'it is true' that he lives is to affirm that someone has *correctly judged* that he is alive. For truths last only as long as the human race, whereas facts have no such dependence on humanity. A great many things which philosophers have said about truths (e.g. that they are eternal) should really, according to Meinong, have been said about facts.

How are we to recognize the factuality of an objective? Meinong's reply is that certain of our judgements have a peculiar property – that of 'evidence': such judgements are directed towards objectives which are facts. 'Evidence', it should be observed, is a character of the judgement; it has a family resemblance to Descartes' 'clarity and distinctness'. Meinong does not mean that objectives are factual only when, in the ordinary sense of that word, we have 'evidence' for them. Such 'evidence' would only consist of further facts – and the question would remain: how did we recognize that *they* are facts? This regress can be avoided only if certain of our judgements carry their own 'evidence' with them.

Enough has now perhaps been said, if not to do justice to the subtlety and intricacy of Meinong's views, at least to indicate what in them particularly attracted the attention of British philosophers. First, the objectivity of facts, of things, of numbers, of universals, of relations, of modal distinctions, has been rigorously maintained. None of these is a property of the mind which contemplates them or affirms them. But secondly, this objectivity has been preserved at a considerable cost. The Universe, it would appear, is populated by a variety of entities with the most surprising properties. It includes, for example, the fact that golden mountains are golden and the fact that they are non-existent, just as much as the fact that men are mortal. Some of its ingredients exist, but many are real without existing and others are neither real nor existent. Was it possible, philosophers were to ask, to reject subjectivism without arriving at these odd, and indeed incredible, consequences?

On what might be described as the 'normal' theory of judgement, there are judgements, understood as events in the history of an individual mind, there are the words in which they are expressed, and there is a 'world' which the judgement either reflects, or distorts, or ties together – about this last point the main controversy had turned. But an 'objective' is neither a mental act, nor a set of words, nor (necessarily) a fact. James, to take only one example, immediately protested: 'Surely truth can't inhabit a third realm,' he wrote in a letter to an American colleague, 'between realities and statements or beliefs. . . . I wish you would forget about this mongrel cur of a supposal, begotten upon you by the unspeakable Meinong and his English pals.' Meinong's 'English pals' would reply, as we shall see, that Meinong was at least emphasizing two important and neglected facts: that a belief (what is believed) is not a mental phenomenon, and that (since it can be either true or false) it is also not a 'reality'. But, at the same time, they came to be as disturbed as James was about the conception of a 'third realm'.

In the phenomenology of Edmund Husserl,[11] Brentano's influence is also marked, although there has been considerable controversy about the precise character and importance of that influence. Except during his student days, when he worked under Masaryk and Brentano, Germany, not Austria, was his home and, as we shall see, he eventually returned to the Germanic Idealistic tradition after a relatively brief, if important, flirtation with British empiricism. It is in Husserl's earlier work that Brentano's influence is most conspicuous. Quite certainly, as in Meinong's case, his point of departure was Brentano's elevation of psychology to the position of the supreme science. His first important work *Philosophy of Arithmetic* (1891) was, indeed, an attempt to derive the basic concepts of arithmetic, which he closely associated with logic, from psychological principles. But he soon abandoned that project; the *Prolegomena to a Pure Logic*, which forms the first volume of his *Logical Investigations* (1900–1901), is specifically directed against 'psychologism', understood as an attempt to rest logical and arithmetical conclusions upon psychological premises.[12]

Mill, in particular, is now the villain of the piece; it is his psychological approach to logic which Husserl especially attacks.[13] In his *Examination of Sir William Hamilton's Philosophy*, Mill had written of logic that 'as far as it is a science at all, its theoretic grounds are wholly borrowed from psychology'. Husserl objects – borrowing an argument which Kant had already, in the *Critique of Pure Reason*, directed against the 'psychologism' of his own time – that psychological laws are no more than inductive generalizations, subject therefore to correction in the light of further experience, whereas logical and mathematical principles are 'necessary' – they *must* be true – and therefore cannot be 'grounded' upon inductively derived premises.

Husserl's determination to preserve the necessity of the laws of logic – and of the fundamental mathematical principles which, he thinks, derive from them – led him to attempt the construction of a pure logic, entirely free from merely empirical, psychological, premises and thereby secured against all risk of error. Such a project had already been embarked upon by the 'symbolic logicians'; Husserl was a mathematician by training and might have been expected to cooperate with them. But in fact he is severely critical of the new formal logic, as exhibited in the writings of, say, Schröder. That sort of logic, he maintains, works with concepts which it never examines: it is insufficiently 'critical' in a Kantian sense – it does not examine the 'grounds' of its own operations. At best, it can provide us with a particular calculus, a particular method of solving a particular kind of problem, but a pure logic must go further than this: it must be a theory of every *possible* calculus, every *possible* type of reasoning. Thus, if Husserl rejected Mill's attempt to 'ground' logic in psychology, it was not in order to conclude that logic is a self-sufficient system whose sole 'ground' lies in its internal consistency.

Lotze's conception of logic was much more to his taste. As Lotze conceived it, logic lays down an ideal of thought, to which every inquiry in some measure approximates. Similarly, Husserl defines pure logic as 'the scientific system of ideal theories which are grounded purely ... in the fundamental concepts which are the common province of *all* sciences, because they determine in the most general manner what makes a science a *science*'. Just because it is concerned with concepts common to all science – involved in every employment of Reason – logic can be identified neither with calculation, in the manner of symbolic logicians, nor with a description of the procedures of empirical science, in the manner of 'inductive' logicians. Symbolic and inductive logic, he admits, can be of value in their own particular sphere – and so can the psychological study of thinking processes – but they cannot be logic proper, as Husserl conceives it, because they lack the requisite certainty and generality.

The construction of a genuinely 'pure' logic demands, he argues, the use of the 'phenomenological' method. At first, Husserl sometimes characterized phenomenology as 'descriptive psychology'; that he should think such a phrase appropriate brings out the historical link between Husserl and Brentano. But there is a vital difference, Husserl from the beginning insists, between his and Brentano's 'descriptive psychology'. For Brentano, as we saw, descriptive psychology – nominally at least – is an empirical inquiry; Husserl's phenomenology, on the other hand, neither adopts the standpoint nor employs the methods of the natural sciences, because it is not possible from that standpoint or by those methods to arrive at a *pure* theory, a theory which will be independent of contingent empirical facts.

Of course, the possibility of such a pure, non-empirical, theory is in itself subject to challenge. It was rejected by those 'historicists' who argued that a 'truth' is no more than what at a given epoch men are willing to believe. And Husserl's *Prolegomena to Logic* therefore contains a lively criticism of 'historicism' or 'cultural relativism'. Like Plato in the *Theaetetus*, Husserl argues that the 'relativists' presume the existence of absolute truths in the very act of denying that they exist; even to put forward their own theory the relativists have to treat it, and the evidence for it, as absolutely true.[14]

The empiricists, on different grounds, had also attacked the idea of a pure logic, and Husserl's reply to their objections takes us to the heart of his theory. On the traditional empiricist view, we are directly acquainted only with 'particular existences'; any general theory must be constructed by generalization out of them if it is to bear any relation whatsoever to the facts of experience. A non-empirical theory, then, could be nothing but a fabrication. Husserl, however, rejects what he regards as the 'mere presumption' that we are directly aware only of 'particulars'. 'The truth is,' so he summarized his view in his *Ideas for a pure Phenomenology and phenomenological Philosophy* (1913), 'that everyone sees ideas, "essences", and sees them, so to speak, continuously; they work with them when they think and they also pass judgements about them. But, from their theoretical "standpoint", people explain them away.'

He illustrates this thesis by an examination of Hume's *Treatise*. When Hume is classifying 'mental acts' – perceiving, remembering, imagining and the like – he makes no reference, Husserl says, to the existence or non-existence of particular natural objects, except by way of illustration. He describes perceiving, for example, as 'having an impression', not as 'observing such-and-such properties of physical objects'. Thus, in the first place, Hume shows how it is possible to proceed in a manner 'absolutely independent of the conclusions of every natural science'. He simply draws attention to the essence, the real nature, of an act of perception; no experiment, no physical observation, could have the least relevance to his procedure whether by way of supporting or of undermining it. Hume might reply that this is only to say that he is a psychologist, not a physicist. But if we look at his procedure, Husserl points out, we notice that he does not, in the manner of an empirical psychologist, examine case-histories or refer to comparative observations. Nor, Husserl argues, does Hume ever engage in 'introspection', in the sense in which an empirical psychologist might introspect. For when Hume examines his own mind he is not looking for evidence with which to test an empirical generalization, nor is it his object to describe in detail a particular specimen of a mental act. His object is to 'intuit the essence' of an act of perception: no more and no less. To do this, Husserl is quite prepared to admit, Hume has to consider some particular act of perception, but the particularity of that act has no relevance to his conclusions – his concern is solely with the 'essence' which that act exhibits.[15]

If, then, Hume were right in his general metaphysical presumption that all our experience is of particulars, his own procedure in the *Treatise*, so Husserl argues, would be unintelligible. Hume is so blinded by his own presuppositions that he does not see the implications of what he is doing: he suffers from the delusion that he is an empirical psychologist, when in fact he is engaged in a 'pure' phenomenological analysis of the mind, intuiting directly the essence of the various mental acts. Similarly, according to Husserl, only a self-inflicted blindness prevents philosophers from realizing that every time they examine numbers they are taking a general concept, not a 'generalization from experience', as their subject-matter; and, again, that so everyday an experience as the recognition that, for example, two objects are *both red* carries with it the intuition of a general property, an 'essence'. Any philosophy which is worthy of the name, Husserl concludes, must shake itself free from all metaphysical presuppositions: it must investigate what actually confronts it, not allowing any metaphysical fantasy to distract it from its direct analysis of 'essences' or 'general structures'. And to proceed thus, on Husserl's first understanding of the term, is to be 'phenomenological'.

Husserl's *Logical Investigations*,[16] then, are meant to exemplify a strictly presuppositionless, wholly scientific, phenomenological approach to philosophical questions – which just because it is strict is logically prior to, and must not imitate, the natural sciences. These investigations, in Brentano's manner, are extremely minute in manner, rich in distinctions; indeed, in philosophical style as well as in their choice of topic and, in part, in doctrine, they anticipate much that was to be typical of twentieth-century

British philosophy. To summarize their content is impossible: a brief reference to the first Investigation, 'Experience and Meaning' – the others are on 'Universals and Abstraction', 'The Analysis of Whole and Part', 'The Idea of a Pure Grammar'[17] and 'Experience and Content' – will have to serve as an illustration of Husserl's interests and methods of approach.

As usual, his initial object is to demonstrate that empiricism is untenable. He distinguishes two different aspects of a statement: the statement as an event in the life of a particular person, and the statement as what the person *means*. Now, it is clearly possible for two persons to make the same statement, in the sense of meaning the same thing, even although, considered as a particular event, every statement is a unique combination of a certain intonation, a certain loudness, a certain emphasis, a certain method of pronunciation. Can the empiricist explain, Husserl asks, how two statements can be identical in meaning? On his general nominalist principles the empiricist would have to reply, Husserl suggests, that the identity of meaning consists in the fact that the two statements are in some respect *similar*. But if we look for similarities, Husserl objects, all we can discover is similarity in intonation, emphasis and the like, i.e. a similarity between the statements considered as particular events. We shall never by any sort of point-by-point comparison of such utterances arrive at the meaning which unites them, as distinct from a resemblance in their manner of utterance. It takes 'direct insight', Husserl concludes, to grasp the meaning of a statement. And it follows that meaning is something of which the empiricist, with his rejection of any avenue to knowledge except the comparison of particular experiences, can never give any account. Yet meaning is fundamental to science. Empiricism breaks down, therefore, at a crucial point. (This was a conclusion which more than one of Husserl's successors was to contest: 'logical positivism', in particular, was an attempt to reply to this sort of critique of empiricism by developing an empirical theory of meaning.)

From his analysis of meaning, Husserl makes his way to the conclusion he particularly wishes to sustain: that logic must rest on 'insight', not, as psychologism maintains, on empirical generalizations. For logic, he maintains, is interested in statements *as meaning*, not in individual utterances. In other words, it is a theory of what B. Bolzano[18] had called the 'proposition' – understood as that which unites those various statements or judgements which we recognize as 'having the same meaning'. We may be tempted to ask Husserl: 'Where does this proposition exist? Is it in the mind or has it a place in the external world?' This question, he would reply, 'has no sense' – like the parallel question 'where is redness?' Propositions and universals are not entities, not things that exist here or there: they are the unity, or essence, of a set of entities – redness of red things, propositions of statements. The fact remains, he considers, that we have direct experience of them, an experience, moreover, which contains in itself a peculiar self-evidence.[19] In the intuition of such essences, we attain a certainty which lies far beyond the reach of any empirical science, with its highly fallible 'generalizations from experience'; thus we can understand the necessity of pure logic, which consists wholly in the elucidation of the basic essences – those which are involved in every form of inquiry.

The *Logical Investigations* – and particularly the *Prolegomena to Logic* – have been 'Husserl' to most Anglo-Saxon philosophers. Relatively few British philosophers, although many more in Germany, an active group in the United States, and a somewhat surprising number of South Americans, have been prepared to follow him through the darker ways that followed.

And yet Husserl thought that the point of view adopted in the *Logical Investigations* was inherently unstable. When that work first appeared the comment of neo-Kantians like Natorp (in *Kant Studien*, 1901) was that Husserl had left quite obscure the status of the ordinary world and its relation to 'essences'; and that to clarify it, he would be forced back into something like a Kantian metaphysics. Husserl came to agree with this judgement, but for 'metaphysics' he hoped to substitute the new discipline of 'transcendental phenomenology' – a 'universal philosophy, which can supply an organon for the methodical revision of all the sciences', as he described it in his article on phenomenology in the *Encyclopaedia Britannica* (fourteenth edition, 1929).

The *Logical Investigations* were in fact too empirical in tone for Husserl's taste; he had not yet satisfied, he came to think, the ideal of a pure philosophy. It was necessary, in order to complete his task, to pass quite beyond the Humean method he had so far employed. Although he had rejected the empiricist doctrine that universals, or 'essences', are generalizations from experience, his philosophy was still 'empirical', he thought, in the sense that he simply took experience as it came and tried to describe the general logical features he found within it. What he now wanted to do was to justify his method of procedure, by showing that to take things as they 'appear to consciousness' is to see them as they certainly are. In the tradition of German Idealism he was in search of the Absolute, of something, itself beyond all criticism, on which all knowledge can rest.

He turned for help to Descartes, and particularly to the Cartesian 'method of doubt'.[20] In his *Meditations*, Descartes set out to doubt whatever could conceivably be doubted, in order to arrive at that which lies beyond all risk of doubt. Husserl's 'method of bracketing' – first systematically employed in the *Ideas* (1913) – followed the same pattern. He begins by 'bracketing' the actual world, not actually doubting its existence but 'suspending his judgement' about it, in the Cartesian manner. By taking that step, he automatically suspends his judgement, also, about every science of natural objects – psychology and sociology, because they consider man as a natural object, as well as physics and chemistry.

So extensive a 'bracketing', we might object, leaves nothing behind. If this were so, natural science would be 'absolute'. Its falsity would be unthinkable, and therefore its doctrines would need no 'ground', no support from anything more certain.

But in fact, Husserl argues, 'consciousness in itself has a being of its own which in its absolute uniqueness of nature remains unaffected by the phenomenological disconnexion'. He presumes, that is – as Descartes did – that there is something called 'consciousness' which could exist even if nothing else existed, and which is not a 'natural object', since it forms no part of the subject matter of any empirical science. Not many contemporary British philosophers would be prepared to accept this view; that is sufficient reason, in their eyes, for rejecting the whole programme of 'transcendental phenomenology'.

The existence of consciousness remains unaffected, Husserl further argues, even if we 'suspend our judgement' about the deductive sciences of logic and mathematics as well as the inductive physical sciences. Were there no mathematical or logical science, there would still be consciousness. We have now suspended our judgement about every 'transcendent' act of consciousness, every act which has an object independent of itself, but we are still left with 'immanent' acts, which contain their objects within themselves. The presumption here, of course, is again the Cartesian one: that there are acts of consciousness which have as their object something which is itself a 'mode of consciousness' – acts, therefore, which would still exist even if everything except consciousness were wiped out – and that the existence of such acts is the primary certainty. We cannot without self-contradiction, the argument runs, 'think away' our consciousness, whereas we can 'think away' any object which is independent of the act of thinking. In Husserl's language, we can 'suspend our judgement' about the truths of arithmetic, but we cannot 'suspend our judgement' about whether we are capable of judging.

The process of 'bracketing', Husserl concludes, leads us to the existence of consciousness as the one 'Absolute' – the one thing that *must* exist, that cannot be thought away. From that Absolute we can move back, but from a novel point of view, to the world of objects. We approach them now from the standpoint of a 'transcendental phenomenology', considering them as they 'declare themselves to consciousness', and not taking for granted the conclusions of natural science, for which an object is something entirely independent of consciousness. By that means, by considering objects only in their dependence upon the Absolute – 'consciousness' – we preserve the purity and the certainty of our inquiry. We proceed without presuppositions, we accept only what cannot be thought away.

Thus, for example, a phenomenology of time, as Husserl understands it, is concerned with *time as it appears to consciousness;* it restricts itself to what is there 'given' – to such 'undeniable' facts, for example, as that a melody appears to consciousness as a succession – and it does not in the least presume the truth of the temporal judgements of science. Such a phenomenology seeks to describe the 'structure' of the time that thus 'appears': to discover what 'constitutes' time, what an appearance must be to be temporal. It issues in laws such as 'temporal order is a two-dimensional infinite series', 'temporal relations are asymmetrical'

– in short, laws which detail general properties which *must* belong to every temporal experience. Similarly a phenomenology of society will be an attempt to analyse the structure of *any possible* social experience. There is a striking resemblance, indeed, between transcendental phenomenology and Kant's attempt to lay down the 'conditions of experience'. Husserl, however, is concerned not only with the 'structure' of natural science, as Kant was, but with what constitutes *any* type of 'deliverance to consciousness'.

In the later sections of his *Ideas* and in his subsequent writings Husserl sets out to explain in more detail the nature of transcendental phenomenology, to defend it against its critics, and to work out specific phenomenological analyses. Many disciples, with varying degrees of independence, have followed in his footsteps, first of all, in Germany, in the *Annual Chronicle of Philosophy and Phenomenological Research* (the *Jahrbuch*) and later in the American *Philosophy and Phenomenological Research* (1940–).[21] In particular, they have so far accepted Husserl's teachings as to seek after the 'constitution', the essential structure, of mind, society, religion, nature and the like. But a multitude of critics, many of them warm admirers of his earlier work, have complained that in his later writings Husserl has reverted to Idealism, completely abandoning that emphasis on objectivity which was so notable a feature of the *Logical Investigations*. In such books as his *Méditations Cartésiennes* (1932), Husserl has defended himself against the oft-repeated charge that his philosophy ends in solipsism; his starting-point, he says, is consciousness in general, not the consciousness of any particular individual. But he is more than ready to admit his allegiance to the tradition of German Objective Idealism – his work, he says, puts Idealism on a scientific basis for the first time.

Thus, in Germany, Brentano's emphasis on the object stimulated two very different lines of thought. Meinong pressed objectivity hard, and ended with a Universe which is certainly objective but very strangely constituted; Husserl, in his attempt to establish a really secure presuppositionless foundation for an objective logic, finally made his way back to Idealism.

In England, meanwhile, one of the first to respond to Brentano's work was G. F. Stout.[22] Stout was a Cambridge man, a pupil of

Henry Sidgwick and James Ward. Sidgwick,[23] an influential teacher, is best known for his work in moral and political philosophy. He wrote little on pure philosophy – and that little, included in the posthumous *Philosophy, its Scope and Relations* (1902) and *Lectures on the Philosophy of Kant and other Philosophical Lectures and Essays* (1905), is not of the first importance. But two general features of his work are interesting: his lively criticism of 'historicism' and his defence of commonsense, which led him to stand out firmly against nineteenth-century Idealism. Stout, as we shall see later, was more sympathetically inclined towards Idealism – an Idealism, all the same, which had to be erected on a commonsensical foundation. The appeal to 'commonsense', indeed, came to be as noteworthy a feature of the Cambridge, as it had been of the Scottish, philosophers. It was this side of Brentano's philosophy which attracted Stout.

He defined his relation to Brentano in his *Analytic Psychology* (1896). There he accepted Brentano's definition of 'attitudes of consciousness' – Stout mistrusted the phrase 'mental acts' and explicitly denied that there is a distinct 'cognitive act' – as different modes in which 'a consciousness refers to an object'. But he went on to differentiate, in a way which partly anticipates Twardowski's distinction of 'content' from 'object',[24] between the 'thought reference' of an attitude of consciousness (the 'object') which is, he says, 'not a present modification of the individual consciousness' and that modification of consciousness (he called it a 'representation') 'which defines and determines the direction of thought to this or that particular object'.

This distinction between the 'object of thought' *to* which an attitude of consciousness refers and the 'representation' *through* which it refers, remained with Stout throughout his long philosophical development. There were, however, many changes in detail. Some of these changes consisted in terminological fluctuations – neither 'representation' nor 'ideas' nor 'content' satisfied him as names for what is immediately present to consciousness. Others were of greater consequence; not only the name but also the status of 'representations' caused him difficulty.

At first, Stout's 'representation' was something very like Locke's 'idea' – as Meinong's 'content' was not. Obviously, this meant that Stout had somehow to overcome the classical difficulties of a theory of representation; he had to show how, if what immediately confronts us is always a representation, we can ever pass beyond the representation to what it represents. Stout wanted to discriminate; although he accepted the existence of representations he did not, he said, put forward a representative theory of perception. For in thought, he maintained, we have access to *the object itself*, even although that access has to be 'mediated' by the representation. 'From the outset,' he wrote in 'Things and Sensations' (1905), 'there are features of our immediate experience which perpetually point beyond themselves to actual existence, other than our own or any immediate experiences of ours.' The facts of the case, he thought, were indisputable. Memory was one case he particularly liked to emphasize: when we remember, he said, what we remember is something past, but the remembering nonetheless takes place in the present and demands a *present* representation. This representation is not *what* we remember – just because it is present. Equally, the past cannot be what we now have before us; thus, to give any account of memory, we have to refer both to representation and to object. Similarly, in sensory perception the small silvery disc we have immediately before our mind is not the moon, which is itself neither small, nor silvery, nor a disc, and yet only through such a representation can the moon ever be an object to us. The difficulty lies, not in pointing to the difference between representations and objects, but in giving an account of the status of representations – their place in the world – and in indicating the precise manner in which they 'point' to objects.

Originally, as we said, Stout accepted the traditional post-Cartesian view that a representation is a 'modification of consciousness'; in some ill-defined sense, it is a 'part of the mind'. There are obviously great difficulties, which Berkeley had emphasized, in maintaining that such a 'modification of consciousness' can point to the existence of something which is *not* a modification of consciousness, which is indeed entirely different in nature from consciousness – a material object. These difficulties Stout at first thought he could overcome by taking over from such writers as Leibniz and Lotze, as his master Ward did, the doctrine that there is no sharp contrast between mind and matter, since what we call 'material objects' are minds in disguise. In that way, the diversity in nature between representation and object would vanish. But he came to reject this Leibnizian metaphysics, and with it the description of representations as 'modifications of consciousness'; he came to hold that representations (rechristened 'sensa') are material, although not physical – by which he meant that although they are not mental, they are equally not 'physical objects' in the sense in which such objects form the subject-matter of physics. Only on this view, he argued in *Mind and Matter* (1931), can we understand the way in which our sensa point to the existence of physical objects without *being* physical objects; both sensa and physical objects are 'of a piece', in so far as they are both material. We have no longer to suppose that a 'mental modification' can stand to us for something quite disparate in nature.

The question still remains how the sense-datum can point to something which, if not different in nature, still lies beyond itself. Stout's answer leads him, in various ways, into that Idealist metaphysics which we shall discuss in a later chapter. One suggestion – and in one form or another he always maintained this – is that the sensum is 'by nature' fragmentary and incomplete; we are bound to take it as belonging to a wider whole, if we are to understand it at all. A sensum, as he also expresses the matter, raises questions which it cannot answer; to answer them, we must think of it in its relation to a physical object. This position is most fully worked out in *God and Nature* (posthumous, 1952) and 'Distributive Unity as a Category' (*AJP*, 1947). At other times – in *Mind and Matter*, for example – the stress is pragmatic; we cannot manage our lives, he argues, with sensa alone: to make 'practical adjustments' to our experience, we have to regard 'sensa' as pointing to *things*. But these are details; he is mainly concerned to insist that what the sensum points to is continuous with, not completely other than, the sensum.

To relate sense-datum and object he introduces that conception of a 'complex' or 'distributive' unity, which plays so considerable a role in his metaphysics. Take the case of our perception of a yellow object. Then, so Stout argues in 'Some Fundamental Points in the Theory of Knowledge', it would be absurd to assert that in such a case as this there are *two* yellows – the yellow of the 'presentation' and the yellow of the object. But, equally, the 'presentation-yellow' cannot be *identical* with the yellow of the object; the multiplicity of yellows experienced by different persons at different times cannot possibly be *each* of them the yellow of the object. The only remaining possibility, Stout argues, is that the various yellows of these multiple presentations together make up a unity, of which each can be regarded as a phase – as *that* yellow under such-and-such conditions. The complex unity of these various presentations, then, is what we call 'the yellow of the object'. Thus Stout hopes to maintain the contrast between 'representations' – or sensa – and 'objects' without falling into the difficulties of a representative theory of perception.

As there was a development in his view about the character of presentations, so equally there was a development in his view about the *objectivity* of presentations, and with that, the objectivity of objects of the mind in general. At first, he was quite prepared to admit the existence of what he called 'being for thought'. The paper he contributed to *Personal Idealism* under the title 'Error' is typical of his earlier position. There, he certainly insists that error is always *about something* and so far refers to reality. But he still maintains that error consists in confusing what he calls 'mere appearance' with reality, and 'mere appearances', he says, although not a quality of the mind to which they appear, yet 'have no being independently of the physical process by which they come to be presented to the individual consciousness'. If, for example, we mistakenly suppose a straight stick to be crooked we are confusing a 'mere appearance' of crookedness with a characteristic of a real object. That 'real appearance' is not a property of our apprehending mind – our mind is not itself crooked; at the same time it exists only as dependent upon our mental processes.

In his 'Real Being and Being for Thought' (*PAS*, 1910, reprinted in *Studies*) 'being for thought' is rejected. On the face of it, nothing can be constituted, Stout argues, by its relation to something else; to be related, to a mind or anything else, an object must have 'a distinct being of its own'. But the fact of error leads us to question this general logical principle. We imagine that in this case, at least, something exists – false appearance – which has being only in relation to our mind. Such a supposition,

Stout now argues, does not in fact solve the problem of error; for we can go on to ask how we can wrongly believe that something which has being only for thought has real being. What happens when we judge, he argues, is that we select from one or the other of the alternative properties a thing *might* have the one we think it *actually* has. Abstractly considered, a stick might be straight or crooked – these are 'alternatives' for it. When we judge it, rightly or wrongly, to be crooked we assign to it one of these alternative properties. Thus, he maintains, the question whether there is 'being for thought' comes down to this: are alternative possibilities no more than 'creatures of the understanding'? If they are, we shall have to say that all judgement, true or false, consists in selecting between such mind-dependent objects; if they are not, as Stout himself argues, we can give an account of error without supposing the existence of the mind-dependent.

In affirming the reality of possibilities, Stout sets himself against Bradley.[25] 'How in the world,' Bradley wrote in his *Logic*, 'can a fact exist as that strange ambiguity *b or c*? We shall hardly find the flesh-or-blood alternative which answers to our "or".' Bradley's objection would be unanswerable, Stout is prepared to admit, if 'there were no kind of real being except particular existence'. But he appeals to Meinong: there are kinds of being which are not particular entities – to presume otherwise is to fall victim to the vulgar prejudice in favour of the actual. Universals must be real, he argues, since otherwise there would be no unity in the world; and for universals to be real, possibilities must also be real, since 'man', for example, refers not only to particular men who have existed but to anyone of that kind who *could* exist. Indeed, some universals of the first importance in science – like 'frictionless fluids' – may have no *actual* instances whatsoever. When we assert that 'any triangle is either equal-sided or unequal-sided', we are giving, according to Stout, perfectly definite information; we are saying, he thinks, that a triangle *really* admits only of these alternatives.

Possibilities, then, are real; and error consists in wrongly *believing* that a certain possibility has been realized. What is 'subjective' in this situation is the belief; the object of the belief – the realization of the possibility – is quite independent of the act of belief, as comes out in the fact that we can have *different* attitudes to precisely this same object, can suppose it, deny it and so on.

Stout does not mean that there is a 'world of possibilities' which is quite distinct from the world of particular existences; on the contrary, he insists on their close interconnexion. Every possibility is possible only relatively to certain conditions: it may, for example, be a mathematical possibility but yet be mechanically impossible. But if the possible thus depends on the actual, so also, Stout argues, the actual depends on the possible: to be actual is to be 'possible in all ways'. The actual is a realized possibility.

A fuller exposition of this view must connect it with Stout's theory of universals, and that we shall discuss in a later chapter. The important point, for the moment, is that Stout's work, from the beginning, is closely concerned with the kind of question which Brentano and Meinong had brought to the attention of philosophers. Like them, he was concerned to defend and to examine the concept of objectivity. And Stout, we must remember, taught both Moore and Russell in the days when he was working on his *Analytic Psychology*. In a variety of ways, their philosophy is continuous with Stout's.

CHAPTER 9

Moore and Russell

'MOORE and Russell' – the conjunction is inevitable. Nor is this merely an historian's stereotype. Russell, then completing his undergraduate studies at Cambridge, diverted his younger contemporary, Moore, from classics to philosophy; Moore led that attack upon Idealism, particularly the Idealism of Bradley, which first won for Moore and Russell their reputation as philosophers. 'I do not know that Russell has ever owed anything to me except mistakes,' Moore writes somewhat ruefully, 'whereas I have owed to his published works ideas which were certainly not mistakes, and which I think very important.' Russell gives a different, and more accurate, account of their relationship: 'He took the lead in rebellion, and I followed, with a sense of emancipation.'[1]

Yet the two men were very different. In his *Autobiography* Moore makes a confession which gives us an important clue to the understanding of his teaching and his influence: 'I do not think,' he writes, 'that the world or the sciences would ever have suggested to me any philosophical problems. What has suggested problems to me is things which other philosophers have said about the world or about natural science.' Locke, Berkeley and Hume, in their various ways, begin from Newton; Green, Bradley, Bosanquet and Spencer have Darwin at the back of their minds; Moore's philosophy, on the other hand, is curiously remote from the 'great controversies' of our time. Neither Freud, nor Marx, nor Einstein, so far as one can judge, has affected his thinking in the least. He is a 'philosopher's philosopher' if ever there was one.[2]

Russell's philosophy, on the other hand, moves in an atmosphere thick with science. His first book was on *German Social Democracy* (1896); his second bore the title *An Essay on the Foundations of Geometry* (1897). Philosophy for him is continuous with social, psychological, physical, and mathematical investigation. When he is technical, as in, say, *The Principles of Mathematics* (1903), his free use of mathematical symbols produces in the ordinary reader the feeling that if this is incomprehensible, it is for only-too-familiar reasons. Moore is almost never technical, in this sense; no writer has ever sought so desperately to achieve utter clarity and utter simplicity, unless it be Gertrude Stein. And yet, sturdy defender of common sense though he is, the point and the method of Moore's philosophy are scarcely intelligible to the ordinary educated reader. W. B. Yeats wrote to T. S. Moore:[3] 'I find your brother extraordinarily obscure'; that is the reaction of a literary man, who expects a philosopher to discuss large questions in a large way. As John Wisdom points out, the scientist is likely to be no less disconcerted. 'Moore offers a game of Logic, and a peculiar one at that for it lacks much that gives satisfaction in ordinary logic and mathematics. In it no architecture of proof is possible, and with that goes too the Q.E.D. with its note of agreement achieved and triumphant discovery'.[4] Yet Moore has a great deal to offer to those who have felt the fascination of his drastic honesty – difficult though it is to convey that fascination, or that honesty, by means of summary.

When he brought together, in his *Philosophical Studies* (1922), those of his contributions to philosophy which he thought worthy of preservation, he included neither his early articles in *Mind* and the *Proceedings of the Aristotelian Society* nor his contributions to Baldwin's *Dictionary of Philosophy and Psychology*, which, indeed, he condemns in his Autobiography as 'extraordinarily crude'. But he also tells us that he 'took great pains' over those early writings; and if the theory they expound was one he rapidly abandoned, it has nevertheless made its mark on English philosophy, partly through Russell's adherence to it. In important respects, furthermore, it set the problems which many twentieth-century philosophers were particularly to explore.

Of those early articles the most important is 'The Nature of Judgment' (*Mind*, 1899). Bradley's *Principles of Logic* is its point of origin. Bradley, Moore thought, had not been sufficiently ruthless in his dealings with Locke's doctrine that judgements are about 'ideas'. Although he had at times written as if judgements are about *what ideas mean*, at other times one would gather that *the idea itself* – as a psychic phenomenon – is an ingredient in our judgement. The former, Moore argues, is the only tenable view: judgements are not about 'our ideas' but about what those ideas point to – what Bradley called a 'universal meaning' and Moore a 'concept'.

The 'concept', Moore maintains, is 'neither a mental fact nor any part of a mental fact'. No doubt it is what, *in our thinking*, we take as our object: but if it did not exist independently of our thinking, there would be nothing for us to think about. Like a Platonic form, which it closely resembles, the concept is eternal and immutable; that is why, Moore says, it can appear as an identical ingredient in a number of different judgements, linking them in chains of reasoning.

Moore's purpose, in this essay, is much like Brentano's and Meinong's: to maintain the objectivity and the independence of objects of thought. His starting-point, one must again insist, is Bradley, not the British empirical tradition; there was in Bradley's *Principles of Logic*, as we have already noted, an anti-psychological tendency to which Moore fell heir. The break with British empiricism in Moore's early work could, indeed, scarcely be a cleaner one. According to the empirical tradition a concept is an 'abstraction', which the mind manufactures out of the raw material supplied by perception. Moore argued, in complete contrast, that 'conceptions cannot be regarded fundamentally as abstractions either from things or from ideas, since both alike can' if anything is to be true of them, be composed of nothing but concepts'. A 'thing', on this view, is a colligation of concepts; a piece of paper, for example, is whiteness and smoothness and . . .

Yet a relation between concepts, Moore also says, is 'a proposition'; he is prepared to accept the inevitable consequence that a 'thing', a 'complex conception', a 'proposition', are different names for the same entity. On this foundation, he constructs his theory of truth. According to the conventional view a proposition is true when it corresponds to reality. There is here involved a contrast between the true proposition – commonly thought of as a set of words or a set of ideas – and the 'reality' it represents. Moore, on the other hand, identifies true proposition and reality. 'Once it is definitely recognized,' he wrote in his article on 'Truth' in Baldwin's *Dictionary*, 'that the proposition is to denote not a belief (in the psychological sense), nor a form of words, but the object of belief, it seems plain that it differs in no respect from the reality to which it is supposed merely to correspond, i.e. the truth that "I exist" differs in no respect from the corresponding reality "my existence".'

What then, if not 'correspondence to reality', is the distinguishing characteristic of a true as distinct from a false proposition? Moore answers that truth is a simple, unanalysable, intuitable property, belonging to certain propositions and not to others, a thesis which Russell also defended in his articles on Meinong (*Mind*, 1904). 'Some propositions,' he there wrote, 'are true and some false, just as some roses are red and some white.'

Any other view, Moore argues, presumes that we can somehow get beyond relations between concepts to a reality which sustains them – and this is impossible in principle. To 'know' is to be aware of a proposition, i.e. a relation between concepts; thus we cannot possibly know anything which 'lies beyond' concepts. This is true, he maintains, even in the case of knowledge by perception. Perception is simply the cognition of an existential proposition – for example, the proposition that 'this paper exists'. Such a proposition, on Moore's analysis of it, relates concepts; it asserts that the concepts which make up *this paper* are related to the concept of *existence*. Whereas Brentano had argued that all propositions are existential in form, Moore regards them all as asserting relations between concepts.

This, then, is the theory of reality and the theory of truth from which Moore and Russell set out, and against which, in certain respects although not in others, they were strongly to react. The world is composed of eternal and immutable concepts; propositions relate concepts one to another; a *true* proposition predicates 'truth' of such a relation of concepts, and is 'a fact' or 'a reality'.

One other striking feature of *The Nature of Judgment* deserves attention: the stress Moore places on 'logic' – and what goes with it, his willingness to follow his dialectic wherever it leads him. 'I am fully aware,' he wrote of his theory of existence, 'how paradoxical this theory must appear. But it seems to me to follow from premises generally admitted, and to have been avoided only by lack of logical consistency. . . . I have appealed throughout to the rules of logic; nor if anyone rejects these, should I have much to fear from his arguments. An appeal to the facts is useless.' Moore was to move a very long way from the sentiments expressed in this passage.

Russell, in his *Autobiography*, has made it clear what Moore's earlier theory meant for Moore and for himself. It was above all a liberation from Bradley's 'Absolute' and Bradley's relegation, from the standpoint of the Absolute, of the world of everyday life to the realm of appearances. 'With a sense of escaping from prison,' Russell wrote, 'we allowed ourselves to think that grass is green, that the sun and the stars would exist if no one was aware of them, and also that there is a pluralistic timeless world of Platonic ideas. The world, which had been thin and logical, suddenly became rich and varied and solid.'

Russell's own world, as we shall see, was to become progessively more 'thin and logical'. But Moore never lost his sense of wonder and relief at being able to believe in the reality of the everyday world; and he was determined not to be driven out of his hardly-won Paradise. Those who, like most of his younger critics, have never felt the attraction of Idealism, those for whom it has never been a 'living option', find it difficult to understand Moore's philosophy; they convert him into a defender, in their own and Wittgenstein's manner, of 'ordinary usage'. But it is ordinary *beliefs*, not usage as such, that he wants to defend. Unlike his critics, he thinks they *need* defence. Moore had himself argued in his earliest writings (*Mind*, 1897–8) that 'time is unreal'. He had heard McTaggart say that 'Matter is in the same position as the gorgons and the harpies'. He was not to be persuaded that he and McTaggart were merely 'recommending a change in our ordinary linguistic habits'.[5]

At the same time, there were serpents in this Paradise, and they soon made their presence obvious. In a series of lectures, delivered (and studied, in part, by Russell) in 1910–11 although not published until 1953,[6] Moore explains why he abandoned, for all its advantages, his identification of true propositions and facts. When we assert, for example, that 'lions do really exist', we are saying more, he came to think, than that a proposition we happen to believe has the unanalysable property of being true; the 'substance' of a fact, as we might loosely express the matter, does not consist in a proposition together with its truth. A second, and more fundamental, objection is that *there do not seem to be propositions at all, in the sense in which the theory demands them.*[7]

The case of the false belief led Moore to this conclusion. On the propositional theory, there must *be* a proposition for us falsely to believe in, even although this proposition has the peculiar property of being false. In fact, however, so Moore argues, it is the very essence of a false belief that we believe *what is not*. As Russell put the same point in *The Problems of Philosophy* (1912), when Othello falsely believes that *Desdemona loves Cassio* his belief is false just because there is no such object as *Desdemona loves Cassio*; if there were such an object, as on the propositional theory there has to be, Othello's belief would be true, not false. Once we come to realize that a false belief is not a belief in a proposition, it seems natural to deny, also – or so both Moore and Russell thought – that a *true* belief has a proposition as its object. 'Belief,' so Moore sums the matter up, 'never consists in a relation between ourselves and something else (the proposition) which is believed.' In fact, 'there are no propositions'.

Moore admits that although he is now quite convinced that 'I believe *p*' does not assert a relation between an act of belief and a proposition, he cannot discover any alternative analysis which is not open to serious objections. Yet he does know, he thinks, in what range of possibilities a solution must be found. It is indisputable, he argues, that the truth of *p* consists in its 'correspondence' to a fact, and that to believe *p* is to believe that it thus corresponds; the philosophical problem is to give a clear account of this correspondence. We must not, he exhorts us, let any philosophical argument, however difficult it may be to answer, convince us that 'there is really no such thing' as correspondence; we *know* there is, although we do not know – this is our problem – how to describe its nature.

Thus the general movement of Moore's thought is away from *giving answers* towards *setting problems*. Metz described him as a good questioner but a bad answerer, and Moore pleads guilty to the charge. But he is convinced, at least, that he has come to see what the problem is, and that this is a point of the first importance. 'It appears to me,' he wrote in *Principia Ethica* (1903), 'that in Ethics, as in all other philosophical studies, the difficulties and disagreements, of which its history is full, are mainly due to a very simple cause, namely the attempt to answer questions, without first discovering what question it is which you desire to answer.' If Moore was to be a questioner, he was determined to be a *good* questioner, no easy matter.

Moore's attitude to the classical 'problem of the external world' underwent a transformation parallel to his theory of truth. In this case, too, he began from a point of logic. 'To say that a thing is relative,' he roundly asserts in his article on 'Relative and Absolute' in Baldwin's *Dictionary*, 'is always to contradict yourself.' By this he did not mean that relations in themselves, as Bradley had thought, are self-contradictory. On the contrary, it is the Bradleyian conception of 'relative existence' which Moore is attacking. To assert that a thing 'has no meaning apart from its relations' or 'would not be what it is apart from its relations' is, Moore argues, to distinguish the thing itself (as *it*) from its relations, in the very act of denying that such a distinction is intelligible. Moore is here defending 'external' relations, as against the theory of 'internal' relations which he ascribes to the British Idealists.[8] 'The writers influenced by Hegel,' he says, '(hold) that no relation is purely "external", i.e. fails to affect the essence of the things related, and the more nearly it is external, the less real are the things it relates.' Moore, in contrast, is arguing that the *essence* of a thing is always distinct from its relations. Nothing, therefore, can be 'constituted by the nature of the system to which it belongs' – this is the main point which Moore and Russell urge against Bradley's monism. To be at all is to be independent. Moore chose as the epigraph to *Principia Ethica* a quotation from Butler: 'a thing is what it is and not another thing,' a quotation which summarizes the character of his opposition to monism.

This is the background to Moore's classical 'The Refutation of Idealism' (*Mind*, 1903, reprinted in *Studies*).[9] The importance of that essay to the Realist movement can scarcely be overestimated, even if Moore, ever his severest critic, was to write (1922) that 'it now appears to me very confused, as well as to embody a great many downright mistakes'. And it is historically important in another respect: it is the first example of that minute philosophical procedure, with its careful distinction of issues, its insistence that *this*, not *that*, is the real question – where *this* and *that* had ordinarily been regarded as alternative formulations of the same problem – which was to be Moore's distinctive philosophical style, exercising, as such, a notable influence on his successors, particularly at Cambridge.

Thus he begins by explaining precisely what in *The Refutation of Idealism* he hoped to accomplish. He is not, he says, directly criticizing the central Idealist thesis – that 'Reality is Spiritual'. His objective is a more limited one. There is, he thinks, a certain proposition which is essential to all Idealist reasoning, although it is not sufficient to establish the Idealist conclusion. It is this proposition – that *to be is to be perceived* – which he sets out to criticize. If he can show that it is false then, he says, the Idealist thesis may still be true, but certainly can never be *proved* to be true.

The Refutation of Idealism, then, is an attempt to demonstrate the falsity of *to be is to be perceived*. But there are further distinctions to be made: the Idealist formula, Moore says, is highly ambiguous. He concentrates upon what he takes to be its philosophically important interpretation. The formula asserts, on this interpretation, that if anything x is known to exist, the consequence immediately follows that *it is perceived*. Thus understood, *to be is to be perceived* is not a mere identity: if *being perceived* follows from *being*, these two cannot be identical. Idealists, Moore argues, have not generally recognized that this is so. Although they profess to be giving information when they announce that *to be is to be perceived*, they have at the same time proceeded as if *being* and *being perceived* are identical, so that the basic Idealist formula needs no proof. And this means, he says, that they have not clearly seen the difference between, for example, *being yellow* and *being a sensation of yellow*.

Some Idealists, Moore will admit, have explicitly maintained that there is such a difference. But they have at the same time tried to suggest that it is 'not a real difference', yellow and the experience of it being so connected in an 'organic unity' – Moore's bête noire – that it would be 'an illegitimate abstraction' to distinguish them at any but the level of phenomenal appearance. Moore will have none of such facing-two-ways. 'The principle of organic unities,' he writes, 'is mainly used to defend the practice of holding *both* of two contradictory propositions, whenever this may seem convenient. In this, as in other matters, Hegel's main service to philosophy has consisted in giving a name to, and erecting into a principle, a type of fallacy to which experience had shown philosophers, along with the rest of mankind, to be addicted. No wonder that he has followers and admirers.' Contempt for Hegel, and for Hegelian 'subterfuges', was indeed to be a regular feature of the movement of thought which Moore led at Cambridge – for all that, or perhaps partly because, it was McTaggart's University. As against the Hegelian 'it is, and it isn't', Moore demands a plain answer to a plain question 'is it, or is it not?'

Moore admits, however, that there are special reasons why one may be persuaded that *yellow* is identical with *the sensation of yellow*. When we examine our cognitive acts, he says, 'that which makes the sensation of blue a mental act seems to escape us; it seems, if I may use a metaphor, to be transparent – we look through and see nothing but the blue'. For all this transparency, Moore is confident that the difference between act and object nonetheless exists: *a sensation of blue* and *a sensation of red* have something in common, consciousness, and this must not be confused, as both Idealists and agnostics confuse it, with what differentiates them – their object, *blue* or *red*.

The 'true analysis', he argues, of *a sensation* or *an idea* is that it is a case of 'knowing' or 'being aware of' or 'experiencing' something. To say that we are 'having a sensation of red', on this view, is not to describe our consciousness as red, nor is it to assert the existence of some kind of 'mental image' – to *have a sensation of red* is just to *be aware of something red*. The traditional problem of epistemology: 'how do we get outside the circle of our ideas or sensations?' is, Moore concludes, no problem at all. To have a sensation is already to be outside the circle: 'it is really to know something which is as really and truly not a part of *my* experience, as anything which I can ever know.' If this were not so, if being aware were not an awareness *of* something, we could never come to be aware even of our awareness; there would only be *a certain kind of awareness*, without our even being aware of that fact.

The question still remains: what is this 'something' of which I am aware? In *The Refutation of Idealism* it can be, although it is not always, a physical object. But in 'The Nature and Reality of Objects of Perception' (*PAS*, 1905, reprinted in *Studies*), Moore distinguishes sharply between what we 'actually see' and that physical object which we ordinarily believe that we directly perceive. When we assert that we 'see two books on a shelf', all we 'actually see', according to Moore, are coloured patches existing side by side – these being examples of what he later came to call 'sense-data'. He explains in *Some Main Problems of Philosophy* why he prefers this expression 'sense-data' to the more usual 'sensations'. 'Sensation', he says, is misleading because it may be used either to mean *my experiencing of*, say, a patch of colour or to mean the patch of colour itself; Moore is most anxious to distinguish the experiencing from the experienced. For he has not abandoned the principal doctrine of *The Refutation of Idealism*: it is not the essence of a sense-datum to be perceived. It is at least conceivable that the patch of colour which I perceive should continue to exist after I cease to perceive it, whereas it is a mere identity that my experiencing of the patch ceases when I cease to experience the patch.

In this respect, then, Moore's 'sense-datum' is quite unlike Locke's 'idea'.[10] It is not 'in the mind'. Moore has still to meet, all the same, the objections which Berkeley brought against Locke. If all that we see is a coloured patch, what evidence can we have that there are three-dimensional physical objects?

Moore's answer is that we do not need evidence that there are physical objects, since this is something we *already know*. In 'The Nature and Reality of the Objects of Perception' he is already writing with approval of Thomas Reid; in his later articles he has more obviously thrown Reid's mantle over his shoulders, particularly in 'A Defence of Common-Sense' (1925) and 'The Proof of an External World' (*PBA*, 1939).[11]

He knows with certainty, he writes in 'A Defence of Common-Sense', that the common-sense view of the world – which he sets out in some detail – is true; he knows, for example, that there are living human beings with whom he can communicate. Any philosopher who tries to deny that anyone exists except himself presumes that there is such a person in the very act of trying to communicate his denial. Indeed, even to speak, however slightingly, of the 'common-sense view' is already to admit its truth: this phrase has no sense unless there are *people who hold views in common*, i.e. unless the common-sense view is true.

In his *Proof of an External World* Moore's argument is more direct – so direct, indeed, that it created something of a scandal.

It 'appeals to fact', in the manner he had, in his earlier writings, condemned as quite inappropriate in philosophy. But the form of his argument had been foreshadowed as early as the 1910–11 lectures. Then, in criticizing Hume, he had reasoned thus: 'if Hume's principles were true, I could never know that this pencil exists, but I do know this pencil exists, and therefore Hume's arguments cannot be true.' This, he admits, looks like a mere evasion, a begging of the question; but in fact, he says, it is a perfectly good and conclusive argument. We are much more confident that what confronts us exists than we are that Hume's principles are correct; and we are entitled to use the facts we are confident about as a refutation of his argument. Similarly in his *Proof of an External World* Moore describes as a 'good argument' for the existence of things external to us the fact that we can indicate such objects. 'I can prove now,' he wrote, 'that two human hands exist. How? By holding up the two hands, and saying, as I make a certain gesture with the right hand "Here is one hand", and adding, as I make a certain gesture with the left hand "and here is the other".'

But even if it be possible, in this fashion, to demonstrate that physical objects exist, the question still remains how they are related to what we 'actually see' (or taste, or feel, or smell). Two things seem to him, as to Stout, to be perfectly clear: that the immediate objects of our perception are sense-data and that we know there are physical objects. What puzzles him is how what we immediately perceive is related to what we immediately know. Take such a statement as 'this (what I am directly perceiving) is part of the surface of my hand'. There is, Moore feels confident, *something* which we are immediately perceiving; and he is confident also that there is a hand, and that the hand has a surface. But he sees difficulties in saying either that what we immediately perceive is *itself* part of the surface of the hand, or that it is an 'appearance' of such a part, or, in Mill's manner, that the 'surface of the hand' is no more than a compendious name for a series of actual and possible sense-data. Different people confronting the same surface at the same time experience sense-data which cannot, Moore thinks, *all* be a part of the surface of the hand – some see a smooth patch, some a rough patch, and the surface cannot be both rough and smooth. And there seems to be no good reason for giving preference to one such sense-datum and calling it 'the surface itself'. Yet to regard the sense-data as 'appearances' of the surface is to raise all the familiar problems of 'representative perception'. Mill's solution, Moore considers, is no better; impossibly complicated in detail, it has the additional disadvantage of conflicting with our 'strong propensity' to believe that the existence of the hand is independent of any actual or possible perception of it. 'The truth is,' Moore wrote in 'Some Judgments of Perception' (*PAS*, 1918, reprinted in *Studies*), 'I am completely puzzled as to what the true answer can be.' Nor has he ever subdued that sense of puzzlement.

Yet, as in the case of truth and belief, he is not going to be browbeaten by philosophers into denying what he *does* know: that there are sense-data and that there are physical objects. Once more, he would express his uncertainties by saying that although he knows quite well that propositions like 'this is the surface of a hand' can be true, he does not know in what their 'correct analysis' consists. In this distinction between true propositions and their analysis, many of Moore's followers thought they could detect a theory about the nature of philosophy. Thus John Wisdom wrote of Moore, to his indignation, that according to him 'philosophy is analysis'. And it is easy to see why Wisdom should come to this conclusion.

Not only does Moore constantly employ an analytic method, not only does he suggest that the real problem, in a variety of cases, is that of 'discovering an analysis', but in 'The Nature and Reality of the Objects of Perception' he explicitly argues that differences in their mode of analysis are what distinguishes philosophers one from another. All philosophers agree, he there maintains, that 'hens lay eggs'; one affirms, however, and another denies that such propositions can be analysed into statements about relations between sets of spirits. Nevertheless, Moore hotly denies that he identifies philosophy with analysis. And clearly the defence of common-sense, to take only one instance, is not in itself analysis. The fact remains that Moore's use of the analytic method did much to fix the philosophical style of a generation of Cambridge philosophers.

What does Moore mean by 'analysis'? That is not an easy question to answer; perhaps the best explanation is contained in

Moore's reply to a critical article by C. H. Langford – 'Moore's Notion of Analysis' – in *The Philosophy of G. E. Moore*. To give an analysis of a concept, Moore there suggests, is to discover some concept which is the same as the concept being analysed, but which can be expressed in a different way, by referring to concepts which were *not* explicitly mentioned in the expressions used to refer to the original concept.[12] An example may make this explanation clearer: *male sibling* is a correct analysis of *brother*; the two concepts are identical, and yet the concepts mentioned in the expression 'male sibling' are not mentioned in 'brother'. Moore does not agree with those of his successors for whom to 'give an analysis' is to describe 'how to use a certain expression'. It is concepts, not expressions, which are analysed, he thinks, and they are analysed by concepts, even although analysis would be impossible were it not that different verbal expressions are used to refer to the same concept. He frankly admits, however, that he cannot explain at all clearly how it happens that by pointing to the identity of two concepts we can provide information about one of them. Nor can he sharply distinguish what he asserts, and what he denies, to be 'an analysis', so as to explain why, for example, *having twelve edges* is not 'a correct analysis' of *being a cube*. Dissatisfaction with Moore's uncertainties on these points, it would appear, did something to drive his successors in a more 'linguistic' direction.

Dissatisfaction with Russell[13] had the same effect; but arose from somewhat different sources. Russell and Moore grew ever further apart as they developed philosophically: the vast murals of Russell's *History of Western Philosophy* or of *Human Knowledge: Its Scope and Limits* (1948) are as remote as can be from Moore's carefully wrought miniatures. In this matter the sympathy of very many of the younger philosophers is with Moore. Russell – for all his criticism of over-bold generalizations* – belongs in

*Most notably in *Our Knowledge of the External World as a Field for Scientific Method in Philosophy* (1914). The new spirit in philosophy, he says, consists in 'the substitution of piecemeal, detailed and verifiable results for large untested generalities recommended only by a certain appeal to the imagination'. This is an admirable statement of the point of view of a great many of his contemporaries, but Russell's own philosophy certainly does not consist of 'piecemeal results', whether or not it is composed of 'large untested generalities'.

spirit to that tradition of philosophy which conceives it as 'the science of sciences'. To the austere minds of his younger contemporaries there is something almost indecent in so bold a display of speculative ambition. They will admit the importance of 'the earlier Russell', the Russell of the early years of the century, but pass by his later books with averted eyes.

Yet there has been no great change in Russell's manner of approach to philosophy; from the very beginning, in his *A Critical Exposition of the Philosophy of Leibniz* (1900), he displays those characteristics which now provoke shock and dismay. He sees in Leibniz's physics, for example, something continuous with, not cut off from, philosophy. It is at once obvious that Russell is trying to link together apparently diverse phenomena as instances of a general law, in the manner of that scientific tradition which first came into vigorous growth, in modern Europe, in the seventeeth century, and in striking contrast to the differentiating habits of the scholasticism against which it forcibly reacted and into which, in philosophy at least, it shows some signs of returning. It would not be absurd to proclaim Russell 'a modern Descartes' or 'a modern Leibniz', a description which no one, for better or worse, could possibly apply to Moore.

A second, immediately apparent, feature of Russell's *Leibniz* is his unusual appreciation of Continental scholarship and Continental speculation. There is no trace of insularity in Russell; and he is always ready to admit, even at times to exaggerate, his indebtedness to his predecessors. His work displays, indeed, a quite unusual capacity for *learning* from his fellow-philosophers, even when they are foreigners, a capacity which has brought a certain amount of opprobrium about his head and certainly complicates the task of a historian.

Thirdly, Russell had from the beginning special views about philosophy, which closely associate it with logic and with mathematics. 'That all sound philosophy should begin with an analysis of propositions is,' he writes, 'a truth too obvious, perhaps, to demand a proof.' Thus whereas for most previous commentators Leibniz had been pre-eminently the creator of an imaginative world-view which 'reconciled science and religion', for Russell the clue to the understanding of Leibniz's *philosophy* – as distinct from the fairy-tales he concocted for the delectation of his royal correspondents – lies in his belief that all propositions can be reduced to the subject-predicate form, i.e. that relations are reducible to properties of the terms between which they hold*. Once this step is taken, Russell thought, Leibniz's metaphysical conclusions inevitably follow – or, at least, the only alternative is Absolute Idealism. If, in the proposition *x is related to y*, *x*'s relation to *y* is an attribute – what Russell calls a 'predicate' – of *x*, then the consequence immediately follows that *x* and *y* are not really distinct; *x*'s environment, in other words, is an aspect of *x* itself, as Leibniz had argued. And the Absolute Idealist carried this doctrine further by maintaining that *x*, too, is an attribute – of Reality as a whole. Leibniz's importance, as Russell sees it, consists in his having thought out in detail the metaphysical implications of the substance-attribute analysis of the proposition. Thus he drew the attention of other philosophers to consequences which might have escaped their notice: he got them to see how important it is to insist, as Russell does – following Moore's 'The Nature of Judgment' – upon the 'externality' of relations, or in other words upon the irreducibility of relational propositions.

Russell's emphasis on the primacy of logical questions is converted into a theory about the nature of philosophy in the chapter entitled 'Logic as the Essence of Philosophy' in *Our Knowledge of the External World*. 'Every philosophical problem,' Russell there wrote, 'when it is subjected to the necessary analysis and purification, is found to be not really philosophical at all, or else to be, in the sense in which we are using the word, logical.' By 'logical' he means 'arising out of the analysis of propositions', or, as he also puts the matter, out of the attempt to determine what kinds of fact there are, and how they are related one to another.

Russell, then, deserts the British empiricist tradition that the essence of philosophy is psychological – although it is interesting to observe that in his later work he manifests a certain tendency to reinstate psychology, and to return in more ways than one to a philosophy very like Hume's. As well, he is contesting the not uncommon view that philosophy consists of the defence of a

---

*By the 'subject-predicate form' Russell and most of his successors mean what could be less misleadingly described as 'the substance-attribute' form.

parti pris – an ethical, religious, or social outlook which philosophy exists to justify and must not question. The philosopher, he maintains in his 'Scientific Method in Philosophy' (1914, reprinted in *Mysticism and Logic*, 1917), must be 'ethically neutral', scientific, impartial. Any other sort of philosophy he describes as 'pre-Copernican' on the ground that it proceeds as if the human being, with his special ethical interests, were the clue to the understanding of the Universe. Thus Russell stands firmly for that 'submission to fact' which Clifford had extolled and James had condemned as neither possible nor desirable.

Although there was much in *The Philosophy of Leibniz* to attract the eye of an attentive reader, *The Principles of Mathematics* (1903) first made it perfectly clear that a new force had entered British philosophy. The rigorous philosophical examination of logico-mathematical ideas was a genuine novelty, and there was an atmosphere of intellectual adventure about the whole book which stamped it as an achievement of the first order.

Once more, Russell's indebtedness is primarily to Continental ideas. He tells us that on his first introduction to geometry he had been distressed to find that Euclid began from axioms which had to be assumed without proof: the idea of a mathematics which was absolutely certain, which contained no loophole through which error could wriggle in, obviously attracted him from his earliest days. Mathematicians like Weierstrass showed him what mathematical rigour could be like; Peano opened his eyes to the possibility of constructing a single deductive system of mathematics, resting on a bare minimum of definitions and elementary propositions. But like Frege before him – although at first in ignorance of Frege's work – Russell could be content with nothing less than the definition of Peano's primitive mathematical conceptions in wholly logical terms. *The Principles of Mathematics* sets out to show how this can be done; in particular, Russell there tries to formulate the logical principles and methods which, so he thinks, must be involved in any construction of mathematics. No work since Aristotle's time has had so striking an effect upon the logic ordinarily taught at universities. Then Russell went on, now in conjunction with his former mathematics teacher A. N. Whitehead, to undertake in detail the construction of mathematics out of logic in the three volumes of *Principia Mathematica* (1910–13)[14] – a classical contribution to symbolic logic which, however, by its very intricacy persuaded most philosophers that this sort of logic was not for them.*

Like Husserl, Russell distinguishes sharply between logic and psychology. 'It is plain,' he writes, 'that when we validly infer one proposition from another, we do so in virtue of a relation which holds between the two propositions whether we perceive it or not'; this relation – 'implication' – not the human activity of inferring, is the principal subject-matter of logic. That is the crucial point of opposition between Russell's logic and the Idealist 'morphology of knowledge' or Dewey's 'logic of inquiry'. In inferring, according to Russell, the human being is 'purely receptive'; he simply 'registers' the fact that an implication is present. For Bradley and for Dewey, on the contrary, inference is a 'construction' which arises out of, and is only discussable within the context of, the attempt to undertake an inquiry. But Bradley's own development had been in the direction of emphasizing the 'objectivity' of inference, and Russell was simply pushing that objectivity harder.

The *Principles of Mathematics* begins with an extraordinarily audacious sentence: 'Pure Mathematics is the class of all propositions of the form "p implies q"', where p and q are propositions containing one or more variables, the same in the two propositions, and neither p nor q contains any constants except logical constants.' A 'constant' is defined as 'something absolutely definite, concerning which there is no ambiguity whatever.' Thus *Socrates* in 'Socrates is a man' is a 'constant', as contrasted with the x of 'if x is a man, x is mortal', which does not refer to any specific person and is therefore a 'variable'.

Russell admits that it is difficult to make precise what is meant by a 'variable'. The same is true, he also grants, of a 'logical constant' – that special type of constant which, on his view, is the only sort to be found in the propositions of pure mathematics.[15]

---

*Russell agrees with them. 'Logic,' he says in the Preface to *Human Knowledge* (1948), 'is not part of philosophy.' This does not mean that he now rejects the view that 'logic is the essence of philosophy'. 'Logic' in *Human Knowledge* means the construction of deductive systems; the 'logic' which is the essence of philosophy, as we saw, is an attempt to describe what kinds of facts there are.

(We could put his point roughly by saying that mathematical propositions assert that whatever has a certain general structure must also have a certain other structure; they make no reference to this or that particular entity. As he says later, 'proper names play no part in mathematics'. This is Russell's version of the Platonic-Cartesian doctrine that mathematics is about 'essences', not about 'existences'.)

If 'logical constants' are too fundamental to be defined, they can, Russell thinks, at least be enumerated. Russell's first list reads as follows: 'Implication, the relation of a term to the class of which it is a member, the notion of *such that*, the notion of relation, and such further notions as may be involved in the general notion of propositions of the same form.' These further notions are 'propositional function, class, denoting, and *any* or *every* term'. Of these constants, we shall be able to comment only on five of the most important – propositional function, implication, relation, class and denotation.

By a 'propositional function' Russell means an expression like 'x is a man', which in itself is neither true nor false; it is converted into a proposition by substituting, say, *Socrates* for x. His theory of implication rests on this distinction between proposition and propositional function. There are, he says, two types of implication – 'material' and 'formal'. A proposition p materially implies a proposition q, if it is not the case that p is true and q is false; thus material implication is a relation between propositions. A formal implication, on the other hand, relates propositional functions; thus 'x is a man' formally implies 'x is mortal'. And just as a propositional function can be regarded as a class of propositions – all those propositions with 'is a man' for their predicate – so also a formal implication is a class of material implications. Thus 'x is a man formally implies x is mortal' asserts the class of material implications, 'Jones is a man materially implies Jones is mortal, Smith is a man materially implies Smith is mortal. ...'

Russell recognizes no other variety of implication. He argues that 'q can be deduced from p' means exactly the same thing as 'p materially implies q' – even although it then follows, as we have already seen,* that any proposition can be deduced from a

*See p. 140 above.

false proposition – and that a true proposition is deducible from any proposition whatsoever. Moore, however, in his essay on 'External and Internal Relations' characterized Russell's identification of *is materially implied by* with *is deducible from* as 'simply an enormous howler'. He introduced the word 'entails', now in common use amongst philosophers, to refer to that relation between p and q which entitles us to say of q that it must be true if p is true.

Russell himself, in the first of his Meinong articles, shows some signs of uneasiness, particularly over the consequence that 'there is a mutual implication of any true propositions'. 'It must be admitted,' he writes, 'that one-sided inferences can practically be made in many cases, and that consequently some relation other than that considered by symbolic logic must be involved when we infer.' But he seems to think that the illegitimate consequences of his dealings with implication can be laid on the doorstep of epistemology, so that symbolic logic can be left free to live its gay and unfettered life.

On relations, Russell adds little to Peirce except clarity of exposition.[16] But it is certainly as a result of Russell's emphasis on relational propositions that they came into their own amongst philosophers. His theory of classes and of class-membership, likewise, at first follows closely in the footsteps of his immediate predecessors. It is in terms of classes that he proposes to define natural numbers, and through that definition all the fundamental notions of arithmetic. Arithmeticians like Peano had already maintained that all other numbers could be defined in terms of the natural numbers; if Russell can define the natural numbers in terms of classes, he has proved, he thinks, that mathematics has no need of *numerical*, as distinct from merely *logical*, constants.

Russell defines a cardinal number – which is always, he says, the number of a class – as 'the class of all classes similar to the given class'; a class has six members, on this definition, if it belongs to the class to which all classes similar to it belong. 'Similar' has a special technical sense – it means 'having the same number as'. Russell had therefore to meet the objection that his definition is circular, that he is defining the number of a class as that class to which all classes with the same number belong. His reply is that he can define 'similarity' or 'having the same number' in non-numerical terms, two classes having the same number when they can be correlated one-to-one. Nor do we need the number one, he further maintains, to establish a 'one-to-one' correlation; a relation is one-to-one when if x stands in this relation to y and so does x^1, then x and x^1 are identical, and if x has this relation to y and to y^1, then y and y^1 are identical. For example, to say that there is a one-to-one correlation between legal wives and legal husbands in a christian community is to assert that if x is the legal husband of y and x^1 is the legal husband of y, then x and x^1 are identical; and if x is the legal husband of y and y^1, then y and y^1 are identical. Thus, Russell maintains, his definition of numbers in terms of similar classes involves no circularity.

In this definition of number is illustrated one of the central techniques of Russell's philosophical method – what he calls 'the principle of abstraction' and might have less misleadingly named 'the principle of *dispensing with* abstractions'. On the normal view, a 'number' is picked out, by abstraction, from a set of groups which possess a common numerical property. But Russell objects that there is no way of showing that there is only one such property – the one we have picked out: abstraction leaves us, indeed, with a class of properties, when we were in search of a single property. The 'principle of abstraction' – which can be employed whenever certain formal conditions are satisfied[17] – avoids this difficulty: it defines by reference to a class consisting of all the classes which have a unique relation (for example, one-to-one correspondence) to each other. Such a definition does not rule out the possibility, Russell will freely grant, that there is a property common to all the members of these classes, but *it does not need to make that presumption*. Here, for the first time, there clearly emerges what was to become a principal driving-force behind Russell's philosophy – the desire to reduce the number of entities and properties which *must* be presumed to exist in order to give a 'complete account of the world'.

Even if the definition of numbers in terms of classes is not para-doxical in itself, it threatened, Russell soon discovered, to produce paradoxes; there were difficulties, in particular, in the notion of 'a class of all classes'. This, it seemed obvious, is itself a class; it follows that it is itself a member of the class of all classes, i.e. that it includes itself as a member. And it is not unique in this respect: the class of things which are not men, to mention another case, is itself something which is not a man. On the other hand, there are classes which do not include themselves. The class of things which *are* men, for example, is *not* itself a man.

It appears, then, that classes can be of either of two types: those which are members of themselves, and those which are not members of themselves. Now suppose we consider the class which consists of all the classes which are not members of themselves. Is this class a member of itself or not? If it is a member of itself, then it is not one of the classes which are not members of themselves; and yet to be a member of itself, it *must* be one of those classes. Here, then, there is a manifest contradiction. But equally if it is not a member of itself, then it is not one of those classes which are not members of themselves – again a contradiction. Thus we are led to an antinomy; either alternative implies a contradiction.

Paradoxes, of course, were no novelty. One of them, the paradox of the liar, is almost as old as philosophy. Russell restates it as follows: Suppose a man says 'I am lying', then if what he says is true he is lying, i.e. what he says is not true, and if what he says is not true, then also he is lying, i.e. what he says is true. Such familiar paradoxes had usually been passed by as mere ingenuities; but the paradox of 'the class of all classes' could not be so lightly regarded, and the same was true of other paradoxes which had raised their head in mathematics and in logic.

Russell, by now aware of Frege's work, sent him his paradox.[18] Frege was greatly perturbed. 'Hardly anything more unfortunate can affect a scientific writer,' he wrote in an Appendix to his *Fundamental Laws of Arithmetic*, 'than to have one of the foundations of his edifice shaken after the work is finished' – and Russell's paradox, he thought, did shake the foundations. The difficulty, as Frege saw it, is that if the logistic construction of arithmetic is to be carried through, we must be able to pass from a properly constituted concept to its extension, so that in the present case we ought to be able to talk without contradiction about the members of the properly constituted class of classes which are not members of themselves. Yet this is just what Russell's paradox seemed to rule out. Frege attempted a solution of the difficulty: he so modified his previous account of 'equal extensions' as to exclude the extension of a concept from the class of objects which fall under it. It will then be no longer permissible to say that the class of things which are not men – the extension of the concept 'not-men' – is itself not a man, or that the class of classes which are not members of themselves is a member of itself. In general, he believed, the addition of limiting conditions to his proofs would enable him to avoid Russell's paradoxes.

Russell's own solution is more radical – the introduction of a theory of types.[19] Not that he was ever wholly satisfied with it. He describes it, indeed, as chaotic and unfinished. But it has had important effects on the development of contemporary philosophy.

The paradoxes all arise, he argues, out of a certain kind of vicious circle.[20] Such a vicious circle is generated whenever it is supposed that 'a collection of objects may contain members which can only be defined by means of the collection as a whole.' To take a case: suppose we say 'all propositions have the property X.' On the face of it, this is itself a proposition, so that the class of propositions has among its members one which presumes that the class has been completed – because it talks of 'all propositions' – before it has itself been mentioned. This contradiction – that the class must at once have been completed and not been completed – brings out the fact that there is *no such class*. 'We shall therefore have to say,' Russell concludes, 'that statements about "all propositions" are meaningless.' Then how are we to develop a theory of propositions? The pseudo-totality 'all propositions', Russell replies, must be broken up into sets of propositions, each capable of being a genuine totality, after which a separate account can be given of each such set. This 'breaking up' is the object of the theory of types; it is, however, applied to propositional functions rather than to propositions, because they, Russell thinks, are more important for mathematics.

Properly speaking, there are *two* theories of types – the simple and the ramified. The simple theory depends upon the conception of a 'range of significance'. In the propositional function 'x is mortal', Russell argues, x can be replaced by certain constants in such a way as to form a true proposition, by others so as to form a false proposition, but in certain cases the resulting proposition will be neither true nor false, but meaningless.* The constants which, when substituted for x, form a meaningful proposition are said to constitute the 'range of significance' or 'type' of the function. In the case of 'x is mortal' the range of significance is restricted to particular entities. It is always sensible, even if false, to assert of any particular thing that it is mortal, but it is without meaning, Russell now says, to describe, say, 'the class of men' or 'humanity' as being mortal. The general principle is that a function must always be of a higher type than its 'argument'. That is why 'mortal' can take 'Socrates' as its argument, but cannot be meaningfully predicated of 'the class men', and that is why, also, a thing can be a member of a class but a class cannot be and cannot fail to be – the denial would be as meaningless as the affirmation – a member of anything less than a class of classes. (Just as an individual can be a member of a club, but a club cannot be a member of anything less than an *association* of clubs.) In the paradox of the class which is a member of itself, this rule, Russell says, had been ignored. It had been presumed that all classes are of a single type, and that any class could be a member of another class. But this supposition gives rise, he argues, to a vicious circle: 'the class of all classes' would then be a *class* additional to the 'all classes' of which it is the class. Once the distinction between types is firmly maintained, it will be obvious nonsense to say of a class either that it is or that it is not a member of itself. Thus the dreaded antinomy vanishes.

Russell thinks that distinctions between types have been unconsciously respected in everyday speech, unconsciously because no one would *want* to say, for example, that 'Humanity is not a man'. But whereas the difference in type between 'Humanity' and 'a man' is an obvious one, the fundamental notions of logic – such notions as truth, falsity, function, property, class – have, he says, no fixed or definite type. We have been accustomed to talk simply about 'truths', whether we mean first order truths (x is y) or second-order truths (x is y is true) or third-order truths

*There was, it should be observed – for the contrary is sometimes asserted – no novelty in the trichotomy, true, false, meaningless. As Russell himself points out, it was to be found even in the older logics – quite explicitly in Mill's *System of Logic* – and we have already had occasion to refer to it in talking about Frege, for example.

('x is y is true' is true). Paradoxes are then inevitable; we are led to imagine that propositions about truths are, as true, about themselves, whereas they are really second-order truths about first-order truths, and we are soon floundering in a sea of nonsense. The only way out, Russell thinks, is always explicitly to mention what *order* of truths, or classes, or functions we are talking about.*

The simple theory of types, according to Russell, does not suffice to remove all risk of paradox. It is necessary to make further distinctions, he thinks, *between* types. Compare the two propositional functions, 'x is a general' and 'x has all the properties of a great general'. They have the same range of significance; 'Napoleon' could be sensibly substituted for x in both cases. But the predicate 'all the properties of a great general' is an illegitimate totality, since it itself would be one such property. This totality can be avoided, Russell argues, only by distinguishing differences of order within each type; then 'has all the properties of a great general' will be of a higher order than 'is a general', and will not itself *be* a property. Such a 'ramified' theory of types is essential, he considers, if every variety of logical antinomy is to be successfully avoided.

Obviously the original hierarchy of types is greatly complicated by the introduction of the ramified theory. But a much more serious handicap, in the eyes of Russell and his critics, was that the ramified theory seemed to rule out certain varieties of mathematical analysis which made use of what, according to the ramified theory, were illegitimate totalities.[21] Russell thought he could overcome this difficulty with the help of 'the axiom of reducibility'; this asserts that corresponding to any assertion of

*Russell later confessed to some uneasiness about *type* itself. Is this, too, of different types? But how is it possible to say that *Socrates* and *mankind* are of different types, unless there is some single general sense of type? Are we not sinning against the theory of types in ascribing a single function *are of different types* to arguments of different types? For this sort of reason, Russell welcomed the 'linguistic' interpretation of the theory of types offered by writers like R. Carnap; it is a mistake, he came to think, to speak of *entities* as being of this or that type, it is *expressions* which differ in type. And it can be said without any contradiction, in a language of the second order, that the *words* 'Socrates' and 'Humanity' have different syntactical functions. See on this Russell's 'Reply to his Critics' in *The Philosophy of Bertrand Russell*. See also J. J. Smart: 'Whitehead and Russell's Theory of Types' (*Analysis*, 1950); P. Weiss: 'The Theory of Types' (*Mind*, 1928).

the form 'x has all the properties of a y' there exists a formally equivalent assertion which does not contain any reference to 'all the properties' but which, just because it is formally equivalent, can replace the original assertion in mathematical reasoning. But this axiom stood out awkwardly in the deductive system of *Principia Mathematica;* and it lacked the 'self-evidence' which mathematicians are accustomed to demand. Not surprisingly, other logicians attempted to avoid the paradoxes without recourse to the ramified theory of types.

The best known of these attempts is contained in F. P. Ramsey's essay on 'The Foundation of Mathematics',[22] and in the second edition of *The Principles of Mathematics* Russell accepts Ramsey's solution. According to Ramsey, Russell has grouped together paradoxes which are quite different in character – those which (like the paradox about classes) arise within the attempt to construct a logical system and those which (like the paradox of the liar) are 'linguistic' or 'semantic' in their origin, i.e. which arise only when we try to *talk about* that system. The simple theory of types, Ramsey argues – following Peano – suffices to resolve paradoxes of the first sort, and they are the only ones which really matter to the logician as such. Paradoxes of the second type can be removed by clearing up ambiguities; they depend upon the ambiguity of everyday words like 'means', 'names', 'defines'. Thus the ramified theory of types is in neither case necessary, and the much-despised 'axiom of reducibility' can be abandoned.[23]

The effect, then, of Russell's theory of types is that, like Moore's account of 'analysis', it encouraged the view that linguistic inquiries, of one sort or another, are of special importance to the philosopher. The same effect, even more obviously, flowed from Russell's theory of *denoting:* and the discussion of this 'logical constant' will lead us into the heart of Russell's philosophy.

As we have already seen, Russell's early metaphysics derived from Moore. 'On fundamental questions of philosophy,' he wrote in *The Principles of Mathematics*, 'my position, in all its chief features, is derived from Mr G. E. Moore. I have accepted from him the non-existential nature of propositions (except such as happen to assert existence) and their independence of any knowing mind – also the pluralism which regards the world, both that of existents and that of entities, as composed of an infinite number of mutually independent entities, with relations which are ultimate and not reducible to adjectives of their terms or of the whole which these compose.' These entities are the 'terms' in propositions.

With this ontology is associated a theory of language. 'It must be admitted,' he wrote, 'that every word occurring in a sentence must have some meaning ... the correctness of our philosophical analysis of a proposition may therefore be usefully checked by the exercise of assigning the meaning of each word in the sentence expressing the proposition.' Every word a meaning, every meaning an entity – these are the principles on which Russell at first worked.

He is already recognizing, however, in his analysis of 'denoting,' as Frege had before him, that the grammatical structure of a proposition can be misleading. A concept may occur in a proposition which is not, in spite of appearances, *about* that concept but about 'a term connected in a certain peculiar way with the concept'. Thus 'I met a man', for example, does not mean 'I met the concept "man"'; 'a man' here 'denotes' some particular human being. Similarly, although less obviously, 'Man is mortal' is not about the concept 'Man'. 'We should be surprised to find in the *Times*,' Russell writes, 'such a notice as the following "Died at his residence in Camelot, Gladstone Rd., Upper Tooting, on the 18th of June, 19–, Man, eldest son of Death and Sin".' And yet that announcement ought to provoke no surprise if 'Man' is mortal.

In *The Principles of Mathematics*, however, propositions like 'the King of England is bald' are not subjected to any considerable transformation; this proposition means, Russell says, that 'the man denoted by the phrase "the King of England" is bald'. It was the consequences of this interpretation which provoked the new theory of denoting presented in Russell's 'On Denoting' (*Mind*, 1905).[24] The years which intervened between *The Principles of Mathematics* and 'On Denoting' Russell had devoted to the study of Meinong. At first, he was confirmed in his allegiance to the philosophy he had learned from Moore. But doubts crept in: Meinong's 'objects' began to look like a *reductio ad absurdum* of Moore's 'concepts'. It was all very well for Meinong to talk with scorn of 'the prejudice in favour of the actual'; that 'prejudice', rechristened 'a robust sense of reality', is essential,

Russell came to think, to any scientific philosophy. 'The sense of reality,' as he eventually summed the matter up in his *Introduction to Mathematical Philosophy* (1919), 'is vital in logic, and whoever juggles with it by pretending that Hamlet has another kind of reality is doing a disservice to thought.'

Yet what is to be said, in terms of 'reality', about such assertions as, in a Republican age, 'the King of France is bald'? This cannot mean that 'the man denoted by the phrase "the King of France" is bald', because there is no such entity for the phrase to denote. Meinong had said that it refers to an object which lies 'outside of being', an object to which the law of contradiction does not apply, since one can say of it, with equal truth, that it has and that it has not any property we care to mention. Of a non-existent King of France we are entitled to say that he is bald or that he is not-bald, just as strikes our fancy. This is the point at which Russell's new-found sense of reality revolted. There must, he thought, be another way out, a way which does not involve interpreting the phrase 'the King of France' as referring to any entity whatsoever. And that is what he sought in his new theory of denoting, and, in particular, in what he came to call 'the theory of descriptions'.

By a 'denoting phrase', he first of all explains – and it is worth observing that it is now *phrases*, not *concepts*, which denote – he means such phrases as the following: 'a man, some men, any man, every man, all men, the present King of England, the present King of France, the centre of mass of the Solar System at the first instant of the present century, the revolution of the earth around the sun, the revolution of the sun around the earth.' He offers no general characterization of such phrases, but it is clear, at least, that they are none of them 'proper names', and yet that they can stand as a grammatical subject in a sentence.

The fundamental principle of Russell's theory of denoting, indeed, is that – in opposition to Mill – these denoting phrases *are not names for entities*, even although their being used as the subject of sentences makes them look as if they were. He tried to prove his point by so reformulating sentences containing denoting phrases as to retain the meaning of the original sentence without employing any denoting phrase. If this can be done, the presumption is, it will no longer be necessary to suppose that a denoting phrase names some specific entity; then Meinong's unreal 'objects' can be abandoned – on the principle of 'Occam's razor', that entities ought not to be multiplied except of necessity.

We can illustrate Russell's general procedure from the 'most primitive' cases – 'everything', 'nothing', 'something'. Such a proposition as 'everything is c', Russell says, does not assert that there is a mysterious entity *everything* which can be truly described as c. That there is no need to suppose the existence of such an entity comes out in the fact that 'everything is c' can be re-formulated as 'for all values of x, "x is c" is true', which makes no mention of 'everything' and yet which fully expresses what was originally asserted.

A more complex, and a more important, case is what Russell later called 'the definite description' – denoting phrases which contain 'the'.* On the face of it, a phrase like 'the so-and-so' *must* refer to an entity: Frege, for example, had thought that 'the' was the sign *par excellence* that an 'object' was being referred to. But such a proposition as 'the author of *Waverley* is Scotch', which one would ordinarily suppose to predicate a property of a particular entity, 'the author of *Waverley*', is not, Russell argues, about the author of *Waverley* at all. This proposition asserts, he tries to show, a conjunction of three propositions: '(a) at least one person wrote *Waverley*, (b) at most one person wrote *Waverley*, (c) whoever wrote *Waverley* is Scotch.' Or, more formally, 'there is a term c such that (1) "x wrote *Waverley*" is equivalent, for all values of x, to "x is c" and (2) "c is Scotch".'

This reformulation does not mention 'the author of *Waverley*'; that means that we could intelligibly assert that 'the author of *Waverley* is Scotch' even if *Waverley* in fact had no author. In that case, our assertion would be false, since proposition (a) – 'at least one person wrote *Waverley*' – would be a false proposition, but it would not be nonsensical. Now we can understand, then, how an assertion like 'the King of France is bald' – which is precisely parallel to 'the author of *Waverley* is Scotch' – can have a sense, even although there is no entity named by 'the King of France', no Meinongian object.

*As distinct from *indefinite* descriptions, containing 'a'. See particularly Russell's *Introduction to Mathematical Philosophy* on descriptions.

Russell was by now well embarked upon what was to be his main philosophical occupation. 'Occam's razor' dealt destruction like a sword – unnecessary entities were miraculously cut down right and left. Numbers, as something distinct from classes of of classes, had been the first to go; but the victory over Meinong's 'objects' had been a more sweeping one. And they were soon to be joined in Hades by more commonplace-looking victims.

Definite descriptions, Russell had argued, are 'incomplete symbols' – what Frege had called 'names of a function' – as distinct from 'complete symbols', i.e. proper names (the names of arguments). They have a use in sentences, but they do not name entities. The same is true, *Principia Mathematica* suggests, of 'classes'; classes, too, are 'symbolic linguistic conventions', used in order to make statements about functions of propositional functions. The assertion 'the class "man" is included in the class "mortals"' looks like a statement about the relation between two entities, the class 'man' and the class 'mortals'. But in fact, Russell maintains, it is no more than a shorthand formulation of the proposition ' "x is a man" formally implies "x is mortal".' There is no entity, as Russell had at first supposed, which is named by the phrase 'the class as one'.

Similarly, whereas in such early articles as 'Is Position in Time or Space Absolute or Relative?' (*Mind*, 1901), Russell had operated freely with spatial 'points' and temporal 'instants' – ultimate units of space and of time – Whitehead now persuaded him that sentences which apparently refer to such entities can, without loss of meaning, be translated into statements about the relations between 'events'. Points, instants, particles, shared the fate of numbers, classes, the author of *Waverley* and the present King of France.

So far, however, the ordinary objects of everyday life, tables, chairs, our own and other people's minds, had been left untouched. But the process by which they are gradually disintegrated into classes of 'sensibilia' is already under way in *The Problems of Philosophy* (1912). In the preface to that book, Russell acknowledges his indebtedness to those lectures of Moore which were published in 1953 as *Some Main Problems of Philosophy;* he agrees with Moore, in particular, that what we are immediately acquainted with are sense-data, not physical objects.

But there are notable differences between Russell's epistemology and Moore's; the existence of physical objects, to Russell, is a scientific hypothesis – parallel, say, to an hypothesis in physics – which we accept as being true because it allows us to give a 'more simple' account of the behaviour of our sense-data than any other hypothesis which has occurred to us. It is not, as it was for Moore, something that we 'immediately know'. And Russell's argument in favour of the view that we do not directly perceive physical objects appeals to 'what science tells us' about the nature of perception, in contrast with Moore's appeal to 'commonsense' and to familiar sensory illusions. Furthermore, the whole atmosphere of *The Problems of Philosophy* is logico-mathematical, in the Cartesian style; Russell sets out in search of the indubitable, of what it is *impossible* to doubt, and criticizes our everyday beliefs from that standpoint. It is already clear that Russell, although he makes certain concessions to 'commonsense' in the form of 'what we instinctively believe', will not be permanently satisfied by the loose and somewhat precarious structure of Moore's 'defence of commonsense'; it is science, not commonsense, which he is anxious to defend and it is science, too, which must sit in judgement on that defence.

The search for the indubitable, in *The Problems of Philosophy*, is formulated as an attempt to discover those objects with which we are immediately 'acquainted'. Russell takes over from James, who had in turn, oddly enough, learnt it from Grote – so that this doctrine travelled from one Cambridge man to another via Cambridge, Mass. – his distinction between knowledge by acquaintance and knowledge by description; this is the point at which Russell's analysis of denoting bears directly on his general philosophy.[25] We have 'knowledge by acquaintance' of an object if we are 'directly aware' of it. The most obvious case, Russell thinks, is the sense-datum: I can be directly aware that I am experiencing a certain sense-datum. And it follows, he more hesitantly concludes, that I am also directly aware of the 'I' that does this experiencing, and of its mental states.

Mental states, our own self, and sense-data are the only 'particulars', he thinks, with which we have direct acquaintance. But we are also acquainted with 'universals' – with whiteness and beforeness and diversity. When we experience one sense-datum as *before* another one, for example, we are acquainted with a universal, the relation 'before'.

We are not acquainted, he argues, with physical objects; we know such an object as a table as that to which a certain description applies – as, say, 'the thing which causes these sense-data' – and it is only by inference, not by direct perception, that we know that there is any such thing. Nor are we acquainted with other human beings, even with those whose 'personal acquaintance' we are accustomed to claim. Such human beings, he thinks, are in the same position as physical objects: they are inferences from our sense-data. As for people with whom we are not in the ordinary sense 'acquainted' – Julius Caesar, for example – we know them, more obviously, through descriptions: as, to keep the same instance, 'the man who crossed the Rubicon'.

On the face of it, this is an odd doctrine. 'Julius Caesar' is not the sort of thing we should ordinarily call 'a description', and in such assertions as 'Julius Caesar crossed the Rubicon' Julius Caesar seems to be *what* we are describing, not a description. But, Russell objects, we cannot possibly talk about anything which lies beyond the reach of our acquaintance; this proposition, therefore, cannot be *about* Julius Caesar, grammatical appearances to the contrary notwithstanding. 'Every proposition which we can understand,' he says, 'must be composed wholly of constituents with which we are acquainted.' A proposition which appears to be about Julius Caesar must really be about certain sense-data (something, in this case, that we have been told or have read) and certain universals. Thus just as the author of *Waverley* is not the true subject of propositions like 'the author of *Waverley* is Scotch', so, too, according to Russell, Julius Caesar is not the true subject of propositions like 'Julius Caesar crossed the Rubicon'. Although the details are complicated, such propositions, he thinks, can be reduced by the methods characteristic of his 'theory of descriptions' to propositions which, without mentioning Julius Caesar, still manage to convey all that the original proposition asserted.

The problem now arises – what about our knowledge of general principles? Is that reducible to statements about objects with which we are acquainted? There is no difficulty, on Russell's view, about mathematical propositions; these, he thinks, relate universals, and we are acquainted with universals. But the inductive principle he finds more puzzling. Like Hume, he thinks that if this principle is unsound, 'we have no reason to expect the sun to rise tomorrow, or to expect bread to be more nourishing than a stone'; but, also like Hume, he does not see how the inductive principle can either be a relation between universals or an inference from experience. He is forced to the conclusion, highly uncomfortable although it is, that 'all knowledge which is based upon what we have experienced is based upon a belief experience can neither confirm nor refute and yet which seems to be as firmly rooted as any of the facts of experience'. This was one of the sore places in his philosophy; his attempts to heal it were finally to lead, in his *Human Knowledge: Its Scope and Limits* (1948), to a position considerably remote from *The Problems of Philosophy*.

Another sore place was the status of the physical object. Physics is supposed to be an empirical science, yet – as Russell pointed out in his essay on 'The Relation of Sense-Data to Physics' (*Scientia*, 1914, reprinted in *Mysticism and Logic*, 1917) – physics itself tells us that what we perceive is something entirely different in character from the entities which form the subject-matter of physics. 'Molecules have no colour, atoms make no noise, electrons have no taste, and corpuscles do not even smell' – yet what we directly experience is always a colour, a sound, a taste or a smell. How then, Russell asks, can the existence of physical objects be verified by the sense-data we experience? He had so far presumed that the existence of such entities can somehow be inferred from sense-data. But he came to agree with Berkeley that such an inference – to entities quite different in nature from anything we can experience – is in principle impossible. Unless physical objects are in some way reducible to sense-data, physics must, he thinks, be a mere fantasy.

The difficulties in such a reduction were, on the face of it, insuperable. Sense-data, as they had ordinarily been defined, are subjective and discontinuous; physical objects are objective and continuous. Different persons experience incompatible sense-data; how can a penny, say, consist of the round sense-datum you experience and the elliptical sense-datum I experience? With the help of lessons he had learnt from the New Realists – especially T. P. Nunn and S. Alexander in England and E. B. Holt in the United States[26] – Russell thought he could overcome these objections.

The major points[27] are, first, that a sense-datum is not 'subjective' – it is neither a mental state nor a constituent in such a state; secondly, that once this is recognized, there is in principle no difficulty in supposing that there are 'sensibilia' – objects 'which have the same metaphysical and physical status as sense-data but which are not actually being perceived by anybody'; and thirdly, that the supposed 'incompatibility' of sense-data rests on a simple-minded conception of space and time. Since sense-data are objective, the argument then runs, physical objects can be defined as series of sense-data, linked together by sensibilia. The supposedly 'incompatible' sense-data will be different members, in different 'private spaces', of such a series of sense-data. Thus, according to Russell, a penny, for example, consists of the elliptical sense-datum which occurs in your private space and the round sense-datum that occurs in my private space, together with various other sense-data in other private spaces. These various appearances, he says, form 'one thing', in the sense that they 'behave with respect to the laws of physics, in a way in which series not belonging to one thing would in general not behave' – at least, this is true of the 'things' with which physics is concerned. The 'things' of commonsense, according to Russell, are conceived with so little precision that a satisfactory account of their construction is scarcely possible.

Physics, Russell concludes, stands in no need of 'physical objects' understood as something wholly distinct in nature from sense-data. And it is, he says, the supreme maxim of all scientific philosophizing that '*wherever possible, logical constructions are to be substituted for inferred entities*'.[28] Thus if physical objects can be constructed out of sense-data, a 'scientific' philosopher ought obviously to abandon the doctrine, which Russell had held in *The Problems of Philosophy*, that their existence has to be 'inferred' as a relatively simple explanation of the sense-data we experience.

At this stage in Russell's philosophy, then, the world as the scientific philosopher sees it consists of sense-data, universals, and mental facts. Russell had by now rejected the view that we are directly acquainted with a self over and above particular mental facts; he still held, however, that mental facts are quite distinct from sense-data. Believing, willing, wishing, experiencing, he thought, are mental facts; what is experienced, willed, wished for, in contrast, is a series of sense-data.

Belief, however, was an embarrassment to him, as became particularly clear when, partly under Wittgenstein's influence, he tried to formulate what he called 'the philosophy of logical atomism.'[29] The philosophy of logical atomism, as Russell conceives it, is an attempt to describe the kind of facts there are – just as zoology tries to describe the different types of animal. He still, that is, accepts Moore's view that philosophy tries to give 'a general description of the whole universe'. Russell begins with a description of the fundamental *constituents* of facts – the logical atoms. These, Russell not surprisingly maintains, are of two kinds, sense-data and universals. An 'atomic fact' – a typical example is *A is before B*, where *A* and *B* are sense-data – has these basic elements as its constituents.

Facts can be particular, like 'this is white', or universal, like 'all men are mortal'. It is impossible to regard the world as wholly composed of particular facts, Russell says, because that view would itself involve the *general* fact that atomic facts are all the facts that there are. And once this general fact is admitted, there seems to be no good reason for not admitting others. Again, a fact may be either negative or affirmative. Some facts are 'completely general' – referring not to particular entities but only to the general form (or 'syntax') of statements – these, he thinks, are the facts of logic. And then there are facts about facts and so on.

There are not, however, true facts and false facts – only propositions can be true or false and a proposition, Russell now says, is a symbol, not a fact. 'If you were making an inventory of the world,' he writes, 'propositions would not come in. Facts would, beliefs, wishes, wills, would, but propositions would not.' It is in the classification of 'propositions' that Russell's troubles about belief arise.

Propositions, according to Russell, fall into two classes – atomic and molecular. All molecular propositions can be ex-

234

pressed as 'truth functions' of atomic propositions i.e. their truth or falsity is wholly determined by the truth or falsity of the atomic propositions which make them up. The truth of an atomic proposition, on the other hand, can be decided only by passing beyond the proposition to the fact which it depicts. Thus, to take the simplest case, the molecular proposition *p and q* is true if the atomic propositions *p*, *q* are both true and is false if either of them is false, but the truth of *p* is independent of the truth of any other proposition.

The problem for Russell is to fit propositions about mental facts into this classification. Is 'I believe that *x* is *y*' an atomic or a molecular proposition? It looks like a molecular proposition with two constituents – *I believe* and *x is y*. But the difficulty with this view is that the truth or falsity of *x is y* is quite irrelevant to the truth of 'I believe that *x* is *y*'; *x is y*, therefore, is not a 'constituent' in 'I believe that *x* is *y*' in the sense that *p* is a constituent in '*p and q*'. A belief, Russell has to conclude, is 'a new species for the zoo'. Yet there is something unsatisfactory about this conclusion; mental facts do not seem to be marked off from other facts by *logical* peculiarities.

If, on the other hand, 'I believe that *x* is *y*' can be reformulated, in the behaviourist manner, as 'when I encounter an *x*, I react in such and such a way' – if, for example, 'I believe that snakes are dangerous' is a way of saying such things as that 'when I see a snake, I pick up a stick' – then there will be no need to distinguish beliefs, or other 'mental facts', as a peculiar logical species. Thus it is not surprising that Russell moved in this direction in *The Analysis of Mind;* significantly, he asked the behaviourist J. B. Watson and the realist T. P. Nunn to read his proofs.[30]

Russell is now in violent reaction against the whole pattern of ideas within which his own and Moore's earlier theories had been worked out; in particular, he rejects outright Brentano's definition of psychic phenomena. He no longer believes that the essence of such a phenomenon consists in the fact that it 'points to an object'; indeed he can see no reason for maintaining that there are either 'acts' or 'objects'. 'Instead of saying "I think", it would be better,' he writes, in a passage which echoes Mach, 'to say "*it thinks in me*" or better still "there is a thought in me".' The form of the sentence 'I think of *x*' suggests immediately that there is an act of thinking and an object of that act: but in reality, Russell is now arguing, there is only the thought, which is 'in me' in the sense that it forms part of that series of events referred to by the word 'I'. Whereas he had previously, like Moore, insisted on the distinction between sensation and sense-data he now rejects sensation as a purely mythical 'act'.

This is as far as Russell ever went in the direction of neutral monism; in *The Analysis of Matter* – in which he comes to terms with Einstein's 'new physics' – he turns hard a-port to something more like, although very different from, that 'inferential' theory of physical objects which he had maintained in *The Problems of Philosophy*. The sense-data of *The Analysis of Mind*, even although they do not depend for their existence on something mental, are yet 'subjective' in a wider sense; they exist only in relation to a human nervous system. Indeed, Russell identifies them with states of that human brain which is ordinarily said to 'experience' them. It is obvious, he says, that the actual process of sensing is in the human brain; the process of sensing, he has argued, is identical with the sense-datum sensed; it follows that the sense-datum, too, must be 'in the brain'.[31] When the physiologist examines a brain what he is *immediately* considering must be states of his own brain, not of the brain which he is attempting to describe.

Russell came to feel, however, that the physical objects *themselves* cannot be thus dependent on the existence of our nervous system, i.e. that physical objects are not, after all, sets of sense-data. He had already admitted 'sensibilia' over and above sense-data. Why stop at that point, he began to ask? 'It is impossible to lay down a hard-and-fast rule,' he wrote, 'that we can never validly infer something radically different from what we observe ... unless indeed we take up the position that nothing unobserved can ever be validly inferred. This view ... has much in its favour, from the standpoint of a strict logic; but it puts an end to physics.' And physics, Russell was determined to retain.

The problem, as he sees it, is the old one: how is the sun I am now seeing related to the sun of the astronomer, which is not 'now' but eight minutes away, not hot or bright, and very different in its structure from anything I can hope to experience? We can infer the existence of the astronomer's sun, Russell argues, only because there is a continuous single causal chain[32] linking events in our nervous system with events in the sun. The inference can never be an exact one, because the causal chain is not *completely* isolated; it is interfered with, in various ways, by other similar chains, and these disturbances prevent us from inferring precisely what lies at the end of any process terminating in our nervous system. But if it were not for the possibility of *some* such inference, Russell argues, we could never pass beyond what he calls 'a solipsism of the moment': we would take nothing to exist except the transient sense-datum – a position, he says, which although it is logically unassailable no human being can consistently maintain.

The twists and turns in Russell's argument after *The Analysis of Matter* we cannot follow in detail. But a few points can be picked out for special consideration, because they bear on those continual preoccupations of Russell's philosophy which we have particularly emphasized. He is still trying to work towards a satisfactory theory of belief, still worried about the relation between physics and perception, but he sees new difficulties, as well, in his earlier views. From the beginning Russell has presumed that there are in our experience 'particulars', which are named by 'logically proper' names. At first, 'I', 'that table', 'Julius Caesar' were all regarded as logically proper names, each referring to some unique entity with which we are acquainted and which we can describe by means of universals. But as his theory of denoting developed, these all ceased to be proper names; each, it was argued, is a descriptive phrase in disguise. Only 'this' survived the scrutiny.

In his articles on logical atomism, Russell pointed out that 'this' played the same part in his philosophy as 'substance' in traditional philosophies – it named entities, 'logical particulars', which 'stand entirely alone and are completely self-subsistent'. But it only gradually occurred to him that if this is so then the classical objections to 'substance' might also apply to 'logical particulars'. Once he noticed this fact, his whole theory of universals and particulars took on a new complexion.

His general view – it is most fully worked out in his article 'On the Relations of Universals and Particulars' (*PAS*, 1912) – had always been that a sharp distinction can be made between logical particulars and universals. He had more than once been tempted by the doctrine that universal *qualities* can be reduced to sets of similar particulars, but he had always drawn attention to the fact that even in such a case there is still at least one universal *relation* – similarity. And why not others?

But in *Meaning and Truth*, he writes as follows: 'I wish to suggest that "this is red" is not a subject-predicate proposition but is of the form "redness is here"; that "red" is a name, not a predicate; and that what would commonly be called a "thing" is nothing but a bundle of coexisting qualities such as redness, hardness, etc.' On any other view, he now thinks, 'this' becomes an 'unknowable somewhat in which predicates inhere, but which nevertheless is not identical with the sum of its predicates'.

Russell is not, it should be observed, defining a thing as a 'meeting-place of universals', in the manner of some Idealists. On the contrary, he is maintaining that *the qualities of a thing* are themselves particular; a 'red thing' is the occurrence in a certain place of a specific shade of colour, which ought to have a proper name. Qualities, now, are particulars, and 'things' are collections of such qualities occurring at such and such a set of spatio-temporal co-ordinates; the 'here' in 'redness is here' refers to a set of qualities by which shades of colour are 'placed' in our visual field as having a certain absolute position there.[33] But this view, he willingly admits, is 'tentative'.

A further question to which he often recurs, particularly in *Human Knowledge*, is a familiar one: how are the general propositions of science to be justified?[34] And with this is linked another problem: what is the minimum departure from empiricism that the philosopher is forced to admit? Russell had never been an empiricist, in the strict sense; even in *The Problems of Philosophy* he had rejected the view that all knowledge can be derived from experience. Mathematical propositions cannot be so derived, he had argued, nor can the inductive principle. Yet at the same time, Russell's conscience is uneasy – as if his secular-godfather Mill were exercising his spiritual rights – whenever he passes beyond experience. If there are limits to empiricism, these limits must still be passed with trepidation.

The outcome of his argument in *The Analysis of Matter* had been, however, that a strict empiricism – since Russell never questions that experience is of 'sense-data' – would be a 'solipsism of the moment'; it would deny that anything is real except our present sense-datum. The question, now, for Russell is to lay down the 'postulates' which have to be added to empiricism if it is to be a satisfactory philosophy of science. The 'inductive principle' is one such postulate, but Russell thinks that its importance has been exaggerated. It is only one postulate, and not the fundamental one. Russell uncovers quite a collection; their general nature can be illustrated from the 'postulate of quasi-permanance' which asserts that 'given any event A, it happens very frequently that, at any neighbouring time, there is at some neighbouring place an event very similar to A'. This is a way of saying that there are continuous things, without invoking the forbidden conception of substance. And without 'things', Russell considers, physics cannot be worked out. His canons, in general, are an attempt to lay down the principles which have to be adopted if scientific inference is to be possible; they are very like the 'general rules' of Hume's philosophy.

Such canons, according to Russell, cannot be inferred from experience. Nevertheless, he also thinks, they have their *foundations* in experience. They derive out of reflection on 'animal inference' – the habits of expectation which the human organism exhibits; they pick out the principles implicit in these habits. And if their mere existence demonstrates that empiricism, as a complete theory of knowledge, is untenable, that very discovery, Russell argues, has been inspired by the empirical spirit, which recognizes 'that all human knowledge is uncertain, inexact and partial'. This is a long way from the optimism of *The Problems of Philosophy*. Russell's philosophical development, it is not too much to say, is the passage from Descartes to Hume epitomized.

CHAPTER 10

Cook Wilson and Oxford Philosophy

THROUGH all the triumphs of Idealism at Oxford, a Resistance Movement had continued to state the case for Realism. Thomas Case, a sturdy Aristotelian who was Professor of Metaphysics and Morals at Oxford from 1899 until 1910 and President of Corpus Christi College until 1924, published his *Physical Realism* in 1888, at the height of Idealism's successes. Not Case, however, but his somewhat younger contemporary, John Cook Wilson,[1] Professor of Logic at Oxford from 1899 to 1915, swung Oxford opinion against Idealism. Too influential a philosopher to be ignored, Cook Wilson is an historian's nightmare. His disciples speak of him with the affection and the admiration reserved for a great teacher; but they are the first to admit that his only important publication – the lectures, manuscript remains, and correspondence posthumously published as *Statement and Inference* (1926) – is fragmentary and inconclusive. Yet on that book the historian must rest his judgement.

Statement and Inference does not even possess the minor, but comforting, virtue of internal consistency. His disciples tell us that Cook Wilson was only just, at his death, 'finding himself'. His important unorthodoxies took shape relatively late in life; naturally enough, he does not consistently sustain them: he relapses into one of the logics in which he was trained – Aristotelian, or neo-Kantian, or Lotzean – out of sheer habit.

Cook Wilson's main theme is logic, but logic conceived in the Oxford manner, as a philosophical investigation into thought rather than as the construction of a calculus. The Boole-Schröder logic, indeed, Cook Wilson condemned as 'merely trivial', in comparison with 'the serious business of logic proper' – inquiry into 'the forms of thought'. Even within its trivial limits, he also tried to show, the Boolean logic is grossly defective. Considered as a calculus – Cook Wilson spent much time on the construction of examples which would prove his point – it is clumsy and tedious; as a logical theory, it is a tissue of misleading mathematical analogies. If it *seems* to work in certain favourable cases that is only because, so Cook Wilson argued, it contains within itself remnants of a better logic. It is neither as mathematical nor as anti-traditional as its proponents imagine.

Of Russellian, as distinct from the Boole-Schröder, logic Cook Wilson had little to say, and that little was finely contemptuous. Thus, of the paradoxes about classes, he wrote to Bosanquet: 'I am obliged to think that a man is conceited as well as silly to think such puerilities are worthy to be put in print: and it's simply exasperating to think that he finds a publisher (where was the publisher's reader?) and that in this way such contemptible stuff can even find its way into examinations.'

Yet he was also dissatisfied with, although less contemptuous of, the logic of the Idealists. Idealist logic begins from the 'judgement'; Cook Wilson criticized it on the ground, sufficiently uncompromising, that there are no judgements, in the Idealist sense of the word. The Idealist error, he argues, arises in the following way: traditional logic takes as its unit the statement; the Idealist, recognizing that logic is concerned with thought and not, primarily, with its verbal expression, substitutes for the statement the judgement, defined as that act of mind which expresses itself in statements. But it is a serious error, according to Cook Wilson, to presume that there is some single act of mind which every statement expresses. Some statements express knowledge, some opinion, some a supposition, some an inference. And these, Cook Wilson argues, are not different varieties of 'judgement'; they are quite distinct acts of thought. The special weakness, in Cook Wilson's eyes, of the Idealist theory of judgement is that it runs together acts of thought which must at all costs be kept distinct: knowledge, on the one hand, and on the other hand those various stages on the road to knowledge – opinion, belief, supposition and the like – which although they all in the end depend on knowledge, and can only be defined in terms of it, must never be confused with it.

What is 'knowledge'? That question is unanswerable, Cook Wilson would reply, if it is a request for a definition of knowledge. Knowledge is simple, ultimate, indefinable; any attempt to define it, or to 'justify' it, or to 'prove that it is possible', will inevitably be circular. The most the philosopher can do is to exemplify it; and the best way of exemplifying knowledge, according to Cook Wilson, is to point to mathematics. That mathematics is objective knowledge is a simple fact, he maintains, which needs neither defence nor demonstration. The full fury of his polemical wrath was reserved for those geometers who dared to suggest that there could be more than one geometry, or that the 'certainty' of a mathematical system might consist solely in the fact that no contradiction has yet been discovered within it.[2]

Thus armed with a direct insight into the nature of knowledge, Cook Wilson can make his second point: all other forms of thinking involve knowledge, although knowledge does not involve them. Knowledge, that is, is not merely one of many coordinate species of thought; it is the basic form of thought, on which every other level of thinking rests.[3] We can have an opinion, for example, only when we *know* that the evidence in favour of our point of view is stronger than the evidence in favour of any alternative; we can 'wonder' only when we *know* what we are wondering about. Logic, as Cook Wilson conceives it, will indicate in detail the ways in which opining, believing, wondering, work towards, but differ from, knowledge. Such a logic he never wrote; but his interest in the various forms of thought was 'caught' by his students and by *their* students, even if what he called 'logic' they came to describe as 'epistemology' or as 'philosophical psychology'.

Another question which interested Cook Wilson is the connexion and the distinction between grammatical and logical analysis. He had a great respect, like so many of his Oxford successors, for ordinary usage: this, again, is Aristotelian. 'Distinctions current in language,' he wrote, 'can never be safely neglected.' And again, in a letter to Bosanquet: 'It is the business of the student of logic to determine the *normal* use of an idiom or a linguistic expression. Everything depends upon that.'

And what Cook Wilson preached he also practised. *Statement and Inference* abounds in careful linguistic analyses. Thus, as part of his criticism of the Idealist theory of judgement, he argues that if we consider the kind of sentence in which the word 'judgement' ordinarily occurs we soon see that a judgement is an inference – not, as the Idealist maintains, a simple assertion. To 'judge' that Jones will win a race, for example, is to infer from evidence at our disposal that Jones will be the victor; to 'exercise our judgement' is to employ our powers of drawing conclusions. This is the only ordinary sense of the word 'judgement'; and obviously neither knowledge nor supposition is a variety of 'judgement', thus understood. Usage, then, tells against the Idealist theory of judgement, and usage ought to be respected.

Another point at which the Idealist Logician has disregarded the claims of usage, Cook Wilson thinks, is in his reduction of the universal to a hypothetical form. According to the Idealist, 'all X are Y' asserts no more than that 'if anything is x, then it is also y'. Cook Wilson objects to this analysis, on the ground that the 'if ..., then ...' form cannot express the full meaning of a categorical statement. 'The question,' he argues, 'is linguistic and can only be answered by investigating the normal habit of a particular language.' The normal habit in English, according to Cook Wilson, is to assert that 'all X are Y' only when we believe that there are in fact such things as X; the 'if ..., then ...' form carries with it no such commitment. Certainly, he will admit, there are *idiomatic* uses of 'if ..., then ...' in which it is categorical, and *idiomatic* uses of 'all X are Y' from which the existential commitment is absent – but normal usage must be the determining factor. Cook Wilson's own conclusion is that all genuine statements are categorical; the hypothetical relates problems, as distinct from making a statement. For example, the hypothetical 'if this liquid is acid, it will turn litmus red' asserts that the solution to the problem whether this liquid is acid can be found by considering whether it turns litmus red. A hypothetical undoubtedly *rests upon* true statements (for example, the true statement that all acids turn litmus red) but it is not itself a statement: if it were, it would be categorical. This theory of Cook Wilson's is intrinsically interesting, but the point of greater historical importance is its respectful attitude to ordinary usage.

If Cook Wilson demands of the philosopher that he shall take grammar seriously, he is equally insistent upon the need for distinguishing clearly between logical and grammatical issues. Mill's theory of denotation and connotation, to take one case, he dismisses as a fragment of grammatical analysis, part of an investigation into the working of nouns, not a contribution to logic. The great source of all such confusions, he thinks, is the failure to recognize that logic is a theory of the forms of thought.

The traditional logician deliberately begins from the verbal formulation, and is therefore bound to amalgamate grammar and logic; the Idealist professedly begins from the judgement, but since there *are* no judgements, he is compelled in practice either to make merely linguistic points or else to pass beyond logic to metaphysics – without realizing what he is doing. Only by holding apart grammar, logic and metaphysics, Cook Wilson considers, can the logical issues be clarified – although that 'holding apart' is not incompatible with a close examination of such grammatical and metaphysical questions as happen to throw light on logic.

A point of particular importance, in this connexion, is Cook Wilson's criticism of the subject-predicate logic. First of all, he sharply distinguishes between the *grammatical* subject and the *logical* subject, which the traditional logic is content, with a faint demurrer, to identify. Take, for example, such a statement as 'glass is elastic'. On the ordinary analysis, 'glass' is obviously the subject and 'elastic' the predicate. But in fact, Cook Wilson argues, the matter cannot be settled with such address. Everything depends upon what question this statement is answering. Suppose it had been asked: what is an example of elasticity? Then 'elasticity' is the logical subject and 'glass is elastic' expresses our belief that it can truly be predicated of 'elasticity' that it is 'exemplified in glass'. If, on the other hand, the question had been 'how does glass differ from steel?' then, certainly, in 'glass is elastic' 'glass' is the logical as well as the grammatical subject. In ordinary speech, Cook Wilson points out, we employ a variety of devices, of which stress is the most obvious, to indicate the true logical subject: we may say either '*glass* is elastic' or 'glass is *elastic*'. But stress and context are ignored by the traditional logic; thus there arises what Cook Wilson regards as the absurd presumption that the noun which is nominative to the principal verb in a statement is bound to indicate the logical subject.

To make matters still more confused, this grammatical analysis is then metaphysically interpreted, as having application to those things to which a statement refers. The distinction between logical subject and logical predicate, according to Cook Wilson, is, like all other logical distinctions, one which holds only within our thinking. The logical subject, on his analysis, is an object as we conceive it *before* we know what the predicate tells us about it; the logical predicate is 'a kind of being asserted in the given statement to belong to the object, but not comprised in what was *before* conceived to belong to the object'. It follows that the distinction between subject and predicate exists only in relation to the order in which our knowledge develops, in accordance with what we happen to know or not to know at a given time.

To talk, in the Idealist manner, as if a thing could be in its own nature a 'predicate' is blatantly to confuse, Cook Wilson argues, distinctions proper to logic and distinctions proper to metaphysics. There are *substances* which are what they are independently of our thinking; but nothing is in its own metaphysical nature a *subject* or a *predicate*, nor does the relation of predication exist except as a way in which we connect our thoughts.[4] And this confusion between subject and predicate on the one hand and substance and attribute on the other is worse confounded when logical and grammatical predicate are silently identified. Philosophers in fact – and this is Cook Wilson's main accusation against them – have muddled together the three different ways in which a statement can be considered: as expressing a form of thought (the logician's point of view), as a verbal structure (the grammarian's point of view), and as saying something about the world (the metaphysician's point of view). The ordinary doctrine of 'predication' is the most notable by-product of this muddle.

Obviously, Cook Wilson's contrast between 'forms of thought' and 'relations between things' carries with it a rejection of the conventional Idealist doctrine, most fully expounded by Green, that relations – and, indeed, 'things' – are themselves nothing but forms of thought. 'Even for the extremest idealistic view,' Cook Wilson wrote, 'there is an object to be distinguished always from our apprehension of it.' He came, in his epistemology, to make that distinction more and more sharply; the tendency of his work is towards Realism.

Knowledge, he argued, is not, as Green had sought to show, a form of 'making' – the unification of elementary 'feelings' into an intellectual whole. To make is one thing, to know what we have made is something quite different. From the very nature of knowledge, it follows that what we know must be *there to be known*, independently of our knowledge of it. The question how it came to be before our mind is a subsequent one; the main point is that its coming before our mind is one thing, its being known quite another thing.

The possibility remains, so far as this argument is concerned, that what we know is always a 'modification of our mind', although it cannot be a modification of the act of knowledge. But, Cook Wilson argues, if we look at the historical antecedents of the view that we know nothing except our own mental states, we at once observe that it arose out of an attempt to show 'how knowledge is possible'; for knowledge to be possible, the argument ran, what we know must be 'in our own mind'. Once we recognize that there is *in principle* no way of proving that knowledge is possible – since any such proof would have to assume that there are certain things we already know – this argument collapses. And it is certainly not in the least *plausible* to maintain that our knowledge is restricted to mental states.

Cook Wilson came to his Realist conclusions only slowly and doubtfully. For Realism involves a distinction, as he presents it, between the act of apprehension and the object it apprehends; and he feared that the act of apprehension would vanish into nothingness were it not given its content by its object. A closer analysis of relations soothed his qualms. Consider, he says, a collision. No doubt, there can be no collision apart from the colliding bodies, just as there can be no apprehension without an apprehended object. The fact remains, he points out, that the colliding bodies must exist independently of the collision, if they are ever to collide; similarly, he thinks, there can be no 'apprehension' unless what is apprehended is independent of the apprehension of it.

In arguing thus, of course, Cook Wilson is committed to rejecting Bradley's argument that relations are self-contradictory. Bradley's dialectical method, so Cook Wilson maintains, consists in asking 'unreal' questions, questions which cannot intelligibly 'arise'. In particular, to ask 'what is the relation of a relation to its terms?' is to demand an answer where no answer, in the nature of the case, is possible. Cook Wilson illustrates by the relation of equality. Suppose A and B are equal. Then if we ask 'how is A related to the relation of equality?' the answer must run thus:

'equality is the relation which A has to B.' Or more precisely: 'the relation of A to A's equality to B is that it is A's equality to B.' We can do no more, that is, than reassert the original relation. There is no second relation, between A and its relation to B, which could serve as the starting point of an infinite regress. Bradley thinks that there is, only because he insists on asking meaningless questions.

Cook Wilson applied his general line of reasoning to problems of perception in a long letter on *Primary and Secondary Qualities*, written in criticism of an article by G. F. Stout (*PAS*, 1903). Epistemologists have wrongly supposed, he argued, that because we can sensibly talk of an object as 'appearing' to us, there must be an entity called an 'appearance', something merely subjective, which is what we actually see. The fact is that an 'appearance' is no more than, and no less than, 'an object appearing'. 'That is,' he sums up, 'we have the nature of an object before us, not only some affection of our consciousness produced by it.'

His account of this 'object', however, brings him closer to Locke (and to Case) than to any sort of 'naïve realism', particularly in his discussion of secondary qualities. Taking heat as a typical secondary quality, he argues that in experiencing heat we are ordinarily aware of nothing but our own sensation – unless we actually touch the body we call 'hot', when we also perceive its extension. We then infer, but do not actually perceive, a power in the body to produce heat in us, the true 'secondary quality'.

The primary qualities, on his view, are in a quite different category. Berkeley's theory of vision had made it appear that all we are aware of in this instance, too – when we talk of perceiving 'a certain shape' or 'a certain size' – is some kind of tactual or muscular sensation, from which we infer the spatial properties of the physical object. But such an inference Cook Wilson rejects as impossible in principle, on the ground already urged by Case that the existence of extended physical objects could never be inferred from the experience of unextended sensations.[5] We must suppose, then, that in our perception of spatial properties, although not in our perception of colours, tastes, heat, we are directly aware of the nature of a physical body. This is as far as Cook Wilson's Realism carried him; and it was further, in the end, than his followers were prepared to go.

Of those who stood particularly close to Cook Wilson, at least in their earlier writings, the two best known are H. A. Prichard and H. W. B. Joseph. Prichard,[6] Professor of Moral Philosophy at Oxford, was a vigorous controversialist who developed his views, for preference, through the medium of criticism. He published only one book on epistemological topics, *Kant's Theory of Knowledge* (1909), although a selection of his essays was posthumously printed as *Knowledge and Perception* (1950). *Kant's Theory of Knowledge* was the means through which Cook Wilson's philosophy first reached an audience outside Oxford. In particular, the chapter on 'Knowledge and Reality' is a clear and lively statement of Cook Wilson's case against Idealism.[7] 'The very nature of knowledge,' Prichard writes, 'unconditionally presupposes that the reality known exists independently of the knowledge of it ... it is simply *impossible* to think that any reality depends on our knowledge of it.' Whether it is a stone or a toothache, the object of knowledge must first *be*, before it can enter into the relationship of knowledge. It may still, he emphasizes, depend for its existence upon us – it may be 'of such a kind as to disappear with the disappearance of the mind' – but its existence cannot depend upon *our knowledge* that it exists.

Thus the only conceivable form of Idealism, in Prichard's opinion, is subjective Idealism. It is possible sensibly to maintain that *as a matter of fact* we know nothing but our own mental states; it is unintelligible to suggest, with the Objective Idealist, that what we know is dependent, not on the existence of a mind, but on *being known* by a mind. But he follows Cook Wilson in arguing that subjective Idealism has no plausibility once the presumption is abandoned that knowledge has to be 'justified'; it is then a matter of special inquiry whether this or that object of perception is dependent on us for its existence. Such an inquiry, he considers, is bound to lead us to Cook Wilson's conclusion that while tastes, colours, and the like, are thus dependent, spatial qualities are not.

Prichard's later explorations of the same problem led him to different and less familiar conclusions. Once again, the approach is usually polemical: the essays and addresses which make up *Knowledge and Perception* are mainly directed against Russell's theory of sense-data or against traditional empirical epistemology. But in a paper on 'Perception', not elsewhere published, he summarizes his positive conclusions.

There are, he says, two points he wishes to emphasize. The first is that perception is never knowledge, the second is that 'in the special cases of seeing and of feeling or touching, what is ordinarily called perception consists in *taking* i.e. really *mis*taking, something that we see or feel for something else'. On the first point, Prichard is departing from Cook Wilson's teaching, for Cook Wilson had maintained, if hesitantly, that *some*, although certainly not all, varieties of perception are knowledge. And this departure depends upon another: Prichard now denies that we 'directly see' physical bodies. The mere existence of sensory illusions is, he thinks, sufficient to show that visual perception cannot be direct.

What then, do we immediately see? The conventional answer, variously formulated, is that we see 'a visible appearance'. But Prichard objects that an 'appearance' (or an 'idea') is always *of* something, so that the use of this terminology inevitably suggests that we *somehow* see that object which the appearance is 'of'; those who employ it – G. F. Stout, Prichard says, is a conspicuous offender – slip backwards and forwards between asserting and denying that we directly observe physical objects, playing upon the ambiguity of 'appearance'. Furthermore, to call what we see an 'appearance' does nothing to indicate the *nature* of what appears; the status of an 'appearance' is left intolerably vague. Prichard's own view, which abandons all talk of 'appearances', is that we really see 'extended, and consequently spatially related, colours'.

Then, we naturally ask, if we 'really see' nothing but coloured extensions, how does it happen that we judge them to be physical objects? Prichard offers a twofold answer. First, although we 'really see' coloured extensions, we do not *know* them to be coloured extensions – indeed, we do not *know* them at all. According to the sense-datum theory, to 'perceive directly' is to know the nature of what we perceive; our awareness of the immediate objects of sense is, indeed, the paradigm of complete knowledge. This Prichard is denying: we do not, he says, ordinarily have any knowledge of what we immediately see. And then, secondly, since we do not *know* the extended colours which we see, there is no question of our 'judging' or 'inferring' that they are, or are caused by, or refer to, bodies; such a judgement, Prichard argues, could only be based on knowledge, and in this case there is no knowledge.

Prichard's view sounds somewhat paradoxical. He tells us that we really see coloured extensions; there is no doubt that we ordinarily believe that we see physical objects. How can this belief arise, we naturally ask, unless we judge the coloured extensions to be the objects? To remove the appearance of paradox, Prichard makes use of a distinction which Cook Wilson had suggested in *Statement and Inference* between 'judging' that X is Y and 'being under the impression' that it is Y. Suppose we see a stranger in the street, and greet him as an acquaintance. Then we are not, Cook Wilson says, *judging* that the stranger is an acquaintance: to say this would imply that we greeted him after having duly considered the evidence. No such consideration took place. What happened, rather, was that we perceived a person and 'took him without reflection' to be a friend, or were 'under the impression' that he was a friend. We did not *judge* him to be a friend, we took him – and, in the event, *mis*took him – for one.

Something very similar happens, Prichard suggests, in all our perceptions of physical objects. We 'actually see' a coloured extension (or feel a tactual extension) but we mistake it for a physical body. Only after subsequent analysis do we come to realize what we are 'actually seeing'; at the uncritical level of everyday perception we are 'under the impression' that we see physical bodies.

Only by accepting some such theory of perception, Prichard tries to show in his critical articles, can we hope to bring to an end the traditional epistemological controversies, which are interminable so long as it is presumed that we *know* what we immediately sense. For if we know what we sense, what we sense must exist independently of the act which knows it – so far Prichard supports Cook Wilson. This consideration drives epistemologists into naïve realism. But they are forced to beat a hasty retreat when they are confronted by the harsh facts of illusion and error. They do not escape unscathed, however, for they find themselves with queer entities on their hands – 'ideas' or 'sense-data' – which, Prichard argues, have none of the characteristics of objects of knowledge and yet which *must* be known if it is true, as the epistemologist presumes, that we *know* what we immediately perceive. There is only one way, Prichard is suggesting, of avoiding once and for all the traditional episte-mological see-saws between realism and representationalism; we must reject the assumption which underlies both alternatives – the assumption that immediate perception is a variety of knowledge.

Closely connected with Prichard's epistemology is his sharp-shooting against 'empirical psychology', by which he means, particularly, the psychologies of Stout and Ward. In the last half-century, Oxford has won for itself the reputation of being the most notable adversary of the advance of psychology. Often enough, the Idealists are praised (or blamed) for Oxford's apparent, if now much diminished, hostility to the work of psychologists. But in fact Bradley, as we have seen, was quite sympathetic to, and actively interested in, psychological inquiry, even if he was less kindly disposed towards the attempt to solve philosophical problems by invoking psychological mechanisms. It was Prichard and Joseph who led the battle against psychology, in the name of the primacy of knowledge.

Empirical psychology, Prichard argued, is an attempt to con-struct knowledge out of some mode of thought which is prior to, and more elementary, than, knowledge – a prospect from which any Cook Wilsonian must recoil in horror. At best, according to Prichard, psychology is a hotch-potch of loosely related inquiries, not a 'proper science'. (Ryle was later to pass the same judgement upon it in his *The Concept of Mind*.)

Prichard's attacks were strongly supported by H. W. B. Joseph[9] in his articles on 'The Psychological Explanation of the Development of the Perception of External Objects' (*Mind*, 1910–11). He interprets Stout as if he were a follower of Mill, as if he were arguing, that is, that our belief in the existence of independent objects arises out of the operation of psychologically-describable processes upon simple sensations – an interpretation Stout warmly contests in his 'Reply to Mr Joseph' (*Mind*, 1911).

In most of his argument, Joseph keeps to the paths traced out by Prichard in his *Kant's Theory of Knowledge*. But he is already uneasy about the realist ingredients in that book. 'In questioning altogether,' he writes, 'the view that what we initially apprehend is something "in the mind" or "mental", I am conscious of many difficulties, for which at present I see no solution; in particular, I am not happy about supposing that space is real independently of all consciousness; I do not understand what I mean by solidity, nor by what fills space; nor by the magnitude of anything.' Now only the solid, on Cook Wilson's view, is independent of mind; Joseph's doubts on this crucial point gradually led him back into something very like the Idealism which Cook Wilson had criticized – as is particularly apparent at the end of his essay on 'A Comparison of Kant's Idealism with that of Berkeley'.[10] Cook Wilson's Realism had always been tentative, hesitant; the rise of the 'new Realism' with its more revolutionary attitude to the Idealist tradition drove back the waverers into the older ways of thought or else forced them forward into the arms of Cambridge.

Joseph's logic, too, is a compromise between Cook Wilsonian and Idealist ways of thought. Joseph shares Cook Wilson's hostility to 'symbolic logic', and in a series of articles entitled 'A Defence of Freethinking in Logistics' (*Mind*, 1932–4) he attacked Russell and his followers – against the stalwart defence of Susan Stebbing – much in the manner in which Cook Wilson had criticized Boole. In 'What does Mr W. E. Johnson mean by a Proposition?' (*Mind*, 1927–8) Joseph's criticism of Johnson is, more than anything else, a criticism of the formal approach to logic; Joseph is maintaining that inference, not implication, is the proper starting-point for logic. This is the fundamental point in dispute between the formal logicians and their critics. His best-known work, *An Introduction to Logic* (1906), is an attempt to formulate without 'traditional' accretions and misunderstandings a genuinely Aristotelian logic. In so far as it rehabilitates Aristotle,[11] it shows the influence of Cook Wilson's own Aristotelianism, and as well it is indebted to Cook Wilson's lectures, as Joseph explains, on a good many points of detail. But even in the second edition (1916) it is sufficiently clear that Joseph has not fully grasped the nature of Cook Wilson's critical logic: *An Introduction to Logic* is mainly, and rightly, read as an Aristotelian, not as a Cook Wilsonian, logic.

Cook Wilson's influence, passed on by Prichard, Joseph and other Oxford tutors, is still very much alive; we shall meet it again in the chapters to come. However, the best known of recent Oxford epistemologists – H. H. Price, Professor of Logic at Oxford since 1935 – in his *Perception* (1932)[12] wove together threads which had so far been separately spun. The influence of Cook Wilson is apparent: Price accepts, for example, the Cook Wilsonian distinction between knowledge and belief[13] and freely employs his notion of 'being under the impression that'. This degree of allegiance did nothing to mollify Prichard: writing on 'The Sense-Datum Fallacy' (*PASS*, 1938 and *Knowledge and Perception*) he counts Price as a follower of Russell – and is perfectly correct in so doing.* For Price agrees with Russell on the crucial point that sensing is a form of knowing, and that what we immediately know is a sense-datum.

A large part of *Perception* is critical; Price considers in detail, and gives reasons for rejecting, most of the theories of perception which have so far attracted our attention and many of those we have still to consider. But he salvages from the wreck the conception of a sense-datum, and with it the view that it is the central problem of epistemology to explain in what manner a sense-datum 'belongs to' a material object – as it must, he thinks, if it is to be of any use to us in our everyday dealings with the world. Russell's 'causal' theory of perception he rejects as clearly untenable; no causal inference could conduct us from sense-data to material objects, unless we already had independent evidence that there are such things. Considering the matter 'historically' (genetically), it is quite obvious, Price argues, that we do not arrive at our belief in the existence of material objects by means of causal reasoning. Unless sense-data somehow directly 'belong to' material objects, there is no way, he concludes, in which they could advance our knowledge of the world around us.

A sense-datum, he maintains – unless it be a 'wild' sense-datum, an hallucination – is a member of a 'family'. The head of the family, if we may so express the matter, is, in the case of visual perception, the 'standard solid'. Suppose, to use the

*Price went so far as to spend a year at Cambridge as a Research Student. Note also, although Price only rarely mentions Husserl, that *Perception* sets out to be a 'phenomenological' description of consciousness, in Husserl's manner. Price hopes to describe what is 'given to consciousness' without importing considerations which derive from physiology or from physics.

language of common-sense, we 'look at a thing from various points of view'. Then we shall experience sense-data, Price argues, which differ considerably in shape and size. Yet these sense-data, he also maintains, all 'fit together', if we think of them as distortions or differentiations of a single volume from which they deviate to different degrees and in different manners: this volume is the 'standard solid' and its shape is the 'standard figure' of the system of sense-data. The standard solid is what we ordinarily describe as 'the real volume of the thing'; other sense-data 'belong to the same thing' if they form part of a series which converges from one direction or another upon the standard solid. A 'family' of sense-data, as Price defines it, consists of the standard solid together with the various series of sense-data which thus converge upon it.

The reference here to a *series* is important. Russell had described a thing as a class of similar sense-data. Price objects that sense-data may be very similar – as the blue of a feather is similar to the blue of an emerald – even although they belong to quite different things, and may be very different – the blue of the same emerald seen under a white and a yellow light, for example – while still recognizably belonging to a single thing. The sense-data which make up a family must, he argues, be both qualitatively and geometrically *continuous*, i.e. they must shade into one another and must also 'adjoin' one another. Of course, Price will admit, the family as it is actually experienced by an individual person contains gaps – a point he discusses more fully in his *Hume's Theory of the External World* (1940). It follows that the family cannot be identified with anyone's actual experience; it consists, as well, of 'obtainable' sense-data, i.e. of those sense-data which that person *could* experience of his point of view were different. Since such 'obtainable' sense-data may actually be obtained by somebody else, the family is 'objective' or 'public' as well as continuous. The analogy between Price's 'family of sense-data' and Mill's 'permanent possibilities of sensation' will be obvious; Price emphasizes it himself. But he criticizes Mill on the ground that, not having arrived at the conception of a 'family', he could not give a satisfactory account of the systematic character of our sense-data.

Furthermore, Mill was a phenomenalist: he identified the

material thing with the permanent possibility of sense-data. This identification Price hopes to avoid. In pursuit of a non-phenomenalist theory he begins by distinguishing between 'a family of sense-data' and a 'physical object'. The most obvious feature of a physical object, he says, is that it can *resist*; an area is 'physically occupied' or 'occupied by a physical object' when any 'families of sense-data' which reach that area are modified in some way, by being, for example, broken up or distorted. A second, connected, characteristic of physical objects is that they operate causally. Price is not content to define the physical object as the family of sense-data which lies within and around the area 'occupied by a physical object' because, he argues, 'the family' does not exist as a particular entity, as a physical occupant does. This is a consequence of the fact that a family contains sense-data which are 'obtainable' but not actual. A family, to put the matter differently, is a 'construct', in a sense in which a physical object is not a construct.

Suppose, for example, I take a red coal out of a fire and look at it. Then, Price argues, only the front* of it is actually 'present to the senses' – 'in all the region reserved for sense-data only one sense-datum is actual at the moment'. On the other hand, the causal properties of the coal are exhibited in all directions. 'A piece of butter is melted here, a piece of paper is curled up over there, somewhere else a handkerchief is scorched, and the eyebrows of the observer are singed – all at the same time.' Similarly the coal resists penetration *from any direction*, not merely from the point at which there are sense-data. These and other considerations show, Price thinks, that there is not a point-to-point correspondence between the family of sense-data and what occupies the area, and hence that the family is not a physical object.

Yet Price admits that he can say nothing about the physical object except that it possesses certain 'powers'; he reinstates the

*Price denies, however, that all sense-data are two-dimensional: sense-data can, on his view, be 'bulgy' i.e. voluminous. He is, he says, astonished to find that sense-data theorists are criticized on the ground that for them the immediate objects of perception are two-dimensional. Why, he asks rhetorically, should they, of all people, deny obvious phenomenological facts? But the fact that visual sense-data have usually been described as 'patches' suggests that the critics of sense-data have not always been beside the mark.

neo-Kantian agnostic doctrine that the 'intrinsic qualities' of the physical object are, and must remain, wholly unknown to us. Even although the physical object and the family of sense-data are not identical, and even although, furthermore, sense-data depend for their existence on physical objects, the fact remains that physical objects can be described and defined, according to Price, only by referring to the kind of family with which they coincide.

When in our everyday life we refer to 'things', Price argues, 'we mean neither the family alone, nor the physical object alone, but something which consists of both; we mean a certain sort of family *together with* the physical object which is coincident with it' – this complex is what Price calls a 'material thing'. Lockian representationalism, on his view, confuses between the material thing and the physical object, phenomenalism between the material thing and the family of sense-data. Of the two, he much prefers phenomenalism: the 'physical object' is a shadowy sort of entity, the 'family' is at least concrete. But he thought he had avoided this choice: not everyone, however, was convinced that he had succeeded – *Perception*, indeed, has been a source-book for phenomenalists.

Price's later work, summed up in *Thinking and Experience* (1953),[14] turns aside from problems of perception to consider the nature of thinking. In part, it is a criticism of those theories of thinking which, under positivist influence, assert that thinking can be defined as the use of symbols. Price tries to show both that there are forms of thinking which do not involve the use of symbols – as when we look at black clouds and think it will rain* – and also that thinking 'overflows' the symbols it uses, in the sense that only part of our thinking ever finds explicit expression in the words or images we employ. The particular image of a dog we have before our mind when we think about dogs, for example, does not wholly express what we think about them; if we 'image'

---

*There can obviously be some dispute whether such processes which, as Price emphasizes, are as much characteristic of other animals as they are of human beings, are really a form of thinking. Price tries to show that they are; he argues that they have a *logic*, that 'if . . . then' and 'or', for example, have a meaning at the level of non-symbolic thinking. His argument on this point has rung strangely in the ears of his reviewers, but it is in the Cook Wilson tradition that logic is a theory of the forms of thought.

a poodle, it does not follow that only poodles are occupying our thoughts.

Yet, at the same time, Price does not want to be forced back upon what he calls the 'classical' theory of thinking – the view that thinking consists in the apprehension of a special class of objects 'which are variously called universals, concepts, or abstract ideas'. He tries to show that we can *use* concepts – 'we all agree', he says, 'that thinking is rightly described as conceptual cognition' – without having them explicitly before our mind as objects. His theory of thinking is a description of 'concepts at work'. The approach, as in *Perception*, is phenomenological. Price is emphasizing what he regards as 'phenomenological truths' about the way we think – truths which, so he suggests, have ordinarily been sacrificed to the needs of some *a priori* theory. And so far Price is still writing in the tradition, for all the differences in detail, of Cook Wilson's *Statement and Inference*. Cook Wilson's logic may have had few imitators; but his soul goes marching on in Oxford theories of knowledge.

CHAPTER 11

The New Realists

IN the early years of the present century, it could no longer be presumed that Realism was intellectually disreputable, a mere vulgar prejudice. What a mind knows, Brentano and Meinong had argued, exists independently of the act by which it is known; Mach, and James after him – if they were still, from a Realist point of view, tainted with subjectivism – had at least denied that what is immediately perceived is a state of mind; and then Moore, seconded by Russell, had rejected that thesis which Idealists like Bradley and phenomenalists like Mill had united in regarding as indisputable: that the existence of objects of perception consists in the fact that they are perceived. The 'New Realism' brought together these converging tendencies; it owed much to Meinong, more to Mach and James, and it acknowledged the help of Moore and Russell in the battle against Idealism.

The first, in England, to formulate the characteristic doctrines of the New Realism was T. P. Nunn.[1] Best known as an educationalist, Nunn wrote little on philosophy, but that little had an influence out of all proportion to its modest dimensions. In particular, his contribution to a symposium on 'Are Secondary Qualities Independent of Perception?'[2] was widely studied both in England where, as we have already noted, it struck Bertrand Russell's roving fancy, and in the United States. Nunn there sustained two theses: (1) that both the primary and the secondary qualities of bodies are really in them, whether they are perceived or not; (2) that qualities exist as they are perceived.

Much of his argument is polemical in form, with Stout's earlier articles[3] as its chief target. Stout had thought he could begin by presuming that there are at least *some* elements in our experience which exist only in being perceived – he instanced pain. But Nunn objects that pain, precisely in the manner of a material object, presents difficulties to us, raises obstacles in our path, is, in short, something we must reckon with. 'Pain,' he therefore concludes, 'is something outside my mind, with which my mind may come into various relations.' A refusal to admit that *anything* we experience depends for its existence upon the fact that it is experienced was to be the most characteristic feature of the New Realism.

The secondary qualities, Stout had also said, exist only as objects of experience. If we look at a buttercup in a variety of lights we see different shades of colour, without having any reason to believe that the buttercup itself has altered; if a number of observers plunge their hands into a bowl of water, they will report very different degrees of warmth, even although nothing has happened which could affect the water's temperature. Such facts demonstrate, Stout thought, that secondary qualities exist only as 'sensa' – objects of our perception; they are not actual properties of physical objects.

Nunn's reply is uncompromising. The contrast between 'sensa' and 'actual properties' is, he argues, an untenable one. All the shades of colour which the buttercup presents to an observer are actual properties of the buttercup; and all the hotnesses of the water are properties of the water. The plain man and the scientist ascribe a standard temperature and a standard colour to a thing and limit it to a certain region of space, because its complexity would otherwise defeat them. The fact remains, Nunn argues, that a thing has not one hotness, for example, but many, and that these hotnesses are not in a limited region of space but in various places around about the standard object. A thing is hotter an inch away than a foot away and hotter on a cold hand than on a warm one, just as it is a paler yellow in one light than it is in another light. To imagine otherwise is to confuse between the arbitrary 'thing' of everyday life and the 'thing' as experience shows it to be.

In Nunn's theory of perception, then, the ordinary conception of a material thing is revolutionized; that is the price he has to pay for his Realism. A 'thing', now, is a collection of appearances, even if every appearance is independent of the mind before which it appears. Nunn's realism, at this point, is very like Mach's phenomenalism. The same is true of American New Realism.

Scottish 'common-sense philosophy', as we have already observed, dominated the American Universities during the greater part of the nineteenth century; nor was it entirely swept out of existence either by James's pragmatism or by Royce's idealism.

Peirce, to take the most notable case, continued to admire that 'subtle and well-balanced intellect, Thomas Reid'; his 'critical commonsensism'[4] owed much to Reid and his school. When Peirce criticized Reid, furthermore, it was from a Realist point of view; Reid, he complained, had not wholly shaken himself free from the Cartesian doctrine of representative perception. 'We have *direct experience of things in themselves*,' Peirce wrote in 1896. 'Nothing can be more completely false than that we can experience only our own ideas. That is indeed without exaggeration the very epitome of *all* falsity.'

The American tendency towards Realism, however, had been vigorously opposed by Royce in *The World and the Individual* (1900). Realism was there defined as, above all, a defence of independence, and Royce criticized it as such. 'The world of fact,' Royce describes the Realist as maintaining, 'is independent of our knowledge of that world . . . the vanishing of our minds from that world would make no difference in the being of the independent facts we know.' Royce's counter-argument, lengthy, robust and ingenious, is designed to show that if independence is ultimate – not mere 'appearance' – then all relations, including the relation of knowledge, are impossible in principle. In trying to preserve the independence of the objects of knowledge the Realist ends, according to Royce, by destroying the very possibility of knowledge.

Royce's attack provoked an immediate reply from two of his former pupils, R. B. Perry and W. P. Montague.[5] Relatedness and independence, they argued, are perfectly compatible. The task of explaining in what 'independence' consists is not, however, an easy one; in England, Schiller had attacked Nunn on this very point. To give a satisfactory account of independence was one of the two main problems which confronted the New Realists; the other was to explain, without abandoning Realism, how reality is to be distinguished from illusion – that rock on which so many hopefully-launched Realisms have foundered.

American philosophical journals, in the first decade of the present century, contain a multitude of attempts to sketch a Realist philosophy which would deal satisfactorily with these problems. But New Realism did not come of age until the publication in 1912 of *The New Realism*, a cooperative volume with contributions by E. B. Holt, W. T. Marvin, W. P. Montague, R. B. Perry, W. B. Pitkin and E. G. Spaulding.

The *New Realism* is the Realist equivalent of Idealism's *Essays in Philosophical Criticism.* A number of philosophers, by no means unanimous on every point, felt that they had in common a method of approach to philosophy, with the help of which they could satisfy their diverse aims. A manifesto,[6] it begins with a long explanatory preface and ends with a series of brief policy-speeches. The world of philosophy could no longer pretend ignorance of the fact that a new and revolutionary spirit of Realism was abroad.

In many respects, however, *The New Realism* had little to add except liveliness of statement to Moore's *Refutation of Idealism.* In other ways, again – in maintaining, for example, that philosophy is 'peculiarly dependent upon logic' and in defending the validity of analysis against the Idealist doctrine that 'the truth is the whole' – the New Realism is mainly important as a medium through which Russell's conception of philosophy was naturalized in America. Yet one must not overestimate the New Realism's indebtedness to English philosophy. Russell, after all, had learnt many of his most characteristic doctrines from William James, whom he describes as 'the most important of all critics of Monism'. The point most vital in the logic of *The New Realism* – that relations are external – James had particularly urged. Marvin summed up that doctrine with rare succinctness. 'In the proposition "the term a is in the relation R to the term b", aR in no degree constitutes b, nor does Rb constitute a, nor does R constitute either a or b.' From this it follows, presuming that knowledge is a relation, that the known is not constituted by its relation to the knower, or the knower by its relation to the known, or either knower or known by the fact that it is a constituent in the knowledge relation.

On so much, the New Realists agreed. There was not the same agreement about the nature of the knower or the nature of the known. When Russell referred favourably to the 'new Realism' he meant the 'neutral monism' which Perry and Holt had worked out under the influence of Mach, James and Nunn.[7] Other New Realists, Montague especially, were highly critical of neutral monism.

The Holt-Perry variety of realism is an out-radicalizing of James's radical empiricism. James had denied that there is such an entity as 'consciousness'; its adherents, he wrote, 'are clinging to a mere echo, the faint rumour left behind by the disappearing "soul" upon the air of philosophy'. There are only 'experiences'; knowing is a relation between portions of pure experience. F. J. E. Woodbridge,[8] however, had objected that 'experience' can only be defined as that of which a conscious being is aware; to talk of 'experience', therefore, is already to presume the reality of consciousness. Perry and Holt recognized the force of Woodbridge's criticism, which they tried to meet by defining experience without making any reference, explicit or implicit, to consciousness.

For this purpose, they adapted to their ends another facet of James's many-sided philosophy. James had emphasized – this had been the theme of one of his earliest essays, 'Spencer's Definition of Mind' (1878) – that a human being is an organism which has to maintain itself in an environment which sometimes favours, and sometimes threatens, its survival. Perry took over from James this emphasis on the human organism, and united with it a theory of perception which Bergson had sketched in his *Matter and Memory*: a mind's 'content', Bergson had argued, consists of that part of its environment to which its attention is momentarily directed. Mind, Perry concluded, is 'an interested response by an organism'. Our 'consciousness of a table', for example, consists simply in the fact that our nervous system is interested in the table. No entity, 'consciousness', is here involved, not even in the form of a 'mental act'.

Thus the familiar distinction between the 'private' contents of a particular consciousness and the 'public' world of science is, on the Holt-Perry view, quite unwarranted. James, in his 'How Two Minds can Know One Thing' (*JP*, 1905), had suggested that an experience is 'mine' only as it is *felt* as mine, and 'yours' as it is *felt* as yours – which does not prevent it from being in fact both mine and yours. Following up this hint, Perry condemns as 'the fallacy of exclusive particularity' the argument that because something is in your mind it cannot be in my mind; if it were not for the fact that the contents of minds intersect, he maintains, any sort of inter-human communication would be impossible.

No doubt, Perry admits, other people sometimes find it difficult to decide what I am thinking about – that is why it is plausible to suggest that the contents of my mind are private to me – but this difficulty, he says, never amounts to an impossibility. Even in the hardest of all cases, the case where I am remembering something, a careful observer, according to Perry, *could* apprehend what I have before my mind. 'My remembering London,' he says, 'consists of such elements as my central attentive process, certain persisting modifications of my cerebrum, my original dealings, practical and neural, with London – and London itself.' All of these are open to public observation, in principle at least.

The central teachings of neutral monism ought by now to be clear. 'Consciousness' is abandoned; and so also are the 'act of awareness' and the 'sense-datum', in the form they take in Moore's theory of perception. Nothing exists except objective 'elements'. Knowing is a relation between such elements, a relation peculiar only in that at least one of its terms must be an organic process.

The usual objection springs to our lips. 'But what of error and hallucination? Are pink rats and bent sticks objective elements?' Holt is perfectly willing to accept this consequence. 'Every content,' he writes, 'subsists in the all-inclusive universe of being.' But surely, we protest, some contents are real, others unreal. 'As to what reality is,' Holt aloofly replies, in a passage which gave rise to more than a little shocked comment, 'I take no great interest.'

This is a natural enough answer, for on Holt's view the difference between the real and the unreal is an arbitrary convention. We set up a system of connected perceptions which, as Hume expressed the matter, we 'dignify with the name of reality'; we call a perception 'real', according to Holt, if it has a place in such a system, and 'unreal' if we wish to deny it the right of entrance to this exclusive society. As Russell mischievously put the same point, some perceptions form part of the 'official biography' of a thing – its staid, respectable behaviour under normal circumstances – whereas others are wild, abnormal, best forgotten, unless the epistemologist insists upon acting as a muck-raker. The philosopher, Holt is saying, cannot be expected to bother his enlightened head with so merely respectable a distinction.

On the ordinary account of the matter, there is a sharp distinction between, say, those properties of a tree which 'really belong to it' and those, such as its perspective foreshortenings, which are 'unreal' or 'subjective'. But Holt follows Nunn in arguing that the innumerable geometrical projections of the tree – to any of which the nervous system may react – have each of them an equal right to be regarded as belonging to it, even if it is convenient for practical purposes to describe a certain shape as its 'real shape'. The projections, it is clear, are all actual relations of the tree, and there is no precise way, Holt argues, of distinguishing between 'the tree' and 'its relations'. As in Nunn's case, then, the Holt-Perry defence of the commonsense view that the objects of perception exist independently of the perceiver culminates in what is anything but a commonsense view about the nature of the objects themselves.

American New Realism was, indeed, severely criticized on just this point. There was something suspect in the very ingenuity which Perry and Holt brought to bear upon their epistemology. The original group disintegrated; Holt became a distinguished psychologist, Perry a moral theorist and a scholar, Pitkin made his reputation by advising a multitude of readers how to be happy though forty; Montague continued to philosophize, but in a manner certainly not New Realist; neither Marvin nor Spaulding made substantial contributions to philosophy.[9] Yet the movement had made its impact. As Perry suggests in his *Realism in Retrospect* (*CAP*, 2) it was an important wing of the contemporary battle against Cartesianism; the New Realism attacked dualism in the interests of a theory more sympathetic to the empirical spirit of the age than Absolute Idealism could ever be. And whatever the difficulties in which the New Realists found themselves, the force of their polemics against Cartesianism and Absolutism was unaffected. Few philosophers, nowadays, would *wholly* reject the name of 'Realist'.

Marvin's contribution to *The New Realism* had borne the title 'The Emancipation of Philosophy from Epistemology'. An odd-sounding title; for Realism had ordinarily been, above all else, an epistemology. But in Marvin's eyes, a Realist epistemology is important mainly because it leaves the philosopher free to undertake the study of 'metaphysics' – understood as an attempt to discover 'the highest generalizations warranted by our present knowledge'. If, as philosophers since Descartes had been accustomed to maintain, all knowledge is based upon knowledge of the contents of our own mind, then it seemed plausible to conclude that an inquiry into the human mind ought to precede any inquiry into reality itself; and the final effect of this circuitous approach to metaphysics had been the actual absorption of metaphysics, at least in empirical philosophies, into epistemology. If, on the other hand, knowing is merely one of the many external relations which link our experience, there is no reason to believe that a detailed epistemology is an essential propaedeutic to metaphysics. The metaphysician is thus emancipated, Marvin thought, from his servile dependence upon the epistemologist.

It was left to a British philosopher, Samuel Alexander, to work out a recognizably Realist metaphysics. His *Space, Time and Deity* was published in 1920, at the beginning of a decade remarkably productive of metaphysical systems; the first volume of McTaggart's *The Nature of Existence* appeared in 1921 and Whitehead's *Process and Reality* in 1929. *The Nature of Existence*, however, belongs in its essentials to the British 'neo-Hegelian' movement; *Space, Time and Deity*, like *Process and Reality*, has the New Realism behind it, even although it is by no means unaffected by Bradley and Bosanquet. And there is another vital difference between *Space, Time and Deity* and *The Nature of Existence*; McTaggart is trying to construct a strictly deductive metaphysics, Alexander to 'give a plain description' of the world in which we live and move and do our thinking. In his 'Some Explanations' (*Mind*, 1921), Alexander goes so far as to assert that he *dislikes* arguments, a strange pronouncement from a philosopher. 'Philosophy,' he says, 'proceeds by description: it only uses argument in order to help you to see the facts, just as a botanist uses a microscope.' In an earlier article on 'Sensations and Images' (*PAS*, 1910) his affiliations with Husserl are even more obvious; his method, he says, is 'an attempt to exclude philosophical presuppositions, and to state what is actually present in a given experience'. Nothing could be more remote from *The Nature of Existence*, which is argument through and through.

Alexander's method makes *Space, Time and Deity* a peculiarly difficult book to read and to discuss; in many respects, it is more like a work of literature than a philosophy. We expect from a philosopher a running thread of argument, interspersed with polemics. But there is very little of this in Alexander; he simply puts a hypothesis before us and then tells us to look and see how reasonable it all is, how admirably it squares with our experience. He does not exhort us, he does not argue with us, he merely bids us cast off our sophistication and look at the world through the naïve eyes of absolute innocence; yet the world he thus presents to us is complex and sophisticated in the extreme. Most philosophers have refused to follow his guidance; for all the acclaim which greeted its appearance, *Space, Time and Deity* is not now widely read. But it has its staunch admirers, some of them prepared to maintain that it is the most important contribution to philosophy our century has known.

When Alexander reached Oxford from Australia in 1877[10] his first contacts were with men of note in the Idealist movement – Green, Nettleship and A. C. Bradley were all tutors at Balliol in Alexander's time. He was naturally influenced by their teachings; and even when he broke with the Idealists, they continued to speak of him with a respect they rarely showed to New Realists – although this charity did not survive the bleakness of Cambridge where McTaggart, forgetting his own blackened pots, complained of *Space, Time and Deity* that 'in every chapter we come across some view which no philosopher, except Professor Alexander, has ever maintained'. It would be inhuman to expect the arch-enemy of Time to praise its arch-prophet.

Influences of a distinctly different sort were also at work on Alexander; the new biology and the new experimental psychology won his admiration. Stout and Alexander, indeed, collaborated in the defence of psychology against its Oxford critics. Alexander's friends did not know whether to be amused or alarmed by his psychological experiments. This was not merely the enthusiasm of youth; *Space, Time and Deity* appeals more often to experimental psychology than to any other form of empirical inquiry. Similarly, the influence of biology, so apparent in Alexander's first book *Moral Order and Progress* (1889) – which belongs to the school of Leslie Stephen – was never wholly to be dissipated;

conceptions derived from biology play an important part in *Space, Time and Deity*.

First, however, Alexander was to make his name as an epistemologist, in a long series of articles culminating in 'The Basis of Realism' (*PBA*, 1914). The immediate stimulus which provoked Alexander's paper was the appearance of Bosanquet's *The Distinction between Mind and its Objects* (1913). In that book Bosanquet welcomed Realism as an ally in the Idealists' battle against the theory of representative perception and, what is ordinarily associated with it, the 'brickbat theory of matter'. But his final verdict on Realism was nevertheless adverse: it sinned gravely, he argued, by speaking of mind as if it were simply one particular entity in a world of particular entities. 'I should compare my consciousness to an atmosphere,' Bosanquet wrote, 'not to a thing at all. Its nature is to include. The nature of objects is to be included. ... I never seem to think in the form "my mind is here and the tree is there".'

In sharp opposition, Alexander maintains that consciousness is a property of certain organic structures; the tree, for him, is not *in* my consciousness but *before* it, as an object 'compresent' with a conscious being. Alexander, indeed, was permanently influenced by Moore's 'Refutation of Idealism'; although he was attracted by the neutral monist reduction of the 'mental act' to an organic response he could never persuade himself wholly to reject the act-object analysis. For Alexander, however – and this brings him closer to Holt and Perry than to Moore – an act of mind is a *conation*, a response to an object. It is such a conation, not a cognitive act, which cognizes an object.[11] And the 'content' of a mental act, for Alexander, is not a pale copy of its object; it consists in those psychological features peculiar to the mental act as a process – its intensity and its direction.

If this is the real situation, if knowledge is nothing more than the 'compresence' of a mental act and an object, how account, we might ask, for the very existence of views like Bosanquet's? What confuses Bosanquet, Alexander argues, is his acceptance of the common assumption that in contemplating an object we are at the same time contemplating the act which knows it. Then the consequence follows that in perceiving X my real object is not X but 'my consciousness of X', within which X is somehow an ingredient. Since, however, X is obviously not 'in my consciousness' in that sense of 'consciousness' in which it is identical with an individual mind, 'consciousness' has to be converted into a general 'medium' or 'atmosphere' within which things exist.

Alexander, however, is determined to retain the common-sense distinction between individual minds and their objects; he cuts the ground from under the Idealist argument by denying that we ever contemplate a mental act. Acts cannot be contemplated, but only 'enjoyed' – 'lived through', as it is sometimes put. Thus 'our consciousness of an object' is never, for us, an object of contemplation; what we contemplate is the object, simply – although we at the same time enjoy the act which is conscious of it.[12] The mental act and its object are sharply sundered. Objects cannot be enjoyed, mental acts cannot be contemplated. From 'an angel's point of view' – the point of view of a being higher than ourselves – our conscious act would be an object; an angel would contemplate our conscious act as something compresent with its object. But we are not angels; for us the mental act exists only as an enjoyment.

To know an object, for Alexander, is to be a mental act compresent with it. The familiar question inevitably occurs to us: if its objects are compresent with the mind, how can it fail to apprehend them as they are? In reply, Alexander, following Nunn, first of all admonishes us not to confuse between selective apprehension and error. A mind is conscious only of what stirs an impulse in it; its 'object' is not the complete thing with which it is compresent, but only a selection from that complete thing. This incompleteness is not, by itself, error. If two people see a table, one as a flat edge, the other as a corner, neither is in error, Alexander argues, unless he wrongly believes that what is true of his 'object' is true of the table as a whole. In general – a point Royce had also stressed – there is no error involved merely in *having* an object before our mind. If we look at a distant mountain, for example, we have blue before our minds; so far all is well: we make a mistake only if we go on to ascribe the blue to the distant mountain. Then we are confusing, according to Alexander, between one thing and another; we are imagining that an object lies within a certain spatio-temporal contour when it actually lies outside it. The error does not consist in our having a

THE NEW REALISTS

non-existent object before us but in our *misplacing* a real object.

The same analysis applies in principle, he tries to show, to more difficult cases. Suppose we wrongly believe that a patch of grey paper against a red background is green. In this case, there is no green anywhere in the neighbourhood of the paper, as there was blue in the neighbourhood of the mountain. But the important point, to Alexander, is that green at least exists *somewhere*, and it is there spread out over an expanse just as we now suppose it to be spread over the paper. Both the object apprehended and its mode of combination with other objects already exist in the world; our error lies in misplacing or mistiming them: we do not create a wholly novel object. This theory of error, which is essential to Alexander's Realism, is worked out in *Space, Time and Deity* with a wealth of detail which can here only be mentioned, not conveyed.

'The temper of Realism,' Alexander wrote in *The Basis of Realism*, 'is to de-anthropomorphize; to order man and mind to their proper place among the world of finite things; on the one hand, to divest physical things of the colouring which they have received from the vanity or arrogance of mind; on the other, to assign them along with minds their due measure of self-existence.' Thus Realism, as he conceives it, is naturalistic; for it, the human being is one finite thing amongst others, not the ruler and lord of the finite universe. Such a naturalism is usually condemned on the ground that, as Alexander expresses the accusation, it 'degrades mind and robs it of its richness and its value'. Alexander's aim in *Space, Time and Deity* is to put mind in its place without degrading it. For this purpose, a useful instrument lay near at hand: the theory of 'emergent evolution'. The conception of 'emergence' goes back at least as far as G. H. Lewes' *Problems of Life and Mind* (1875); but it had more recently been worked up into a theory of evolution by the philosopher-biologist C. Lloyd Morgan.[12] Lloyd Morgan hoped to tread a midway path between 'mechanism' and 'vitalism'. The mechanists had set out to show that organisms are 'nothing but' physico-chemical structures, which have assumed their present shape as a result of the operations of natural selection. For the vitalist, on the contrary, an organism possesses a 'vital force'; it is, indeed a medium through which life struggles towards perfection.[13]

Lloyd Morgan had no patience with vitalism as a biological theory. 'With all due respect,' he wrote in *Instinct and Experience*, 'for M. Bergson's poetic genius – for his doctrine of Life is more akin to poetry than to science – his facile criticisms of Darwin's magnificent and truly scientific generalizations only serve to show to how large a degree the intermingling of problems involving the metaphysics of Source with those of scientific interpretation may darken counsel and serve seriously to hinder the progress of biology.' Vitalism, he argues, is not a scientific hypothesis, it is a metaphysics – a theory about the 'Source' of evolution, not a description of evolutionary processes. The theory of emergent evolution, on the other hand, purports to be a careful description of what actually happens in evolution, a description which at the same time brings to light the inadequacy of the 'mechanical' view that living processes are merely physico-chemical. In a genuine evolution, Morgan maintains – as distinct from the routine repetition of an established habit of action – there is always 'more in the conclusions than is contained in the premises'; in other words, the resultant process is never 'nothing but' the processes out of which it has evolved. Thus it is that modes of behaviour – consciousness, for example – can evolve out of physico-chemical processes without themselves being reducible to, although they are continuous with, such processes.

This doctrine of emergent evolution supplies the framework for Alexander's *Space, Time and Deity*. It might seem strange that a theory developed by a biologist for biology should be thus employed in a metaphysics; metaphysics is most often envisaged as a supra-scientific inquiry, in which science is, if not superseded, at least transcended. But for Alexander, metaphysics is itself a science, distinguishable from, say, physics only by its greater degree of comprehensiveness. Although its *method* differs from that of a natural science yet its conclusions must accord with the conclusions of scientists, and it can well take a hint from their discoveries. For its subject-matter is simply those pervasive features of things which are variously exemplified in the different fields of science: Space, Time, and the Categories.

Space and Time come first: 'it is not too much to say,' Alexander writes, 'that all the vital problems of philosophy depend for their solution on the solution of the problem what Space and Time are and, more particularly, how they are related to each other.' Philosophers have usually depreciated time; this is obviously true of Bradley and McTaggart, amongst recent philosophers, and the same can be said, to a large degree, of Russell. 'There is some sense,' he had written in *Our Knowledge of the External World*, 'in which time is an unimportant and superficial characteristic of reality. Past and future must be acknowledged to be as real as the present, and a certain emancipation from slavery to time is essential to philosophical thought.' Any philosopher who approaches philosophy through logic is likely to argue in this way: on the face of it, implication is not a temporal relation and 'truth', as logic understands it, is eternal. One may note, in contrast, that for Alexander 'truth' is relative. 'Truth,' he says, 'varies and grows obsolete or even turns to falsehood'; to be 'true' is to be accepted by the 'social mind' and what that mind accepts varies from time to time.[14] And of inference, which like the Idealists he takes to be the subject matter of logic, he writes that it 'betrays most plainly that truth is not merely reality but its unity with mind, for inference weaves propositions into a system, and system and coherence belong not to reality as such but only in its relation to a mind.' Not even truths, then, and not even logical relations are eternal; Alexander is 'taking time seriously' with a vengeance.

Bergson had already sought to rehabilitate time. But Bergson elevated time, Alexander thought, at the expense of Space, and in the process left it completely mysterious. In this respect, the opposition between Bergson and Alexander is complete: Bergson's philosophy is a protest against the interpretation of time in spatial terms, whereas Alexander maintains that this is how it *must* be interpreted, although equally, he grants, space must be interpreted in temporal terms. Neither space nor time, indeed, is intelligible in itself; each can be understood only by reference to the other, as an aspect of Space-Time.[15]

Alexander did not think it necessary to show in detail that time and space by themselves are unintelligible. In their negative arguments, he was prepared to follow Bradley and McTaggart: pure time would have to be at once pure succession and pure duration. But he does not conclude, as they did, that time is 'unreal'; we meet it in our experience, Alexander argues, and must describe it as we find it there. In that experience, however, it is never *pure* time; our experience is of the spatio-temporal. The succession we encounter in our concrete experience is the successive occupation of a place; the space with which we have dealings is not an undifferentiated inert mass but is at different instants diversely occupied. Once we recognize these facts, the 'contradictions' in Space and Time, Alexander thinks, lose their terrors.

On the naïve view of Space and Time, they are twin boxes within which things move about; in reaction against the 'box' theory, philosophers have attempted to identify Time with the relation of temporal succession and Space with the relation of spatial coexistence. But the relational theory of Space and Time, Alexander argues, ignores the fact that the terms in such relations are *themselves* spatial and temporal, and that it would involve a vicious infinite regress to try to reduce such spatio-temporality to a further set of relations. Furthermore – an objection which carries him to the heart of his metaphysics – 'relation', like any other category, is intelligible only if it is interpreted as a mode of spatio-temporality. To use it to give an account of Space-Time is to reverse the true order of dependence.

Alexander proposes a third view of Space-Time: it is, he says, the 'stuff' out of which things are made (although in a Pickwickian sense of 'stuff', since matter is subsequent to Space-Time). This is not an easy theory to comprehend, nor do Alexander's elucidations and elaborations always relieve his readers' bemusement. Perhaps what he wants to say will be a little clearer in another form: Space-Time, he argues, is identical with Pure Motion; to say that Space-Time is the stuff of which things are made is to affirm that a thing is a complex of motions. 'Motion' is 'the occupation of points which successively become present'; and this occupation of a point by a succession of instants is precisely what Alexander means by 'Space-Time'. He would, he says, happily speak of the ultimate Stuff as Motion instead of Space-Time, were it not that we find it harder to represent to ourselves the idea of an all-encompassing Motion than that of an all-encompassing Space-Time. Alexander's metaphysics, indeed, is in many ways akin to that of Heraclitus; 'the universe', he says, 'is through-and-through historical, the scene of motion'.[16] A spatio-temporal universe, for him, is by its nature a universe in growth: this is the point at which Alexander's theory of Space-Time unites with the doctrine of emergent evolution.

The part of *Space, Time and Deity* on which Alexander particularly prided himself is Book II, *Of the Categories*. As we have seen, he regards the categories as the pervasive characters of things; this pervasiveness, he thinks, needs some explanation; it arises from the fact that the categories are properties or determinations of the primordial stuff, Space-Time. They belong to everything, just because everything is a complex generated in Space-Time.

We can illustrate the manner of his procedure by reference to two categories which have already occupied our attention in other contexts – universality and relation. There are, he argues, no 'particulars' and no 'universals'; everything is an 'individual', i.e. is both particular and universal. It is 'particular' in so far as it is distinguishable from other things of the same 'general plan of construction'; its 'universality' consists in the fact that the same plan of construction is repeated elsewhere, whether as the construction of that same finite being (as a marble keeps the same form as it rolls along the ground) or of different finite beings (as the marbles in a bag all have the same general construction). This possibility of repetition, Alexander argues, depends upon the uniformity of Space-Time, which enables a thing to change its place while retaining the same plan of construction. In that respect, to talk of 'universality', according to Alexander, is simply a way of drawing attention to Space-Time's uniformity. Furthermore, a 'plan' is simply a regular mode of behaviour; the universal, as Alexander describes it, is not a Platonic form, changeless, immutable and eternal, but a pattern of motions, 'instinct with Time'.

Relations, similarly, are essentially spatio-temporal. Alexander defines a relation as 'the whole situation into which its terms enter, in virtue of that relation'. Thus the maternal relation, for example, is a set of actions on the part of the mother and a set of actions on the part of the child, considered in so far as they 'establish a connexion' between mother and child or 'initiate a transaction' between them. A relation, therefore, is a concrete whole, not a vaguely-conceived 'link' between terms. Often, Alexander maintains, it is more important than the terms; as when, in time of war, although we are aware that the conflicts taking place involve men, we envisage the conflict-situation clearly, the individual men scarcely at all. But these are, comparatively speaking, matters of detail: the important point, for Alexander, is that a 'relation' is a spatio-temporal transaction between spatio-temporal constituents, the transactions having a 'sense' or a 'direction'. To put the same point differently, a relation is motions passing between systems of motions.[17]

From the Categories, Alexander passes in Book III to 'The Order and Problems of Empirical Existence' which many of his critics have considered to be the most profitable section of *Space, Time and Deity*. So far it has simply been said that the empirical qualities a thing possesses are 'correlative with' their underlying motions. But 'correlation' is an intolerably vague conception; the problem now is to make it more precise. The clue, he thinks, comes from the mind-body relation.

This is an unexpected suggestion; most philosophers have seen in the mind-body relation one of the most intractable of all philosophical problems. Alexander does not agree. Observation and reflection make it perfectly apparent, he thinks, that certain processes with the distinctive property of being conscious occur in the same places and at the same times as 'highly differentiated and complex processes of our living body'. The 'correlation' of mind and body consists, then, in the fact that *the very same process* which is experienced from within, or 'enjoyed', as a mental process can be 'contemplated' as a neural one.

Physiological processes of a certain type and complexity, according to Alexander, are conscious processes. Consciousness, to express the matter in terms of evolution, 'emerges' at a certain point in the development of living processes. No knowledge of physiology, he considers, could enable us *prior to experience* to predict that this quality would emerge, even although, after the event, we can determine the degree of complexity exhibited by those physiological processes which are conscious. 'Consciousness' is a novel, unpredictable quality, for all that it has its roots in, and is determined by, physiological processes.

Working with this 'clue to quality', Alexander describes the general pattern of emergence. When Space-Time or motion reaches a certain degree of complexity qualities emerge: first, the so-called 'primary qualities' such as size, shape and number, which are 'empirical modes of the categories', then secondary qualities like colour, which stand to the primary qualities as mind stands to body, then living processes, then mind – and deity. In each case, we must accept with 'natural piety' the fact that new qualities emerge; there is no 'explanation' of this fact, it just is the case.[18] The determination of the sequence and number of stages is, he says, a problem for natural science: the metaphysician must be content to sketch the general conception of a 'level of existence', and to illustrate the relationship holding between such levels.

We can now summarize Alexander's theory of finite existences. Every finite existence, in the first place, is compresent with (spatio-temporally connected with) other finite existences. A finite existence is a substance, i.e. a volume of Space-Time with a determinate contour; it is the scene of movements, which have each of them a history. They appear in time, exist through time, and end in time. There are three distinguishable aspects of a thing: its spatio-temporality, the processes which occur in it, and its plan of construction, or configuration. The first, from our point of view, is the thing's place, date, duration and extent; the second its qualities, perceived as sensibilia; the third is its 'nature', which we take as the object of our thought.

Alexander's theory of knowledge now finds its home within this metaphysical framework, as a special exemplification of it. A mind, like anything else, is a particular finite existence, and is 'compresent' with a variety of other finite existences. 'Compresence', it is important to observe, does not connote simultaneity. Many of the events with which a mind is 'compresent' – or which, as Alexander also expresses the matter, form part of its 'perspective' – occurred a very long time ago, the events it perceives in the distant stars being a striking example. This, however, is not peculiar to mind; everything reacts to events which have already passed away. We can think of anything whatsoever as the point of departure for a 'perspective', which will include all those events in various places and of various dates to which it is related, with which, that is, it 'has transactions'.

Space-Time, indeed, is built up of such perspectives, not of simultaneous cross-sections.[19]

How does Deity fit into this metaphysics? That is the question Alexander sets out to answer in Book IV of *Space, Time and Deity*. Deity, Alexander argues, is the next stage in evolution; it bears the same relation to mind as mind does to living processes and living processes to the physico-chemical. For us to predict its nature is impossible. To call Deity 'mind', for example, would be comparable to asserting that living processes are nothing but physico-chemical processes: Deity must no doubt *be* mind, but its distinctive properties will not lie in that fact.

Considered thus, Alexander admits, God is ideal rather than actual, in the making but not yet made. If we demand an actual God, that can only be 'the infinite world with its nisus towards deity'. Why, we may object, should we not describe Space-Time – which is both infinite and creative – as God? One reason, according to Alexander, is that no one could worship, or feel a religious emotion towards, Space-Time; and it is the object of a metaphysics of deity to discover an entity towards which such an emotion is appropriate. He admits the abstract possibility that metaphysics might lead the philosopher to the conclusion that there is no such entity; but his own metaphysics, he considers, leads towards deity, not away from it. And this, he argues, is a point in its favour, for 'a philosophy which leaves one portion of human experience suspended without attachment to the world of truth is gravely open to suspicion'; the presumption must always be, he thinks, that to every appetite there corresponds an object which could satisfy it, and the religious emotion, on his account of it, is such an appetite, to be satisfied with no object less than Deity. That this Deity was very different from the God of ordinary religion, not least in the fact that there is no reason for regarding Deity as the last stage in evolution, did not seriously perturb Alexander.

A number of other philosophers were prepared to describe themselves as Realists, and felt the impact of Alexander's philosophy, without making the transition from epistemology to metaphysics. John Laird,[20] in such works as *A Study in Realism* (1920) expounded a 'down-to-earth' Realism – he liked to remember that his birth-place was near Reid's – in which the emphasis was critical and analytic rather than metaphysical. He admired Alexander greatly, and thought that Alexander's work overshadowed his own, but the atmosphere of his philosophy is that of Moore's Cambridge, where he had been a student; he did not move easily amid Alexander's abstractions. From his own Gifford Lectures *Theism and Cosmology* (1940) and *Mind and Deity* (1941) very little emerges in the way of a definite conclusion: no more than that a transcendental theism is 'not proven' although an immanent theism has some measure of attractiveness for a reasonable man.

Another Scottish professor, the scholar N. Kemp Smith, author of classical commentaries on Descartes, Hume and Kant, stood much closer to Alexander, for all that he described himself as an 'Idealist'. His *Prolegomena to an Idealist Theory of Knowledge* (1924) is an attempt, as he expresses the matter, to formulate 'an idealist theory of knowledge along realist lines.' [21] There is, he argues, no necessary connexion between Idealism and subjectivism; subjectivism is metaphysically neutral, lending itself as much to the purposes of a Mach as to the purposes of a Berkeley. The Idealist can also be a realist; what he has to show, according to Kemp Smith, is not that reality is mind-dependent but that it incorporates 'spiritual values', that these, indeed, operate 'on a cosmic scale'. Thus much of Kemp Smith's argument is an attempt to demonstrate the many-sidedness of Nature, its richness and resourcefulness, quite in opposition to the tendency of many idealists to deaden Nature in order to make of mind the one enlivener.

Kemp Smith is able to absorb into his Idealism both Alexander's critique of subjectivism and his theory of natural processes. But he does not go all the way with Alexander, particularly in regard to the independence of secondary qualities. He agrees that sensa are not in the mind; he still thinks that they exist only in dependence upon an organism. They are on his view a biological device, enabling the organism to deal with an environment so complex that to see it accurately would be to find it overwhelming. When we look at water, for example, we see something continuous and stable, not a dervish-dance of molecules; and if we were not thus deluded, it would wholly bewilder us. We are deceived only because Nature is taking care of our interests.

Another philosopher who saw virtue in the resurgence of realism was C. E. M. Joad, who moved with it from 'The Refutation of Idealism' to *The Analysis of Matter*. But *The New Realism* was too pale and emaciated to claim a permanent lien over Joad's wide-ranging affections. Within a seam-bursting eclecticism, Russell, Bergson and Plato had somehow all to make room for themselves, as the representatives, respectively, of matter, life and value.[22] The result was a conglomeration of considerable popular appeal but little philosophical consequence. The fact remains that Joad – an invigoratingly polemical broadcaster, essayist and lecturer at a time when the ideal of 'good taste' was threatening to destroy personality – represented 'philosophy' to a large segment of the British public. What this proves, either about philosophy or about the British public, I should not care to say.

CHAPTER 12

Critical Realism and American Naturalism

IF the patents law had application to philosophical trademarks, 'critical realist' would have given rise to some pretty legal battles. To be a realist, and yet to be free from any suspicion of naïveté – that was a prospect which attracted a variety of philosophers, however diverse their objectives in every other respect.

British[1] critical realism was generated in Scotland in the last quarter of the nineteenth century. There, as in America, Reid's 'Common-sense' philosophy had not been wholly submerged beneath the wave of enthusiasm for exotic metaphysical systems. We note its persistence, for example, in the writings of that highly idiosyncratic Scot, S. S. Laurie,[2] who, for all his Idealism, was prepared roundly to assert that 'I am conscious of an object at a distance, which is extended, localized, configurated, coloured, and of a certain mass'. Another Scot, Andrew Seth (Pringle-Pattison) was, as we have already seen,[3] no less insistent upon Nature's independence of Man, although his long discipleship to Kant made it impossible for him to return whole-heartedly to the Scottish tradition of 'natural realism'. It is to mark the fact that he hoped to be a realist without ceasing to be a Kantian that Seth described himself as a 'critical realist'.

'The conscious being,' he writes in opposition to any form of naïve realism, 'cannot in the nature of things overleap and transcend itself'; what we are directly aware of, he therefore argues, must be 'in our mind,' even although it points to a world independent of ourselves. He was naturally accused, as American critical realists were to be, of attempting to reinstate Locke's theory, universally condemned, of representative perception. Locke, Seth replies, made a serious blunder; he thought that knowledge is *of* ideas, whereas in fact it takes place *through* ideas. Although we are directly *aware* of ideas, they are not what we *know*. At this point, Seth joins hands with Stout, to whose early work he freely refers.

Seth's main critical attack is directed against phenomenalism: were experience not referred to objects, he argues, it would be an incoherent succession of merely transitory states. If, on reading Mill's phenomenalist epistemology, we imagine that we understand it, this is because, he suggests, we automatically read 'things' whenever Mill writes 'permanent possibilities of sensation'. Something similar is true generally; Idealism and phenomenalism can offer us a substitute for an objective external world only in virtue of their secret borrowings from realism. No one can work out a coherent philosophy without at some stage speaking as a realist – that, Seth, thinks, is the principal argument in realism's favour.

A different version of post-Kantian critical realism is hinted at by another Scot, Robert Adamson. Best known as a scholar, Adamson never presented his theory of knowledge in a rounded form; it has to be laboriously extracted from the lectures and essays brought together by W. R. Sorley as *The Development of Modern Philosophy* (1903).[4] Clearly, however, it belongs within the neo-Kantian ambit.

Experience, Adamson argues, does not initially contain any clear-cut distinction between mind and its objects – the 'inner' and the 'outer'. At the same time, experience is not intrinsically indifferent to this distinction; the fact that only certain of our perceptions are spatial provides a starting-point for our recognition of an independent world. (This is Adamson's reinterpretation of Kant's 'space is the form of the outer sense'.) We gradually come to realize, according to Adamson, that our experience is two-sided: a moment in the life of a finite being, it yet has a content which is not part of the life of such a being. Since the distinction between inner and outer proceeds *pari passu*, one must not say either that all our knowledge is of the 'inner', as the subjectivist maintains, or that what we know is known as independent of the 'inner', as the naïve realist contends. Thus critical realism, as Adamson presents it, is a compromise between naïve realism and subjectivism. With the realist, Adamson denies that experience is knowledge of the mind-dependent – with the subjectivist, that it is knowledge of the mind-independent. The fact is, he argues, that what is experienced is not experienced as having *any sort of relation whatsoever* to mind, because 'experience' is prior both to knowledge of mind and to knowledge of objects.

The most subtle and ingenious of the British critical realists was one of Adamson's pupils at Manchester – G. Dawes Hicks.[5] Unlike Adamson, however, he had to defend his position not only in opposition to Idealism but also, and more importantly, in opposition to the sense-datum theories of Moore and Russell and to the realism of Nunn and Alexander. His preoccupation with polemics may be one reason why Dawes Hicks did not produce a continuous work on epistemology; his most important publication, *Critical Realism* (1938), is a collection of essays and addresses.

He had read Meinong with care, and it is in terms of 'content' – by which he means 'a group of qualities' – that he formulates his theory of perception. Any satisfactory analysis of perception, he argues, must recognize not one but three 'contents': the content of the object, the content we immediately apprehend, and the content of the perceiving act. Whereas, however, the object and the perceiving act are distinct entities, qualified by their contents, the content we immediately apprehend does not qualify some third entity – say, a sense-datum. On Moore's account of visual perception, there is first a bare act of awareness, secondly a patch with certain properties, and thirdly an object, to which this patch is somehow related. According to Dawes Hicks, however, there is no 'patch', no 'appearance', no entity of any sort except the act of awareness and the object, one of which, therefore, the content apprehended must qualify.[6] One might object that there must be 'appearances' because it is sensible to say of things that they 'present different appearances' to different people. In such a sentence, Dawes Hicks replies, 'an appearance' is not the name of an entity. To say that things 'present different appearances' is just a somewhat misleading way of saying that they *appear differently* to different persons. That there should be differences of this sort, he further argues, is not in the least surprising.

Perception, Dawes Hicks agrees with Adamson, is an act of discrimination, a selection from within the immense complexity of our environment. Placed in the same environment, different observers will pick out different sets of qualities. Thus it is, according to Dawes Hicks, that errors arise. One observer fails to distinguish the black feathers of a bird singing in a tree from the leaves which surround them and therefore supposes the singing bird to be green; another's eye is caught by a dazzle of yellow, where the sun strikes upon the leaves, and supposes that yellow to be the colour of the bird. If a dispute arises in such a case, Dawes Hicks argues, there are regular methods for settling it, methods which give us all the certainty we are entitled to expect in an empirical issue. Thus, he concludes, there is no ground for asserting either, in the naïve Realist manner, that one perception is as good as another or, like Moore and Russell, that what the observers apprehend is a peculiar kind of entity – an 'appearance' or 'sense-datum' – not the actual qualities of the bird.

The evidence from physics for 'sense-data', he maintains, is no more convincing than the evidence from error. The colour of a thing, so it is commonly asserted, has been 'shown by physics' to be nothing more than a vibration of particles. Yet the colour we perceive is certainly not such a vibration; therefore, the conclusion is drawn, what we perceive must be a sense-datum, not a property of a physical object. But physics has not demonstrated, Dawes Hicks argues, that the vibrations of particles are either the physical equivalent of, or the cause of, the colour of an object. 'A luminous body,' he writes, 'may *both* shine with a red light *and* consist of particles vibrating at the rate, roughly, of four hundred billion times a second.' We fail to see the vibrating particles, we succeed in seeing the colour; it follows that we do not ordinarily perceive certain of the qualities that physical objects possess; it does not follow that they are really properties of a quite different entity – the sense-datum.

Thus, Dawes Hicks concludes, there is no positive reason for believing that what we immediately apprehend is a sense-datum. On the other side, the sense-datum theorist, so Dawes Hicks argues, can provide no fixed place of residence for his pseudo-entities; like a poor relation, they drift between the human organism and the physical object, scorned by both yet having no alternative but to trade upon their charity. Asked to explain how a sense-datum can be an 'appearance' of, say, a vibrating particle, the sense-datum theorist discovers that he has an important engagement elsewhere. These difficulties vanish, according to Dawes Hicks, without any violence to the scientific evidence, if we suppose that the vibrating particles *stimulate us to perceive* the colour of the object, without themselves *being* the colour.

Dawes Hicks' critical realism, then, rests on a sharp distinction between qualities and objects: the quality is what we immediately apprehend, the object is what stimulates us to that apprehension; the qualities are not entities – whether 'existent' or 'subsistent' – whereas the object and the apprehending act of mind *are* entities. Some of the American critical realists rested their case on this very same distinction; others maintained that the immediate object of apprehension, although not a physical object, is nevertheless an entity in its own right.

As expounded in *Essays in Critical Realism: A Cooperative Study of the Problem of Knowledge* (1920) – with contributions by D. Drake, A. O. Lovejoy, J. B. Pratt, A. K. Rogers, G. Santayana, R. W. Sellars, C. A. Strong – American critical realism is in large part a counterblast against the New Realism. In opposition to any sort of naïve realism, the critical realists agree on one vital point: that there are three distinct ingredients in perception – the perceiving act, something given (the 'datum' or 'character-complex') and the object perceived.

Holt and Perry had maintained that what we directly apprehend are character-complexes, and had then gone on to identify thing and character-complex, defining a thing as the meeting-place of the properties we perceive. The critical realists reject this identification of character-complex and thing, on the ground that it destroys the ordinary common-sense conception of a thing as something which has one, and only one, place and shape. The only way of saving the 'things' of everyday life from the disintegration they suffer in the New Realism, they argue, is to reject the identification of character-complexes and things (or 'physical objects'); the character-complex, on their view, is no more than a 'guide to' or 'sign of' the presence of a thing.

Obviously, then, the critical realists have somehow to meet Berkeley's familiar objection that if what we immediately apprehend is always a character-complex, it is impossible in principle to know that it is a sign of something which is *not* a character-complex. Berkeley's argument, the critical realists reply, assumes – partly because Locke went badly astray on this point – that we first of all apprehend the character-complex as a distinct entity and then ask ourselves to what it could guide us. In fact, however, every such complex is apprehended *from the very beginning* as pointing beyond itself to a physical object.

So much, the critical realists were all of them ready to affirm. About the precise nature of the character-complex there was not the same unanimity. Santayana and his followers – Strong, Drake, Rogers – took the character-complex to be a set of universals or essences, which can be exemplified in a particular existence but of itself neither exists nor subsists. To ask 'where does a character-complex exist?' is, on their view, wholly to misapprehend its nature. For the more conservative wing, in contrast, analysis, although not immediate apprehension, reveals the character-complex to be the property of a particular mental state; to the question where it exists, there is a clear answer – 'in the mind'.

This point of difference inevitably brought another with it, about the precise way in which a character-complex points beyond itself. Sellars, for example, likes to refer for support to Ward, to Stout, and to the Gestalt psychologists, and could equally have referred to Adamson. The conception of an independent external thing gradually evolves, he argues, out of that vague reference to externality which is present from the beginning in our perceptions; this process of evolution genetic psychology can describe in detail. Santayana, in contrast, is not psychologically-minded. We 'instinctively feel', he argues – feel as animals, not as psychologists – that things exist independently of us, things in which some of the character-complexes we apprehend are exemplified. This instinctive feeling of ours cannot be 'justified', but it is of such force as not to need justification.

The divergencies between the two wings of the critical realist movement were too many and too marked for it to have a long history as a group. At the same time, the main endeavour of critical realism – to follow the New Realists in rejecting Idealism, without abandoning the familiar conception of a physical object – persisted in the numerous independent publications by members of the group.

Thus Lovejoy composed in *The Revolt against Dualism* (1930) the most effective of all the polemical works produced by the critical realist movement.[7] Lovejoy accuses the New Realists of winning easy dialectical victories by pommelling men of straw quite arbitrarily labelled 'Locke' or 'the theory of representative perception'. He tries to show in detail that modern anti-representationalists - Kemp Smith and Whitehead as well as Russell and the New Realists – have been quite unable to find a way out of those notorious dilemmas which originally led all reflective men to accept some variety of the representative theory of perception. Such everyday phenomena as errors and illusions, memories and expectations, so he argues, are not satisfactorily accounted for by the tortuous ingenuities of the New Realists, who are also incapable of coming to terms with the evidence from physics and physiology that we do not perceive things as they really are. Posing as the defenders of commonsense, the New Realists have totally destroyed the everyday 'thing', on which our commonsense view of the world must rest, replacing it by an incredible congeries of incompatible qualities. Only the critical realist, Lovejoy maintains, can uphold the convictions of a reflective man; Lovejoy is less concerned to work out in detail the form such a realism ought to take than to attack those philosophers whose realism, on his view, is quite uninformed by a critical spirit.

Of the other critical realists, Strong,[8] in a long series of books which began in 1903 with *Why the Mind has a Body* and terminated, after many shifts on points of detail, with *A Creed for Sceptics* (1936), had as his main object the construction of a pan-psychist ontology: 'critical realism', in his eyes, was merely one ingredient in such an ontology. For the most part ignored, Strong made a notable convert in Drake, whose *The Mind and its Place in Nature* (1925) is the clearest exposition of the philosophical faith they share.

Strong and Drake agree with the New Realists that there is a single 'stuff' out of which everything is composed, although not that this stuff consists of properties. They distinguish sharply between stuff and structure. Physical science, they argue, describes the order, or structure, of things; and this is all that can possibly be inferred from the data we immediately apprehend. Only in one case have we knowledge of stuff as distinct from structure – in our observations of our own mind, of the 'way things feel'. (This is not a psychologist's knowledge; the psychologist looks to 'structure', to the brain and the nervous system.) Since we know no other stuff, it is a reasonable inference that this is also the stuff of which material things are made; and on no other view, Strong and Drake try to show, can we give a satisfactory account of the relation between minds and other things, of mind's place in Nature.

Both Strong and Drake were happy to call themselves 'naturalistic' or 'materialistic', because they denied that mind stands outside the natural order. Studied as a psychologist studies it, mind is reaction by an organism; looked at introspectively, it shares its 'stuff' with natural objects. In neither case, then, is it an interloper, a supernatural centre in a natural world.

A quite different version of naturalistic critical realism was defended by R. W. Sellars,[9] in a considerable number of books and articles – most notably, perhaps, in *A Philosophy of Physical Realism* (1932). By 'physical realism' he means the doctrine that 'everything which exists is spatial and temporal and is either a physical system or is existentially inseparable from one'. Thus he adopted what he calls an 'under-the-hat' theory of mind; mind, he argues, cannot possibly 'transcend' the organism, since it exists only in connexion with brain-states. For that reason, any sort of naïve realism is untenable: the mind cannot get outside the organism in order to make direct contact with physical objects. This is the point of connexion between Sellars' naturalism and his critical realism.

Earlier varieties of naturalism, he argues, broke down because they did not make use of the conception of levels. Like Alexander, Sellars advocates a theory of emergent evolution – with this difference, that what evolves is not Space-Time but only this or that particular physical system. Thus we are not to suppose, according to Sellars, that mind and value are 'reducible' to something else; the theory that everything is natural must be carefully distinguished from the theory that there is a single 'nature' which everything manifests. Nor is Sellars any more sympathetic to Dewey's than he is to Haeckel's naturalism. Dewey makes the mistake, he argues, of beginning from the merely human conception of 'experience', whereas any adequate naturalism must be 'physicalistic', i.e. its starting-point must be the physical object.

Many, although not all, of the critical realists, then, were naturalistic in their ontology. The best known of those whose critical realism was a facet of their naturalism is certainly Santayana, a philosopher of considerable importance in the intellectual life of the United States. His influence in England, on the other hand, has been very slight indeed. Although he won the admiration of Bertrand Russell and had a certain vogue in literary circles, his claim to be considered a philosopher of any consequence would certainly not, in Great Britain, go undisputed.[10] Certainly if philosophy is defined as the 'analysis' or the 'clarification' of everyday concepts Santayana is only occasionally a philosopher. One naturally classifies him with Schopenhauer – to whom he is much indebted – or with Nietzsche, rather than with either Moore or McTaggart. For all that his works are conceived on a grand scale, he is an episodic thinker, remarkable for his *aperçus* rather than for a sustained philosophical effort. His power lies in his capacity to shock, illuminatingly, a particular reader; and just at what point the illumination will come depends upon the 'set' of the reader's mind. This fact obviously constitutes a problem for the historian, which is intensified when, as in the present volume, ethics and aesthetics are excluded. It is as hard in Santayana's case as it is in the earlier Platonic dialogues to determine where ethics ends and metaphysics begins. What interests him is the human mind and human culture; his metaphysics fades into obscurity as it moves away from that central point. That he wrote a widely-read novel, *The Last Puritan* (1935), is not in the least surprising.

These comments apply particularly to Santayana's most influential book, or series of books, *The Life of Reason* (1905–6). Santayana's metaphysics is there little more than an atmosphere surrounding a concrete study of the mind in action. The striking point about *The Life of Reason* is that it took a platitude seriously: for Santayana man is, quite genuinely, a rational animal. A certain kind of life, the rational life, he thinks, is man's great contribution to the world; the rational life is lived, however, not by a quasi-supernatural being but by an animal organism. Thus Santayana offered United States philosophers a third alternative in a situation in which the choice had seemed to lie between the 'moralism' of a Royce and the reductive materialism of a Haeckel.[11] In part, it must be confessed, Santayana was influential just because he was misunderstood. For most of his readers, as he wryly recognized, 'naturalism and humanism meant no popery, the rights of man, pragmatism, international socialism and cosmopolitan culture'.[12] When Santayana denied that any human institution has Nature on its side, he was taken to be affirming that human institutions are based on nothing more substantial than a passing fancy, whereas in fact his sense of the importance of tradition was such that he was prepared to subscribe himself, although certainly in a novel sense, a Catholic. One does not honour Man, he thought, by decrying his most substantial and most stable creations – his social institutions. He was, indeed, a conservative, although the effect of his teaching was radical.

In *The Life of Reason* and the articles which immediately succeeded it, Santayana's metaphysics was sketched in sufficient detail for it to serve as an inspiration to the critical realists. But it did not take a formal shape until 1923 when he published *Scepticism and Animal Faith* (1923) as a preface to the four volumes (1927–40) which together compose *The Realms of Being*. They are of unequal value. From volumes with such titles as *The Realm of Essence* and *The Realm of Matter* the philosopher is entitled to demand a degree of precision appropriate to the subject matter. This he does not get: 'both in the realm of essence and that of matter,' Santayana confesses, 'I give only some initial hints.' And the hints are certainly dark ones.

In *Scepticism and Animal Faith*, the most widely read of his later works, Santayana, like Russell and Husserl before him, approaches metaphysics through the method of Descartes' *Meditations*, doubting whatever can be doubted in order to see what residue of certainty remains. But whereas Descartes thought he could thus arrive at an existential proposition *I exist as a thinking being*, Santayana, again like Russell and Husserl, tries to show that a strict application of the method of doubt leaves us with 'data' or 'essences', not with existences. That anything 'exists', i.e. that it has a past and a future and enters into a variety of external relations with other things around about it can, he thinks, always be doubted; what cannot be doubted is that we are apprehending a certain 'essence'.

This may remind us of Plato; but Plato, Santayana thought,

approached essences in a 'moralistic' vein, excluding whatever was lowly or unpleasant. For Santayana, in contrast, every possible predicate is an essence. From the realm of essence nothing is ruled out; the sinner has equal rights with the saint, the dreamer with the scientist. The rational animal, however, makes use of essences as signs, indices of the world that lies around him. The theory of indices Santayana learnt from Peirce: Peirce taught him how essences could be a guide to existences without being 'pictures' of them, pale copies of the real world.

If we ask Santayana how we can ever pass from essence to existence, from the bare apprehension of properties to the belief that there are existences which these essences characterize, his answer, as we have already seen, is that this belief arises in the course of our animal dealings with things. We eat and we drink, are hurt and are surprised. Things happen to us, in other words; and what we thus suffer is our clue to the realm of matter, of motion and change.

Santayana is quite prepared to admit that we can never reach the point of contemplating the realm of matter as we do the realm of essences.[13] The fact remains, he considers, that we have knowledge of things; we know a thing when we can apply to it a description which 'fits' it, i.e. which brings out some aspect of the way in which our animal life has to cope with it. These descriptions, which may take the form of a scientific theory, never, on Santayana's view, *copy* material objects. Thinking is creative, poetic, not a catching in a mirror. Descriptions which serve the animal as effective 'signs', warnings of the dangers by which he is beset, are for the nonce 'true'. It is reasonable to regard them as 'scientifically established', although with a note of irony in one's voice.

The rational man, as Santayana describes him, confronts the world around him in a cool and appropriate manner, a manner learnt very largely by participation in the great human institutions. Beyond rationality, Santayana thought, lies the life of the spirit. At this point, most of his admirers dropped away; the apostle of naturalism, they thought, had changed his allegiance, and they refused to move with him. Santayana denied that there was anything anti-naturalist in his recognition of spirit. For naturalism, as he defines it, is the view that only the material can act; and spirit, so he argues, is not a power. The 'psyche' – the everyday self which psychology describes – can no doubt act; that is evidence, to Santayana, that it is material, not spiritual. The spiritual life is not a life of action; indeed Santayana returns to the doctrine of Schopenhauer that only in so far as it frees itself from the pressure of will can spirit realize its own potentialities. Reaction against the pragmatic emphasis on action and energy could scarcely go further.*

Another, and a more predictable, leader amongst American naturalistic philosophers, a man very different from Santayana in temper and interests, yet not unfavourable towards a good many of his conclusions, is Morris Cohen.[14] Like Santayana, he went in search of a naturalism which would be a genuine ontology, in opposition to what he called the 'anthropocentric' naturalism of John Dewey; yet also, and again like Santayana, the social institutions in which human beings live their diverse lives lay at the centre of his interests.[15]

Cohen's philosophical ideas never took final shape as a single continuous contribution to philosophy. His most notable book, *Reason and Nature* (1931), is compounded out of periodical articles; that same manner of composition, with its inevitable defects, is employed in *A Preface to Logic* (1944). *Reason and Nature* bears the subtitle: 'An Essay on the Meaning of Scientific Method.' That is an admirable summary of his metaphysical procedure. He begins from scientific method – the practice of rational human beings – and asks what the successes of that method imply about the general nature of the world. First of all, however, he has to describe the method itself. At once he is on the attack – his enemy the view that science is essentially 'induction', the inferring of general conclusions from particular cases. The progress of knowledge, so he argues, is from the vague to the definite, not from the particular to the universal. 'We perceive trees,' he writes, 'before we perceive birches,' i.e. we recognize that something has the general, and vague, property of being a tree before we have the least notion of what kind of tree it is.

The careful discrimination of particulars, Cohen therefore

*Compare James's description of Santayana's philosophy as 'the perfection of rottenness'.

argues, is a product of scientific inquiry, not its point of departure. Similarly, a vague recognition that there is a general connexion between one kind of thing and another is the starting-point for the discovery of scientific laws. Scientific laws, on this account of the matter, are by no means abbreviations for sets of experiences, as Mill had sometimes argued; rather, they relate concepts to one another – concepts more precise, more suitable for scientific purposes, than those with which experience begins.

Such a theory of science has, like Santayana's, a Platonic ring about it, which may well surprise us since naturalism and Platonism are odd bed-fellows. But the resemblance to Plato is a superficial one; Cohen rejects the fundamental tenet of Platonism – that there is a sharp distinction between sensation and thought. Plato and the empiricists, he argues, made the same bad mistake. They defined experience as the passive 'having' of sensations, contrasting it with 'thought', which on their account of it actively relates universals one to another.

This dualism of particular and universal, passive and active, experience and thought, Cohen hopes completely to overthrow. In experience, he argues, we encounter things which exhibit invariant modes of behaviour, and which are transformed into other things in regular ways. Once this is realized, he considers, the bifurcation of the world into a realm of universals, or 'essences', and a realm of existences loses all its plausibility.

One difficulty, however, gives him pause. On the face of it, physics concerns itself with entities – a perfectly rigid body, for example – which experience never reveals to us and never could reveal to us. Does not this fact indicate that science takes as its subject-matter a world of ideal non-natural entities? Even although, however, we can never experience a perfectly rigid body, it is still possible for us, Cohen points out, to arrange bodies in the order of their rigidity; 'fictional' scientific laws, he suggests in his *Preface to Logic*, describe relationships, modes of transformation, between one such order and another. The 'ideal case' is simply a way of referring to the general nature of the order involved.

Cohen applies a similar method of analysis to the most abstract-looking of all laws – the laws of logic and the laws of pure mathematics which, following Russell, he identifies. The laws of logic, so he argues, are 'the rules of operation or transformation by which all possible objects, physical, psychical, neutral or complexes can be combined'. Thus logic, too, fits within the framework of a naturalistic theory, as informing us of the ways in which objects can be combined or set asunder.

Cohen's naturalism, then, is logical rather than biological; we are bound to be naturalists, he thinks, if we take seriously the implications of scientific method. Scientific materialism – the doctrine that 'all natural phenomena depend on material conditions' – is not a shaky generalization from experience but 'the requirement of an orderly world, of a cosmos that is not a chaotic phantasmagoria'. Naturalism emphasizes the interconnectedness of things; that is what particularly attracts Cohen to it and that is why he is so intent upon disengaging it from that atomic-sensationalist theory of experience which has so often, if so oddly, been its accompaniment. Cohen's naturalism, indeed, stands closer to the 'objective idealism' of Caird, Bosanquet and Royce than it does to Locke or to Hume.

As we have already seen, Cohen rejects a good many conventional antitheses – the antithesis between thought and experience, for example. This rejection hardened into the 'principle of polarity'.[16] A thing, he argues, never exhibits a single pattern of behaviour; opposite tendencies are always at work within it. It acts and suffers, lives and dies, is actual without ceasing to be ideal, is at rest and yet in motion. Cohen's formulation of the principle of polarity is not exact; at his hands, it is as much a mode of approach, a methodological principle, as a metaphysics. It admirably accords with the critical bent of his mind, enabling him to assail empiricism and rationalism alike, according as the danger seems to him to lie in one direction rather than another. As well, however, Cohen's emphasis on polarity suggests a way out of the traditional impasses of philosophy – a plague, and at the same time a benison, upon all philosophical houses.

In a variety of ways, then, recent American philosophy has been naturalistic. The cooperative volume *Naturalism and the Human Spirit* (ed. Y. Krikorian, 1944) – which opened with an essay by Dewey, was dedicated to Cohen, and freely refers to Santayana – reveals at once the diverse interests and the very considerable abilities of American naturalistic philosophers. Some of the contributors, like S. P. Lamprecht and H. W. Schneider, are well-known scholars; others, like S. Hook, are mainly interested in social philosophy; A. Edel defends a naturalistic ethics, E. Vivas a naturalistic aesthetics. What metaphysics unites them, however, it is not easy to say.

That is a point taken up by W. R. Dennes[17] in his essay on 'The Categories of Naturalism'. Naturalism, as he points out, has ordinarily attempted to show that there is a single substance – matter or Space-Time or mind-stuff – of which everything is a particular modification. Contemporary naturalism, however, is a theory of categories, not of substance; it leaves to the physicist, the biologist, the moral theorist, the aesthetician, the task of describing his own 'matter', the stuff with which he particularly concerns himself. The naturalist insists, only, that every inquirer must approach his task scientifically; the principal tenet of modern naturalism, as Dennes interprets it, is that there is 'no knowledge except of the type ordinarily called "scientific"'. Its method is analytic; it examines and elucidates, in Cohen's manner, the basic categories of scientific inquiry. Therapy is its main aim: to find a cure for the illusion that there are unbridgeable gaps between different realms of knowledge. If that illusion were ever to lose its potency, philosophy would, without regrets, bow itself out and leave the world to science.

Of those whose naturalism has taken this form, Ernest Nagel is one of the best known. His chosen medium, as in Dennes's case, has been the essay,[18] not the book; this is precisely what we should expect from a philosopher who conceives his task to be critical and analytical. One of his main objects has been to give an account, which shall be satisfactory to a naturalist, of the nature of logic: to all appearances, logic does not employ the ordinary scientific method of observation and experiment, and it therefore presents a difficulty for the view that this is the only method by which knowledge can be attained.[19]

Nagel had collaborated with Cohen in a widely-read textbook, *An Introduction to Logic and Scientific Method* (1934), but he is not satisfied with Cohen's doctrine that logic describes the most general structure of, and most general relations between, the objects of experience. That way of looking at logic, he argues, can make nothing of the fundamental logical relation – the relation of inconsistency. Only statements, he says, not things, can be inconsistent; and similarly it is *statements* which logic enables us to transform – logic does not concern itself in the least with the conditions under which one *thing* is transformed into another.

Nagel is even more dissatisfied with Mill's naturalistic defence of logical laws; logical principles, Nagel argues, are certainly more than strongly established scientific generalizations. For it is only with logic's help that strongly established can be distinguished from weakly established generalizations. Yet, on the other side, Nagel is not prepared to conclude from Mill's or from Cohen's failure that logic must lie outside the field of reference of a naturalistic metaphysics. The so-called 'laws of thought', he suggests, set up an ideal of precision; the logician, in affirming them, is maintaining that communication and inquiry are most likely to be effective at the hands of those who approximate to that ideal – a claim which can be tested, naturalistically, by studying the actual behaviour of inquirers at work. Similarly, the various logics which modern logicians have constructed are, to Nagel, alternative proposals for habits of inference, not alternative accounts of a single subject-matter – 'the relation of implication'. To justify any such logic, Nagel argues, is to show that the habits of inference it proposes would in fact be useful in this or that scientific investigation. It will be apparent by now that Nagel's naturalistic logic carries him closer to Dewey than to Cohen, although he continues, like Cohen, to deplore as irrelevant to logic Dewey's references to biological origins.

The older barriers, then, have been breaking down. Cohen was a naturalist who admired Hegel; Nagel a mathematician and formal logician who had some sympathy with pragmatic interpretations of logic. An even more striking case of this meeting of extremes is the philosophy of C. I. Lewis. He is neither a naturalist nor a critical realist; he is sometimes described as an Idealist. Yet it is not inappropriate to choose this, rather than some other, occasion to refer to his contributions to philosophy.

Lewis studied under Royce, who directed his attention to symbolic logic. Discontented with the paradoxes of material implication, he worked out a logic of 'strict implication' from which these paradoxes vanished.[20] In Lewis's system, p implies q if and only if it is logically impossible for p to be true and q to be false: the notion of logical impossibility as distinct from the notion of 'not both true' is taken as fundamental. Lewis admits, however, that although he can construct a calculus on this basis, his system is in no way superior from a purely formal point of view to the system of material implication – or to a host of possible alternative logics which no one has bothered to work out. Neither system contains any contradictions, and therefore both systems satisfy the only critical tests a logician has at his disposal. How then, Lewis went on to ask, is it possible to choose between one calculus and another? Logic cannot, by itself, make the decision; the logician must therefore pass beyond logic into epistemology.

At this juncture, Lewis thought, justice can be done to Dewey, without abandoning the formality of logic itself. In the construction of a calculus, none but formal considerations is relevant; the choice between systems, however, must be made on pragmatic grounds. Out of these reflections grew *Mind and the World Order* (1929).[21] There Lewis distinguishes sharply between the 'presentations of sense' – the merely given – and the *a priori* categorical principles in terms of which these presentations are interpreted and judged, emphasizing in particular the principles by which they are discriminated into 'real' and 'unreal'. Experience, he argues, cannot sit in judgement on its own content; only the mind, working with its own criteria, can judge experience, just as only the mind can choose between logical systems. The business of philosophy, according to Lewis, is the formalization of the categories the mind employs in such judgements, a business which will be critical, not merely descriptive, in so far as it attempts to clear up the obscurities and to smooth out the inconsistencies which mar our ordinary use of categories.

There is not, he considers, a single set of categories with universal application to experience; a dream, for example, is 'real' to the psychologist although it is 'unreal' to the physicist. Every scientist employs the categories most suitable as guides to action in his own field of inquiry. When he puts the matter thus, Lewis does not mean that the scientist consciously brings categories to the world; the distinction between what is given to the mind and what the mind contributes has to be discovered in the world – it is not itself given. The world we actually experience, he agrees with Green, is one in which the mind has already been at work. Were that not so, it would be wholly indescribable; nothing less than a pattern or an order can be named. From this it follows, Lewis points out, that we can never say of anything that it is 'the given'. To know at all is to categorize, he argues; Russell's 'knowledge by acquaintance' is impossible in principle. Yet that there *is* a given – something which no activity of thought could alter – is, according to Lewis, beyond all question. No philosopher has ever succeeded, he maintains, in doing without the given, whatever his professions to the contrary. So far the critical realists were right, and they were right also in recognizing the importance of essences. But, he thinks, they confused between what is given – the 'unspeakable' sensory elements – and the categories through which it is categorized, describing both indifferently as essences. Had they seen that it is only the categories which serve as guides, their theory, Lewis is prepared to admit, would have partly coincided with his own.

The problem which beset them also arises: how do we know that experience will fit into our categorical types? In a sense, Lewis replies, this question is unanswerable – if it means, how do we know that what we experience is not quite different from what we take it to be? For we could know this only by taking experience to be something else, and about this new 'taking' the same questions would arise. But in another sense, the question can be answered by saying that experience *must* 'really' be the sort of thing which satisfies our categorical principles, because those principles are the only thing which can determine what is 'real' and what is not. Categorical principles, according to Lewis, describe the way in which we interpret our experience; nothing that could happen, therefore, could overthrow them. They may alter if our interests, and with them our methods of interpretation, are modified; but they can never be refuted.

Similarly, experience can do nothing to refute an *a priori* truth, for such truths do no more than analyse and relate the categories we employ. They can be criticized, and can be amended, only on the formal ground that they lead to contradictions. In this way Lewis hopes to preserve *a priori* truths, and logic in particular, from pragmatic erosion. But when it comes to the application of categories to experience, formal considerations no longer avail and the pragmatic test comes into its own.

The precise nature of that test Lewis explored further in his *An Analysis of Knowledge and Valuation* (1946).[22] There, as in the writings of John Dewey, empirical propositions and valuations are closely linked one with another: Lewis sets out to show that ethics is the 'cap-stone' of epistemology and the theory of meaning. At the same time, he tries to incorporate within this pragmatic framework a doctrine of the *a priori* which allows that in some sense there are 'necessary truths'; in this admixture of the formal and the pragmatic the peculiar interest of Lewis's philosophy consists.

CHAPTER 13

Recalcitrant Metaphysicians

OF idealists, little has now been said for several chapters past. But they were not wholly submerged beneath the successive waves of Realist criticism. Bosanquet combated Realism – and Idealist heresies – in his *The Meeting of Extremes in Contemporary Philosophy* (1921); Muirhead, Hoernlé and many others kept the British Idealist tradition alive into the nineteen-forties. New varieties of Idealism, too, first saw the light of day in these critical years.

Some of the younger Idealists were Christian theologians, looking for a safe route between Bradley's Absolute and the scarcely less disconcerting heterodoxies of the Personal Idealists. Thus, for example, C. C. J. Webb, in such books as *God and Personality* (1919), sought to show against Bradley that the Absolute must be a Person, and against the exponents of a finite God that an ultimate Person must be infinite and all-embracing. He shocked Bosanquet mightily by writing as if the human being could enter into personal relations with the Absolute[1] but his Christian Idealism was congenial to less sensitive readers.

Other Idealists sustained and developed the principal theses of Idealist logic. Of these, the most notable was H. H. Joachim, to whose *The Nature of Truth* (1906) we have already had occasion to refer.[2] As Professor of Logic (1919–35) in the University of Oxford, he exercised his acute critical powers on generations of students, although he published little of any moment. He did, however, prepare for publication a commentary on Spinoza's *Tractatus de Intellectus Emendatione* (posthumously published, 1940) and certain of his lectures were edited by L. J. Beck as *Logical Studies* (1948).

Logical Studies is logic in an Idealist, certainly not in a formal, sense of that word. For the most part, it is a criticism, in familiar vein, of the concept of the 'given' – a criticism directed as much against Descartes as against Russell. Both Descartes and Russell, in their different ways, went in search of truths which would be immediately self-evident; Joachim maintains, in the sharpest possible contrast, that no proposition is wholly true. True in so far as it leads us towards knowledge of the system to which it belongs, it is false in so far as it is bound to express that system imperfectly.

Joachim admits that his analysis of what he calls 'truth-or-knowledge' is not an easy one to sustain. Falsity seems to be very different from incomplete knowledge – a geometrical error, for example, is not merely, on the face of it, an imperfect knowledge of the geometrical system. Yet an Idealist cannot admit that error and incomplete knowledge are ultimately distinct. In the second place, there is a certain tension within the Idealist theory of 'truth-or-knowledge'. It is, Joachim insists, something which grows, as thought gradually realizes its own possibilities; yet at the same time, as an ideal, it lies beyond all growth, all change. If he emphasizes the first aspect of the matter, the Idealist seems to be asserting that 'progress' is simply movement from one error to another ; if the second, he elevates truth beyond all human aspiration – this path leads to Bradley's Absolute, to an ideal of thought which is mystical, ineffable. But the dialectic, Joachim believes, can reconcile truth's timelessness with its gradual development – for dialectical 'development' is a logical transition from ground to consequent, not a temporal transition from predecessor to successor. To say that one stage in the history of thought develops out of another, on this view, is just to affirm that the first is logically grounded on the second; and the relation of ground to consequence is a timeless one. Joachim's Idealism, then, leads him back at point after point to Hegel's dialectic.

If Joachim thus kept the Hegelian flag flying at Oxford, his colleague, J. A. Smith, Professor of Moral and Metaphysical Philosophy from 1910 until 1935, turned south for his Idealism, to the writings of B. Croce and G. Gentile.[3] He, too, wrote little; well-known as an Aristotelian scholar, and a teacher often referred to with affection, he was content to announce his general allegiance to the Croce-Gentile 'philosophy of the spirit'.

Italian Idealism, like its British counterpart, was a reaction against nineteenth-century naturalism, which was represented in Italy by such voluminous positivists as R. Ardigo; and at first, as in the writings of B. Spaventa, it took Hegel as its master.[4] The Italian Hegelians soon made it apparent, however, that they would wear their discipleship with a difference. Hegelianism in Italy was interpreted concretely, as a philosophy of history rather than as a 'logic'; Hegel, like so many other Germans, was humanized as he moved toward the Mediterranean.[5]

Out of that humanized Hegelianism grew the Idealism of Croce and Gentile. Croce's[6] interests, it is important to observe, were at first literary and antiquarian; he only gradually turned to philosophy. Nor did he ever cast off his attachment to historical and literary inquiry. Indeed, he has made his mark in England as an aesthetician, a critic, a philosopher of history, a spokesman for Italian liberalism, rather than as a metaphysician, for all the diligence of such warm advocates as J. A. Smith and H. Wildon Carr.[7]

Reality, according to Croce, is 'spirit'; to be real, that is, is to play a part in one of mind's diverse activities. Croce opposes any sort of 'transcendence', any suggestion that there is an entity which lies wholly outside the human spirit, whether it be Kant's thing-in-itself, or the Christian 'God', or the naturalist's 'Nature'. Whatever mind cannot find within itself Croce rejects as mythical. 'Finding', however, is not, for Croce, a matter of simple introspection; it is in and through action that the mind discovers its own resources.

To act is to struggle: Hegel's great achievement, so Croce argues in his *What is Living and What is Dead in the Philosophy of Hegel* (1907)[8] was to give formal expression to that intuition. Yet although he pays homage to Hegel, Croce resents being described as a neo-Hegelian. For he spurns the Hegelian ideal of a final system: development, he says, is all – reality is a 'provisional dynamic system developing through provisional and dynamic systematizations'.

Nor is that development, as Croce describes it, the annulment of opposites in a higher synthesis. Hegel confused, Croce thinks, between 'opposites' and 'distincts'. Good and evil, truth and falsity, are, no doubt, genuine opposites, in dialectical conflict and cooperation one with another; goodness and truth, on the other hand, are 'distinct' forms of mental development, which do not conflict and cannot be synthesized in any higher principle.

Croce distinguished four such distinct 'grades' of mind, and devoted the first three of the four books which make up his

Philosophy of the Spirit to a description of their nature and inter-relation. He begins with a book on aesthetics (1902): a strange way to initiate a philosophy, to English eyes, for in England aesthetics is generally regarded as a dubiously legitimate cadet member of the philosophical family. The philosophical import-ance of aesthetics, according to Croce, consists in the fact that in creating and appreciating a work of art the mind works at an 'intuitive' level. Croce wishes particularly to emphasize that level of mental activity – aesthetics, for him, is the analysis of intuitive apprehension – just because, he thinks, it has so often been ignored by philosophers. They have tended to move directly to the second, theoretical, 'grade' – the level of conceptual or logical thinking, described by Croce in his *Logic as the Science of the Pure Concept* (1909) – without realizing that all fruitful concepts rest on intuitions.

Similarly, in the sphere of 'the practical', philosophers have ignored the 'economic' level of thought – or, as Croce later came to call it, the 'vital' level – in favour of the ethical, at which our 'economic' activities are conceptually described. They have judged ways of life to be good or bad without really under-standing *in what those ways of life consist*. By thus losing touch with the concrete, Croce argues in his *The Philosophy of the Practical* (1909), philosophy fades into phantasy, into empty conceptual constructions.

The mind, according to Croce, perpetually moves through these different 'grades', conceptualizing what it intuits and then returning to the intuitive level for fresh inspiration; or again, discovering in practice the test of theory and in theory the under-standing of practice. The movement of mind, then, is cyclical, not the progressive zig-zag of dialectic. Yet the cycle is not, as Vico[9] had thought, a pattern of bare recurrence: mind *advances* by means of its constant return to its source.

To what level of mind does philosophy itself belong? Philoso-phy, so Croce argues in his *Theory and Practice of Historiography* (1917), can be nothing more than a description of the general principles exhibited in the movements of mind – philosophy, in other words, is 'the methodology of history'. History exhibits the actual workings of mind; philosophy describes the methods of history. Not a few philosophers have thought that philosophy is the methodology of the natural sciences. But the natural sciences, according to Croce, suffer from abstractness; only if the sciences are studied *historically*, as part of the movement of the human mind, do we understand their real content. To understand is to see historically – that is the central point in Croce's teaching.

According to Croce, then, there is a double movement of mind – the dialectical movement through opposites and the cyclical movement through 'distinct' levels. Other Italian Idealists, Gentile in particular, condemn this duplicity as leading inevitably to contradictions. It is no accident that Gentile was a spokesman for Mussolini[10] – his thinking is at once activist and totalitarian. Nothing is real, according to Gentile's *Theory of Mind as Pure Act* (1916), except the pure act of thought, the *pensiero pensante*, which is at the same time an act of creation. 'Nature' is simply dead thought – *pensiero pensato*. Only if Nature is thus assimilated to thought, he argues, can mind's apprehension of Nature be made intelligible; otherwise Nature, conceived as a thing-in-itself, must be for ever unknown to mind. Thus the restraints of objectivity, in Gentile's philosophy, entirely vanish. The diverse forms of human thinking all coalesce into 'action'; 'Reality' exists only as the act of seeking it. Bosanquet was moved to protest against this short way with objectivity; not surprisingly, Gentile's philosophy has been regarded with even less sympathy by the followers of Moore and Russell.

Of English philosophers, the one who stands closest to the Italian school, and to Croce in particular, is R. G. Collingwood,[11] J. A. Smith's successor in the Chair of Metaphysical Philosophy at Oxford. In certain, although not in all, respects Collingwood conforms to the Continental rather than to the British philosophical ideal; human culture is his main theme, his logic and his metaphysics take shape within his aesthetics and his theory of history. He is prepared to stand out against the ordinary British presumption that physics is the very type of genuine knowledge; for him, as for Croce, history rather than physics introduces us to the real nature of things. But that was a conclusion to which he only gradually arrived.

The only philosophy which is of any conceivable use, so Collingwood argued in his *Speculum Mentis* (1924), is a 'critical review of the chief forms of human experience'. That sounds familiar enough; we naturally take Collingwood to mean that the philosopher is an epistemologist. But Collingwood's intention is very different. 'We find people practising art, religion, science and so forth,' he writes, 'seldom quite happy in the life they have chosen, but generally anxious to persuade others to follow their example. Why are they doing it, and what do they get for their pains?' This is the sort of 'experience' which Collingwood takes as his starting-point – the diverse experience of the artist, the saint, and the scientist, not the 'sensation' or the 'perception' of traditional epistemology.

How is the philosopher to proceed in such an inquiry? He may be tempted to model himself on a Boundary Commissioner, allocating this territory to science, that to art, this other, if any at all, to theology. But a self-appointed Boundary Commissioner, Collingwood points out, cannot expect to have his decisions respected. For one thing, the philosopher has his own claim to stake out; and he will soon discover that the 'impartiality' on which he prides himself is universally condemned as the unction of a hypocrite. More important still, neither art nor science nor religion will admit that it *has* boundaries, that there are areas of human conduct which lie outside its reach. Collingwood defends this intransigence. The fact is, he argues, that art, science and religion are different maps, in different degrees distorted, of precisely the same territory – 'the world of historical fact, seen as the mind's knowledge of itself'.

Are we to conclude that the philosopher is cartographer-in-chief, secure in the possession of the One True Map? Not at all. The philosopher, according to Collingwood, has no guide to reality except 'the toil of art, the agony of religion, the relentless labour of science' – even if neither the artist, nor the theologian, nor the scientist, understands quite what it is that he is revealing. Each of them shows the philosopher a reflection in a distorting mirror – a work of art, or God, or Nature, or History – and tells him that *there* lies reality. The philosopher, as Collingwood envisages him, sees the reflection as a reflection; he knows that there is no reality except the spirit, which discovers itself only by creating worlds in which it can see its own image. He knows, too, that some mirrors distort less than others, the mirror of the historian least of all, but he knows this only by having observed that history takes up into itself the lower grades of spiritual activity, not by comparing its reflections with those revealed in some wholly accurate mirror of his own.

Speculum Mentis announces the main themes of Collingwood's philosophy. Yet he could not remain content with the way in which they were there developed. The position of philosophy, in particular, was left obscure. Every mode of spiritual activity, so he had argued, coalesces into philosophy, for each such mode is a route by which the mind comes to a knowledge of itself. But if philosophy is thus elevated into a position of supreme importance, it has still no province and no method of its own; philosophy is simply art, science and religion made conscious of their limitations.

In *An Essay on Philosophical Method* (1933), on the other hand, philosophy is conceived as a specific inquiry; Collingwood there attempts to distinguish its method, or 'logic', from the logic of natural science and mathematics. Considering in turn such logical processes as classification, definition, deduction, he tries to show that within philosophy they assume a form peculiar to that subject. Thus, for example, whereas natural science classifications attempt to group objects into mutually exclusive species, philosophical concepts, in contrast, are not coordinate species: reality and goodness, for example, cut across all classifications. Even the classifications of formal logic, so he argues, exhibit this peculiarity. Every judgement both affirms and negates; judgements are at once singular and universal, hypothetical and categorical; a judgement is also an inference.

Similarly, a philosophical definition, quite unlike a natural science definition, is not an attempt to differentiate a genus. Plato's procedure in the *Republic*, so Collingwood argues, is typical of philosophical definitions. Beginning from the minimal idea of the State as a primitive economic structure, he slowly works his way towards the ideal, which is at the same time the *real*, State. A philosophical definition, indeed, is the discovery of the ideal form, by reference to which its imperfect embodiments can be 'placed' – just as in *Speculum Mentis* Collingwood had 'placed' art, religion, science, and history by relating them to philosophy, understood as the ideal of self-knowledge. Definition and classification, thus understood, are the principal methods of philosophy. For philosophy, according to Collingwood, seeks to place a concept in a scale of forms, working in a manner which is neither deductive nor inductive – since it neither begins from nor ends in generalizations – but has nevertheless its own kind of rigorous logic.

There is little sign in the *Essay* of the 'historicism' which Collingwood was shortly to advocate.[12] Certainly, his method is historical, in the sense that he asks himself how philosophers have *actually* proceeded, what method they have *in fact* adopted. But he still presumes that there are persistent philosophical problems; he describes philosophy, indeed, as 'a single sustained attempt to solve a single permanent problem' – a view he was later to reject with scorn, on the ground that Plato's problems, for example, are totally different from those which confront the modern political theorist.

In his *Autobiography* (1939), Collingwood made public his conversion to historicism. Like other philosophical autobiographies Collingwood's account of his intellectual development is to be read as an ideal possibility rather than as a historical narrative. According to Collingwood, his philosophical ideas developed in a continuous line from his archaeological and historical studies to his final metaphysics – if this is so, his published work is remarkably unrepresentative of his true beliefs. He has little to say, too, about the influence of Croce, which has obviously been considerable.[13] But at least he explains just why he was dissatisfied with the Realism to which his Oxford tutors had directed his attention.

He was taken aback, in the first place, by the unhistorical approach of the Realists; Moore and Cook Wilson, he maintains, were condemning as 'Bradley' and as 'Berkeley' philosophical theories which exist only in their horrific imaginations. He was at first inclined to excuse them, on the ground that they were philosophizing, not doing history. But he soon came to feel that such an excuse was quite inadequate; not to understand what Bradley and Berkeley are trying to do, he considered, is to be an incompetent philosopher.

By concentrating, Collingwood thought, on the most trivial examples, such as 'this is a red rose', the Realists had managed to persuade themselves that knowledge is 'transparent', i.e. that it consists, merely, in the confrontation of the mind by an object. But as soon as we ask ourselves how our knowledge grows at, say, an archaeological excavation we realize, Collingwood argues, that mere staring would get us nowhere. To 'know', in any important sense of that word, is to *seek the answer to a question*; knowledge is a process – of which questioning is one stage and answering is another. This is true even in trivial cases, he considers, although answer then follows so rapidly on question that we can easily fail to realize that any question was asked.

Out of this theory of knowledge, Collingwood's logic naturally developed. He rejected the Russellian propositional logic, and the theory of truth which goes with it, on the ground that it dissociates question and answer. A proposition, Collingwood argues, exists only as an answer to a question; it is true when it is the 'right' answer within a question-answer complex, i.e. when it is the answer which helps inquiry to proceed. Neither the proposition nor its truth, then, exists independently of the process of inquiry, as the Russellian propositional logic presupposes.

In *An Essay on Metaphysics* (1940) Collingwood makes his question-and-answer logic the starting-point for a fresh account of the nature of metaphysics. He now rejects the traditional doctrine that metaphysics is a theory of 'pure being', of the ultimate resting-point in a scale of forms. Such ultimacy – the ultimacy of a form which contains no peculiarities and therefore cannot be 'grounded' by any higher form – is indistinguishable, Collingwood argues, from nonentity: a form of which nothing further can be said is itself nothing. Thus 'pure being' is not a subject for investigation.

On the other hand there are, he thinks, 'ultimate presuppositions', which are sufficiently concrete. Every statement, every proposition, he has already argued, answers a question. But every question, in its turn, rests upon a presupposition, without which the question would not arise. When, for example, an archaeologist asks 'What does that inscription mean?' he presupposes that the inscription *has* a meaning. Such a presupposition Collingwood describes as 'relative' because it, too, can be regarded as an answer to a question – to the question: 'Has that inscription a meaning?'

In contrast, the presupposition that events have causes, according to Collingwood, is 'ultimate'; it does not arise out of scientific inquiry; it is not the answer to a question which scientists have asked: it is rather a presupposition of their questioning. Or at least, it *used* to be such a presupposition; Collingwood is more than ready to recognize that presuppositions change from time to time. At a certain historical period, he thinks, a 'constellation' of presuppositions governs this or that form of inquiry. (The presuppositions of biology may be different from the presuppositions of physics.) These presuppositions must be 'consupponible', i.e. it must be possible to hold them simultaneously. At the same time, Collingwood suggests, there is bound to be an element of strain in their relations one to another and to the progress of inquiry; to overcome that strain, presuppositions are changed. They are not rejected on the ground that they are false – the notions of truth and falsity do not apply to them, since they are not propositions, not answers to questions; they are merely dropped.

A good many metaphysicians before Collingwood had asserted that their concern was with ultimate presuppositions; but they had usually supposed that the metaphysician must demonstrate the truth of such presuppositions, or must find a place for them in a deductive system. If Collingwood is right, such ambitions rest on a misunderstanding. Presuppositions are not propositions; there cannot be a science of presuppositions. By their nature they do not admit of proof – to attempt to relate them one to another as conclusion to premises is to think of them as being less than ultimate. All that metaphysicians can do, on Collingwood's account of the matter, is to proceed historically, disentangling the presuppositions of a certain form of inquiry at a particular historic period. This, he also considers, is what they have actually done, without realizing it. Aristotle was a great metaphysician because he brought to light the presuppositions of Greek science, Kant because he performed the same office for Newtonian physics. When the Greek philosophers talked about 'God' as opposed to 'the Gods', he argues, they were obliquely referring to the unification of a variety of particular inquiries in a single science. 'Nature' played a similar role in the seventeenth century; and when Spinoza asserted that 'God is Nature', he was doing no more than pointing to the identity of these two sets of presuppositions.

Collingwood, then, exemplifies that genetic approach to philosophical ideas which we noted in nineteenth-century thought. Whereas, however, genetic inquiry for the nineteenth century was psychological or biological, Collingwood takes the fundamental genetic science to be history. Even natural science, so he maintains in *The Idea of Nature* (posthumously published, 1945), is essentially historical. Its 'facts' consist in this: that at a certain time and in a certain place certain observations have been made. To show whether this is so, he argues, one must undertake an historical inquiry. Scientific 'theories', similarly, are somebody's thinking; to understand the classical theory of gravitation is to interpret the records of Newton's reflections. Thus, Collingwood concludes, 'natural science as a form of thought exists and has always existed in a context of history, and depends upon historical thought for its existence . . . no one can understand natural science unless he understands history and no one can answer the question what nature is unless he knows what history is'.

Hume had tried to show that metaphysical questions are unanswerable until they are resolved into a psychological form. 'What is the true nature of a cause?' he converts into 'How do we come to believe that A is the cause of B?' Psychology, Collingwood objects, is the science of feeling and sensation, not of thought; as such it is valueless in the discussion of metaphysics. The true question, a question both answerable and relevant, can be put thus: 'What presuppositions of a causal sort did scientific inquirers presume at such-and-such a stage in the history of thought?' History, then, wholly replaces metaphysics. In *Speculum Mentis* history, while the nearest of spiritual activities to philosophy, still fell below its level; now, however, history is the only form of inquiry in which the human spirit is completely at home.

A more orthodox variety of Idealism, closely related to the conventional preoccupations of British philosophy, was worked out by G. F. Stout.[14] His *Mind and Matter* (1931) is probably the most quoted of recent writings in the British Idealist tradition, and it has recently been supplemented by the posthumous publication of *God and Nature* (1952) in which his metaphysics is more fully elaborated.

As we have already seen, the leading idea in his metaphysics –

playing the same sort of role as the theory of the concrete universal in Idealism – is the 'distributive unity', most familiar as an ingredient in his theory of universals. Stout's theory of universals[15] – a good deal influenced by Cook Wilson[16] – begins by rejecting the traditional view that things are particulars and their qualities universals. A 'thing', Stout argues, is not an entity over and above its qualities; if qualities are universals, then whence could a thing derive its particularity? Room can be made for particularity only if qualities are themselves particular. The qualities of two billiard balls, he therefore maintains, are as particular as the billiard balls themselves; each ball has its own whiteness, its own roundness, its own smoothness. So far he agrees with the nominalists; but he does not conclude, as they do, that qualities share nothing but their name. The various whitenesses, he argues, 'belong to the same kind' and thereby form a unity – a unity, however, which involves multiplicity. 'Whiteness', on this view, is the unity of particular whitenesses, not something over and above that unity, just as 'a thing' is a unity of properties, not a 'substance', and the self is a unity of experiences, not a 'pure ego'. In every case, a postulated entity lying over and above the unity of the particulars is replaced in Stout's philosophy by the 'distributive unity' of the particulars.

Is there an all-embracing unity in which these various special forms of unity all take their place? Stout thought there must be; and in *God and Nature* argued the point against Russell. He accepts Russell's statement of the Idealist position: 'everything short of the whole is obviously fragmentary and obviously incapable of existing without the complement supplied by the rest of the world.' Nothing short of the Universe, that is, is self-contained. Russell, however, had tacitly identified that thesis with another: that from any single segment of the Universe it is theoretically possible to argue to the nature of the Universe as a whole. It is against the second thesis, which Stout rejects, that Russell's argument is mainly directed.

Every segment, Stout maintains, raises questions which it cannot answer and in so doing exhibits itself as a fragment of a larger unity; but the answer to the questions it raises cannot be discovered by further contemplation of that solitary segment. To give an adequate description of the nature of the Universe we must take into account *all* our experience. Even then, Stout considers, we cannot hope wholly to pass beyond an attitude of interrogation; to that extent, Stout is happy to describe himself as an 'agnostic' and to take his stand by Bradley's side. But he does not accept Bradley's contention that the segments are self-contradictory. To Stout, they are genuinely parts of the Universe, simply as they stand, for all their incompleteness. Thus Stout hopes to be an Idealist without ceasing to be an empiricist.

The problem, now, is to explain how the diverse unities to which experience leads us can together constitute a single unity. The only serious problem, he considers, is set by the apparent discontinuity between mind and matter. This discontinuity is certainly not absolute, since the actions of my mind flow into the world around me; I can carry out my plans as a tennis player, say, only with the cooperation of ball and racquet. Yet there does seem to be at least a *measure* of discontinuity at this point – for material objects are not selves.

The materialist achieves unity, but only at the cost of regarding the mind as a product of matter. Much of *Mind and Matter* is devoted to a criticism of the materialist solution; Stout's fundamental argument is that matter could never produce anything so different from itself as mind. To make this point Stout defends, against Hume's criticisms, the view that a cause is not only an antecedent to, but is an 'intelligible ground' of, the effect. 'A cause,' he argues, 'is such a reason, so that if we had a sufficiently comprehensive and accurate knowledge of what really takes place, we should see how and why the effect follows from the cause with logical necessity.' The cause and the effect, he concludes, must have the same 'generic nature'; thus, as against Hume, it is not true that 'abstractly considered' anything might cause anything. In particular, the non-mental could never cause the mental.

Another way of achieving unity is the monadistic way, to which Stout, under Ward's influence, was at one time inclined; material objects, it might be argued, are selves in disguise. But the world as it is experienced by us, Stout argues, is certainly not a set of selves, and that simple fact the monadist cannot explain.

Stout's own solution is that mind is *embodied* mind, not the 'pure spirit' of Cartesian dualism; and every material object, he also maintains, must be infused by mind, even although it is not itself a mind. Only thus, he thinks, can the distinctness of mind and matter be reconciled with their continuity. Nature, so he concludes in *Mind and Matter*, expresses a universal and eternal mind. The working out of that view he left to *God and Nature*, which he did not publish in his long life-time and never wholly completed. The fact is that he did not feel at home in speculations remote from daily experience. It is clear, all the same, that his whole metaphysics leads towards the conception of a Mind which is the 'ground of unity' of nature as a whole. Our presentations, he has argued, are essentially incomplete, pointing towards an object of which they are phases; that object itself is only a segment of Nature, raising questions which nothing short of the unity of the universe can satisfy; our own mind, similarly, is unified only in virtue of the fact that it has a single object of thought – the Universe as a whole – however inadequately it may apprehend that object. The Universe, then, must be a unity. Yet it cannot be a unity, he has also argued, unless it is a Mind, for otherwise its unity is broken by a sharp division between selves and material objects. The unity of the Universe, however, does not annul the parts; it is a distributive unity. Thus Stout's Universal Mind stands closer to the God of Christian theology than to Bradley's Absolute.

Other British metaphysicians, in recent years, have sought inspiration in one variety or another of Continental philosophy. H. J. Paton has been mainly concerned to re-interpret the work of Kant; his *Kant's Metaphysic of Experience* (1936), in particular, is a remarkable exposition of Kant's *Critique of Pure Reason*.[17] In his *Aeternitas* (1930),[18] H. F. Hallett expounded and defended the teachings of Spinoza, undertaking *en route* a criticism of Alexander and Whitehead. His main object is to show that philosophy cannot stop short at the description of experience – at what, although not in Husserl's sense, Hallett calls 'phenomenology' – but must attempt to deduce the features of experience from the character of ultimate reality. Hallett, in short, bids defiance to positivism. So, in their various ways, do many other philosophers; at the Scottish Universities, particularly, Idealism is still the predominant tendency in philosophy.[19]

In the United States, Idealism has continued to flourish in a bewildering variety of forms, although no modern Idealist has the authority once possessed by Royce. Merely to list names would be fruitless, and to discriminate in a satisfactory way between the different types of American Idealism is a task calculated to bring the historian to an early grave. If three writers – W. E. Hocking, B. Blanshard and W. M. Urban – are here selected for brief consideration, it is in the hope, rather than the assured belief, that they represent the most notable trends in recent American Idealism.[20]

Hocking's many books, of which *Human Nature and Its Remaking* (1918) is one of the best known, express that ethico-religious impulse which lies behind so much American Idealism. There is no parallel here to the rigid dialectic of a Bradley or a McTaggart; Hocking's approach is at once eclectic and 'moralistic', in Santayana's sense of the word. The starting-point of his philosophy is the presumption that 'the universe has a meaning'; to deny this, as the naturalist does, is, he thinks, to abandon all claim to be considered a philosopher. There are, for Hocking, no 'brute facts'; everything has a 'meaning' or, as he otherwise puts it, a 'value'. The 'meaning', he grants, is not always obvious; experience shows us, however, that if we enlarge our vision of things, as the poet and the mystic help us to do, values emerge which we had previously overlooked. It is not merely arbitrary, then, for the philosopher to believe that it is his blind-ness, not any ultimate contingency in the facts, which sometimes prevents him from seeing the meaning of the experiences which daily crowd in upon him.

To see the 'meaning' of the Universe, Hocking further argues, is to see it as a self; in this respect, he considers, the insight of the mystic carries us nearer to the truth than does the logic of the Absolute Idealist. Hocking, like Webb, will not admit that there can be anything more ultimate than the self. The self, he maintains, is a 'value'; that is why science is unable to give a satisfactory account of it, except in the most superficial way: here the meta-physician steps in to point to the 'values' which science ignores.

A very different kind of Idealism is formulated by Brand Blanshard, whose *The Nature of Thought* (1939)[21] is in many respects the best presentation of that theory of thinking which British Idealists had expounded as 'logic'. There are two points, according to Blanshard, at which the work of writers like Bosanquet needs to be supplemented; they paid too little attention to psychology[22] – which, indeed, they ordinarily denied to be of any relevance to a theory of thinking – and they did not exhibit the ideal of thought in sufficient detail. To repair the first omission, Blanshard tries to describe the development of human thinking in terms which are at once psychological and logical. The transition from elementary perception to systematic knowledge is, he says, one which the psychologist is certainly competent to describe; yet, at the same time, the psychologist must recognize that human thinking is dominated throughout its development by a logical ideal. Thinking grows through psychologically-describable phases, and yet in a way which reveals a logical pattern.

In his description of the ideal of thought, Blanshard owes more than a little to Joachim, to whom his work is part-dedicated. The coherence theory of truth, he tries to show, depicts, as no other theory can, the ideal towards which all human thinking strives – a system in which the constituent members are necessarily connected one with another. Whereas the empiricist, Blanshard says, tries to explain necessity away, and the formalist to confine it to logic and mathematics, the idealist sees it everywhere. Once again, formidable criticisms have to be met; and Blanshard defends his thesis at length. Like Stout, he is particularly concerned to overthrow Hume's theory of causality. Causality, he argues, is necessary connexion; from the omnipresence of causality, indeed, Blanshard hopes to make his way to the omnipresence of systematic necessity. Thus Blanshard's philosophy, for all that he is respectful to the claims of psychology, belongs in essence to the British school of Absolute Idealism. At some points he stands close to Royce, certainly, but to Royce the logician rather than to Royce the moralist.

W. M. Urban[23] prefers not to be described as an Idealist; one of his books bears the title *Beyond Realism and Idealism* (1949). It is *epistemological* idealism, however, which Urban, partly under Hegel's guidance, hopes to transcend; his object is to work out a philosophy which is Idealist in so far as it affirms that the Real is also the Ideal but which denies that what we immediately apprehend depends for its existence and character upon the mind which apprehends it. Such a philosophy, Urban argues, will accord with 'the natural metaphysics of the human mind'; it will be a contribution to the 'perennial philosophy' exemplified in the writings of Plato and Aristotle, Anselm and Aquinas, Spinoza and Leibniz, and opposed only by extreme naturalists who, he agrees with Hocking, do not deserve to be called philosophers. The struggle between naturalism – with its divorce between facts and values – and the perennial philosophy, not the futile battles of epistemological idealists and epistemological realists, is, he argues, the crucial controversy in modern thought.

The 'natural metaphysics of the human mind' accepts the common-sense conception of an everyday thing, and the categories – the category of substance and attribute, for example – which natural languages employ; no theory, Urban tries to show in *Language and Reality* (1939), can in the end do otherwise. A certain difficulty arises, he admits, when the categories of a natural metaphysics are applied beyond experience. There is some plausibility in the view that the supra-empirical metaphysics of the perennial philosophy – its conception of God as the supreme reality – is hopelessly anthropomorphic. But this plausibility vanishes once we realize that the metaphysician is talking in symbols; it is only because he took the metaphysician literally that Kant was able to construct so striking a case against the possibility of a transcendental metaphysics. Theories of God, according to Urban, are inevitably symbolical, analogical,[24] which does not mean that they are nonsensical.

When Urban retired from his Chair at Yale in 1941, that University went in search of a successor who could carry on the tradition he had there established; they found their man in Ernst Cassirer, since 1932 an exile from his native Germany. At that time none of his major works except *Substance and Function* (1910) and *Einstein's Theory of Relativity* (1921) – translated as a single volume in 1923 – had appeared in English dress. In the last few years, however, there has been a spate of Cassirer-translations. His *Essay on Man* (1944), a brief restatement for English readers of his *Philosophy of Symbolic Forms* (1923–9), has been several times reprinted, and *The Library of Living Philosophers* has devoted a volume to his work.[25]

Yet Cassirer's status as a philosopher is by no means firmly established, in England at least. None of the contributors to the *Living Philosophers* volume, one observes, is an Englishman, and none of them, except Urban, has made an independent reputation as a metaphysician. The *Mind* (1953) reviewer of *Problems of Knowledge* (1950) was, too, unusually blunt: 'a very bad book,' he wrote.

The reviewer, G. C. J. Midgley, was prepared to concede, however, that Cassirer had opened up new ground as a historian of culture, even if he had tilled it imperfectly. This reaction is typical: Cassirer's reputation in England is as a philosophical historian, not as a philosopher. In Cassirer's eyes, however, this is a distinction without a difference. Philosophy, for him as for Croce, is 'self-knowledge', and self-knowledge is the knowledge of the human spirit at work in culture.

Cassirer grew up philosophically as a member of the neo-Kantian School at Marburg, a pupil of Cohen's; for the rest, his spiritual ancestors include Hegel's *Phenomenology of Spirit*, Herder's philosophy of history, and Hertz's 'symbolic' interpretation of physics. From these sources, he derived the conclusion that none of the great areas of human culture – science, religion, art, myth, language – ever offers us a picture of 'reality', considered as an 'external world' which the human being has simply to apprehend. Each of them, he argues, is 'a form of apprehension', not a bare perception of a given world but rather the construction of a way of dealing systematically with our experience – a mode of apprehension made tangible in symbolic structure and saved from arbitrary subjectivity by its rationality and orderliness.

Cassirer began from the case of physics. Very obviously, he thought, the development of physics has been from a crude naïve realism to a highly symbolic structure, which no longer depicts but only 'orders' a world. Philosophers concentrate their attention unduly on physics, he thought, because they wrongly believe that it gives access, uniquely, to 'reality'; once we recognize its creative, symbolic character, we see that physics is one constituent, only, in a human culture which everywhere exhibits the same movement away from concrete particularity towards an ideal, abstract, system – a system in which the human spirit sees itself expressed. The central clue to the understanding of man, Cassirer came to think, is not his science but his *language*: man is the symbolizing animal. And human language, too, develops away from the sensuous and the direct towards the abstract and the universal.

If, from within the British tradition, we ask the questions which Cassirer's neo-Kantian metaphysics naturally stimulates – What belongs to 'the given' and what to the 'form of apprehension'? In what lies the difference between truth and falsity? – Cassirer's work will scarcely supply an answer; or perhaps one should rather say one can extract various answers, which are hopelessly in conflict.[26] That is the justification for denying that he is a 'philosopher', as that word is now commonly understood by British philosophers; only if his work is read as a study in the development of human culture, simply, does it spring to life. Already, he has had considerable impact upon historians of philosophy; he was the first to draw attention, for example, to the importance of Newton, Boyle, Galileo for the history of epistemology.[27] Yet even then, there must be reservations: one cannot read him as a historian in the strict sense. His bold and imaginative analyses of human culture have, indeed, the same sort of suggestiveness as Toynbee's *The Study of History*, and comparable limitations.[28]

When he described his metaphysics as a defence of 'the perennial philosophy', Urban was appropriating a phrase which neo-scholastics have been accustomed to apply to the philosophy of Aquinas. Urban is more than ready to admit Aquinas to a place of honour in his philosophical pantheon, but will not concede that Thomism *is* the perennial philosophy. This independent attitude has also been characteristic of British admirers of Aquinas. Writers like Webb, Taylor, Emmet, with a special interest in the philosophy of religion, have all borrowed freely from Aquinas, without granting him absolute supremacy. Most of the better-known British and American philosophers have gone further; they have ignored neo-scholasticism, just as they have ignored dialectical materialism, on the ground that it is the ideology of an organization rather than a product of the free workings of the philosophical spirit.[29]

On the Continent of Europe, on the other hand, neo-scholasticism – and neo-thomism in particular – has been a prominent feature of the intellectual scene ever since the papal encyclical *Aeterni Patris* (1879) laid it down that the works of Aquinas were to be the foundation of philosophical teaching in Roman Catholic seminaries. If the importance of a philosophy be estimated by the number of its professional adherents, neo-thomism has no serious rival except dialectical materialism.[30]

Naturally, the neo-scholastics have devoted much of their energy to the preparation of editions of, and commentaries on, medieval philosophers, whose works have gradually been made available to the modern reader in admirable editions and translations. Many other neo-scholastics, for example F. J. Copleston in England, have undertaken critical studies in the history of philosophy – ancient, medieval and modern. In Belgium, the *Institut supérieur de philosophie* at Louvain, founded by Cardinal Mercier, has not only acted as a centre for neo-thomistic philosophy but has also published extensive philosophical bibliographies.

Not all neo-scholastics, it is worth noting, have been content to restate the position of their medieval masters. P. J. Maréchal, in his monumental *The Point of Departure for Metaphysics* (1923–6), tries to reconcile Thomism with other trends, especially the Kantian, in modern philosophy. Under the leadership of A. Gemelli, editor of the *Rivista di filosofia neo-scolastica*, a group of Italian writers have sought to absorb the results of modern science and philosophy into the general structure of Thomistic thought. German neo-scholasticism has rarely been purely Thomistic: at the hands of such philosophers as J. Geyser it has entered into alliance with phenomenology.

Numerically, however, these writers are an insignificant minority within a philosophical movement which has been for the most part content with orthodox neo-thomism. In France that orthodoxy achieved its most notable intellectual expression at the hands of Jacques Maritain.[31] Like so many Roman Catholic intellectuals a convert, Maritain was at first an ardent Bergsonian but he lived to denounce both Bergson and the French Idealists in the interests of neo-thomism. Outside France, he is best-known for his writings on art and politics; of his more narrowly philosophical writings *The Degrees of Knowledge* (1932) is perhaps the most widely read. He there distinguished between scientific knowledge, metaphysics and mystical experience, as different, although connected, forms of knowledge – in opposition to any attempt to argue that one of them, and one only, leads to reality.

British (and Irish) neo-scholastics have been largely occupied with the preparation of text-books for use in seminaries; the manuals of J. Rickaby and the more substantial text-books of P. Coffey are well-known examples of their kind. Two Oxford Jesuits, L. J. Walker and M. C. D'Arcy, have been somewhat more ambitious. Walker's *Theories of Knowledge* (1910) critically analyses the main varieties of epistemology, with the object of showing that the elements of truth they contain are already present within an Aristotelian-Thomistic metaphysics; D'Arcy's *The Nature of Belief* (1931) is a re-examination of the questions which had agitated Newman in *The Grammar of Assent*, considered now, as Newman had not considered them, from a neo-scholastic point of view.

Other varieties of metaphysics have flourished on the continent in these last fifty years, without attracting much attention in England. Léon Brunschvicg[32] in such works as *The Development of Thought in Western Philosophy* (1927) belongs to the same stream of thought as Croce and the later Collingwood. He attacks the doctrine, which he ascribes particularly to the mathematical logicians, that it is the philosopher's task to arrange and define concepts which are already 'given'; on such a view, he says, the human mind could, in principle, be replaced by a calculating machine. The fact is, he argues, that concepts are part of the work of the mind, arising out of its attempts to interpret Nature. To study concepts philosophically, one must examine the operations of the mind. But that does not mean, as he carefully explains in *Self-Knowledge* (1931), that philosophy is introspection: to know the mind is to watch it in operation in the endless variety of its interests.

In Germany, meanwhile, the ferment was at work which finally issued in existentialism; that movement of ideas, most conspicuously represented by M. Heidegger, can for the moment be left aside. Mention should be made, however, of the massive ontology of N. Hartmann.[33] His *Ethics* (1925) has been translated into English (1932); his ontological writings, on the other hand, of which five volumes appeared between 1933 and 1950, have not been widely read in Great Britain or in America. That is not surprising. In the predominantly critico-analytic atmosphere of contemporary British philosophy, Hartmann's ambitious attempt to construct a 'theory of being' is scarcely likely to be read with sympathy, even if his attack on the Cartesian tradition might be more favourably received. But it is worthy of note that philosophy on a grand scale, if almost dead in England, is still vigorous on the Continent of Europe.[34]

CHAPTER 14

Natural Scientists turn Philosophers

IN the nineteenth century, natural science came of age as a social institution: it began to invade schools and universities, to demand that laboratories should stand side by side with libraries, to proclaim that it, and not classics or philosophy, was the true educator. Naturally, these claims did not go uncontested; science could win for itself a place in the sun only at some cost to vested interests. The belligerence of Haeckel, of Huxley, of Clifford, was science on the offensive. These writers drew public attention to the emergence of a new and, as it was to turn out, immensely powerful social force – somewhat as the brashness of an adolescent gives notice that a new person has now to be reckoned with.

Other scientists, meanwhile, were manifesting a different symptom of adolescence: introspective analysis, self-criticism. At first, this self-criticism concentrated upon the expulsion from science – and particularly from mechanics – of whatever might perturb a positivist conscience. Scientists, indeed, were compiling a footnote to neo-Kantianism.

The preface to G. R. Kirchhoff's *Principles of Mechanics* (1874) sums up the programme of scientific positivism. 'Mechanics,' Kirchhoff wrote, 'is the science of motion; we define as its object the *complete* description in the *simplest* possible manner of such motions as occur in nature.' Kirchhoff is intent upon denying that science explains 'why' things happen as they do. For the scientist, he maintained, every 'why' is a 'how' – by discovering new connexions between phenomena, not by passing beyond phenomena to 'underlying reasons', the scientist completes his task.

Ernst Mach's *The Science of Mechanics* (1883, English translation 1893) has been widely regarded as the most important application of Kirchhoff's principles, although Mach had in fact arrived independently at similar conclusions as early as 1872. Indeed, the Mach-Kirchhoff species of positivism arose quite naturally out of the scientific and philosophical atmosphere of the time. A science beginning to be mistrustful, for reasons internal to its development, of such conceptions as 'atom', 'force',

..lute space', a science determined to set itself sharply in contrast with speculative metaphysics, naturally drew its weapons from the neo-Kantian arsenal. 'The *Critique of Pure Reason*,' Mach wrote in his *Popular Scientific Lectures* (1896), 'banished into the realm of shadows the sham ideas of the old metaphysics.' His object is to exercise the same surgery upon the old mechanics.

Science, so he argues, is an attempt to deal economically with experience. By describing a large number of diverse experiences in a single concise formula, which is widely applicable, it diminishes the risk that we shall find ourselves in a wholly unfamiliar situation. In a sense, he considers, science disillusions us, 'takes away the magic from things', for it shows us that what appeared to be wholly strange and unfamiliar is but a special manifestation of some very familiar mode of connexion between experiences. Such a disillusionment, such a reduction of the unfamiliar to the familiar, is at the same time precisely what we need for what Berkeley called 'the conduct of life'.[1]

Mach's criticism of traditional mechanics begins at this point. A mechanics which goes beyond experience – by speaking, for example, of 'electrical fluids' or of 'atoms' – is failing, he says, to perform its proper task. Considered as a mathematical model, he is prepared to admit, the atomic theory may facilitate our dealings with experience. But if the scientist is led by its successes to suppose that atoms have a reality of their own then he is crossing the boundary which marks off the fruitful fields of science from the marshy wastes of metaphysical speculation.

Absolute space, absolute time, causality even, so Mach thought, must go the way of atoms. In Nature, there is neither cause nor effect; Nature merely 'goes on'. A developed science will express its conclusions as functional relationships; aseptic formulae replace the 'causal links' of metaphysics. As for absolute space and absolute time, these concepts, according to Mach, are medieval remnants. It is meaningless, he protests, to talk of a body's spatial or temporal position except in relation to some other body. The physicist can compare the movements of a pendulum with the revolution of hands on a clock-face, but never with the progress of absolute time. To talk of the absolute duration of a process, or of its absolute date, is 'idle metaphysics'; and precisely similar considerations apply to absolute space. This is the side of

Mach's thought which was to influence Einstein and, after him, logical positivists.

Another persistent theme in Mach's philosophy of science was to be important in the sequel. He attacked what he regarded as the excessive emphasis on *demonstration* in the writings of physicists, an emphasis, he thought, which led them to take as their ideal 'a rigour that is false and mistaken'. A scientific hypothesis – or, as he alternatively described it, 'a new rule' – need not be artificially deduced, he argued, from so-called 'first principles'; if it stands up to testing, that is all we can demand of it. 'When after a reasonable period of time,' he wrote, 'a hypothesis has been suffi- ciently often subjected to direct testing, a science ought to recog- nize that any other proof has become quite needless.' The vague- ness here – in such phrases as ' a *reasonable* period of time' and '*sufficiently* often subjected to direct testing' – will be only too obvious. The fact remains that Mach's attack on the Platonic- Cartesian conception of science as strict demonstration was an important contribution to the subsequent development of methodology.

In England, where Mach's books rapidly became familiar in translation, somewhat similar views had already been maintained by W. K. Clifford and, in greater detail, by his friend and pupil, the biologist-statistician Karl Pearson. In his lecture *On Theories of Physical Forces*[2] Clifford, in the course of suggesting that many sentences which have an interrogative form are not genuinely questions, had exemplified his general point by reference to the sentence: 'Why do things happen?' This, he argued, is a pseudo- question, not a genuine request for information. We can properly ask, because we can hope to answer, only the genuinely scientific question: 'What precisely *does* happen?' Again, in his *Mind* article 'On the Nature of Things in Themselves' (1878), he threw out the remark that 'the word "cause" has no legitimate place either in science or in philosophy'.

One can see which way the wind is blowing: the fact remains that these are little more than *obiter dicta*. Clifford's *Common- sense of the Exact Sciences* (1885), which Pearson edited and completed, is a much more substantial work.[3] Clifford is here reflecting upon the consequences of the new non-Euclidean geo- metries, consequences which had already been more than hinted at by the German philosopher-scientist H. von Helmholtz in his lecture on 'The Origin and Meaning of Geometrical Axioms'.[4] No longer could it be presumed that there is a single geometry, Euclidean geometry, which is at once a purely demonstrative branch of mathematics and an ideal description of the paths taken by particles in space. 'Pure' geometry is now sharply distinguished from 'applied' geometry. Considered as a branch of pure mathematics, Clifford argues, geometry is a game, like dominoes. It is as improper to describe one geometry as 'correct', and another as 'incorrect', as it would be to assert that dominoes is correct and ludo incorrect. Within dominoes, no doubt, a particular operation can be condemned as 'incorrect', i.e. as not being in accordance with the rules of dominoes; in the same way, a pure geometer can 'make mistakes' by deviating from the rules of his particular geometry. But a geometry *as a whole* is 'correct' or 'incorrect' only when it is 'applied', when it is considered, that is, as a description of the paths taken by moving particles. Then it at once ceases to be mathematics, in the very act of leaving itself open to empirical tests. This sharp distinction between mathematics and its applications was largely to prevail in the decades that followed, whatever qualms might be felt about the precise manner in which geometry 'applies' to the world around us.

Karl Pearson[5] was largely content to accept Clifford's theory of mathematics; his own interest, like Mach's – who dedicated his *Science of Mechanics* to Pearson[6] – lay in the field of mechanics. In those parts of *The Grammar of Science* which concern themselves with the concepts of mechanics Pearson is, as he says, developing the hints which Clifford had dropped; but Pearson, not Clifford, supplied the details. *The Grammar of Science* (1892) in which Pearson worked out his theory of mechanics in a more systematic way, has been widely influential; something of its status can be gathered from the fact that it has been reprinted in *Everyman's Library*. No doubt, like many other of the contributions of scientists to philosophy, *The Grammar of Science* will not stand up to philosophical scrutiny – the epistemology which runs through it is an unholy compromise between Locke and Berkeley – but it often surprises us by its modernity; very many of the theses which were later to become familiar as 'logical positivism' are here clearly expounded.

...st place, Pearson, like his successors, insists upon the ... all-comprehensiveness of science. 'The whole range of ph.. ..ena, mental and physical – the entire universe – is its field.' When theologians and metaphysicians demand that science 'restrict itself to its proper business', they are imposing limits, Pearson argues, which no scientist can accept; nothing whatever lies beyond the reach of scientific investigation.

Thus Pearson uncompromisingly denies that religion or metaphysics provides us with supra-scientific knowledge. There is only one way of arriving at the truth, so he argues – and that is by classifying facts and reasoning about them. If we employ this scientific method we are bound in the end all to arrive at the same conclusions; the mere fact that each metaphysician has his own system, therefore, is enough to demonstrate that metaphysics has no contribution to offer to human knowledge. The metaphysician, Pearson agrees with Lange, is a kind of poet – but a dangerous one, because he pretends to be engaged in rational discussion.

Finally, like Mach and Kirchhoff, Pearson denies that science 'explains'. A scientific law, according to Pearson, is a brief description of the order of our perceptions. When the physicist says, for example, that he has arrived at a 'mechanical explanation' of a phenomenon, all he can properly mean is that 'he has described in the language of mechanics a certain routine of experiences'. Mechanics, in fact, is a convenient language in which to summarize our experiences – no more and no less.

Pearson's work is also interesting from a somewhat different point of view; to an even greater extent than Mach, he was dissatisfied with the mechanics of his time. 'There is need for a strong breeze,' he wrote, 'to clear away our confused notions of matter, mass and force.' One must not imagine that nineteenth-century positivism was an attack on philosophy by arrogant and self-satisfied scientists; to an important degree, it prepared the way for the twentieth-century revolution within science itself, the revolution associated with the name of Einstein.

Before we consider the nature and the effects of that revolution, however, something should first be said about the writings of a number of philosopher-scientists who, in their various ways and in various degrees, were at once influenced by and critical of Mach's positivism. The German physicist H. Hertz was a pupil of

Helmholtz who lived to write the preface to Hertz's incomplete and posthumously published *The Principles of Mechanics Presented in a New Form* (1894, English translation 1899). Hertz there set out to distinguish in detail between what is *a priori* and what is empirical in mechanics; he carried out his task in a manner which was to influence his fellow-engineer Wittgenstein, and, after him, a number of contemporary British philosophers of science.

Pure, or *a priori*, mechanics, according to Hertz, consists of 'images' or 'conceptions'. These 'images', however, are not to be regarded as copies, or as simple reflections, of experimental facts. They must, he admits, *accord* with the facts, but this is not the 'accordance' of a picture with the object it represents. Provided only that the images enable us to make the necessary predictions, that is all the 'agreement with reality' we can reasonably demand from them. It follows, Hertz thinks, that any of a number of 'images' can be equally satisfactory, if we judge them only from the standpoint of their empirical applicability. Thus in his *Electrical Waves* (1892, English translation 1893) he argues that the electrical theories of Maxwell, of Helmholtz, and those he is there presenting, for all their great difference in form, 'have the same inner significance'; they lead to the same equations and must therefore 'comprise the same possible phenomena'.

If a physicist prefers, then, one 'image' to another, when each leads to the same equations, this can only be because some images are 'more appropriate' or 'simpler' than others: they picture, better than other images, the 'essential relations of the object' and contain 'a smaller number of empty and superfluous relations'. Any picture we construct is bound to have some characteristics which are not essential to the job it does – as certain features of a map, for example, derive from the nature of the paper it is printed upon and not from the geography of the terrain it represents. The fewer such irrelevancies a picture contains the better; it is on this ground that Hertz would prefer his theory of electrical waves to Maxwell's; he does not pretend that his theory is 'right' at some point where Maxwell's is 'wrong'. In general, Hertz rewrites mechanics to achieve greater clarity and simplicity, not greater accuracy.

The system he constructed does not recommend itself to working physicists;[7] what mattered was his sharp distinction between the 'images' by means of which mechanical facts are represented and the facts themselves – and what went with it, the attempt to demonstrate that there is in mechanics a purely *a priori* ingredient. *The Principles of Mechanics* is divided into two parts: in a prefatory note to the first book Hertz expresses the conviction that the subject-matter of that book is 'completely independent of experience'. This, if it were true, rules out the possibility of a wholly empiricist mechanics in Mill's manner. At the same time, the *a priori* ingredients, according to Hertz, are no more than a set of images we construct to deal more effectively with experience; they are not in any sense a 'necessity of reason'. Thus Hertz's analysis of mechanics pioneers a route between traditional empiricism and traditional rationalism.

In such works as *Science and Hypothesis* (1902, English translation 1905) Henri Poincaré,[8] by training a mathematical physicist, put forward a somewhat similar position in a form much more popular and, in consequence, more immediately influential. Poincaré is particularly concerned to dispute the view that science, in principle, could be mechanically constructed by extracting consequences from axioms. In that respect, he belongs in spirit to the same movement of thought as Bergson and the pragmatists; he defends spontaneity and 'intuition' against any attempt to mechanize thought. For this reason he violently attacked the mathematical logic of Russell and his coadjutors: he thought that to reduce mathematics to logic would be to destroy that element of spontaneity and intuition which he particularly valued in it.

This is the background to the 'conventionalism' which is associated with Poincaré's name. When he maintained that the laws of mechanics are 'conventions', this was because a 'convention' is a free creation of the human spirit. If a law, as the positivists had argued, is a bare summary of experiences, then the role of the scientist is restricted to the recording and summarizing of his observations; the scientist, indeed, is no more than a sensitive machine. But if, on the contrary, laws are conventions, definitions in disguise, a language we deliberately construct in order to talk about the movements of particles, then the scientist is a creator.

On the face of it, however, this doctrine destroys the objectivity of science, converts it into a species of poetry. Some of his disciples,[9] Poincaré thought, pushed his conventionalism too far in that direction and lapsed into idealism. So he tried to show that a convention, although a free creation, is not arbitrary. Experience, if it does not compel the scientist to adopt a specific convention, at least guides him in one direction rather than another. If, in choosing between a Ptolemaic and a Copernican description of the movement of the planets – Poincaré's favourite example – the scientist is selecting a convention, not recording a fact, he does not hesitate for a moment in his choice. The objectivity of science derives from the fact that, a convention once hit upon, scientists agree upon its superiority. Thus Galileo, Poincaré thought, was fighting for the truth, even if Truth is not quite what Galileo took it to be.

Whether Poincaré really succeeds in reconciling the conventionalist and the empirical elements in his work is another matter; certainly he failed to convince his fellow-scientist Pierre Duhem that he had done so.[10] Duhem grants that scientific theories are abandoned with great reluctance, sometimes long after experimental evidence points to their defectiveness; he will not admit, all the same, that they are *pure* conventions, that no experiment can *in principle* refute them. His object is to give an account of scientific theories which subjects them to the test of experience, while yet granting that this test is not direct and immediate.

Methodologists, according to Duhem, fall into a beguiling, but dangerous, error; they assimilate physical theories to the empirical hypotheses of sciences like physiology or, indeed, of everyday life. But whereas such a hypothesis describes the properties of observable particular entities, a physical law, so Duhem argued, is abstract, symbolic. It refers to masses, pressures, volumes, not to physical entities. If a scientist talks of 'observing' a pressure or a temperature he needs to remember, Duhem warns, that his 'observation' presumes a theoretical relationship, e.g. a relationship between temperature and a change in the volume of a column of mercury. Thus, it is quite wrong to suppose that physical science consists of empirical hypotheses which can be conclusively established or conclusively refuted by 'observations'; the so-called 'observations' themselves involve scientific theories, and it may be one of these theories, not the hypothesis, which is in conflict with our observations.

The procedure of physics, as Duhem describes it, falls into four phases. First, the physicist picks out what seem to him – of course he may be wrong – the simplest constituents in physical processes, those which he does not know how to decompose but out of which he can construct more complex processes. He symbolizes these in a mathematical form; here there is certainly an element of pure convention (as when the physicist chooses to symbolize temperature by so many degrees on a centigrade scale). Then, by the exercise of the creative mathematical imagination, he links these symbols together into a general theory. So far, experience is powerless to correct the physicist; unless his work contains internal contradictions it is impregnable. But eventually he returns to 'experience'; not, however, to bare facts but to experimental laws. If known experimental laws can be deduced from his theory, he accepts it as true; if the results he deduces are inconsistent with experimental laws (to whatever degree of accuracy his instruments permit) he abandons his theory as false – or at least introduces some modification into it. At this stage, then, experimental laws are decisive.

Duhem's approach is in certain respects Machian; a physical theory, he argues, is not an 'explanation'; explanation should be left to the metaphysicians.* A theory, he says, is 'a system of mathematical propositions which attempts to represent as simply, as completely, and as exactly as possible a whole group of experimental laws'. At the same time, he is by no means a simple follower of Mach: his originality consists, first, in his sharp distinction between theories and experimental laws, secondly, in his abandonment of the ideal of a 'crucial experiment', and thirdly, in his insistence that physical theories must take a mathematical form – his rejection, that is, of 'mechanical models'.

In the writings of E. Meyerson,[11] the opposition to Mach is more definite and uncompromising. Perhaps it is not without

---

*Duhem, however, was a Catholic: if he sharply separated physics from metaphysics this was as much in the interest of metaphysics as of physics. A striking feature of recent philosophy, indeed, has been the readiness of Catholic philosophers to accept positivist accounts of science, on the ground that they 'leave room for' religion.

significance that Meyerson was trained as **a** chemist; in a sense, his theory of science might be described as a defence, against Machian positivism, of traditional chemical 'realism'. He is considerably junior to Pearson and to Duhem; indeed, his most extended contribution to philosophy, *The Progress of Thought*, was not published until 1931. The fact remains that his thinking was formed in the pre-Einstein period; it belongs in atmosphere to a time earlier than bare chronology would suggest.

The title of his first important book – *Identity and Reality* (1908, English translation 1930) – suggests the two main themes of Meyerson's work. In opposition to the positivist thesis that science 'orders sensations', he maintains that it is the object of science to penetrate to realities, to *things* – that, indeed, the ontological impulse, the attempt to discover what 'really is', is the prime mover in scientific inquiry. The atomic theory, for Meyerson, is the very type of a scientific theory. Secondly, against the view that science restricts itself to the discovery of constant conjunctions, he argues that science is the search for *identities*; science demonstrates that what superficially appear to be processes of creation and destruction are actually no more than readjustments within a substance which retains its identity through apparent changes; in that respect, Meyerson thought, conservation laws are the typical outcome of scientific investigation. Indeed, if science were wholly successful, it would collapse into a set of tautologies – a fate from which it is saved, paradoxically enough, only because it never wholly overcomes 'the irrational', i.e. distinctions which it fails to reveal as identities.

Meyerson's work obviously cuts across the main tendencies of contemporary philosophy; he is nowadays more highly regarded as a historian of science than as a philosopher proper. In contrast, the other writers we have been considering – Mach, Pearson, Clifford, Hertz, Duhem, Poincaré – between them sketched most of the 'philosophies of science' which have attracted the attention of contemporary philosophers. Meanwhile, however, physicists themselves have been led into the very depths of metaphysical speculation.

In the last few decades, indeed, a notable change of tone has appeared within the writings of philosophically-minded scientists. Duhem and Mach, if for very different reasons, both insisted upon the entire independence of physics from metaphysics; physics, they maintained, owed nothing and could contribute nothing to traditional philosophy. In sharp contrast, such writers as Eddington and Whitehead, mathematicians by training, are metaphysicians through-and-through, in an age in which metaphysics is generally spurned by professional philosophers.

Changes in the character of physics, changes which we can do no more than date and name,[12] are responsible for this revolutionary modification in the attitude of scientists to philosophy. In a variety of ways, so it appeared, physics fell heir to the responsibilities of metaphysics.

First, in regard to space and time. Einstein's special theory of relativity (1905) was interpreted as settling, in favour of relativity, the much disputed philosophical problem whether spatial position and temporal duration are absolute or relative. A philosophical controversy had at last been brought to an end – but by a physicist, not by a metaphysician. Secondly, physics had thrown quite new light, so it was argued, on the old determinist controversy. Classical determinism can be formulated thus: given a complete description of a physical system at a given moment and of the external forces operating upon it, it is always possible in principle to predict future states of the system. Quantum mechanics, issuing in Heisenberg's 'principle of uncertainty' – which Eddington rechristened 'the principle of indeterminacy' – undermined classical determinism by rejecting the possibility of complete description, at least in the case of submicroscopic processes. In the very course of determining with complete accuracy the position of an electron, Heisenberg argued, the physicist automatically rules out the possibility of determining, with the same degree of accuracy, its velocity. Many physicists took this to mean that the principle of causality had been overthrown; once more, it appeared, an important philosophical conclusion had emerged out of the reflections of physicists.

Thirdly, the new physics was to a striking degree epistemological; its successes, so it was argued, settled once and for all the traditional disputes of epistemologists. The test case, which now has the status of a 'classical example', is Einstein's critique of the conception of 'absolute simultaneity'. How can one possibly show, Einstein asks, that two distant events are absolutely simultaneous? Any operation by which one might hope to establish their simultaneity involves, so he tries to prove, a vicious regress. Suppose we suggest, for example, that two events are simultaneous if they occur at the same time as measured on clock-faces. How, in the case of distant objects, can one determine that the hands on the clock-faces reach the same point *at the same time*?

The conception of 'the absolute simultaneity of distant objects' Einstein concludes, has no meaning. Epistemological analysis – Einstein tells us that his reading of Hume and Mach influenced him decisively – is here employed within the framework of physical theory, no longer, as in Locke's case or in Berkeley's, as an 'outsider's' critical device. It is now one of the physicists' working-tools, to be justified like any other tool by its success in fashioning solutions to physical problems. On this criterion, so it is argued, the only acceptable epistemology is one which defines concepts in terms of 'operations', rejecting all concepts as meaningless which do not lend themselves to operational definition.

Not all physicists, of course, greeted with joy the philosophical transformation of physics, the re-emergence, as Eddington put it, of 'natural philosophy'. Experimentalists like Rutherford were distinctly suspicious of the new tendencies. On the whole, however, the mathematical physicists, to whom epistemological analysis is more congenial than laboratory experimentation, have been the spokesmen for modern science.[13] Even they, however, have been by no means unanimous about the philosophical implications of modern physics. Einstein and Planck[14] are neither of them prepared to admit that Heisenberg's 'uncertainty principle' has finally overthrown the principle of causality; not all physicists have accepted Einstein's theory of space and time, at least without certain reservations; and, as we shall see, the relation between 'concepts' and 'operations' has been variously envisaged. But whatever the extent of these disagreements, the fact remains that very many of the traditional problems of philosophy are now freely discussed within the context of physical theory. Physicists regard themselves as bringing expert knowledge to bear upon disputes which they would at one time have dismissed as 'barren metaphysics'.[15]

Professional philosophers, as distinct from philosophical journalists, have been singularly little affected by the revolution in physics. They have been inclined to suspect that, like a great many other revolutions, the revolution in physics raised no new philosophical problems and settled no old ones, for all the dust and fury. As well, it must be confessed, professional philosophers have been intimidated by the mathematics into which philosophical physicists so gratefully sink at crucial points in their reasoning; nor has the philosophical crudity of what they could understand led philosophers to expect any considerable degree of illumination from what passes their comprehension. There have, of course, been exceptions. That very remarkable philosopher-statesman, R. B. Haldane, in his widely read *The Reign of Relativity* (1921),[1] attempted to incorporate Einstein's theory within the Hegelianism to which he so faithfully adhered; Alexander welcomed what he took to be a partial confirmation of his theory of space-time; Russell wrote popular expositions of the new physics and shows traces of its influence; and a number of Cambridge philosophers, such as C. D. Broad, coped manfully with the attempt to make philosophical sense out of contemporary developments in physics. On the whole, however, one must turn to the philosopher-scientists, of whom there have been more than enough, for philosophically-toned accounts of recent science.

Amongst English writers, the astronomer Sir Arthur Eddington is the best-known.[17] His *Space Time and Gravitation* (1920) first displayed his remarkable gifts as a vivid – some would say *too* vivid – expositor of modern scientific ideas; in *The Nature of the Physical World* (1928) and *The Philosophy of Physical Science* (1939) he appears as a full-blown 'natural philosopher'. His philosophy exhibits the widespread tendency to interpret modern physics in what can vaguely be described as a 'personal idealist' manner.[18] Eddington presumes, as beyond all question, that we are directly aware of nothing except 'the contents of our consciousness'; in this respect, as in many others, his philosophical ideas spring directly from those of W. K. Clifford. He does not seem to realize, even, that this *is* an assumption – a fact which, more than any other, arouses the scepticism of the philosopher when he is told that Eddington's philosophy is a 'direct consequence' of modern science, and not at all, say, a product of the Cartesian tradition in modern philosophy.

Thus for Eddington, Einstein's 'operational' definition of physical concepts is an appeal to the contents of consciousness: 'experiences' or 'operations' wholly consist of such contents. Yet at the same time, the human being inevitably attempts to arrive at the knowledge of something which lies beyond his own consciousness – the 'external world'. Eddington is confronted, then, by the characteristic problem of subjectivism; he must show how knowledge which is restricted to our own consciousness can at the same time be knowledge of something which is external to consciousness. His solution is neo-Kantian: only if the 'external world' is of the nature of consciousness, he argues, can experience acquaint us with its character. The 'external world', then, is consciousness, life; all knowledge of the external world, all 'objective' knowledge, is knowledge of spirit; the purely objective world is the spiritual world, which physics can do no more than 'shadow' or 'symbolize'.

We need not be surprised that philosophers, confronted with this sort of doctrine and noting the embarrassing amateurism with which it is expounded and defended, have refused to take Eddington's metaphysics seriously. His philosophy of science, in a narrower sense, has greater interest in it: it draws attention, in a striking way, to the implications of a good deal of recent argumentation in physics.

Physicists, according to Eddington, are still not sufficiently rigorous in their rejection of 'unobservables', concepts the presence of which in a particular situation can never be verified. Once the implications of Einstein's method are taken seriously, it will become apparent, he argues, that physics does no more than coordinate 'pointer-readings', i.e. metrical observations. These pointer-readings, and not unobservable processes or entities, are the true subject-matter of physical science. The physical world – the world of protons, electrons and the like (which must not be confused with the *external* world of life and consciousness) – can only be defined as the world which pointer-readers are interpreted as describing.

The physical world, so Eddington considers, is *not* objective: the laws which the physicist thinks of as 'governing', or more properly, as 'constituting', the behaviour of physical entities are not descriptions of something which is 'really there'; all natural laws are 'subjective'. By calling them 'subjective' Eddington means that they are deducible from epistemological principles, or are *a priori*: he is out-Kanting Kant. Even 'natural constants' – the number of particles in the universe, for example – can, he writes, 'be deduced unambiguously from *a priori* considerations, and are therefore wholly subjective'. This is a startling doctrine; one cannot, however, dismiss it as wholly arbitrary or eccentric. Eddington is drawing very forcibly to our attention the role played in recent physical theory by arguments from what, in given circumstances, *it is possible for us to know.* His detailed illustration of that point, rather than the epistemological and metaphysical constructions he builds upon it, has made Eddington's work particularly important for the philosopher of science.

Eddington, one can readily see, is juggling precariously with the notions of 'subjective' and 'objective', 'physical world' and 'external world': he is unwilling to be driven to the extreme of asserting that 'the physical world' is at once subjective and the only world there is. The 'external world', in his philosophy, is a way of 'leaving room for values', while still paying his respects to the ideal of objectivity. Eddington's fellow-physicists, however, were not unnaturally dissatisfied with the view that knowledge is 'objective' only in so far as it lies beyond physics.

Of those who rejected Eddington's 'external world', while remaining in other important respects within the orbit of his philosophical ideas, we may mention two: H. Dingle and P. W. Bridgman. Dingle's monograph on *The Sources of Eddington's Philosophy* (1954) brings out very clearly the distinction and the connexion between Dingle's and Eddington's philosophy of science. Eddington, according to Dingle, quite failed to realize the implications of his own work; he did not see that he had reduced to meaninglessness what Dingle calls the 'Victorian' conception of the external world – oddly, considering how many 'Victorian' physicists were phenomenalists. Recognizing that physical science fails to reveal an external world, Eddington concluded that it must be revealed *in some other way*: the proper conclusion, Dingle protests, is that there is *no* external world. Science, Dingle agrees with Mach, is 'the correlation of experiences': in the case of physics, these experiences take the form of pointer readings, and the correlation consists in constructing out of such readings a world of electrons, protons, wave functions, and the like; in the case of biology, the experiences are biological observations, which are correlated in a 'world' containing evolutionary development, heredity and similar biological concepts; religion and ethics, in the same way, coordinate religious and moral experiences. Neither physics nor biology, neither metrical nor non-metrical observation, can carry us beyond 'the world of science' – a world containing nothing but correlated experiences – to an external world, envisaged as lying beyond any possible scientific coordination. Nor do morality and religion necessitate the construction of such a supra-experiential world. Experience is all – and quite enough.

Bridgman's 'operationalism' – first fully expounded in his *The Logic of Modern Physics* (1927) – abounds, like Eddington's philosophy of science, in epistemological tangles: what has been most influential in it[19] is its pragmatic doctrine that 'the concept is synonymous with the corresponding set of operations'. The concept of length, to take the example Bridgman works out in most detail, is identical with the set of operations by which, as we commonly say, 'length is measured'. It follows that astronomical 'length' is a quite different concept from 'length' as calculated by a theodolite; it follows also that 'all knowledge is relative' – Bridgman refers with approval to Haldane's *The Reign of Relativity*. These conclusions, Bridgman thinks, are an inevitable consequence of Einstein's theory of relativity; unless we accept them we have quite failed to appreciate the revolutionary character of Einstein's teaching.

Of all the scientists – if one can properly describe a mathematician in that way – who have converted themselves into philosophers the best-known is certainly A. N. Whitehead. There are those who would maintain that he is the outstanding philosopher of our century – even if there are others who would dismiss his metaphysical constructions as obscure private dreams. Whatever the final verdict of history, which it would be imprudent to anticipate, one can say this much: no one will ever succeed in writing a short account of his work which is not, in a high degree, arbitrary. The shifts of opinion which are everywhere apparent, not only as between the diverse and substantial works which he produced in the course of his long life but even within the confines of a single chapter; the obscurity and looseness of expression which too often prevail; the elusiveness of his multitudinous references to science, to art, to society, to the history of philosophy; these together produce in the chronicler of contemporary thought a feeling of desperation. The best that can be done is to construct a bare framework which the reader can adorn with his own interpretations.[20]

Whitehead began, as we said, as a mathematician, but his mathematics displayed what was to be the leading characteristic of his work as a philosopher: his passion for arriving at the most extensive of possible generalizations. In his first major work, *A Treatise on Universal Algebra* (1898),[21] he carried further that generalization of algebra, the freeing of it from any special relationship to arithmetic, which we have already observed in the work of George Boole. Whitehead hoped to construct an algebra which would be truly 'universal', an algebra of which ordinary numerical algebra would be a sub-species. At the same time, his *Treatise* bears the sub-title 'with applications'; he was not content to operate with uninterpreted symbols – he liked to make use of his symbols in specific fields of inquiry. If one compares him with other contemporary British philosophers one notices that he differs from them as much in concreteness as in abstractness: if on the one side he generalizes where they distinguish, on the other side he attempts to interpret his generalizations as theories of physics, or of education, or of art, whereas their distinctions, for the most part, have no point except within philosophy itself.

The years of Whitehead's life which immediately followed the composition of the *Universal Algebra* were largely devoted to working out, in collaboration with his ex-pupil Bertrand Russell, the ideas which found expression in *Principia Mathematica*.[22] But he also found time to compose a remarkable memoir for the Royal Society: 'Mathematical Concepts of the Material World' (1905),[23] an attempt to make use of the language of symbolic logic to describe 'the possible relations to space of the ultimate entities which (in ordinary language) constitute the stuff in space.'

Two points in that memoir especially deserve attention. Philosophers, Whitehead complains, work with a wholly inadequate logical apparatus, admitting no more than substances, qualities, and (at most) two-termed relations. Any adequate account of the relation between material objects and space must, he maintained, make use of many-termed (polyadic) relations; the various traditional theories break down, he sought to show, just on account of their over-simplification of the logical possibilities. This was to be a recurrent theme in his philosophy.

Secondly, one can see in this *Memoir* why Whitehead was dissatisfied with 'the classical concept of the material world' and, in embryo, what kind of ontology he hoped to substitute for it. With its sharp distinction between three kinds of entity – points of space, particles of matter, instants of time – the classical theory failed to satisfy Whitehead's demand for complete generality. As yet, he does not so much as suggest the possibility that instants of time might be dispensed with, but he is already toying with the idea that points of space might be defined in terms of material particles. The classical theory, he considers, works admirably so long as it confines itself to pure geometry, for which the universe is static, but it fails as a physics, because it cannot give an adequate account of change. Obviously, fixed points in absolute space cannot change; and so the physicist has on his hands an irresolvable dualism between changing particles and unchanging points. The occupation of a point by a particle at an instant is, as we might express the matter, wholly *arbitrary*, not in the least deducible from the nature of the point, the particle, or the instant; that element of arbitrariness obviously perturbed Whitehead.

It is also apparent from his *Memoir* that Whitehead was very much under the influence of Russell's philosophical ideas, as is only to be expected. Indeed Russell's *Philosophy of Leibniz* – at that time his major contribution to philosophy – never ceased to fascinate Whitehead, even if, at the end, he was more sympathetically inclined towards Leibniz's philosophy, as Russell expounded it, than to Russell's own views.

In 1906, however, Whitehead was still, on most matters, a Russellian, even if a wavering one. When, after 1914, he turned from mathematics to philosophy, he still began from a typically Russellian problem – how 'the neat, tidy exact world' of science is related to the 'rough' world of everyday experience – and he tried to solve that problem in Russellian terms: physical concepts and physical objects are, he thought, 'constructions' out of 'fragmentary individual experiences'.[24]

His books of the next period, however – the books that first made his name as a philosopher and which many would regard as the highwater mark of his philosophical achievement – break away from the British tradition to which Russell has been faithful. In *An Enquiry Concerning the Principles of Natural Knowledge*[25] (1919), he worked out a new philosophy of physical science; in *The Concept of Nature* (1920) he expounded that philosophy in less technical terms; in *The Principle of Relativity* (1922) he tried to show that a general theory of relativity is directly deducible from his natural philosophy, without recourse, in Einstein's manner, to 'special facts' about clocks, measuring-rods, and the velocity of light.

These books, it should be emphasized, have a limited aim. Whitehead accepted the definition of philosophy formulated by the Idealists, and particularly by Haldane, with whom Whitehead was accustomed to discuss philosophical questions. The philosophical ideal, Whitehead writes in *The Concept of Nature*, is the 'attainment of some unifying concept which will set in assigned relations within itself all that there is for knowledge, for feeling, and for emotion'. For the moment, Whitehead is leaving 'feeling and emotion' out of the picture: his concern, solely, is with the principles which unify science.

At the same time, one can find enunciated in Whitehead's philosophy of science what were to be the main themes of his metaphysics. In the first place, there is his emphasis upon relatedness. 'The so-called properties of things,' he writes, 'can always be expressed as their relatedness to other things unspecified, and natural knowledge is exclusively concerned with relatedness.' Russell had complained that Leibniz reduced relations to qualities; in Whitehead's philosophy, relations have their revenge.

Secondly, a connected point, Whitehead now wholly rejects the view that perception presents us with isolated 'sensations': perception, according to Whitehead, is experience from within nature of the system of events which make up nature – the 'self-knowledge enjoyed by an element of nature respecting its relations with the whole of nature in its various aspects'. Certainly, Whitehead grants, we never experience the whole of nature simultaneously; our experience, nevertheless, is of events which are related to (or 'signify') such a system. It will be observed that Whitehead's epistemology already incorporates a biological theory of perception – the perceiver is a natural organism reacting to the world around him – and this is the germ of Whitehead's 'philosophy of the organism'.

Thirdly – and once more Whitehead is attacking any sort of atomism – our experience is of durations ('events') not of point-instants. On no other view, he maintains, is change intelligible; in change the past flows into the present, as durations can but instants cannot. At the same time, Whitehead is not prepared wholly to relinquish the conception of 'Nature at an instant' – what he calls 'a moment' – because it is, he thinks, essential in scientific analysis. But it is 'the fallacy of misplaced concreteness', he says, to conclude from the fact that science needs instants that instants must be actual ingredients in our experience. Yet Whitehead does not wish to argue, either, that an instant is a 'fiction' or a 'convention'; to speak thus, he thinks, is to cut all connexion between science and experience. By 'the method of extensive abstraction' Whitehead defines instants in terms of experience without actually identifying them within experience; instants are defined as a class of sets of durations with certain special extensive relations one to another.[26]

Fourthly, Whitehead's Platonism is now full-blown. He distinguishes sharply between 'events' and 'objects'. An event is unique; by its nature it can never recur. Events, we might say, are the stuff, the particularity, of Nature. 'Objects', on the other hand, are what we *recognize* in Nature, its permanent features. Neither object nor event can exist in isolation; every event is of a certain character, i.e. an object has 'ingressed' into it, and every object characterizes some event. Nevertheless, according to Whitehead, although we can properly ascribe a specific 'situation' to an object, it is a great mistake to think of it as being 'simply located' in that region. We may say, for example, that a gale is situated in the Atlantic. So it is; but nervous passengers in England cancel their berths; the gale is in England, therefore, as well as in the Atlantic. 'An object is ingredient throughout its neighbourhood,' he writes, 'and its neighbourhood is indefinite.'[27]

Fifthly, and this side of his philosophy was widely influential – particularly as it came to full expression in *Science and the Modern World* – Whitehead attacks what he calls 'the bifurcation of Nature'. This is the Galileo-Locke distinction between a world of immediate experience, containing colours, sounds, scents, and the world of 'scientific entities', colourless, soundless, unscented, which so act upon the mind as to produce in it the illusions in which it delights. For science, Whitehead argued, the red glow of sunset is as much 'part of Nature' as the vibration of molecules; if the scientist dismisses the sunset as a 'psychic addition' he is confessing that he has failed in his task of giving a coherent account of whatever Nature contains. Science must correlate whatever is known without making any reference to the fact that it is known: that is what Whitehead meant when he wrote, in a widely quoted and widely misinterpreted phrase, that 'Nature is closed to Mind'.

In the overtly metaphysical writings which Whitehead wrote in his later years, after his appointment (1924) at the age of sixty-three to the Chair of Philosophy at Harvard, the themes of his 'philosophy of Nature' were both restated and developed. Of all these later writings, *Science and the Modern World* (1925) has been the most widely read, not so much for its metaphysics as for its contributions to the understanding of human culture; *Adventures of Ideas* (1933) shared that popularity, for similar reasons. It is in *Process and Reality* (1929) that Whitehead's metaphysical impulse finds its most complete, if its most baffling, expression.

One naturally compares *Process and Reality* with Alexander's *Space, Time and Deity*, which Whitehead greatly praised: the admiration was mutual. Both writers see in the relation of particular things to space and time the central problem of philosophy, even if their solutions diverge. Further and more important still, they make use of the same philosophical method – what we might disrespectfully describe as the 'I'm telling you' method. Neither argues, in any ordinary sense of that word. A metaphysics, Whitehead wrote in *Religion in the Making* (1926), is a description: the metaphysician discerns in some special field of interest what he suspects to be the general characters of reality; he sets these up tentatively as categories; then he seeks to discover whether they are in fact general by considering whether they are exemplified in other areas of human interest. It is impossible to deduce experience from general principles – to suppose otherwise is, he thinks, the fatal error of metaphysicians; but we can hope to describe the most general features of experience. *Process and Reality* attempts such a description.

The starting-point, for Whitehead, is the theory of perception. Whereas in his natural philosophy his approach is 'homogeneous', i.e. makes no reference to the human activity of perceiving or thinking, his metaphysics is 'heterogeneous', i.e. he is analysing our *thinking* about Nature. 'The philosophy of organism,' he writes, 'accepts the subjectivist basis of modern philosophy ... the whole universe consists of elements disclosed in the experience of subjects.' Thus he deliberately links his metaphysics with the Idealist tradition; his object, he says, is 'the transformation of some of the main doctrines of Absolute Idealism on to a realist basis'. He stands closer, however, to the synoptic tendencies of Bosanquet and Haldane than he does to Bradley, for all that he confesses his indebtedness to Bradley's theory of 'feeling'; he accepts Haldane's principle that 'we ought to be prepared to believe in the different aspects of the world as it appears'. The crucial point of coincidence between Whitehead's philosophy and Absolute Idealism – and nothing could mark more definitely Whitehead's complete break with all that Russell stood for – lies in his acceptance of the principle that 'every proposition refers to a universe exhibiting some general metaphysical character ... and must, in its complete analysis, propose the general character of the universe required for that fact'. This conclusion is the natural outcome of the doctrine that all a thing's properties are reducible to its relations with a system.

The biological tone of Whitehead's philosophy,[28] however is certainly not in the Idealist tradition; at this point, perhaps, Whitehead was influenced by American pragmatism. Having first analysed perception in biological terms as the grasping – 'prehension' – of part of its environment by an organism, he detects this same 'prehension' in the relations between things in general, organisms or not: the universe, as he describes it, is composed of 'unities of existence' built into unities ('feelings') by prehensions. Philosophers have been misled, Whitehead suggests, because they have supposed that sight is the typical mode of relationship; Whitehead exhorts them to reflect upon their visceral sensations. Then they will come to see, he thinks, that appropriation and resistance – not 'the having of a blue sense-datum' – are the characteristic features not only of perception but of all the relationships which together make up the universe.

CHAPTER 15

Some Cambridge Philosophers;
and Wittgenstein's Tractatus

THE fruitfulness of the Cambridge Moral Science Faculty during the first decades of the present century has already been abundantly illustrated. A university which can lay claim to Moore and Russell, McTaggart and Whitehead, Ward and Stout, need fear no accusations either of sterility or of narrowness. Yet our tale is still incomplete. Other Cambridge-bred philosophers added to the University's philosophical fame; and it gave hospitality, first as an advanced student, later as a Professor, to the most remarkable – many would say the greatest – philosopher of our century, the Austrian Ludwig Wittgenstein.

Of W. E. Johnson, one of the more notable of the home-grown products, we have already spoken briefly (Chapter 6). His articles on 'The Logical Calculus' (1892) anticipated the tone, and in part the detail, of much that was later to be written in Cambridge. In the years that followed he exercised great influence as a teacher, but published nothing. Not until the nineteen-twenties did he publish his major work, with the simple title *Logic*.[1] Even then, the force of character of one of his students, rather than any impulse of his own, brought him to the point of publication. His *Logic*, indeed, is a series of manuscripts collected together to make a book – not a composition ruled by some governing idea. Its value lies in its detail; all that can now be attempted, however, is a characterization of the most general sort.

Although Johnson was trained as a mathematician, his *Logic* is essentially philosophical, not mathematical, in character. Sympathetically inclined to the logistic programme of deducing mathematics from logic, he yet does not participate in it; except for a detailed and somewhat severe criticism of Russell's theory of propositional functions, indeed, he scarcely refers to the work of logicians junior to J. N. Keynes – whose renovated traditional logic he absorbed into his own work.

He begins, we have already pointed out, from the proposition. At the same time, his break from Idealist logic is not a wholly

343

sharp one; the proposition, he writes, 'is only a factor in the concrete act of judgement'. In spite of Johnson's emphasis on the importance of clear distinctions, his various accounts of the relation between judgement and proposition are impossible to bring into consistency; this fact, touching the very heart of his *Logic*, does much to explain why that book does not leave a single impression on his readers. Unlike the Idealists, he concedes a certain autonomy to formal logic, considered as a theory of propositions; at the same time, this autonomy is so hedged with reservations that formal logic is little more than a puppet-kingdom, the real power lying in the hands of epistemology.

Johnson's *Logic*, in consequence, ventures into unexpected fields; it contains, for example, an elaborate analysis of the mind-body relationship. Logic, he argues, as 'an analysis and criticism of thought' cannot ignore probability and induction; any adequate discussion of induction must explore the conceptions of cause and substance; such an exploration, if it is at all serious, must take account of, and resolve, the special problems set by the mind-body relationship. Johnson, in short, follows his argument wherever it leads him; his *Logic* is a contribution to general philosophy, not only to logic in the narrower sense of the word. But it manifests to a notable degree what one thinks of as 'Cambridge' characteristics; his philosophical discussions are clear, analytic, discriminating, but rarely decisive.

At a few points, however, Johnson has been widely influential. His neologisms, as rarely happens, have won wide acceptance: such phrases as 'ostensive definition', such contrasts as those between 'epistemic' and 'constitutive', 'determinates' and 'determinables', 'continuants' and 'occurrents', are now familiar in philosophical literature. Nor does this mean, only, that Johnson was a clever coiner of words; he demonstrated the usefulness of his innovations in sharpening and reshaping philosophical controversies.

He sets out to show, for example, that there is not one process of definition, or one process of induction, but many; if he then gives a name to these newly-discovered species, this is not for merely decorative purposes. Or again he rebukes logicians for carelessness in discriminating logical forms. In particular, he thinks, they have wrongly grouped together, as being of the same type, such propositions as 'Red is a colour' and 'Plato is a man'; in order to make the distinction they have overlooked he introduces his contrast between 'determinates' and 'determinables'. Whereas 'Plato is a man', so he argues, asserts class-membership, 'Red is a colour' relates, not a member to a class, but a 'determinate' to a 'determinable'. Red, green, yellow are all determinates of the determinable *colour*, just as square, circular, elliptical, are all determinates of the determinable *shape*. What unites a set of determinates is not that – like the members of a class – they agree in some respect, but rather, Johnson suggests, that they differ in a peculiar manner. Determinates of the same determinable 'exclude' one another, in the special sense that they cannot simultaneously characterize the same area; the one area can be both red and circular, but cannot be both red and green. Furthermore, he argues, their differences are 'comparable', as differences between determinates of different determinables are not. One can sensibly assert, he means, that the difference between red and green is greater than the difference between red and orange, but not that it is greater than, less than, or equal to, the difference between red and circular.

Johnson's talents, it will be obvious, lay particularly in his capacity for making careful distinctions. Recalling also his mathematical powers, one is not surprised to find that he was attracted towards the theory of probability where, if anywhere, careful analysis of problems on the borderland between mathematics, formal logic, and epistemology can reap a rich harvest. His writings on probability, however, are fragmentary and not altogether coherent; they were not published until eleven years after another Cambridge man, J. M. Keynes,[2] had completed *A Treatise on Probability* (1921) which in part incorporated Johnson's teachings, in part went beyond them in ways which Johnson did not quite know how to estimate.

Keynes' indebtedness to Johnson – whom he knew first as a close friend of his father, J. N. Keynes, later as a teacher, and then as a colleague – is sometimes supposed to consist merely in the fact that Keynes took over certain of Johnson's theorems. In fact, however, the spirit of the philosophical parts of the *Treatise* is certainly Johnson's.[3] In his introduction Keynes coupled Johnson's name with those of Moore and Russell, as philosophers who 'are united in a preference for what is matter of fact, and have conceived their subject as a branch rather of science than of creative imagination, prose writers, hoping to be understood'. Moore had said in his *Principia Ethica* that good is indefinable: Keynes was emboldened to say the same of probability. Russell had deduced arithmetic from logic; Keynes set out to do the same for probability theory. But the peculiarly epistemologico-logical atmosphere of the *Treatise* may fairly be regarded as deriving from Johnson.

In Johnson's manner, Keynes begins from the proposition, not, as Venn had done, from a 'happening' or an 'event'. On Venn's version of the 'frequency' theory, the statement 'the next ball from the urn will probably be black' is an assertion about the percentage of draws from the urn in which a black ball appears; for Keynes, on the other hand, the problem is to ascribe a probability to the proposition 'the next ball will be black'. Unless probability theory is prepared to surrender all claims to be useful in everyday determinations of probability, Keynes argues, it must extend its interest into areas where the frequency theory, which looks plausible enough in the case of ball-drawing, would be obviously inapplicable.

To assign a degree of probability to a proposition, on Keynes' theory, is to relate it to a body of knowledge. Probability is not a property of the proposition-in-itself; it expresses the degree to which it would be rational, on the evidence at our disposal, to regard the proposition as true. Thus probability is always relative; it is nevertheless 'objective', in the sense that a proposition *has* a certain probability relative to the evidence, whether or not we recognize that probability. What precisely, we may ask, is this relation of 'making probable' which holds between evidence and conclusion? A unique logical relation, Keynes answers, not reducible to any other; we apprehend it intuitively, as we apprehend implication.

Unlike implication, however, the probability relation admits of degrees. On given evidence, one conclusion may be 'more probable' than another. Recognizing this fact, some probability-theorists have jumped to the conclusion that probabilities must always be quantitatively comparable. Once again, Keynes thinks, they have generalized from a quite untypical case – the case where, as in drawing balls from an urn which contains none but black or white balls, the alternatives are exclusive, equiprobable and exhaustive. Then, no doubt, probability can be numerically estimated; but if we look at the matter more broadly, Keynes thinks, we soon see that even comparisons of order, let alone precise quantitative formulations, are often completely out of the question. Consider the relation between sets of experiments and a generalization: suppose that in *Case A* the experiments are more numerous, in *Case B* more varied, and in *Case C* the generalization is wider in scope. In terms of what units, Keynes asks, are we to compare the probabilities of the generalization in relation to these different sets of evidence?

On Keynes' theory of probability, there is a close connexion between probability and induction. To say that a proposition has been arrived at by a 'justifiable induction' is, he thinks, identical with saying that it is 'highly probable'. The classical problem – how is induction to be justified? – thus turns into another: when are we entitled to assert that a generalization is highly probable? Keynes tries to show that any such conclusion depends upon a general postulate, which he calls the Principle of Limited Variety – a revised version of Mill's 'Uniformity of Nature'. 'We can justify the method of perfect analogy,' he writes, 'and other inductive methods so far as they can be made to approximate to this, by means of the assumption that the objects in the field, over which our generalizations extend, do not have an infinite number of independent qualities; that, in other words, their characteristics, however numerous, cohere together in groups in invariable connexions, which are finite in number.'

In other words, induction is justified because the qualities of things carry other qualities with them. Whether this principle is more effective than Mill's in 'saving induction', Keynes' successors gravely doubted.

Of other Cambridge philosophers who took a lively interest in the processes of scientific thinking one of the best known is that modest but voluminous writer, C. D. Broad.[4] Broad, in his *Scientific Thought* (1923), estimates his talents thus: 'If I have any kind of philosophical merit, it is neither the constructive fertility of an Alexander, nor the penetrating critical acumen of a Moore; still less is it that extraordinary combination of both with technical mathematical skill which characterizes Whitehead and Russell. I can at most claim the humbler (yet useful) power of stating difficult things clearly and not too superficially.' To this can be added what Russell wrote in his review of Broad's *Perception, Physics and Reality* (1914); 'This book does not advance any fundamental novelties of its own, but it appraises, with extraordinary justice and impartiality and discrimination, the arguments which have been advanced by others on the topics with which it deals.' What more is there to say? One cannot describe 'Broad's philosophy' for, as he freely admits, 'there is nothing which answers to that description.' To summarize his clear and meticulous summaries would be to gild the lily. We shall content ourselves, therefore, with an outline of his views about the nature of philosophy, partly to correct a not uncommon misapprehension, partly because this is the easiest way to place him in the context of Cambridge philosophy.

Broad[5] distinguishes between 'critical' and 'speculative' philosophy. Critical philosophy is philosophy in what he takes to be the Moore–Russell manner; its object, according to Broad, is to 'analyse' the basic concepts of science and of everyday life – concepts like *cause, quality, position* – and to submit to cross-examination the general propositions which the scientist and the ordinary man daily presume, such propositions as 'every event has a cause' or 'Nature is uniform'. Most of Broad's work, then, is analytic in its intention; although, often enough, it is analytic at second remove. It does not so much analyse 'the conception of a material thing' as describe the views which have been, or might be, held about its correct analysis. The final chapter in *Mind and its Place in Nature* (1925), in which Broad distinguishes seventeen possible theories of the mind-matter relation, is the finest flower – or should one say the *reductio ad absurdum*? – of this method.

Yet Broad is not, as some have thought, an enemy of speculation. 'If we do not look at the world synoptically,' he writes, 'we shall have a very narrow view of it'; a purely critical philosophy, he thinks, is arid and rigid. He praises Idealism, because it at least attempts to incorporate within a single theory the findings of art, of science, of religion, of social theory. It is certain types of speculative philosophy, only, which Broad attacks.

Thus, in the first place, those for whom philosophy is by its nature suggestive, metaphorical, poetic, are not likely to regard Broad with sympathetic affection. 'What can be said at all,' he writes, 'can be said simply and clearly in any civilized language or in a suitable system of symbols.' Secondly, he will not allow that speculative philosophy can ever aspire to the heights of strict demonstration. By its nature, he thinks, it must be tentative, fluid, ready to adjust itself to new findings in science, new paths in art, new experiments in social life. It cannot determine *a priori* what is the case; its materials come to it from outside.

Then, thirdly, a sound speculative philosophy must always rest, Broad thinks, upon a foundation of critical philosophy; the speculative philosopher who is content to take over uncriticized whatever anyone cares to affirm is at the mercy of fantasies. Broad's own work is meant as a propaedeutic to, not as a sub-stitute for, speculative philosophy – and to a certain degree it is itself speculative. *Scientific Thought* is an attempt to clarify some of the concepts used in the natural sciences; at the same time it might be described as an attempt to combine into a single theory whatever is viable in physics, in epistemology, and in common-sense. *Mind and its Place in Nature* undertakes an analysis of psychological concepts; yet in so far as it attempts to 'place' mind within Nature, it passes beyond criticism to speculation. (Broad defends a species of 'emergent materialism'.) Indeed, we begin to wonder whether the distinction between analysis and speculation can be as sharp as Broad at first suggests.

Many of Broad's readers were shocked because, in *Mind and its Place in Nature*, he took seriously and discussed in detail the findings of psychical research; this, they felt, is not the sort of conduct to be expected from a Cambridge philosopher. Broad's defence in his essay on 'Psychical Research and Philosophy'[6] throws considerable light on his approach to philosophy.

First of all, he condemns unsparingly those for whom 'philos-ophy consists in accepting without question, and then attempting to analyse, the beliefs that are common to contemporary plain men in Europe and North America, i.e. roughly, the beliefs which such persons imbibe uncritically in their nurseries and have never found any reason to doubt'. As he wrote elsewhere, 'it is now abundantly evident that little can be done for commonsense'.

349

Analysis thus understood is, he thought, 'a trivial academic exercise'. In this respect, he stands close to Russell, and at the remotest pole from Moore. His starting-point is science, rather than commonsense; if there is a conflict, commonsense must give way. He seeks to imitate, all the same, Moore's meticulousness rather than Russell's audacity. Once he lamented thus: 'si Moore savait, si Russell pouvait'; this may be read as nominating his ideal – Russell's knowledge conjoined with Moore's analytic powers.

Commonsense, then, has no rights against the findings of psychical research; nor can an *a priori* metaphysics rule out ghosts, if only for the very good reason that there is no such metaphysics. Psychical research, he concludes, must be left to speak for itself, subject of course to the control of critical philosophy. This is Broad's characteristic attitude.

Of all metaphysicians, Broad most admires McTaggart, for all that McTaggart attempted the impossible, the construction of a deductive metaphysics. Broad devoted several years of his life to the writing of his vast three-volumed *Examination of McTaggart's Philosophy* (1933–8), a book which as well as commentary contains many striking examples of Broad's own philosophical work. Two things delighted Broad in McTaggart: his coolness and his clarity. No metaphysician has been less dithyrambic, none has made so desperate an effort to be clear. For once, Broad remarks, 'definite premises are stated in plain language and definite conclusions are drawn from them by arguments we can all follow and accept or reject'. That Broad considered McTaggart to be worthy of so extensive an examination is further evidence at once of his sympathy with speculation and of the special character of that sympathy.

'I shall watch with a fatherly eye,' Broad wrote in the Preface to *The Mind and its Place in Nature*, 'the philosophical gambols of my younger friends as they dance to the highly syncopated pipings of Herr Wittgenstein's flute.' That was in 1925, and Wittgenstein's *Tractatus Logico-Philosophicus* had first appeared in English[7] three years previously (the German version was published in 1921). Broad's comment, then, bears witness to the immediate impact of the *Tractatus* upon certain of the younger philosophers at Cambridge, for all that it was by no means widely read in England until the late nineteen-thirties, and was not until the nineteen-sixties made the subject of detailed criticism and commentary.

It is a book, indeed, which one sets out to describe with more than ordinary diffidence.[8] Partly this is a consequence of the enthusiasm Wittgenstein inspired in his pupils. If there is now nobody, if indeed there never has been anybody, who would subscribe to all the leading doctrines of the *Tractatus* – Wittgenstein, as we shall see later, came to criticize it severely – there is still in many quarters a reluctance to believe that Wittgenstein could have been mistaken in ways that were not somehow wiser, more penetrating, than the mistakes of his contemporaries. Again, delicate questions of discipleship are involved: the question, 'What did Wittgenstein mean?' is closely linked with another, 'Who can truly claim to be carrying on his work?' On the other side, there are still those who would dismiss Wittgenstein as a charlatan. It will be apparent that no account of the *Tractatus* is likely to win universal acceptance.

Apart from these extrinsic difficulties, which the chronicler must learn to regard with relative equanimity as the perils incident to his profession, the *Tractatus* itself is sufficiently intimidating. It discusses questions of a peculiarly intricate kind – meaning, the nature of logic, facts and propositions, the task of philosophy – in a manner which disconcertingly combines the Romantic, not to say apocalyptic, and the precisely formal.

The preface at once displays these two streaks. The opening sentence – 'this book will perhaps only be understood by those who have themselves already thought the thoughts which are expressed in it, or similar thoughts' – is in the best tradition of Romanticism, in so far as it suggests that only a chosen few, sympathetic souls, will *really* understand. Yet Wittgenstein goes on to tell us that the 'whole meaning' of the *Tractatus* can be summed up as follows: 'what can be said at all can be said clearly; and whereof one cannot speak thereof one must be silent.' Here at once the central paradox of the *Tractatus* leaps to the eye; it tells us what, it says, cannot be said, and tells us obscurely, in metaphor and epigram, that what can be said at all can be said clearly. The very form of the *Tractatus* reflects this paradox. Each paragraph is numbered in accordance with an elaborate system, as if now at last we were dealing with a philosopher who would aid our comprehension in every possible way. Yet the paragraphs thus numbered are composed in a style so enigmatic, with sentence-links so tenuous, that scarcely one of them does not raise serious problems of interpretation.

An elucidation of the *Tractatus*, then – even supposing that I felt competent to undertake it – would need to be lengthy and minute. All that I can hope to do, within limits at all reasonable, is to select for slight consideration those points at which the *Tractatus* has, so far, been mainly influential.

Something should first be said about the intellectual background of the *Tractatus*. Wittgenstein was trained as an engineer, not as a philosopher, so that one cannot presume in him an ordinary acquaintance with academic philosophy. Like many another amateur, he was interested in Schopenhauer; if there is sometimes a Kantian flavour in his work, that is perhaps the explanation. He knew something of Mach and Hertz, and perhaps he had dipped into, or heard somebody discuss, Meinong and Husserl. All one can say with confidence is that in writing the *Tractatus* Wittgenstein was taking as a point of departure some of the things he had read in the works of, or picked up in discussion with, Frege and Russell. Quite what he owed to, and quite what he contributed to, Russell's 'philosophy of logical atomism' it is difficult to say. He nowhere refers to any of his predecessors except in an elusive and off-hand fashion; what he says even about Frege and Russell is sometimes very puzzling. In short, this is not a case in which the detailed pursuit of influences is likely to prove at all rewarding.

Now for the *Tractatus* itself. It begins with a series of staccato pronouncements: 'The world is everything that is the case. The world is the totality of facts, not of things . . .' Yet this, it is fairly clear, is not the real beginning. Wittgenstein has ordered the paragraphs of the *Tractatus* in what he judges to be the most artistic, the most striking, sequence; if we hope to understand *why* he says what he does, we have to move backwards and forwards through their serried array. His real starting-point is a theory of meaning, not a directly-intuited ontology.

Wittgenstein's crucial assumption is that every proposition has a clear and definite sense; and conjoined with that, the assumption that this sense lies in the proposition's relation to the 'world'. Now the propositions of everyday life contain complex expressions, expressions which are certainly not what Russell called 'logically proper names'. Such complex expressions can always be replaced by descriptions. If, for example, somebody asks us what it means to say that 'all millionaires are stubborn', we can answer by substituting descriptions for 'millionaires' and 'stubborn', by saying, for example, 'all persons who possess more than a million pounds are difficult to persuade'. But by offering this sort of elucidation, we have still not made the sense perfectly 'clear and definite' in Wittgenstein's sense of that phrase; we could sensibly be asked to substitute further descriptions for the complex expressions in our new assertion. To arrive at a determinate sense for the proposition – to give the 'one and only complete analysis of the proposition' – we must, according to Wittgenstein, define the complex sign by means of (logically proper) names. 'It is obvious,' he writes, 'that in the analysis of propositions we must come to elementary propositions, which consist of names in immediate combination.' At that point we can no longer ask that the sense be made clearer to us; a name cannot be defined. Nor do we *need* to make this request, for a proposition containing no expressions except names points immediately to the world – its sense is given directly to us as the combination of simple entities to which it refers.

There must be simple entities, then – what Wittgenstein called 'objects'[9] – because there are names; and there must be names because propositions have a definite sense. Wittgenstein was not interested in nominating examples of simples. The point, for him, is that there *must be* simples; *what* they are is a matter of secondary importance. 'Even if the world is infinitely complex,' he writes, 'so that every fact consists of an infinite number of atomic facts and every atomic fact is composed of an infinite number of objects, even then there must be objects and atomic facts.' This is much more in the spirit of Leibniz than of Hume.

Names, Wittgenstein argues, have no sense except in the context of a proposition; correspondingly, we cannot think of an object except as having various possible connexions with other objects; such possible connexions between objects are 'atomic facts'. This sounds very strange – to call *possible* connexions 'facts'. We ordinarily think of a fact as actual, by its very nature.

Yet it is difficult to find any other translation for the German 'Sachverhalt'. The strangeness diminishes slightly if we think of an atomic fact as 'that which makes a proposition true or false'. A proposition is true if certain atomic facts 'exist', false if they 'do not exist': the atomic facts must, then, be of such a kind that the question whether they 'exist' or 'do not exist' ('obtain' or 'do not obtain') can always be raised. Atomic facts are realized possibilities if the proposition which pictures them is true, un-realized possibilities if it is false, but their 'existence' as possi-bilities is unaffected by the question whether they are realized or not, by the question, that is, whether they are 'facts' in the harder sense of that word. In studying logic, according to Wittgenstein, we are not really interested in the hardness of facts: 'all possibili-ties are its facts.' This is inevitably so, he thinks, because false propositions – propositions which assert possibilities which are not realized – are as much part of the field dealt with by logic, as much capable of being asserted and denied, of implying or not implying, as true propositions.

How exactly are propositions related to facts? Wittgenstein's answer is that they are 'pictures' of the fact. Various anecdotes are told about the circumstances in which this view first occurred to him, anecdotes which agree in one respect: he was impressed by a model which had been constructed to illustrate some cal-amity, let us say a motor accident. 'There,' he thought as he looked at the miniature cars, the miniature road, the miniature hedges, 'is a proposition.'

The problem, as Wittgenstein saw it, was to give an account of the proposition which will allow, first, that we are free to con-struct false propositions as well as true ones, and secondly, that the point of a proposition lies in its relation to the world. The 'picture' analogy seemed to be satisfactory in both respects. Obviously, by means of miniature motor-cars we can give a false picture of what actually happened; obviously again, the point of our manipulations with the motor-cars is to 'convey something about the world'.

The motor-cars, of course, are not in themselves a proposition; we could use them in a game as well as to picture an accident. Only when they are arranged in a certain way do they convey what has happened. Thus arranged, according to Wittgenstein, they are a 'propositional sign'; the 'proposition' is such a sign 'projected on the world', i.e. used to affirm or deny that something is the case. But what about the case – the normal case – where the propositional sign consists of words? Wittgenstein admits that such a proposition is not, superficially, the sort of thing we should ordinarily describe as a 'picture'. Even although, however, our ordinary language is no longer hieroglyphic, it has kept, he thinks, what is essential in hieroglyphic writing. It retains its power of conveying to us what it represents, even although we have never actually observed what is thus conveyed – and indeed in that case where the proposition is false, we could not possibly have observed what it conveys. This power of conveying depends, he maintains, on the fact that the proposition has precisely the same structure as what it represents. 'One name stands for one thing,' he writes, 'and another for another thing, and they are connected together; in this way, the whole, like a *tableau vivant*, presents the atomic fact ... in the proposition there must be as many things distinguishable as there are in the state of affairs which it represents.'[10]

One objection which naturally occurs to us is that this theory could apply, at most, to elementary propositions. Ordinary propositions do not picture atomic facts: they contain such expressions as 'all', 'some', 'or', 'not', none of which can have any analogue in an atomic fact. For in calling such facts 'atomic' what Wittgenstein means above all is that they are logically independent; from the 'existence' of an atomic fact, nothing whatever follows about the 'existence' or the 'non-existence' of any other atomic fact. Thus there can be no negative atomic facts – let alone universal atomic facts – since the 'existence' of *X is not Y* is not logically independent of the 'non-existence' of *X is Y*.

'My fundamental thought,' Wittgenstein therefore wrote, 'is that the "logical constants" do not represent.' Although they occur within propositions, he means, logical constants are not one of the elements in the picture. He discusses in considerable detail the crucial case of 'not'. It is obvious, he thinks, that 'not' is not the name of a relation, in the sense that 'right' and 'left' name relations. Indeed, 'not' cannot be a name at all; if it were, 'not-not-*p*' would be a quite different assertion from '*p*', as naming two *nots* which '*p*' does not mention. Then – a conclusion he regards as ridiculous – from the single fact that *p*, an infinite number of other facts could be made to follow, by the process of adding double-negations. 'Not', then, is no name; it does not refer to an object. What it does is to indicate – and the same is true of all the other logical constants – that an operation has been performed upon '*p*', in this case the operation of denial.

As a result of his consideration of the role played by 'logical constants' in propositions, Wittgenstein is led to conclude that every non-elementary proposition is a 'truth-function' of elementary propositions. In his paper* 'Some Remarks on Logical Form' (*PASS*, 1929) he puts the matter thus: 'If we try to analyse any given propositions we shall find in general that they are logical sums, products or other truth-functions of simpler propositions. But our analysis, if carried far enough, must come to the point where it reaches propositional forms which are not themselves composed of simpler propositional forms. We must eventually reach the ultimate connexion of the terms, the immediate connexion which cannot be broken without destroying the propositional form as such. The propositions which represent this ultimate connexion I call, after Russell, atomic propositions. They, then, are the kernels of every proposition, *they* contain the material, and all the rest is only a development of this material.'

Suppose we consider the proposition *p or q*. Then the word 'or' does not represent 'an ultimate connexion'; as comes out in the fact that the sense of *p or q* can be wholly given by referring to its 'truth-grounds', in which 'or' plays no part. It will be true if *p* and *q* are both true, true if *p* is true and *q* is false, true if *p* is false and *q* is true, false if *p* is false and *q* is false. Set out these results in a diagram – a 'truth-table' – and the result is a propositional sign which clearly pictures the sense of *p or q*.[11] Every non-elementary proposition can be analysed by this method, according to Wittgenstein, even when – although this presents special difficulties – it contains the universal quantifier 'all'. This result can be alternatively expressed by saying that all propositions

---

*Wittgenstein was so dissatisfied with this paper, his only publication after the *Tractatus*, that he refused either to read or discuss it when the time came for its delivery. But I do not think he was then dissatisfied with the passage I have quoted.

have the same general form: that of a selection out of the range of atomic facts, a selection made by negating certain combinations.

There are two extreme cases in such a selection: the case where no combination whatever is ruled out, and the case where every combination is ruled out. Thus suppose we substitute *not-p* for the *q* in *p or q*, then the resulting expression *p or not-p* is true for all possibilities: the only possibility ruled out by *p or q* is the case where *p* and *q* are both false, and this case cannot occur when *q* is replaced by *not-p*. An expression such as *p or not-p* Wittgenstein calls a 'tautology'; *p and not-p*, which allows no possibilities, he calls a 'contradiction'. Tautologies and contradictions are 'without sense' because they do not picture the world. 'I know nothing about the weather,' Wittgenstein writes, 'when I know that it is either raining or not raining.' Yet they are not useless; they form 'part of the symbolism'.

All the truths of logic, indeed, are classed by Wittgenstein with 'tautologies'. This follows directly from the truth-functional analysis. Take, for example, the logical truth that *p or q* together with *not-p* implies *q*. Set out the truth-grounds for *p or q* and the truth-grounds for *not-p* and we shall be able to read off immediately that *p or q* and *not-p* cannot both be true except in the case where *q* is true. This fact can be alternatively expressed, on Wittgenstein's theory of 'sense', by saying that the sense of *q* is included in the sense of *(p or q) and not-p*. In an adequate symbolism – in an ideal language – this, according to Wittgenstein, would be immediately obvious. We are not, then, saying something about the world when we assert that *p or q* and *not-p* together imply *q*; in making this assertion we are not excluding some genuine possibility. All we are doing, according to Wittgenstein, is drawing attention to a feature of our symbolism, something the symbolism itself should show. 'It is a characteristic mark of logical propositions,' he writes, 'that we can perceive in the symbol itself that they are true.'

If logic consists wholly of tautologies, we might ask, why do we find it necessary to construct proofs of the propositions of logic? A 'proof', Wittgenstein answers, is nothing but a mechanical expedient for recognizing tautologies more rapidly; the view that there are 'primitive propositions' of logic from which all the other propositions of logic ought to be deduced is a delusion. All the propositions of logic, he argues, stand on exactly the same footing; they all say the same thing, i.e. nothing at all.

What of mathematics? That consists, Wittgenstein argues, of equations; from which it follows directly that the propositions of mathematics, too, are without sense. For it is always nonsense, he maintains, to say of two distinct things that they are identical; and to say of one thing that it is identical with itself is to say nothing. Mathematics says, what in its symbolism we can see, that certain expressions can be substituted for one another; that this can be done *shows* us something about the world but does not *picture* the world. Thus the propositions of mathematics are 'senseless'.

Senseless, but not nonsensical; on the other hand, Wittgenstein argues, the metaphysician talks nonsense, in the fullest sense of the word. There is no novelty in this accusation: as we have already seen, it formed part of the regular stock-in-trade of nineteenth-century positivism, to trace it no further back. What was novel, however, was the accusation that metaphysics arises out of the fact that philosophers do not understand 'the logic of our language'.

In the most obvious case, the philosopher is misled, according to Wittgenstein, by the fact that the grammatical form of our propositions does not always reflect their logical form. Merely because 'millionaires are non-existent' resembles in grammatical form 'millionaires are non-cooperative', the philosopher is led to suppose that 'non-existent' is a quality, and is then well embarked upon a metaphysical inquiry into 'the nature of non-existence'. In a perfect language, one in which every sign immediately indicated its logical function, such misunderstandings, Wittgenstein thinks, would vanish; what we now write as 'millionaires are non-existent' would be so expressed that 'non-existent' would no longer look like a predicate. Such a language, we might say, would make logic unnecessary and metaphysics impossible.

In other instances, Wittgenstein thinks, metaphysics arises out of the attempt to pass beyond the boundaries of language – by talking, as we have been doing, about the relations between language and the world. No proposition, Wittgenstein maintains, can represent what it has in common with the world – that form in virtue of which it is an accurate picture. To do this, it would have to include within itself a portion of the world in a non-pictured form – so as to be able to make the comparison between the world and the picture. But this, according to Wittgenstein, is impossible; to talk about the world is at once to picture it. To suppose otherwise is to imagine that we can somehow say what lies beyond language, i.e. beyond anything that can be said.

What, then, *can* the philosopher say? Wittgenstein's answer is uncompromising – 'nothing at all!' 'The right method of philosophy,' he tells us, 'would be this: to say nothing except what can be said, i.e. the propositions of natural science, i.e. something that has nothing to do with philosophy: and then, always, when someone else wishes to say something metaphysical, to demonstrate to him that he had given no meaning to certain signs in his propositions.' Philosophy, on this view, is not a theory but an activity: the activity of making clear to people what they can, and what they cannot, say.

By way of reply, we might be tempted to assert that there are at least *some* non-metaphysical, sensible, philosophical assertions, namely those which arise out of the analysis of scientific method. This Wittgenstein denies. Such propositions, he says, are either propositions about the psychology of human beings or else turn out, on analysis, to be propositions of logic, propositions which 'belong to the symbolism'. Of the first type, the most important example is 'the so-called law of induction'. Induction, as defined by Wittgenstein, is 'the process of assuming the *simplest* law that can be made to harmonize with our experience'; and, he argues, 'there are no grounds for believing that the simplest course of events will really happen'. It is 'only a hypothesis,' he says, that the sun will rise tomorrow; we do not know that it will rise. We should only *know* it will rise if this were a *logically necessary* consequence of our experience; there is no sort of necessity, he presumes, except logical necessity, no sort of inference except 'logical' (i.e. tautological) inference. 'In no way,' he writes, 'can an inference be made from the existence of one state of affairs to the existence of another entirely different from it . . . superstition is the belief in the causal nexus.' It follows that 'the law of induction' is certainly not a proposition of logic; on Wittgenstein's view it says merely – and so it is a proposition of psychology, not of philosophy – that human beings ordinarily prefer simpler to more complex explanations.

As for the law of causality, that, according to Wittgenstein, is a proposition of logic in disguise – an attempt to say what can only be shown in our symbolism, that 'there are natural laws'. We do not discover that there are uniformities, he argues, by inspecting the world around us; these uniformities already show themselves in our talk about the world, in the mere fact, indeed, that we are able to think. Similarly, what Hertz picked out as the *a priori* laws of mechanics are simply descriptions of our symbolism, descriptions which our symbolism itself ought to 'show'. If we think of science as an attempt to describe the world by means of a fine mesh, *a priori* laws, Wittgenstein says, are not part of the results at which we thus arrive: on the contrary they are the characteristics of the mesh (although it *shows* us something about the world, Wittgenstein thinks, that it can be described in such-and-such laws).[12] So, Wittgenstein argues, his general conclusion remains – all propositions which picture the world belong to the natural sciences, and those which do not picture the world, if they are not nonsense, are tautological. Nowhere is there any room for a peculiar class of philosophical propositions. This was certainly a disconcerting conclusion.

Of those Cambridge men who were immediately influenced by the *Tractatus*, the most remarkable was F. P. Ramsey. Ramsey died at the age of twenty-six, and the few years of his mature life were divided between economics, mathematical logic and philosophy; nor was he one of those who light in early life upon a system to which they are thereafter faithful. Thus he wrote no major work, and the essays and fragments collected for posthumous publication by R. B. Braithwaite as *The Foundations of Mathematics* (1931) represent different stages in the development of a mind rather than varied aspects of a single point of view. They have been none the less influential for that.

In the essay (1925) which gave its title to *The Foundations of Mathematics* Ramsey takes his stand with the logistics of Whitehead and Russell against Hilbert and Brouwer; but at once displays his independence. In opposition to Wittgenstein, he maintains that the propositions of mathematics are tautologies, not equations, and is thus enabled still to uphold the doctrine that mathematics is deducible from logic; at the same time, of course, it was from Wittgenstein that he learnt to think of logic as being composed of tautologies. His general object is to show, with the help of Wittgenstein's truth-functional analysis of general propositions, that it is possible to derive mathematics from a logic which contains no empirical propositions, no propositions like the Axiom of Reducibility or the Axiom of Infinity, and yet which does not collapse into paradox.* In attempting to continue, with aid from the *Tractatus*, the sort of inquiry which Whitehead and Russell had initiated, Ramsey was almost unique amongst British philosophers of the between-wars period. For the most part, philosophers – whose other interests are usually literary, historical, or linguistic, rather than mathematical – when faced with the formidable symbolism of *Principia Mathematica* decided that formal logic was no longer for them; they retreated into the more congenial territory of epistemology.

Ramsey moved in the same direction, partly under the influence, it would seem, of Johnson, partly because he had now read Peirce, partly following in Russell's footsteps. Thus the final conclusion of his 'Facts and Propositions' (1927), although he largely derives his logical apparatus from Wittgenstein, is pragmatic in tendency. One can see this most clearly in his analysis of negation: he agrees with Wittgenstein that *not-not-p* is the same proposition as *p*, and hence that 'not' is not a name, but he is unwilling to leave the matter at this point. The word 'not', he argues, expresses a difference in feeling, the difference between asserting and denying. It will follow that 'disbelieving *p*' is identical with 'believing *not-p*': and this conclusion Ramsey tries to justify in a typically pragmatic manner, by identifying the causes and the consequences of these two apparently different attitudes of mind.

Similarly, in his 'Truth and Probability' (1926) he rejects Wittgenstein's doctrine that we 'have no grounds' for inferences which are not tautological. Induction he describes, after Peirce,

*See, for the details, Ch. 9 above. He later had qualms about the possibility of 'saving' the whole of pure mathematics by a logic which contains no empirical propositions; so much the worse for pure mathematics, he seems to have concluded.

as a 'habit of the human mind', one which cannot, he admits, be justified by any purely formal methods – not even, as Keynes had thought, by the theory of probability – but which it is none the less 'unreasonable' not to adopt. A logic of induction, a 'human logic', will describe, he concludes, the degree of success with which inquirers employ different methods of arriving at the truth. Induction, he thinks, is pragmatically justified; and this is a rational justification, not, as Wittgenstein had argued, a mere matter of psychology.

The same movement towards pragmatism can be discerned in 'General Propositions and Causality' (1929). Ramsey now rejects the view, which he had previously taken over from Wittgenstein, that a general proposition is a conjunction of atomic propositions, although a conjunction with the peculiar property that we cannot, for lack of symbolic power, enumerate its constituents. (On which Ramsey comments: 'But what we can't say we can't say, and we can't whistle it either.') At the same time, he is still convinced that all propositions are truth-functions; the conclusion he draws is that general propositions are not, properly speaking, 'propositions'. We ought not to distinguish them, he argued, into the true and the false, but rather into those which it is 'right' or 'wrong', 'reasonable' or 'unreasonable', to maintain. They are ways of meeting the future: to say that 'all men are mortal', on this view, is to announce that any man we meet we shall regard as mortal. People may try to wean us from this way of regarding men, they may condemn it as unreasonable. But it cannot be proved to be false, Ramsey thinks, just because it makes no definite statement about the properties of objects.

As opposed to Wittgenstein, again, Ramsey considers that philosophy issues in a particular class of propositions – elucidations, classifications, definitions, or, at least, descriptions of the way in which a term *could* be defined. The difficulty for philosophy, he thinks, is that its elucidations involve one another; we cannot, for example, begin our elucidation by presuming that the nature of meaning is completely clear and then go on to use meaning to elucidate space and time, because to clarify the nature of meaning we must already have attained to some understanding of space and of time. The great danger of an elucidatory philosophy, Ramsey says, is scholasticism – 'the essence of which is treating what is vague as if it were precise and trying to put it into an exact logical category'. With that remark, however, we have crossed the border between the older and the newer Cambridge.

For the time being the emphasis was still on clarity. Russell, Moore, Wittgenstein, Broad, Johnson, were all read as making the same point: that philosophy is analysis, clarification. A typical product of the period is the journal *Analysis*, which first appeared in 1933, under the editorship of A. Duncan-Jones, and with the collaboration of L. S. Stebbing, C. A. Mace,[13] and G. Ryle. The object of *Analysis*, so it was laid down, was to publish 'short articles on limited and precisely defined philosophical questions about the elucidation of known facts, instead of long, very general and abstract metaphysical speculations about possible facts or about the world as a whole'. This was clearly a reformulation of Russell's demand for 'piece-meal investigations', as represented in practice rather by Moore's philosophical articles than by Russell's books. When the then editor of *Analysis*, Margaret Macdonald, published a selection of articles from *Analysis* as *Philosophy and Analysis* (1954) she chose her epigraph, however, from the *Tractatus*, not from the work of Moore or of Russell: 'The object of philosophy is the logical clarification of thoughts. ... The result of philosophy is not a number of "philosophical propositions" but to make propositions clear.' Wittgenstein was preaching, it was thought, what Moore had practised: the *Tractatus* was read as a sort of analyst's handbook.

Naturally, however, certain difficulties arose out of this conflation of Russell, Moore and Wittgenstein. What exactly, it was asked, does analysis analyse – a sentence, a proposition, a concept, or a word? More important still, what does it analyse them into? These questions were much discussed;[14] analytic methods, it is fair to say, were more freely employed in the analysis of analysis than in the analysis of anything else.

The variations through which this discussion moved can be illustrated in the work of L. S. Stebbing.[15] Her 'The Method of Analysis in Philosophy' (*PAS*, 1931) begins from a distinction between the 'immediate reference' of a proposition – what we all understand when we hear it uttered – and its 'exact reference', which includes everything which must be the case if the proposition is true. The 'immediate reference' of the proposition 'All

economists are fallible', for example, does not include the fallibility of Keynes; we can understand this proposition without ever
having heard of Keynes. But the fallibility of Keynes forms part
of its 'exact reference', Stebbing says, since if the proposition is
true Keynes must be fallible.

Metaphysical analysis, according to Stebbing, works with two
assumptions; first that we understand quite well, at the level of
immediate reference, quite a variety of propositions, secondly,
that such propositions make 'exact reference' to basic propositions, ultimate sets of elements, the ultimacy of which consists in
the fact that their immediate reference and their exact reference
are identical. Obviously, she has in mind Moore's doctrine that
'we all know quite well' that hens lay eggs, but differ about the
'ultimate analysis' of this proposition; at the same time, her 'set
of elements' is, she says, identical with Wittgenstein's 'combination of elements' or 'atomic facts'. Thus, on her interpretation,
Moore and the *Tractatus* are saying much the same thing: that
philosophical analysis consists in unveiling those basic propositions to which an everyday proposition ultimately refers.

Fairly clearly, however, not all 'analysis' satisfies this definition. In her 'Logical Positivism and Analysis' (*PBA*, 1933)
Stebbing distinguishes, therefore, between four different kinds of
analysis. First, there is the analysis of sentences with the object
of clarifying their logical form, the sort of analysis typified in
Russell's theory of descriptions; secondly, the analysis of a concept, illustrated in Einstein's analysis of simultaneity; thirdly,
the mathematician's 'postulational analysis', the definition of
terms by analytic methods; and then fourthly, the sort of analysis,
now christened 'directional analysis', she had described in 'The
Method of Analysis in Philosophy'. That, she thought, is the
peculiarly philosophical sort of analysis – in opposition, say, to
Ramsey for whom Russell's theory of descriptions was the
'paradigm of philosophy'.

By the time Stebbing came to write her essay on 'Moore's
Influence' for *The Philosophy of G. E. Moore* (1942), she had
begun to feel suspicious of the metaphysics which is presumed by
directional analysis. It now seemed to her that there are no 'basic
facts'; the doctrine of basic facts, she suggests, is a relic of the
days when philosophers thought they had to justify the beliefs

of commonsense by setting them on a solid 'ultimate' foundation. The important sort of analysis, she came to think, is 'same-level' analysis, in which expressions are defined by expressions and concepts are defined by concepts – an analysis which makes no metaphysical assumptions. In thus reacting against 'directional analysis' Stebbing reflects the general tendency of the 'thirties.

The earlier writings of John Wisdom may serve as a second example of the analytic controversy. In his 'Is Analysis a Useful Method in Philosophy?' (*PASS*, 1931), he distinguishes three sorts of analysis: material, formal and philosophical. Russell's theory of descriptions is 'formal' analysis; the ordinary definitions of science are examples of 'material' analysis. Both of these are 'same-level'; philosophical analysis, in contrast, is 'new-level', replacing the less by the more ultimate. He explains, by the use of examples, what he means by 'more ultimate'. 'Individuals', he says, 'are more ultimate than nations. Sense-data and mental states are in their turn more ultimate than individuals.' It turns out, then, that philosophical analysis consists in trying to show how statements about minds can be reduced to statements about mental states, and statements about material objects to statements about sense-data: in short, it is the practice of what a foreign observer has described as 'the favourite English parlour-game' – reductive epistemology. Wisdom wrote an elementary textbook *Problems of Mind and Matter* (1934) in order to illustrate the usefulness of analytic methods; there is very little in it which would read strangely to Broad or even to Stout.

The long series of articles on 'Logical Constructions' (*Mind*, 1931–3) is a different matter: these we might describe as the most whole-hearted of all attempts to set out the logical assumptions implicit in 'philosophical analysis'.[16] In what respects, he asks, is an ordinary proposition an unsatisfactory 'picture'? There is a sense, it is obvious, in which 'England declared war on France' is already a perfectly satisfactory picture: we understand that assertion quite well. The analyst has to show that there is another sense in which such a 'picture' is *not* satisfactory. This Wisdom attempts by a vertigo-inducing alternation of small and capital letters. The ordinary sentence 'shows' in so far as it tells us something, but it does not 'Show' us the ultimate logical structure of what it shows; it points to a 'fact', but not to a 'Fact', not that is, to what is ultimately the case. A similar duplicity is exhibited, he suggests, by all the other words which we would wish to employ in an account of the functioning of propositions. Wisdom's *Logical Construction* articles display an astonishing degree of virtuosity, but their very ingenuity had the effect of persuading philosophers that something had gone wrong somewhere. They mark, indeed, the end of an epoch at Cambridge.

CHAPTER 16

Logical Positivism

IN 1895, Mach was appointed to a newly created professorship in the philosophy of the inductive sciences at the University of Vienna, an appointment which was at once a testimony to the strength of the empirical tradition at Vienna and the means by which that tradition was confirmed and strengthened. In 1922 the same chair was offered to Moritz Schlick, who had already made a name for himself as a philosopher-scientist – in particular as an interpreter of Einstein; around Schlick as nucleus 'the Vienna Circle'[1] rapidly took shape. For the most part, its members were scientists or mathematicians, already anti-metaphysical Machians. Except for Schlick himself they knew little about, and cared less for, the classical philosophers. The novel doctrines espoused by Wittgenstein, as the Circle read them in the *Tractatus* or heard them reported by Schlick and Waismann, were a different matter.[2] He, too, was a scientist, an anti-metaphysician, and was worthy, then, to be heard with respect.

Wittgenstein, so the Circle thought, showed empiricists the way out of what had threatened to be an impasse. How, empiricists had anxiously inquired, could the certainty and the 'ideal' character of mathematics be reconciled with the empiricist doctrine that all intelligible propositions are based upon experience? Not many empiricists had the hardihood to argue, with Mill's *Logic*, that the propositions of mathematics are empirical generalizations.[3] If only they could be interpreted, in Wittgenstein's manner, as identities, all would be well.[4] The empiricist need only amend his original thesis slightly: now he would maintain that every intelligible proposition rests upon experience *unless it is an identity*. Since no metaphysician would be prepared to admit that his propositions 'tell us nothing about the world', such an amendment did not seriously impede the empiricist criticism of metaphysics – which is what really interested the Vienna Circle.

'Metaphysics', for the members of the Circle – 'logical positivists' as they came to be called[5] – is the attempt to demonstrate that there are entities which lie beyond the reach of any possible experience, Kantian 'things-in-themselves'. So they were naturally attracted by 'the principle of verifiability' – the principle that the meaning of a proposition lies in its method of verification. They saw in it a way of eliminating, as meaningless, all references to entities which are not accessible to observation; metaphysics, then, could be dismissed out of hand as nonsense. To argue against metaphysics in detail, they concluded, was a complete waste of time: if one metaphysician says 'Reality is the Absolute' and another that 'Reality is a plurality of spirits' the empiricist need not trouble himself to reply to their arguments. He need only say to them – 'What possible experience could settle the issue between you?' To this question metaphysicians have no answer; and from this it follows, according to the verifiability principle, that their assertions are quite without meaning. It is as senseless, on this view, to say that 'Reality is not the Absolute' as to say 'Reality is the Absolute'; for neither assertion can be verified. Thus metaphysical disputes are wholly pointless.

The principle of verifiability, too, the logical positivists thought they had derived from Wittgenstein's *Tractatus*. Now certainly Wittgenstein there wrote that 'to understand a proposition means to know what is the case, if it is true'. However, it is quite a step from that almost platitudinous dictum to the identification of a proposition's meaning with its method of verification. According to Wittgenstein, the positivists misunderstood remarks he had let drop in conversation. 'I used at one time to say,' he is reported[6] as remarking, 'that, in order to get clear how a certain sentence is used, it was a good idea to ask oneself the question: How would one try to verify such an assertion? But that's just one way of getting clear about the use of a word or sentence. . . . Some people have turned this suggestion about asking for the verification into a dogma – as if I'd been advancing a *theory* about meaning.'

Whatever its origin – and it does little more than formalize the techniques of Mach and Pearson – the verifiability principle soon came to be regarded as the leading tenet of logical positivism. It was first explicitly stated by F. Waismann in his 'Logische Analyse des Wahrscheinlichkeitsbegriffs' (*Erk*, 1930); disputes arose almost immediately about its status, its meaning, and its plausibility.[7]

The points at issue can be summarily set out thus:

(1) The principle of verifiability itself, on the face of it, is neither an empirical generalization nor a tautology. What, then, is its status?

(2) We ordinarily inquire into the meaning of words or sentences. A proposition is what a sentence means, not something that *has* a meaning. On the other hand, it is propositions which we verify, describe as true or false. How, then, can verifiability be identified with meaning?

(3) Propositions may be unverifiable either because we cannot, for the moment, think of any way of verifying them, or because it is physically impossible to verify them, or because any attempt to verify them is ruled out for purely logical reasons. Which of these species of unverifiability carries meaninglessness with it?

(4) 'Verify' is ambiguous: it can mean 'prove the truth of' or 'test the truth of'. Are we to say that a proposition is meaningless unless there is some way of proceeding which, if successful, would *prove* it to be true, or is it demanded only that there should be some way of *testing* its truth? Furthermore, is this method of procedure, in either case, *identical* with the proposition's meaning, or merely a way of showing that it has a meaning?

(5) The principle of verifiability leads towards ultimate verifiers. If a proposition's meaning consists in what verifies it, these 'verifiers' cannot themselves be propositions; or, alternatively, they must be propositions whose meaning somehow lies in themselves. What are they?

The complex history of the logical positivist movement, shaped by the attempt to resolve these issues, can best be illustrated by a study of two leading members of the Circle, Schlick and Carnap, and its principal British exponent, A. J. Ayer. Schlick, as we have already seen, had some acquaintance with the history of philosophy and did not deny that philosophy had its value – but not, he thought, as a branch of knowledge. His fellow-positivists, he argued, quite misunderstood the situation when, following in Russell's footsteps, they set up a 'scientific philosophy', or proposed, even, to replace the word 'philosophy' by 'such colourless and unaesthetic expressions' as 'the logic of science'.[8] They were wrong in thinking that their own work was completely cut off from the philosophical tradition; but wrong, too, in imagining that any sort of science could 'replace' philosophy. Philosophy, Schlick agrees with Wittgenstein, is an activity, not a theory – the activity of seeking for meanings. Since it says nothing, although it helps us to understand more clearly what we wish to say, it is quite different in character from science.

To this position there is an obvious objection: Schlick himself is putting forward philosophical theses – for example, the verifiability theory of meaning. How, then, can he deny that philosophy is a branch of knowledge? Wittgenstein tried to anticipate criticisms of this sort by admitting that the propositions of the *Tractatus*, in so far as they are philosophical, are nonsensical; their nonsensicality, he nevertheless suggested, is of a queer sort, enlightening, in contrast with the dark nonsense of metaphysics. Schlick is not prepared thus to discriminate between different types of nonsense. The verifiability principle, he prefers to suggest, is a 'truism'; it tells us nothing new, it does no more than draw our attention to what we have always known. Thus to call it a 'theory' is a gross misdescription. Not surprisingly, neither his nor Wittgenstein's conclusion satisfied his fellow positivists: a 'truism', they argued, is still a truth; and 'nonsense' cannot enlighten. So they looked for an alternative account of philosophical truths.

On the face of it, too, Schlick's distinction between the pursuit of meaning and the search for truth is an untenable one. To discover a meaning, we naturally object, is to arrive at a true proposition – one in which the correct meaning of a proposition is elucidated. But elucidations, Schlick replies, cannot be expressed as propositions. If someone asks us what 'troglodyte' means, we may no doubt answer ' "troglodyte" means "cave-dweller" '. This, however, is only a preliminary reply, for it still leaves open the question: 'Yes, but what does "cave-dweller" mean?' To give 'the ultimate meaning' of an expression, the elucidation which rules out any further inquiry, Schlick therefore argues, we must pass beyond words altogether: we must directly indicate, by gestures, the properties to which our expressions refer.

It will be observed that although the verifiability principle purports to be a method of discovering the meaning of a *proposi-*

tion, what Schlick here describes is the method of defining a *word*. Schlick still has to show how the meaning of a word is connected with the meaning of a proposition. This he attempts in his 'Facts and Propositions' (*Analysis*, 1935), where he formally defines a proposition thus: 'a series of sounds or other symbols (a "sentence") *together with the logical rules belonging to them*, i.e. certain prescriptions as to how the sentence is to be used.' 'These rules,' he continues, 'culminating in "deictic" definitions, constitute the "meaning" of the proposition.'

But how, we might well ask, can a proposition, thus defined, be *verified*? Neither a symbol nor a rule can be *true*, nor does it improve matters in this respect to take them in conjunction. Furthermore, how can a conjunction of the symbols and the rules 'mean' the rules by themselves?

Perhaps in consequence of such difficulties, Schlick laid it down in 'Meaning and Verification' (*PR*, 1936) that only sentences, not propositions, have a meaning; the rules, he now says, are the meaning of the symbols, not of the symbols plus the rules. Yet this does not prevent him, on the very next page, from reaffirming the verifiability principle in its original, propositional, form. There is, indeed, an unresolved tension in Schlick's philosophy between traditional positivism, for which meaning is verifiability, and the novel ideas – the identification of meaning with use – he had picked up from the later speculations of Wittgenstein.

This duality is clearly revealed in Schlick's discussion of 'unverifiability'. For nineteenth-century positivists, the 'meaningless' is that which science knows no way of testing. This definition led them to condemn as 'meaningless' many propositions present-day scientists accept as scientific truths – propositions, for example, about the chemical structure of the stars. Schlick wishes so to define 'meaningless' that the question whether a proposition has a meaning is independent of the state of scientific knowledge at a given time; a proposition is meaningless, he says, only if it is 'unverifiable in principle'. As an example, he cites 'the child is naked but is wearing a long nightgown', which is meaningless, on Schlick's view, because the rules for using the word 'naked' forbid us to apply it to persons who are wearing a long nightgown. When we come to examine metaphysical assertions, he argues, we see that they are meaningless for precisely this sort of reason:

they 'offend against logical grammar'. Alternatively, as Wittgenstein put the matter in the *Tractatus*, we observe that the metaphysician 'has given no meaning to certain signs in his expression'. In either case his expressions, as not being linked with rules, are 'unverifiable in principle'.

Decisions on verifiability, one would naturally conclude, are to be decided on purely 'logical' grounds, i.e. by reference to the rules governing the use of the symbols which make up the sentence submitted for consideration. Schlick sometimes says as much. 'Verifiability, which is the sufficient and necessary condition of meaning,' he writes, 'is a possibility of the logical order; it is created by constructing the sentence in accordance with the rules by which its terms are defined. The only case in which verification is (logically) impossible is the case where you have made it impossible by not setting any rules for its verification.'

This reads like a complete abandonment of the empirical-positivist criterion of meaning. But Schlick will not admit that he has changed his mind. Linguistic rules, he says, refer ultimately to ostensively-defined experience; to discover meanings, then, we have to observe the world. 'There is no antagonism,' he writes, 'between logic and experience. Not only can the logician be an empiricist at the same time; he must be one if he wants to understand what he himself is doing.' This conclusion – that the search for meanings is at once a logical inquiry and an empirical investigation – did not satisfy everybody.

In any case, serious difficulties arose when Schlick tried to explain what he meant by 'experience'. To understand these difficulties, we must return to Schlick's earlier version of the verifiability principle, which identified verifiability – and, hence, meaning – with 'reducibility to experience'. 'To understand a proposition,' he wrote in 'A New Philosophy of Experience',[9] 'we must be able exactly to indicate those particular circumstances that would make it true and those other particular circumstances that would make it false. "Circumstances" means facts of experience; and so experience decides about the truth or falsity of propositions, experience "verifies" propositions, and therefore the criterion of the solubility of a problem is its reducibility to possible experience.'

Schlick here distinguishes, like Mach, between answerable and unanswerable questions. Unanswerable questions – questions like 'What is the meaning of life?' – are characterized by the fact that there is no way of deciding between the 'solutions' that are proffered to them, no way of bringing such solutions to the 'test of experience'.

Now, an 'experience', for Schlick, is a state of my mind – not originally given as 'mine', since the ego, he agrees with the neo-Kantians, is itself a construction out of experience – but nevertheless revealed by analysis to be mine and mine only. It makes no sense to assert, then, that other people have, or have not, minds; the question whether they have minds is 'unanswerable', because such minds cannot, in principle, be reduced to 'experiences of mine'. Thus 'verifiability by experience' means verifiability by mental states *which I alone can experience*. There is in principle, it will follow, no way of determining whether a proposition is verifiable – or unverifiable – for anybody except myself. Since meaning and verifiability are identical, we are apparently forced to the odd conclusion that only I can know what a proposition means; indeed, to say of anybody else that 'he knows what that proposition means' will be meaningless.

Schlick tries to avoid this conclusion by taking over the Russell-Poincaré view that scientific knowledge is always knowledge of 'structure' and distinct from the 'enjoyment' – or 'living through' – of experience. When we 'enjoy', say, the sensation of green, this experience, according to Schlick, is private. Other people, no doubt, use the word 'green' when they look at a leaf; it does not follow, he argues, that they experience what we experience – the same 'content'. All we can know – and all that for scientific purposes we need to know – is that the structural relations between *their* experiences are identical with the structural relations between *our* experiences. For the physicist, on this view, 'green' is the name, not of an experience, but of a place in a system of relationships, say a colour chart. In a developed physics, Schlick argues, words like 'green' are entirely replaced by mathematical expressions; the propositions of pure physics are entirely formal.[10]

But what do such propositions mean? On the one side, we find Schlick arguing that, as structural, they can mean nothing but structures, something quite public and intersubjective. At the same time, he is not unmindful of the dictum that form without content is empty. So we also find him maintaining that the empty frame of a scientific system 'has to be filled with content in order to become a science containing real knowledge and this is done by observation ("experience")'. Real knowledge, he thinks, as distinct from mathematical identities, must somehow point to contents, for all that it cannot mention them.

Such contents, it must be remembered, are incommunicable and private: 'every observer,' Schlick writes, 'fills in his own content ... thereby giving his symbols a unique meaning, and filling in the structure with content as a child may colour drawings of which only the outlines are given.' Thus, it would seem, the 'ultimate meaning' of scientific statements is, after all, ineffable – a strange conclusion for a positivist! On Schlick's definition of metaphysics as the attempt to get beyond structure to content, his discussion of content, his fellow-positivists thought, must certainly be condemned as metaphysical.

Carnap's determination to avoid this form-content dichotomy played a large part in the development of his philosophy. At first, in his *Logical Construction of the World* (1928),[11] he had adopted Schlick's doctrine, even if his philosophical method was already quite different from Schlick's. As befitted one who liked to think himself a disciple of Socrates, Schlick's method is informal, literary; Carnap, a pupil of Frege, is a system-builder, a formalist, one of the few contemporary philosophers to make use of symbolic logic for philosophical purposes.

Thus he attempts to construct the world out of 'primitive ideas' linked by 'primitive relations'. As his primitive ideas he selects cross-sections of the stream of experience, not, in Russell's manner, sense-data. Being 'primitive', he argues, such cross-sections do not admit of further analysis. What we ordinarily regard as ingredients within such a cross-section – colours, for example – must therefore be constituted out of them by means of the primitive relation, 'recognition of similarity'.

Inventing a number of ingenious technical devices for this purpose, Carnap relates segments of experience, on the ground of their recognized similarity, into quality-classes, and these in turn into sense-classes. Two quality-classes belong to the same sense-class, he tries to show, if they are connected by a chain of similars: any two colours, for example, can be linked by intermediate colours, whereas a colour and a tone, which are not so related, belong to different sense-classes. Sense-classes in turn fall within a 'sensory field', definable, according to Carnap, in dimensional terms. The 'visual sense-field' is the sensory class with five dimensions, the 'auditory sense-field' is the sensory class with two dimensions. In this manner, he thinks, qualities can be defined in a wholly 'formal' or 'structural' manner: the colour 'red', say, is definable as the class of similars which have a certain location in a five-dimensional system. Carnap then goes on to outline in general terms a procedure by which 'things', as distinct from 'qualities', can be 'formally constituted'; this part of his book, however, is merely a sketch.

Carnap's formal construction is beset with considerable difficulties; that may be one reason why he never returned to complete the project sketched in his *Aufbau*. The more fundamental reason, however, is that he was dissatisfied with its starting-point; the public world of scientific knowledge, he came to think, cannot be constituted out of cross-sections of private experiences. In thus abandoning the earlier tenets of logical positivism, he was greatly influenced by the arguments of the most radical member of the Circle, its most ardent metaphysics-destroyer, Otto Neurath.

Playing Berkeley to Schlick's Locke, Neurath argued that sentences can be compared only with sentences, never with an 'inexpressible reality'.[12] Verification, it now appears, is a relation between sentences, not between sentences and experience: sentences are to be verified by means of 'protocol sentences'. Such sentences can be characterized, Neurath suggests in his 'Protokoll-sätze' (*Erk*, 1932), in a quite formal way as sentences with the structure: 'Otto's report at 3.17 p.m.: Otto's speech-thought at 3.16 p.m. was – in the room at 3.15 p.m. a table was perceived by Otto.' Protocol sentences are not incorrigible; to suppose that there are unquestionable 'atomic' or 'basic' sentences is, he says, to persist in the metaphysical search for 'ultimate foundations'.

Schlick had admitted that all scientific propositions are corrigible; it followed, he thought, that the incorrigible foundations of science are not propositions but direct non-verbalizable encounters with experience ('constatations'). Rejecting 'the inexpressible' as metaphysical but accepting Schlick's view that empirical statements are always corrigible, Neurath was bound to conclude that 'protocol statements' are in this respect in the same position as every other empirical proposition. 'If a new sentence is presented to us,' he writes, 'we compare it with the system with which we are concerned; we examine that system to see whether the new sentence agrees with it. If the new sentence stands in contradiction to the system we abandon it as inapplicable (false) ... or else we accept it and then alter the system so that it remains self-consistent after the new sentence is added to it.' Thus Neurath's attack on metaphysics leads him back to that coherence theory of truth already familiar to us in the writings of the Absolute Idealists – not surprisingly, since for them, too, 'transcendence' was the great enemy.[13]

Neurath's 'protocol sentences' contain a reference to acts of perception – which, however, are to be interpreted behaviouristically as biological processes. That is why, indeed, Neurath's protocol sentences ascribe such acts of perception to named, publicly recognizable, persons, not to the 'I' of subjectivist epistemology. By this means he hopes wholly to exclude all reference to inaccessible 'experiences'. At his hands, logical positivism allies itself with behaviourism; all statements about 'experiences', he argues, can be expressed in 'the language of physics', i.e. by reference to processes in space and time. This is the essence of Neurath's 'physicalism', which is closely related to his 'thesis of the unity of science'. Since all empirical statements, according to Neurath, can be expressed in the language of physics – what cannot be thus expressed is either tautologous or nonsensical – there are no 'spiritual sciences', to be contrasted with 'natural sciences'; all sciences are equally 'natural' and for this reason form a unity.[13]

Neurath's innovations aroused considerable hostility within the Circle, but he won a powerful, if a critical, ally in Carnap. Carnap accepted Neurath's physicalism and his thesis of the unity of science, although he took a different view about protocol sentences. In The Unity of Science,[15] to which Neurath's 'Protokollsätze' was intended as a reply, he had defined protocol sentences as sentences which 'refer to the given, and describe directly given experience or phenomena' – or (in what he calls 'the formal mode') as 'statements needing no justification and serving as the foundation for the remaining statements of science'. They are, then, incorrigible 'foundation sentences', of the sort Neurath condemns as metaphysical. Furthermore, although Carnap is uncertain about the precise form of protocol statements, none of the possibilities he canvasses makes any reference to an observer; protocol sentences, on his view, 'record experience' but do not nominate an experiencer.

Carnap's theory of protocol sentences sets for him the major problem of *The Unity of Science*. Every protocol sentence, he has argued, records a private experience; how then can such sentences serve as a 'foundation' for the public, inter-verifiable, sentences of science? In his attempt to solve that problem, he begins by maintaining that 'science is a unity, that all empirical statements can be expressed in a single language, all states of affairs are of the one kind and are known by the same method'. Now, on the face of it, nobody has ever denied that all empirical statements 'can be expressed in a single language', say in English; a 'language', however, has in Carnap's writings a special sense, a sense in which 'the language of economics' is a different language from 'the language of physics'.

A language is constituted by the fact that it has a distinctive vocabulary – a set of 'primitive ideas' or 'basic concepts' – and a 'syntax', a set of rules for 'translating' the sentences of the language into other sentences, either within or outside the language. 'All empirical statements can be expressed in a single language' asserts, then, that there is a single set of basic expressions into which all other expressions can be translated, and a single method of translation which can be applied to all empirical statements.

Following Neurath, Carnap argues that this fundamental language is the language of physics, in which 'a definite value or range of values of a coefficient of physical state' is attached to 'a specific set of coordinates'. All the propositions of science, he is confident, can be formulated in this language; the problem for him is whether the same is true of 'protocol statements', those 'records of direct experience' upon which scientific statements rest. Science is impossible, on Carnap's view, unless protocol statements are thus translatable; it is not enough to say, as Schlick did, that science is interested only in structure. Scientific propositions, he argues, have ultimately to be tested by reference to experience; and this means that 'structure' and 'experience' must be expressible in a single language.

To show how protocol sentences can be scientifically expressed Carnap invokes the aid of Neurath's 'physicalism'. Every protocol statement, Carnap argues, can be translated into a statement about states of my body. We have ways of deciding whether it is true that 'the body S is now seeing red' (e.g. by telling S to press a button when he sees red); and 'the body S is now seeing red' is, he says, logically equivalent to the protocol statement 'red, now'. This equivalence, Carnap thinks, gives him all that he needs; if somebody objects, 'Yes, but what I *mean* by "experiencing red" is something quite different from what you observe when you see me reacting to a red stimulus' he is not, according to Carnap, using 'meaning' in its scientific sense. If two statements are logically equivalent – if each can be inferred from the other – that shows, Carnap says, that they *have the same meaning*. Any differences between the two statements will be a matter not of meaning, but of purely personal associations.

When Neurath attacked Carnap for continuing to hold that some propositions are 'direct records of experience', Carnap replied ('Über Prokollsätze', *Erk*, 1932) that there was no real dispute between Neurath and himself: they were simply suggesting *different methods of constructing the language of science*. Carnap was saying that protocol sentences lie outside the language of science, that their structure, therefore, is not laid down in the language, although there are special rules for translating them into the language; Neurath that they fall within the language, have a fixed form, and that therefore no question of translation arises. This is not a genuine difference of opinion, Carnap argues, which could be decided as an empirical issue. A consistent language, he thinks, can be constructed either in his manner or in Neurath's, so that the choice between the two languages will depend on which is the more convenient – no other consideration can possibly affect the issue. Carnap admits, however, that his language is more likely than Neurath's to lead to metaphysics; his own inclination turned towards the view, derived from conversation with Karl Popper, that, as opposed to Neurath, any singular proposition – not only propositions which refer to the perceptions of an observer – can act as a 'protocol sentence', but also that, here in agreement with Neurath, these sentences are already expressed in the language of science.

The 'conventionalist' tendency of Carnap's reply to Neurath reaches its peak in Carnap's most influential book *The Logical Syntax of Language* (1934) where Carnap, under the influence of recent developments in logic (cf. Chapter 18, below), espouses what he calls the 'principle of tolerance'. 'In logic,' he writes, 'there are no morals. Everyone is at liberty to build up his own logic, i.e. his own form of language, as he wishes.' And philosophy, according to Carnap, is a branch of logic – he calls it 'the logic of science'. Philosophy, he argues, does not give us information about transcendental entities, since all sentences containing what purports to be a reference to such entities are senseless; most of its propositions – the propositions of ethics as well as of metaphysics – express and stimulate feelings (they are, in Lange's words, a 'kind of lyric poetry') but tell us nothing whatsoever about the world; those of its propositions which do tell us something, e.g. certain of the propositions of epistemology, properly belong to the empirical science of psychology, not to philosophy. Those philosophical propositions which remain after his wholesale purge are, he tries to show, either descriptions of the language scientists employ or else recommendations for the modification of that language. Mach had said 'there is above all no Machian philosophy but at most a scientific methodology'; Carnap proclaims that 'the logic of science takes the place of the inextricable tangle of problems which is known as philosophy'.

This linguistic interpretation of philosophy is a difficult view to maintain, since the propositions of philosophy seem to be about kinds of entity – relations, quality, number, meaning, and the like – which are not, on the face of it, linguistic forms. To answer this objection, Carnap distinguishes between three classes of sentences – syntactical sentences, object sentences and pseudo-object sentences. A syntactical sentence, as he defines it, describes a language; an object sentence describes a physical object; pseudo-object sentences, of which philosophical sentences are a species, *look* like object sentences but are revealed by analysis to be syntactical.

Thus the philosophical sentence: 'five is not a thing but a

number' is, he argues, not really parallel to the 'object' sentence 'water is not an acid but an alkali'. The absence of parallelism comes out in two ways: first, there are no empirical tests to determine whether five is a thing or a number, nothing which corresponds to the use of litmus paper in distinguishing acids from alkalis; secondly, the philosophical sentence can be translated into syntactical terms – expressed in the 'formal mode' – as 'the word "five" is not a thing-word but a numerical expression', whereas there is no such syntactical translation of 'acid' and 'alkali'. Philosophers ordinarily employ the 'material mode' i.e. they talk in terms of 'things' rather than 'thing-words', 'numbers' rather than 'numerical expressions'. This procedure, Carnap grants, is harmless in itself. But it leads very easily, he thinks, to metaphysics, to pseudo-problems about, for example, 'the nature of a number'.

Similarly, Carnap argues, all statements about 'meaning', or 'content', are pseudo-object sentences. Thus, he says, the sentence: 'yesterday's lecture treated of Babylon', which appears to relate yesterday's lecture to a particular physical entity, Babylon, in fact tells us nothing about Babylon, only something about the appearance of the word 'Babylon' in a certain set of sentences. It should be reformulated in the formal mode, therefore, as 'In yesterday's lecture the word "Babylon" (or a synonym) occurred'. Again, 'the word "daystar" denotes the sun' will appear in the formal mode, according to Carnap, as 'the word "daystar" is synonymous with the word "sun"'. If philosophers will only keep in mind the possibility of such translations, Carnap considers, all controversies about 'what meanings are' will vanish for ever.

Clearly, however, the words 'daystar' and 'sun' could be synonymous in one language but not in another – as 'fin' and 'excellent' are, in certain contexts, synonymous in French but not in English; statements about synonymity, then, are relative to a language. The same is true, according to Carnap, of all philosophical theses. Wittgenstein, Schlick, Carnap in his earlier writings, presumed that all sentences form part of a single language – 'the language' – so that a sentence is absolutely tautologous or non-tautologous, meaningful or meaningless. In *The Logical Syntax of Language*, in contrast, Carnap argues that whether a sentence is tautologous depends on what language we happen to be employing. There are as many languages as we choose to construct and nothing, except convenience, to determine what rules shall govern them. A philosophical statement, Carnap concludes, is not fully expressed, even in the formal mode, unless it contains reference to the language, or languages, to which it applies. Once that condition is satisfied, he considers, philosophical disputes will vanish: they are seen to be, like Carnap's argument with Neurath, alternative recommendations for language-forms, not disputes about the facts.

When, for example, one mathematical philosopher asserts that numbers are classes of classes, another that they are primitive expressions, either, Carnap tell us, each is describing his own language, or else each is recommending to mathematicians a particular mode of construction for mathematical systems: they are not, then, contradicting one another. As for philosophical expressions which obstinately defy restatement in a syntactical form – Carnap instances Wittgenstein's 'there is indeed the inexpressible', or Schlick's assertions about 'unutterable contents' – these must, he says, be rejected as nonsensical.

Philosophy now has a subject-matter of its own. Wittgenstein, as we have already seen, came to the conclusion that the propositions of the *Tractatus* are without sense. 'My propositions are elucidatory in this way,' he wrote, 'he who understands me finally recognizes them as senseless when he has climbed out through them, on them, over them.' This conclusion naturally struck his readers as being paradoxical in the extreme. Thus the poet Julian Bell in his *Epistle on the Subject of the Ethical and Aesthetic Beliefs of Herr Ludwig Wittgenstein* complained that

'he talks nonsense, numerous statements makes,
Forever his own vow of silence breaks'

and saw in the doctrine of 'showing' a reversion to the mystical:

'He smuggles knowledge from a secret source;
A mystic in the end, confessed and plain,
The ancient enemy returned again;
Who knows by his direct experience
What is beyond all knowledge and all sense.'

For Wittgenstein had written: 'There is indeed the inexpressible. This *shows* itself; it is the mystical.'

Not surprisingly, the scientifically-minded positivists were dissatisfied with this doctrine. Russell in his preface to the *Tractatus* had suggested one way out: perhaps, he said, although a language cannot describe its own form, its form can be described in another language, the form of that language in yet another language and so on – the effect being that a language's form is always describable, although not in the language which exhibits that form. Russell's conception of a hierarchy of languages played an important part in the development of logic, and Carnap himself did much to introduce it to a wider philosophical public. Yet although he places great stress at the beginning of *The Logical Syntax of Language* on the importance of distinguishing between statements in a given language and statements which describe such statements, these forming the 'metalanguage', he nevertheless maintains that propositions describing a language can form part of the language they describe. One can see why. He had somehow to show that statements which describe the language of science fall within that language. For they are not tautological – we cannot deduce from rules that a particular language contains a particular rule – and he was not prepared to regard them as nonsensical. Thus either they form part of science or else Carnap's trichotomy – scientific, nonsensical, or tautological – is broken down.

Carnap thought he could show, in opposition to Wittgenstein, that the form of a language can be described within that language itself. For Wittgenstein, the form of a language is that which is common to it and to the reality it depicts; for that reason form – as involving a reference to something which lies beyond language – can never be depicted within language. In Carnap's *Logical Syntax of Language*, however, the 'form' of a language consists in the rules it lays down – 'formation' rules which determine whether a sentence is 'well-formed' or 'grammatical', and 'transformation' rules which describe the manner in which one sentence can be derived from another. The language of science, Carnap argues, can contain such rules within itself. Those general rules of syntax which refer to the possible forms a language can assume belong to arithmetic – to combinatorial analysis; those syntactical propositions which describe in formal terms the structure of a specific language are propositions of applied mathematics; those which refer merely to the symbols – for example 'the symbol "the" occurs twice on this page' – are propositions of physics. 'The sentences of the logic of science,' he writes, 'are formulated in syntactical sentences about the language of science; but no new domain in addition to that of science itself is thereby created ... syntax, pure and descriptive, is nothing more than the mathematics and physics of language.' In this way, a home is found for philosophical propositions within a world parcelled out between the sciences.

What, by now, has become of the verifiability theory of meaning? Its chequered history can best be illustrated by reference to Carnap's 'Testability and Meaning' (*PSC*, 1936–7). The verifiability principle is there regarded neither as a truism nor as a significant piece of nonsense but as a recommendation for the construction of the language of science. As a recommendation, it is addressed to empiricists, who will naturally wish to construct the language of science in such a way that metaphysical propositions cannot be expressed within it. Empiricists, according to Carnap, ought not to make such assertions as 'all knowledge is empirical' – assertions which profess to tell us something about the world; they ought to make it clear that what they are doing is to recommend certain restrictions on the use of language, restrictions which do not exist within a 'natural' language like English. Their object, then, is to work out an 'ideal language', defined as one which would enable them to assert whatever an empiricist wishes to assert – scientific and mathematico-logical propositions – but would rule out as meaningless all metaphysical assertions. A metaphysician will naturally pursue a different ideal; if the metaphysician can work out a language alternative to empiricism, the empiricist, provided only that the language is consistent, can have no grounds for objection to it although he will not wish to adopt it himself.

Within the general framework of an empiricist language, however, there are still various possibilities, varying in their degree of strictness. An empiricist must maintain that the 'primitive predicates' of science – those which appear in its 'basic assertions' or 'protocol statements' – are all of them observable, but he may either decide to admit into his language, Carnap considers, only predicates of the 'thing-language', or may prefer also to include 'psychological' predicates.* In this second case, there are again alternatives: the psychological predicates may be phenomenalistic in form, referring to private states of consciousness, or they may be 'physicalistic' predicates – predicates referring to psychological acts, like *being angry* or *perceiving a dog*, which only the agent himself can observe, but the presence or absence of which can be confirmed by independent observers. Carnap himself, following Popper, decides in favour of the 'thing-language', as against his earlier phenomenalist or Neurath's physicalistic protocols, on the ground that no other language can preserve the absolute objectivity of science. Naturally, some positivists have greeted his decision with indignation, as a retreat from positivism into realism.

Positivists had usually agreed – this is stated explicitly in the early writings of Schlick – that all non-primitive predicates must be definable in terms of the primitive predicates; Carnap had taken this same view when he had asserted in *The Unity of Science* that all empirical statements can be 'translated' into the language of physics. Once more, in *Testability and Meaning* he moves away from this stringent requirement: not translatability but only reducibility through 'reduction pairs' is all, he thinks, that the empiricist need demand. What leads him particularly to this conclusion is that he does not see any way of defining 'disposition-predicates' (predicates such as 'soluble', 'visible', 'audible') as conjunctions of primitive predicates. On the other hand he thinks that the empiricist can 'introduce' the predicate 'soluble' into his language by means of the pair of propositions: 'if x is put into water at time t, then if x is soluble in water, x dissolves at time t' and 'if x is put into water at time t, then if x is not soluble in water, x does not dissolve at time t.' Thus we have a test for solubility, although not a method of *translating* propositions of the form 'x is soluble' into propositions about x's

*The 'thing-language' is made up of such everyday language predicates, including 'warm', 'quadrangular', 'blue', as are used to describe material objects. Carnap thinks that this 'thing-language' is what he really had in mind when he maintained that 'the language of Physics' is the fundamental language. See G. Bergmann: *The Metaphysics of Logical Positivism* (1954) for an ideal language which includes psychological predicates.

observable predicates – since x may be soluble even although no one ever puts it into water.[16]

A similar shift from translatability to testability had already been presaged in Carnap's account of verifiability in *Philosophy and Logical Syntax* (1935). There he had distinguished between two sorts of verification – direct and indirect. Only protocol statements, he had argued, can be directly verified, because they alone restrict themselves to the recording of an experience. Other propositions – singular propositions like 'this key is made of iron' as well as universal propositions like 'if any iron thing is placed near a magnet it is attracted by it' – can be verified only *indirectly*. Thus singular statements, as well as the universal laws of science, 'have the character of hypotheses'.[17] Indirect verification, as Carnap defines it, consists in taking the proposition to be verified along with other already-verified propositions in such a way as to deduce directly verifiable propositions. For example, 'this key is made of iron' is verified by combining it with the already verified law 'if an iron thing is placed near a magnet, it is attracted by it' and deducing the directly verifiable proposition 'this key is attracted by the magnet'. 'Verification,' obviously, no longer means 'shown to be true' – or rather it still has this meaning in the phrase 'directly verified' although not in the phrase 'indirectly verified'. For by indirect verification we certainly do not *prove* the truth of the verified proposition. Not surprisingly, then, in his *Testability and Meaning* Carnap abandoned the word 'verifiable' in favour of 'testable' – in the case where a method of experimental verification is actually at our disposal – or 'confirmable' – in the case where we cannot nominate such a method.

The crucial point, for our present purposes, is that a proposition can have a meaning even although it is not 'verifiable' in the original positivist sense of that word – even although, that is, it is not equivalent to a finite set of 'atomic propositions' or 'experiences'. The older positivist doctrine, according to Carnap, was 'inconvenient', because it ruled out as nonsensical all propositions which have unrestricted generality – all physical laws – and, indeed, all propositions which contain predicates which are not reducible to primitive predicates. Schlick had tried to overcome this inconvenience in Ramsey's manner, by maintaining that physical laws are not assertions but instructions for the formation of assertions – to which Carnap replies that physical laws are manipulated by scientists in the manner of sentences, not in the manner of rules. His own 'recommendation' is that propositions of unrestricted generality should be admitted into science.

This leads him to the conclusion that the most suitable language for science has rules of the most liberal sort: the empiricist need only demand that 'every synthetic proposition must be confirmable'. Such a rule, he thinks, is strong enough to expel metaphysics, since metaphysical propositions do not lend themselves to any sort of empirical confirmation, and yet at the same time it does not restrict the development of science. Clearly Carnap has moved a long way from his earlier *identification* of meaning with translatability into experience; now the most he is prepared to say is that a proposition is meaningless *unless* it has some empirical consequences. Carnap still saw difficulties, however, both in 'meaning' and in 'confirmation'; his attempt to solve these difficulties led him still further away from logical positivism into the controversies we shall describe in a later chapter.

In England A. J. Ayer was the leading exponent of logical positivism; his *Language, Truth and Logic* (1936) – a young man's book, lively, uncompromising, belligerent – is, indeed, the most readily accessible defence of classical, phenomenalistic, logical positivism.[18] Naturally, however, it reflects the difficulties which had already arisen in settling upon the precise form of the verifiability principle. Ayer distinguishes a 'strong' verifiability principle, which lays it down that a proposition is meaningless unless experience can conclusively establish its truth, and a 'weak' principle, which requires only that some observation should be 'relevant' to the determination of a proposition's truth or falsity. He accepts the verifiability principle only in its weak sense, on the ground that he does not wish to condemn as nonsensical universal laws or statements about the past, neither of which are reducible to present experiences. The principle in this form, he agrees with Carnap, is quite sufficient to destroy metaphysical propositions; no observation is relevant, by the nature of the case, to such a metaphysical proposition as that 'the world of sense-experience is unreal', nor could any observation help us to determine whether the world is a single 'ultimate substance' or a plurality of such substances.

Once we reject philosophy's claim to be a purveyor of metaphysical truths, we see, Ayer argues, that its real function is analysis – the function that Locke, Berkeley, Hume and Russell had principally exercised. One is not to conclude, however, that philosophy consists in 'breaking up' objects into atomic entities; the view that the Universe is 'really' a collection of elementary entities is metaphysical nonsense. Philosophical analysis, according to Ayer, is linguistic: it provides us with modes of defining a symbol by translating it into sentences which contain neither that symbol nor any synonymous symbol. Russell's theory of descriptions is an instance of it, and so is the phenomenalist translation of sentences about material objects into sentences about sense-data.

In thus conjoining Continental logical positivism and British philosophical analysis, Ayer was drawing attention to a genuine historical connexion: at the same time, he led many to believe that 'analysis' and logical positivism are actually identical, a view which still, I suppose, prevails amongst educated readers who are not professionally engaged in philosophy.[19] In fact, however, logical positivists were very little interested in the epistemological problems upon which British analysts concentrated; analysts, for their part, paid little attention to the structure of scientific or mathematical theories. British analysts and Continental positivists are both anti-metaphysical, both empiricist in tendency, but in their conception of the positive role of philosophy they stand poles apart.

For Ayer, one may say, philosophy consists of British empiricism restated in linguistic terms, as becomes still clearer in his *The Foundations of Empirical Knowledge* (1940). That book is wholly concerned with the classical British problem – 'our knowledge of the external world'. At the same time, his discussion shows the effect of his Continental explorations. No observations, he tries to demonstrate, can settle the dispute between realists and sense-datum theorists. When the upholders of sense-data maintain that the changes which take place in our perceptions of objects and the divergences between the perceptions of different observers cannot be reconciled with the view that we directly perceive material objects, the realist, Ayer thinks, can always reply that the sense-datum theorist takes too narrow a view of 'material objects'. The question at issue, then, is whether it is more 'convenient' to say with the realists that material objects can, or with the sense-datum theorists that they cannot, possess different colours at the same time – a question to which observation is not in the least relevant. Since, he considers, we can talk sensibly and consistently about the world in either 'the sense-datum language' or 'the material object' language, we have only to decide which language flows most easily from our lips.[20]

Ayer's own preference is for 'the sense-datum language'; *The Foundations of Empirical Knowledge* has been widely read as a defence of phenomenalism. The British empiricists went astray, Ayer argues, because they thought that 'sense-datum', 'idea', and the like, were *names of entities*, whose properties can be considered in precisely the same manner as any other entity – so that we can sensibly ask, for example, whether sense-data have properties which we do not perceive them to have. To proceed thus, he considers, is to lose the whole advantage of the sense-datum terminology: the classical problems of illusion will break out all over again in regard to sense-data. If someone asks us, for example, *how many* stars a person sees when he 'sees stars', we must, Ayer thinks, refuse to answer this question, on the ground that it makes no sense; from the fact that the person who sees the stars could not tell us how many he saw, we are not to infer that his 'sense-data' had properties he did not notice but only that 'sense-data stars', unlike real stars, are not denumerable.[21]

Phenomenalism, Ayer thinks, is best formulated as follows: everyday sentences about material objects can be translated into sentences which refer exclusively to sense-data – including hypothetical sentences of the form 'if I were to do such-and-such, I should experience such-and-such sense-data'. One familiar objection to this position is that no set of statements about sense-data is equivalent to a statement about a material object; this comes out in the fact that statements about material objects are always corrigible – further experience could lead us to reject them as false – whereas a set of statements about sense-data is by definition incorrigible. Ayer concedes this absence of equivalence; but it does not follow, he says, that material-object statements are about something *other* than a sense-datum. 'Someone is at the door', he argues, is not equivalent to a set of statements about particular persons, 'either x or y or z is at the door'. Yet 'someone' is not the name of an entity over and above any particular person.

All we are entitled to say, Ayer concludes, is that sense-datum statements can never 'precisely specify' a material object; in consequence, it is impossible to analyse, say, a statement about a table into a set of statements about sense-data. We can, however, in Hume's manner, point to those relations between sense-data which induce us to construct out of our experience assertions about material objects. It is interesting to observe that in his attempt to rewrite Hume, Ayer falls back into the traditional 'material mode' of British empiricism: 'I have found it convenient,' he remarks, 'to deal with this problem as if it were a question of constructing one sort of objects out of another; but strictly it should be viewed as a problem about the reference of words.' His readers were not always convinced that his discussion could readily be translated into the formal mode: the fact remains that the novel feature of Ayer's book was his attempt to restate phenomenalism in linguistic terms.[22]

Ayer's preface to the second edition (1946) of *Language, Truth and Logic* can serve as the last word on logical positivism; it reveals with exceptional clarity the difficulties which have bedevilled it. We find him distinctly uneasy, for example, about *what it is* that is verified. He introduces yet a third candidate – the 'statement' – to dispute the honour with the 'sentence' and the 'proposition'. A 'sentence' he defines as a grammatically significant set of words, a 'statement' as what such symbols express, a 'proposition' as a sub-class of 'statements' containing only such statements as are expressed by 'literally meaningful' sentences. Thus the phrase 'meaningless proposition' is, according to Ayer, a contradiction in terms; it is *sentences* which are 'literally meaningful' and statements, it would seem, that are verifiable. Whether matters are thus mended, or still further confounded, is a point we shall leave to the discretion of the reader.

Again, Ayer is troubled about the nature of verifiability. Interpreted in its 'strong' sense, the verifiability principle rules out, he thinks, all but 'basic' propositions (defined in the manner of

Schlick's 'constatations'), and yet in its 'weak' sense it is not sufficiently positivist, since experiences are certainly 'relevant', in the wide sense of that term, to some metaphysical propositions.[23] This, indeed, is the dilemma in which the logical positivists, like Hume before them, constantly found themselves – throw metaphysics into the fire, and science goes with it, preserve science from the flames and metaphysics comes creeping back.[24] Ayer attempts to deal with the situation by means of an elaborate reformulation of the verifiability principle, too complex for description here.[25] Indeed, the great charm of logical positivism lay in the simplicity of its dealings with metaphysics: once admit, as Ayer now does, that the verifiability principle needs to be supported by detailed analyses of metaphysical arguments and its magic has vanished.

The general tendency of Ayer's preface was to move with logical positivism in a linguistic direction; where once he blasted, he now discreetly recommends. In one fundamental respect, indeed, he seemed to be working away from linguistic interpretations – by denying that *a priori* propositions are linguistic rules. Such rules, he says, are arbitrary, whereas the rules of logic are necessary truths.[26] Since the linguistic approach to philosophy was generated out of the *Tractatus* discussion of mathematical and logical truths, second thoughts on this point are likely to be historically important. But Ayer still maintains that the necessity of logical truth is a *consequence of*, even although it is not identical with, the adoption of a set of rules.[27]

In essentials, then, Ayer was in 1946 still a positivist of the linguistic generation. But as logical positivism was gradually transformed, at Carnap's hands, into physicalism, Ayer more and more retreated into a British-empiricist type of epistemology, even if in a spirit chastened by the criticisms of such of his contemporaries as Wittgenstein, Ryle and Austin. In *The Problem of Knowledge* (1956) the enemy to be routed is scepticism rather than metaphysics.*

---

*He still, however, stands by his rejection of metaphysics, and even, for all the difficulty of formulating it, the verifiability principle. See *The Concept of a Person* (1963). See reviews of *The Problem of Knowledge* by P. F. Strawson (*Phil.*, 1957); G. P. Henderson (*PQ*, 1958); W. Doney (*PR*, 1960). See also H. H. Price: 'Professor Ayer's Essays' (*PQ*, 1955).

The traditional reply to scepticism had been that there are propositions of such a nature that it is logically impossible for us to be mistaken in taking them to be true, either because they are *a priori* or because they are records of immediate experience. Ayer freely admits that if a proposition is an *a priori* truth it is logically impossible for it to be false. But it by no means follows, he points out, that it is logically impossible for us to be mistaken in supposing it to be *a priori*. So the mere existence of *a priori* truths does not act as a guarantee against the risk of error.

Then what of the 'basic statements' of logical positivism – such statements as 'this looks to me red', 'I have a headache'? As statements, Ayer argues, these are clearly not incorrigible; I can suppose today, even if wrongly, that when I said yesterday 'I have a headache' I was mistaken in so doing. But, it might be objected, at least I could not have been mistaken at that time at which I said, of a headache I then had, 'I have a headache'. The statement 'At the present moment I am experiencing a headache', that is, cannot possibly be false at that time at which it is uttered. If, Ayer replies, this statement means: 'I am now experiencing the sort of thing which other people call a headache' it can certainly be false: perhaps other people would call what I am experiencing 'a tight head'. Even in a 'private language', I could make a similar mistake: I might wrongly say to myself, 'This is the sort of experience I ordinarily call a headache'.[28] Nor will it do to object – as Ayer had himself once suggested – that in such a case I am making a mistake about the right words to use, not about the facts of the case. For what I am wrong about is the *kind of experience it is*.

So Ayer is led to reject the view, which he had sustained as late as the second edition of *Language, Truth and Logic*, that there are 'basic propositions', incorrigible ultimate verifiers. He grants to the sceptic that it is always *logically possible* that we are mistaken.[29] He does not grant, however, that we never have 'knowledge' – if this is taken to mean that we never have the right to be fully confident that a proposition is true. It is quite exceptional for us to be wrong in thinking that we have a headache. We can quite properly, therefore, use such statements as 'I have a headache' to verify others, for even if it is always logically possible that they are false, they are nevertheless the sort of statements which we have the best possible grounds for believing to be true. In that sense they are 'basic'.

What about the sceptical arguments against induction? Once again, the sceptic is right, according to Ayer, in so far as he rejects the possibility of providing a formal, deductive, justification of induction. But this is only to say that there is no *better* argument than induction, which could be used to justify it. This reply to the sceptic is particularly important to Ayer. For both our knowledge of the past and our knowledge of other minds rest, so Ayer argues, on inductive reasoning. It is logically impossible, he says, for us to have direct knowledge either of the past or of other people's experiences. In both cases our knowledge rests on inferences from what we observe. In the case of our knowledge about the past it rests on our observation of what is now happening – inferences about the past being in this respect parallel to predictions about the future – in the case of our knowledge of other people's experiences it rests on our observation of the behaviour, the displays of feeling, the manner of acting, of other people. It is logically possible that all our statements about the past are mistaken, and it is logically possible that other people have no minds, but all the same we can rightly claim to be sure that the Battle of Waterloo was fought in 1814 and that our wife feels affection for us – although only in so far as our claims have a good inductive basis. Ayer now wholly rejects the view to which he had subscribed in *Language, Truth and Logic*, that statements about other people's minds are really statements about their bodies and *a fortiori* rejects the 'physicalist' doctrine that statements about our own minds, too, are logically equivalent to statements about our own bodies.[30]

The most troublesome sceptical objections, Ayer thinks, relate to our perception of external bodies. On this question, Ayer still defends the general position of *The Foundations of Empirical Knowledge*, but with much less emphasis on the idea of a 'sense-datum language'. The sceptic is right, Ayer admits, in denying that statements about my sense-data can be either equivalent to, or logically conclusive proof of, such assertions as 'the book is on the table'. It by no means follows, however, that they do not *justify* such assertions; indeed, it is by reference to sense-data that such statements are to be justified.[31]

In general terms, then, logical positivism has marched in two different directions. At Carnap's hands, towards a realist account of perception and a physicalist account of minds; at Ayer's hands, back to the British empiricism out of which it developed. What has been discarded, in both cases, is the conception of a kind of empirical knowledge which is wholly trustworthy, free of any risk of error. Reichenbach once wrote of Carnap that 'his theory may be regarded, after a fashion, as a modern fulfilment of Descartes' quest for an absolutely certain basis of science'.[32] In as far as that was his ambition, most logical positivists would now admit, he certainly failed to fulfil it.

CHAPTER 17

Logic, Semantics and Methodology

AFTER the publication of *Principia Mathematica* symbolic logic was little cultivated in England; the leadership passed to Germany, Holland, Poland and the United States – and, even then, to mathematicians rather than to philosophers.[1] At first, the emphasis was on amendments to *Principia Mathematica*. Its axioms were reduced to a single axiom, and it was purged of such extraneous elements as the Axiom of Reducibility and the theory of types.[2] Not all mathematicians, however, were satisfied that mathematics could be founded on logic, in the Russell-Whitehead 'logistic' manner, or indeed that the consistency of logic could be established independently of the consistency of mathematics.

Two schools of anti-logistic mathematics soon established themselves: the formalists, led by Hilbert, and the intuitionists, who took Brouwer as their master.[3] In his writings on the foundations of mathematics,[4] Hilbert set out to construct a 'completely formalized' mathematics, i.e. a mathematics with a logical structure which is entirely independent of the meaning of the expressions it employs. Such a pure calculus, unlike *Principia Mathematica*, contains no explicit definitions, since it does not specifically refer to a particular class of entities. Definitions are replaced by 'formation' rules, which lay down the mode in which the symbols of the system operate, and 'transformation' rules, which regulate the methods of deriving formulae from axioms. Although these rules appear among the 'axioms' of the system, they are not 'self-evident truths'; they function in the same manner, Hilbert suggests, as rules of chess. The 'symbols', too, are to be considered, simply, as (actual or possible) marks on paper, not as symbolizing anything in particular.

Russell complained that 'the formalists are like a watchmaker who is so absorbed in making his watches look pretty that he has forgotten the purpose of telling the time'. An arithmetic, he argues, must begin from the natural numbers, not from uninterpreted symbols, and it must issue in arithmetical truths, not in arbitrary rules. Hilbert was quite ready to agree with Russell that we ordinarily use arithmetical symbols in order to count. But his own purpose is not an ordinary one. He is setting out to demonstrate the consistency of arithmetic; for that special purpose, he thinks, he must first convert arithmetic into a formalized axiomatic system. The construction and examination of such formal systems, according to Hilbert, is the task of 'metamathematics', as distinct from mathematics. In 'metamathematics' mathematical systems are discussed, not used; that is why mathematical symbols, for the metamathematician, are only marks on paper. Having formalized mathematics the metamathematician can go on to consider whether the deduction of consequences from this particular set of axioms will engender contradictions, i.e. whether contradictory formulae can be derived within the system. If no such contradictions can be derived, the formal system is consistent. But furthermore, and now the metamathematician proves his worth, any system which interprets the symbols, by means of correlative definitions, as standing for a particular class of entities – the natural numbers, for example – must also be consistent. Thus the consistency of ordinary mathematics, Hilbert thinks he has shown, can be proved *via* the consistency of a completely formalized system.

To carry out this programme, the formalist needs a general method of determining whether a formula is 'valid' (provable) in his system. For it is not enough to wait and see whether contradictions eventually reveal themselves; the formalist has to show that contradictions *cannot* arise within his system, and he can do this only if he can say definitely of any given formula that it is or is not 'provable' in the system. So more than a little stir was created when Kurt Gödel demonstrated (in 1931) that a system like *Principia Mathematica* – or indeed any system rich enough to contain arithmetic within it – must contain propositions which are not 'provable' within that system. It was clear, now, why the formalists had encountered such difficulty in proving the consistency of arithmetic; this task, as they had envisaged it, can never, by its very nature, be brought to completion.[5] Even if they abandoned their more extreme ambitions, however, the formalists have had a lasting effect on symbolic logic. Many logicians are convinced that no logical theory is worth a moment's consideration unless it has been set out as a formal, axiomatized, system.

Hilbert's philosophy of mathematics takes as its mathematical norm a purified axiomatic geometry; for the 'intuitionists', on the other hand, the norm is 'mathematical induction'. Two features of mathematical induction particularly attracted the intuitionists: first, although it is a method of arriving at conclusions about *all* numbers, it nowhere presumes that there is an actual *totality* of numbers, a 'real infinite'; secondly, it makes use only of processes like addition which we know how to perform, and refers to no numbers except those which, like *the successor to n*, we know how to construct. Hilbert had argued that although metamathematics must restrict itself to procedures the validity of which is intuitively obvious, mathematics itself has a freer hand; the intuitionists, in contrast, are not prepared to admit any but intuitively obvious processes into mathematics itself, even at the cost of rejecting certain branches of pure mathematics. Only thus, they argue, can mathematics be secured against paradox.

Mathematics, according to the intuitionists, rests on the possibility of making selections from experience and then indefinitely repeating such selections; they admit no numbers except such as can be constructed in this manner.[6] Thus, they conclude, mathematics cannot be founded on logic, since logic already presumes the *mathematical* fact that symbols are repeatable. The consistency of logic and the consistency of mathematics, indeed, have to be established *pari passu*.

The classical mathematician, if asked to prove that 'there exists an *n* with the property *P*' may do so by deducing contradictions from the proposition 'for all *n*, it is not the case that *n* has the property *P*'. In asserting that a number 'exists' only if we know how to construct it, the intuitionist is rejecting the validity of all such indirect proofs of 'existence'. This puritanism has the somewhat startling consequence that the classical 'principle of excluded middle' must also go by the board. For if the intuitionist were to admit the validity of the transition from 'it is false that for all *n* it is not the case that *n* has the property *P*' to 'at least one *n* has the property *P*', he is at once granting that the 'existence' of a number can be indirectly established. The proposition, 'at least one *n* has the property *P*', according to Brouwer, is in such a case neither true nor false – he calls it 'undecidable' – since no rule has been laid down for constructing the n in question. So a logic which runs parallel to arithmetic – the only logic the consistency of which can be demonstrated – must be 'three-valued': Brouwer replaces the familiar dichotomy, true or false, by a trichotomy – true, false, or undecidable.

In Poland, meanwhile, an interest in three-valued logics had arisen out of a concern with quite different philosophical problems.[7] The background of the Polish logicians was Aristotelian, and it was Aristotle's 'problem of the sea-battle' – or, more generally, what came to be christened 'the problem of future contingents' – which led Lukasiewicz to question the principle of excluded middle.[8] Suppose, before the event, somebody makes the assertion that 'the battle of Salamis will take place'. Obviously this assertion is not false. Yet if it is true, Lukasiewicz thought, we are bound to conclude that the future is pre-determined, since it must have been true *before* the battle took place that it *would* take place. There is only one way of avoiding this fatalist conclusion, according to Lukasiewicz: we must admit a 'third-value' over and above truth and falsity – the value he calls 'neuter'. Then we shall be able to maintain that 'the battle of Salamis will take place' is neither true nor false, thus neatly sidestepping the either-false-or-fatalism dilemma. Once three values were admitted into logic there seemed to be no good reason for stopping at this relatively ungenerous point; the Polish logicians were soon hard at work on the construction of n-valued systems.

In another respect, too, their interest in Aristotle led them away from the traditional two-valued logics – towards, this time, the construction of modal logics, in which propositions are characterized as 'necessary' or 'possible' or 'impossible', as well as 'true' or 'false'.[9] Encouraged by the Polish spirit of revolution, other logicians have attempted to extend the range of logic by working out a 'logic of imperatives' additional to the traditional logic of statements; inquiries have even been made into the possibility of constructing a logic of interrogatives.[10]

These developments naturally delighted formalistically-minded logicians: system after system to formalize and test for consistency! An immense amount of energy has been expended on the axiomatization of n-valued and modal systems and the solution of 'decision problems' within them. Lewis's system of 'strict implication', too, has been examined in detail as a pure calculus, and the same methods have been applied to Boole's algebraic logic and even to the logic of Aristotle. Not surprisingly, few philosophers have felt inclined, or indeed have had the necessary mathematical capacity, to pursue logicians through these symbolic mazes. Granted the value of formalization as an exercise in the purest sort of pure mathematics, its philosophical importance, most philosophers have been inclined to say, is negligible. Nevertheless, as we have already seen, the formalized approach to logical problems had a considerable direct effect on the work of Carnap and the logical positivists. And it has had indirect effects, too: for 'ordinary language' philosophies can often be best understood as a reaction against the method of formalization. There are signs, one should add, that the new logics might yet stimulate philosophy in a variety of directions.[11]

Perhaps the best known of the Polish logicians, in English countries, is A. Tarski, whose *Introduction to Logic and to the Methodology of Deductive Sciences* (1936) appeared in an English edition in 1941. Tarski's name is particularly connected with two things: the distinction between logic and metalogic, and the 'semantic' theory of truth. 'Metalogic' talks about and formalizes logical systems, just as 'metamathematics' talks about and formalizes mathematics. There is, however, an important point of difference between Hilbert's metamathematics and Tarski's metalogic: metamathematics, according to Hilbert, is an *informal* discussion of mathematics, whereas Tarski set out to construct a formalized metalogic, free from the 'vague and imprecise' expressions of ordinary language and not dependent for its validity upon that 'direct intuition' to which Hilbert appealed.

Carnap's *Logical Syntax of Language* is an example of Tarski's method in practice. Even the most highly formalized logic books had always contained passages of exposition in ordinary language, in order to explain the method of constructing logical formulae and to describe the relations holding between them. Only if these passages can themselves be formalized, Carnap argues, will logic be wholly exact. *The Logical Syntax of Language* purports, therefore, to describe an exact method for the construction of such 'sentences about sentences'. But also it was Tarski – this time in his work on semantics – who finally persuaded Carnap to relax the severity of *The Logical Syntax of Language*, in which he had damned as metaphysical all references to 'meaning' which cannot be expressed as a relation between sentences. Under Tarski's influence, he embarked upon his less self-denying *Studies in Semantics*.

The word 'semantics', in its short history, has covered an extraordinary variety of intellectual activities. M. Bréal coined the word in his *Essai de sémantique* (1897) as a name for philological inquiries into meaning; Chwistek meant by it what Carnap called 'logical syntax'; it is often used to refer to such inquiries into meaning as Peirce's theory of signs, Frege's distinction between sense and reference, and Wittgenstein's picture theory; at a more popular level, any attempt to analyse the manner in which we can be confused and misled by language is 'semantics'.[12]

This latter species of semantics stems from *The Meaning of Meaning* (1923) by C. K. Ogden and I. A. Richards who, however, had read with care certain of Peirce's papers, to which they devote a lengthy appendix, and had some acquaintance (by way of Russell) with Frege. In general terms, they welded together a version of Peirce's theory of signs and a behaviourist psychology of the sort presented in Russell's *Analysis of Mind*.

Two features of *The Meaning of Meaning* caused a particular stir: its nominalism and its theory of 'emotive meaning'. As so often happens in contemporary philosophy, Ogden and Richards appeal to the horrid example of Meinong's theory of objects: *that* is what happens, they warn us, if we dare to suppose that abstract nouns name entities.[13] Ogden and Richards swing to the opposite extreme, to the sort of position Wittgenstein was to criticize in his *Philosophical Investigations*. A 'proper symbol', they argue – as distinct from a 'symbolic accessory' – is always the name of a spatio-temporal event, or can be expanded into a set of such names. This side of their work was adopted with enthusiasm by such writers as A. Korzybski in his *Science and Sanity* (1933) and Stuart Chase in *The Tyranny of Words* (1938). Never have abstractions been assailed with such violence; whole areas of human thinking were dismissed with ignominy as congeries of empty abstractions.

The distinction between 'emotive' and 'descriptive' language, too, won converts everywhere; often enough, it was used to damn whatever is not a proposition of physical science. But it also had wider philosophical consequences.[14] Of the proposition 'this is good' Ogden and Richards had written: 'the peculiarly ethical sense of "good" is a purely emotive sense ... "is good" has no symbolic function; it serves only as an emotive sign expressing an attitude ... and perhaps evoking similar attitudes to other people or inciting them to actions of one sort or another.' This approach to ethics – worked out more fully by C. L. Stevenson in his article on 'Persuasive Definitions' (*Mind*, 1938) and his *Ethics and Language* (1944) – helped to destroy the view that every statement of the form *S is P* offers a description of *S*. Thus it opened the way to a free consideration of the diverse functionings of statements, even if the original dichotomy 'descriptive or emotive' was soon abandoned as being altogether too little discriminating.

Of those semanticists whose work stands close to *The Meaning of Meaning* the most thorough and systematic is C. W. Morris.[15] He, too, is greatly indebted to Peirce – indeed his work is a detailed commentary on Peirce's theory of signs – and he, too, is a philosophical behaviourist. In his *Foundations of the Theory of Signs* (*US*, 1938) he distinguished, in a way which has helped to fix the usage, within 'semiotics', the general theory of signs, three subsciences: 'syntactics', which describes the relations of signs one to another, 'semantics', which describes the manner in which they designate, and 'pragmatics', which describes the relation between signs and their interpreters. Morris himself is mainly interested in interpretation; he hopes to show, in particular, that the interpretation of signs is not a 'private' mental performance but a mode of publicly-observable behaviour. In the end, indeed, he is led to reconsider his original description of 'semiotics'. He had placed altogether too much stress, he came to think, on language; the proper approach to a theory of signs is Peirce's – to take as primary those modes of behaviour in which our action is a consequence of our 'interpretation' of a situation. The characteristic 'sign-using behaviour', on this view, is exemplified in our putting on a coat at the sight of rain clouds rather than in our reading a book; in Morris's *Signs, Language and Behaviour*, indeed, 'semantics' moves over into social psychology.

Semantics of the more narrowly philosophical sort derives from

Tarski rather than from Ogden and Richards. In strict historical justice, we should first describe the work of Leśniewski and T. Kotarbinski, to which Tarski is greatly indebted. But this is still unpublished or else has been published only in Polish; for the world outside Poland, Polish semantics begins with the appearance in a German translation of Tarski's 1933 essay on the semantic conception of truth.[16]

If the demon of metaphysics is to be exorcized, Carnap and Neurath had presumed, expressions like 'meaning', 'truth', 'designation' must be defined in purely syntactical terms (i.e. as referring to the properties of sentences in a formal system). In *The Logical Syntax of Language* Carnap's attempt to carry through this programme to its bitter end reduces him to desperate measures: he interprets 'yesterday's lecture treated of Africa', for example, as a misleading way of asserting that 'yesterday's lecture contained the word "Africa"'! Carnap welcomed Tarski's semantics because it removed the necessity for such forced 'translations' – even if some of the more obdurate positivists remained convinced that Tarski was a metaphysician in formal dress.

Furthermore, Tarski promised a way out of the 'semantic paradoxes'. These paradoxes, he argues, cannot be resolved in any language which is 'semantically closed', i.e. which contains within itself not only sentences but the names of sentences – '*snow is white*', for example, is the name of *snow is white* – and such sentence-designations as 'true', 'false', 'synonymous'. For in any such language sentences can be constructed of the form 'all true sentences are X' – sentences which refer to themselves; the paradoxes, according to Tarski, arise immediately and inevitably once such self-referential statements are admitted into a language. Tarski's arguments have been a useful weapon in the struggle of formalists against 'ordinary language' philosophies; since ordinary language does contain such 'self-referring' expressions it is bound to be infected, the formalists maintain, with irresolvable paradoxes.[17]

Tarski's best-known contribution to semantics, his definition of truth, begins by laying down conditions for the 'material adequacy' of any such definition; an adequate definition of truth, he says, must imply the equivalence: 'The sentence "snow is white" is true if and only if snow is white.' More generally, where

401

p is a sentence and *X* is the name of the sentence, the definition must imply all equivalences of the form '*X* is true, if and only if *p*'. This equivalence, it should be observed – for the contrary is sometimes supposed – is not in itself a definition of truth; it does no more than establish the conditions which a definition of truth must satisfy.

In order to avoid self-reference, Tarski continues, 'truth' must be defined in a metalanguage, a metalanguage rich enough to include every sentence of the object-language – since any such sentence can be substituted for *p* in the class of equivalences the definition implies – names for all these object-sentences, and such general logical expressions as 'if and only if'. Within this metalanguage Tarski finally arrives at a definition of truth – it is too technical for description here – which satisfies, he believes, the requirement of material adequacy without leaving any loophole through which paradoxes can creep.

Many philosophers have been doubtful about the value of such exercises in formal semantics, but Carnap had no qualms; he seized with enthusiasm upon the new methods Tarski was exploiting.[18] Thus in Carnap's later work philosophy is identified with 'semiotic' – he takes over Morris's terminology – not with syntax; many of the questions, for example the 'problem of meaning', which he had previously discussed in syntactical terms he now regards as primarily semantic issues.[19] But this does not mean that his work diminishes in formality; on the contrary *The Formalization of Logic* (1943) is an attempt to formalize such semantic expressions as 'true', 'false', 'truth-value', 'value of a variable', which logicians, so Carnap complains, had ordinarily used in an informal way. They had relied on nothing better than instinct and commonsense to save themselves from error. Carnap promises them the security of definite and exact rules.

In *Meaning and Necessity* (1947), the third of Carnap's *Studies in Semantics*, Carnap takes up once more the favourite themes of Mill and Frege.[20] Modern philosophical logicians, according to Carnap, have commonly supposed that every expression in a well-formed language is the name of a concrete subsistent entity whereas in fact, he argues, expressions 'mean' in virtue of their possessing an extension and an intension – in Frege's language, a 'reference' and a 'sense'. On the basis of this theory of designation – worked out in considerable detail – Carnap sketches the outlines of a modal logic, in which modal statements are interpreted as asserting semantical properties of sentences. ('*A* is necessarily *B*,' for example, asserts that 'the sentence "*A* is *B*" is a necessary one'). Thus modal logic, too, turns out to be a branch of semantics. Indeed, if Carnap is right, semantics is a discipline of fundamental importance in every branch of logic.

Throughout his writings, for all their variety in other respects, Carnap insists upon the distinction between 'logical' and 'factual' truth; he was distressed to observe that Tarski took this distinction very lightly. A number of leading American logicians, of whom W. V. O. Quine is the best known, have carried Tarski's heterodox suggestions to a striking extreme.

Unlike most of the logicians we have recently been discussing, Quine has remained faithful to the Russell-Whitehead 'logistics'. Although in his 'New Foundations for Mathematical Logic'[21] he abandons the theory of types and works with a smaller number of elementary logical notions than the *Principia* had employed, his 'new foundations' are a modification, not a wholesale rejection, of the Whitehead-Russell philosophy of mathematics. Quine is faithful, as well, to the ideal of an extensional logic, and sceptical about the possibility of constructing modal logics, except at great theoretical cost.[22] Yet if he is conservative as a logician, his philosophical observations are of a distinctly fresh, not to say revolutionary, character.

Two of his brief essays in particular – 'On What There Is' (*RM*, 1948) and 'Two Dogmas of Empiricism' (*PR*, 1951)[23] – have astonished his British contemporaries. 'On What There Is' sets out to discover in what respects our acceptance of a specific logical theory commits us ontologically – a project which most British philosophers would rule out *a priori* on the ground that logic is ontologically neutral. The mere use of names, he argues, does not commit us to asserting that the names we are using – say 'Pegasus' – all refer to entities, nor does the use of predicates imply that there must be universals. On the other hand, according to Quine, the use of 'bound variables' *does* commit us. Take the statement 'some dogs are white': to assert this, he argues, is to be committed to maintaining that '*there is something* which is both a dog and white', although not to the existence of 'whiteness' or 'dogginess'. Similarly, Quine considers, to say that 'some zoological species are cross-fertile' is to commit ourselves, *prima facie* at least, to the existence of species.

This commitment is only *prima facie*, he thinks, because a logician might devise a method of reformulating these statements – a method parallel to Russell's theory of descriptions – so that they do not mention species. The reformulated statement will still commit us to the existence of *something*, but not, perhaps, to the existence of species. A logician cannot compel us to accept his reformulations; but it is important to see whether a logic can be worked out which is not committed to the existence of species and yet can formalize biological statements. Then if for other reasons – because, say, it provides us with a simpler and broader conceptual scheme – we think it better to adopt a species-free ontology, we shall know at least that there is nothing in logic to force us to reject such an ontology. Quine himself would like so to reformulate mathematical propositions that they do not commit him to the existence of universals; but no one need feel the least obligation, he fully admits, to follow him in his asceticism.[24] The only point he wants to insist upon is this: if we do accept a particular mode of formalizing, we are at the same time compelled to accept the ontology which goes with it. 'It is wrong to admit abstract entities,' so he sums up this point, 'and gloss over their admission.'

In 'Two Dogmas of Empiricism', Quine attacks two distinct but, he thinks, related 'dogmas': the first that there is a fundamental distinction between incorrigible (or analytic) and corrigible (or synthetic) propositions, the second that every meaningful statement is a construction out of immediate experiences. Quine follows Duhem in arguing that the scientist brings to the test of experience a set of propositions, not an isolated assertion; a proposition, on this view, is an ingredient in a scientific system, as distinct from a mere 'summary of experiences'. If experience turns out unexpectedly, Quine argues, no one can say in advance which of the set of scientific propositions will be abandoned – any one of them is in principle corrigible, synthetic. Some of them, no doubt, *look* unassailable; we cannot imagine any circumstances in which we would give them up. But, he points out, the discovery of quanta phenomena, which no one could have imagined in advance, has led many scientists to abandon such apparently impregnable propositions as the principle of causality and the law of excluded middle. This should be a warning to us, Quine argues, not to imagine that *any* proposition is intrinsically unmodifiable by experience.

Formal tests for analyticity, he also maintains, are no more satisfactory than epistemological tests. Consider the following common line of reasoning: 'no bachelors are married' is analytic because it can be converted into a tautology by substituting 'unmarried men' for its synonym 'bachelors'. How are we to tell, Quine asks, that 'bachelors' and 'unmarried men' are synonymous? Often enough, analyticity is used as a proof of synonymity: two expressions x and y are said to be synonymous if 'x is y' is analytic. But anyone who proposes to use the method of substituting synonyms as a test for analyticity will have to give an independent definition of synonymity. No interpretation of synonymity, he tries to show, will do the trick; and he concludes that neither by the method of substitution of synonyms nor by any other means can a class of propositions be picked out as analytic.[25] He is quite ready to admit that there are some propositions – the propositions of arithmetic, for example – which we should abandon only as a last resort, but not that there is any proposition which cannot *in principle* be rejected in the light of further experience.

One of the most independent of recent logicians – although he, too, has been much influenced by Tarski – is Karl Popper, whose logical writings have so far appeared only as articles. In his 'New Foundations for Logic' (*Mind*, 1947),[26] he sets out from what he regards as the fundamental problem of logic: how valid can be distinguished from invalid inferences. Following Tarski, he defines a valid inference as one which is so constructed that any interpretation of it which makes its premises true will also make its conclusion true. Thus, for example, *if p and q, then p* is a valid inference because if any true propositions are substituted for the p and the q of *p and q* then, on the same interpretation, the conclusion p will also be true.

In this case the validity of the inference is trivial; we may be inclined to object that *if p and q, then p* 'isn't an inference at all'. But Popper's choice of trivial examples is deliberate – it is his object to complete what in his address to the *Tenth International Congress of Philosophy* (1948) he called 'the trivialization of mathematical logic'. Earlier attempts to trivialize logic by means of the truth-table method broke down; Popper adopts a quite different line of attack. He sets out to show, in the first place, that all the leading notions of mathematical logic can be defined in terms of a single primitive notion – the transitive and reflexive relation of deducibility. Even quantification and identity, neither of them definable by the truth-table method, Popper thinks he can define in terms of deducibility. Then, making use of none but trivial inferences, the complex structure of mathematical logic can be wholly derived, he tries to show, from these definitions; in that way it is possible to construct what Popper calls 'a logic without assumptions'. It has no need of axioms, since the general notion of deducibility is by itself a sufficient starting-point.

Popper first made his name in English-speaking countries with *The Open Society and Its Enemies* (1945) which created something of a sensation by the violence of its attacks on Plato and Hegel; that book, although it discusses in passing a variety of logical and methodological questions, lies for the most part outside our ambit. His *The Logic of Scientific Discovery* (1935) did not appear in a (much-enlarged) translated version until 1959 and was for many years hard to come by. Its leading doctrines had all the same a considerable impact on British methodological writings.[27]

Popper takes as his point of departure what he calls 'the problem of demarcation', the problem of distinguishing between science and 'pseudo-science'. 'Pseudo-science', according to Popper, includes not only transcendental metaphysics but also astrology – which claims to be empirical – and, more important still, such ostensibly scientific theories as psycho-analysis and the Marxist philosophy of history. Popper is not concerned to discuss whether these theories are true, but only whether, as they claim to be, they are *scientific*. That is the motive behind his 'thesis of refutability': an hypothesis is 'scientific', he argues, if and only if it is possible in principle to refute it.

Although Popper was never a member of the Vienna Circle, he was in close contact with it, and his 'thesis of refutability' has often been interpreted – by Carnap, for example – as a revised version of the verificationist theory of meaning.[28] He was read as saying: 'No, not verifiability in principle but refutability in principle is the test of meaningfulness.' In fact, however, Popper was convinced that 'the problem of meaning' is of no real importance; the positivist attempt to find a 'criterion of significance', he thought, led to no positive results, but only to the setting up of quite arbitrary stipulations. Refutability, as he conceived it, is not a criterion of meaning but a method of distinguishing between science and its simulacra.

It had sometimes been said that a scientific hypothesis is one which can be confirmed; sometimes again that a hypothesis is scientific if it is highly probable; or even that it is scientific in so far as it 'explains everything which can possibly happen'. The thesis of refutability is directed against all these views. If an hypothesis 'explains' every possibility, Popper argues, it explains nothing; it must be incompatible with some possible observation if it is to explain *any* observation. On this ground, Popper rejects the claims of Marxism to be scientific. Whatever happens, the Marxist says, *must* confirm his hypotheses about the course of social development, but if this is so he can never explain why things work out in one way rather than in another – his 'hypotheses', then, are completely unscientific in character.

Again, there is no difficulty in thinking of a 'highly probable' hypothesis. All we have to do is to make some trivial or vacuous suggestion; the less it commits us to, the more probable it is. Thus if we want to explain, say, why someone has a fever, the explanation 'there must be something wrong with him', is highly probable, much more probable than 'he has measles', but it is entirely without scientific value. The scientist, so Popper argues, does not look for a highly probable hypothesis but for one which commits him to definite expectations – and will be *definitely* ruled out if they are not realized. It is a useful exercise, he suggests, to think of every scientific statement in terms of what it rules out, as 'all tigers are carnivorous', for example, rules out the existence of non-carnivorous tigers. In that way we understand its force; and we see just how it could be refuted – by the discovery of such tigers.

Finally, it is not enough to say that a scientific hypothesis is one which can be confirmed, since it is nearly always possible to find confirmations of a hypothesis. The real question is whether a hypothesis has been thoroughly tested, i.e. whether thorough efforts have been made to refute it. That is Popper's ground for objecting to the scientific claims of astrology. Astrological hypotheses – e.g. that people born in September are sensitive – can no doubt be confirmed in innumerable cases; but the astrologer does not subject them to the test of attempting to refute them. Thus, to sum up, refutability is the distinguishing mark of scientific hypotheses; and there is science only where there are systematic attempts (successful or unsuccessful) to refute.

If a hypothesis stands up to severe tests, it has been 'corroborated'. Popper has worked out a calculus of corroboration,[29] mainly in order to demonstrate that it is not a probability calculus. He tries to show, indeed, that it is self-contradictory to identify 'highly corroborated' with 'having a high degree of probability'. Degree of corroboration, he suggests, is a measure of the extent to which the corroborated hypothesis has stood up to severe testing and, therefore, of the rationality of accepting, tentatively, that hypothesis; it is not a measure of the probability of its being true.

The 'severity' of a test is, however, definable in terms of probability. Hypotheses are tested against a background of accepted beliefs. Duhem, and after him Quine, drew the consequence that what is tested is not the new hypothesis alone but the whole system of accepted beliefs.[30] This 'holistic' doctrine Popper rejects; it is essential to the progress of science, he argues, that a single hypothesis can be tested separately. But in measuring the severity of a test background knowledge is taken into account. If certain consequences follow from the hypothesis when, in the light of our background knowledge alone, the probability is low that they would occur, then it will be a severe test of the hypothesis to see whether they in fact occur.[31]

A good theory, for Popper, is one which can be severely tested; and this means that it has a 'high informative content' and 'great explanatory power' – these being closely related.[32] For the more, if true, it would add to our knowledge, the easier it will be to distinguish its consequences from the consequences of what we already believe to be true, and the more readily, therefore, shall we be able to subject it to severe tests.

It will be obvious that Popper has abandoned the 'inductive' analysis of scientific method, according to which science begins from 'pure observations' which it gradually builds up by induction into generalizations. Scientists gradually come to believe in the existence of regularities, on this view, as a result of their having repeated experiences of similar patterns of events. But in fact, Popper objects, we are all of us born with expectations, inborn reactions, of which the expectation of regularity is the most important. What we have gradually to develop is a *critical attitude* – not a propensity to generalize, but a willingness to subject our generalizations to testing.

Observations, he argues, are not the 'raw material' of theories; on the contrary, theory guides us to observations. 'At no stage of scientific development,' he writes in *The Poverty of Historicism*, 'do we begin without something in the nature of a theory ... which *guides* our observations, and helps us to select from the innumerable objects of observation those that may be of interest.' To Hume's suggestion that our expectations arise out of the resemblance between our experiences, Popper objects that 'resemblance' is always *similarity in some respect that is important to us*: to recognize a similarity, then, is already to have expectations.

The starting-point of science, according to Popper, is the critical examination of myths – myths which flow from our inborn dogmatism – not the collection of observations. So, he concludes, the scientist is not called upon to explain how he 'makes the transition from observations to theories'; there is no problem of induction. Beginning with hypotheses, the scientist attempts to eliminate the false ones by showing that they lead to false conclusions. The logical justification of his procedure lies in the fact that universal propositions – the only propositions Popper admits within the corpus of science – can be falsified by propositions which assert the existence of observable events at particular points in space and time. Propositions of this sort are 'basic', not in the sense that they represent some sort of 'immediate experience', but just because it is by means of them that a hypothesis is tested. If we 'accept' a basic proposition – there is, Popper thinks, an element of convention in our procedure at this point – we are bound to reject any hypothesis it contradicts. An hypothesis, he argues, cannot be 'constructed out of' a set of basic propositions, for the very good reason that no such set could be equivalent to a universal proposition, i.e. a proposition which, as we have already seen, *denies* existential propositions. (The set of propositions 'this is a carnivorous tiger, that is a carnivorous tiger, etc.', cannot together be equivalent to 'there are no non-carnivorous tigers'.) So general hypotheses cannot possibly be 'established by induction'.

In *The Logic of Scientific Discovery* Popper laid such stress on the importance of refutation that he has not unnaturally been accused of adopting a 'negative attitude' to science, of quite ignoring the fact that the progress of science has involved a gradual accumulation of knowledge. In his later writings, most obviously in 'Truth, Rationality and the Growth of Scientific Knowledge', Popper has to some degree modified his views, although the title of the volume in which that essay first appeared – *Conjectures and Refutations* (1963) – makes it apparent that this shift of emphasis is not to be taken as implying an abandonment, as distinct from a development, of his earlier ideas.

In his earlier writings, Popper seemed to be more concerned with whether a theory is interesting than with whether it is true. Like many of the logical positivists, indeed, he was somewhat reluctant to speak in terms of 'truth'. Under Tarski's influence, however, he came to feel that it is possible to develop an objective theory of truth – as distinct from a theory of 'acceptability' – and to define in terms of truth the progress of science. But whereas for 'inductivists' scientific progress consists in the gradual accumulation of truth, for Popper it consists in the replacement of theories by better theories. 'Better', Popper now emphasizes, contains as an ingredient 'closer to the truth'; the better theory has greater 'verisimilitude'. Popper defines 'verisimilitude' by reference to what he calls the 'content' of a theory, the class consisting of all its logical consequences. This can be divided into its 'truth-content' – i.e. the true propositions which follow from it – and its 'falsity content' i.e. the false propositions which follow from it (this may, of course, be an empty class). Theory t_2 has greater 'verisimilitude' than theory t_1 if the truth-content but not the falsity-content of t_2 exceeds that of t_1, or if the falsity-content of t_2 but not its truth-content exceeds that of t_2. So even after theory t_2 is eventually refuted, we can still properly say of it that it was a better theory – had greater verisimilitude – than theory t_1. This allows us to understand how science can progress, even although that progress takes the form of refuting existing theories. At the same time it helps us to see why science proceeds by seeking to refute, i.e. by trying to find out whether a theory has a 'falsity-content', and why, too, it looks for wider theories – theories which have a greater 'truth-content' than have narrower theories. So that to say that science seeks 'verisimilitude' is not at all to say that it proceeds cautiously, or accumulates facts one by one, or prefers highly probable to less probable theories.

Popper now contrasts his methodology not only with 'inductivist' methodologies, but, no less sharply, with that theory of science which takes as its ideal an axiomatized, fully deductive system. Formalizing a theory is helpful, Popper suggests, just in so far as it assists us to compare the theory with its competitors and to see at what point it can be most severely tested. But it is not the final aim of science to produce such systems – its aim, rather, is to lead us to deeper and more interesting problems.

A third important feature of Popper's work is his criticism of what he calls 'essentialism', i.e. the attempt to answer questions of the form: 'What is a so-and-so?' by means of propositions which expound the 'real nature' or 'essence' of the thing in question. More generally, 'essentialism' is the view that it is the task of science to offer 'ultimate explanations' – a view which, Popper thinks, holds up inquiry and encourages obscurantism. Now, of course, Popper is not the first to criticize essentialism, but its critics, for example, Berkeley and Mach, have usually thought that the only alternative to essentialism is 'instrumentalism'; scientific theories, they have argued, are 'instruments' for coping more effectively with the world, not descriptions of it. But instrumentalism, Popper thinks, cannot account for our method of testing scientific hypotheses. An 'instrument', he argues, can break down, or can go out of fashion, but it certainly cannot be *refuted*. Furthermore, instrumentalism encourages a purely technological approach to science, engendering a complacency about the 'useful applications' of scientific theories, which in the end is fatal to scientific advance.

Popper hopes, then, to find a way between essentialism and instrumentalism. A scientific theory, he argues, is 'an informative guess about the world', a guess which is subjected to severe critical tests. This is as true of hypotheses about, say, electrons, as it is of hypotheses about living organisms. The 'essentialist', according to Popper, wrongly supposes that the electronic theory of matter 'destroys the reality' of tables and chairs by showing that in their 'real nature' they are 'only a collection of atoms'; the instrumentalist is no less mistaken in maintaining that the electronic theory is only an instrument for dealing with reality, not a description of it. Tables are not the 'real nature' of electrons, any more than electrons are the real nature of tables; both tables and electrons have equal claims to be considered real.[33]

A number of problems arise out of Popper's work. One of the most obvious, especially since the rise of statistical mechanics, is that although probability-statements play an important part in science they do not seem to be refutable: no existential proposition (e.g. *it is raining today*) could refute the hypothesis that, say *the probability of its raining in Canberra has the value p*. Popper has devoted considerable attention to this difficulty. He argues, first, that although quantum laws are tested by statistical observations, they are not themselves statistical, and secondly that, appearances to the contrary notwithstanding, probability hypotheses are in principle refutable, since they make assertions about frequencies in finite classes. But we shall understand this side of Popper's theory better – in any case it has not been widely influential – if we consider it in the general context of recent work on probability.[34]

Much of this work, like recent mathematical logic – with which indeed it is often closely associated – is of a highly technical character; it is not easy to discern and explain the philosophical points at issue. One naturally begins by drawing a broad contrast between two schools of probability: those who, like Keynes, define probability as a logical relation between propositions, for whom, then, probability propositions are of the form: 'in virtue of its relationship to the set of propositions n, the proposition s has the probability p', and those who follow Venn in advocating a frequency theory of probability; on their interpretation, probability statements are of the form 'the class of events b occur within the class of events a with the frequency f'. But the boundaries, as we shall see, are not so sharp and clear as this preliminary classification might suggest, and the sub-species are almost endless.[35]

Of recent methodologists, Harold Jeffreys stands closest to Keynes. Beginning from the Keynesian 'comparative' analysis of probability, Jeffreys tries to show in his *Scientific Inference* (1931) that a strictly quantitative probability-analysis, with the help of a conventional assignment of numerical values, can be founded on axioms which refer only to comparative probabilities. Jeffrey's work is rigorously axiomatic in form. Not at all designed for the casual reader, or for the philosopher who is not mathematically-inclined, it is a notable restatement and development of the Keynesian approach.

A theory of a somewhat similar kind, deriving in the end from Bolzano and more recently from J. von Kries's *Principles of the Calculation of Probabilities* (1886), was suggested by Wittgenstein in the *Tractatus* and worked out more fully by Waismann in his contribution to the first volume of *Erkenntnis* (1930)[36]. Every proposition, this theory begins by presuming, has a certain 'range' ('spielraum'), i.e. it leaves open certain possibilities. For Wittgenstein, a proposition's range is identical with its 'truth-grounds'. If the number of truth-grounds of the proposition r is represented by the symbol Tr, and the number of truth-grounds the propositions r and s have in common by Trs, then the ratio of Trs to Tr is the measure of probability r gives to s. Thus, for example, the probability of p in relation to p or q is $\frac{2}{3}$ since, from the truth-tables, p and $(p$ or $q)$ is true in two-thirds of the cases when p or q is true. Similarly, the probability of any atomic proposition p on the evidence of any other atomic proposition q is $\frac{1}{2}$, since this is the ratio of the number of truth-grounds of p and q to the number of truth-grounds of q.

Wittgenstein agrees with Keynes, it will be observed, that there is no sense in talking about the probability of a proposition *simpliciter*: the question, always, is to determine its probability in the light of the circumstances known to us. And this probability is defined *a priori* as a formal relation between logical possibilities. Only on such a view, Wittgenstein argues, can we understand how there can be a *calculus* of probability. That, say, the number of black balls drawn out of an urn gradually approximates to the number of white balls drawn out is an empirical

413

fact; on Wittgenstein's analysis of mathematical propositions it cannot, therefore, 'belong to mathematics'. Thus frequency theories, he argues, fail to explain the logico-mathematical character of probability relationships.

For Wittgenstein, empirically determined relative frequencies have only a negative importance in probability analyses. Suppose that on the basis of the information – all the relevant information at my disposal – that an urn contains an equal number of black and white balls, I have calculated the probability that a black ball will be drawn from the urn. Then I find that in fact the number of white balls drawn approximates to the number of black balls drawn; this confirms me in my belief that the drawing of the balls is not being influenced by circumstances unknown to me. But the actual calculation of probabilities is always a matter of logical deduction, simply. Waismann, similarly, will admit that our measurement of the degree of overlap between ranges is not always wholly determined by logical considerations – for in choosing between different possible estimates of the overlap we try to bring our results into accord with statistical experience – but still maintains that *the probability itself* consists in the relation between ranges.

Frequency theorists, on the contrary, *identify* probability with frequency. The frequency theory, its supporters say, brings probability down to earth, away from the mysterious areas inhabited by *a priori* possibilities and into the closest possible connexion with the practical work of the statistician. Indeed, R. von Mises in his *Probability, Statistics and Truth* (1928)[37] tried to work out a frequency theory of probability which would be as empirical as theoretical physics. But the actual effect of his work has been to cast doubts upon the empirical character of frequency theories. Frequentists had been accustomed to maintain that 'the probability of a penny turning up heads is $\frac{1}{2}$' is equivalent to 'in a long series of runs a penny turns up heads in half the total number of throws'. Obviously, however, 'in the long run' is inexact. And there is another difficulty. Suppose it always happened that every fifth penny was a tails and every tenth penny a heads. Then, although it would still be the case that half the throws in a long run are heads, it would no longer be natural to talk generally about 'the probability of a penny turning up heads', without any reference to its position in a series of throws. Probability theory, as we saw, grew out of work on gambling odds; obviously the odds are completely altered if it can be predicted in advance that a particular throw will always, and another throw never, turn up heads. Thus frequency, it would seem, cannot be identical with probability.

Von Mises attempts to meet both these objections. He introduces the conception of a 'collective', defined as an infinite class of observations which fulfils the following two conditions: first, the frequency with which a particular attribute characterizes particular members of the collective converges towards a limit, and secondly, the value of this limit will be unaffected if we consider, instead of the whole set of members of the collective, a sub-set distinguishable by the presence of some special characteristic. (This is the requirement of 'randomness', which von Mises also calls 'the principle of the impossibility of gambling systems'). Granted, however, that the notion of a collective, as von Mises claims, facilitates operations with the mathematical calculus of probabilities, it raises very serious problems about the empirical status of frequency-propositions. If frequency-assertions define probability by reference to convergences in an infinite class, how can they be confirmed or falsified by empirical investigation, we naturally ask, restricted as it is to *finite* classes?

Popper thought he could restore the frequency theory to an empirical footing by substituting the notion of a 'condensation point' of relative frequencies for von Mises' 'limit'. Unlike a limit, the condensation point is an *actual* frequency in a finite segment of the series – a frequency from which the frequency in other segments differs by only slight amounts. This frequency is the 'probability'; we then assert, as a hypothesis, that frequencies within future segments of the series will not differ from the value of the condensation point by more than assigned amounts. Thus – with reservations – probability assertions are testable.[38]

The most thoroughgoing upholder of the frequency theory, however, is certainly H. Reichenbach.[39] The principal novelty in Reichenbach's epistemology, which otherwise follows along traditional positivist lines, is the use he makes of the conception of 'weight' as a third truth value – indeed, in the end, as a substitute for truth-value. Very few propositions, he argues, can be characterized as true or false; we are never in a position, for example, thus to describe a proposition about the future. Every proposition, however, has a determinate 'weight' which, unlike truth, is measurable against a continuous scale. 'Truth' and 'falsity', according to Reichenbach, are abstractions from such a scale, ideal limiting cases. Like Keynes, Reichenbach believes that the 'weight' of a proposition is always relative to the state of our knowledge, but unlike Keynes he thinks that any meaningful proposition has a *determinate* weight – 'having a determinate weight' is, indeed, his criterion of meaningfulness – which can be calculated by reference to frequencies.

Keynes had rejected the frequency analysis of probability on two grounds: that it cannot account for our ascription of a probability to a *single* case, and that it can make nothing of the probability of propositions, as distinct from the frequency of events. Reichenbach admits that the frequentist will regard as inexact any reference to 'the probability' of a single event. For the assertion 'the probability that John Smith will die within a year is one in twenty' has, according to the frequency theory, only an elliptical meaning: it means 'on the basis of the fact that he is a member of a certain sub-class, and not of any narrower sub-class concerning which we have statistical knowledge, the "posit" that he will die has a probability of one in twenty'. Knowing, for example, that John Smith is a tubercular male of twenty-one and that one-twentieth of such males die before the year is out, and not knowing him to be a member of any narrower sub-class – say the class of tubercular males of twenty-one with a weak heart – about which we have accurate statistical knowledge, we can 'posit' (bet) that he has one chance in twenty of dying. Our 'posit' might be completely altered, Reichenbach points out, if the state of our knowledge were to change, e.g. if we were to discover that John Smith rides a motor-cycle. This proves, Reichenbach thinks, that statements about the probability of a single event have only a 'transferred' probability – a 'weight' on certain evidence – in contrast with statements like 'one in twenty among twenty-one-year-old tubercular patients die within the year', the truth of which remains unaffected by the discovery that such patients have this or that additional characteristic in common.

Nevertheless, although probability statements about individuals are 'fictitious', practical reasons force us to make such statements as 'posits'; we are justified in using statistical evidence for this purpose because there is no better way of proceeding. Since the statement that a certain event is probable can also be expressed, according to Reichenbach, in the form 'the proposition "this event will occur" is probable', his frequency analysis, he thinks, can as readily account for our ascription of probability to propositions as for its ascription to events; Keynes's second objection to frequency theories, then, falls with his first objection.

Formalizing his frequency analysis of probability, Reichenbach constructs a multi-valued probability logic, in which the two values 'true' and 'false' are replaced by the multi-valued concept of 'weight'. Such a formalized probability logic can be constructed, according to Reichenbach, just because, by way of the frequency interpretation, it reduces to arithmetic. It has no longer to be supposed, then, that when we make statements we do not actually know to be true – 'posits' about the future – we are making use of a special informal 'inductive' logic. Reichenbach's probability logic, he thinks, completes the empirical task of formalizing logic; he believes that he has shown – as against, say, Russell – that there is no need to invoke non-formalizable, inductively apprehensible, *a priori* principles in order to explain how we can make statements about the future.

A probability logic, however, is a mode of calculating with general probability statements. The question still remains, how do we establish such general statements? All we can actually observe is a limited set of cases. Suppose that within this set a characteristic recurs with a certain frequency; how does this prove that its frequency in all similar sets will converge towards the same, or indeed towards any, limit? For Reichenbach, this is the proper way of stating the classical problem of induction. Induction, he answers, is a *policy* – the policy of selecting a certain value for the limit of the frequency when (omitting complications) this limit is approached within the sets we have observed, and then correcting this value in the light of subsequent experience. The inductive policy is a justifiable one, he argues, because if there is any limit to the frequency, this is the best way of discovering what it is.

Reichenbach, then, is a determined and whole-hearted frequentist. Carnap, in his usual manner, prefers the role of a mediator.[40] He draws a sharp distinction between two sorts of probability: frequency-probability and confirmation-probability. The first, he says, is the province of statisticians, the second of logicians; nothing but chaos can result if, in Reichenbach's manner, we try to amalgamate them into a single theory. It is quite futile to suggest, he argues, that frequency is the only 'real' sort of probability; and it is equally futile to maintain that probability statements *never* assert frequencies. According to Carnap, then, frequentists and anti-frequentists are 'talking about different things' – about two quite different concepts of probability.

Confronted by a particular probability statement, we cannot always determine by inspection, according to Carnap, which concept of probability it incorporates. Suppose, referring to a loaded die, somebody says: 'The probability of this die turning up a six is 0.15'. Asked for his evidence, he replies: 'In a lengthy series of 1,000 throws – the only cases I know about – 150 throws yielded a six.' One may be inclined to conclude that he is using the frequency concept of probability. But if we probe further, Carnap suggests, we see that he is not simply *counting* a frequency: rather, he is *basing* a probability estimate on a frequency. His statement amounts to this: 'In respect of the evidence at my disposal, there is a high probability for the prediction that the relative frequency of sixes in a long series of future throws with this die will lie within an interval around 0.15.' So, Carnap argues, it is not an empirically corrigible statement about relative frequencies but an analytic statement about the logical relation between certain evidence and a conclusion.

Thus although Carnap is prepared to admit that probability statements may sometimes do no more than assert frequencies, the frequency interpretation, on his view, has an extremely limited area of application, much more limited than its exponents ordinarily imagine. In general, Carnap agrees with Keynes that probabilities are assigned to a particular event on purely logical grounds. But, unlike Keynes, Carnap hopes to work out a quantitative method of assigning a probability to an hypothesis. And unlike Waismann, he thinks that a measurement of the overlap of ranges or, as he puts it, of the 'degree of confirmability' of one proposition by another can be worked out by purely logical methods, which do not depend in the least upon statistical observations. Such methods, he considers, constitute the foundations of an inductive logic.

No logic, Carnap agrees with Popper, can tell us how to arrive at correct hypotheses. But in this respect, he argues, inductive logic and deductive logic are strictly comparable. There is no procedure, given certain axioms, for finding new theorems, although there is a procedure for testing the claim that such-and-such a theorem follows from the axioms; similarly, although given evidence e, there is no procedure for lighting on a hypothesis h which will explain e, there are, Carnap thinks, methods of testing any argument which professes to prove that the degree of confirmation of h, on the evidence e is, say, r (where r is a real number). These methods of testing – which correspond in function to the rules of syllogism in Aristotelian logic – constitute the 'logic of induction'. It is clear that inductive logic has, on Carnap's view, a very restricted function; his predecessors, Carnap says, were not philosophers like Mill, who confused logic and methodology, but rather the probability theorists. So far, Carnap has only sketched his theory of induction; some features of it are by no means clear.[41]

Four other recent works deal at length with this same theme of probability and induction: D. C. Williams's *The Ground of Induction* (1947), W. Kneale's *Probability and Induction* (1949), G. H. von Wright's *The Logical Problem of Induction* (1941), and R. B. Braithwaite's *Scientific Explanation* (1953). Williams is the most optimistic of them all; induction, for him, is simply a particular species of formally valid reasoning, with the peculiarity that the conclusion follows from the premises, not absolutely, but with a high probability. Suppose, for example, confronted with a load of apples, we wish to determine how many of them are worm-eaten. By purely mathematical reasoning, Williams argues, we can prove that if we select any reasonably-sized sample from the load the probability is very high that the proportion of worm-eaten apples in the sample will not differ by more than a small amount from the proportion of worm-eaten apples in the whole set. If, for example, 30% of the apples in the sample are worm-eaten, we are entitled to conclude that it is highly probable that somewhere between 25% and 35% of the whole load will be worm-eaten. Thus, he argues, we can justify our inductively-derived conclusions by purely logico-mathematical reasoning. No doubt there is a residue of risk; the sample *could* turn out to be an untypical one. But the risk is a calculated one, the sort of risk no rational man would fear to take.[42]

In a way, too, von Wright's[43] *The Logical problem of Induction* is a conservative book. He considers in turn each of the traditional modes of justifying inductive inferences: first, by setting out inductive methods; secondly, by basing them on some such general principle as the uniformity of Nature; thirdly, by arguing, in the conventionalist manner, that propositions established by induction are 'true by definition'; fourthly, by maintaining that inductively-derived propositions, if not demonstrably true, are at least highly probable. In each case, von Wright sets out the 'justification' in a more rigorous form than had been customary,[44] deploying the full resources of symbolic logic; his general conclusion is that the 'justification' never 'demonstrates the validity' of induction, but that each method of justification may properly be appealed to under certain circumstances. On the whole, however, von Wright is more interested in formalizing the traditional 'justifications' than in detailing the contexts in which they might properly be said to 'justify' induction.

Similarly, von Wright's discussion of probability, especially in his *A Treatise on Induction and Probability* (1951), is mainly concerned with the construction of an axiomatic system; very little is said about its interpretation. Indeed, his own conclusion is that when we formalize arguments from 'inductive probability' we observe that they are 'utterly trivial and void of practical interest'; the theory of probability, he thinks, is much more interesting as a calculus than as a practical instrument in inquiry. But to point this out, he also thinks, is an important piece of 'mental hygiene'; for it will disabuse the probability-theorist of any belief that he has found a magical method.

Kneale,[45] like Williams, hopes to construct a 'logical' theory of probability. Probability, he holds, is an objective relation connecting propositional functions: probability statements assert that X's being of the kind R makes it probable that it is of the kind *S*. The importance of such statements, he thinks, lies in their relationship to rational action; any satisfactory theory of probability must help us to understand – as, he says, the frequency theory does not – why it is *rational* to use a probabilified proposition as a basis for action.

A striking feature of Kneale's argument is that he rejects the now orthodox identification of 'principles' and 'well-attested facts'; principles, he argues, determine what the facts can be but are not themselves facts. Some principles – for example, the principle that nothing can be red and green all over at the same time – are, Kneale says, apprehended directly by 'intuitive induction'; other principles, including laws of nature, cannot so be apprehended. Yet they are clearly principles; for such a law of nature as '*P is Q*' does not assert, simply, that 'every *P* is a *Q*' but much more – that nothing can be *P* without being *Q*.* The 'inductive problem', for Kneale, is to explain why it is rational to believe such non-intuitive principles as laws of nature.

Kneale accepts a modified version of the 'range' theory of probability. The probability that *X*, by being a *P*, has the property *Q* is a function of the 'range' of *P* in relation to the range of *Q*. Now Wittgenstein in the *Tractatus* could express the range of a proposition as a conjunction of atomic propositions – comparing ranges, for him, was a simple matter of 'numbering off' atomic propositions. Kneale grants, in contrast, that a propositional function such as 'being an apple' leaves open an infinite range of possibilities; there is no end to the possible ways of describing an apple. But these possibilities, he tries to show – his argument at this point is highly abstract and difficult – can be grouped into sub-ranges, so that the set of alternative ways of being an apple can be compared, in principle, with the set of alternative ways of being, say, worm-eaten. Such a grouping, he grants, is possible only under conditions which are not usually satisfied; but his task, he says, is to *define* probability – he does not have to claim that he always knows how to measure it.

The range of a propositional function, according to Kneale, is limited by logical and scientific laws; only principles can establish what possibilities *P* leaves open, and with what it is incompatible. It is meaningless, he concludes, to talk about 'the probability'

*Compare Chapter 18, Note 21.

of natural laws. Natural laws are what determine probabilities – they are themselves neither probable nor improbable.

No doubt, Kneale admits, we sometimes ascribe probability to a hypothesis, i.e. to a proposition we suspect of being a natural law. But in doing so, he argues, we are making use of a concept of probability quite different from that which is involved in the calculation of chances – as comes out, he says, in the fact that we cannot sensibly assign a numerical value to 'the probability' of a hypothesis. It would be better, he therefore suggests, to talk of the 'acceptability' rather than the 'probability' of a hypothesis. The central inductive question can then be expressed thus: under what conditions is a hypothesis 'acceptable', i.e. under what conditions is it rational to use it in action as if it were a principle? Kneale answers that a hypothesis is 'acceptable' if it is reached with the the aid of 'the inductive policy', i.e. the policy of generalizing the frequencies experience has so far revealed to us (thus if we we know of no X's that are not Y, it is inductive policy to assert that all X's are Y) while at the same time – Kneale is a good deal influenced by Popper – keeping a sharp look-out for any experiences which might tell against our generalizations. But how, we might ask, is this policy itself to be justified? By showing, Kneale thinks, that it is the best policy to adopt if, as we do, we wish to predict the future.[46]

Kneale's work is thoroughly Cook Wilsonian in atmosphere; R. B. Braithwaite, on the contrary, is through-and-through a Cambridge man in interests and point of view. His *Scientific Explanation* discusses a very large number of methodological issues; he tries to show againt Kneale, for example, that laws of nature appear to have a peculiar necessity only because they fill a special role in the structure of scientific systems, and again he discusses at length the use of 'models' in scientific theory. But we shall have to concentrate on his analysis of probability and induction.

An important feature of Braithwaite's book is that he brings into the philosophical arena the work of the 'Neyman-Pearson' school of statisticians, and the 'theory of games' which has been developed under their influence.[47] Faced with the problem how it is possible either to demonstrate or to refute probability-statements, Braithwaite argues that it is possible to lay down a 'rule of rejection' for probability statements ('the k rule') although with the proviso that the rejection is never final; when we reject a probability-hypothesis on this view, it is always with the reservation that subsequent experience may lead us to reinstate it. The fact they can be thus provisionally rejected – Braithwaite, too, has felt Popper's influence – preserves the empirical character of probability-statements.

The k rule lays it down that the hypothesis that an a is a b with the probability p is to be rejected if, and only if, the number of b's in n observations of a is less or greater than p by an amount which is a function of the small number k. The value to be ascribed to k cannot be determined within the calculus of probabilities; if the hypothesis is one which is of great practical importance, we assign to k a very low value, so that the hypothesis will be rejected only if the percentage of b's in n observations of a differs from p by a very large amount; if the hypothesis is of theoretical interest, only, we shall assign to k a very high value. Thus 'ethical' interests – considerations of relative importance – enter into the very heart of the decision whether to reject a hypothesis. Only with the aid of such considerations, Braithwaite further argues, can we possibly decide between alternative hypotheses, when none of them can be refuted by the k-rule.

This does not mean that the decision between hypotheses is an arbitrary one; for it is possible in principle, Braithwaite thinks, to *calculate* what we stand to gain or lose by adopting a particular hypothesis. Our choice is a rational one when we select the most profitable hypothesis. In the end, then, utility, not pure logic, must guide our choice; and even utility can guide us only if the relative utilities of alternative hypotheses can be mathematically compared.[48]

CHAPTER 18

Wittgenstein and Ordinary Language Philosophy

IN his preface to the *Tractatus*, Wittgenstein expressed himself thus confidently: 'the truth of the thoughts communicated here seems to me unassailable and definitive.' 'I am of the opinion,' he continued, 'that the problems have in essentials been finally solved.' One need not be surprised, then, that he abandoned philosophy for a number of years. He had turned philosopher, in his engineer's way, in order to drain what seemed to him a swamp. The task was completed; there was no more to be said.

In his years of silence, however, he was not left entirely alone. Ramsey and Braithwaite sought him out in his Austrian retreat and, for some part of the time, he was in close contact with Schlick and Waismann.* Round about 1928, his interest in philosophy revived. The stimulus may have been Brouwer's lectures on the foundations of mathematics, the set of problems which had originally led Wittgenstein to philosophy. In 1929, he returned to Cambridge.

His paper on 'Logical Form', his last public statement of the views he was later unreservedly to condemn, was published in the *Proceedings of the Aristotelian Society* (Supplementary Volume) for that same year. Philosophy, Wittgenstein there argued, attempts to construct an 'ideal language', a language the terms of which are all of them precisely defined and the sentences of which unambiguously reveal the logical form of the facts to which they refer; such a perfect language must rest upon atomic propositions; the fundamental philosophical problem is to describe the

---

*His conversations with Ramsey, Wittgenstein tells us, woke him from his dogmatic slumber. We can as yet only guess what these discussions were about; but it is worth noting that there is a distinct pragmatic streak both in the later writings of Ramsey and in *Philosophical Investigations*. Professor D. A. T. Gasking has suggested to me that some of the ideas about science contained in N. Campbell's *Physics: The Elements* may also have been brought to Wittgenstein's notice by Ramsey. Wittgenstein was also greatly influenced, he tells us himself, by the criticisms of the economist P. Sraffa – I do not know in what respects.

structure of these atomic propositions. His subsequent writings are in large part a reaction against this Russellian 'philosophy of logical atomism'.[1]

Philosophers, Wittgenstein came to think, had made the mistake of trying to model their activities on those of scientists – as indeed, the very phrase 'logical atomism' suggests; that is why they had tried to lay down strict definitions and to discover true, if unusually abstract, universal propositions. When, for example, Socrates asked Theaetetus to tell him what knowledge is and Theaetetus replied by mentioning various cases in which we would ordinarily be said to 'have knowledge', Socrates refused to accept this answer even as a starting-point; nothing less would content him than an attempt to state 'the essence of knowledge' by offering a strict definition of it. Yet such a strict definition, Wittgenstein argues, is neither possible nor desirable.

Of course, we could *make* our definitions strict at the cost of arbitrarily ruling that this or that is 'not really knowledge'; but to proceed thus, according to Wittgenstein, is quite to misunderstand the nature of a philosophical issue. For philosophical purposes, in order to find our way out of that tangle of puzzles philosophers have been accustomed to call 'the theory of knowledge', we need to undertake a detailed concrete examination of the cases in which people *actually* use the word 'knowledge' – the roles that word plays in ordinary, everyday language, not in a purified super-refined language. These various roles, according to Wittgenstein, cannot be summed up in a brief formula, a 'strict definition': the words which interest philosophers are 'handyman' words, with a variety of jobs, but no rigidly definable responsibilities. (Quite unlike such a word as 'lithium' which has a narrow, professional job to do.)

But how are these various ways of using the word 'knowledge' linked with one another, we may ask, if not through a formal definition? Look at a concrete case, Wittgenstein exhorts us, to see how word-uses can be linked without being describable in a single comprehensive formula. Consider the word 'game' for example. Board-games have many points in common with card-games, but share only some of these similarities (rigidly-defined rules, for example) with football; ring-a-ring-a-roses has something in common with football, but what with chess? The result of our survey, Wittgenstein argues, is that 'we see a complicated network of similarities overlapping and criss-crossing: sometimes overall similarities, sometimes similarities of detail'. Such a network he calls a 'family'.[2] The 'essence' of a game will consist in these complex, interlacing ways of using the word 'game' – a conclusion Wittgenstein sums up in an epigram: 'essence is expressed by grammar: grammar tells us what kind of object anything is.'

'Grammar' is here a technical expression; there are others in the *Philosophical Investigations*, like 'language-game' and 'criterion'. His readers – and still more his expositors – are disconcerted because Wittgenstein does not pause to explain how he is using these expressions.* This failure to explain, whether justifiable or not, is a direct consequence of Wittgenstein's conception of philosophy. Exact definitions would make philosophy look like a species of science; philosophy, as Wittgenstein envisages it, explains nothing, analyses nothing – it simply describes.

Furthermore, he considers, even its descriptions are important only as an ingredient in a process of therapy. Certain features of the way we use words like 'knowledge' generate philosophical disorders, making us feel intellectually dizzy or frustrated. Nothing less can cure us, Wittgenstein thinks, than an exact description of our actual usage, a description which, however, is of no intrinsic interest. 'The philosopher's treatment of a question,' he writes, 'is like the treatment of an illness.' To take a different metaphor: the philosopher shows the bewildered fly how to get out of the bottle into which he has flown. ('The philosopher', in such contexts, means the good philosopher, i.e. the philosopher who makes use of Wittgenstein's methods; most philosophers, he would say, have spread disease rather than cured it, have helped to lure the fly into the bottle.[3])

*Compare Moore's comment: 'I still think he was not using the phrase rules of grammar in any ordinary sense, and I am still unable to form any clear idea as to how he was using it.' And Malcolm: 'With some reluctance I will undertake to say a little bit about the notion of "criterion", a most difficult region in Wittgenstein's philosophy.' See R. Albritton: 'On Wittgenstein's Use of the Term "Criterion"' (*JP*, 1959); C. Wellman: 'Wittgenstein's Conception of a Criterion' (*PR*, 1962); M. Garver *et al.*: 'Wittgenstein on Criterion' in *Knowledge and Experience* (ed. C. D. Rollins, 1964).

If then, we wish to understand Wittgenstein's treatment of a philosophical question, we must first ask ourselves: from what particular temptations is he trying to deliver us? Take his discussion of meaning. Wittgenstein there concentrates his attention on two principal temptations: the first, to regard every word as a name, a temptation which leads us, in Meinong's manner, to postulate mysterious pseudo-entities to serve as the objects of reference for, say, abstract nouns; the second, the temptation to think that 'understanding a word', 'learning a word's meaning', is some sort of mental process, involving the contemplation of what Locke called an 'idea' or Schlick a 'content' – an analysis of meaning which leads inevitably to the puzzles Schlick's writings so abundantly exemplify.[4]

If we keep calm, and look without prejudice at the way words are actually used, Wittgenstein considers, the 'mystery of meaning' will evaporate. We can more easily preserve our balance, he also thinks, if we begin by considering possible, rather than actual, languages. Now this is Carnap's view too, but whereas Carnap's 'possible' languages, as he describes them in *The Logical Syntax of Language*, are complex artificial formulae, calculi, which we could not possibly use in the ordinary affairs of life, Wittgenstein describes a mode of social behaviour – although sometimes the behaviour of an imaginary tribe rather than of a real community – and asks us to consider the sort of language which would be practically useful within such a 'form of life'.[5] Suppose, for example, a builder is working with a labourer: he teaches his labourer to bring him a slab when he says 'Slab!', a brick when he says 'Brick!' and so on. Then this, Wittgenstein thinks, is the kind of language philosophers must have had in mind – he quotes Augustine – when they wrote of language as if it wholly consisted of names.

Such a language, he points out, is obviously very much simpler than the English language; it is of use in far fewer social situations. But furthermore – and this is the fundamental point – even in this simplified language words are not mere names. To understand, say, the word 'slab' is to grasp how it is used in a certain 'language-game' – in this case the 'game' of receiving and giving orders. To obtain this grasp we might have to undertake such procedures as listening to the builder while he points to certain objects and says '*that* is a slab'. Alternatively, a way of looking at the matter which, Wittgenstein thinks, brings out the fact that a name is a label, the word 'slab' might actually be printed on the slabs; then we should have to learn how to read this word before we could obey the builder's instructions. But such processes – we might call them 'learning the names of objects' – are, according to Wittgenstein, preliminaries to the use of a language, not examples of it. 'Naming is not so far a move in the language-game,' he writes, 'any more than putting a piece in its place on the board is a move in chess.'

'The meaning of "slab", then, does not consist in the objects it names, but in the way it is used in a language.' If the actual slab – the physical object – were part of the meaning of 'slab', Wittgenstein argues, we ought to be able to say things like: 'I broke part of the meaning of the word "slab"', 'I laid a hundred parts of the meaning of the word "slab" today'. Such sentences are obvious nonsense – which helps us to see, Wittgenstein suggests, that the 'naming' theory of meaning is also nonsense. (Wittgenstein's argument at this point is an example of what he regards as an important therapeutical method: 'converting concealed nonsense into *overt* nonsense'.)

In certain special cases, Wittgenstein admits, we might say to somebody: 'the word "slab" means *this* sort of building material', accompanying our remarks by pointing to a slab. But then, he considers, we are talking to someone who already understands our particular language-game, telling him to use the word 'slab' – not the word 'brick' – at a certain point in that game. The 'naming' theory of meaning, Wittgenstein is suggesting, derives its plausibility from those atypical cases in which we are extending our vocabulary within an already familiar language or learning a foreign language, whereas an adequate analysis will have to concentrate its attention upon the ways in which we come to understand *our own* language. Approaching the matter in this way, he thinks, we shall soon see that learning what labels to put on objects is no more 'understanding a language' than repeating words after a teacher is 'speaking a language' – although both labelling and repeating may be useful, or even essential, preliminaries to understanding.

Why had theories of meaning, Wittgenstein asks, placed such

stress on pointing, or 'ostensive definition'? Because philosophers had thought, he answers, that pointing clears matters up, that it takes us beyond the risk of misunderstanding by indicating precisely what is being talked about. But, Wittgenstein argues, there is no way of removing the risk of misunderstanding: we can misunderstand what somebody is pointing at, just as we can misunderstand a formal verbal definition. If, for example, a teacher points to a red square and says 'red', his pupils might conclude that he is telling them the name of a square. Philosophers had supposed – Wittgenstein has particularly in mind the *Tractatus* and Russell's logical atomism – that there must be an 'ultimate analysis' of an expression's meaning, an analysis consisting of simple elements to which we would point in order to make that meaning perfectly clear. But there are no 'simples', he now thinks, in the sense that logical atomism requires them.

For the purposes of a given language-game, he is ready to admit, we can take certain objects to be 'simple' – their names would then be unanalysable elements in our sentences – but such objects are not 'simple' in the metaphysical sense; they are not 'the ultimate constituents of the world'. Russell's search for a 'logical proper' name, a name which should refer to something by nature unanalysable, led him in the end to the conclusion that the demonstrative 'this' is the only name that fills the bill. Yet the word 'this', Wittgenstein points out, is not a name at all. The correct conclusion, he thinks, is that there are *no* logically proper names, from which it follows that the analytic theory of meaning, and with it the view that it is the special task of philosophy to offer ultimate analyses, must be wholly rejected.

What leads us astray? What sends us in search of 'simples' and 'ultimate analyses'? We are accustomed to clear up misunderstandings, Wittgenstein suggests, by substituting a clearer expression for a misleading one. Such a substitute-expression can reasonably be described as an 'analysis' of the original expression. Thus we are led to suppose that there could be a completely exact, crystalline language, one which would contain no expressions except such as are 'ultimate analyses'. In pursuit of this language, he thinks, we are led to ask the sort of question which had preoccupied him in the *Tractatus* – such questions as 'What is the real form of a proposition?', 'What are the constituents of the ultimate language?' – and so on. We are held captive, driven into metaphysical perplexity, Wittgenstein suggests, by an ideal; his first task, therefore, is to destroy the attractiveness of that ideal. His critics, he knew, would accuse him of destroying whatever is 'great and important'. In fact, he says, he is 'destroying nothing but houses of cards'. And these houses of cards will collapse of their own accord as soon as we come to a clear understanding of 'the ground of language on which they stand' – an understanding of the ways in which we actually use words like 'knowledge', 'proposition', 'name', in our everyday language.

So much, although with none of Wittgenstein's subtlety, for the view that we understand a language if and only if we can point to the objects the words in that language name, whether proximately or ultimately. Now for the harder problem: how to overcome the temptation to suppose that 'understanding' is a mental process. Consider a case where we might say of a person that he 'understands'. Suppose a teacher writes down the series: '3, 9, 27' and then says to his pupil: 'continue!' The pupil writes: '81, 243'. The teacher is content; his pupil understands. Or suppose we watch somebody write '1, 3, 6', and feel puzzled, expecting the '6' to be '5'. Then he writes '10'. The next numbers will be 15, 21', we might say, 'now I understand.'

To such a 'process of understanding', there may be many different accompaniments: we might feel a sense of tension, and then of relief; we might say to ourselves 'the difference increases by one'; we might have mental images of the numbers we expect. But none of these, according to Wittgenstein, is necessary or sufficient for understanding. Even if we normally have visual images when we understand, these images, he argues, could always be replaced by something else – e.g. having a red image could be replaced by looking at a colour chart – without our ceasing to understand. Even if, again, we normally say formulae over to ourselves, it would not affect our understanding if, instead, we said them aloud. On the other side we could have the image, could say a formula to ourselves, and still not understand. Thus, Wittgenstein concludes, 'in the sense in which there are processes (including mental processes) which are characteristic of understanding, understanding is not a mental process'.

'If understanding is not a mental process,' we naturally ask,

'what is it?' Now this is an 'essence' question, to be transformed
therefore, on Wittgenstein's general view, into a problem in
'grammar'. He absorbs the special problem about 'understanding' into a more general problem about 'psychological words'.
How, he asks, do such words function? How can we possibly tell
whether we are or are not using them correctly? These are
questions which Wittgenstein sets out to discuss in the latter part
of the *Investigations*. But we must not expect to find there a
precise and definite answer; that would be quite out of keeping
with Wittgenstein's method. His object, once again, is therapeutic; in this case to cure us of our tendency to suppose that
psychological words must name 'private experiences which we
alone can know' or, as he puts the matter, to imagine that we
each of us make use of a private language, the words of which
name events in a secret mental life.

The very idea of such a 'private language', Wittgenstein tries
to show, is an unintelligible one.[6] A language uses names in
accordance with an implicit or explicit *rule*; that it proceeds in
accordance with rules is precisely what distinguishes a language
from mere noises or from marks on paper. But how are we to tell,
Wittgenstein asks, that the names in our private language are
used consistently? 'Sensations', 'impressions', or what you will,
are, by hypothesis, fleeting; we cannot bring them back to compare them with our present experiences, so as to see whether they
ought to be given the same name. It is not enough to reply, Wittgenstein argues, that 'they seem to me to be the same'; the criterion that I am using my language rightly cannot consist in the
mere fact that I seem to myself to be doing so. A criterion is used
to determine whether what seems to be the case is in fact the
case – that is its whole point; 'seeming', then, cannot itself *be* a
criterion. The reply 'I remember it to be the same' is in no better
case, according to Wittgenstein, unless, as when I claim to
remember public events, there is some independent way of
checking my memory. Otherwise, to appeal to memory is 'as if
someone were to buy several copies of the morning newspaper
to assure himself that what it said was true'. There is in fact no
criterion for determining whether the so-called 'private language'
is being used properly or improperly; and this amounts to saying
that *there is no such language*.

431

Are we to conclude that words *cannot* refer to sensations? That, according to Wittgenstein, would be an absurd conclusion: 'don't we talk about sensations every day and give them names?' The only real question is *how* they refer – in other words, how we *learn to use* sensation words, like, for example, 'pain'. 'Here is one possibility,' he suggests, 'words are connected with the primitive, the natural expressions of the sensation, and are used in their place. A child has hurt himself and he cries; and then adults talk to him and teach him exclamations and, later, sentences. They teach the child new pain behaviour.'

The possibility Wittgenstein is here contemplating, it should be observed, is that 'I am in pain' *replaces* crying and moaning; even although it has the form of a statement, that is, it is in fact a variety of pain-behaviour rather than a descriptive statement. We might be inclined to reject such an interpretation outright, on the ground that a person always uses language in order to 'convey a thought', to 'express a proposition', or to 'make a judgement'.[7] But this is just what Wittgenstein is contesting: judging, he is saying, is one, but only one, of the very many ways in which we use language. It may turn out, he further suggests, that 'I am in pain' has a different point in different contexts. 'We surely do not always say someone is complaining', he writes, 'because he says he is in pain. So the words "I am in pain" may be a cry of complaint and may be something else.' The crucial point, however, is that they *need not be a statement*. Similar considerations apply to such a 'psychological statement' as 'I am afraid'. If, when we say 'I am afraid', we are asked whether our utterance is a cry of fear, or an attempt to convey how we feel, or a reflection on our present state of mind, sometimes we would give one answer, sometimes another, sometimes we would not know what to say. The question 'What does "I am afraid" really mean?' then, has no straightforward answer. We have always to take account of the context, the language-game, in which the words are uttered. Certainly we cannot presume – and this is the point on which Wittgenstein particularly wants to insist – that whoever makes such an assertion must be 'describing a state of mind'.

Epistemologists have commonly argued that 'I am in pain' describes a 'private state', and have gone on to draw the conclusion that 'only I can *know* I am in pain'. But, Wittgenstein objects, this is clearly not so; it is a matter of everyday experience that other people can know that I am suffering. Indeed, he says, I cannot *know* that I am in pain at all; 'I know that I am in pain' is meaningless. It would make sense, he argues, only if we could contrast 'I know I am in pain' with 'I *rather think* I am in pain', 'I *strongly believe* I am in pain' and so on. Other people can sensibly say of me 'I know he is in pain,' just because, according to Wittgenstein, under other circumstances they can 'rather think' or 'strongly believe' I am in pain, as distinct from 'knowing' that I am – but we can say none of these things of our own pain. I cannot *doubt* whether I am in pain, but it does not follow – quite the contrary – that I can *know* I am in pain.

When a philosopher tells us that we cannot *really* be sure that other people are in pain he must mean, Wittgenstein suggests, something like this: 'Couldn't you imagine the possibility that although he cries, and moans, and groans and . . . still all the time he is only pretending!' Wittgenstein is quite prepared to admit that we can easily *imagine* how one *could* be doubtful in such a case, but not the supposed consequence, that we can never be 'really sure'. One can also imagine, he says, a person who never opens his front door without doubting whether the ground outside the door will be solid – and recognize, as well, that on a particular occasion such a person might in fact step into an abyss; yet *we* do not doubt whether the ground is solid. 'Just try in a real case,' Wittgenstein admonishes us, 'to doubt someone else's fear or pain.' 'But,' somebody may object, 'if you are certain isn't it that you are shutting your eyes in face of doubt?' Wittgenstein's reply is uncompromising: 'They are shut!' We cannot rule out the possibility that we are wrong; but it is *folie de doute* to conclude that we can never be certain.

It had been Wittgenstein's original intention to include as part of *Philosophical Investigations* his final thoughts on the philosophy of mathematics. What he intended to say can in part be gathered from the manuscripts – some of them mere jottings, some relatively well-developed – now published as *Remarks on the Foundations of Mathematics* (1956).[8] Discontinuous, obscure, inconsistent, these *Remarks* have by no means received the attention which has been devoted to the *Tractatus* or the *Philosophical*

Investigations. Commentators on Wittgenstein not uncommonly ignore them, and even his more sympathetic critics dismiss large segments – for example, Wittgenstein's lengthy discussion of Gödel's theorem and of the Dedekind cut – as substantially worthless.[9]

Yet the *Remarks* contain many of the most revealing – nowhere is he more radical – of Wittgenstein's 'philosophical remarks'. What, he asks, is the nature of the logical 'must', the necessity attaching to mathematical and logical propositions? Naturally, he rejects any Platonic-type philosophy of mathematics, according to which mathematics discovers the eternal and immutable relationships which hold between timelessly subsistent mathematical objects. Whereas for Russell, and even more obviously for such pure mathematicians as Hardy, the mathematician discerns or discovers mathematical relations, Wittgenstein depicts him as essentially an inventor, not a discoverer. (A typical mathematician, in Wittgenstein's eyes, is the man who invented the decimal notation.)

So far Wittgenstein falls into the conventionalist camp. But conventionalists like Carnap replace the traditional conception of a necessary truth by the conception of a necessary consequence. Mathematical necessity, in their eyes, attaches to a mathematical proposition in virtue of its being the necessary consequence of the adoption of certain axioms, certain definitions, certain rules. Rules, Wittgenstein objects – at this point his *Remarks* overlap with *Philosophical Investigations* – never compel absolutely. Suppose we draw a consequence by means of rules of inference and that consequence is rejected as an inadmissible use of the rule. What determines, Wittgenstein asks, that it is inadmissible? Another rule? Then the same difficulty can arise in the application of *that* rule. No rule can determine of itself how it is to be applied; it does not, as it were, contain within it, only needing to be unfolded, all its applications.

Then are we to say, simply, that the supposed necessity of applying a mathematical rule in a particular way consists in this: we do in fact make use of certain mathematical techniques, we do in fact interpret the instruction 'add 2' in a particular way? That is certainly not, for Wittgenstein, the whole story. For one thing, we are not wholly free to apply or not to apply a mathematical rule in a particular way. Anyone who acts differently finds himself in difficulties, difficulties of the same sort as he will encounter if he does not accept any way of acting current in his own society. It may properly be said, even, of such a rebel that he 'cannot think', or 'cannot calculate'. But this is because what he does is not what we *call* 'thinking' or 'calculating'; for us it is an 'essential part' of what we call thinking or calculating that it involves, for example, interpreting the order 'add 2' in a particular way. The line between thinking and not thinking, however, is not a 'hard and fast one' – we may change our minds about what we consider as 'thinking' or 'calculating'.

It does not follow, according to Wittgenstein, that the propositions of mathematics are 'anthropological propositions saying how we men infer and calculate'. A mathematical proposition is no more an anthropological proposition than the statute book is a set of anthropological propositions; it is *normative*, not a simple description of what we do. At the same time, we can (in principle) change mathematical rules for practical reasons, just as we can change the laws in a statute book.

What about proofs? A proof, according to Wittgenstein, is a picture, a picture which convinces us that if we follow a certain rule, things will come out in a particular way. When we are convinced by a proof, we work with a new technique. But the same point can be made by saying that we have accepted a new concept, or that we are now treating a relation as an 'internal' one or that, for us, a certain connexion is now a 'grammatical' one. One example Wittgenstein gives is the addition of 200 and 200. If we were to add 200 apples to 200 apples and then count 400 apples, this would not serve, he argues, as a proof that $200 + 200 = 400$. Mathematical propositions cannot be proved experimentally. One needs for a proof – it will be obvious that Wittgenstein uses the word 'proof' is an unusually broad sense – a picture which includes the fact that the apples *behave normally*, i.e. that none of them is lost or conjoined in the process of adding them up. Such a picture gives us the concept of 'counting 200 and 200 objects together'; it convinces us of a grammatical proposition about 'counting', it shows us the essence of 'counting together'. As an expression of this result we 'accept a rule'. We have not, in accepting the rule, acquired a new piece of knowledge. Rather, we have come to a decision, the decision to adopt a particular technique.

In its general approach, Wittgenstein's philosophy of mathematics is 'finitist' or 'constructivist', in Brouwer's manner. However, he does not regard himself as a finitist, any more than he regards himself as a behaviourist. Finitism and behaviourism, he says, are alike in wanting to reach a conclusion of the form 'but surely, all we have here is . . .' They both 'deny the existence of something' – consciousness or infinite sets – in order to escape from a confusion. In contrast, Wittgenstein hopes to escape from confusion by asking what *point* there is in using such an expression as 'private feelings' or 'infinite sets'.

Similarly, in his discussion of those paradoxes which were for Russell, Frege and their followers the clinching evidence that something was wrong with a calculus, Wittgenstein's approach is, in general terms, pragmatic. He does not at all deny that a contradiction *can* be important; it can involve us in practical difficulties. What he wholly rejects is the doctrine that we cannot regard a calculus as 'trustworthy' unless we can prove it to be free of contradictions. Suppose a contradiction were discovered in arithmetic, he asks, would that demonstrate that we were wrong to have relied on arithmetic all these years past? Does it matter that arithmetic, any more than it matters that English, allows us to say something paradoxical? Only, he suggests, at the points at which it *does* matter. The Russellian contradiction about classes, for example, emerges only within what is already a 'cancerous growth' on mathematics; it does not affect the trustworthiness of any useful mathematical or logical technique. What mathematical propositions stand in need of, what the philosopher of mathematics can hope to provide, is not a foundation 'to prove mathematics free from contradictions' but, rather, a conceptual analysis which will enable us to understand 'the nature of their grammar', how they are useful to us in our thinking.

In general, Wittgenstein's pupils followed the example of their master during his years of silence: it is quite obvious that he did not care to have his views reported at secondhand. But there were Cambridge philosophers, of whom the best-known is John Wisdom,[10] who worked out in their own way what they had learnt from Wittgenstein – and from Moore – thereby keeping open lines of communication between Cambridge and the outside world.

Unlike many other contemporary philosophers, Wisdom is deeply interested in art, religion and personal relationships, about all of which he has made illuminating remarks. Perhaps that explains why, in some measure, he is sympathetic towards metaphysics; nobody who takes literature (or psycho-analysis) seriously is likely to succumb to the doctrine that whatever is worth saying can be said clearly and precisely, or to be satisfied that only true statements can be illuminating. Wisdom hopes to show that metaphysics can be valuable without reverting to the pre-positivist doctrine that it provides us with a description of supra-empirical entities.

In order to bring out the special character of metaphysical controversies, Wisdom distinguishes between three different types of dispute. 'Empirical' disputes – e.g. a controversy about the inflammability of helium – are, he says, settled by observation and experiment, 'logical' disputes by reference to a 'strict rule of usage'. Thus to settle the dispute whether '$2 + 2 = 4$' is a rule, we need only point out, he argues, that a 'rule' cannot, in strict usage, be either true or false, whereas a mathematical proposition can be either. Suppose, however, somebody sets the following problem: 'if when a dog attacks a cow she keeps her horns always towards it, revolving as fast as the dog rotates, does the dog go around the cow?'[11] Then it is no use referring to the ordinary way of using 'around'; this, according to Wisdom, is a 'conflict' dispute, which can be resolved only by establishing a new convention – by deciding to use, or not to use, 'around' in these circumstances.

The queer thing about philosophers, Wisdom suggests, is that they hold views which, considered from the point of view of strict logic, are obviously false. They go on telling us that the laws of mathematics are really rules of grammar, even after we point out to them that a rule cannot be either true or false; they still insist that material objects do not exist even when, in Moore's manner, we hold up our hand and say: 'There, that's a material object.' How can we account for their blatant refusal to accept the regular methods of settling a dispute? The fact is, Wisdom suggests, that philosophers are *dissatisfied* with our ordinary usage, and so will not accept as decisive an appeal to it. They are advocating a linguistic innovation; where we see a 'logical' dispute, they see a 'conflict'.

The philosopher's obduracy is valuable, Wisdom thinks, in so far as it draws attention to a similarity we should otherwise overlook. Suppose a psychologist says: 'Everybody is neurotic.' We might at first imagine that this proposition expresses an empirical discovery, to the effect that more careful psychiatric observation will always reveal a neurosis where, at first sight, none appears to be present – as a pathologist might discover that every living organism has cancerous cells within it. But we should miss the whole point of the psychologist's statement, Wisdom suggests, if we were to reply: 'that isn't true, a careful investigation has shown that only 14% of the population has a neurosis', i.e. if we were to regard it as an empirical proposition, to be combatted at that level. For even if it is suggested by the discovery that the neurotic and the non-neurotic are less easily distinguishable than is ordinarily supposed, 'everybody is neurotic', according to Wisdom, is *a priori*, not empirical: the psychologist is recommending that we change our way of using the word 'neurotic'. We can 'dispute' what he says only by drawing attention to the inconvenient results of his verbal recommendation. Similarly, Wisdom thinks, if a philosopher tells us that 'all mathematical statements are rules of grammar', the bare response: 'Of course, they are not rules', while true, misses the point; the proper reply is rather: 'Yes, I see they are like rules in some ways but ...' Then we have not missed the illumination the philosopher's paradox can cast.

What recommendations, we might ask, fall particularly within the philosopher's province? To what similarities does he wish particularly to draw attention? The traditional reply, Wisdom suggests, would run something like this: the philosopher interrelates realms of being – material objects and sense-data, facts and values. But this reply may mislead us into believing that there are strange entities – 'sense-data', 'values' and the like – which the philosopher has to relate to facts, as the medical scientist might relate viruses to diseases. It will be less misleading, according to Wisdom, to think of the philosopher as one who 'describes the logic' of different classes of sentences – tells us how they are verified, supported by reasons, argued about. A philosopher can profitably discuss 'the different logics' of 'this is red', 'Napoleon was a man', 'Mr Pickwick was a good man', whereas he will be led completely astray into the wilds of metaphysics or the deserts of logical analysis if he sets out to consider 'the relation between fictional and real beings' or 'the difference between facts and values'.

The similarities in which the philosopher is interested, then, are similarities and dissimilarities in the use of sentences. His paradoxes are useful, Wisdom considers, just in virtue of the light they throw on these similarities. When, for example, the positivist tell us that 'metaphysical propositions are meaningless', his paradox usefully draws attention to differences between the logic of scientific and the logic of philosophical assertions; when he maintains that 'we can never really know that other people have minds' he helps us to see that we do not verify statements about other people's minds in the same way as we verify statements about chairs and tables – a point Wisdom illustrates at length in his articles on 'Other Minds'. Yet, Wisdom admits, it is difficult to account in these terms for the peculiar excitement and intensity of metaphysical disputes. Why should verbal recommendations engender such heat? Faced with this problem, Wisdom turns for help to one of his special interests, psycho-analysis.[12] Listening to philosophers who obstinately persist in such assertions as 'we can never really know what other people think and feel', we are at once reminded, he considers, of the neurotic's chronic doubts. 'In the labyrinth of metaphysics,' he writes in a characteristic passage, 'are the same whispers as one hears when climbing Kafka's staircases to the tribunal which is always one floor higher up.' The philosopher thinks of himself as striving towards a goal – towards, for example, the *direct* apprehension of other people's minds – even when, as in the neurotic's case, no conceivable experience would persuade him that he had reached his goal. But if we forget about the goal, Wisdom suggests, and think of the philosopher's work as a re-description of the point he has already reached, we shall see in what its true value consists.

My account of Wisdom's philosophical position is, in one important respect, misleading. I have made him out to be more definite, more explicit, than he actually is. His characteristic method consists in first making a distinction – say, the distinction between a 'logical' and a 'conflict' dispute – as if it were a sharp one, and then blunting its edges; or first making an assertion – say, that philosophical paradoxes are verbal recommendations – and then asserting its contradictory. 'I have said that philosophers' questions and theories are really verbal,' he wrote in his paper on 'Philosophical Perplexity' (*PAS*, 1936), 'but if you like we will not say this, or we will also say the contradictory.' Wisdom's elusiveness is not merely freakish or irresponsible; it flows from his firm conviction that philosophical theories are at once illuminating and misleading, *and that both these points need to be made*. There is no hope of transcending this awkward situation and thus arriving at philosophical conclusions which cannot mislead; all the philosopher can do is to mislead and then – elaborately – to draw attention to the points at which what he has said is misleading – and not misleading.

In his introduction to M. Lazerowitz's collection of essays, *The Structure of Metaphysics* (1955), Wisdom remarks that 'when people listened to Wittgenstein they often found it difficult to get a steady light giving an ordered view of what they have wished to see and that when they now read him they still have this difficulty.' Not a few readers would feel the same about Wisdom's own writings; but the general tendency of recent post-Wittgenstein philosophy, one might say, is to revert to definiteness, if in a spirit chastened by Wittgenstein's critique. We can see that tendency clearly enough in Lazerowitz's book; he operates with Wisdom's main thesis – that philosophical paradoxes are verbal recommendations, backed by unconscious motives – as if it were a scientific theory to be verified by applying it to a variety of philosophical disputes.[13] Wisdom is obviously uneasy about the result; he wants to add: 'Yes, but on the other side . . .'

For similar reasons – because they find them insufficiently subtle, over-explicit – not all ex-students of Wittgenstein look with kindness on the 'ordinary language' philosophies[14] which have latterly dominated the philosophical scene at Oxford, for all that they show clear signs of Wittgenstein's influence. At Oxford, Wittgenstein's ideas entered a very different philosophical atmosphere from that which prevailed at Cambridge. Oxford philosophers, for the most part, have learnt their philosophy as part of a course of study which is based upon classical scholarship; in particular, the influence of Aristotle has been strong at Oxford as it has never been at Cambridge, where in so far as any classical philosopher has been influential it is Plato, not Aristotle – and this is as true of Wittgenstein as it is of Moore.

Now when Aristotle considers such a question as 'whether the virtues are emotions', he makes use of what it would be natural to call 'an appeal to ordinary language'. The virtues are not emotions, he argues, since '*we are not called* good or bad on the ground that we exhibit certain emotions but only in respect of our virtues and vices'; again, he argues, an emotion *is said to* 'move' us whereas a virtue or vice *is said to* 'govern' us. What 'we say', then, is the decisive factor. Arguments of this sort are everywhere to be found in Aristotle's *Nicomachean Ethics*, and were freely employed by the most influential Oxford Aristotelians. Cook Wilson, as we have already seen, always laid great stress on the importance of determining 'the normal idiom'; in the ethical writings of W. D. Ross – in sharp contrast to Moore's *Principia Ethica* – the appeal to 'what the ordinary man would say' plays a conspicuous part. Add to these special influences the quite general consideration that classically-trained men are always likely to place great stress on 'correctness', which has a reasonably definite meaning within a dead language, and it will no longer seem surprising that 'ordinary language' philosophies made such rapid headway at Oxford. At Oxford, then, Wittgenstein's ideas were grafted on to an Aristotelian-philological stock; the stock has influenced the resultant fruits which, amongst other things, are considerably drier and cooler than their Cambridge counterparts.

Oxford philosophy displays, too – most notably in the writings of J. L. Austin – an interest in language for its own sake, quite foreign to Wittgenstein. A study of 'the use' of words like 'mind', 'knowledge', 'perception', so a good many Oxford philosophers think, is interesting in itself, quite apart from its therapeutic, antimetaphysical, powers. Philosophy for them has a positive and systematic task; in the eyes of many of the Cambridge 'old guard' of Wittgensteinians, Oxford philosophy has desiccated into scholasticism.

The best known of Oxford 'ordinary language' philosophers is Gilbert Ryle. Ryle was educated in the Cook Wilson tradition; Aristotle is always his natural point of departure. But he was also interested in continental philosophy, at first in Husserl and Meinong, later in the logical positivists. He is a trained academic philosopher, as Wittgenstein was not – a philosopher 'in the tradition', whatever his unorthodoxies. That is one reason why his ideas have been widely discussed, even by philosophers who can 'make nothing' of Wittgenstein.

In his 'Systematically Misleading Expressions' (*PAS*, 1931 and *LL* I) Ryle announced his conversion – although, he said, a reluctant one – to the view that the task of philosophy is 'the detection of the sources in linguistic idioms of recurrent misconstructions and absurd theories'. Distinguishing – like Bradley, Frege and Russell – between the syntactical form of an expression and the form of the facts it depicts, Ryle argues that a great many of the expressions of everyday life are, in virtue of their grammatical form, 'systematically misleading'. Merely because, for example, a sentence like 'Mr Pickwick is a fiction' is grammatically analogous to 'Mr Menzies is a statesman', we are tempted to read it as if it were a description of a person – a person with the property of being fictitious. In fact, however, this statement is not about a fictitious person, Mr Pickwick, with odd properties but about a *real* person, Dickens, or a *real* book *Pickwick Papers*. How is this to be shown, if the point be not immediately granted? If 'Mr Pickwick is a fiction' were about a person by the name of 'Mr Pickwick', then, Ryle argues, it would imply such propositions as 'Mr Pickwick was born in such-and-such a year' – consequences which *actually contradict* the original assertion. 'Paradoxes and antinomies,' he more generally concludes, 'are the evidence that an expression is systematically misleading.'

Ryle willingly grants that such expressions as '. . . is a fiction' do not mislead us in everyday life. But metaphysicians, with their special interest in 'the structure of facts' or 'the categories of being', are enticed into their strange theories because they take the grammatical forms of statements at their face value. They are led to believe that there are 'universals' – remember that Ryle had been reading Meinong and Husserl – because they wrongly presume that 'Punctuality is a virtue' is grammatically parallel to

'Hume is a philosopher', i.e. that like 'Hume', 'Punctuality' is a name. Or again, merely because we can sensibly say 'the idea of taking a holiday has just occurred to me', philosophers are led to conclude that there is an entity – 'the idea' – which the phrase 'the idea of taking a holiday' names.

To avoid the misleading suggestions of everyday speech, Ryle argued, the philosopher must learn to restate sentences – in the manner of Russell's theory of descriptions, which for Ryle as for Ramsey was 'the paradigm of philosophy' – so as clearly to exhibit 'the form of the facts into which philosophy is the inquiry'. 'Philosophical analysis', he thought, issues in such reformulations. Obviously, Ryle held both that philosophy is therapeutic and that it has a positive task – to reveal 'the real form of facts'. 'Systematically Misleading Expressions', in fact, belongs to the first Wittgenstein period, the period which culminated in Wisdom's 'Logical Constructions'. That an Oxford man, at a time when Cook Wilson's followers held the centre of the stage at Oxford, should proceed in a manner so obviously 'Cambridge' was a portent. (Although Price, it should be remembered, has already created some dismay at Oxford by sympathizing with Russell's theory of sense-data.)

Ryle wrote a considerable number of philosophical articles in the years that followed. Two of them are especially important for an understanding of *The Concept of Mind* – 'Categories' (*PAS*, 1937) and his inaugural lecture *Philosophical Arguments* (1945). In his 'Categories' Ryle defined 'a category' in a way which, he thinks, preserves whatever was of value in Aristotle and Kant, while laying down, as they did not, a definite way of proving that two expressions differ in category.[15] Consider such an incomplete expression (a 'sentence-frame') as '... is in bed'. Then, Ryle argues, we can without absurdity insert 'Jones' or 'Socrates' in the gap the sentence-frame leaves unfilled, but not 'Saturday'. This is enough to prove that 'Jones' belongs to a different category from 'Saturday'.[16] It still does not prove, however, that 'Jones' and 'Socrates' belong to the *same* category; for there might be other sentence-frames, Ryle says, into which 'Jones' could be inserted but 'Socrates' would not fit without absurdity. Thus although either 'he' or 'the writer of this book' can be inserted in '... has read Aristotle' they nevertheless belong to different categories; for only 'he' – not 'the writer of this book' – will fit without absurdity into the sentence-frame '. . . has never written a book'.

In such a case, Ryle thinks, the absurdity resulting from the inappropriate completion of a sentence-frame is obvious; but it is *not* obvious, in contrast, that we shall fall into antinomies and contradictions if we fill the gap in '. . . is false' by the phrase 'the statement I am now making'. Such un-obvious absurdities are the philosophically interesting ones.[17] Indeed philosophers, Ryle thinks, are led systematically to distinguish between categories only because they light on unexpected antinomies; then they go on to seek out concealed antinomies in cases where they suspect that a category-distinction lies concealed.

Two general characteristics of Ryle's paper on 'Categories' are important for the understanding of his philosophical point of view: first, that although he talks throughout of 'expressions' – he will not allow that either a belief or a concept can properly be described as 'absurd' – he is not, he says, conducting a philological investigation; he is telling us something about 'the nature of things' or, at least, about 'concepts'. He has continued to stress this point; many critics who are otherwise sympathetically inclined towards his work complain that his conclusions are misleadingly expressed in the 'material' rather than in the 'formal' mode.[18] Secondly, category-distinguishing, as Ryle describes it, involves philosophical argument, ratiocination: a point overlooked, he suggests, by those who define philosophy as 'analysis'.

To this theme his inaugural address was devoted. Philosophical arguments, he says, are neither inductions nor demonstrations; the philosopher has his own methods of procedure, of which the most characteristic is the *reductio ad absurdum*. By 'deducing from a proposition or complex of propositions consequences which are inconsistent with each other or with the original propositions' the philosopher demonstrates the 'absurdity' of the proposition or complex of propositions in question. Ryle is not suggesting that philosophical arguments are purely destructive. The *reductio ad absurdum*, on his view, acts as a sieve; or, to vary the metaphor, by determining the boundaries at which absurdity appears it outlines the actual field of application of a proposition.

Every proposition, Ryle says, has certain 'logical powers'. For the most part, he thinks, we are conscious only of a limited number of the logical powers of the propositions we use, and so have only a 'partial grasp' of their meaning. Yet we can use propositions like '3 × 3 = 9' or 'London is north of Brighton' without falling into those arithmetical or geographical errors which would be evidence that we did not understand what we were saying; if we cannot state the rules which govern the use of these propositions, at least we know how to use them in practice under ordinary circumstances. If this were not so, Ryle says, the philosopher would have no starting-point.

When propositions have something in common, it is sometimes convenient, Ryle thinks, to abstract this common factor as a 'concept'. Thus, for example, from the set of such propositions as 'Jones behaves intelligently', 'Brown thinks intelligently', we might wish to pick out 'the concept of intelligence'. Moore, in his earlier writings, had written as if a concept were a building-block out of which propositions are constructed; Ryle argues, in opposition to Moore, that a concept is merely a handy abbreviation for a 'family' of propositions. When, then, Ryle goes on to talk of 'a concept's logical powers' this is intended as a brief way of referring to the logical powers of all those propositions which are similar in virtue of possessing a certain common factor.

The Concept of Mind (1949) analyses the logical powers of 'mental concepts'.[19] In everyday life, he thinks, we work quite well with these concepts: we know how to decide, say, whether Jones is intelligent or stupid, whether he is making a joke or thinking out a problem. But we become puzzled when we try to discover the category to which such expressions belong, i.e. the logical powers of the propositions into which they enter. To overcome our puzzles, Ryle suggests, we have to 'map' the various mental concepts, thus determining their geographical position in a world of concepts – in other words, the limits of their application.

First, however, a myth has to be destroyed: the 'official', or Cartesian, myth that mental-conduct expressions refer to a queer sort of entity, 'mind' or 'soul', distinguishable from the body in virtue of being private, non-spatial, knowable only by introspection. Recognizing that words like 'intelligence' do not name entities which obey mechanical laws, philosophers have been led to conclude, Ryle suggests, that they must therefore name entities which obey non-mechanical, spiritual laws. In fact, however, it is a 'category mistake' to suppose that they name *any entity whatsoever*. The function of the word 'intelligence' is to describe human behaviour, not to name an entity. According to Descartes and the epistemologists who followed in his footsteps, a human being is compounded of two disparate entities – a mind and a body, a ghost and a machine.[20] Then at once the epistemologists are beset by a host of problems: How can an immaterial spirit influence the workings of a material body? How can the ghost peer through the machine to the world around it? To such questions as these, Ryle thinks, there can be no answer; yet we must not try to avoid them by maintaining, with the Idealist, that in reality man is a ghost, or with the materialist, that in reality he is a machine. The human being is neither a ghost, nor a machine, nor a ghost in a machine; he is a human being, who sometimes behaves intelligently and sometimes stupidly, sometimes notices things and sometimes overlooks them, sometimes acts and sometimes is quiescent. 'Man need not be degraded to a machine,' Ryle writes, 'by being denied to be a ghost in a machine. He might, after all, be a sort of animal, namely a higher mammal. There has yet to be ventured the hazardous leap to the hypothesis that perhaps he is a man.'

Philosophers have tended to suppose that 'acting intelligently' is synonymous with 'theorizing' or 'discovering the truth'. Since thinking is usually carried on in private – once we have learnt the trick in childhood – it is then an easy step to the conclusion that every exercise of intelligence belongs to a secret, private, world. But in fact, Ryle argues, theorizing is only a *species* of intelligent behaviour – the species he calls 'knowing that'; most intelligent action consists in 'knowing how' to carry through some action to its conclusion, 'knowing how' to play a game, or to speak French, or to build a house, which is very different from *theorizing* about games, or about language-speaking, or about house-building. If, indeed, we try to maintain that practice *can* be intelligent only when it is preceded by intelligent thinking, we are at once involved, Ryle argues, in an infinite regress; if there were any good reason for supposing that intelligent cricket-playing must be preceded by intelligent theorizing about cricket, there would be exactly as much reason for supposing that intelligent theorizing must in its turn be preceded by intelligent theorizing about theorizing, and so on *ad infinitum*. At some stage – and why not at once? – we have to recognize that a form of activity is intelligent, whatever precedes it or fails to precede it.

But, the objection may be raised, we cannot tell by bare inspection of an act that it is intelligent; it might be a mere fluke. The worst of chess-players will occasionally make a truly formidable move. For that reason, Ryle grants, we have to 'look beyond' the isolated act in order to determine whether it displays 'intelligence'. This 'look beyond', however, does not consist in trying to penetrate to a secret, intelligent mental performance – which is, indeed, by hypothesis quite inaccessible to us. Rather, we inquire into the agent's general abilities and propensities. Does he make similar moves in similar situations? Can he appreciate such moves when they are made by others? Can he tell us why he made the move? If the answer to such questions as these is in the affirmative, then he 'knows how' to play chess.

'Knowing how,' Ryle concludes, is 'dispositional.' He is not suggesting, in thus describing it, that it is the name of a special sort of entity – a 'disposition'. The proposition 'glass has a disposition to break', he argues, is shorthand for a (vaguely-limited) range of hypothetical propositions: 'if you drop glass, or hit it with a stone, or try to bend it, it will break.' If glass never did break, if there were in our experience no 'episodes' of glass-breaking, then, no doubt, we should not call it 'breakable'; in thus describing it, all the same, we are not naming an episode but stating hypothetical propositions.[21] Similarly, then, although we should say of a person that 'he can read French' only if he sometimes performs the sort of action we expect of French-readers, or that he is irritable only if he sometimes gets angry. or that he is 'amiable' only if he is sometimes friendly, there is no particular episode the occurrence of which is a necessary and sufficient condition for the application to a person of these dispositional descriptions.* To look for the entity, or the episode, named by a

*Compare what Wittgenstein says about 'understanding' (p. 430 above).

disposition is to hunt the unicorn. To say we have a certain dis-position, in Ryle's view, is to assert, simply, that our conduct is 'law-like', i.e. that it follows a regular pattern.

Ryle's analysis of motives proceeds along similar lines: acting with a motive, he suggests, is like acting from habit – as comes out in the fact that we are often uncertain whether a particular person has acted 'from habit' or 'with a certain motive'. Just as to ascribe an action to 'the force of habit' is not to unveil its secret cause but to deny that it is peculiar or unexpected, so also to ascribe a motive to an action is merely to subsume it under a general type, as distinct from causally explaining it. To 'act from ambition' is to exemplify the ambitious sort of action; 'ambition' is not a peculiar non-mechanical cause.[22]

As for such so-called 'mental processes' as 'acts of volition', these, Ryle argues, are not in the least like 'processes'. None of the ordinary ways of describing processes is in this case applic-able: it is useless to ask whether volitions are continuous or interrupted, how they can be speeded up or slowed down, when they begin and when they end. The difference between voluntary and involuntary behaviour does not lie in the fact that voluntary behaviour is preceded, whereas involuntary behaviour is not preceded, by an 'act of volition'.

Similarly, although there is certainly a difference between seeing and not-seeing, recalling and not-recalling, there are no 'mental processes', Ryle argues, properly describable as 'acts of seeing' or 'acts of recalling'. 'Seeing' and 'recalling', indeed, are 'achievement-words', not 'process' words; to 'see' is to succeed in a task – it is parallel to *winning* a race, as distinct from *running* in one. If Moore was puzzled by the elusiveness of 'mental acts', this is for the very good reason that he was looking for what is not there to be found.

Many philosophers who are in general sympathy with Ryle's demolition of the Cartesian myth have boggled at his analysis of imagination.[23] Yet this analysis is vital to his general thesis that 'when we characterize people by mental predicates, we are not making untestable inferences to any ghostly processes occurring in streams of consciousness which we are debarred from visiting; we are describing the ways in which those people conduct parts of their predominantly public behaviour'. He has to show that 'imagining' is not the process of contemplating a class of intrinsically private entities – 'images'. Just as, he argues, to pretend to commit a murder is not *really* to commit a queer sort of murder (a 'mock-murder') so, equally, to 'imagine' seeing Everest is not *really* to see an 'Everest image'. If somebody imagines seeing Everest there is neither a real mountain in front of his real eyes, nor a mock-mountain in front of mock-eyes; he is utilizing his knowledge of Everest so as to 'think how it would look'. Imagining, Ryle contends, may be a form of rehearsing – anticipating the future – or it may be a form of pretending, but it is certainly not an 'inner seeing'. In so far as rehearsing and pretending are *in principle* public so, too, is imagining. Thus the inner bastion of privacy – the 'world of images' – proves, after all, not to be impregnable.

In *The Concept of Mind* Ryle reformulated and solved in his own way some of the problems in philosophical psychology which had perturbed Wittgenstein; his *Dilemmas* turns to another of Wittgenstein's main themes: the problem how we are to overcome the apparently irresolvable dilemmas which beset the philosopher. The philosopher is confronted, often enough, by two conclusions, each of them reached, it would seem, by an impeccable chain of reasoning, yet so related that one of them must be wholly wrong if the other is only partly right. Considering in turn a number of such dilemmas, Ryle tries to show that in each case the conflict is only an apparent one – a pseudo-conflict between theories which are 'in a different line of business', and stand in no need, for that reason, of being reconciled.

Take, for example, the familiar problem how the world of science is related to 'the world of everyday life'. On the one side, the physicist assures us that things are really arrangements of electrons in space, that they are not 'really' coloured, solid or sharply-defined; on the other side, we are quite convinced that chairs and tables are real and that they really have the colour, the solidity, the shape, we ordinarily ascribe to them. How is this dilemma to be resolved? The conclusions of the physicist, Ryle tries to show, do not really conflict with our everyday judgements, so that the supposed dilemma turns out to be no more than a difference in interest.

He makes his point by means of an analogy. A College auditor may tell an undergraduate that the College accounts 'cover the whole life of the College' – its games, its entertainments, its teachings are all there depicted. The auditor is not deceiving the undergraduate, for indeed the accounts are comprehensive, accurate and exhaustive. Yet the undergraduate is convinced that the accounts 'leave something out'. That, Ryle thinks, is precisely our position *vis-à-vis* the physicist. Any physical change can be represented as a movement of electrons; in that respect physics is 'complete'. Yet, somehow, the world we love and fear has escaped the physicist's net.

The undergraduate, Ryle suggests, should look more closely at the auditor's claim that his accounts 'cover the whole life of the College'. No doubt they do, in the sense that every College activity is represented in the account books as a debit or a credit; but his accounts do not describe, do not even attempt to describe, precisely those features of College life which the undergraduate finds so fascinating. For the accountant, a new library book is a debit of twenty-five shillings, not the precious life-blood of a master spirit. Similarly, Ryle argues, although physics covers everything, it does not give a complete description of what it covers. The physicist is interested only in certain aspects of the world around us. Just as the accountant has his business and the undergraduate a different business, so the physicist has a different business again. Each can go on his way, according to Ryle, without any fear of meeting a dilemma around the corner. This doctrine of 'spheres of influence' has recently attracted a good many admirers, particularly amongst those who desire to be uncritically religious without ceasing to be critically philosophical.[24]

Ryle, we said, always insists that his work is not in the least philological; and certainly, he does not engage in close linguistic analyses. For such analyses we must look to the work of J. L. Austin[25] who, until his premature death in 1960, exercised in postwar Oxford an intellectual authority nothing short of remarkable. Even amongst his closest associates, however, there is more than a little controversy about what Austin was trying to do and its relevance to the traditional pursuits of philosophy.

One thing is clear: at no time did Austin believe, as he is not uncommonly supposed to have believed, that 'ordinary language' is for all philosophical purposes the final court of appeal. 'Our common stock of words,' he certainly wrote in 'A Plea for Excuses' (*PAS*, 1957), 'embodies all the distinctions men have found worth drawing, and the connexions they have found worth making, in the life-times of many generations'. In relation to everyday practical matters, he therefore thought, the distinctions which ordinary language incorporates are likely to be sounder than 'any that you and I are likely to think up in our arm-chairs of an afternoon'. They are to be neglected at our peril; if not the end-all, they are certainly the 'begin-all' of philosophy.

But he freely admits that even although 'as a preliminary' the philosopher must track down in detail our ordinary use of words, in the end he will always be compelled 'to straighten them out to some degree'. The ordinary man's authority, furthermore, extends only to practical affairs. Whenever the philosopher's interests are 'more intellectual and extensive' than those of the ordinary man it will be necessary to point to new distinctions, to invent a new terminology – as Austin himself did with extreme, even excessive, freedom.

Austin's lecture on 'Ifs and Cans' (*PBA*, 1956) will serve to illustrate both the subtlety of the grammatical distinctions he was accustomed to make and the two rather different views he took about the philosophical importance of such distinctions. In that lecture he set out to dispute Moore's analysis of 'could have' in his *Ethics*. Moore wrongly suggests, according to Austin, first, that 'could have' simply means 'could have if I had chosen'; secondly, that for 'could have if I had chosen' may properly be substituted 'should have if I had chosen': thirdly – this by implication rather than expressly – that the *if*-clauses in these revised statements refer to a causal condition.

In opposition to Moore, Austin tries to show that it is a mistake to suppose that 'should' can be substituted for 'could'; that the *if* in such statements as 'I can if I choose' is not the *if* of condition but some other *if*, perhaps the *if* of stipulation; and that the supposition that 'could have' means 'could have if I had chosen' rests on the false presumption that 'could have' is always a past conditional or subjective, whereas it may be – and in the relevant cases in fact is – the past indicative of the verb 'can'. (At this point, Austin takes his evidence from Latin as well as from

English.) By means of such arguments he concludes that Moore was mistaken in supposing that determinism might be consistent with what 'we ordinarily say and presumably think'.[26] But Austin tells us that, rather than shows us how, this general philosophical conclusion follows.

Part of the 'importance' of what he is doing, according to Austin, derives from the fact that 'if' and 'can' are words which constantly turn up in philosophy – especially, perhaps, at those points at which the philosopher fondly imagines that his problems have been solved – so that it is vital to be clear about their use. By studying such linguistic distinctions we become clearer about the phenomena they are used to differentiate; 'ordinary-language philosophy' would be better called, he suggests, 'linguistic phenomenology'.

But he goes on to make another point, which gradually came, one suspects, to be nearer to his heart. Philosophy has commonly been the breeding-ground of sciences; perhaps, Austin conjectures, it is on the point of giving birth to a new science of language as it has recently given birth to mathematical logic. Austin clearly hoped to act as one of the midwives of such a science. Following James and Russell, Austin even suggests that a question is philosophical just in so far as it is in a state of confusion; once men are clear about a problem it ceases to form part of philosophy and is converted into a question for science.[27] Perhaps that is why he is prepared to assert, as he does more than once, that over-simplification is not so much the occupational disease of philosophers as their occupation, and why he is willing, too, to condemn the mistakes of philosophers in such unrestrained epithets as, for example, 'extraordinarily perverse', 'not even faintly sensible', 'grossly exaggerated'. These are all, it would seem, the trade-marks of philosophy, as distinct from a merely personal weakness of some particular philosopher.

Austin's polemical style is most fully deployed in *Sense and Sensibilia*. His shafts are particularly directed against A. J. Ayer's *Foundations of Empirical Knowledge* (1940), but Price's *Perception* (1932) and G. J. Warnock's *Berkeley* (1953) do not go unscathed. Austin chose those particular books for consideration, so he told his undergraduate audience, for their merits and not for their defects, because they provide 'the best available exposition' of a view which is 'at least as old as Heraclitus'. But their merits Austin scarcely made visible. He announced his intention of exposing 'a mass of seductive (mainly verbal) fallacies' and 'a wide variety of concealed motives' and he did so with relish – although not always, perhaps, with complete fairness.[28]

Austin hoped to destroy two doctrines: the first, that what we 'directly perceive' are sense-data[29] and the second that propositions about sense-data serve as the incorrigible foundations of knowledge. To achieve the first end, he is content for the most part to attack the classical argument from illusion. That argument, he suggests, fails to distinguish between *illusions* and *delusions* – as if in an illusion, as in a delusion, we were 'seeing something', in this case a sense-datum. But in fact when we look at a straight stick in water we see a stick, not a sense-datum; if under those very special circumstances the stick sometimes looks rather like a bent stick this need not perturb us.

As for incorrigibility, Austin argues that there are no propositions whose nature it is to be 'the foundation of knowledge' – propositions which by their very nature are incorrigible, directly verifiable, and evidence-providing. Nor, on the other side, do 'material-object statements' need to be 'based on evidence'. We need, in general, no evidence that there is a book on the table; on the other side, we may, taking another look, come to doubt whether we were correct in saying that the book 'looks heliotrope'.

Austin does not seriously raise the general question why the sense-datum theory in one or the other of its many varieties has had, as he himself emphasizes, so long and honourable a philosophical career. In particular, Austin says nothing whatever about that argument from physics – from the disparity between things as we ordinarily take them to be and things as the physicist describes them – which many epistemologists have thought to be the most fundamental of all arguments for sense-data.[30] He turns his attention, rather, to such questions as the precise functioning of the word 'real', which in phrases like 'the real colour' has played a very large part in sense-datum theories. 'Real,' he argues, is not at all a normal word – a word, that is, which has a single, specifiable meaning. Nor is it ambiguous. It is, he says, 'substantive-hungry' – it cannot stand alone as a description, as 'pink' can, but like 'good' only has meaning in the context of 'a real such-and-such'; it is a 'trouser-word' – it excludes the possibility of something's *not* being real, in any of a variety of possible ways; it is a 'dimension-word', in the sense that it is, again like 'good', the most general of a set of words all of which perform much the same function – words such as 'proper', 'genuine', 'authentic'; it is an 'adjuster-word' permitting us to cope with new and unforeseen situations, without inventing a special new term. Such discriminations are highly relevant, in general terms, to the issues which Austin is ostensibly discussing, but they come at Austin's hands to have a life of their own, not as a mere propaedeutic to, or instrument in, the criticism of sense-data theories.

Of all Austin's writings, his contribution to a symposium on 'Other Minds' has won the most unqualified acclaim.[31] In particular the analogy it incorporates between 'knowing' and 'promising' – usually formulated by saying that 'knowing' is a performative word – has come to be thought of as, unmistakably, a major contribution to philosophy.[32] Knowing, it had not uncommonly been presumed, is the name of a special mental state and to assert that 'I know that S is P', therefore, is to assert that I am in that mental state in relation to 'S is P'. This doctrine, Austin argues, rests on 'the descriptive fallacy', the supposition that words are used only to describe. To claim to know is not to describe my state but to take a plunge – to give others my word, my authority, for saying that S is P, just as to promise is to give others my word that I will do X.*

Yet when P. F. Strawson (criticizing Tarski), put forward a performatory analysis of 'true' – to assert that *p* is true, he suggested, is to confirm *p*, or to grant that *p*, as distinct from saying something about *p* – Austin protested. No doubt, he argued, '*p* is true' has a performatory aspect, but it does not follow that it is a performatory utterance.

To assert that *p* is true, according to Austin, is to maintain, in a sense which, he freely admitted, needs clarification, that '*p* corresponds to the facts'. This, he says, is 'a piece of standard English',

---

*Pritchard had already suggested that 'I promise . . .' is neither true nor false, but 'a sort of incantation, a linguistic device by which the speaker imposes an obligation on himself'.

and as such 'can hardly be wrong'. Austin tried to clarify the meaning of 'correspondence' in terms of *descriptive* conventions, which relate words to types of situations, and *demonstrative* conventions, which correlate sentences with the actual historical situations which are to be found in the world. To say of 'S is P' that it is true, he suggests, is to say that the situation to which it refers is of the sort that is conventionally described in the manner in which it is now being described. (To put the matter roughly: 'the cat is on the mat' is true if and only if that is a correct description of the sort of situation which we have before us.)[33]

In his William James Lectures on *How to do Things with Words* Austin re-examined the whole doctrine of performatives. These lectures are as near as Austin ever got to 'a science of language'. It is clear that he conceived this science in an odd way, reminiscent of Bacon's *New Atlantis*.[34] It was to involve neither experiment nor fieldwork, but, rather, the cooperative discussion of examples derived from a variety of literary sources and from personal experience. These were to be examined in a completely theory-free intellectual atmosphere, with no problem in mind except the problem of describing.*

Austin begins *How to do Things with Words* by restating his 'performative-constative' distinction in a neat and tidy form.[35] (He now prefers 'constative' to 'descriptive', since he thinks he has shown in 'How to talk' that 'descriptive' has only a very limited use.) Performative utterances, he suggests, are 'happy' or 'unhappy' but they cannot be true or false; constative utterances are true or false. Thus although 'I name this ship *Queen Elizabeth*' cannot be false it is 'unhappy' if I am not entitled to name ships, or if this is not the right time to do it or if I am using the wrong formula. 'He named that ship *Queen Elizabeth*' is, in contrast, true or false, not happy or unhappy.

*The contrast between Austin and Popper is instructive. For Popper, there is no such thing as theory-free description, and any worthwhile contribution to knowledge begins from a problem. Whereas Austin is suspicious of talk about 'importance' and suggests that the only thing about the 'importance' of which he is confident is 'truth', Popper argues that what we have always to seek are *interesting* truths, interesting in relation to important problems. The contrast between Austin and Wittgenstein is scarcely less obvious.

But now the doubts begin to creep in. First, on the side of performatives. When we come to look more closely at 'happiness', Austin points out, we see that it always involves something's being true, e.g. that the formula is in fact the correct one, that the person using it has in fact the right to use it, that the circumstances in which it is being employed are in fact the right circumstances. This difficulty might seem to be easily met by the reply that even although the happiness of the performative utterance presupposes the truth of certain statements, the performative utterance is in itself neither true nor false. But the same interplay of truth and happiness, Austin remarks, applies to statements – to the statement 'John's children are bald', for example, if it refers to John when John has no children. It is then not false, but 'unhappy', improperly uttered. And, on the other side, such a performative as 'I warn you that the bull is about to charge' is surely open to criticism on the ground that it is false that the bull is about to charge. So it is not as easy as it at first seemed to be to distinguish between statements and performatives by contrasting what is true or false with what is happy or unhappy.

Then can, perhaps, performatives be distinguished from constatives on some other grounds – grammatical grounds, for example? We might be led to hope so, since performatives are so often expressed in a special sort of first person indicative: 'I warn you', 'I name you'. But, Austin points out, they do not always have this grammatical shape: 'You are hereby warned' is as much a performative as 'I warn you'. Furthermore, 'I state that . . .' also has the first person grammatical form, and that, surely, is a constative!

Austin looks, therefore, for a different mode of distinguishing utterances, in terms of the kind of act they perform. He distinguishes three sorts of sentence-using act; the 'locutionary' act of using a sentence to convey a meaning, as when somebody *tells us* that George is coming, the 'illocutionary' act of using an utterance with a certain 'force', as when somebody *warns* us that George is coming, and the 'perlocutionary' act of producing a certain effect by the use of a sentence, as when somebody, without actually telling us that George is coming, *succeeds in warning us* that he is on his way. Any single utterance combines, Austin came to think, locutionary and illocutionary functions.[36]

On the face of it, locutionary acts correspond to constatives and illocutionary acts to performatives. But Austin has rejected the view that a particular utterance can be classified as a pure performative or a pure constative. To state, as much as to warn, is, he says, to *do* something, and my action in stating is subject to various kinds of 'infelicity'; statements can not only be true or false, they can be fair, precise, roughly true, rightly or wrongly uttered and so on. On the other side, considerations of truth and falsity apply directly to such performative acts as a judge's *finding* a man guilty, or a watchless traveller *estimating* that it is half past two. So the distinction between performatives and constatives must be abandoned – except as a first approximation.

Have these distinctions – and the many other distinctions which in *How to do Things with Words* Austin makes, exemplifies, and names – any importance as a contribution to the solution of traditional philosophical problems, as distinct from problems in a science of language? Very much so, if Austin is right. Elucidation, he suggests, is always of the total speech act; so there is no question, as 'logical analysts' thought there was, of analysing the 'meaning' as something sharply distinguishable from the 'force' of a statement. Stating and describing are, simply, two kinds of illocutionary act, devoid of the special significance with which philosophy has commonly endowed them. Except by an artificial abstraction which may be desirable for certain special purposes 'truth' and 'falsity' are not, as philosophers have commonly supposed them to be, names for relations or qualities; they refer to a 'dimension of assessment' of the 'satisfactoriness' of the words used in the statement in relation to the facts to which they refer. ('True', as we might put it, means 'very well said'.) From this it follows that the standard philosophical distinction between 'factual' and 'normative' must go the way of many other philosophical dichotomies.[37]

Characteristically, however, these somewhat startling conclusions are only *asserted* to follow, not shown in detail to do so; Austin's detailed care is devoted to linguistic distinctions. Only by taking such care, Austin might have replied, is it possible to advance philosophical discussion. Philosophers have attacked the stronghold when they ought to have been reconnoitring the foothills. Only after they have classified and clarified all the possible

ways of *not exactly doing things,* for example, will it be time for
them to ask themselves in what human action consists, and long
after that how such actions are to be explained.[38] But it is hard to
resist the conclusion that Austin thought he already knew that the
stronghold was empty, but the foothills fertile.

Austin's line of reasoning is taken over, to cite one of many examples, by S. E. Toulmin – of Cambridge origins but subsequently
an inhabitant of Oxford – in his 'Probability' (*PASS*, 1950).
Philosophically-minded probability-theorists, he argues, fascinated by the intricacy of puzzles about infinite classes or by the
elegance of the calculus of probability, begin their analyses at
too elevated a point. They should start by considering how we
ordinarily use such expressions as 'I shall probably come'.[39]
Then it will be clear, he thinks, that to say '*S* is probably *P*'
is to make a guarded and restricted statement: it is to commit ourselves to a certain degree – for 'we are prohibited from saying',
for example, 'I'll probably come, but I shan't be able to' – but
only with reservations, which we often make explicit. ('I'll probably come, but it depends on what time we get back from the
Zoo'.) There is no particular 'thing', Toulmin concludes, that
probability statements are about – neither 'frequency', nor 'an
overlap between ranges'; a probability statement is not distinguished from other statements by having a special subject-
matter, but by involving a special degree of commitment.
Frequencies or overlaps might be appealed to, he admits, as a
backing for a claim that this or that will probably happen – but
they are not *what* we are claiming. Thus, Toulmin suggests,
Reichenbach, Carnap and von Mises are contending in vain.
Each of them has gone in search of what simply does not exist –
an entity named by 'probability'. Unwilling to admit the fruitless-
ness of their quest, they bring us back not probability but something quite different, and then quarrel about which of these
substitutes is *really* probability.

Probability is not the only area of dispute which 'ordinary
language' philosophers have declared wasteland. Consider, for
example, D. Pears' article on 'Universals' (*LL* II). Each of the
traditional theories of universals, he argues, fails for precisely the
same reason; it attempts a *general* answer to the question 'why
do we name things as we do?' In so doing, it inevitably presumes

that the answer is already known; it is no accident that all the traditional 'theories of universals' turn out to be circular. For although we can explain why *particular* things are called by the same name, why, for example, Pomeranians and Alsatians are both called 'dogs', the more general question why we use names at all, Pears argues, could be answered only by overstepping – in language! – the bounds of language. Such a pursuit of the impossible, he admits, may have its value, for we may learn how language works by trying to defeat its workings, but it certainly cannot lead to definite answers to definite questions.

The justification of induction, too, has gone the way of 'probability-theory', most clearly perhaps in P. F. Strawson's chapter on 'Inductive Reasoning and Probability' in his *Introduction to Logical Theory* (1952).[40] It is absurd to suppose, he argues, that induction can be 'justified' by showing that it is *really* a variety of deductive reasoning – whether reasoning from an ultimate 'inductive premise' or from the axioms of the calculus of probability – and to attempt to justify it by 'its success' is to rest induction on induction, for any such attempt involves the presumption that what was successful in the past will be successful in the future.

Suppose, instead of seeking a justification, we ask, simply, whether it is 'reasonable' to rely on inductive arguments. Then, Strawson argues, the answer is bound to be 'Yes', because 'being reasonable' *means* 'having a degree of belief in a statement which is proportional to the strength of the evidence in its favour' – the reasonableness of induction is, then, analytic. So there can be no question of *showing* that induction is 'reasonable' or 'justifiable'. We can properly ask whether we are 'justified' in accepting *this or that belief:* but we can no more ask whether inductive reasoning *in general* is justified, Strawson argues, than we can ask whether the law of the land is legal.[41]

Philosophers, Strawson admits, tend to be dissatisfied with this line of reasoning; they complain that their qualms about induction have not been allayed. Somehow, they feel sure, they are being cheated. They are inclined to object: 'isn't it possible that a man might discover *another* method of finding things out, and mightn't it then be rational to prefer this method to induction? So, after all, isn't it necessary to show that induction is the rational method to adopt?' This 'possibility', Strawson argues, is not a real one. For if asked to support the claim that he had discovered a new method better than induction, the inventor could do so only *by inductive reasoning*; he would have to defend such propositions as 'I always get the right answer be doing so-and-so' – propositions which could themselves be based only on induction. In fact, Strawson argues, the phrase 'successful method of finding things out which has no inductive support' is self-contradictory.

Strawson, it will be observed, makes very free use of the expressions 'analytic' and 'self-contradictory'; perhaps nobody since Leibniz has used them with such confidence. Not surprisingly, then, he has vigorously defended the distinction between analytic and synthetic against Quine's attacks on it.[42] Strawson and Quine, indeed, are the leading figures in the battle between 'informal' and 'formal' logic.

Ultimately, perhaps, the quarrel is between Strawson and Russell; always somewhat suspect at Oxford, Russell's philosophical ideas have recently been the main target of attack amongst Oxford logicians, who see in them the source of that Germanic-American formalization they so deeply mistrust. The *locus classicus* is Strawson's 'On Referring' (*Mind*, 1950) – an irreverent attack on that sacred doctrine of formalists, Russell's theory of descriptions.[43]

Russell, according to Strawson, made two connected mistakes; he overlooked the fact that a sentence can have a variety of uses, and he wrongly supposed that if a significant sentence is not being used to make a true statement it must be making a false statement. Russell's trichotomy – true, false or meaningless – collapses, Strawson thinks, once we realize that a sentence can be meaningless or significant but is never true or false, that a statement can be true or false but is never meaningless, and that on a great many of the occasions on which a sentence is being used the question of truth or falsity 'simply does not arise'. By a 'sentence' Strawson means a set of words or expressions. The same sentence, he argues, can be used to make quite different statements: 'the king of France is wise', for example, might be used to make a statement either about Louis XIV or about Louis XV; and it can also be used to crack a joke – as if I say, 'the king of France is the only wise ruler in Europe' – or to tell a story. In these latter cases, anyone who replies 'but that's false' is quite misunderstanding, Strawson argues, the way I am using the sentence; he is assimilating all sentence-uses to statement-making.

Equally, Strawson thinks, to reply 'but there is no King of France' to someone who says, in a Republican age, that the king of France is wise is not, as Russell imagines, to *contradict* the speaker; if there is no king of France the question whether it is true or false that he is wise *simply does not arise*. Russell's theory of descriptions begins from the presumption that since 'the king of France is wise' is neither true nor meaningless it must be false; and again that since it obviously does not describe 'the king of France' – when there is no such person – it must *really* describe something else. After desperate philosophical struggles, Russell finally came to the conclusion that all propositions *really* ascribe predicates to 'logically proper' names, only to meet the complication that there are no such names. But if we recognize, Strawson argues, first, that the question whether 'the king of France is wise' has a meaning is quite independent of the question whether there is in fact such a king – it has a meaning if it *could* be used to talk about somebody – and secondly, that this sentence is not used to *assert*, although no doubt it ordinarily 'implies' or 'presupposes', that there is in fact a king of France, the ground is cut from under the theory of descriptions.

Formal logicians, Strawson complains, have concentrated all their attention on relatively context-free sentences – such sentences as 'all whales are mammals', which are not ordinarily used except to make the statement about whales that they are mammals; this explains why they have ignored the difference between sentences and statements. If they had looked rather at sentences containing such words as 'I' or such phrases as 'the round table' – sentences which can obviously be used on different occasions to make entirely different statements – the difference between sentences and statements would have been bound, he thinks, to strike them forcibly.

As Strawson explains in his *Logical Theory*, he has no objection to the construction of formal systems as such. Formal systems, he thinks, are useful in appraising 'context-free' discourse, as exemplified, say, in mathematics and physics. A formal logic, however, needs to be supplemented by a logic of everyday discourse, for it is incapable, he tries to show, of coping with the complexities of ordinary speech. The 'if ..., then ...', the 'and' and the 'not' of the logician, he argues, are only a selection from 'the ordinary use' of these expressions; there are many kinds of entailment which the formal logician overlooks; the formal logician cannot deal effectively with arguments which depend on temporal relationships or are otherwise 'tied' to specific places and times. These defects, according to Strawson, can be overcome in an 'ordinary language' logic, which begins by asking such questions as 'what are the conditions under which we use such-and-such an expression or class of expressions?' Not so elegant or systematic as formal logic, such a logic can still, he thinks, 'provide a field of intellectual activity unsurpassed in richness, complexity and the power to absorb.'[44]

Of other philosophers teaching at Oxford in the post-war period, one of the best known is F. Waismann.[45] Waismann began as a logical positivist, but always stood particularly close to Wittgenstein. His *Erkenntnis* article on probability (1930), as has already been pointed out, was a development and clarification of Wittgenstein's ideas, and the same is true in some measure of his *Introduction to Mathematical Thinking* (1936).[46] Waismann entirely rejects the view that mathematics can be 'founded on logic'. Mathematics, he argues – even the arithmetic of natural numbers – 'rests on nothing'. It begins from conventions, not from necessary truths; its propositions are neither true nor false. We can say of them, only, that they are compatible or incompatible with certain initial conventions. If we were so to choose, there is nothing to prevent us from constructing a *different* arithmetic, with *different* conventions; we can easily imagine a world, Waismann thinks, in which such an arithmetic would be preferable to the one we now ordinarily use. A philosophy of mathematics, then, must be content to describe arithmetic, abandoning the attempt to provide a foundation for it. 'Only the convention,' Waismann writes, 'is ultimate.'

Numbers, he suggests in Wittgenstein's manner, form a 'family of concepts' – 'number' is not a single strictly definable concept. Exactly the same is true of 'arithmetic'. What we are prepared to call 'a number' or 'a kind of arithmetic' depends on our traditions, not on formal definitions. Their 'openness' is a point in favour of these concepts, he suggests, because it leaves us free to incorporate new mathematical work within our already existing terminology – a possibility which fixed, pre-defined, concepts would rule out.

Waismann's conventionalism, together with his related emphasis on 'open texture', runs through his philosophical essays, achieving perhaps its best known expression in his contribution to a Symposium on 'Verifiability' (*PASS*, 1945, and *LL* I). He begins by criticizing, from a novel point of view, the earlier, phenomenalist, version of logical positivism: the fundamental objection to phenomenalism, he argues, is that the terms in a material-object sentence have an 'open texture'. If, then, we try to set out a collection of sense-datum statements which are sufficient and necessary to establish the truth of, say, the material-object statement 'that is a cat', we shall immediately be met with objections of the following sort: 'Suppose all these conditions were fulfilled, but the thing you have described as a cat were suddenly to develop into a creature of enormous size, what would you say then?' To these questions, Waismann thinks, there is no definite answer, just because 'cat' has an 'open texture'. We do not know what we should say; there is nothing to compel us to say that the suddenly-gigantic creature is or is not a cat. It is not just through somebody's oversight, Waismann argues, that the concept 'cat' lacks definite boundaries: the fact is that we can never know all about an empirical object, can never give a complete description of it. There is always the chance that it will turn out to have quite unexpected qualities.

An empirical statement, Waismann concludes, is never 'completely verifiable', since no battery of tests can establish its truth. This conclusion is not very startling; by the time Waismann wrote 'Verifiability' it was sufficiently agreed upon. But Waismann wants to go further: an empirical proposition, he argues, does not even *entail* specific observational propositions. If it did, it could be refuted by coming into conflict with observations; in fact, he considers, such a conflict is never sufficient to overthrow an empirical proposition. A discrepancy between our expectations and our observations can always be explained away by saying, for example, 'I can't have looked carefully enough'. All we are entitled to say is that an experience 'speaks for' or 'speaks against', 'strengthens' or 'weakens' a proposition, never that it proves or disproves it.

More generally, he argues, such traditional logical relations as contradiction hold only between statements which belong to 'the same language-stratum' – between, say, two theorems in mechanics or two observations of the same pointer-movement.[47] Within a stratum propositions may conflict *simpliciter*, and, again, may be conclusively proved or disproved. The logical relations between two different strata, e.g. between laws and observations, are, he argues, quite different, and much looser – we ordinarily refer to them by such expressions as 'is evidence for', 'tells against', as distinct from 'contradicts' or 'proves'.

Waismann questions, too, the positivist doctrine that 'reality is made up of facts in the sense in which a plant is made up of cells, a house of bricks, a stone of molecules'. Language, no doubt, is made up of separate sentences, but such sentences, according to Waismann, make cuts through reality; they do not merely picture facts which are already there, waiting to be recognized. How we make our cuts will very largely depend, he argues, on the structure of the language we are using; merely because the Englishman says 'the sky is blue' rather than, as in some other European languages, 'the sky blues', he is bound to see the world differently. Facts do not 'speak for themselves', even although, equally, we do not *invent* them.

This general point of view is a little more fully worked out in a long series of articles on 'Analytic-Synthetic' (*Analysis*, 1949–52). Waismann never completed this series of articles and their outcome is not entirely clear. But it has been widely read as a plea for a loose and liberal attitude to language, as opposed to the tendency of 'ordinary language' philosophers to emphasize 'rules' and 'correctness'. ('I have always suspected,' writes Waismann, 'that correctness is the last refuge of those who have nothing to say.')

Like Quine, he questions the orthodox view that there is a precise distinction between 'analytic' and 'synthetic'. He tries to show, in the first place, that none of the distinguishing criteria ordinarily suggested is *itself* precise – that, for example, anyone who argues that analytic propositions are 'grounded on definitions' has failed to observe that 'definition' has itself an open texture – and in the second place, that there are very many propositions which, like 'I see with my eyes', we should hesitate to describe either as analytic or as synthetic, as necessary or as contingent. Once again, then, edges are blurred; an apparently sharp, formalizable, distinction leaves us uncertain what to say.

This uncertainty, Waismann will not admit to be a sign of imperfection; it is the great virtue of language, on his view, that it leaves room for us to say something unexpected, unconventional. The philosopher who plays the schoolmaster, castigating all departures from 'correctness', inevitably moves within the narrow set of categories implicit in the forms of his own language; thus he quite fails to perform the philosophic task: 'philosophy *begins* with distrusting language.' No doubt the philosopher should pay some attention to the 'stock use' of expressions; but if he has anything to say, Waismann thinks, he will very quickly be obliged to depart from that stock use.

CHAPTER 19

Existentialism and Phenomenology

I F, working within my self-imposed limitations, I were to make no reference whatsoever to existentialism, I could not justly be rebuked. For one thing, it has been quite without influence on the main trends in contemporary British philosophy; for another thing, in so far as it has been discussed, existentialism has been taken seriously as a stimulus to ethico-religious thinking, rather than as a metaphysics. Professional philosophers, for the most part, dismiss it with a contemptuous shrug.

Yet there would be a certain cowardice in ignoring it completely, welcome, in some respects, as that decision would be. Existentialism lies on the periphery of British philosophical consciousness; it stands, to British philosophers, for Continental excess and rankness. To sketch its ramifications, then – all that can be attempted in anything less than a large and intricate book – may at least bring into sharper focus that fundamental opposition between British and Latin-Teutonic philosophy on which I have several times insisted, but in somewhat general terms.[1]

At this point, one may be tempted to preach a sermon on British insularity; certainly the attitude of contemporary British philosophers to their Continental colleagues is sometimes reminiscent of the famous newspaper poster announcing a fog in the British Channel: 'Continent Isolated.' Yet, in the sphere of logic and epistemology at least, the British philosopher may well object that it is his Continental colleague, not he, who is insular; for whereas the British philosopher knows his Descartes, his Leibniz, his Kant, the Continental philosopher is likely to be almost wholly ignorant of Berkeley, Hume and Russell. If it is difficult for a British-trained philosopher to read with patience the new Continental ontologies, that is because they simply ignore, do not even attempt to answer, empiricist criticisms of Cartesian rationalism and German Idealism. Thus, for example, neither in Karl Jaspers' huge *Philosophy* (1932) nor in his equally inflated *Philosophical Logic* (1947) is there a single reference to Berkeley or Hume; and if Sartre's *Being and Nothingness* (1943) begins by quoting a famous Berkeleian phrase, Sartre soon makes it clear that he cannot have looked closely at Berkeley's works.*

The fact we have to live with, then, is that if most British philosophers are convinced that Continental metaphysics is arbitrary, pretentious and mind-destroying, Continental philosophers are no less confident that British empiricism is philistine, pedestrian and soul-destroying. Even when existentialism reflects certain aspects of British empiricism – as in its emphasis on contingency – it does so in the manner of the distorting mirrors in a Fun Fair; what seemed eminently rational and ordinary suddenly looks grotesque.

Perhaps one can most easily characterize existentialism as a violent reaction against that view of man and his world which is enshrined in Plato's *Republic*. For Plato, 'existence' is a paltry, second-rate manner of being; existent entities are real only in so far as they manifest a 'form' or 'essence'. To see the world as it *really is*, according to Platonists, is to see it as an intelligible system of essences. Similarly, individuality is a defect; man discovers his true nature only if he allows himself to be fully absorbed into a function – so becoming *a* philosopher, *a* guardian, *a* citizen. The good ruler is dominated by the 'forms'; the good citizen by the force of habit. Neither of them has to suffer the agony of choice, neither has ever to *commit* himself; and neither the ruler nor the citizen, the existentialist would therefore say, knows what it is to be *a person*.

Existentialism has its roots in German Romanticism, which was a protest in the name of individuality against the 'rationality' of eighteenth-century Enlightenment; more directly, it derives from, or at least recognizes as forerunners, the Danish theologian Søren Kierkegaard and the German moralist Friedrich Nietzsche. Neither Nietzsche nor Kierkegaard was a systematic philosopher – they were indeed positively *opposed* to systematic philosophy – but this has not prevented them from exercising a powerful influence upon existentialism: indeed, from a British point of view, existentialism itself, in many of its forms, is anti-philosophical.

*He ascribes to him the doctrine that *to be* is *to be perceived*, ignoring Berkeley's limitation of this formula to the being of material objects, and solemnly argues that Berkeley's theory will not suffice since there must also be a perceiver, if there is to be a perceived.

Kierkegaard wrote voluminously,[2] sometimes under his own name, sometimes – because he thought that truth could best be revealed through the dramatic confrontation of opposing habits of life – pseudonymously, in the guise of a magistrate or a seducer. Nowhere, however, does he straightforwardly present his purely philosophical views: his philosophy always arises in an ethico-religious context, as part of his attempt to solve what he took to be the question of questions: 'How can I become a Christian?'[3]

Christianity, he thought, had two powerful enemies: the unreflective church-goer and the Hegelian. The unreflective church-goer would be shocked to hear that he must learn how to *become* a Christian: he is already a Christian, he imagines, in virtue of the fact that he lives in a Christian community. He is a Christian *qua* 'good citizen' – as in different circumstances he would be a Mohammedan or a Hindu – not because he has chosen to attempt to be one. His Christianity, then, is depersonalized – the religion of a functionary. Similarly, the Hegelian tries to depersonalize philosophy; he portentously delivers 'the verdict of philosophy', as if philosophy could ever be anything but the strivings of *individual philosophers*.

Abstract, impersonal thinking has a certain value – so much Kierkegaard is prepared to admit – but it is wholly inapplicable to the human situation. 'Always it leads away from the human being,' he writes, 'whose existence or non-existence, quite rightly from the objective point of view, becomes infinitely indifferent.' Mathematics, for example, cares nothing for my existence or non-existence. But this abstractness, Kierkegaard argues, cannot be carried to its extreme point – to the entire abolition of the subjective – without self-contradiction; for even mathematics is the creation of a human being. In this sense, he argues, *Existenz* – the existence of a human being – is prior to 'essence', prior to the abstractions of impersonal thinking. And the existent 'subject', who is prior to science, cannot himself be converted into a scientific object. 'Let it [science] deal with plants and animals and stars,' Kierkegaard wrote in his *Journal*, 'but to deal with the human spirit in that way is blasphemy, which only weakens ethical and religious passion.'[4] 'The subject', he argues, 'is by his very nature an historical being, living here and now, passionately involved in his own future, his own salvation; and, for all Hegel's pretence to the contrary, abstract 'objective' inquiry can make nothing of the change, the movement, the individuality, inherent in this historicity.

When philosophers urge us to be 'objective', to abandon our 'merely individual' point of view, what they mean, Kierkegaard thinks, is that we should ignore *Existenz* and concentrate all our attention on essences. But if we are to arrive at 'truth', Kierkegaard is suggesting, we must move in precisely the reverse direction. It is not enough, he says, to live 'aesthetically', content to toy with possibilities without committing ourselves to their reality, or to live 'intellectually' – to be absorbed, in a Platonic manner, in the contemplation of essences.[5] In that way, the 'truths' which really concern us – and, of course, Kierkegaard is thinking particularly of Christian 'truth' – will always escape us; for 'truth' is bound up with existence, not with essences. 'Truth', indeed, is 'subjective'; only that is 'true', according to Kierkegaard, which we have grasped by our own efforts, encountering it through commitment and making it part of our own nature. Society, he considers, presses us to be objective; it wants us to allow our individuality to be absorbed into a type and our knowledge into abstract generalizations. We do not find it easy, therefore, to be 'subjective' – but in no other way can we break through abstractions to *Existenz*.

What we commit ourselves to is, for Kierkegaard, less important than *how* we commit ourselves: 'the energy, the earnestness, the feeling with which we choose.' For if we choose wrongly, the energy of our commitment, he thinks, will make our mistakes clear to us, whereas the 'indifferent', 'objective', man never commits himself with enough zeal to find out how wrong he is. We can discover ourselves, and can come to understand the human situation, he further argues, only through leaps, decisions, not by means of rational deductions from first premises. For a 'first premise', Kierkegaard argues against the Hegelians, is 'first' only because we make it so; because we determine – by a deliberate act of choice – that at that point we shall begin. Similarly, each major step on the way to truth is a free decision. Our progress, according to Kierkegaard, from the aesthetic to the scientific point of view, and then again from the scientific to the ethical and from the ethical to the religious, cannot be rationalized into an orderly, formally justifiable, step from premises to conclusions: it is in each case a leap to a quite new way of looking at things.

The human situation, as Kierkegaard sees it, is paradoxical by its very nature; for a temporal 'existent' yet belongs to eternity. No bare contemplation of essences, he argues, could lead us to this *existential* paradox, nor again to the specifically Christian paradox of the incarnate God; our guide, now, is not 'speculative philosophy' – he attacks, particularly, Hegel's attempt to rationalize Christianity – but rather our deep feelings of despair, which are ontologically revealing. The Philistine tries to escape from despair: he pretends that he is wholly temporal, wholly devoted to narrow and practical ends, and that in striving after them he can hope to achieve everything of which man is capable. But to maintain this pretence he has to force himself to live in a fashion which is intolerably petty and narrow – and even then his despair breaks through in the great crises of his life. The man who attempts to be a Christian, however, comes to 'know himself' – Kierkegaard thinks of himself as continuing the Socratic mission – just by facing his despair, and seeing its implications.

The core of Kierkegaard's thinking, then, is Christian; Nietzsche,[6] in contrast, begins from the presumption that 'God is dead'. Men must learn to re-examine the human situation, he argues, in the light of the fact that it is no longer possible to believe in God's existence. If Kierkegaard's problem is: 'How can I become a Christian?' for Nietzsche it is rather: 'How am I to live as an atheist?'

Yet there are important points of resemblance between Nietzsche and Kierkegaard, so that it is not merely an accident that their influence has converged in existentialism. Both philosophers concern themselves passionately, if diversely, with the human situation; they both reject as a delusion all abstract, objective, systematic, philosophy; for both of them 'life is more than logic'. 'It makes all the difference in the world,' Nietzsche wrote, 'whether a thinker stands in personal relation to his problems, in which he sees his destiny, his need, and even his highest happiness, or can only feel and grasp them impersonally, with the tentacles of cold, prying thought.' That might be Kierkegaard talking – or any existentialist. Again, both Kierkegaard and

Nietzsche see in 'essences' a device men use to tame the world, to reduce it to something indifferent and stable. The 'real' world, they tell us, is historical, 'existential', revealed as such to the courageous human agent, but lying beyond the understanding of abstract thought, which always, by its nature, deals in types. And Nietzsche, like Kierkegaard, bitterly attacks the Philistine, the mediocre man, whose highest ideal it is to submerge himself – to do 'what is done', to be 'Man' as distinct from 'a man'.

The bracketing of Kierkegaard and Nietzsche is now an historical commonplace, but it dates back only to Karl Jaspers' *The Psychology of World-Views* (1919), the book in which – for all that it was originally designed as a contribution to psychology – the principal themes of existentialism were first announced. Twelve years later, in his *Man in the Modern Age*,[7] Jaspers officially defined existentialism as 'a philosophy which does not cognize objects' but 'elucidates and makes actual the being of the thinker'.

'It does not cognize objects' – in other words, philosophy, as the existentialist conceives it, is not a variety of science, in however extended a use of that term. Jaspers was originally a medical man, and made his way only gradually into philosophy by way of psychopathology. He does not share the Philistine contempt for science, the confusion of it with mere technology, which many of his fellow-existentialists exhibit. Indeed, he goes so far as to maintain that 'any philosopher who is not trained in a scientific discipline or who fails to keep his scientific interests alive will eventually fall into confusions'. But it is, he thinks, the worst of mistakes – a mistake Jaspers attributes to Descartes – to suppose that science and philosophy are, or could be, identical or, as Husserl did, that philosophy could be converted into a specialized 'strict science'.[8]

Jaspers is particularly opposed to Marx and Freud because, he says, they put forward 'a world-view in the guise of science' – in Freud's case 'a barren hateful world-view concealed behind a humanitarian form'. But is it worth noting that Darwin, too, lies beyond the limits of Jaspers' toleration; his work, according to Jaspers, 'implies the destruction of all authentic life'. Indeed, Jaspers goes so far as to suggest that man has always existed, although perhaps in a different biological form, and that the ape is a degenerate man! For all Jaspers' professed respect for science, he completely rejects scientific conclusions not only when they are philosophy in disguise, which is his official ground for objecting, but whenever they threaten the conception of a man-centred universe.

The English reader, if he knows his *Tractatus*, will find the main lines of Jaspers' philosophy familiar; they are summed up in those passages of the *Tractatus* from which English commentators on Wittgenstein ordinarily avert their eyes. 'The sense of the world must lie outside the world'; 'the feeling of the world as a limited whole; it is this that is the mystical'; 'if a question can be framed at all, it is possible to answer it'; 'when all possible scientific questions have been answered, the problems of life remain completely untouched'; 'there are things that cannot be put into words; they make themselves manifest; they are what is mystical'. (The common source, of course, is the German Kantian tradition; Jaspers takes over from Kant almost all of his leading tenets, parting company with him only at those points at which Kant professes to be proceeding deductively to philosophical conclusions or to have arrived at a universally applicable theory about the structure of thought.)

Naturally, then, that difficulty recurs in Jaspers which readers of the *Tractatus* have so often felt. Is not Jaspers, by the very nature of his task as a teacher, compelled to talk about what he says cannot be talked about, to treat as knowledge what he so paradoxically calls 'the non-knowledge of philosophical exploration'? In a controversy with the theologian, Rudolf Bultmann, Jaspers rebukes him for trying to convert existentialism, under Heidegger's influence, into a body of conceptual knowledge. Bultmann's reply is a natural one: Jaspers' own writings, he points out, abound in statements which are presented as objective truths about the human being. How else is it possible to talk at all?[9]

According to Jaspers there are two boundaries at which we pass beyond the limits of knowledge, beyond the limits, that is, of what can be expressed in words or can have questions asked about it: these are at the boundary of 'Transcendence' and at the boundary of *Existenz*. We are brought to these two boundaries as a result of our encounter with 'ultimate situations' – in our personal life the ultimate situations of suffering, guilt and death; in scientific thought the ultimate situations represented by paradoxes and antinomies. (That is why the philosopher needs to be a scientist – to encounter its paradoxes.) These experiences bring home to us the shallowness of our knowledge of the empirical self and the unreliability of all 'worldly existence'. Suffering, guilt and death reveal to us our *Existenz*, that capacity of our self for free decisions in virtue of which the self is inexhaustible by scientific knowledge, not because it is too complex to be fully described, but because there are no limits to what it can make of itself. 'Transcendence' we come to recognize through the incapacity of science to achieve that unification which it takes as an ideal but to which it can never attain. Restricted as it is to the understanding of specific situations by the use of purely scientific methods, science, according to Jaspers, can never lead us to a knowledge of the whole. In our tradition philosophers ordinarily give content to the idea of the transcendent by making use of the biblical representation of God, but they cannot properly claim, Jaspers argues, to *know* that the transcendent has this, or any other, content, any more than they can properly claim to know in what our *Existenz* consists.

Then what is the philosopher to do, if not to give us knowledge about *Existenz* and the 'transcendent'? According to Jaspers, philosophy – and in this it resembles poetry, mythology, mysticism and, even, madness* – sees all natural objects as 'ciphers', as a system of signs, as the language of God. The philosopher helps us to read these signs, as Jaspers sets out to do in the system of categories he propounds in his large-scale philosophical works. But it is wrong to imagine, according to Jaspers, that the help the philosopher offers us in 'reading' the natural world can be expressed as a set of eternally valid interpretations or that any philosopher can provide us with a wholly dependable method of interpretation. Nor is philosophy, according to Jaspers, a gradual progress towards better and better interpretations.

*So Jaspers defends mythology against Bultmann (although not, of course, in so far as it professes to give us *knowledge*) and, even more strikingly, in his *Strindberg and Van Gogh* (1922), condemns the habit of using the description 'mentally ill' in a disparaging sense. Strindberg and Van Gogh, he suggests, show us how in madness there can be revelations which the sane, ordinary man never experiences.

When Jaspers came to write *The Great Philosophers* he did two significant things: he began his 'history' with an account of Socrates, Buddha, Confucius, Jesus, even although he admits that (except for Socrates) they are not usually described as philosophers, and he largely ignored chronology. It does not in the least trouble him that Kant is discussed at length in the first volume of *The Great Philosophers* whereas Descartes and Hume are reserved for the third volume. For Jaspers, there is not a sharp distinction between sage and philosopher, and chronology is unimportant, seeing that philosophers learn nothing – since there is nothing to be learnt – from their predecessors. (A particularly odd view when one remembers how much Jaspers himself learnt from Kant.)

Especially after Heidegger and Sartre began to develop the radical forms of existentialism, Jaspers came to be very conscious of the anarchical implications inherent in a doctrine of *Existenz*, if that is conceived of as an isolated centre of action. He makes more and more use of three unifying concepts, the Encompassing, Reason and Communication. The encompassing has two aspects – or, as Jaspers puts it in his *Reason and Existenz* (1935, English translation 1956) – it 'appears and disappears for us in two opposite perspectives'. From one point of view it includes us; it is the whole of Being of which we form part. From another point of view *we ourselves* are the Encompassing – the Encompassing is Being as it is for us, as forming 'part of our consciousness'.[10] To use a favourite word of his own, Jaspers 'glides' from one to the other of these perspectives.

He is not afraid of accusations of circularity or self-contradiction; circularity and self-contradiction, he argues, are inevitable in metaphysics. A philosophy which tries to get rid of its circularities and self-contradictions, so Jaspers tells us, 'falls flat on its face and becomes totally empty'. The only question is whether its contradictions and its circles are 'significant'. The circle of *Existenz* and the Transcendent is 'significant', according to Jaspers, because without it the Transcendent would collapse into emptiness as a mere Unknowable, indistinguishable from nothing, and *Existenz* would become a 'sterile, loveless and demoniac defiance'. Neither *Existenz* nor Transcendence can stand alone; in the Encompassing they find one another, each by its own method of approach.

In his *Reason and Anti-Reason in our Time* (1950, English translation 1952) Jaspers went so far as to declare, in reaction against Sartre, that his own philosophy should be called a 'philosophy of reason' rather than an 'existentialism'. 'Reason', in Jaspers' writings, has its characteristic German sense, which distinguishes it sharply from 'the Understanding'. The Understanding, i.e. what in English is called 'rational thinking', is condemned by Jaspers as 'nihilistic' because it separates, distinguishes. 'Reason,' in contrast, unifies. It forbids us to rest content with that merely specific knowledge to which science is limited; it gives us confidence that we shall in the end arrive at 'the attitude of transcendence', at a concept of the world-as-a-whole. In what Jaspers says of Reason – that it is, for example, 'the existential absolute which serves to actualize the primary source and bring it to the instant manifestation' – he most conspicuously passes beyond the comprehension of empirically-minded philosophers. They are unlikely to be convinced that Jaspers' 'Reason', with its search for 'fulfilled, conquered non-knowledge' is anything but irrationality in a very thin disguise.

On the other hand, Jaspers' eloquent plea for communication has struck a sympathetic chord in Anglo-Saxon hearts, so far at least as it is expressed in such essays as *The Idea of a University* and *The European Spirit*.[11] But further examination shows that what Jaspers means by 'communication' is not what ordinarily goes under that name. Bultmann has said of Jaspers' criticisms of him: 'They have little in common with the spirit of genuine communication. His style is not that of a Socratic-Platonic dialogue, but rather that of an *ex cathedra* pronouncement.' Jaspers resents this characterization of his approach, claiming as he does that his task is to awaken, not to make pronouncements. But he freely grants that in philosophical discussions – which are, for Jaspers, 'discussions concerned with matters of faith' – one can do no more than 'convey inner dispositions, claims and decisions, to express one's own views and reply to questions'. This, above all, is why it is so difficult for (most) Anglo-Saxon and (most) Franco-German philosophers to communicate with one another; they have quite different conceptions of 'communication'.

For most contemporary Franco-German philosophers, particularly since Hitler's successful destruction of German empiricism*, to communicate is to express one's views, inviting questions but not criticism; for most Anglo-Saxon philosophers, to communicate is to engage in a critical discussion. To Anglo-Saxon eyes, Jaspers' philosophical approach rules out the very possibility of that 'communication' of which he is so eloquent a spokesman; his 'communication' is no more than an emotional relationship. For how is it possible, the Anglo-Saxon would ask, even to 'point the way', as distinct from merely arousing emotions, except by making objectively-testable claims? And in philosophy, according to Jaspers, there is no room for such claims.

Jaspers seldom refers to Martin Heidegger; when he does, it is to suggest that there is in Heidegger's work an uneasy vacillation between the traditional conception of philosophy as an attempt to construct a system of truths and Jaspers' own view that all one can do in philosophy is to 'point the way'. The intellectual background of the two men was very different.[12] Heidegger is quite innocent of science: he was trained, first as a Jesuit seminarian, then in an academic department of philosophy under the supervision of Heinrich Rickert. His interest in that 'question of Being' which was to be his major intellectual concern was first aroused by Franz Brentano's academic essay *On the Manifold Meanings of Being in Aristotle* (1862); his own 'habilitation' thesis was on *Duns Scotus' Doctrines of Categories and Meanings* (1915). Under Husserl's influence he made his way out of scholasticism. But Heidegger came to feel that Husserl had overemphasized the self. Whereas for Husserl the 'wonder of all wonders' is 'the pure ego and the pure consciousness', for

---

*It is odd to observe that existentialists often speak of logical positivism as if it were a peculiarly Anglo-American phenomenon with offshoots in Scandinavia. In fact, of course, it was born in Austria and many of its leading spokesmen were German. It is undoubtedly true that German philosophers, and in some measure French philosophers, are still obsessed by that nineteenth-century Romanticism which was in England no more than a passing phase; the 'return to objectivity' was never widely welcomed. But it is only necessary to recall the names of Brentano, Frege, the early Husserl, Schlick, Carnap, Feigl, Popper to dispel any suggestion that there is something in the German national character which makes any form of empiricism wholly uncongenial to it.

Heidegger it is 'that there are things in being'. Heidegger never abandoned, that is, the Aristotelian-scholastic emphasis on Being.

In England, Heidegger is most often referred to as a horrible example of just how meaningless metaphysics can be. A passage which Carnap quoted from Heidegger's *What is Metaphysics?* in order to illustrate the nonsensical character of metaphysics has assumed the status of a classical example. Certainly such sentences as 'Nihilation is neither an annihilation of what-is, nor does it spring from negation. ... Nothing annihilates itself' leave one with the impression that something has gone very wrong indeed.

Heidegger, Ayer assures us in his *Language, Truth and Logic*, has been led astray because he wrongly presumes that every word is a name; since there is a word 'Nothing', Heidegger has jumped to the conclusion that there must also be an entity, Nothing, which this word names. But Ayer's pleasantly straightforward explanation of Heidegger's ontology will scarcely suffice: for Heidegger explicitly maintains that 'Nothing is neither an object nor anything that is at all. Nothing occurs neither by itself nor apart from what is, as a sort of adjunct'. So Heidegger is not, after all, reifying 'Nothing'; we must look elsewhere for the roots of his metaphysics.

Yet Heidegger's major work, *Being and Time*[13] was not, on its first appearance, universally condemned by empirically-minded philosophers. Gilbert Ryle, reviewing it in *Mind* (1929), wrote with some enthusiasm of Heidegger's 'subtlety' and 'boldness', and drew attention to the 'unflagging energy with which he tries to think beyond the stock categories of orthodox psychology and philosophy'. The rejection of stock categories is, indeed, the most striking feature of *Being and Time* – especially when one contrasts it with that scholastic and neo-Kantian setting within which it arose. Although Heidegger, it would seem, knows nothing whatever of Anglo-American philosophy, *Being and Time* can profitably be read as an attack upon the ontological assumptions which lie behind British empiricism, to which, as we have already observed, neo-Kantianism was closely allied.

Neo-Kantianism and British empiricism have two fundamental assumptions in common: the first is that 'the problem of knowledge' rather than 'the problem of being' is the central problem of philosophy, the second is that a sharp distinction can be drawn between what we experience and the 'importance' or 'value' we attach to it. Professing to be ontology-free, such an 'empiricism', Heidegger argues, in fact rests on an ontology which, if taken seriously, gives rise to insuperable problems. Roughly speaking, empiricism presumes that the world falls apart into two classes of entities – 'subjects' whose principal task it is to perceive and 'objects' whose character it is to be perceived. So perception, according to the empiricist, is the link between two ontologically isolated forms of substance. But then, according to Heidegger, it is impossible to show how any link could possibly connect substances so disparate, how, for example, a 'spiritual substance' could ever perceive an 'external world'.

Whereas for Kant, 'the scandal of philosophy' is that it has never succeeded in demonstrating the existence of an external world, the real scandal, Heidegger maintains, is that philosophers should continue to attempt such a demonstration, as if in answer to a genuine problem, instead of realizing that the problem only arises within an ontology which renders a solution to it impossible. As soon as we ask *what it is* that is demanding a proof of the external world, we see at once, according to Heidegger, that it is already a 'being-in-the-world'. Only the impossible ontological presumption that questions about the external world could be asked by an isolated self enables the empiricist to suppose that the existence of the external world could ever be a real problem.

Similarly, Heidegger argues, the classical problem of truth[14] arises out of the presumption that truth is a property of some entity, or set of entities, which lies between us and the world; the insuperable problem which then arises is how such entities could 'correspond' to anything in the world. In fact, according to Heidegger, truth is a 'revelation', a 'showing forth': 'That hammer is too heavy', for example, is true if the hammer reveals itself as being too heavy – there is no third entity between ourselves and the heaviness of the hammer to which the 'too-heaviness' of the hammer somehow 'corresponds'.

Heidegger's choice of example is significant. British empiricism takes as its typical instances of what we notice in the world such facts as 'the grass is green', or, in the more sophisticated forms of empiricism, 'that thing over there looks green'. These examples at once suggest that our interest in the world is that of a spectator, a looker-on. 'The hammer is too heavy', in contrast, suggests as typical a quite different, more practical, attitude to the world, for which the things around us are tools, 'equipment', things which are 'ready-to-hand', as distinct from merely 'present-at-hand'.

The 'being-in-the-world' characteristic of 'Human Existence',* is not simply, according to Heidegger, a matter of the human body's standing in a spatial relationship to other beings; the human being *inhabits* a world, finds a home in it, displays a 'care' for it.† The world is phenomenologically revealed to the human being as *his* world, not in the sense of being the world which he perceives but as being the world he cares about, made up of things which are usable or unusable, hindrances or helps, potentially useful or potentially troublesome. Perception, being content to be a looker-on, is, for Heidegger, a rare form of 'care', not the typical mode of being-in-the-world. (Contrast Berkeley

*I have ventured to use this phrase (capitalized) as a translation of Heidegger's *Dasein*, in the contexts which particularly interest us. Literally, *Dasein* means as a verb 'to be there' and as a noun 'Existence', but either translation would be misleading. It is characteristic of the difficulty in translating Heidegger that translators have suggested as translations of *Dasein* words as remote in meaning as 'being-there' and 'transience'; it has been said of *Dasein*, even, that 'it is roughly equivalent to Kant's pure reason, although without the rationalistic overtones of this term' (*Hamlet* without the Prince of Denmark?). Untypically, Macquarrie and Robinson retain the German in their translation – as is no doubt the only alternative if one hopes to translate *Dasein* by the same expression in all the contexts in which it occurs. My 'Human Existence' is roughly equivalent to Sartre's translation – 'Réalité humaine' – but it obviously will not do in those contexts in which Heidegger speaks, as he does, of the *Dasein* of God.

†Heidegger's special use of the German language and of German etymology can be illustrated from the fact that he derives 'in' from a (postulated) old German word 'innen' with the meaning of 'inhabit'. In German the word 'bei' already means not only 'by' but 'at the home of', so that it seems more natural in German than it is in English to suggest that the things which are 'by us' are all of them 'in our home'. The word 'care' should be read as implying both 'care' in the sense of 'he really cares for her' and 'care' in the sense of 'proceed with care'. As has often been noted, Heidegger's criticism of empiricism is in many respects like Dewey's. On his attitude to language, compare Austin's remark that 'a word never – well hardly ever – shakes off its etymology' ('A Plea for Excuses', *PAS*, 1956).

for whom the whole being of objects consists in their being perceived.)

Nor is it, according to Heidegger, the essence of the mind to
perceive – to look at things impartially. When we look at the
world, he argues, we are always 'in a certain mood'. Men talk of
overcoming their moods, but what really happens in such cases,
according to Heidegger, is that one mood overcomes another.
Even apathy is a mood, not the absence of a mood. We encounter the world as something 'attuned' to our mood; the
world for us is always something we value or despise. We do
not first see it and then attach a value to it; what we see and how
we see it depends on what we are at that moment taking to be
valuable.

We encounter other people, too, not as inferences from what
we perceive, but as owners of, and fellow-users of, 'equipment'.
Other people are not just there to be looked at. Even when they
are 'standing around', this – unlike the immobility of a statue –
is itself a way of behaving, a rejection of what surrounds them
as inutilizable. 'The others,' so Heidegger sums up, '*are what
they do*' – we know them as agents, and in the process of observing their agency we come to know our own powers as an
agent.

Indeed, in its most characteristic, 'everyday' form, Human
Existence consists not in being oneself – revealing one's own
Existenz – but in being 'They' (or as the German illuminatingly
has it, *Man*). In our everyday 'average' life we act as 'the others'
act, not because we have *deliberately chosen* to conform to 'the
tasks, the rules, the standards, the urgency' of others, but simply
because 'acting as They do' is the typical mode of behaviour of
Human Existence.

'Acting as They do', however, although 'everyday' is nonetheless 'inauthentic'. Like Kierkegaard and Jaspers, Heidegger
suggests that we are aroused out of this inauthenticity by encountering 'ultimate situations' and, in particular, by our realization that we must die, a realization which has to Heidegger a
crucial significance. Most of the situations in which we can
contemplate our finding ourselves are of such a kind that we can
easily think of its being someone else rather than ourselves who
is involved in them; we can easily imagine that it is a friend,

rather than ourselves, who takes a holiday in Rome, or writes a successful book, or, even, suffers the death of his child. But the case of our own death, according to Heidegger, is very different; in death it is *my* Human Existence which comes to an end, it is *my* potentialities which are exhausted. Nobody else can – in the sense which is now in question – die for me. I can, of course, try to forget that I will die, in the 'idle chatter' of everyday existence; but only by not forgetting it, by holding tight to the fact of mortality, can I preserve my authenticity.*

In the phenomena of guilt and conscience, too, we come to recognize our own *Existenz*. Conscience, Heidegger argues, cannot be reduced to 'the voice of God' or 'the voice of the people'; these are attempts to cope with conscience inauthentically, to convert it into something 'They' say to us. There is, Heidegger admits, some excuse for such an interpretation of conscience. Phenomenologically, conscience calls to me as if it were both from me and from beyond me; that is why it is natural, concentrating on the second aspect of its manner of calling, to ascribe that call to somebody else. But the call of conscience seems alien to us only because we are ordinarily so absorbed within that impersonal life which 'one' lives, I do not recognize that in conscience I am calling myself, because the call comes not from my everyday self, but from my 'uncanny' self.

What is the 'uncanny' self? Heidegger first introduces this concept as part of his phenomenological analysis of 'anxiety'. He distinguishes sharply between anxiety and fear, on the ground that in anxiety we are not afraid of a definite possibility, as we might be afraid of being run over when we cross the Place de la Concorde; we are afraid of nothing in particular. Or as we might also put the matter, we are anxious about 'what the world might do to us' – we no longer feel at home in the world. (Heidegger exploits the fact that the German word for 'uncanny' is '*unheimlich*', from the root-word '*heim*', meaning 'home').

Now we begin to see how Heidegger introduces the conception of Nothing. In anxiety what are we afraid of? Nothing. And what is the authentic self, in its permanent character? Nothing. What, in conscience, calls to us? Nothing. This at least, so Heidegger

---

*Tolstoy's short novel *The Death of Ivan Ilyich* (1886) is a literary expression of this same theme; it is often referred to in existentialist writings.

suggests, is how we must reply to such questions so long as we are expected to reply in an everyday, 'worldly' way – for we cannot answer them by referring to that sort of definite particularized entity which is the staple of everyday 'being-in-the-world'. Our authentic 'self' is a potentiality for action, not an agent in the ordinary sense of the word; 'conscience' is the call of our potentialities, not the call of a person. The guilt for which conscience rebukes us, Heidegger argues, is not a 'worldly-guilt' for not having done what 'They' want us to do – not having paid a debt, for example – it is a guilt for what we have not done, for our failure to be what we might have been. We feel guilty, that is, about 'nothing'.

A central phenomenological fact about Human Existence, according to Heidegger, is its temporality, its historicity. This, he suggests, is one of the points at which both phenomenology and scholasticism break down; they neither of them recognize the historicity of Being. Just for that reason they are powerless against Marxism, which to some degree does so. But to say that Human Existence is 'historical' is to say a great deal more than that, as Marxists suggest, human beings are 'a more or less important atom in world-history'. Human Existence, according to Heidegger, is through-and-through temporal. It lives in anticipation – in particular in the anticipation of its own death; it finds things 'useful' for the future or 'worn-out' from their past.

On the traditional view, human beings live in the present and reach towards the past and the future only by way of recollection or prediction. For Heidegger this is true, and even then with reservations, only of inauthentic Human Existence – which, indeed, tries to think of the future and the past as if it were only the present all over again. But the fundamental mode of being of Human Existence, according to Heidegger, is in the future. This conclusion follows directly from Heidegger's phenomenological analysis of Human Existence, for which 'care' is central, and from his emphasis on our own future death as the critically-important 'ultimate situation'. But the past is, on his view, of scarcely less vital import than the future. Human Existence is not merely fatalistic in its attitude to the fact that it must die; out of its recognition of its mortality, out of its sense of guilt, of not having achieved what it might have been, it develops 'resoluteness'. And this 'resoluteness', although directed towards the future, derives its confidence, Heidegger suggests, from a return to the past, from the possibility of taking a 'hero' from the past, of 'repeating' what has been done before, not in the sense of doing just that thing again, but as responding to those possibilities which were inherent in it but which were not realized. It is characteristic of the 'hero' that in his deeds or in his thoughts there is this reserve of as yet unrealized possibilities. We have not exhausted what, for example, Parmenides can mean to us. No doubt the 'everyday' present, Heidegger admits, already in some measure absorbs the past. But the 'resolute' self finds itself compelled to 'disavow' the present in order to return to the past, to see the past in terms of the unrealized possibilities it still presents. This, it becomes clear in the outcome, is Heidegger's 'vision' of his own 'destiny' as a philosopher. More and more he returns to the past, especially to the early Greek philosophers, but not in the spirit of a scholar: his object is to complete the task which they initiated but which men later 'forgot'.

What has so far been said about *Being and Time* is in a fundamental respect highly misleading; for it would suggest that *Being and Time* is purely and simply a contribution to existentialism. But Heidegger has explicitly denied that he is an existentialist. 'My philosophical tendencies,' he wrote in a letter to Jean Wahl, 'cannot be classified as existentialist; the question which principally concerns me is not that of man's *Existenz*; it is Being in its totality and as such.' That fact, indeed, is made perfectly clear at the very outset of *Being and Time*.

Heidegger takes as his point of departure, not Kierkegaard's analysis of *Existenz*, but a passage from Plato's *Sophist* – a passage which he translates as follows: 'For you have long been aware of what you mean when you use the expression "being". We, however, who used to think we understood it, have now become perplexed.'

Everybody, Heidegger agrees with Plato, must in some sense know what he means when he says of something 'it is'. But philosophy, Plato says, has become perplexed about the meaning of being; it is that perplexity which Heidegger hopes to understand and to resolve. Philosophy, he argues, must return to the problem of Being; a problem which Plato himself put fatally in the wrong light in so far as he identified Being with certain particular beings – the Forms.

Heidegger is well aware that the question 'What is Being?' has been denounced as senseless. Nietzsche, who is in Heidegger's eyes the culminating figure in Western metaphysics, had explicitly maintained that Being is an empty idea – 'the last cloudy streak of evaporating reality'.[15] In his *Introduction to Metaphysics* (1953, English translation 1959) Heidegger set out to answer Nietzsche. Man cannot do without the conception of Being, according to Heidegger; without it he would be speechless. 'There would, indeed, be no language at all' and in consequence no Human Existence, since man is essentially a language user. In order to speak at all, we have to be able to say of things that they 'are'.[16] No doubt, they 'are' in quite different fashions – the 'is' of 'the lecture is in the Auditorium' is not identical with the 'is' of 'the book is mine' or of 'the red is the port side' or of 'God is' – but that is only to say, according to Heidegger, that Being manifests itself in various ways.

If its real theme is 'the meaning of Being', why is so much of Heidegger's *Being and Time* devoted to Human Existence? Human Existence, Heidegger argues, is peculiarly important to ontology, just because the human being has – in the sense to which Plato drew attention – 'a vague average understanding of Being'. By his nature as a language-user, as an inquirer, as the only being who is conscious that he is one day not to be, as 'solicitous' for others, solicitous for what they have it in them to be, the human being 'cares' for Being. So, by studying Human Existence the philosopher is led directly to Being.[17]

One reason why *Being and Time* has so often been read as a variety of existentialism is that it is incomplete; Heidegger never published those final sections, although he several times directs his readers to them, in which the meaning of Being was to be made clear. So the first sections of *Being and Time*, which were intended only as a foundation for a 'hermeneutics' in which the nature of Being would be 'read off' from the analysis of Human Existence there provided, constitute, in the outcome, its whole. Thus it is that Heidegger becomes, one might say, an existentialist in spite of himself.

Nor does Heidegger in his later writings – essays and lectures, many of them very brief – supply the missing *finale* to *Being and Time*. The 'quest for being' traditionally takes the form of ontology and metaphysics. But although in *Being and Time* Heidegger is happy to describe what he hoped to achieve as 'ontology', he came to feel that this was a misleading description of it; so he was led to reject ontology. Metaphysics, he argued in his introduction to the 1949 edition of *What is Metaphysics?*[18], has also to be 'overcome'. 'Due to the manner in which it thinks of being,' he there writes, 'metaphysics almost seems to be, without knowing it, the barrier which keeps Man from the involvement of Being in human nature'. The difficulty, in Heidegger's eyes, is that both metaphysics and ontology substitute a particular characteristic or a particular entity for Being itself; in the typical 'worldly' fashion they confuse Being with a being, whether they identify it with God or the form of the good or the 'highest genus'. This does not mean that metaphysics and ontology have simply to be condemned; there is much to be learnt from them, Heidegger thinks, but in the end one must disavow them and return to their grounds. Even philosophy, he suggests in his *Woodman's Trails* – if that, rather than *Blind Alleys*, is the best translation of *Holzwege* (1950) – is the 'enemy of thinking'. ('Thinking' now has the special meaning of 'thinking about Being'.) If we were to say of these late writings, as many of us would like to do, that in them Heidegger is 'not a philosopher at all', Heidegger would, it seems, be in perfect agreement with us.

Then what path does Heidegger recommend to us? *Being and Time* tried to approach Being through Human Existence, and in his essay on *Identity and Difference* (1957, English translation 1960) Heidegger still argues that 'only in Man can Being be domiciled', that 'Man alone has made himself accessible to Being'. But Being is not to be reached, it would seem, by the path of phenomenological analysis. We shall not find it by a painstaking search but rather by letting it reveal itself to us. Heidegger turned then to poetry, and especially to the poetry of Hölderlin.[19] 'Poetry,' so he wrote in an essay on Hölderlin, 'is the establishment of Being by means of the word.' He never abandons that view; in Heidegger's later writings, the poet has the same authority as the philosopher, and Parmenides' poem about being, not the Platonic dialogue, is the exemplar of philosophy.

But 'the word', rather than poetry as such, comes more and more to the fore. Language, especially the Greek language, is, according to Heidegger, the principal method by which Being 'discovers itself'. Greek and German, he had written in *The Introduction to Metaphysics*, are the most 'spiritual' languages – it would not in the least trouble Heidegger that he cannot be wholly translated into English – but Greek has the advantage of taking us 'back to the roots'. 'The Greek language', Heidegger went so far as to write in *What is Philosophy?* (1956, English translation 1958), 'is no mere language like other European languages. The Greek language and it alone is *logos*'. Greek, in other words, is the language in which Being speaks to us.

Heidegger's etymological disquisitions on the Greek language and his interpretations of Greek philosophy are often nothing short of extraordinary.[20] He makes scarcely a reference to professional philology or professional scholarship – none at all, of course, to British or American philology or scholarship. But this is characteristic of the radicalism of his thinking, a radicalism, which, if we may adopt Heidegger's etymological style, is a 'root-finding'. The traditional translations and interpretations of scholars, their grammatical analyses, their philology, even the logic they employ, all of them reflect, according to Heidegger, an untenable ontology, which is 'forgetful of Being'. They must be 'overthrown', logic not least of all. Going back to their roots, to that Greek language out of which they arose – approaching them in that 'resolute' manner he described in *Being and Time* – is the only way of discovering Being. But what is revealed is not a particular entity; Being is a light in which things are revealed, or a light which reveals things to us, not a particular entity which is revealed in that light. In his *Zur Seinsfrage* (1956) he even suggests that 'Being' itself is an inadequate description of what he is seeking; he has '*Sein*' printed in his later works with crossing-out marks superimposed on it – as ~~Sein~~. There are fluctuations, too, in his views about whether Being can exist apart from beings, In a postscript to the fourth edition of *What is Metaphysics?* (1943) he had explicitly asserted that 'Being can indeed be without beings'; in the fifth edition (1949) – 'containing only minor corrections'! – this becomes 'Being never is without beings'.

What of science? Cannot science, as Jaspers had suggested, provide us with a clue or a 'cipher' to Being? In *Being and Time* Heidegger exhibits no special hostility to science; he was prepared to describe his own work, as, in a broad sense of the word, 'scientific' – as a contribution to the 'science of Being as such'. But in the 1930s science comes more and more under attack. In his *Introduction to Metaphysics* Heidegger writes with scorn of those who see in science a 'cultural value'. Science, he argues, is 'a technical, practical business'; it is quite impossible for 'an awakening of the spirit' to take its departure from science; science, in fact, is an 'emasculation of the spirit'.[21]

In that same review in which Ryle spoke with modified enthusiasm of the phenomenological analysis in *Being and Time* he went on to remark: 'It is my personal opinion that ... phenomenology is at present headed for disaster and will end either in a self-ruinous subjectivism or a windy mysticism'. Ryle would certainly think of that prophecy as having been borne out by the subsequent course of events. But Heidegger would not admit the impeachment. His thinking, he would argue, is completely objective; for it is, so he tells us in *What is Thinking?* (1954), 'bound by Being'. He offers his interpretations with the confidence of a man who has Being on his side. But whether Being has in fact revealed itself to him, he leaves us with no conceivable way of determining. Thinking, he tells us, is 'non-conceptual'; it is a kind of 'reverential listening'. 'In this sphere,' according to *Identity and Difference*, 'nothing can be proved but much can be hinted.' How does this differ from mysticism? That thought is different from mystical experience, Heidegger certainly believes. But how they differ never becomes clear.

In Jaspers' philosophical writings, 'God' had always played a part as a transcendent being; in his later work, his references to 'God' take on unmistakably biblical overtones. Heidegger, on the other hand, is usually read as a Nietzschian atheist, but he rejects this interpretation. 'Because we drew attention to Nietzsche's aphorism that "God is dead",' he complained in his *Letter on Humanism* (1947),[22] 'they say that we teach atheism. For what is more "logical" than to assume that anyone who experiences "the death of God" (in the present age) is a thoroughly godless person?' In fact, he argues, he has set his face only against that conception of God which sees in him 'the supreme value', and refuses to face the problem of his Being; Heidegger's own ontology, however, is by no means definite on 'the Being of God'.[23]

The religious issue in French existentialism is much more clearcut: Gabriel Marcel[24] is a convert to Catholicism, Jean-Paul Sartre an uncompromising atheist. Existentialism, indeed, has been in France a storm centre of violent theologico-philosophical controversies, with the Marxists joining in to damn existentialism as the ultimate expression of 'bourgeois individualism'.

Although he greatly admires Jaspers, Marcel arrived independently at his existentialism, as a result of his struggle to free himself from absolute Idealism.[25] That struggle is depicted in diary-form in his *Metaphysical Journal* (1947) – a work which, for all its tentativeness, its personal character, and its obscurity, or perhaps one should rather say *in virtue* of these characteristics, best represents Marcel's philosophical ideal: a persistent struggle, never wholly successful, to penetrate to the metaphysical level – a struggle obscurely depicted, not through wilfulness, but because the metaphysical level lies beyond clarity. He is dissatisfied, he tells us, with the two volumes of his *Gifford Lectures*,[26] just because they are too explicit, too systematic – although not many of his British readers would wish to make *that* complaint about them.

The doctrines obscurely suggested in Marcel's *Metaphysical Journal* are in some measure clarified in his 'Existence and Objectivity.'[27] That essay begins, in Kierkegaard's manner, with an attack on 'Idealism', understood Platonically as the identification of the real with 'the rational', i.e. with 'essences' or 'values'. Idealism, Marcel argues, converts things into pure objects; it loses sight of the 'presence' of things, the fact that they are not simply *before* us as embodiments of an essence, but intimately affect our nature by the impact of their existence upon us.

In the end, indeed, the Idealist questions even the 'reality' of existence: existence is condemned as self-contradictory and is wholly absorbed, so far as its reality goes, into essences, or even into a single essence – the Absolute. But, Marcel argues, one cannot really doubt whether 'anything exists'; we can doubt whether 'Jones is honest' because his honesty is separable from his existence, but there is no such separation between 'existents' and 'existence'. The Idealist proceeds, then, merely by *fiat*: he simply *refuses to recognize existence*; typically, he reduces every assertion to the hypothetical form – as if categorical, existential, statements 'really' did no more than assert connexions between general possibilities.

Such a way of talking about the world, Marcel agrees with Jaspers, has a certain value. But there is a tremendous gulf between, say, the general propositions of psychology and 'integral human experience with its life that trembles with tragedy' – the existence of this gulf brings home to us the inadequacy, in certain fundamental respects, of generalized thinking.

Suppose, as against Idealism, the philosopher takes his stand on this: that 'existence is beyond all doubt'. What can he mean? Certainly not, Marcel argues, that there are some empirical statements which are indubitable; nor, again, that it is 'existence in general' which we cannot doubt, for 'existence in general' is an empty, mythological, abstraction. What is indubitable, Marcel argues, is the existence of the Universe, considered not as an entity, but as the negation of specificity – in short, Bradley's 'experience' or what Marcel calls 'absolute presence'.

The human being, according to Marcel, plays his part in this Universe immediately. He does not apprehend it indirectly, *via* 'messages' or 'sensations', but *directly* through his unity with his body. So far, Marcel would wish to describe himself as an empiricist. On the ordinary view, the body is a sort of instrument which records messages from things and passes them on to the mind; this suggests that I am related to my body as I might be to a radio-set. In speaking of my body thus, Marcel suggests, I am adopting the point of view of a *third person*, who distinguishes my 'personality' from my 'body' by a sort of imaginary disincarnation. Further reflection, however – what Marcel calls 'second reflection' – soon shows me, he argues, that this distinction is a wholly artificial one: my body is *mine* in a sense in which no *object* can be mine.[28] 'Thus the role of reflection,' he writes, 'does not consist in dissecting and dismembering but, on the contrary, in re-establishing in all its continuity that living tissue which imprudent analysis tore asunder.'

Once again, the influence of Bradley is apparent: Bradley, too, had said that philosophical reflection is a healing of the breach which thinking makes in experience. But whereas for Bradley 'second reflection' drives us to the Absolute, Marcel is content for it to lead us to a plurality of 'mysteries'. At first, he says, we suppose that there is a 'problem' in relating mind to body – an intellectual puzzle to be resolved by intellectual means. But we soon see that this puzzle is not at all parallel to, say, a puzzle about the relation between sun-spots and atmospheric disturbances, a puzzle into which we enter only as a disinterested observer. For to understand the relation between mind and body, we are driven back to reflect upon *ourselves*, upon the implications of our own situation in, and attitude to, the world.

This is characteristic of a 'mystery' – that it cannot be solved at the objective level of 'first reflection', because it drives us back to consider our own existence. Another example is the existence of God: God's existence, too, according to Marcel, does not admit of intellectual proof – Marcel is no Thomist. 'First reflection' may lead us to imagine that God's existence is a 'problem' – comparable to a problem about whether there is life on Mars – but 'second reflection' shows us that God's existence is intimately bound up with our own; meditation on our own ontological nature, not formal proof, is the path to God.[29]

On the socio-ethical side, Marcel participates in the general existentialist attack on the 'typing' of the human being by society. 'I need hardly insist,' he writes, 'on the stifling expression of sadness produced by this functionalized world. It is sufficient to recall the dreary image of the retired official, or those urban Sundays when the passers-by look like people who have retired from life.' Alarmed, however, by what he condemns as the undisciplined and irrational aspects of Sartrean existentialism, he has recently been emphasizing the value and importance of tradition, somewhat in T. S. Eliot's manner.[30] For existentialism as the world ordinarily understands it, then, we must turn rather to that *enfant terrible* of philosophy, J-P. Sartre.[31]

Sartre, in English-speaking countries, is not uncommonly dismissed as a pamphleteer, a 'literary man', interesting, perhaps, as illustrating the decadence of post-war European culture, but of no consequence as a philosopher. In France, however, he is known as the author of an immense ontological work, *Being and Nothing-*

ness (1944), which is highly esteemed, partly because it has 'beaten the Germans at their own game' of ontologizing, partly as the medium through which the ideas of such German philosophers as Husserl, Jaspers, Heidegger – to say nothing of Hegel[32] – have been transmitted to French culture.

Granting the central importance of *Being and Nothingness*,[33] we shall still do best to approach Sartre through his first novel, *La Nausée* (1938) – a thinly disguised spiritual autobiography – in which the main themes of Sartre's existentialism are stated in an emotional, rather than an ontological, context.[34] The enemy, once again, is the attempt to rationalize the world; in part, Sartre is doing no more than assert dramatically what British empiricists had more coolly maintained: that contingency, brute factuality, cannot be explained away as necessity in disguise.

Sartre is not content, however, simply to *recognize* contingency; he is enough of a rationalist to conclude from the contingency of existence to its being absurd, irrational, even obscene.* 'A circle,' reflects Roquentin in *La Nausée*, 'is not absurd . . . but also it does not exist. That root [he is looking at the root of a tree] on the contrary exists in proportion as I cannot explain it. Knotty, inert, nameless, it fascinates me, fills my eyes, constantly leads me back to its own existence. It is no use my saying "that is a root. . . ." I see clearly that it is impossible to make one's way from its function as a root, a suction-pump, *to that*, to that hard and compact seal-skin. . . . The function explained nothing. . . .' Those qualities of a thing which make up its very existence, Sartre is suggesting, are from the point of view of rationality *de trop*, superfluous. The same point is summed up more technically thus: 'By definition, existence is not necessity. To exist is *to be there*, simply; existents appear on the scene, let themselves be *met*, but can never be deduced'. To lose sight of contingency by absorbing the world

---

*Compare the English phrase 'brute fact'. Hume's somewhat melodramatic conclusion to Book I of the *Treatise* can be interestingly contrasted with Sartre's profound unease. Hume bids us forget our scepticism in social relationships; that it induces such forgetfulness, we might say, is precisely what Sartre has *against* society. The 'absurdity' of the world is even more strongly emphasized by A. Camus in *Le Mythe de Sisyphe* (1942). But Camus is not an existentialist: he does not believe that absurdity can be ontologized. See L. Roth: 'A Contemporary Moralist: Albert Camus' (*Phil.*, 1955).

into a set of rational functions is to blind oneself, Sartre argues, to what the world is really like.

Similarly, to allow oneself to be absorbed into functions and duties is to lose sight of oneself; *La Nausée* is a bitter attack on the middle-class conception of 'duty' – as exhibited by what Sartre calls 'the serious people, glowing with rectitude' – which he condemns as death to the spirit. There is no novelty in such an attack on 'bourgeois morality'. Sartre is working within that French tradition of harsh, coarse, individualism which is profoundly disturbing to the Englishman – as distinct from the Irishman* – but which is common enough in France to be summed up in a descriptive phrase: 'pour épater le bourgeois.'

The experience Sartre calls 'la nausée', then, is his version of Heidegger's 'boredom' – the experience through which we come to see 'what-is': in Sartre's case, to see the world as a mass of solid brute facts. This world weighs heavily upon the human being, he thinks: it is a world within which it seems impossible for a human being to move, to breathe. But if I courageously face its contingency, Sartre suggests, I shall at the same time see that there *is* room for me in it, precisely because, one might say, I need no space; I am *free*, and this means that I am a bare capacity for action, a being whose very nature it is not to be anything in particular. (Compare Jaspers on the 'authentic self'.)

The *absoluteness* of Sartre's conception of human freedom is the source of many of the strangest features of his philosophy. The 'hero' of *La Nausée* is a historian; and in the course of his spiritual pilgrimage he comes to recognize not only the contingency of the world but, what is even more astonishing to him, his disconnectedness with the past. He had been fascinated by the past, because it seemed to give a second dimension to the fleeting present. 'Each event,' he had once thought, 'when its role had ended, took up its position, soberly, in a box and became an honorary event – so difficult it is to imagine nothingness.' But he came to think very differently; 'now I know – things are entirely what they appear to be – and *behind* them – there is nothing.' Not only God, but the past, is dead. It is a mistake to

*Thus, for example, there is a good deal in common between Sartre's 'Roquentin' and Joyce's 'Stephen Daedalus'; and one is also reminded of Swift.

suppose, Sartre concludes, that we can be *made* by the past; each of our acts is free in the sense that it is wholly disconnected from what has previously happened – separated from it by nothingness. Our 'nature' consists in our choice of a future, not in a structure which has been built up in the past and now wholly determines us. Only in virtue of this fact, he thinks, can we be free.

On the traditional view, free-will exhibits itself in an occasional departure from a nature which ordinarily determines us; for Sartre, in contrast, man is wholly free or wholly determined. If he has 'a nature' in the ordinary sense of that phrase – a fixed character, no longer of his choosing – then that nature must determine him: he can be free, Sartre concludes, only if his 'nature' is a bare capacity. In *Le Sursis* – the second novel in Sartre's novel-sequence *Les Chemins de la Liberté* – the central character, Mathieu, meditates thus: 'for a human being, to *be* is to choose himself; nothing comes to him either from without or from within himself that he can receive or accept – thus freedom is not a being, it is the being of man, that is to say his non-being'. A man 'exists', that is, as *nothing*; if he were anything, he would not be free.

This picture of the world as something composed on the one side of brute facts and on the other of absolute freedom is, Sartre admits, in many ways a terrifying one. 'Serious people' – those whom Sartre collectively dismisses as 'les salauds' – refuse to recognize its truth. They seek refuge in a more stable world of their own making – whether it be the world of science or the world of religion. But they do not achieve true stability in science or religion; in fact their world, far from being solid, is a 'viscous' or 'slimy' one.

'Le visqueux' is described at length in a remarkable section of *Being and Nothingness*; there it is the type of all evil – it is what we at first confidently imagine we can appropriate, freely deal with, but are in fact entrapped by. (If Wittgenstein hopes to show the fly the way out of the bottle into which he has flown, Sartre hopes to release him from the fly-paper.) 'Sliminess' is a characteristic not only of things but also of human beings, of that handshake or smile which entices us into a friendship which turns out to be a deadly entanglement – of our own thoughts, even, in so far as they stickily hold us to the past. It is deceptive, precisely because it is a compromise between the genuine solidity of contingent things, brute facts, and the fluidity of freedom; it does not resist us firmly as the solid does. We know where we are with the solid, but the slimy swallows us up like a bog. Sartre's emphasis upon such unpalatable features of the world as sliminess has won him the reputation of being dismal and depressing. But it is the bourgeois, he replies, who is gloomy. What could be more dismal, he asks in *L'existentialisme est un humanisme* (1946),[35] than such favourite bourgeois aphorisms as 'charity begins at home'?

In such a novel as *La Nausée*, and even in *Les Chemins de la Liberté*, we are looking at the world through the eyes of distinctly eccentric characters; the hero of *La Nausée*, for example, has never known what it is to attach himself to a person or to a cause. We read Sartre's novels, then, as psychological studies; it is quite another matter to express this schizophrenic point of view as an ontology, as Sartre attempts to do in *Being and Nothingness*. Indeed, an existentialist ontology, it might be argued, has been ruled out in advance. We allow Roquentin to communicate 'the incommunicable', we allow Mathieu to tell us that 'There is no within. There is nothing. I am nothing. I am free', because a novelist is entitled to describe what his characters *feel* to be the case. But if we are asked to interpret these statements as literal truths, our philosphical conscience is at once aroused. How can we recognize our emptiness, we ask, without *being something* to recognize it? And must not our 'emptiness', to be recognized, be a positive state of feeling, i.e. not an emptiness in any ontological sense?

Certainly, for all that it contains a multitude of interesting observations on human nature – the very thing it ought not to contain – Sartre's *Being and Nothingness* must appear to an ordinary philosophically trained English reader to be arbitrary in the extreme. Sartre's starting-point, indeed, is familiar enough. There are, he argues, no 'transcendental objects' beyond 'appearances'. An 'appearance' can be distinguished from an 'object', only because the object is *an infinite series* of perceptions. But what, Sartre asks, of the *being* of appearances? Their being, he argues, cannot itself be something that merely appears: 'the being of the phenomenon cannot be reduced to the phenomenon of being'. So at once, even in the analysis of appearances, we are forced to recognize something which has intrinsic *being*.

The view which Sartre ascribes to Berkeley, that 'to be' simply is 'to appear', is self-contradictory, he argues, because if there are appearances there must also be a being *to which what appears appears*. This being, according to Sartre, is consciousness: consciousness is the 'transphenomenal being of the subject'. All consciousness, he agrees with Brentano and Husserl, is 'intentional' – it reaches out towards an object.[36] And in so reaching out, he argues, consciousness must at the same time be conscious of itself. (His argument at this point is extraordinarily primitive. If my consciousness were not consciousness of being conscious of the table,' he writes, 'it would then be consciousness of that table without consciousness of being so. In other words, it would be a consciousness ignorant of itself – an unconscious consciousness, which is absurd.') This consciousness-of-itself, according to Sartre, is self-consciousness, not consciousness *of* the self as an object: it is prior to the Cartesian *cogito*, which is a reflection on our own being, as distinct from *that being itself*. The existence of such a self-conscious being, he further argues, is a condition of the being of essences. There are essences because a self-conscious being exists: it does not exist by the grace of essences. So 'existence is prior to essences'.

Sartre is now well embarked on his 'pursuit of being'. After a very few pages of *Being and Nothingness* we are confronted by such sentences as 'Being is. Being is in-itself. Being is what it is' – sentences which read like a parody of positivist parodies of metaphysics. Two things, however, distinguish this ontology from any of its predecessors; first, Sartre's analysis of not-being, and secondly, his attempt to translate psychological theories into ontological terms.

Not-being, he agrees with Heidegger, cannot be identified with the negative judgement – for we have an 'intuition' of nothingness, an intuition which is prior to the judgement. Suppose, he says, I am expecting to see a friend at a café: I look around and say 'Peter is not here.' Then this is not in the least like such an arbitrary, unspontaneous, negative judgement as 'The Archbishop of Canterbury is not in this café'. Peter's absence 'haunts this café' – such a felt absence, according to Sartre, is the primordial root of the negative judgement. 'Nothingness', he concludes, comes from our being: we are the nihilators, for it is only *for us* that Peter is absent. In all our judgements, according to Sartre, we 'nihilate'. For to judge is to distinguish, to treat this thing as being other than, and hence as 'not being', that thing. As Hegel had expressed the matter in his *Phenomenology of Mind*, nihilation 'lies at the heart of our Being'. In thinking, we do not, however, create Being as such. So much follows, Sartre argues, from the intentionality of our consciousness; consciousness is a consciousness of something other than itself, of Being.[37] But by means of the act of judging we transform Being into the world we ordinarily suppose ourselves to live in, a world of causally connected individuals. We do not create Being, but we make beings out of Being.

What about our everyday self? How is that created? It derives, Sartre argues, from our experience of others, our experience of them as subjects. 'The others' gaze at me – and in virtue of their gaze I find myself a person. I acquire a Nature.[38] That nature I cannot disown; 'I bear it around as a burden'. But only in 'bad faith' can I identify this empirical self with my own consciousness – my 'Being-for-itself' as contrasted with my 'Being-for-others'. Like Heidegger, that is, Sartre is suggesting that my 'everyday self' is governed by 'They', not by 'I', and that it is always *possible* for me to cast it off.

Heidegger's mistake, Sartre argues, lay in his treating the experience of Nothing as a relatively rare one, in his not recognizing that all my experience is an experience of Nihilating. But what is it, we naturally ask Sartre, that does the nihilating? It is at once obvious that what nihilates cannot be a particular entity, since 'particularity' is itself the product of nihilating. Consciousness, Sartre concludes, must itself be Nothing. 'It is nothing but the pure nihilation of the In-itself; it is like a hole of being at the heart of Being'. Its special relationship to objective Being - 'Being-in-itself' – derives from that very fact; if Consciousness were itself a 'Being-in-itself' it could not be that which is directed towards Being-in-itself.

The extreme strangeness of this doctrine, when it is couched in terms of Nothingness, will perhaps be a little mitigated for the British reader if he recalls G. E. Moore's description of acts of consciousness and their objects in 'The Refutation of Idealism' (see p. 209 above). When we examine any mental act, according to Moore, what makes it an act of consciousness always evades us. When, for example, we look at a sensation of blue the act of sensing the blue escapes us – we see only the blue. Yet consciousness of blue, Moore nonetheless argues, must not be identified with the blue of which it is conscious.

This difficulty in picking out consciousness led James, and after him Russell, to assert the 'non-existence of consciousness'. But Sartre has already argued that as a consequence of the existence of objects consciousness *must* exist.[39] So the alternative for him is that it exists as Nothing. If we look for it we shall find nothing except the beings it is conscious of, including the empirical self, never consciousness itself. Yet on Sartre's view it is essential, in order to avoid the morasses of subjectivism, that we preserve the concept of a naked consciousness – 'the consciousness the scientist has always had, of being a pure nothingness, a simple beholder'.

At the same time Sartre, inevitably, ascribes positive characteristics to this Nothingness. It has, he says, a 'passion for being'. It passionately desires itself to become substantial, even although this is a logically impossible ambition, and in trying to fulfil this same ambition it sets up an 'In-itself which creates contingency' i.e. God. 'But,' according to Sartre, 'the idea of God is contradictory and we lose ourselves in vain. Man is a fruitless passion.' It is impossible to escape contingency; our 'dreadful freedom' is the nearest thing we have to a 'real nature', our 'nothingness' to 'Being'. The idea of God is contradictory, just because it conjoins in one entity both Being and Nothingness.

The purity of our consciousness is identified by Sartre with the absoluteness of our freedom, an identification which is, he says, natural to anyone working in a Cartesian tradition. It is pure consciousness, not our empirical self, which is absolutely free and it must be free because it creates all causal connexions. It is impossible to talk of our consciousness as being made, or as being influenced, by something outside it, because this would suggest that it is logically possible for that in relation to which things exist as 'made' to itself be made. What we call 'obstacles' to our freedom, similarly, are only obstacles in relation to the choice we have made; the height of Everest, for example, restricts our freedom of action only because we have decided to climb it. No being is in itself, in virtue of its mere existence, an obstacle to our freedom; we are always free to overcome it by reshaping our purposes. The existence of such obstacles, therefore, does nothing to diminish our freedom, although they – and particularly the obstacles created by the existence of other people and the 'nature' they impose upon us – may induce us, in 'bad faith', to conceal our freedom from ourselves.

Sartre's ontological reflections, then, are a deliberate attempt to push to its extreme the doctrine of metaphysical freedom: it is in the cause of absolute freedom that he juggles so obscurely with the twin ideas of being and not-being. This 'freedom', we are bound to feel, has something pathological about it; as if a neurotic had persuaded himself that his anxiety is courage, that his impulse to destroy is creative. Again and again, as Sartre writes, we feel ourselves forced into Freudian interpretations of his metaphysics. So little does what he says make any literal sense, that we are enticed into interpreting it as a dream, a private phantasy.

But Sartre has forestalled us; he is, indeed, deliberately forcing the Freudian interpretation on us. He writes, for example, of 'the slimy' in what are all-too-obviously sexual terms. Thus he prepares the way for his final *tour de force*: the sexual impulses themselves, he argues, are no more than symbols of ontological needs. If the Freudian sees sexual symbolism everywhere in Sartre's ontology this is only because, Sartre suggests, the Freudian is trying to disguise his ontological loneliness – the loneliness of a self which exists only in its free acts, in an obscene, contingent, godless world, with no values, except those which he himself creates. The Freudian seeks refuge in the comfortable doctrine that this loneliness is no more than a sexual need, not, then, beyond human skill to satisfy. This is Sartre's reply to the Freudians – a reply worked out in detail as an 'ontological psychoanalysis'; quite what he would say to his 'ordinary language' critics had better, considering the resources of Sartre's vocabulary, be left to the imagination.

'Cursed lucidity' is not a description which the British reader would naturally apply to Sartre's philosophy. But when his erstwhile close associate, Maurice Merleau-Ponty, attacked Sartre's 'cursed lucidity', it was not entirely without justification: Sartre is still at heart a Cartesian.[40] Merleau-Ponty's own philosophy can certainly not be accused of 'cursed lucidity'; it has been characterized, indeed, as a 'philosophy of ambiguity'. Only in 'bad faith' can a Sartrean subject fail to understand its objects; for Merleau-Ponty, in contrast, objects are by their very nature enigmatic, 'ambiguous'.

His rallying-cry, like Husserl's, is 'back to the things' – or, what he takes to be equivalent – 'back to perception'. In a summary of his philosophical ideas, prepared as part of his candidature for a professorship at the Collège de France,[41] he criticized the rationalistic tradition he was attacking thus: 'We never cease to live in the world of perception but we by-pass it in critical thought ... critical thought has broken with the naïve evidence of *things*.'

To restore the 'primacy of perception' is, he suggests, the task of phenomenology. But the phenomenology which Merleau-Ponty professes in his major work *The Phenomenology of Perception* (1945, English translation 1962) is very different from what ordinarily goes under that name.[42] Whereas for the Husserl of *Cartesian Meditations* 'truth dwells in the inner man', Merleau-Ponty, like Heidegger before him, rejects the concept of an 'inner man'. Man, he argues, is essentially a 'being-in-the-world'. Phenomenology, on Merleau-Ponty's interpretation, is an attempt to recapture the lived experience, to go back beyond science, back beyond all forms of propositional truth, to the world as we actually encounter it in perception. The 'transcendental reduction', the 'bracketing' of science, leads not to a pure Ego, as Husserl had thought, but to a body-subject involved in perception.

The percipient subject is embodied; Heidegger's philosophy is defective, according to Merleau-Ponty, just because he places insufficient stress on the body.[43] The same could scarcely be said of Sartre, to whose analyses Merleau-Ponty's own phenomenological account of bodily relationships is much indebted. But Sartre's phenomenology of human behaviour, so Merleau-Ponty argues, cannot be reconciled with his ontology, identifying as that does the subject with pure Consciousness. The objects of a pure Consciousness must be revealed to it, once and for all, as being just what they appear to be. But the objects of our lived experience, according to Merleau-Ponty, are always ambiguous; we can suddenly see them in a totally new way; the picture we saw as a duck suddenly appears to us as a rabbit; the stranger we saw as menacing we suddenly see as friendly.

The influence of Gestalt psychology is at this point obvious.[44] In his first book, *The Structure of Behaviour* (1942), Merleau-Ponty set out to demonstrate in detail that neither classical behaviourists nor classical Gestalt psychologists succeed in constructing a science of behaviour.[45] But he did not reject either approach as wholly useless; he converted their experimental evidence to his own purposes. His principal arguments against behaviourism, indeed, are Gestalt in inspiration. Normal human behaviour, he argues, is not a reaction to a physical stimulation acting mechanically on an organism; we react to situations which the organism has already 'endowed with meaning'. Whether, for example, we react to a stimulus with hunger depends not on the physico-chemical structure of the stimulus but on whether we *see it as food*, i.e. as the sort of thing which we are accustomed to eat. So far the Gestalt psychologist is correct. But the Gestalt psychologist makes the mistake of simply substituting 'forms' or 'wholes' for the atomistic stimuli of behaviourism; he writes as if the 'wholes', the 'forms', to which the organism responds were themselves causal agents. 'Form', Merleau-Ponty complains, 'is placed amongst the events of nature; it is used like a cause or a real thing'. The real relationship between 'form' and ourselves, he goes on to argue, is 'dialectical', not mechanical or causal. What does this mean? Merleau-Ponty sets out to explain in *The Phenomenology of Perception*. He has a delicate path to tread, between traditional empiricism and traditional rationalism. He attacks traditional empiricism[46] on the ground that the 'sensations' which according to empiricists serve as the starting-point of all knowledge are scientific abstractions, not objects of experience. Our perceptual field, he argues, consists not of sensations, but of things with spaces between them. Nor could the things we perceive be 'constructed out of' sensations with the help, as empiricists have often suggested, of associative mechanisms; like Bradley before him, Merleau-Ponty argues that only things, not sensations, can be associated by 'resemblance' or 'contiguity'.

The traditional alternative to empiricism has been some form of 'intellectualism', according to which perceptual experience is nothing more than a means of 'triggering-off' the activity of pure thought. But then it becomes impossible to understand, Merleau-Ponty argues, why experience should be needed at all. For how can pure thought ever be ignorant? '"Empiricism", Merleau-Ponty sums up, 'fails to see that we need to know what we are looking for, since otherwise we would not be looking for it; "intellectualism" fails to realize that we must be ignorant of what we are looking for, or else, once more, we should not be searching.'

The starting-point of Merleau-Ponty's 'middle way' between empiricism and intellectualism is the 'body-subject'. The 'body-subject' is neither a pure object nor a transparent subject; it is 'ambiguous'. In certain contexts it is perceived as an object, in other contexts it is the perceiving subject. It does not judge; its mode of relationship with the world is 'older than intelligence'. But on its 'lived experience' of the world all judgements ultimately rest.

The 'body-subject', so Merleau-Ponty tells us, always perceives more than is 'there', more than can be analysed in terms of light-waves and retina; it sees houses, not façades; it perceives what lies behind as well as what lies in front. To put the matter thus, however, at once suggests that we have some way of contrasting what is 'actually there' with the 'something more' that we perceive. If such a contrast can properly be made, is it not after all science, one naturally asks, which gives us the truth about what is 'there'? In seeing things as having meaning, are we not 'mis-seeing' them, endowing them with qualities which as 'actually there' they do not possess? Yet if to avoid such conclusions Merleau-Ponty were to identify what is 'there' with what, in perception, we take to be there, he would be driven into those extremes of subjectivity which Sartre set out to avoid.[47]

Once again, Merleau-Ponty hopes to find a 'middle way', in this case between realism and subjectivism. That is the purpose of his 'dialectical' description of the relationship between body-subject and the world. To revert to our previous example, if a hungry body-subject sees what he takes to be food, and then, in eating it, discovers it to be inedible, that discovery influences what he will in future see. The body-subject encounters a world which already has 'meanings' incorporated in it – as a member of a particular society he perceives this substance as food and that substance as inedible – but he can also give new 'meanings' to what he encounters. Thus he can discover new foods, or reject as inedible what is ordinarily accepted as food. So he neither merely makes nor merely encounters the world he lives in, just as he neither merely makes nor merely perceives the duck in that picture he might alternatively perceive as a rabbit.

By means of this same conception of dialectic, Merleau-Ponty sets out to 'tread' yet another 'middle way', this time between determinism and the Sartrean conception of absolute freedom. Sartre had argued that freedom must be either wholly non-existent or total. But in fact, Merleau-Ponty replies, it is neither. If freedom were total, we could not distinguish, as we do, certain of our acts as free from others in which our situation determines our action. Merleau-Ponty emphasizes that we are born into a social situation; the Marxist is right, he thinks, in insisting that our condition as social beings in large part determines how we act, just as it largely determines what we see.[48] We are not free wholly to throw off our historically-conditioned self. But our social situation does not *wholly* determine our modes of action, any more than the ready-made 'meanings' we encounter in the things around us entirely determine what 'meanings' we shall find in them.

Language, according to Merleau-Ponty, is a perfect illustration of the dialectical relationship between ourselves and our world. We encounter our language as a set of fixed rules and fixed meanings, of the sort described by grammarians and dictionary-makers. We cannot use words just as we like. But we can still, in that language, develop a new style. Every great work of literature, so Merleau-Ponty suggests, does as much. It is always written in a language which existed before it was written; but that language is not the same after a new style has been introduced into it.

But problems still remain, problems of which Merleau-Ponty is very conscious. How can we add to the stock of objective truths on the basis, merely, of new 'lived experiences'? How, again, is it possible to say anything at all about such experiences – to construct a phenomenology of perception – without making those sharp distinctions between ourselves and the world, between objects and the meanings we ascribe to them, which Merleau-Ponty does not allow?

Merleau-Ponty worked for many years on a book, originally entitled *The Origin of Truth*, in which he proposed to explain how objective truths could be derived from perceptual experiences. But he succeeded in completing only its introduction, published posthumously as *The Visible and the Invisible* (1965). The problem of perception still, in that introduction, preoccupies him; indeed, his difficulties become more rather than less apparent. Philosophy, he says, asks what the world is like before we begin to talk about it, and it addresses that question to the 'mixture of the world and ourselves' which precedes all reflection. Then how, we naturally ask, can the philosopher *say* what he finds? Whatever he tells us will inevitably be a description of the world as it is talked about, not of the world before it is talked about. Merleau-Ponty falls back at this point on his description of the 'ambiguity' of language; through our language, he argues, we can suggest more than we can explicitly say. But, of course, what this 'more' is cannot be said.

In Merleau-Ponty's philosophy, then, only-too-familiar problems recur. How is it possible, in language, to contrast experience as we live it with experience as we conceptually describe it, seeing that to talk at all is to make use of concepts? And how else, if not in language, can such a contrast be made? With this goes another dilemma: how is it possible to reject the view that the world is simply 'given', at least in certain types of experience, without being forced to conclude that it is wholly made by us? If one sometimes despairs of philosophy's tendency to fluctuate between absurd extremes, this fluctuation is no accident; a 'middle way', as Merleau-Ponty's philosophy illustrates, is not easy to find or to persist in.

CHAPTER 20

Description, Explanation or Revision?

FIRST published in 1959, P. F. Strawson's *Individuals* bore the startling sub-title: 'an essay in descriptive metaphysics' – startling, because Strawson had been so prominent a spokesman for 'ordinary language' philosophy. And even although, unlike logical positivists, ordinary language philosophers did not officially denounce metaphysics, their emphasis on careful analysis, on detailed description, on the peculiarities of particular 'language-games', had strongly suggested that metaphysics, with its inherent generality, lay distinctly beyond the pale.

No doubt, Strawson's break with 'ordinary language' philosophy was by no means an absolute one. 'Up to a point,' he was still prepared to write, 'the reliance upon a close examination of the actual use of words is the best, and indeed the only sure, way in philosophy.' But the philosopher must pass beyond that point, he also argues, if he hopes to 'lay bare the most general features of our conceptual structure'. For that structure is taken for granted, not expressed, in the answers men give to questions about their manner of using expressions.

What, we naturally ask, does Strawson mean by 'our conceptual structure'? *Whose* conceptual structure – the Australian aboriginal's, the humanistically-educated European's, or the theoretical physicist's? To that question Strawson replies that 'there is a massive central core of human thinking which has no history' – it is this massive core which he hopes to 'lay bare'. The 'categories and concepts' which make up this perennial structure of human thinking are, he says, 'the commonplaces of the least refined thinking' as well as 'the indispensable core of the conceptual equipment of the most sophisticated human beings'. Thus the faith in the 'ordinary man', typical of 'ordinary language' philosophies, persists in Strawson's descriptive metaphysics. The metaphysician need pay no special attention to physical science, which Strawson scarcely mentions, for whatever would be of interest to him in the thinking of scientists can be as readily detected in the most commonplace thoughts of the most commonplace 'man in the street'. Nor is it the metaphysician's task to modify or correct the structure of commonplace thinking, any more than it is the ordinary language philosopher's task to correct commonplace idioms. Descriptive metaphysics, in Wittgenstein's phrase, 'leaves everything as it is'.

Thus it has to be distinguished from 'revisionary metaphysics', as exemplified, according to Strawson, in the works of Descartes, Leibniz, Berkeley – all of whom are extensively criticized in *Individuals*. Whereas 'descriptive metaphysics', with Aristotle and Kant as its exemplars, 'is content to describe the actual structure of our thought about the world', the revisionary metaphysician 'is concerned to produce a better structure'. Strawson does not wholly condemn revisionary metaphysics, but he admits its usefulness only in so far as 'it is at the service of descriptive metaphysics' i.e. in so far as it helps us to understand the *actual* structure of our thought. Whether attempts to revise our everyday concepts have so subordinate a significance is one of the main points at issue in contemporary philosophy.[1]

Strawson's *Individuals*[2] is divided into two sections, which are closely linked with one another in so far as the idea of 'referring to an object' is central throughout. But they differ greatly in philosophical character and in the degree of confidence they exhibit. In general terms, the second half is a reconsideration and development of Strawson's doctrine of presuppositions. It proceeds polemically by way of a criticism of Frege, Geach and Quine to the conclusion that subject-expressions are 'complete', in the sense of presenting a fact in their own right, whereas predicate-expressions are incomplete. Thus, to take the simplest case, if I assert 'that person there is smiling' I presuppose as a fact that 'that person is there', whereas the use of the predicate 'is smiling' does not of itself presuppose any fact. The traditional association between 'subjects' and 'particulars' is justified in these terms: the paradigm use of a subject is to introduce a particular, i.e. something which is complete for thought in that it unfolds into a fact and incomplete in that, so introduced, it is thought of as a constituent of a further fact.

Far more striking, for our present purposes, is the confident metaphysics of the first half, in which Strawson sets out to discover which are the 'basic particulars'. As an ambition this connects historically with the traditions of British empiricism. But in British empiricism, at least after Berkeley, the ground for calling certain particulars 'basic' is that all other particulars are 'ultimately' reducible to them; sense-data, for example, are 'basic particulars' if and only if everything else we ordinarily call a particular – e.g. a particular table, or a particular person – is 'in the ultimate analysis' a 'construction out of' such sense-data. For Strawson, on the other hand, a 'basic particular' is a particular by means of which other particulars are identified; it is not an element out of which they are constructed.[3]

He begins from the simplest case – the identification of those particulars at which, in principle, we can point, as we can point at 'that man in the centre of the row'. In such instances, we identify a particular by placing it in the 'scene', the particular spatial region in which we are at that time present. But how is it possible to identify something which is not in that scene? To accomplish this end, we ordinarily use an identifying phrase such as 'the man in a black hat'. Clearly, however, it is always logically possible that this description, however much detail we add to it, will be taken by an auditor to refer to some person other than the person we hope to identify by means of it. Are we to conclude that we can never identify, without any risk of ambiguity, a particular which is not now present in our scene?

We can always link an identifying description, Strawson argues, to a place in the spatio-temporal system and so, indirectly, to the scene we inhabit. We can identify the particular we are talking about by substituting for 'the man in a black hat' the description 'the man wearing a black hat standing two feet north of University House on November 10, 1965 at 10.05 a.m.' It does not follow that every identifiable particular is in space and time; it does follow, according to Strawson, that every identifiable particular must be *uniquely related* to a spatio-temporal particular.

The particulars which make up the framework of space-time, according to Strawson, are material objects. These, then, are the basic particulars through the identification of which all other particulars are identified. Neither private experiences, as in traditional empiricism, nor events and processes, as in some forms of revisionary metaphysics, nor the atomic particles of physics can fill the role of basic particulars, since none of them can be identified except by way of their unique relationship to a material object.[4]

Philosophers have often professed to feel a special difficulty about the possibility of identifying 'states of consciousness' by reference to material objects. But how else is it possible to identify them? Strawson considers two alternatives.[5] The first, which he calls the 'no-ownership' theory, is that states of consciousness do not, properly speaking, belong to the person who has them. In fact, they do not 'belong' to anything at all – unless this means nothing more than that they are causally dependent on the state of a particular body. This, Strawson argues, is an incoherent doctrine. For the 'no-ownership' theorist is obliged to assert the existence of the allegedly contingent causal relationship in some such form as 'All my experiences are dependent on the state of the body B'. But what does 'my' mean in this context? It cannot mean 'the experiences dependent on body B'; if it did, the allegedly contingent fact would collapse into the analytic statement that 'experiences dependent on body B are experiences dependent upon body B'. It turns out, indeed, that the use of 'my' cannot be understood without the help of that very concept of ownership which the 'no-ownership' theorist professes to abandon. Underlying this objection, according to Strawson, is the fact that an experience can be identified only as *somebody*'s experience – it owes its identity to the logical impossibility of its being anyone else's experience. The no-ownership theory leaves us with no way of identifying particular experiences, no way of referring to them.

The second alternative is a Cartesian-type theory, for which states of experience belong not to a person but to a private ego. This encounters a parallel difficulty. If states of consciousness are wholly private there is no possible way in which we could ascribe them to anybody but ourselves, no way of identifying them as 'so-and-so's experience'. It would, indeed, be impossible to ascribe them even to ourselves, since 'there is no sense in the idea of ascribing states of consciousness to oneself unless the ascriber already knows how to ascribe at least some states of consciousness to others'. To say that 'I am in pain', for example, is to say that it is I, not you, who is experiencing the pain; the possibility of contrasting your pain with my pain is essential to the ascription of a particular pain to myself.

The only way out of such difficulties, Strawson concludes, is to take the concept of a person as a primitive unanalysable concept. A person, that is, must be thought of not as a compound of body and mind but as a single particular to which we can ascribe not only such 'M-predicates' (material object-predicates) as 'weighs ten stone' but also such 'P-predicates' (person-predicates) as 'is going for a holiday', 'is in pain', 'believes in God'.[6] These latter predicates are ascribed to other people 'on the strength of' our observation of their behaviour; their modes of behaviour provide us with logically adequate criteria for the ascription of P-predicates to them. Exactly the same concept – e.g. the concept of being depressed – covers the depression which X feels but does not observe and the depression which persons other than X observe but do not feel. To deny this, Strawson argues, is 'to refuse to accept the structure of the language in which we talk about depression'. The sceptic, in his attempt to deny that we have any right to ascribe P-predicates to other persons, simultaneously accepts and does not accept that language. He pretends to point to a logical gap between my depression and the depression you observe. But if his scepticism were to be taken seriously, even the concept of 'my depression', on which the sceptical argument rests, could not exist.

It will now be apparent in what sense Strawson's metaphysics is descriptive, conservative. We end our reading of *Individuals* with fresh views about the nature of the world only if we have been seduced by some form of revisionary metaphysics and have therefore to be reconverted to commonplaces. That does not mean that we have learnt nothing; we now have, if Strawson is right, *good grounds for believing* that the 'basic particulars' are, as in commonplace thinking they are taken to be, things and persons in a spatio-temporal framework, persons being distinguishable from other material objects in virtue of the applicability to them, as not to tables and chairs, of P-predicates.

Such a common-sense metaphysics is also defended in Stuart Hampshire's *Thought and Action*, published in the same year as *Individuals*.[7] 'I am in effect arguing,' Hampshire writes, 'that we must unavoidably talk of reality as consisting of persistent things of different types and kinds.' We 'must' do so because otherwise it would be impossible to use language in order to identify. There could not possibly be a language, Hampshire argues, in which only sensations were referred to and described. In any such a language it must be possible at least to distinguish one *person* from another, and to distinguish persons is to be able to distinguish objects, as distinct from sensations. For Hampshire, as for Strawson, persons are 'continuing things producing changes' – no less persons for being characterized in corporeal terms as well as in terms of states of consciousness.

Like Strawson, too, Hampshire has not broken sharply with the analytical tradition. He suggests, only, that there are some philosophical purposes which cannot be met by 'a concrete and step-by-step analysis'. So that 'even in philosophy' – Hampshire's mode of expression bears witness to the extent to which the 'analytic' conception of philosophy had come to seem the normal one – there is room for 'a more general survey' and for 'more tentative opinions'. In particular, Hampshire suggests, the method of analysing everyday concepts is no longer decisive at those points at which conflicts about the nature of human personality arise most acutely. At such points, it is not enough merely to describe the structure of our thinking, for our thinking is at odds with itself. In deciding how to employ such concepts as action, responsibility, will, the philosopher, Hampshire therefore suggests, is forced to exercise his moral judgement. So, it would seem, Russell's demand that the philosopher be 'ethically neutral' cannot, in the long run, be acceded to; it goes the same way as his insistence that philosophy should concentrate on 'piecemeal results'.

In *Thought and Action* one of Hampshire's principal concerns is with human freedom in its relation to knowledge, a theme to which he returns in *Freedom of the Individual* (1965).[8] He wholly rejects the conventional view that as we come to know more about the workings of the human mind the area of free decision narrows, to a vanishing-point at which it would wholly disappear. On the contrary, he argues, the more I know about my mind, the less likelihood there is that I will mistakenly announce that I am going to act in a manner which does not in fact lie within my power. And the leading characteristic of a free agent is that he can tell us in advance – not by inference from his past but directly and immediately – what he is going to do.

Whatever knowledge we possess, according to Hampshire, we can always step back from that knowledge and ask ourselves: 'How, in the light of that knowledge, shall I decide to act?' This possibility of stepping-back, this 'recessiveness of the I', no increase in our scientific knowledge could possibly destroy. There is, Hampshire says – or at least there now seems to be, for Hampshire, unlike Strawson, admits that our concepts could change – an irreplaceable distinction between 'the observed natural course of events' and 'a man's decisions about the natural course of events'. Your *knowing why* I want X is no substitute for my *deciding that* I want X. A deterministic theory leaves no room, Hampshire argues, for the fundamental distinction between a man's explaining to us, in terms of norms, why he has certain desires, certain intentions, certain attitudes, and some other person's explanation, in terms of causes, why he has those desires, intentions and attitudes. At least, this is true for any form of determinism 'which entails that the commonplace scheme of explanation of conduct be replaced by a neutral vocabulary of natural law.'

Neither Hampshire nor Strawson refers at all, in their discussions of human action, to the writings of psychologists. One of the most striking features of Ryle's *The Concept of Mind* had been the limited responsibility – the classification and diagnosis of our 'mental impotences' – which it allocated to psychology. It was perfectly in order, on this showing, for Freud to offer an explanation of our slips of the tongue, mistakes, lapses of memory. But it is not in order for a psychologist to offer us an explanation of what happens when we speak correctly, get things right, remember correctly, notice accurately. 'Let the psychologist tell us why we are deceived; but we can tell ourselves and him why we are not deceived.'[9]

Such a degree of resistance to the claims of psychology to be a general explanatory theory of human behaviour was not peculiar to Ryle. G. F. Stout left Oxford for St. Andrews in 1902 because he found it so unsympathetic to the claims of psychology; William Macdougall left Oxford in 1920 for the United States; Prichard, as we have already noted, anticipated Ryle's view that psychology is a hotch-potch of miscellaneous investigations, not a proper science; Joseph attacked it no less severely; Collingwood condemned it as 'the fashionable fraud of the age'.

Outside Oxford, until about 1950, this attitude to psychology was generally regarded as an aberration, one more proof, if any were needed, of Oxford's supremacy as 'a home of lost causes'. Philosophers generally presumed – certainly the logical positivists did – that psychology had established itself as an independent science, at least in its structure and its ambitions, even if not as yet in its accomplishment.[10] As late as the 1940s the phrase 'philosophical psychology' had as old-fashioned a ring as 'natural philosophy' still has.

Wittgenstein's *Philosophical Investigations*, however, proved to be scarcely less critical of psychology than Oxford had traditionally been. It is true that, unlike Ryle, Wittgenstein several times refers to psychologists, especially to the Gestalt psychologist W. Köhler. But *Philosophical Investigations* ends with a judgement on psychology. We are not to explain its barrenness, Wittgenstein suggests, by excusing it as a 'young science'; its defects are not of the sort which maturity can be expected to repair. Psychologists have developed experimental techniques, which they take to justify their expectation that they will, in the end, solve the psychological problems which remain unsolved. In fact, so Wittgenstein argues, the techniques they employ do not bear upon the problems which confront them. Their problems arise out of conceptual confusion, not out of failures to discover laws. For Wittgenstein, what is really needed is a clarification of our everyday thinking about human beings, and experimental investigations are of no help in this task; only more careful conceptual analysis can do the trick.[11]

That is why Peter Geach's *Mental Acts* (1957), the first of a monograph series issued under the general title *Studies in Philosophical Psychology*,[12] is in large part devoted to what are clearly *logical* problems. It is true that Geach does not entirely ignore psychologists. In the course of discussing his main subject – the nature of concepts and their role in judgements – he comments critically, for example, on the account of concept-formation offered by the psychologist G. Humphrey in his *Thinking* (1951). But this criticism takes the form of arguing, in the manner typical of much philosophical psychology, that what Humphrey calls 'concept-formation' and illustrates from the behaviour of rats is quite different from what ordinarily goes under that name. Humphrey, in other words, is revising our ordinary concept of 'concept-formation', while pretending to describe it.

Geach sets out to show that concepts are not formed by abstracting from experience, that they are made by the mind, in no sense discovered by it, and that to judge is to use such mind-made concepts in relation to one another. In developing his argument, Geach makes considerable use of sophisticated contemporary logical techniques. He has much to say about the proper use of quotation marks, the nature of synonymity, the conditions of translatability. He moves backwards and forwards without any sense of incongruity between logical, psychological and epistemological considerations, precisely in the manner of Aquinas, to whom he several times refers.[13] He accepts, as he explicitly says, the 'psychology of the old logic books'. Thus in opposition to Ryle, he maintains that reports of mental acts are categorical, not hypothetical or semi-hypothetical statements about overt behaviour. In particular, *judging* is a mental act, formed by analogy from 'stating'. To judge that 'X is sharper than Y' is to 'say in my heart' something to the same effect as the sentence 'X is sharper than Y'. Geach does not, of course, set out to 'reduce logic to psychology', but the effect of his work is to break down some of the barriers between them.[14]

Norman Malcolm's *Dreaming* (1959)[15] has been described as the *reductio ad absurdum* of Wittgenstein's method in *Philosophical Investigations*. Absurdity or not, it demonstrates to just what radical conclusions, from the standpoint of traditional psychological investigation, the use of that method can lead. It has always been presumed that we dream while we are asleep, that our dream occurs at a certain time during our sleep and lasts for a certain time, that while we are asleep we judge, feel, employ imagery, just as we do while we are awake, although in a less coherent and logical fashion. But, Malcolm asks, what could it possibly mean to say that all these things happen while we are asleep?

It would be self-contradictory to suppose, Malcolm argues, that a person is ever able, while asleep, to judge that he is asleep – anything which counted as evidence that he could make that judgement would serve to demonstrate that he was not in fact asleep. From this it follows that no one can ever judge both that he is asleep at a certain time and that he is at that same time judging that 'it is raining', or experiencing such-and-such feelings, or using such-and-such imagery. No doubt, when he wakes up a person may tell us that he now has the impression that he formed a certain judgement while he was asleep, or that he felt afraid, or that he had a vivid image. But there is no possible way of showing that this impression is a correct one. And if it is impossible to show that anyone has ever correctly used the sentence 'In my sleep I judged so-and-so, felt in such-and-such a manner, had such-and-such an image' then, according to Malcolm, this sentence has no sense.

Malcolm will, of course, allow a person to say 'I had such-and-such images in my dream', just as somebody might say 'In my dream I climbed a mountain'. But in the latter case it does not at all follow that *while he was asleep* he climbed a mountain. Quite the contrary: to say that this happened 'in his dream' is to deny that he did in fact climb a mountain. Similarly, 'I had certain feelings in a dream' amounts to a denial that I in fact had these feelings while I was asleep.

But surely, at least, we can say that we dreamt at, and for, a certain time? Do not experimental psychologists tell us at what point in our sleep a dream occurred and how long it lasted? The experimentalists, Malcolm argues, must be using a quite different concept of dreaming from the one we ordinarily employ; they must, for example, be using the existence of eye movements as a criterion of dreaming, as we do not. They are pretending by experimental methods to establish facts about dreaming when what they are really doing is trying to persuade us to accept a quite new concept of dreaming. Once again then, psychology fails to throw any light on our everyday, properly psychological, concepts – it revises when it professes to be describing.

Another, more influential, type of philosophical psychology is exemplified by G. E. M. Anscombe's *Intention* (1957).[16] It is distinguished by its concern with a set of problems which closely relate to conventional moral judgements – although Anscombe sets out to investigate them for their own sake, in a manner divorced from any moralistic concern.

Philosophers have ordinarily presumed that those actions we mark off as 'intentional' are preceded by, or incorporate, a special kind of internal act – 'the intention to act in that way'. Anscombe, in contrast, takes it to be the distinguishing feature of an intentional act that the question 'Why?', asked in relation to it, can be a request for a reason, not for a cause. Intentional acts, that is, are defined not in terms of psychological processes which precede them but in terms of the sort of question which 'has application' to them.

When has the request for a reason no application? In the first place, according to Anscombe, when the agent does not know that he is performing the kind of action for which we are seeking the reason. If when asked why he was driving at sixty miles an hour a person sincerely replies: 'I did not know that I was doing so', then he was not intentionally driving at sixty miles an hour. Note, however, that had he been asked why he was driving at more than thirty miles an hour, he might have been able to give us a reason. An act, that is, can be intentional 'under a certain description', even although it is unintentional under a different description.

Secondly, the request for a 'reason why', Anscombe suggests, does not apply to an involuntary action of a certain type – that sort of action which we 'know without observation', but the cause of which can only be known by observation.[17] Even with his eyes shut a man knows that his knee kicks when the doctor taps it, but only by observation can he discover why his knee behaves in that way. Asked 'why' in relation to such activities, he cannot give a reason, and may not know the cause.

Suppose, however, that when a man is asked 'Why?' he replies by referring to some past act. Is he offering a reason or a cause? Take the case when we ask him: 'Why did you kill that man?' Then if he replies: 'Because I felt something go snap in my brain' or 'Because I felt I just had to kill somebody' he is, according to Anscombe, telling us the 'mental cause' of his action – that event, not necessarily a mental event, which produced his action.[18] But if he says 'I acted in revenge, because he killed my father', he is giving a reason, the difference being that in this case his action is a response to what he regards as a harmful act and is an attempt to repay that harm.

An intentional action, Anscombe argues, is not 'known by observation' to come under the description in relation to which it is intentional. But surely, it might be replied, we must know by observation that, for example, we are writing on a blackboard when we intentionally do so. How else could we know it? To answer this objection Anscombe – in what is certainly the most obscure section of her never notably pellucid argument – makes use of the Aristotelian distinction between 'theoretical' and 'practical' knowledge. Knowledge of our intentions, she argues, is practical knowledge, not theoretical knowledge. Suppose, with my eyes shut, I write on the blackboard 'I am a fool'. I know that this is what I am doing, even if in fact the blackboard is too wet, and no words visibly appear there. To 'know what I am doing', in this sense, is to have 'practical knowledge'. I do not have a mistaken belief that I am writing on the blackboard if no words appear there; I am only putting up a bad performance, failing fully to perform what I none the less *know* that I am doing.[19]

Except for a passing reference to 'psychological jargon', Anscombe makes no specific reference to psychology. It is one outcome of her argument, however, that psychologists have no light to throw on intentions. For intentions are not 'psychological phenomena'. Other philosophical psychologists have argued, in similar fashion, that psychology, understood as an experimental inquiry issuing in explanations of human behaviour, has nothing to tell us about motives, about reasons, about perceiving. In short, the claims of psychology to be in some sense the 'physics', the fundamental explanatory science, of human behaviour have been wholly rejected by the philosophical psychologists.[20]

One argument runs through the rapidly-expanding literature[21] of philosophical psychology and may reasonably be regarded as fundamental to it. This argument is sketched by D. W. Hamlyn in an article on 'Behaviour',[22] which, characteristically, begins from a distinction of Aristotle's and makes no reference to any subsequent psychologist except Freud.[23] It runs like this: there is a distinction between motions of the body, such as the knee reflex, and activities of the person, or 'behaviour'. Behaviour can never be defined in terms of movements of the body, since the very same set of movements can be present in quite different kinds of behaviour. For example, the same movements of the body can take place in signalling that one is about to turn left or in pointing to an article in a shop-window, and yet these are quite different pieces of behaviour. The physiologist can explain the motions of a body in terms of causes, but he cannot explain human behaviour. Indeed, behaviour has no causes.[24]

To explain a piece of behaviour, on this view, is to give a reason for it, to mention its aim or purpose, or to point to the rules that govern it.[25] (These are, of course, different but related procedures.) Since behaviour is essentially normative, the new teleologists argue, it is logically impossible to explain how men behave if we restrict ourselves to the purely descriptive language available to physical science. There is no way of deducing from a knowledge of physiology, however thorough, that there is a rule in our society to the effect that an extended hand means 'I am about to turn to the right'. So it is impossible to explain in physiological terms a particular piece of behaviour which takes place in order to accord with that rule. No doubt behaviour sometimes fails to fulfil its purpose, is sometimes irrational, sometimes does not follow the rules. But even to explain these abnormalities we have to invoke, not the mechanisms of physiology, but a theory like Freud's – when he forgets that he is a 'natural scientist' – which points to the *hidden* purpose of our action, the *hidden* rules which govern our conduct, not its cause.

So much then, for the contemporary Aristotelians, for whom the task of philosophy is to describe more clearly what we already know to be the case. With the partial exception of Strawson they are interested in man, it should be observed, rather than the world, in relation to which they are usually content to rely upon a vaguely-formulated 'natural realism'. Whereas in the British empiricist tradition the central problem was to reconcile the physicist's and the ordinary man's picture of physical objects, now the problem, as the philosophical psychologist sees it, is to reconcile the ordinary man's with the neurophysiologist's conception of human behaviour. This, indeed, is one objection Wilfred Sellars[26] brings against philosophical psychologists: the proper comparison, he argues, is between the total scientific picture, the picture which science is engaged in constructing, and the total commonplace picture. Only thus can the virtues of the scientific picture be made fully apparent. It is not enough to contrast the two pictures of man, as distinct from man-in-the-world.

The Aristotelians by no means have matters all their own way. In England, never well-disposed to psychology or the social sciences, they dominate the philosophical scene. But that is far from being the case either in the United States or in Australia, although in both countries 'philosophical psychology' is well represented. It is instructive to contrast Strawson's *Individuals* with Quine's *Word and Object* (1960), which is at many points explicitly directed against Strawson.[27] One difference which is apparent from the outset is that whereas Strawson refers not at all to the conclusions of scientific inquiry, Quine makes considerable use of anthropology, of linguistics and of behaviourist psychology – especially as presented by B. F. Skinner in his *Science and Human Behaviour* (1953).[28] He wholly rejects that sharp contrast between philosophy and science which had been common ground to phenomenology, to logical positivism, to Wittgenstein, and to Oxford's 'ordinary language' philosophy. He reverts to the general position of Spencer and Alexander – philosophy differs from the special sciences, he says, only in virtue of its greater generality, in its being concerned, for example, not with whether wombats or unicorns exist but with whether classes and attributes exist.[29] Quine grants, of course, that philosophy often approaches its problems by way of a consideration of language; it is often advantageous, he suggests, for the philosopher to 'make a semantic ascent' or, in Carnap's language, to move from the 'material' to the 'formal' mode. But the same is true, Quine argues, of physical science. That, too, will sometimes, even if less often, profit by a 'semantic ascent'. Either the physicist or the philosopher may clear up a problem by reconstructing his discourse. It does not follow that either physics or ontology is 'really about language'.

In fact, *Word and Object* is very largely concerned with language, but with language considered as a form of human behaviour.[30] Quine begins by defining what he calls the 'stimulus-meaning' of an utterance, that class consisting of the kinds of stimuli which would prompt a person to assent to the utterance. Thus if the utterance is 'Car!' the stimulus-meaning might include dust rising from the road, the sound of a horn, the squeal of brakes, as well as the visible presence of a natural object of a certain shape or size. In terms of this definition, utterances can be divided into two classes – 'occasion sentences' and 'standing sentences'. An 'occasion sentence', such as 'Car', 'Rabbit', 'It hurts', is assented to only when a stimulus recurs; a 'standing sentence' such as 'Cars are dangerous' may be assented to in the absence of the kind of stimuli which originally prompted its utterance – for example, the sight of a car running off the road.

Two sentences are 'stimulus-synonymous', in Quine's terminology, if, for nearly everyone who speaks the language, they have the same stimulus-meaning. This is the case for a large class of standing sentences, which the linguist, analysing a foreign language which is absolutely unfamiliar to him, can therefore translate with reasonable confidence. By studying the circumstances in which native speakers assent to and dissent from utterances, the linguist can make out, too, which expressions are truth-functional connectives – corresponding, for example, to 'and' or to 'if' – and can discover that certain occasion sentences are 'stimulus-synonymous' within the society he is studying. He can observe, too, that some sentences are always assented to, and some are never assented to, whatever the stimulus, i.e. that some utterances are stimulus-analytic and some are stimulus-contradictory. But the linguist cannot *translate* many occasion sentences, Quine argues, without using 'analytic hypotheses', hypotheses in terms of which he breaks up sentences into constituent parts or 'words', as a visitor from Mars might develop the hypothesis that 'whersthcar' consists of four words which can be translated into Martian by two words.

From these premises, Quine draws his conclusion that translation is always indeterminate. To take an illustration, suppose a native language contains the word 'gavegai' and the linguist observes that this word is stimulus-synonymous (or roughly so) with our 'rabbit'. He has not demonstrated that the word 'gavegai' is synonymous with 'rabbit', in that vague intuitive sense in which we ordinarily think of some words as 'having the same meaning'. It could be that the native speaker uses the word 'gavegai' to refer to temporal stages of rabbits or to integral parts of rabbits, not to rabbits-as-a-whole. It might be supposed that the linguist would find this out by asking the native speaker, in the native language, such questions as 'Is this the same rabbit as that?' But the linguist can ask such questions only when he has established a translation, based on certain analytic hypotheses, for 'the same' and 'that one'. And it may be that he is using 'the same as' as a translation for 'the same temporal state as' rather than for 'the same thing as', or 'that one' as a translation for 'that temporal stage' rather than for 'that thing'. In other words, the linguist has no way of discovering the difference in meaning between 'gavagai' and 'rabbit', because the questions he asks with a view to discovering whether the words differ are already so translated as to make it impossible to discover that they do.

What is the philosophical interest of this theory of translation, which Quine takes to apply within English as well as between English and other languages? Quine is suggesting, in the first place, that while we can sensibly ask whether two sentences are stimulus-synonymous, there is no sense in asking whether they 'really mean the same'. We can say of two words that they are synonymous *within the framework of a particular set of analytical hypotheses*, but this is only to say that they possess stimulus-synonymity. Again, we can distinguish certain sentences as 'socially stimulus-analytic', i.e. as being of such a character that all members of a linguistic community will assent to them as soon as they are uttered and will suppose that anyone who seems to be denying them must be misunderstanding the language. But this concept of analyticity includes all sentences which are, in that community, regarded as truisms – it includes, for example, 'that is a car' said in the presence of a car – and does not correspond to the philosopher's idea of 'analyticity'. And there is no other clear way of determining that a proposition is 'analytic'.

Quine's theory of synonymity forms part of his defence of what he calls the 'regimentation of language' into the 'canonical forms' of logic. It is of no importance, he argues, that the logician's 'regimented' way of reformulating an everyday sentence is not 'strictly synonymous' with that sentence. Indeed, 'strict synonymity' is not a clear enough notion for us to be able to say with confidence that it is or is not preserved. What is important is that the logician's reformulation shall be, in some respect, an 'advance' on ordinary language.

What can be meant, in this context, by an 'advance'? With the help of Skinner, Quine looks naturalistically at the way a child learns a language, and asks what purposes the child fulfils by using certain types of logical devices, e.g. how he comes to talk about abstract objects, to 'slip into the community's ontology of attributes'. Then Quine is in a position to raise the question whether we could better fulfil our purposes, more adequately use language as an instrument for referring to the things around us, by changing our linguistic devices and abandoning the ontology implicit in their use. There is no possibility, he argues, of our starting anew, constructing an 'ideal language' afresh, but by working within our language we can hope to reconstruct it so that it will more perfectly fulfil certain, if not all, of our purposes. That task is an impossible one, however, if it is hindered by the presumption that what we come to say must be 'strictly synonymous' with what we have previously been accustomed to say. A philosophical reconstruction 'explicates'; it disposes of certain concepts, substituting others for them, new concepts which will do any real work the original concepts did, while avoiding the confusions arising out of their use.[31] An 'analysis' or 'explication' of an expression does not pretend to make clear 'what its users really had in mind'; it sets out to 'supply lacks'. Having once fixed on 'the particular functions of the explicated expression that makes it worth troubling about', it then devises a substitute, 'clear and couched in terms to our liking', which fulfils that function.

So, as opposed to Strawson's sharp distinction between 'descriptive' and 'revisionary' metaphysics, Quine is suggesting that philosophy, like other forms of inquiry, describes functions in order to revise concepts, revises concepts so that they will more effectively fulfil the functions philosophy has described. If, for example, physical objects and classes of such objects can do all the work that is done by abstract objects, without involving the ambiguities and obscurities of abstract objects, then that is the best of reasons for dispensing with abstract objects. But we must be sure that there are not jobs to do which physical objects and classes of objects cannot perform without the help of abstract objects. Nor does it follow, Quine freely admits, that for all purposes and on all occasions we must purge our discourse of every reference to abstract objects; we do not always need to be as clear and precise as the canonical forms of logic allow us to be on those special occasions when, as in the philosophy of mathematics, clarity and conciseness are particularly called for.

Precisely the same considerations, Quine argues, apply to the concepts employed in our everyday descriptions of human action. We may need to get rid of concepts like 'purpose' or 'intention' in order adequately to describe and to explain human behaviour, but it does not follow that we should do without them in our everyday communication with other human beings. Strawson, Quine freely admits, may be correct in his description of these everyday concepts, but to stop at that point is to stop thinking. It is part of 'the structure of our thought' for our thinking to be 'revisionary'.

The points at issue between philosophical and scientific psychologists are in the long run logico-methodological; many of them turn around the disputed question whether human conduct can be explained by reference to laws which make no mention of purposes, goals, or reasons. The general tendency of empirically-minded philosophers had been, at least until very recently, to work towards a unified concept of explanation, according to which to explain – or, at least, *fully* to explain – a mode of behaviour is to show that it is deducible from a set of laws operating under certain specific ('initial') conditions. That hypothetico-deductive model of explanation has been meticulously worked out by Ernest Nagel in *The Structure of Science* (1961).[32]

Nagel argues in detail that what purport to be irreducibly different types of explanation, teleological and genetic explanations, for example, can always be reinterpreted as special instances of hypothetico-deductive explanation. For his own special purposes, Nagel freely admits, the biologist may wish to concentrate his attention upon the modes of operation of a particular part of an organism in its relation to the activities of that organism; when he does so it is natural for him to express his explanatory conclusions in terms of 'functions', 'purposes', or 'goals' rather than laws and initial conditions. But the teleological form is a convenience, not essential. The practical usefulness in biology of such teleological formulations does nothing to demonstrate that it is impossible in principle to explain the behaviour of living organisms by reference to physico-chemical laws.

Similar considerations, according to Nagel, apply to the 'science of man'. There is no reason in principle, Nagel argues, why propositions asserting general connexions between forms of human conduct – e.g. between particular types of parental attitude and the development of neurosis in children – should not be derivable from the laws of physics and chemistry. It could well be the case that authoritarian parents always exhibit chemical peculiarities and that they produce chemical changes in their children. But such peculiarities could not be observed by social scientists, as they are now trained, and with their practical preoccupations they are more likely to be interested in loose, probabilistic connexions employing everyday social concepts than in the possibility of discovering universal physico-chemical laws from which strictly universal social relationships would be derivable. The fact remains that there is no method of explanation peculiar to the social sciences. The difference, only, is that the social scientist is commonly content with the discovery of necessary, rather than necessary and sufficient, conditions of social phenomena and with probabilistic rather than strictly universal laws.

In particular, Nagel argues, there is not a special sort of explanation describable as 'giving reasons' which is sharply distinguishable from law-citing explanations. Suppose somebody offers us as an example of such a 'rational' explanation: 'Hitler invaded Russia in order to destroy communism'. Then we ask ourselves whether this is a good explanation. It is not enough, according to Nagel, for us to inquire whether destroying communism is a 'good reason' for invading Russia. We want rather to know whether a man of Hitler's type, in the kind of position in which he found himself, would invade Russia except as a means towards destroying communism. To answer that question we have to make use of general, even if only probabilistic, statements about human conduct. Admitting, then, that when we ask the question 'Why?' we are not always seeking for a strict explanation, Nagel would nevertheless insist that whenever we do find a strict explanation it will, in the long run, take the form of a deduction from laws and initial conditions.[33]

If all propositions about human behaviour are, in principle, deducible from statements about physico-chemical laws, does this mean that psychology and sociology are 'reducible' to physics and chemistry? Consider the case in which a person has been accustomed to make temperature discriminations by the methods ordinarily used in everyday life. Later he is told that temperature is 'the mean kinetic energy of molecules'. What is he now to make of such judgements as 'the milk is warm'? He may be attracted to any of three conclusions. The first (reductionism) is that 'really' things are not warm or cold at all: temperature is entirely 'subjective'; 'the milk is warm', so far as it states a truth, must 'really' be a way of affirming that the molecules of the milk have such-and-such a mean kinetic energy. The second (instrumentalism) is that concepts like 'molecules' and 'kinetic energies' are fictions, simply a convenient tool for dealing with relations between temperatures. The third (emergentism) is that temperature is an emergent quality, manifesting itself only at higher levels of nature, not at the molecular level; the kinetic theory, on this view, 'explains' temperature only in the sense of pointing to those physical conditions under which temperature emerges as a quality.

Nagel wants to avoid all three of these conclusions. 'Reduction' he argues, is always a matter of reducing one theory to another; it makes no clear sense to talk of reducing *concepts*.[34] It consists, to put the matter roughly, in showing that one set of confirmable statements – e.g. statements about temperature – are deducible from another such set of statements, in this case about the energy of molecules. But any such deduction of statements about temperature from statements about the energy of molecules involves the use of a connecting statement of some kind, in which the energy of molecules is related to temperatures. It is impossible to deduce statements about temperature merely from statements about molecules. About the precise nature of such connecting statements, Nagel admits, there can be real controversy, but this much, he thinks, is clear: they are not mere statements of synonymity.

It is one thing to assert, for example, that headaches occur only under certain physical and chemical conditions, so that 'I have a headache' is in principle deducible from 'such-and-such physico-chemical changes are going on in my body.' It is quite another matter, and clearly a mistake, to claim that 'headache' is synonymous with some expression in physical theory. Nor are we to conclude, according to Nagel, either that headaches are an illusion or that physico-chemical theory is only a more convenient way of talking about headaches. All we are properly entitled to say is that as a matter of contingent fact headaches occur only when certain physical and chemical conditions are satisfied. Does this commit us to asserting that a headache is an 'emergent'?

Only, Nagel suggests, if by calling headaches 'emergent' we mean nothing more than this: that statements about 'headaches' cannot be deduced from *statements about particles alone*. But this does nothing to suggest that headaches exist at a higher level than particles or that there is a peculiar class of 'higher qualities' which emerge out of the physico-chemical.[35] For what is true in the doctrine of emergence is as true at the physico-chemical level as at any others. There is as good a reason for describing thermodynamical properties as 'emergent' in relation to mechanical properties as there is for saying this of psychological or biological properties.

Nagel's – and comparable – accounts of explanation and reduction have been criticized from a number of different points of view. He is mistaken, it has been argued, in suggesting that it is possible in principle to reduce biology and psychology to physics and chemistry. For it is not enough to grant, as he and Quine both do, that for practical reasons biologists and psychologists, social scientists, historians, will often prefer to make use of explanations couched in teleological terms; this is the only mode of explanation proper to history, to psychology, to biology. In other words, the commonplace concepts we ordinarily use in talking about human beings are the only concepts which can properly be employed in talking about *behaviour*, as distinct from mere bodily movements.[36]

These criticisms, however, do not challenge Nagel's account of explanation as it applies to the physical sciences; in large part, indeed – although in more detail and with greater plausibility – the new teleologists revive the anti-naturalistic arguments put forward by Rickert, Windelband, and Ward at the turn of the century. Much more radical are the criticisms of P. A. Feyerabend.[37]

The hypothetico-deductive model of explanation, Feyerabend

argues, rests on an untenable assumption – the assumption that meaning remains invariant throughout the process of explanation, so that, for example, what is meant by 'warm' is unaffected by the development of the kinetic theory of temperature. More generally it presumes that a theory explains 'established facts'. The actual situation, Feyerabend suggests, is that when we adopt a new theory we at the same time alter the concepts and the 'facts' from which we started.

It has often been suggested that science progresses by inventing new theories in relation to which older theories appear as special applications, so that, for example, Newton's physical theory is simply a narrower theory than Einstein's – Einstein's theory applied to a set of special cases. Following Duhem and Popper, Feyerabend argues that the new theories are always *inconsistent with* the old theories and involve their rejection. The same is true, he says, of facts; in the light of the new theories we come to reject what were previously 'established facts'. Not only that, we now work with a different ontology, with a corresponding change in the meaning of whatever descriptive terms we continue to employ. Thus a new theory of temperature does not simply explain why the milk is warm, in the sense of enabling us to deduce from statements about the mean kinetic energy of molecules, along with certain connecting statements, that the milk is (in the original sense of the word) warm; rather, it involves a change in the meaning of 'being warm'. The statements we deduce from the kinetic theory of temperature are different statements – although we may continue to use the same terminology – from the statements which we made about temperature before that theory was formulated.[38]

A theory, Feyerabend admits, may have been so widely accepted that we find it hard to imagine any way of describing what we observe except in terms of that theory. So it is not surprising that Niels Bohr, for example, has suggested that observation statements can only be formulated in terms of classical physical descriptions, as distinct from, for example, quantum-mechanical descriptions. But it is a defect in science, Feyerabend argues, that it should ever be so committed to a single theory; scientists ought always to be working with *alternative* theories as a protection against dogmatism.

Our everyday language, according to Feyerabend, itself incorporates theories; we cannot avoid theoretical assumptions, as phenomenologists and ordinary-language philosophers have supposed, by making use only of the concepts incorporated in everyday descriptive expressions. It is quite wrong to suggest, for example, that whatever theoretical advances we make, such an expression as 'pain' is bound to keep its present meaning.[39] Indeed, we can hope to make advances in such tangled fields as the mind-body problem, so Feyerabend argues, only if we are prepared to recognize that there may need to be wholesale changes in our ordinary modes of using such expressions as 'thought' and 'sensation'. To suggest, as Strawson does, that there is a common core of concepts which do not have, and could not have, a history, or, in the manner of the philosophical psychologists, that we are for ever committed to those methods of describing behaviour we now commonly employ is, in Feyerabend's eyes, arrant dogmatism.

The points at issue can be more clearly brought out by considering different ways of formulating the thesis of 'central state' materialism to which Feyerabend, with reservations, subscribes – as does Quine. U. T. Place defended the identity-theory in his 'Is Consciousness a Brain-Process?'[40] Place begins from the presumption that the behaviourist account of such concepts as 'knowing', 'understanding', 'intending' is fundamentally sound: these are all of them dispositions to behave in a certain way. The behaviourist theory still leaves to be accounted for, Place suggests, a set of concepts centring around such notions as 'consciousness', 'experience', 'sensation', 'imagery', where it is impossible to avoid talking in terms of processes which are not reducible to overt behaviour. Place tries to find room for such concepts within a naturalistic account of human beings by maintaining that consciousness is a brain-process.

He takes this to mean that consciousness *is empirically identical with* a brain-process in the same sense that a cloud has been discovered to be identical with a mass of tiny particles in suspension, or lightning with a motion of electrical charges. It is simply an empirical fact that the cloud we see as a large amorphous mass is in fact a mass of tiny particles. It could have been the case that clouds are a kind of soft fluffy substance; in fact it turns out that they are made of water (and other) particles. So, similarly, it turns out that states of consciousness are brain-processes.

If the hypothesis that consciousness is a brain-process sounds strange to us – even logically impossible – this, Place argues, is because we easily fall into a certain fallacy, which he calls the 'phenomenological' fallacy, i.e. the fallacy of supposing that when we describe how things look, sound, smell or taste what we are describing are actual properties of objects or events in a sort of 'internal cinema'. If we presume, for example, that a person who reports a green after-image is asserting that there exists within himself an object which is literally green, then 'we have on our hands an entity for which there is no place in the world of physics'. It then seems absurd, as indeed it is, to conclude that what is in fact green is a state of the brain. But what rather happens, according to Place, is that sometimes when we are not perceiving a green object it seems to us as if we were. All that the physiologist needs to explain is why this should be so. To understand a person's ability to make 'introspective reports' we have to ask how he learns to distinguish between cases when it is appropriate for him to report 'that is green' and cases when it is appropriate to report 'that looks green to me'; there is no question of looking for something which is in these latter instances 'the green he really sees'.

Feigl has developed the identity-theory in its least radical version, which accepts the traditional British empirical doctrine that we are directly acquainted with 'raw feels' in our experience and then impute them by analogy to others.[41] 'I am in pain', on this view, whatever else it does, reports that I have experienced a particular feeling. These 'raw feels', Feigl argues, are empirically identifiable with 'the referents of some neuro-physiological concepts'. There is no logical difficulty in identifying the two: to identify them does not involve a 'category-mistake'. To suppose that it does is to confuse, as early positivists confused, between the way we come to know what we know and what we know. We know raw feels by direct acquaintance: we do not know our neural processes by direct acquaintance. But it by no means follows that *what we know* in the two cases must therefore be different. Nor does this follow from the fact that the way in which we ordinarily talk about raw feels is different from the way in which we ordinarily talk about neural processes.[42]

This is not intended as a thesis, simply, about 'raw feels' but about mental states and events in general. As such, it would be criticized by the followers of Brentano, for example, on the ground that it cannot possibly account for the 'intentionality' of our mental acts, for the fact that 'desire', 'belief', 'thinking' and so on all refer to objects.[43] So 'I am thinking about the Battle of Waterloo', for example, can never be expressed in neuro-physiological language. This, Feigl is prepared to admit, is a fatal objection to those varieties of physicalism which suggest that all statements involving mental terms must be translatable into statements about physical events.[44] But the identity-theory is not about translatability. It does, of course, maintain that there is a qualitative or a structural difference between a person who is thinking about the Battle of Waterloo and a person who is thinking about Caesar's crossing the Rubicon, but not that the statement 'I am thinking about the Battle of Waterloo' can be translated into a statement about neural processes. There is a semantic problem in clarifying the relation between intentional and other forms of statement, but the semantical peculiarities of intentional statements do not at all affect the identity thesis.

In Feyerabend's version, it becomes extremely doubtful whether we should talk about an 'identity' theory at all. He himself has expressed considerable doubts on this point.[45] Feigl takes it for granted that there are 'raw feels'; Place does not quite do that, but presumes that he has the responsibility of showing how the subject's report that he is experiencing such-and-such sensations can be interpreted in terms of brain processes. Both would agree that there is a 'mind-body' problem.[46]

Even to presume that there is such a problem, Feyerabend on the contrary argues, is to take for granted the truth of a *theory*; it may well be the case that there are no 'minds' at all in the sense in which this word is commonly used and hence that there is no mind-body relation to be analysed. 'It is no good repeating, as Feigl does,' Feyerabend writes, 'that I experience P'; the question what we experience is not one which can be determined except within a theory. There is no *a priori* reason why our common-place descriptive concepts should not entirely disappear from our thinking, no reason for supposing that we have to take these concepts for granted and then look for a way of correlating them with, or identifying them with, the concepts of a scientific theory. No doubt, as Strawson insists, we arrive at, and at first explain the meaning of, scientific concepts by way of everyday concepts. But there is no reason why in the long run we should not work entirely with the new concepts, just as we no longer speak of oxygen as 'dephlogisticatcd air', as Priestley did, but as a kind of gas.

Everyday concepts, on this view, are like Wittgenstein's ladder, which we must throw away once we have climbed up on it. Or, as Lotze once put it, they are 'like a scaffolding which does not belong to the permanent form of the building it helped to raise but, on the contrary, must be taken down again to allow the full view of its result'. For Strawson, on the contrary, some of them, at least, are the coping-stones of our thinking; try to remove them, and our thought wholly collapses. To determine which of these views is correct is one of the major philosophical problems of our time.

Notes

CHAPTER 1

1. Interest in Hume dates back to the edition of his works by T. H. Green and T. H. Grose (1874); Berkeley was read by 'empirical psychologists' for his theory of vision, but was little regarded as a philosopher until the publication of A. C. Fraser's edition (1871). The successful chronological ordering of Plato's dialogues by W. Lutoslawski in his *Origin and Growth of Plato's Logic* (1897) – following up a line of reasoning initiated by L. Campbell in his editions of Plato's *Sophist* and *Statesman* (1867) – drew attention to the philosophical importance of Plato's later dialogues.

2. For a traditional empiricist's judgement on Mill see A. Bain: *John Stuart Mill: A Criticism with Personal Recollections* (1882). The fluctuations in Mill's philosophy are most fully brought out in R. P. Anschutz: *The Philosophy of J. S. Mill* (1953); see also W. S. Jevons: *Pure Logic and other Minor Works* (1890); J. F. Crawford: *The Relation of Inference to Fact in Mill's Logic* (1916); O. A. Kubitz: *The Development of John Stuart Mill's System of Logic* (1932). For an estimate by a present-day empiricist see K. Britton: *John Stuart Mill* (1953). For biography see M. S. J. Packe: *John Stuart Mill* (1954). The best edition of the *Autobiography* is H. J. Laski's (1949); Mill's *Logic*, in a skilfully abbreviated form, is contained in E. Nagel: *Mill's Philosophy of Scientific Method* (1950).

3. See H. C. Warren: *A History of the Association Psychology* (1921); J. C. Flugel: *A Hundred Years of Psychology* (1933); A. Bain: 'On Association Controversies' (*Mind*, 1887). In the writings of Bain, the British empiricist tradition passes into psychology as we now understand it. For his work, see Flugel, *op. cit.* Bain played a large part in the foundation of *Mind* (1876). Its first editor, Croom Robertson, was an able continuator of the empiricist tradition, whose interests, too, were mainly psychological. He wrote very little; most of his articles were republished as his *Philosophical Remains* (1894).

4. The essay on Bentham, like most of Mill's essays, is included in *Dissertations and Discussions* (4 vols., 1859–75). See also *Bibliography of the Published Works of John Stuart Mill*, ed. M. MacMinn, J. R. Hainds, J. M. McCrimmon (1945). On Bentham and the Mills see E. Halévy: *The Growth of Philosophical Radicalism* (English translation 1928) and L. Stephen: *The English Utilitarians* (1900). On Mill's relation to Bentham and his opponents, see F. R. Leavis: *Mill on Bentham and Coleridge* (1950); the discussions between 'Mr Skionar' (Coleridge) and 'Mr MacQuedy' (J. R. MacCulloch, a friend of Mill's) in T. L. Peacock's *Crotchet Castle*; E. Neff: *Carlyle and Mill* (1924).

5. On this method, see C. K. Ogden: *Bentham's Theory of Fictions* (1932).

6. There is a good brief account of Comte in L. Lévy-Bruhl: *History of Modern Philosophy in France* (1899). See also T. Whittaker: *Comte and Mill* (1908); E. Caird, *The Social Philosophy and Religion of Comte* (1885) – a

criticism from the standpoint of British Idealism; Comte's *Discours su l'ensemble du positivisme* (1848, English translation 1865); Mill's *Auguste Comte and Positivism* (1865); H. B. Acton: 'Comte's Positivism and the Science of Society' (*Phil.*, 1951). For Comte's influence in the United States see R. L. Hawkins: *Auguste Comte and the United States* (1936) and *Positivism in the United States* (1938).

7. One must begin somewhere; and I have arbitrarily decided that Whewell lies before the period with which I am concerned, although in many respects his philosophy of science is more 'modern' than Mill's. His *History of the Inductive Sciences*, from which Mill derived many of his scientific examples, appeared in 1837; his *Philosophy of the Inductive Sciences*, in 1840. In its third edition (1858–60) this latter work is broken up into three volumes: *History of Scientific Ideas, Novum Organum Renovatum, On the Philosophy of Discovery*. See R. Blanché: *Le Rationalisme de Whewell* (1935) which contains very full bibliographical notes on Whewell and his critics. C. J. Ducasse: 'Whewell's Philosophy of Scientific Discovery' (*PR*, 1951); E. W. Strong: 'Whewell *vs.* J. S. Mill on Science' (*JHI*, 1955); R. E. Butts: 'Necessary Truth in Whewell's Philosophy of Science' (*APQ*, 1965); H. T. Walsh: 'Whewell and Mill on Induction' (*PSC*, 1962).

8. Mill's reply to Comte's attack on the 'abstractions' of economics takes much the same form. Economics, he argues in his essay on *The Definition of Political Economy* (1836) – reprinted in *Some Unsettled Questions of Political Economy* (1844) – concerns itself with men in so far as they pursue wealth; in applying it in practice we correct our conclusions by taking into account the additional motives which are likely to be operating, the laws of which we derive from psychology and other branches of social science.

9. See on this point Anschutz and Britton (*op. cit.*); R. Jackson: *An Examination of the Deductive Logic of John Stuart Mill* (1941). Unfortunately, the traditional misinterpretation has been repeated in Packe's biography.

10. For his estimate of the nature of formal logic, see particularly his *Inaugural Address to the University of St Andrews* (1867), reprinted in F. A. Cavenagh: *James and John Mill on Education* (1931).

11. These methods are based upon Sir John Herschel's *Discourse on the Study of Natural Philosophy* (1830). They have been very influential, but also much criticized. See, as well as Britton and Anschutz, Whewell: 'On Mill's Logic' (1849), reprinted in *On the Philosophy of Discovery*; W. S. Jevons: 'Mill's Philosophy Tested' in *Pure Logic* (1890); T. H. Green: 'The Logic of J. S. Mill', *Works*, Vol. II (1886); F. H. Bradley: *The Principles of Logic* (1883); J. Cook Wilson: *Statement and Inference* (1926); M. Cohen and E. Nagel: *Introduction to Logic and Scientific Method* (1934).

12. S. V. Rasmussen: *Sir William Hamilton* (1925); W. H. S. Monck: *Sir William Hamilton* (1881); John Veitch: *Hamilton* (1882); Leslie Stephen's article on Hamilton in *DNB*. Veitch defends Hamilton against Mill's attack. The more important philosophical sections of Mill's *Examination* are included in E. Nagel's *J. S. Mill's Philosophy of Scientific Method* and in *British Empirical Philosophers*, ed. A. Ayer and R. Winch (1951). See also A. Seth's *Scottish Philosophy* (1885). Hamilton's early essay on *The Philos-*

ophy of the Unconditioned (1829), reprinted in his *Discussions on Philosophy and Literature* (1852), conveys the general spirit of his philosophy.

13. The most important member of the Scottish School after Hamilton's death, James M'Cosh, migrated to America and powerfully reinforced the Scottish tradition there. For details see H. W. Schneider's *History of American Philosophy* (1946). In general, Americo-Scottish philosophers were content to write text-books for College use. In France, the 'eclecticism' of V. Cousin (*The History of Modern Philosophy*, 1828–9), which had considerable affiliations with Scottish philosophy, played a very similar role as the official philosophy of the ordinary teacher in the French educational system.

14. Mansel's arguments, which caused a very considerable stir, are substantially identical with those advanced by 'Demea' in Hume's *Dialogues on Natural Religion*. But they were restated in the language of a Hamiltonian metaphysics, and with something of Hamilton's erudition. Not all members of the 'Scottish School' were prepared to accept the agnostic tendencies in Hamilton's work. See, for example, H. Calderwood: *Philosophy of the Infinite* (1854).

15. Compare W. G. Ward: *Essays on the Philosophy of Theism* (1884). Ward, a leading member of the 'Oxford Movement' who was converted to Roman Catholicism in 1845, attacked Mill's phenomenalism in the name of a theory of 'intuitive truths'. This was Mill's *bête noire* stirring into life again.

16. Compare and contrast F. W. Myers' account (*Essays, Classical and Modern*, 1883) of a conversation with George Eliot: 'Taking as her text the three words which have been used so often as the inspiring trumpet-calls of man – the words God, Immortality, Duty – she pronounced with terrible earnestness, how inconceivable was the first, how unbelievable the second, and yet how peremptory and absolute the third.' This was strict Comtian Positivism, as expounded by George Eliot's lover, the philosopher George Henry Lewes, in the eighteen-fifties, and by such influential writers as Frederic Harrison and Harriet Martineau: it found expression in the formation of the *London Positivist Society* (1867). See also R. Carr: 'The Religious Thought of John Stuart Mill: A Study in Reluctant Scepticism' (*J H I*, 1961). General studies of Mill, in which the emphasis is less on his philosophy than on his general outlook and attitudes, include T. Woods: *Poetry and Philosophy: A Study in the Thought of John Stuart Mill* (1963); M. Cowling: *Mill and Liberalism* (1963); A. Weinberg: *Theodore Gomperz and John Stuart Mill* (1963); R. Borchard: *John Stuart Mill the Man* (1959); M. W. Cranston: *John Stuart Mill* (1958).

Notes

CHAPTER 2

1. See F. Lange: *History of Materialism* (1866); J. T. Merz: *History of European Thought in the Nineteenth Century* (1896); R. B. Perry: *Present*

Philosophical Tendencies (1912); P. A. R. Janet: *The Materialism of the Present Day* (English translation by G. Masson, 1865).

2. Thus, for example, Büchner's *Force and Matter* is the preliminary reading recommended by the nihilist Bazarov in Turgenev's *Fathers an Sons* (1862).

3. On these writers generally, see A. W. Brown: *The Metaphysical Society* (1947); W. H. Mallock: *The New Republic* (1877), in which 'Storks' is Huxley, 'Stockton' is Tyndall and 'Saunders' is Clifford; Noel Annan: *Leslie Stephen* (1951); Virginia Woolf's portrait of her father – Leslie Stephen is 'Mr Ramsay' – and his friends in *To the Lighthouse* (1927); George Meredith's *The Egoist* (1879), in which 'Vernon Whitford' is based on Stephen; F. W. Maitland's *The Life and Letters of Leslie Stephen* (1906); M. H. Carré: *Phases of Thought in England* (1949); William James: *Principles of Psychology* (1890). For Huxley see H. Peterson: *Huxley, the Prophet of Science* (1932); E. W. MacBride: *Huxley* (1934); *Huxley's Life and Letters* (ed. L. Huxley, 1900); A. O. J. Cockshut: *The Unbelievers* (1964); C. Bibby: *T. H. Huxley* (1959).

4. Quoted from 'Dr Jenkinson's' (Jowett's) sermon in *The New Republic*. For details about this famous frog see T. H. Huxley's 'Of the Hypothesis that Animals are Automata' (1874) reprinted in *Science and Culture* (1882).

5. L. Eiseley: *Darwin's Century* (1958); G. Himmelfarb: *Darwin and the Darwinian Revolution* (1963 – a hostile witness); J. A. Passmore: 'Darwin's Impact on British Metaphysics' (*Victorian Studies*, 1959).

6. See T. H. Huxley: 'Evolution in Biology' (1878), reprinted in *Science and Culture*; E. Cassirer: *The Problem of Knowledge* (1950); A. O. Lovejoy: *The Great Chain of Being* (1936); R. H. Shryock: 'The Strange Case of Wells' Theory of Natural Selection' in *Studies and Essays in the History of Science and Learning* (1946).

7. 'Science and Morals' (1886) reprinted in *Essays Upon Some Controverted Questions* (1892).

8. R. Flint: *Agnosticism* (1903).

9. The address (1872) is reprinted in his *Addresses* (1886–7). It ends with the word 'Ignorabimus', which became the motto of German agnosticism.

10. W. H. Hudson: *Herbert Spencer* (1908); H. Elliot: *Herbert Spencer* (1917); W. James: 'Spencer's Autobiography' in *Memoirs and Studies* (1911); J. Martineau: 'Science, Nescience and Faith' (*Essays, Reviews and Addresses*, Vol. III, 1891); John Dewey: 'The Philosophical Work of Spencer' (*PR*, 1904); A. S. Pringle-Pattison: 'The Life and Philosophy of Herbert Spencer' (*Qtly. Rev.*, 1904); Josiah Royce: *Herbert Spencer, an Estimate and a Review* (1904); F. C. S. Schiller: 'Spencer' (*Encycl. Brit.*, 1911). Note Laevsky's description of his romance in Chekhov's *The Duel* (1891): 'To begin with, we had kisses, and calm evenings, and vows, and Spencer, and ideals and interests in common', and the part played by Spencer's *First Principles* in Olive Schreiner's *The Story of an African Farm* (1883).

11. cf. Frederic Harrison's vigorous critical attack in *The Nineteenth-Century* (March, 1884) – reprinted in the Pelican volume *Nineteenth-Century*

Opinion (ed. M. Goodwin) – entitled 'The Ghost of a Religion'. Note also F. H. Bradley's comment: 'Mr Spencer's attitude towards the Unknowable seems a proposal to take something for God simply because we do not know what the devil it can be.'

12. cf. J. Kaminsky: 'The Empirical Metaphysics of George Henry Lewes' in *JHI* (1952). His main work was *Problems of Life and Mind* (1874–9). See also A. Bain: 'G. H. Lewes on the Postulates of Experience' (*Mind*, 1876).

13. For a criticism of Spencer's use of this formula see J. Ward: *Naturalism and Agnosticism* (1899); H. S. Shelton: 'Spencer's Formula of Evolution' (*PR*, 1910).

14. In England, similarly, Clifford maintained that 'the universe consists entirely of mind-stuff.' That is the principal thesis of his essay 'On the Nature of Things in Themselves' (first published in *Mind*, 1878, reprinted in *Lectures and Essays*, 1879). His critics pointed out that Clifford's 'mind-stuff' was extraordinarily like what other people meant by matter. G. J. Romanes in *Mind, Motion and Monism* (1895) developed Clifford's view in a pan-psychist direction.

15. M. H. Fisch: 'Evolution in American Philosophy' (*PR*, 1947); H. W. Schneider: *History of American Philosophy* (1946); P. P. Wiener: *Evolution and the Founders of Pragmatism* (1949).

16. To say nothing of the ingenuities of James M'Cosh who, in *The Religious Aspect of Evolution* (1888), interpreted the Darwinian theory of natural selection as a biological expression of Calvinism, with God as the Great Selector.

17. For an exposition see M. Cornforth: *Dialectical Materialism* (3 vols, 1952–4); T. A. Jackson: *Dialectics* (1936). Critics include M. Eastman: *Marxism, is it Science?* (1940); H. Acton: *The Illusion of the Epoch* (1955); K. Popper: 'What is Dialectic?' (*Mind*, 1940); J. Anderson: 'Marxist Philosophy' (*AJP*, 1935). Marx himself never presented his philosophical views in any detail; Engels is the philosopher of Marxism. Note that we are not here discussing 'the materialist conception of history', which is a different matter.

18. S. Hook: *From Hegel to Marx* (1936).

19. Dühring had his own variety of materialism to maintain. See H. Höffding: *History of Modern Philosophy*, Vol. II, English translation 1900.

20. cf. G. Paul: 'Lenin's Theory of Perception' (*Analysis*, 1938).

21. S. Hook's interpretation of Marx, especially in *Toward the Understanding of Karl Marx* (1933), most fully illustrates this affiliation.

22. J. B. S. Haldane: *The Marxist Philosophy and the Sciences* (1938); H. Levy: *A Philosophy for a Modern Man* (1938) will serve as examples.

Notes

CHAPTER 3

1. cf. A. Aliotta: *The Idealistic Reaction against Science* (English edition, 1914); M. H. Carré: *Phases of Thought in England* (1949).

2. This *cri de coeur* is first to be heard in O. Liebmann: *Kant and the Epigoni* (1865).

3. Thus, for example, F. Lange, whose *History of Materialism* (1866) is one of the most important productions of the neo-Kantian school, was a devoted student of British philosophy in general and of John Stuart Mill in particular. See also Ch. V.

4. Translated into English by an extraordinary series of translators, including Green, Bosanquet, Nettleship, the logician E. Constance Jones, and the daughter of Sir William Hamilton. See H. Jones: *A Critical Account of the Philosophy of Lotze* (1895), which is a vigorous attempt, from a neo-Hegelian point of view, to stem the tide of Lotze's influence; E. E. Thomas: *Lotze's Theory of Reality* (1921), or his articles in *Mind* on 'Lotze's Relation to Idealism' (1915); L. Stählin: *Kant, Lotze and Ritschl* (English translation 1889); T. M. Lindsay: 'Hermann Lotze' (*Mind*, 1876); G. Santayana: 'Lotze's Moral Idealism' (*Mind*, 1890); F. C. S. Schiller: 'Lotze's Monism' (*PR*, 1896); J. T. Merz: *History of European Thought in the Nineteenth Century* (1896); For the very considerable German literature see F. Ueberweg: *Grundriss der Geschichte der Philosophie*. There is a lengthy account of Lotze in J. E. Erdmann; *History of Philosophy*, Vol. III (English translation 1890), and see also the essays on Lotze appended to R. Adamson: *A Short History of Logic* (1911). On Lotze's influence in England see P. Devaux: *Lotze et son influence sur la philosophie anglo-saxonne* (1932).

5. Lotze's *System of Philosophy*, which was to be a complete and systematic account of his philosophical views, remained uncompleted at his death, only the *Logic* (1874) and the *Metaphysic* appearing. His *Microcosmus* (1856–64) is a more popular presentation of his whole range of thought.

6. Other philosophers, of course, attacked Huxley from the standpoint of traditional theology. The best known is Robert Flint whose *Theism* (1877) went into thirteen editions. See D. Macmillan: *Life of Robert Flint* (1914).

7. See A. H. Stirling: *J. H. Stirling, His Life and Work* (1912). It is worthy of notice that Stirling, like Caird and Wallace after him, was a Scot. Dissatisfaction with the traditional Scottish philosophy partly provoked the new interest in Continental philosophy.

8. cf. J. H. Muirhead: *The Platonic Tradition in Anglo-Saxon Philosophy* (1931), which gives a detailed account of the introduction of Hegelianism into England and the U.S.A. Among other achievements, the St Louis Hegelians were responsible for the foundation of *The Journal of Speculative Philosophy* (1867), the first journal of its kind in an Anglo-Saxon country. See also P. R. Anderson and M. H. Fisch: *Philosophy in America, from the*

Puritans to James (1939); J. L. Blau: *Men and Movements in American Philosophy* (1952); G. Watts Cunningham: *The Idealistic Argument in Recent British and American Philosophy* (1933). W. T. Harris was the leader of the St Louis Hegelians.

9. On the whole movement from Coleridge to Bradley see, as well as Muirhead, J. Pucelle: *L'Idéalisme en Angleterre de Coleridge à Bradley* (1955).

10. E. S. Haldane: *J. F. Ferrier* (1899); G. F. Stout: 'Philosophy' in *Votiva Tabella* (1911); A. Thomson: 'The Philosophy of J. F. Ferrier' (*Phil.* 1964). His scholarly work is collected in *Lectures in Early Greek Philosophy and other Remains* (1866). Mill's comment on Ferrier is interesting: 'His fabric of speculations is so effectively constructed, and imposing, that it almost ranks as a work of art. It is the romance of logic.' But considered as philosophy rather than as poetry 'the whole system is one great specimen of reasoning in a circle.'

11. See, as well as Muirhead *op. cit.*, F. Houang: *Le néohegelianisme en Angleterre* (1954) and G. Faber: *Jowett* (1957). Jowett came to be very suspicious of the ultimate effect of German Idealism.

12. For Caird and his influence, see H. Jones and J. H. Muirhead: *The Life and Philosophy of Edward Caird* (1921); J. S. Mackenzie: 'Edward Caird as a Philosophical Teacher' (*Mind*, 1909); John Watson: 'The Idealism of Edward Caird' (*PR*, 1909). Jones, Muirhead, Mackenzie and Watson were Caird's most distinguished pupils. For Jones see H. J. W. Hetherington: *Life and Letters of Sir Henry Jones* (1924) and J. H. Muirhead's memoir (*PBA*, 1921). He was an enthusiastic and eloquent teacher, Welsh in origin, who maintained until the end of his life – see his *A Faith that Enquires* (1922) – the full gospel of Caird's Hegelianism against the 'new men', whether they called themselves 'Absolute' or 'Personal' Idealists. His most important polemical work is his *Critical Examination of Lotze's Philosophy* (1895). Watson, like Edward Caird's brother John Caird, was mainly interested in the philosophy of religion. For John Caird see C. L. Warr: *Memoir of Principal Caird* (1926). Muirhead and Mackenzie carried on the tradition of Cairdian Idealism into the third decade of the present century, with an emphasis upon its political, ethical and social implications and a gradual accommodation of it to later developments in science and philosophy. Caird's philosophy was at no time tightly organized or rigorous; at the hands of writers like Mackenzie it developed into a liberal eclecticism. See J. S. Mackenzie: *Elements of Constructive Philosophy* (1917), and Muirhead's memoir (*PBA*, 1935) of Mackenzie. Muirhead's most important work was in ethics and the history of philosophy; as general editor of *The Library of Philosophy* and of the essays included in *Contemporary British Philosophy* (1924–5) he played a conspicuous part in bringing together philosophers of divergent shades of opinion – the Cairdian ideal of reconciliation always lay close to his heart. See Muirhead's autobiography *Reflections by a Journeyman in Philosophy* (posthumously published, 1942) and the memoir by C. G. Robertson and W. D. Ross (*PBA*, 1940). Muirhead's autobiography is important for an understanding of the part played by Idealists in the new social tendencies of the period.

13. On this side of Green see J. Bryce: *Studies in Contemporary Biography*

(1903) and M. Richter: *The Politics of Conscience* (1964). The most illuminating study of Green is still R. L. Nettleship's *Memoir* (Green's *Collected Works*, Vol. III, 1888), an important philosophical production in its own right. Nettleship was himself a promising member of the school, who died at the age of forty-seven. His scattered writings are collected in *Philosophical Lectures and Remains* (1897) with a biographical sketch by A. C. Bradley. See also W. H. Fairbrother: *The Philosophy of T. H. Green* (1896); A. J. Balfour: 'Green's Metaphysics of Knowledge' (*Mind*, 1884); E. Caird's introduction to *Essays in Philosophical Criticism* (1883); H. Sidgwick: 'The Philosophy of T. H. Green' (*Mind*, 1901); H. V. Knox: 'Green's Refutation of Idealism' (*Mind*, 1900); Jean Pucelle: *La Nature et l'Esprit dans la philosophie de T. H. Green* (1960). Green is the 'Mr Grey' of Mrs Humphrey Ward's *Robert Elsmere* (1888).

14. What they are is another matter. See S. Alexander's critical review of Green's works in a now-defunct periodical *The Academy* (1885).

15. Others, of course, fought back. See Green's controversy with Spencer in *The Contemporary Review* (1880).

16. See Muirhead: *Platonic Tradition*; A. E. Taylor: 'F. H. Bradley' (*PBA*, 1924); R. W. Church: *Bradley's Dialectic* (1942); C. A. Campbell: *Scepticism and Construction* (1931); H. Rashdall: 'The Metaphysic of Mr F. H. Bradley' (*PBA*, 1912); the articles on Bradley by G. D. Hicks, J. H. Muirhead, G. F. Stout, F. C. S. Schiller, A. E. Taylor and J. Ward in *Mind* (1925); M. T. Antonelli: *La Metafisica di F. H. Bradley* (1952); R. Wollheim: *F. H. Bradley* (1959); H. J. Schüring: *Studie zur Philosophie von Bradley* (1964). Bradley is 'Cheiron' in Elinor Glyn's *Halcyone* (1912).

17. See his *Presuppositions of Critical History* (1874) where he describes the view that sensory observation is 'the smallest guarantee or test of truth' as 'a wretched superstition, a proof of the most utter philosophical uneducatedness', displaying 'that completest blindness to the experience of everyday life which is possible only to a vicious *a priori* dogmatism'.

18. Of German philosophers, the one who in method, although not in conclusions, comes closest to Bradley, is J. F. Herbart, Lotze's predecessor at the University of Göttingen. Herbart's 'method of relations' is very much the dialectic Bradley employs in some of the most important sections of *Appearance and Reality*. Bradley was a close student of Herbart's work; he recommended him to A. E. Taylor as an antidote against too much Hegel. When Bradley says in his additional notes (Bk 2, Pt II) to *The Principle of Logic* that he was not acquainted with Herbart in 1883 he must be referring, as the context permits, to Herbart's *Psychology*; he had already mentioned Herbart's *Logic* at an earlier point in the text. See J. Ward's article on Herbart in the ninth edition of the *Encyclopaedia Britannica* and G. H. Langley: 'The Metaphysical Method of Herbart' (*Mind*, 1913). Bradley was also much influenced by the Tübingen School of Theology, and particularly by the writings of its leader, F. C. Baur, who defended an Hegelianized Christianity in a number of books published between 1830 and 1860. See R. Mackay: *The Tübingen School* (1863); A. A. Schweitzer: *Paul and his Interpreters* (1911, English translation 1912).

19. G. F. Stout: 'Alleged Self-Contradictions in the Concept of Relation' (*PAS*, 1901).

20. See J. S. Mackenzie: 'Bradley's View of the Self' (*Mind*, 1894).

21. For the 'abstract' and the 'concrete' universal, see N. K. Smith: 'The Nature of Universals' (*Mind*, 1927); M. B. Foster: 'The Concrete Universal' (*Mind*, 1931); H. B. Acton: 'The Theory of Concrete Universals' (*Mind*, 1936–7); and the Symposium (J. W. Scott, G. E. Moore, H. Wildon Carr, G. Dawes Hicks): 'Is the "Concrete Universal" the true type of Universality?' (*PAS*, 1919), as well as the writings of the Idealists themselves, e.g. B. Bosanquet: *The Principle of Individuality and Value* (1912); Bradley: *Principals of Logic*; Hegel: *The Phenomenology of Spirit* (1807).

22. cf. R. F. A. Hoernlé: 'Pragmatism v. Absolutism (1)' in *Mind* (1905) and G. Dawes Hicks: 'F. H. Bradley's Treatment of Nature' (*Mind*, 1925, reprinted in *Critical Realism*, 1938).

23. G. F. Stout: 'Bradley on Truth and Falsity' (*Mind*, 1925) reprinted in *Studies in Philosophy and Psychology* (1930); C. D. Broad: 'Mr Bradley on Truth and Reality' (*Mind*, 1914).

24. See Terminal Essay 2 in *Principles of Logic*; G. F. Stout: 'Mr Bradley's Theory of Judgment' (*PAS*, 1903, reprinted in *Studies*).

Notes

CHAPTER 4

1. For family reasons he later changed his name to A. S. Pringle-Pattison. See the memoirs by G. F. Barbour in the posthumously published *Balfour Lectures on Realism* (1933) and by J. B. Baillie and J. B. Capper (*PBA*, 1931); H. F. Hallett's obituary notice in *Mind* (1933) and E. N. Merrington's in *AJP* (1931). He was a student of A. Campbell Fraser, the editor of Locke and Berkeley, whose *Philosophy of Theism* (1895) itself teaches a variety of Personal Idealism. For the controversy Seth's view aroused see his 'The Idea of God: a Reply to some Criticisms' (*Mind*, 1919).

2. This doctrine, of the essential isolation of the self, is a commonplace of late nineteenth-century and early twentieth-century literature. It is Baudelaire's 'sentiment de destinée éternellement solitaire' transformed from a personal attitude into a judgement on the fate of mankind, each, in the words of T. S. Eliot's *Waste Land*, 'in a prison, waiting for a key'. Eliot began as a philosopher, one who, like the personal idealists, turned to Leibniz for his inspiration, detecting Leibnizian elements even in Bradley (cf. his 'The Development of Leibniz's Monadism' and 'Leibniz's Monads and Bradley's Finite Centres', *Monist*, 1916 as well as his *Knowledge and Experience in the Philosophy of F. H. Bradley*, 1964).

3. Thus Seth's philosophy was admirably adapted to reconciling science, philosophy and religion. He played a leading part in the *Synthetic Society* (founded in 1896) which brought together men of science and men of religion. The atmosphere of this society is very well conveyed in Michael de la Bedoyère's study of the Roman Catholic theologian von Hügel (*The Life of*

Baron von Hügel, 1951). Hügel himself, although he was not a philosopher in the professional sense of the word, exerted a considerable influence on the philosophy of religion; amongst those who felt that influence one of the best known is A. A. Bowman, whose *Studies in the Philosophy of Religion* and *A Sacramental Universe* appeared posthumously in 1938. See N. K. Smith's memoir in the first of these works.

4. In his pioneer work, *A Hundred Years of British Philosophy* (1935, English translation 1938), to which I am much indebted.

5. See particularly his *The Limits of Evolution* (1901). The second edition (1905) is enlarged by a series of replies to his critics. See also J. E. McTaggart's review in *Mind* (1902); J. W. Buckham and G. M. Stratton: *George Holmes Howison: Philosopher and Teacher* (1934); C. M. Bakewell: 'The Personal Idealism of G. H. Howison' (*PR*, 1940). American Personal Idealism developed into 'Personalism' under the influence of B. P. Bowne. See the periodical *The Personalist* (1920), founded by R. T. Flewelling; E. S. Brightman, himself a leading Personalist, on 'Personalism and the influence of Bowne' in *Proceedings of the Sixth International Congress of Philosophy* (1926). Bowne's personal idealism was less radical than Howison's; although he maintains that every empirical entity is either a self or a collection of selves, he also thinks that all such selves are manifestations of a single finite being. For another example of American Lotzean philosophy see the writings of G. T. Ladd, especially *The Philosophy of Religion* (1905). French 'personalism' is something different again: see its leading exponent, E. Mounier, in *Personalism* (1950, English translation 1952) and the journal *L'Esprit* (1932), particularly the 1950 special number on Mounier.

6. Personal Idealism is here quite explicitly linked with the demand for a philosophy which shall be satisfactorily 'democratic'. For a fuller working out of this theme, see an article by Howison's disciple, H. A. Overstreet ('The Democratic Conception of God', *Hibbert Journal*, 1913) in which it is alleged that there is no place in a democratic society for 'such radical class distinction as that between a supreme being favoured with eternal and absolute perfection and the mass of beings doomed to the lower ways of imperfect struggle'. One thing which makes much American philosophy look very strange to European eyes is that it does not even *pretend* to look at its subject-matter *sub specie aeternitatis*. It must be granted to Howison that Indian philosophers have been particularly attracted by Absolute Idealism, keeping Bradley's name alive at a time like our own when he has few disciples in the Western world. See, for example, *The Philosophy of S. Radhakrishnan*, in *Library of Living Philosophers* (ed. P. A. Schilpp, 1952).

7. For Sturt, see C. C. J. Webb in *Mind* (1947). See Chapter 5 on F. C. S. Schiller. The other contributors included G. F. Stout (see Chapter 13); W. R. Boyce Gibson, best known for his translations of, and commentaries on, Continental philosophy (see W. A. Merrylees, *AJP*, 1935); and the ethical theorist Hastings Rashdall (see the *Life of H. Rashdall* by P. E. Matheson, 1928).

8. For a popular presentation of this same thesis see H. G. Wells: *Mr*

Britling sees it through (1916); *God: The Invisible King* (1917); and 'Scepticism of the Instrument' (*Mind*, 1904).

9. cf. C. D. Broad's *Examination of McTaggart's Philosophy* (3 vols, 1933–8). No other contemporary philosopher has been graced by so extensive a commentary. And when Cambridge philosophers analyse metaphysical arguments, they have a strong tendency to take as their typical example McTaggart's denial that time is real. See also G. Lowes Dickinson's *J. McT. E. McTaggart* (1931); S. V. Keeling's study, contained in that memoir, of McTaggart's philosophy; C. D. Broad's memoir (*PBA*, 1927, reprinted with modifications as a preface to the second edition of *Some Dogmas of Religion*, 1930); G. E. Moore's obituary (*Mind*, 1928); and McTaggart's summary of his philosophy in 'An Ontological Idealism' (*CBPI*).

10. See M. Macdonald: 'Russell and McTaggart' (*Phil.* 1936); G. E. Moore: 'Mr McTaggart's *Studies in Hegelian Cosmology*' (*PAS*, 1901) and 'Mr McTaggart's Ethics' (*Ethics*, 1903).

11. For details see Broad's *Examination* and John Wisdom: 'McTaggart's Determining Correspondence of Substances: a Refutation' (*Mind*, 1928).

12. See, as well as previous references, P. Marhenke: 'McTaggart's Analysis of Time' (*California Publications in Philosophy*, 1935); M. Dummett: 'A Defence of McTaggart's Proof of the Unreality of Time' (PR, 1960).

13. See the memoir by his daughter, O. W. Campbell, published as a preface to the posthumous *Essays in Philosophy* (1927); A. H. Murray: *The Philosophy of James Ward* (1937); W. R. Sorley: 'James Ward' and G. D. Hicks: 'The Philosophy of James Ward' (both in *Mind*, 1925); W. E. Johnson: 'James Ward' (*British Journal of Psychology*, 1925); G. D. Hicks: 'James Ward' (*PAS*, 1924); various articles on Ward in *The Monist* (1926). Ward was obviously a fine teacher and a notable personality; his former pupils speak of him with warm admiration even when, like G. E. Moore, they owe nothing to his philosophy.

14. To more than one philosopher, Ward's psychology is still much more interesting than the work of his successors. It provides the psychological foundations for F. R. Tennant's *Philosophical Theology* (2 vols, 1928–30). Bradley – following Hegel – had already attacked the attempt to substitute an associationist psychology for philosophy, but he was surprisingly sympathetic to the associationist tradition within psychology itself. He criticized Ward's psychological innovations, on the ground that they confounded psychology with philosophy. Ward's critique of associationism was carried further by G. F. Stout in his *Analytic Psychology* (1896). See also G. D. Hicks: 'Professor Ward's Psychological Principles' (*Mind*, 1921); G. F. Stout: 'Ward as a Psychologist' (*Monist*, 1926, and *Studies*).

15. Ward's emphasis on 'activity' was what Bradley particularly objected to; for the opposition between the two men see Ward's review of *Appearance and Reality* and Bradley's reply (both in *Mind*, 1894). See also E. E. C. Jones: 'Ward's Refutation of Dualism' and A. E. Taylor: 'Ward's *Naturalism and Agnosticism*' (*Mind*, 1900).

16. Ward's emphatic contrast between history and physics has affiliations

with the views of such post-Lotzean German philosophers as W. Windel-band (*History and Natural Science*, 1894) and H. Rickert (*The Cultural and the Natural Sciences*, 1899, English translation 1962). Once again Ward is rebelling against the Cartesian tradition. Descartes had dismissed history in his *Discourse on Method* as being, by its very nature, a highly selective and therefore inaccurate account of what 'really is'. For Rickert, see M. Mandelbaum: *The Problem of Historical Knowledge* (1938).

17. cf. S. Radhakrishnan: *The Reign of Religion in Contemporary Phil-osophy* (1920) for a detailed consideration of the degree to which Ward's theism drives him into monism. It should be observed that all the 'pluralists' we have discussed in this chapter think of the plurality of selves as together making up a single unified system: thus they leave themselves open to the criticism that after all they affirm the existence of a *single* Reality, i.e. the 'system'. The strains and stresses within their philosophies derive largely from their attempt to reconcile the unity of the system with the distinctness of its ingredients. For Ward's uncertainties, see the letter he wrote to William James in 1899, published in R. B. Perry: *The Thought and Character of William James* (1936).

18. For commentaries, see W. R. Boyce Gibson: *Rudolph Eucken's Philosophy of Life* (1906); M. Booth: *Rudolph Eucken, his Philosophy and Influence* (1913); W. Tudor Jones: *An Interpretation of Eucken's Philosophy* (1912).

19. His philosophical career extended from 1883, when he was one of the contributors to *Essays in Philosophical Criticism*, until 1923, when he wrote an account of his 'Life and Philosophy' for *Contemporary British Philosophy*. See J. H. Muirhead: *Bernard Bosanquet and his Friends* (1935) which con-tains an extensive selection from Bosanquet's correspondence; Helen Bosanquet: *Bernard Bosanquet, a Short Account of His Life* (1924); F. Houang: *De l'humanisme à l'absolutisme, l'évolution de la pensée religieuse du néo-hegelien anglais Bernard Bosanquet* (1954); and *Le Néo-Hegelian-isme en Angleterre: la philosophie de Bernard Bosanquet* (1954); J. H. Muir-head: 'Bernard Bosanquet' (*Mind*, 1923); H. Wildon Carr: 'In Memoriam, Bernard Bosanquet' (*PAS*, 1922); articles on Bosanquet in *PR* (1923); A. C. Bradley and Lord Haldane: 'Bernard Bosanquet' (*PBA*, 1923); C. Le Chevalier: *Éthique et idéalisme* (1963).

20. See p. 68 for the 'Concrete Universal'; and for Bosanquet's logic, Ch. 7. See also G. H. Sabine: 'Bosanquet's Logic and the Concrete Uni-versal' (*PR*, 1912).

21. See the Symposium by B. Bosanquet, A. S. Pringle-Pattison, G. F. Stout and Viscount Haldane on 'Life and Finite Individuality' (*PASS*, 1918); R. E. Stedman: 'An Examination of Bosanquet's Doctrine of Self-Transcendence' (*Mind*, 1931).

22. R. E. Stedman: 'Nature in the Philosophy of Bosanquet' (*Mind*, 1934).

23. See the memoir by D. S. Robinson in the posthumously published *Studies in Philosophy* (1952).

24. His essays are collected together in *Studies in Speculative Philosophy* (1925). Creighton wrote very little, but was an influential teacher. See, for

example, the articles on Creighton by G. H. Sabine and F. Thilly (*PR*, 1925).

25. There is a lengthy account of Royce's philosophy in J. H. Muirhead: *The Platonic Tradition in Anglo-Saxon Philosophy*. See also G. Marcel: 'La Métaphysique de Royce' (*RMM*, 1918–19, reprinted as a book in 1945); George Santayana: *Character and Opinion in the United States* (1920); *Papers in Honour of Josiah Royce* (ed. J. E. Creighton, 1916); R. B. Perry: *The Thought and Character of William James* (1935), and his article on Royce in *Dictionary of American Biography*; D. S. Robinson: 'Josiah Royce – California's Gift to Philosophy' (*Personalist*, 1950); J. E. Smith: *Royce's Social Infinite* (1950); J. H. Cotton: *Royce on the Human Self* (1954); D. Monsman: 'Royce's Conception of Experience and the Self' (*PR*, 1940); the special Royce number of *JP* (1956); J. E. Skinner: *The Logocentric Predicament* (1965); H. T. Costello: *Josiah Royce's Seminar, 1913–14* (ed. Grover Smith, 1963); V. Buranelli: *Josiah Royce* (1964).

26. Whereas Bradley used the infinite regress as a proof that a conception is self-contradictory, Royce feels himself obliged to maintain that infinite regresses are harmless. See the long appendix to *The World and the Individual* (1900) for Royce's reply to Bradley.

27. According to Santayana, American moral ideals were too powerful for Royce's Absolutism. For Absolutism, evil is a necessary ingredient in the total scheme of things; for morality, it is something which could be wiped out, with sufficient good will. Royce never succeeded in reconciling these two points of view – 'he has remained entangled, sincerely, nobly, and pathetically, in contrary traditions, stronger than himself.' His moralism leads him to lay great stress on will; yet he refuses to abandon an Absolutism for which the will – with its implication that someone is striving to make the imperfect better – could never be more than a mere 'appearance'. See also C. M. Bakewell: 'The significance of Royce in American Philosophy' (*Proc. of the Seventh International Congress of Philosophy*, 1930). For Royce's mature criticism of the representationalist and the pragmatic theories of truth, see his article 'Error and Truth' in the *Encyclopaedia of Religion and Ethics* (1912).

Notes

CHAPTER 5

1. In *The Contemporary Review* (1876); republished in *Lectures and Essays* (1879).

2. Schopenhauer did not come into his own until the eighteen-fifties, and even then it was his essays (*Parerga and Paralipomena*, 1851) rather than his systematic *The World as Will and Idea* (1819) which attracted admirers. His attack on Hegelianism – 'The driving forces of this movement are, contrary to all these solemn airs and assertions, not ideal; they are very real purposes indeed, namely, personal, official, clerical, political, in short, material interests' – was a welcome contribution to the general reaction against the

'State philosophy'. And Schopenhauer's pessimism was invigorating, in contrast with the professional optimism of most philosophers. He provided a relatively coherent 'philosophy' for that curiously productive 'Weltschmerz' which is so distinctive a feature of nineteenth-century German culture, where vast music-dramas culminate in 'the twilight of the Gods'. See W. Wallace's *Life* (1890); F. Copleston: *Arthur Schopenhauer, Philosopher of Pessimism* (1946); Thomas Mann: *The Living Thoughts of Schopenhauer* (1939); P. Gardiner: *Schopenhauer* (1963).

3. E. von Hartmann's *Philosophy of the Unconscious* (1869), in which Schopenhauer's 'Will' is transformed into 'the Unconscious', went into eight editions in ten years – an unprecedented popularity which von Hartmann had some difficulty in reconciling with his pessimistic judgement on mankind. This book certainly helped to prepare the way for the acceptance of Freudianism. See (in German) W. von Schnehen: *Eduard von Hartmann* (1929); J. W. Caldwell: 'The Epistemology of Ed. von Hartmann' (*Mind*, 1893); W. L. Northridge: *Modern Theories of the Unconscious* (1924).

4. James, usually so tolerant, was extremely hostile to Schopenhauer but this, I should say, is precisely because he felt his fascination. See in Perry's *Thought and Character* the remarkable letter in which he refused to subscribe to a memorial to Schopenhauer and, in general, Chapter 45 of that book.

5. Kuno Fischer's 'Exposition of Kant's Philosophy' (*History of Modern Philosophy*, 1860) is the first serious scholarly study of Kant. The controversy it provoked with the Aristotelian scholar A. Trendelenburg drew attention to the need for a more accurate account of Kant's teaching. To satisfy this need, H. Cohen wrote his *Kant's Theory of Experience* (1871). On this book Lange's interpretation depends, even although the 'Marburg' school of neo-Kantians under Cohen's leadership were to react strongly against a 'psychologizing', in favour of a Platonic, interpretation of Kant. For Cohen, see E. Cassirer: 'H. Cohen, 1842–1918' (Social Research, 1943). See also H. Dussort: *L'école de Marburg* (1963).

6. In his *The Philosophy of 'As If'* which was substantially completed by 1877, although not published until 1911. See the author's preface to the English translation (1924).

7. See D. Halévy: *The Life of Friedrich Nietzsche* (1909); W. A. Kaufmann: *Nietzsche* (1950); F. C. Copleston: *Friedrich Nietzsche* (1942); G. A. Morgan: *What Nietzsche Means* (1941); A. C. Danto: *Nietzsche as Philosopher* (1965); R. J. Hollingdale: *Nietzsche: The Man and his Philosophy* (1965). The standard work is in French, C. Andler: *Nietzsche, sa vie et sa pensée* (six vols, 1920–31). For a present-day German estimate see Karl Jaspers: *Nietzsche* (1936). See also the Nietzsche-Wagner correspondence (English translation 1922).

8. See the edition with Preface and Introduction by C. F. Harrold (1947); M. C. D'Arcy: *The Nature of Belief* (1931); L. Stephen: *An Agnostic's Apology* (1893); C. Bonnegent: *La théorie de la certitude dans Newman* (1920). It was not until 1879 that the papal encyclical *Aeterni Patris* directed Roman Catholics to Aquinas for their philosophy; Newman's *Essay* shows few signs of scholastic influence – Locke and Berkeley are his masters.

9. A. Seth: 'Mr Balfour and his Critics' in *Man's Place in the Cosmos* (1897); W. Wallace: *Lectures and Essays on Natural Theology*; W. M. Short: *A. J. Balfour as Philosopher and Thinker* (1912); A. Wolf: 'The Earl of Balfour' (*Phil.*, 1930); H. Jones: 'Mr Balfour as Sophist' (*Hibbert Journal*, 1905); K. Young: *Arthur James Balfour* (1963).

10. Renouvier was a considerable force in French philosophy in the latter half of the nineteenth century. A disciple, F. Pillon, was the editor of the influential journal *L'Année philosophique* (founded 1890); another disciple, L. Prat, is the author of *Charles Renouvier, philosophe* (1937). The French literature includes G. Séailles: *La Philosophie de Charles Renouvier* (1905); R. Verneaux: *Renouvier, disciple de Kant* (1945). See also S. H. Hodgson: 'M. Renouvier's Philosophy' (*Mind*, 1881); J. A. Gunn: 'Renouvier' (*Phil.*, 1932).

11. A 'tough-minded' version of British empiricism had been vigorously maintained by a Harvard friend, Chauncey Wright. See W. James: 'Chauncey Wright' (*Collected Essays and Reviews*, 1920); G. Kennedy: 'The Pragmatic Naturalism of Chauncey Wright' (*Columbia Studies in the History of Ideas*, Vol. III, 1935); E. H. Madden: *Chauncey Wright and the Foundations of Pragmatism* (1963). Wright's essays are collected together in *Philosophical Discussions* (1877).

12. See his *Letters* (ed. H. James Jnr, 1920) and the correspondence with Renouvier reprinted in *RMM* (1935). Mill tells us in his *Autobiography* that he went through a similar experience.

13. For biography, apart from Perry's admirable and monumental *Thought and Character of William James*, see C. H. Grattan: *The Three Jameses* (1932) and, for those not in search of information in the more vulgar sense of that word, Henry James: *A Small Boy and Others* (1913) and *Notes of a Son and Brother* (1914). See *Essays Philosophical and Psychological in Honor of William James* (1908); *In Commemoration of William James* (1942); E. Boutroux: *William James* (1911, English translation 1912); T. Flournoy: *The Philosophy of William James* (1911, English translation 1917); T. Blau: *William James, sa théorie de la connaissance et la vérité* (1933); G. Santayana: *Character and Opinion in the United States* (1920); J. Royce: *Willaim James and Other Essays on the Philosophy of Life* (1912); John Dewey: *Character and Events* (1929); F. C. S. Schiller: 'William James and Empiricism' (*JP*, 1928); R. B. Perry: *In the Spirit of William James* (1938) and 'The Philosophy of William James' (*PR*, 1911), reprinted as an Appendix to *Recent Philosophical Tendencies*; A. O. Lovejoy: *The Thirteen Pragmatisms* (1963). On the will to believe in particular see D. S. Miller: 'James's Doctrine of the Right to Believe' (*PR*, 1942); L. T. Hobhouse: 'Faith and the Will to Believe' (*PAS*, 1903).

14. See Peirce's *Collected Papers* (ed. C. Hartshorne and P. Weiss, 1931–50). See the memorial volume of *JP* (1916); J. Buchler: *Charles Peirce's Empiricism* (1939); T. A. Goudge: *The Thought of C. S. Peirce* (1950); ed. P. P. Weiner and F. H. Young: *Studies in the Philosophy of C. S. Peirce* (1952); W. B. Gallie: *Peirce and Pragmatism* (1952); M. H. Thompson: *The Pragmatic Philosophy of C. S. Peirce* (1953); M. Murphey: *The Development of Peirce's Philosophy* (1961); *Perspectives on Peirce* (ed. R. J. Bernstein,

1965); W. P. Haas: *The Conception of Law and the Unity of Peirce's Philosophy* (1964) with bibliography; N. Bosco: *La Filosofia Pragmatica di C. S. Peirce* (1962); E. Nagel: 'Charles S. Peirce: Pioneer of Modern Empiricism' (*PSC*, 1940); R. B. Braithwaite's review of *Collected Papers* (*Mind*, 1934); J. H. Muirhead: *The Platonic Tradition* (1931). For Peirce's letters to James see Perry: *Thought and Character*.

15. H. W. Carr: *Henri Bergson, The Philosophy of Change* (1911); R. T. Flewelling: *Bergson and Personal Realism* (1920); J. A. Gunn: *Bergson and his Philosophy* (1920); A. D. Lindsay: *The Philosophy of Bergson* (1911); J. McK. Stewart: *A Critical Exposition of Bergson's Philosophy* (1911); H. M. Kallen: *William James and Henri Bergson* (1914). Bergson belongs to the school of French 'spiritualist' philosophers, deriving from Maine de Biran (see H. Gouhier: 'Maine de Biran et Bergson' in *Les Études bergsonniennes*, Vol. I. 1948) and represented in the latter part of the nineteenth century by such philosophers as F. Ravaisson, J. Lachelier and E. Boutroux, who conjoined the French tradition with neo-Kantianism. See A. Lovejoy: 'Some Antecedents of the Philosophy of Bergson' (*Mind*, 1913). For Ravaisson, see Bergson: *The Life and Work of Ravaisson* (1904), reprinted in *Creative Mind* (1946); for Lachelier, see the Obituary by A. Robinson (*Mind*, 1919); T. Greenwood: 'The Logic of Jules Lachelier' (*PAS*, 1934); E. G. Ballard (ed. & trans.): *The Philosophy of Jules Lachelier* (translated extracts with an introduction, 1960). Several of the works of Boutroux have been translated into English: the best known, perhaps, is *The Contingency of the Laws of Nature* (1874, English translation 1916). The Cartesian tradition of 'clear and distinct perceptions', which Bergson sought to overthrow, did not lack for defenders: see especially J. Benda: *Belphegor* (1918, English translation 1929) and *The Treason of the Intellectuals* (1928). Bergson's influence on French literature, especially on Proust, has been considerable. See S. Kumar: *Bergson and the Stream of Consciousness Novel* (1963). But Gide remarks that future historians will over-estimate Bergson's influence just because he was the spokesman to so notable a degree for 'the spirit of the Age'. See also *The Bergsonian Heritage* (ed. T. Hanna, 1962).

16. James was much indebted at this and other points to a curious nineteenth-century figure, Shadworth Hodgson, now mainly remembered as the founder of the Aristotelian Society (1880). At first a group of interested amateurs, the Aristotelian Society came to be the home ground of that 'London philosophy' which kept philosophy in touch with the empirical tradition during the long Oxford dalliance with Idealism. The best known of all British philosophical societies, its *Proceedings* are in themselves a continuous history of British philosophy. Hodgson, in some respects, stood for all that James most detested: materialism, determinism and Platonism at once. But the elaborate epistemological analyses in his *The Philosophy of Reflection* (1878) and *The Metaphysic of Experience* (1898) contain many of James's characteristic doctrines, as James himself always freely acknowledged. See H. W. Carr's obituary in *Mind* (1912) and in *PAS* (1911); G. D. Hicks's obituary in *PBA* (1913); G. F. Stout's critical 'The Philosophy of Mr Shadworth Hodgson' (*PAS*, 1892) and Perry's *Thought and Character of William James*.

17. cf. D. Balsillie: 'Prof. Bergson on Time and Free Will' (*Mind*, 1911).

18. This thesis was first clearly stated in James's essay 'Does Consciousness Exist?' (*JP*, 1904), the first of the articles reprinted in *Essays in Radical Empiricism*. See John Dewey: 'The Vanishing Subject in the Psychology of James' (*JP*, 1940, reprinted in *Problems of Men*, 1946).

19. Similar views were maintained, to say nothing of Mill's phenomenalism, by E. Mach: *Analysis of Sensations* (1886); R. Avenarius: *Critique of Pure Experience* (1888–90); K. Pearson: *The Grammar of Science* (1892). Mind and matter are made of the same stuff, which is itself neither mental nor material – that is the essence of their doctrine. They are all attempting to work out a view which avoids the notorious difficulties of dualism, without being either idealist or materialist. But these writers were all positivists, as James was not. In a letter to N. K. Smith (1908) James speaks of Avenarius's 'spiritual dryness and preposterous pedantry'; James was looking for a 'juicier' philosophy. On the other hand, he admired Mach greatly, and must have learnt much from him. See F. Carstanjen: 'Richard Avenarius' (*Mind*, 1897); N. K. Smith: 'Avenarius' Philosophy of Pure Experience' (*Mind*, 1906); W. T. Bush: 'Avenarius and the Standpoint of Pure Experience' (*Archives of Philosophy and Scientific Methods*, No. 2, 1905); C. B. Weinberg: *Mach's Empirico-Pragmatism in Physical Science* (1937); P. Frank: *Modern Science and its Philosophy* (1949).

20. For the historical background to pragmatism, see P. Wiener: *Evolution and the Founders of Pragmatism* (1949); M. Baum: 'The Development of James's Pragmatism Prior to 1879' (*JP*, 1933); A. F. Kraushaar: 'Lotze's Influence on the Pragmatism of William James' (*JHI*, 1940); C. S. Peirce's historical note in *Collected Papers* (5. 11), which brings out his relation to Kant; J. Dewey: *Philosophy and Civilization* (1931); E. C. Moore: *American Pragmatism* (1961).

21. Pragmatism grew out of a careful analysis of scientific method; it is by no means what Ruggiero calls it – 'the philosophy of the business-man'. Certainly, as Royce emphasizes in *The Philosophy of Loyalty* (1908), James deliberately chooses metaphors ('cash-value', for example) which originate in the world of business. But James liked to poke out a Philistine-looking tongue at the solemnities of Absolutism. His notion of 'profit' and 'expediency' is very different from a businessman's.

22. For Idealist criticisms see Bradley's *Essays on Truth and Reality*; McTaggart's review of *Pragmatism* (*Mind*, 1908); R. F. A. Hoernlé: 'Pragmatism v. Absolutism II' (*Mind*, 1905); A. E. Taylor: 'Truth and Practice' (*PR*, 1905). From a realist point of view, see the criticisms in G. E. Moore's 'Professor James's Pragmatism' (*PAS*, 1907), reprinted in *Philosophical Studies*; W. P. Montague: 'May a Realist be a Pragmatist?' (*JP*, 1909); R. B. Perry: *Present Philosophical Tendencies*; Bertrand Russell: *Philosophical Essays* (1910). *The Journal of Philosophy* in the years 1903–9 abounds in articles on, and by, James and his associates.

23. cf. G. T. Fechner's *Zend-Avesta* (1851): 'I believe that nothing can be true which it is not good to believe, and that the truest is the best.' James was much attracted by Fechner's highly speculative variety of pan-psychism. See his *Pluralistic Universe* and W. T. Bush: 'William James and Pan-

Psychism' (*Columbia Studies in the History of Ideas*, Vol. II, 1925). Pan-Psychism was also being advocated by James's friend, C. A. Strong, in his *Why the Mind has a Body* (1903); but James would never be quite convinced.

24. See R. Abel: *The Pragmatic Humanism of F. C. S. Schiller* (1955); R. Marett: 'Ferdinand Canning Scott Schiller' (*PBA*, 1938); J. I. McKie: 'Dr F. C. S. Schiller' (*Mind*, 1938) and R. T. Flewelling and L. J. Hopkins in *The Personalist* (1938). For another British version of pragmatism see the writings of H. V. Knox: *The Philosophy of William James* (1914) and *The Evolution of Truth and Other Essays* (1930). Schiller's impact upon Oxford undergraduates is emphasized in Compton Mackenzie's novel *Sinister Street* (1913).

25. See the long controversy between Schiller and Perry in *Mind* (1913–15); Appendix X to Perry's *Thought and Character*; James's review of Schiller's *Humanism* (*Mind*, 1904).

26. On this, see W. James: 'Bradley or Bergson?' (*Collected Essays and Reviews*, 1920).

27. See P. A. Schilpp: *The Philosophy of John Dewey* (1939); S. Hook: *John Dewey: An Intellectual Portrait* (1939); G. Santayana: *Obiter Scripta* (1936); M. G. White: *The Origin of Dewey's Instrumentalism* (1943); S. S. White: *A Comparison of the Philosophies of F. C. S. Schiller and John Dewey* (1940); J. Ratner's selections with a lengthy introduction: *Intelligence in the Modern World* (1939); B. Russell: *History of Western Philosophy* (1946) and *An Inquiry into Meaning and Truth* (1940); two symposia *John Dewey, the Man and his Philosophy* (1930) and *The Philosopher of the Common Man* (1940); various articles in *JP*, 1939, 1955, 1959, 1960 and *PR*, 1940; G. R. Geiger: *John Dewey in Perspective* (1958); *John Dewey and the Experimental Spirit in Philosophy* (C. W. Hendel ed. 1959); *John Dewey, his Thought and Influence* (J. Blewett ed. 1960); articles in *JHI* (1959); M. H. Thomas: *John Dewey: a Centennial Bibliography* (1962).

28. Dewey's Hegelianism came to him through G. S. Morris. Morris's 'dynamic idealism' was itself a biological and experimentalist version of Hegel's philosophy. See his *Philosophy and Christianity* (1883) and R. M. Wenley: *The Life and Works of G. S. Morris* (1917).

29. Thus Dewey's highly influential writings on education set out to destroy the view that liberal education and vocational education are opposed to one another. Education is training in intelligence – training, that is, in the ability so to assess a situation as to be able to change it for the better. This necessitates an education which is at once practical, since we must know *how* to change the world, and liberal, since we must know in what 'the better' consists. But this, too, can only be discovered experimentally, not by pure contemplation.

30. See, for example, the cooperative volume by Dewey and others: *Creative Intelligence* (1917). G. H. Mead is perhaps the most important of later pragmatists; his *The Philosophy of the Act* (1938, posthumously published) is a detailed analysis of 'action', in the context of Dewey's theory of inquiry. See C. W. Morris: 'Peirce, Mead and Pragmatism' (*PR*, 1938); A. E. Murphy: 'Concerning Mead's *The Philosophy of the Act*' (*JP*, 1939); A. J. Reck: 'The Philosophy of G. H. Mead' (*Tulane Studies*, 1963). As

examples of other pragmatic writings see S. Hook: *The Metaphysics of Pragmatism* (1927); A. F. Bentley: *Behaviour, Knowledge, Fact* (1935); A. W. Moore: *Pragmatism and its Critics* (1910); C. W. Morris: *Six Theories of Mind* (1932).

31. See Perry: *Thought and Character*; G. Megaro: *Mussolini in the Making* (1938). Of course, James had no sympathy with totalitarianism – for which Idealists like G. Gentile supplied the intellectual trimmings – but Fascism in its earlier days, with its call for action, its appeal to enthusiasm, could without absurdity quote James in its support. On Papini, see James's article 'G. Papini and the Pragmatist Movement in Italy' (*JP*, 1906). James also influenced Giovanni Valiati, whose name has become a rallying point for Italian philosophers interested in the philosophy of science. See H. S. Harris: 'Giovanni Valiati 1863–1963' (*Dialogue*, 1963–4).

32. Apart from those works on James referred to above (p. 545), see J. A. Wahl: *Pluralist Philosophies of England and America* (1920, English translation 1925); E. Leroux: *Le Pragmatisme américain et anglais* (1922). For Sorel see R. Humphrey: *Georges Sorel: Prophet without Honour* (1951).

Notes

CHAPTER 6

1. This is a topic which ought to be studied with a delicate and loving exactitude. That would involve details too technical for the purposes of our present exposition. For something more satisfactory see C. I. Lewis: *A Survey of Symbolic Logic* (1918); J. Jørgensen: *A Treatise of Formal Logic* (1931); L. Liard: *Les logiciens anglais contemporains* (1907 edition); A. T. Shearman: *The Development of Symbolic Logic* (1906); P. E. B. Jourdain: 'Development of theories of mathematical logic and the principles of mathematics' (*Quarterly Journal pure and applied Maths*, 1910–12); W. and M. Kneale: *The Development of Logic* (1962); Hao Wang: *A Survey of Mathematical Logic* (1963); J. van Heijenoort: *Source Book in Mathematical Logic 1879–1931* (1964). There are excellent bibliographies by A. Church in *The Journal of Symbolic Logic* (1936) with corrections and additions in 1938 and a continuous bibliography for the years that follow. See also I. M. Bochenski: A *History of Formal Logic* (1956, English translation 1961).

2. Hamilton published only occasional pieces on logic, of which the most important is his 'Logic: The Recent English Treatises on the Subject' (*Edin. Rev.*, 1833, reprinted in *Discussions on Philosophy and Literature*). His *Lectures on Logic*, which consist in large part of quotations or paraphrases from minor post-Kantian logicians, were published posthumously in 1861. An Appendix includes fragments of Hamilton's projected work on logic, of which T. S. Baynes: *An Essay on the New Analytic of Logical Forms* (1850) is an officially approved version. The most important work published under Hamilton's direct influence is W. Thomson: *Laws of Thought* (1842) which introduced new types of immediate implication into the traditional logic, particularly implication by 'added determinants'.

3. George Bentham, to say nothing of Continental writers, had anticipated the Hamiltonian scheme of propositions in his *Outline of a New System of Logic* (1827), a work based on the manuscript remains of his famous uncle, Jeremy Bentham. It is sometimes said, for example by Jørgensen, that Hamilton was 'not aware of Bentham's idea'. But in fact he had reviewed Bentham's book as part of his *Edinburgh Review* article. That he should, in a lengthy controversy with De Morgan, so belligerently have insisted on his priority as a quantifier – dating back his own discovery to that very review article – is one of the curiosities of history. But, in fairness, one should notice Venn's view that Hamilton was the first to make extensive use of quantification: at times, although not always, Hamilton claims no more than this. (See the Appendices to Hamilton's *Discussions* and to De Morgan's *Formal Logic* for the details of the controversy.)

4. G. B. Halsted: 'De Morgan as Logician' (*Jnl. Speculative Phil.*, 1884); S. E. De Morgan: *Memoir of Augustus De Morgan* (1882). C. I. Lewis (*op. cit.*) gives the fullest account of De Morgan's logic. De Morgan's papers have been reprinted as *On the Syllogism And Other Logical Writings* (ed. P. Heath, 1965).

5. Compare G. H. von Wright: *A Treatise on Induction and Probability* (1951). Von Wright remarks that De Morgan's blithe dealing with the formulae he takes over from Bayes and Laplace 'cannot but amaze the modern reader by its complete lack of self-criticism'. See also W. Kneale: *Probability and Induction* (1949) on 'the inversion theorem' and the connected 'Rule of Succession'.

6. See the memoir by R. Harley in *British Qtly. Rev.* (1866), reprinted in *Studies in Logic and Probability* (ed. R. Rhees, 1952), and the 'Note in Editing' in that same volume; J. Venn: 'Boole's Logical System' (*Mind*, 1876) and *Symbolic Logic* (1881); W. S. Jevons: 'Boole' (*Enc. Brit.*, 1876); S. Bryant: 'The Relation of Mathematics to General Formal Logic' (*PAS*, 1901); W. Kneale: 'Boole and the Revival of Logic' (*Mind*, 1948); A. N. Prior: 'Categoricals and Hypotheticals in George Boole and his Successors' (*AJP*, 1949). On Boole's relation to the mathematics of his time, see E. Nagel: 'Impossible Numbers' (*Columbia Studies in the History of Ideas*, Vol. III, 1935); E. T. Bell: *Men of Mathematics* (1937) and *The Development of Mathematics* (1940); A. Macfarlane: *Lectures on Ten British Mathematicians* (1916).

7. See particularly the account of Boole's theory in Lewis, *op. cit.*; and the essays on probability included in *Studies in Logic and Probability* especially 'On the Theory of Probabilities' (1851). See R. A. Fisher: *Statistical Methods and Scientific Inference* (1956) for a modern statistician's estimate of Boole.

8. The economist. Logic and economics were closely associated in England during the years that followed; Johnson, Ramsey and Keynes were all of them philosopher-economists. See Jevons's *Letters and Journal* (ed. H. A. Jevons, 1886); G. C. Robertson: 'Mr Jevons' Formal Logic' (*Mind*, 1876); W. Mays and D. P. Henry: 'Jevons and Logic' (*Mind*, 1953).

9. For his relations to Boole, see his *Remarks on Boole's System* (Ch. XV of *Pure Logic*); his letters to Boole as reprinted, in part, in Jourdain, *op.*

cit.; G. B. Halsted: 'Jevons' Criticism of Boole's Logic' (*Mind*, 1878). There is a full account of Jevons in Jourdain and Jørgensen, *op. cit.*

10. See his 'On the Mechanical Performance of Logical Inference' (read to the Royal Society in 1870, reprinted in *Pure Logic and Other Works*, ed. R. Adamson, 1890); Mays and Henry, *op. cit.* and the articles referred to therein.

11. See Lewis, *op. cit.* The best known is his interpretation of *p or q* as *either p or q or both* as compared with Boole's interpretation of it as *either p or q and not both*. This innovation greatly facilitated the construction of logical calculi.

12. Obviously this sort of logic has close affinities with Hamilton. Since Jevons professed to be restating Boole, this helped to create the myth, now too firmly established in encyclopedias ever to be quite eradicated, that Boole's object was to turn Hamilton into algebra.

13. This attack originally appeared in a series of articles in the *Contemporary Review* (1877–9) and is reprinted in the 1890 edition of *Pure Logic*. Something of the agitation Jevons created can be discerned in *Mind* (1878) to which a number of distinguished philosophers rushed in Mill's defence. See also the vigorous criticism of Jevons in the preface to the third edition of T. Fowler: *The Elements of Inductive Logic* (1869).

14. See Jørgensen, *op. cit.*

15. Taking up the suggestions of Leslie Ellis. See Ellis's papers of 1842 and 1854, published in *Mathematical and other Writings* (1863). Venn's criticism of Bayes and the 'Law of Succession' was historically highly effective. See Fisher: *Statistical Methods*.

16. Lewis Carroll (S. Dodgson) wrote a *Symbolic Logic* (1896), developed an ingenious Venn-like game (1887), and composed a number of puzzles (*Mind*, 1894–5) which still give rise to controversy. See for example, A. W. Burks and I. M. Copi (*Mind*, 1950). In *Studies in Logic by Members of Johns Hopkins University* (1883), C. L. Franklin proposed in the 'antilogism' a method of testing the validity of syllogism (see *Mind*, 1928, and 'Symbolic Logic' in Baldwin's *Dictionary*) and O. H. Mitchell worked out an ingenious and elaborate algebra of logic. H. MacColl in a long series of articles in *Mind* (1880–1906) which were finally incorporated into his *Symbolic Logic and its Applications* (1906) systematized a logic in which propositions, not classes, were taken as fundamental. MacColl arrived independently at many conclusions for which other logicians now have the credit. He was generally accused of 'mixing up psychology with logic' because he described propositions as 'impossible', 'meaningless' and the like, as well as true and false. His refusal to conform to the ideal of 'pure logic' does something to explain why he is neglected. (See Russell's review in *Mind*, 1906, and MacColl's reply, 1907.)

17. On Johnson's earlier work, see A. N. Prior: 'Categoricals and Hypotheticals in George Boole and his Successors' (*AJP*, 1949). See also Ch. 15 below.

18. See, on Peirce's logic, C. I. Lewis (*op. cit.*) who was the first to draw attention to the extent of Peirce's creativeness as a logician; G. D. Berry on 'Peirce's Contributions to the Logic of Statements and Quantifiers' in *Studies*

in the Philosophy of C. S. Peirce (ed. P. Wiener and F. Young, 1952); Paul Weiss: 'C. S. Peirce' in the *Dictionary of American Biography*. Peirce's logical papers are collected, for the most part, in *Collected Papers*, Vol. II, III and IV. Peirce's reading of medieval writings, it is worth observing, was extensive: in logic, medieval philosophy is re-entering the main stream of contemporary thought. At the same time, while Peirce admired the 'minute thoroughness' of the scholastic logicians, he forcibly condemned their 'beast-like superficiality and lack of generalizing thought'. See J. F. Boler: *Charles Peirce and Scholastic Realism* (1963).

19. cf. I. Stearns: 'Firstness, Secondness and Thirdness' in *Studies in the Philosophy of Charles Sanders Peirce* (ed. P. P. Wiener and F. H. Young, 1952). Russell, who made great use of Peirce's distinction between monadic, dyadic and polyadic relations, especially in his theory of truth, refers to Royce, not to Peirce; in particular, he mildly ridicules 'Royce's' emphasis upon triadic relations. Within the context of Peirce's metaphysics, however, that emphasis is not merely arbitrary.

20. cf. the chapters on 'Peirce's Theory of Knowledge' in W. B. Gallie: *Peirce and Pragmatism*.

21. In *Collected Papers*, Vol. VI. A good selection of Peirce's work on this topic is included in J. Buchler: *The Philosophy of Peirce* (1940).

22. N. Lobachevsky's non-Euclidian geometry appeared in 1855; K. Weierstrass developed the conception of rigorous arithmetical proofs in the eighteen-fifties; the theory of 'trans-finite' numbers, of a 'real infinite', grew out of the work of R. Dedekind in the eighteen-eighties and G. Cantor in the last quarter of the nineteenth century. See E. T. Bell: *The Development of Mathematics*; B. Russell: 'Mathematics and the Metaphysicians' in *Mysticism and Logic* (1921), reprinted from *The International Monthly* (1901).

23. B. Russell: 'The Logical and Arithmetical Doctrines of Frege' in *The Principles of Mathematics* (1903); E. E. C. Jones: 'Mr Russell's Objections to Frege's Analysis of Propositions' (*Mind*, 1910); H. R. Smart: 'Frege's Logic' (*PR*, 1945) with A. Church's review of that article in *JSL* (1945); R. S. Wells: 'Frege's Ontology' (*RM*, 1950); P. D. Wienpahl: 'Frege's *Sinn und Bedeutung*' (*Mind*, 1950); W. Marshall: 'Frege's Theory of Functions and Objects' (*PR*, 1953) and M. Dummett's reply (*PR*, 1955), with his further note and Marshall's reply (*PR*, 1956); as well as Jourdain (with notes from Frege) and Jørgensen (for the details of Frege's symbolic system). See also note at end of chapter.

24. It was, however, through Peano that Russell was first led to read Frege. See P. Nidditch: 'Peano and the Recognition of Frege' (*Mind*, 1963).

25. These and other articles together with a brief extract from Frege's *Begriffsschrift* (1879) and *The Fundamental Laws of Arithmetic* are included in P. Geach and M. Black: *Translations from the Philosophical Writings of Gottlob Frege* (1952). Note the corrections in the review by M. Dummett (*Mind*, 1954). It should be observed that from the standpoint of formal logic as such, *Begriffsschrift* – Frege's first important work – is the most notable of all his contributions. But Frege's distinctive symbolism, which uses straight lines and curves to express logical relations, is difficult to follow or to reproduce. For that reason, his logical system has been in some measure

neglected. According to Kneale, Frege 'first presented logic as a deductive system . . . in rigour and elegance his system is superior at many points to *Principia Mathematica*'.

26. See also 'The Thought: A Logical Inquiry' (1918), trans. in *Mind*, 1956.

27. cf. M. Dummett: 'Truth' (*PAS*, 1959).

28. For examples of the difficulties which arise see P. T. Geach's 'On Names of Expressions' (*Mind*, 1950).

29. Work subsequent to 1957 on Frege includes: W. and M. Kneale: *The Development of Logic* (1962); R. S. Grossmann: *The Structure of Mind* (1965) on whether concepts have both sense and reference, together with (all in *PR*) G. Bergmann: 'Frege's Hidden Nominalism' (1958); E. D. Klemke: 'Professor Bergmann and Frege's "Hidden Nominalism"' (1959); H. Jackson: 'Frege's Ontology' (1960); R. Grossmann: 'Frege's Ontology' (1961); C. E. Caton: 'An Apparent Difficulty in Frege's Ontology' (1962). See also G. E. M. Anscombe and P. T. Geach: *Three Philosophers* (1961); B. V. Birjukov: *Two Soviet Studies on Frege* (1964); J. D. Walker: *A Study of Frege* (1965); C. D. Parsons: 'Frege's Theory of Number' (*Philosophy in America*, ed. M. Black, 1965). Geach's *Reference and Generality* (1962) incorporates a considerable discussion of Frege. See also M. Furth's translation and edition of sections of *The Basic Laws of Arithmetic* (1964).

Notes

CHAPTER 7

1. Green condemns him as a Hamiltonian in his essay 'On the Formal Logicians'.

2. F. Ueberweg is now best known for his *Manual of the History of Philosophy* (1862–6), but his *System of Logic and History of Logical Doctrines* (1857) was a widely read text-book, both in Germany and in England. C. Sigwart's *Logic* (1873), which Mrs Bosanquet translated in 1895, is a more ambitious work, attempting as it does 'to reconstruct logic from the point of view of methodology', i.e. to lay down an 'Ideal of Thought' to which inquiry will attempt to conform. In its general character, as a philosophical logic, this book establishes the form which Bradley and Bosanquet follow and they are also much indebted to it on points of detail. On Lotze, the most influential of the group, see R. Adamson: 'Lotze's Logic' (*Mind*, 1885, reprinted in *A Short History of Logic*, 1911). Lotze wrote a *Logic* as early as 1843, but the first part of his *System* (1874) is his major contribution to logic.

3. See for Bradley's metaphysics and its relations to his logic Chapter 3 above; R. Kagey: *The Growth of F. H. Bradley's Logic*, 1931; G. F. Stout: 'Mr Bradley's Theory of Judgment' (*PAS*, 1902, reprinted in *Studies*); G. Ryle's introduction and the article by R. A. Wollheim on 'F. H. Bradley' in *The Revolution in Philosophy* (1956). Ryle brings out clearly the points of resemblance between Bradley and Frege. See also D. S. Scarrow: 'Bradley's Influence upon Modern Logic' (*PPR*, 1962).

4. James referred to Bradley's *Principles of Logic* when it first appeared as 'epoch-making', a book which 'breaks up all the traditional lines'. See also the last chapter of his *Principles of Psychology*.

5. See L. J. Russell: 'The Basis of Bosanquet's Logic' (*Mind*, 1918) and Bosanquet's reply (*Mind*, 1919).

6. 'Among the vagaries of some German logicians of some of the inexact Schools,' wrote Peirce, 'the convertibility of illation [i.e. of *if p, q.*], like almost every other imaginable absurdity, has been maintained; but all the other inexact Schools deny it, and exact logic condemns it, at once.'

7. cf. 'Cause and Ground' (*JP*, 1910).

8. See Royce's *Logical Essays* (ed. D. S. Robinson, 1951); C. I. Lewis: *Survey of Symbolic Logic*.

9. He was a good deal influenced by A. B. Kempe's papers on 'The Theory of Mathematical Form' (*Phil. Trans. Royal Soc.*, 1886) and 'On the Relation between the Logical Theory of Classes and the Geometrical Theory of Points' (*Proc. London Math. Soc.*, 1890). He writes of Kempe's views that they have been 'almost unnoticed'. But Peirce, at least, had paid close attention to them.

10. See above Ch. 5; H. S. Thayer: *The Logic of Pragmatism, an Examination of John Dewey's Logic* (1952); M. R. Cohen: 'John Dewey' in *A Preface to Logic* (1944); 'A Symposium of Reviews of John Dewey's Logic: *The Theory of Inquiry*' (*JP*, 1939); D. A. Piatt and Bertrand Russell in *The Philosophy of John Dewey* (ed. P. A. Schilpp, 1939).

Notes

CHAPTER 8

1. See G. F. Stout's article on 'Introjection' in Baldwin's *Dictionary of Philosophy and Psychology*.

2. See, for example, J. Cook Wilson: 'On an Evolutionist Theory of Axioms', Inaugural Lecture, 1889.

3. See the posthumous edition (ed. O. Kraus, 1924–8) with additional essays (French translation by M. de Gandillac, 1944); O. Kraus: *Franz Brentano* (1919, in German); A. Kastil: *Die Philosophie Franz Brentanos* (1951); H. O. Eaton: *The Austrian Philosophy of Values* (1930); L. Gilson: *Méthode et métaphysique selon Franz Brentano* and *La Psychologie descriptive selon Franz Brentano* (both 1955); *Realism and the Background of Phenomenology* (R. M. Chisholm ed. 1961) which contains in translation two selections from Brentano's *Psychology*. The Appendix to *Our Knowledge of Right and Wrong* (1899) – the first and for a long time the only work of Brentano's to be translated (1902) into English – contains Brentano's essay 'On Subjectless Propositions' and a biographical note by the translator. Brentano's influence on German philosophy has been extensive: Meinong, Husserl, Ehrenfels, Stumpf, Masaryk – to mention only names well-known outside Germany – all came under his influence. Freud, it is worth noting, attended his lectures for some three years. But he was a reluctant

publisher, and in any case was diverted from large-scale philosophical work by his long controversy with Roman Catholic authorities on the issue of Papal infallibility. His letters and manuscripts are still being collected and published.

4. For Brentano's interpretation of scholasticism see E. Gilson: 'Franz Brentano's Interpretation of Mediaeval Philosophy' (*Mediaeval Studies*, 1939). Brentano's general attitude to his predecessors can be gathered from his *Die vier Phasen der Philosophie* (1895); Kant and Hegel represent, in his eyes, the decadence of modern philosophy. His preference for British philosophy was regarded with suspicion by the 'Guardians of the German Spirit'.

5. cf. E. B. Titchener: 'Brentano and Wundt: Empirical and Experimental Psychology' (*Amer. Jnl. Psych.*, 1922).

6. When Hume says in the Appendix to the *Treatise* that a belief differs from a fiction 'in the manner of its being conceived', he is anticipating, in this phrase 'manner of being conceived', Brentano's theory of mental acts. On the other hand, Hume's more usual definition of belief as a 'vivid idea', Brentano vigorously criticizes, just because it attempts to identify an *act* – belief – with the *object* of an act – an idea.

7. On the distinction between 'simple' and 'complex' judgements, see the notes to *The Origin of the Knowledge of Right and Wrong*. Brentano's theory of existential import is very much what Venn was to suggest as the best foundation for symbolic logic. See Chapter 6 above. Brentano's logical innovations were introduced to the English reader by J. P. N. Land's note in *Mind*, 1876. This note is particularly interesting as foreshadowing the logical discussions of a later day; Land maintains against Brentano that although a universal proposition does not assert the existence of its subject it none the less 'presupposes' it.

8. At the same time, Meinong continued to be interested in the problems of a philosophical psychology. See J. N. Findlay on 'Emotional Presentation' in *AJP* (1935) and his 'Recommendations regarding the Language of Introspection' in *PPR* (1948) in which he continues the tradition of Meinong's psychological inquiries. The present account of Meinong is much indebted to Findlay's *Meinong's Theory of Objects* (1933). See also R. Jackson's review of that book in *Mind*, 1934. Bertrand Russell's articles in *Mind* on 'Meinong's Theory of Complexes and Assumptions' (1904) and his reviews of Meinong's works (*Mind*, 1899, 1905, 1907) throw much light on Russell's philosophy and some on Meinong's. See also G. Dawes Hicks: 'The Philosophical Researches of Meinong' (*Mind*, 1922, reprinted in *Critical Realism*, 1938); A. Michaelis: 'The Conception of Possibility in Meinong's Gegendstandstheorie' in *PPR* (1941); J. N. Findlay: 'The Influence of Meinong in Anglo-Saxon Countries' in *Alexius Meinong Gedenkschrift* (1952). Meinong's 'Theory of Objects' has been translated in R. M. Chisholm: *Realism and the Foundations of Phenomenology* (1960). For Meinong's influence see also Chisholm's preface and the second edition (1963) of Findlay's *Meinong*.

9. On Twardowski see Polish number of *JP* (1960) and Z. A. Jordan: *Philosophy and Ideology* (1963).

10. Meinong's way of describing the status of these objects varied from time to time (cf. Findlay, *op. cit.*). For Brentano's comments, see the Appendices to *Von der Klassifikation* and the posthumous supplement on 'The Objects of Thought' (both included in the 1924–8 edition of the *Psychologie*). Brentano there denies that we ever have before our mind an object with the peculiar property of *not being*. If we think of a round square, there is in this case, he says, no 'object' to be considered, there is only the 'thinking mind'. He is obliged, therefore, to modify his view that the act of thinking always involves a *relation* to an object, since this would imply that there must always, in some sense, *be* an object. Now he speaks of the object as standing in a 'quasi-relation' to the mind. He thereby hopes to bring out the fact that there need be nothing present in some cases except a mind. But 'quasi-relation', to most of Brentano's critics, has looked like an attempt to have the best of both worlds by at once affirming and denying the distinction between the mind and its objects; and it involved that Cartesian contrast between what has independent existence and what only exists as the object of a mind which modern 'objectivism' hoped to avoid. See R. Grossmann 'Acts and Relations in Brentano', (*Analysis*, 1960) and the subsequent controversy with R. Kamitz (*Analysis*, 1962); J. Srzednicki: *Franz Brentano's Analysis of Truth* (1966).

11. M. Farber: *The Foundation of Phenomenology: Edmund Husserl and the Quest for a Rigorous Philosophy* (1943) and ed. *Philosophical Essays in Memory of Edmund Husserl* (1940); the Husserl numbers of *RIP* (1939, 1965) with bibliographies; articles in *JP* (1939); Bosanquet's review of *Ideen* (*Mind*, 1914); G. Ryle, H. Hodges, H. Acton: 'Phenomenology' (*PASS*, 1932); *Husserl*, Cahiers de Royaumont, 3, 1959; J. N. Mohanty: *Edmund Husserl's Theory of Meaning* (1964); the volumes published as *Phenomenologica*, especially the collections (vol. 2) *Edmund Husserl 1859–1959* and (vol. 4) *Husserl et la pensée moderne* (1959); H. Spiegelberg: *The Phenomenological Movement* (1960); R. M. Chisholm (ed.): *Realism and the Background of Phenomenology* (1960); L. Landgrebe: *Der Weg der Phänomenologie* (1963); C. V. Salmon: 'The Starting-Point of Husserl's Philosophy' (*PAS*, 1929); articles in *PPR*, from 1940; the Husserl number of *Études Philosophiques* (1954).

12. This reaction, so far as mathematics is concerned, was undoubtedly assisted by Frege's critical review in *Zeitschrift für Philosophie und phil. Kritik* (1894). According to Farber, William James also helped Husserl to emancipate himself from 'psychologism'. The reference is presumably to James's chapter on 'Necessary Truths' in *The Principles of Psychology* where James argues, against Mill and Spencer, that logic and mathematics have as their subject matter 'ideal and inward relations amongst the objects of our thought'. Husserl also refers freely to Natorp's criticism of psychologism as expressed in an article on 'The Objective and Subjective Foundations of Knowledge' (*Philosophische Monatshefte*, 1887). For Natorp's relation to Husserl, see especially Farber, *op. cit.*

13. In Germany, 'psychologism' is particularly associated with the name of J. F. Fries who, in such works as *Neue Kritik der Vernunft* (1807), had worked out a variety of neo-Kantianism in which 'Kritik', considered as

the method of discovering which propositions are necessary – although not of 'justifying' that necessity, which by its nature, he thinks, needs no justification – is depicted as a variety of empirical psychology. Fries's work was revived at the beginning of the present century by the 'neo-Friesian' School, under the leadership of Leonard Nelson. (See the English translation of extracts from Nelson's works, published as *Socratic Method and Critical Philosophy*, 1949). Nelson replied to Husserl's attack on 'psychologism' in his *On the so-called problem of knowledge* (1904). He argues that while we cannot deduce necessary propositions from the propositions of psychology, it is only by means of psychological investigation that we can discover (or *uncover*) what they are, since many of them ordinarily lie hidden from us as 'dark cognitions'. Brentano was also unconvinced by Husserl's arguments against 'Psychologism'. 'As soon as he hears this neologism,' he wrote, 'more than one pious philosopher now crosses himself, as if these sounds contained the devil in person.' If by 'psychologism' was meant 'subjectivism', Brentano was prepared to participate in the new exorcism. But he still insisted that 'knowledge is judgement and judgement belongs to the realm of the mind'. (See his essay on 'Psychologism', in the eleventh appendix, 1911, of his *Psychologie*.)

14. cf. John Wild: 'Husserl's Critique of Psychologism: its Historic Roots and Contemporary Relevance' in *Philosophical Essays in Memory of Edmund Husserl* (ed. M. Farber) for a fuller account of Husserl's arguments, which are subtle and diverse, and a more detailed comparison with Plato. Wild is the leader of a contemporary group of American 'Realists' who follow Husserl in maintaining the reality of 'essences' or 'universals'. See (ed. Wild): *The Return to Reason* (1953).

15. Compare G. Ryle's description of his task in *The Concept of Mind* (1949) as that of determining 'the logical geography of concepts'. See also G. Ryle: 'La Phénoménologie contre *The Concept of Mind*' in *La Philosophie Analytique*, Cahiers de Royaumont IV, 1962; A. J. Ayer and C. Taylor: 'Phenomenology and Linguistic Analysis' (*PASS*, 1959); John Wild: 'Is there a World of Ordinary Language?' (*PR*, 1958).

16. They first appeared in 1901, but Husserl partly rewrote them in 1913 to bring them into greater accordance with his later views: subsequent impressions follow the 1913 text.

17. This may have had some influence on Wittgenstein; at least the idea of a 'logical grammar' is prominent in it.

18. B. Bolzano, a priest who lectured on the philosophy of religion at Prague until he was dismissed in 1819 on political grounds but whose most important work is in logic and the philosophy of mathematics, is best known in England for his *The Paradoxes of the Infinite* (posthumously published, 1851), to which Russell several times refers in *The Principles of Mathematics*. But it is on account of the contributions to logic contained in his *Wissenschaftslehre* (1837) that Husserl praises Bolzano as 'the best of logicians'. In that book Bolzano set up the distinctly Husserlian ideal of a 'pure logic' free from all psychological presuppositions. Logic, he maintains, is the theory of propositions – a proposition being defined as 'any statement that something is or is not, irrespective of whether it be true or false, was ever

formulated in words, or ever entered anybody's mind as a thought'. Thus a proposition is neither a set of words nor a thought; and logic is certainly not, as had been traditionally supposed, a 'science of thought'. The proposition exists independently of statements; at the same time it is what statements mean. It bears a family resemblance to what Meinong was to call an 'objective'. See the Historical Introduction to the English translation (1950) of *The Paradoxes of the Infinite*; H. R. Smart: 'Bolzano's Logic' (*PR*, 1944); Y. Bar-Hillel: 'Bolzano's Propositional Logic' (*Arch. für Math. Log.*, 1952) and 'Bolzano's Definition of Analytic Propositions' (*Methodos*, 1950); J. Berg: *Bolzano's Logic* (1962). On Husserl and Bolzano see Farber, *op. cit.* and H. Fels: 'Bolzano und Husserl' (*Philos. Jarhbuch der Görresgesellschaft*, 1926).

19. For reservations and complications see H. Spiegelberg: 'Phenomenology of Direct Evidence' (*PPR*, 1941). Compare Meinong's 'evidence' and Brentano's 'perception'. The connexion with the Platonic-Cartesian tradition, which distinguishes between 'essence' and 'existence', will be obvious. More recently, Lotze in his *Logic* had defended the conception of an 'immediate certainty which, whether called intuition or by some other name, must be admitted to exist'.

20. See J. S. Fulton: 'The Cartesianism of Phenomenology' (*PR*, 1940).

21. See Chapter 19 below for details. American phenomenologists are generally unwilling to accept Husserl's movement in an Idealist direction. See especially M. Farber: *Naturalism and Subjectivism* (1959). See also J. M. Edie: 'Recent Work in Phenomenology' (*APQ*, 1964) – with extensive bibliographies, and J. Q. Lauer: *The Triumph of Subjectivity* (1958).

42. See the Memoirs by C. A. Mace (*PBA*, 1945); C. D. Broad (*Mind*, 1945), R. Knight (*Br. Jnl. Ed. Psych.*, 1946); J. Passmore (in Stout's *God and Nature*, 1952).

43. See the *Memoir* by A. S. and E. M. S. (1906); J. Bryce: 'Henry Sidgwick' in *Studies in Contemporary Biography* (1903); L. Stephen: 'Henry Sidgwick' (*Mind*, 1901) and in *DNB*; C. D. Broad: 'Henry Sidgwick' in *Ethics and the History of Philosophy* (1952).

24. See his 'Some Fundamental Points in the Theory of Knowledge' (1911), reprinted in *Studies in Philosophy and Psychology* (1930) in which he claims to have worked out his views, although he did not publish them, before Twardowski's article appeared (in 1894). Findlay in his *Meinong's Theory of Objects* draws attention to important points of difference between Meinong and Stout, especially on the nature of 'content'.

25. See also R. F. Hoernlé: 'Professor Stout's Theory of Possibilities, Truth and Error' (*Mind*, 1931) and Stout's reply: 'Truth and Reality' (*Mind*, 1932).

Notes

CHAPTER 9

1. See Russell's autobiography in *The Philosophy of Bertrand Russell* and Moore's in *The Philosophy of G. E. Moore* (both ed. P. A. Schilpp). See also A. R. White: *G. E. Moore* (1958); the Moore number of *Philosophy* (1958); the Moore number of *JP* (1960); R. B. Braithwaite: 'G. E. Moore 1873–1958' (*PBA*, 1961); N. Malcolm: 'G. E. Moore' in *Knowledge and Certainty* (1963); D. Lewis: 'Moore's Realism' in *Moore and Ryle* (Iowa Publications, 2, 1965).

2. Moore's chapter on 'The Ideal' in *Principia Ethica* did, however, greatly affect the cultural life of our century through its influence on 'the Bloomsbury group' – Roger Fry, J. M. Keynes, Virginia Woolf, E. M. Forster. See J. M. Keynes: *Two Memoirs* (1949); R. F. Harrod: *The Life of J. M. Keynes* (1951); J. K. Johnstone: *The Bloomsbury Group* (1954).

3. The poet, Moore's brother. See *W. B. Yeats and T. S. Moore: Their Correspondence* (ed. V. Bridge, 1953), which largely consists of an attempt by Yeats to understand G. E. Moore and by T. S. Moore to explain him, with an occasional admonitory note by G. E. Moore.

4. 'Moore's Technique' in *The Philosophy of G. E. Moore.*

5. See his 'Reply to My Critics' in *The Philosophy of G. E. Moore.*

6. At John Wisdom's instigation, as *Some Main Problems of Philosophy.*

5. One of the most controverted points in recent philosophy. See H. Joachim: *The Nature of Truth* (1906); G. E. Moore: 'Mr Joachim's *Nature of Truth*' and Joachim's Reply (*Mind*, 1907); B. Russell: 'On Propositions: What They Are and How They Mean' (*PASS*, 1919); F. P. Ramsey and G. E. Moore: 'Facts and Propositions' (*PASS*, 1927); G. Ryle: 'Are There Propositions?' (*PAS*, 1929) and the subsequent discussion with R. Robinson (*Mind*, 1931); M. Schlick: 'Facts and Propositions' and C. G. Hempel: 'Some Remarks on "Facts" and Propositions' (*Analysis*, 1935); C. A. Baylis: 'Facts, Propositions, Exemplification and Truth' (*Mind*, 1948); A. Kaplan and I. Copilowish: 'Must There Be Propositions?' (*Mind*, 1939); A. Church: 'On Carnap's Analysis of Statements of Assertion and Belief' (*Analysis*, 1950).

8. For a later discussion of the same problem see Moore's 'External and Internal Relations' (*PAS*, 1919, reprinted in *Studies*). Stebbing reports, in her contribution to the *Philosophy of G. E. Moore*, that Moore later 'expressed himself as unable to understand what he could *possibly* have meant by the views that he had previously stated and was quite convinced that they were wrong'. See Ch. 3 for Bradley and Ch. 5 for James on this same distinction. See also A. C. Ewing's *Idealism* (1934) which draws attention to the manifold ambiguities in the whole controversy, and Russell's 'The Monistic Theory of Truth' (*Philosophical Essays*, 1910).

9. See C. A. Strong: 'Has Mr Moore refuted Idealism?' (*Mind*, 1905); A. K. Rogers: 'Mr Moore's Refutation of Idealism' (*PR*, 1919); J. Laird's

review of *Philosophical Studies* (*Mind*, 1923); C. J. Ducasse: 'Moore's Refutation of Idealism' (in *The Philosophy of G. E. Moore*); B. Bosanquet: *The Meeting of Extremes in Contemporary Philosophy* (1921).

10. See the symposium by Stout and Moore on 'The Status of Sense-Data' (*PAS*, 1913); J. B. Pratt: 'Mr Moore's Realism (*JP*, 1923); M. C. Swabey: 'Mr G. E. Moore's Discussion of Sense-Data' (*Monist*, 1924); A. E. Murphy: 'Two Versions of Critical Philosophy' (*PAS*, 1937); John Wisdom: 'Philosophical Perplexity' (*PAS*, 1936); T. P. Nunn: 'Sense-Data and Physical Objects' (*PAS*, 1915).

11. See the articles in *RM*, 1963; A. E. Murphy: 'Moore's Defence of Common Sense' in *Reason and the Common Good* (1963); A. F. Holmes: 'Moore's Appeal to Common Sense' (*JP*, 1961); N. Malcolm's article in *The Philosophy of G. E. Moore*. Moore's later essays are collected in *Philosophical Papers* (*1959*).

12. See also 'The Justification of Analysis' in *Analysis* (1934). That journal was founded (1933) as a medium of publication for short studies in the analytic manner, and should be consulted for examples of, and papers on, analysis. On analysis generally see Ch. 15 below; J. O. Urmson: *Philosophical Analysis* (1956); M. Black, John Wisdom and M. Cornforth: 'Is Analysis a Useful Method in Philosophy?' (*PASS*, 1934); A. E. Duncan-Jones and A. J. Ayer: 'Does Philosophy Analyse Common-Sense?' (*PASS*, 1937); L. S. Stebbing: 'The Method of Analysis in Metaphysics' (*PAS*, 1932) and 'Some Puzzles About Analysis' (*PAS*, 1938); M. Black: 'Philosophical Analysis' (*PAS*, 1932), 'The Paradox of Analysis' (*Mind*, 1944, 1945), 'How Can Analysis be Informative?' (*PPR*, 1945) and his introduction to *Philosophical Analysis*, 1950; A. C. Ewing: 'Two Kinds of Analysis' (*Analysis*, 1935) and 'Philosophical Analysis' (*Philosophical Studies: Essays in Memory of L. Susan Stebbing*, 1948); C. Lewy: 'Some Remarks on Analysis' (*Analysis*, 1937); M. Macdonald's Introduction to *Philosophy and Analysis* (1954).

13. See particularly *The Philosophy of Bertrand Russell* (ed. Schilpp, 1944); C. A. Fritz: *Bertrand Russell's Construction of the External World* (1952); E. Riverso: *Il pensiero di Bertrand Russell* (1958); articles in *Phil.*, 1960; H. Gottschalk: *Bertrand Russell* (in German, 1962); A. Wood: *Bertrand Russell: The Passionate Sceptic* (1958 – a somewhat journalistic biography); G. Santayana: 'The Philosophy of Bertrand Russell' in *Winds of Doctrine* (1913); the chapter on 'The Philosophy of Logical Analysis' in Russell's *History of Western Philosophy* (1945); P. E. Jourdain: *The Philosophy of Mr Bertrand Russell* (1918); the Russell number (1953) of *Rivista Critica di Storia della Filosofia*; A. Dorward: *Bertrand Russell* (1951) and Russell's *My Philosophical Development* (1958).

14. Russell had also been influenced by the French logician-mathematician L. Couturat. It is difficult to distinguish what is Whitehead's and what Russell's in *Principia Mathematica*, except that Whitehead disclaims all responsibility for the introduction and appendices to the second edition (1925). See also Russell's 'Whitehead and Principia Mathematica' (*Mind*, 1948); W. V. O. Quine: 'Whitehead and the Rise of Modern Logic' (*Philosophy of A. N. Whitehead*, ed. Schilpp, 1944); H. Reichenbach: 'Bertrand

Russell's Logic' (*Philosophy of Bertrand Russell*); S. Waterlow: 'Some Philosophical Implications of Mr B. Russell's Logical Theory of Mathematics' (*PAS*, 1909); P. E. B. Jourdain: 'Mr Bertrand Russell's First Work on the Principles of Mathematics' (*Monist*, 1912); F. P. Ramsey: *The Foundations of Mathematics and Other Logical Essays* (1931); F. Waismann: *Introduction to Mathematical Thinking* (1936); J. Jørgensen: *A Treatise of Formal Logic* (1931); E. J. Nelson: 'Whitehead and Russell's Theory of Deduction' (*Bull. Am. Math. Soc.*, 1934).

15. See J. A. Chadwick: 'Logical Constants' (*Mind*, 1927).

16. See particularly the summary in the second lecture of *Our Knowledge of the External World* (1914).

17. See *Principles of Mathematics*, Ch. XXVI, for details.

18. For the Frege-Russell correspondence see J. van Heijenoort: *Source Book in Mathematical Logic 1879–1931* (1964).

19. First in Appendix B to *The Principles of Mathematics*, then in articles on 'Mathematical Logic as Based on the Theory of Types' (*Am. Jnl. Maths.*, 1908) and 'La Théorie des types logiques' (*RMM*, 1910), but most fully in *Principia Mathematica*. There is a relatively popular presentation in Russell's articles on 'The Philosophy of Logical Atomism to July 1919' (*Monist*, 1918–19). His hesitancies are most marked in his *Introduction to Mathematical Philosophy* (1919). Since the theory of types was presented independently by Russell in these various places, it is reasonable to refer to it as 'Russell's' although Whitehead no doubt had some effect upon its method of formulation.

20. For subsequent criticisms of Russell's account of vicious circles, see Kurt Gödel: 'Russell's Mathematical Logic' (*Philosophy of Bertrand Russell*).

21. Particularly 'the Dedekind cut'. See Gödel, *op. cit.* and G. H. Hardy *A Course of Pure Mathematics* (1908).

22. In *Proceedings of the London Mathematical Society*, reprinted in the posthumous collection *The Foundations of Mathematics and Other Logical Essays* (ed. R. B. Braithwaite, 1931). See also R. Carnap's discussion of 'The Antinomies' in *The Logical Syntax of Language* (1934, English version 1937), the article on 'Logical Paradoxes' by A. Church in *The Dictionary of Philosophy* (ed. D. D. Runes), and the lengthy account in Vol. III of Jørgensen, *op. cit.* On the Axiom of Reducibility, see W. V. O. Quine: 'On the Axiom of Reducibility' (*Mind*, 1936).

23. There were, of course, other proposals for dealing with the paradoxes. The 'intuitionists' – of whom the most prominent were L. J. Brouwer and H. Weyl – were willing to abandon as unsound those parts of mathematical analysis within which the paradoxes – or at least the more intractable ones – arose. E. Zermelo in an article entitled 'Investigations into the Foundation of the Theory of Sets' (*Mathematische Annalen*, 1908) approached the problem by distinguishing those predicates which do, and those that do not, have an extension. W. Quine in his 'New Foundations for Mathematical Logic' (*American Math. Monthly*, 1937) and later in his *Mathematical Logic* (1940) tried to bring together Russell's theory of types and Zermelo's theory of sets. See Quine's *Set Theory and its Logic* (1963); A. A. Fraenkel

and Y. Bar-Hillel: *Foundations of Set Theory* (1959) and the symposium in *Logic, Methodology and Philosophy of Science* (ed. E. Nagel, P. Suppes, A. Tarski, 1962). See also K. Grelling: 'The Logical Paradoxes' (*Mind*, 1936), A. Fraenkel and Y. Bar-Hillel: 'Le problème des antinomies et ses développements récents' (*RMM*, 1939). On the relation between Quine's solution and Frege's see W. V. O. Quine: 'On Frege's Way Out' (*Mind*, 1955).

24. See Chapters III and IX in L. S. Stebbing: *A Modern Introduction to Logic* (2nd ed., 1933); J. W. Reeves: 'The Origin and Consequences of the Theory of Descriptions' (*PAS*, 1933); R. J. Butler: 'The Scaffolding of Russell's Theory of Descriptions' (*PR*, 1954); G. E. Moore: 'Russell's Theory of Descriptions' in *The Philosophy of Bertrand Russell*, and other contributions to that volume; Russell's innovations are criticized by the logician, E. E. C. Jones, in several articles in *Mind* (1910–11). Russell replies in *Mysticism and Logic*; for recent criticisms see P. T. Geach: *Reference and Generality* (1962); M. Lazerowitz: 'Knowledge by Description' (*PR*, 1937); P. F. Strawson: 'On Referring' (*Mind*, 1950); articles in *Analysis* (1957–9).

25. Although Russell acknowledges his indebtedness to James, his way of making the distinction is different from James's. Russell's essay on 'Knowledge by Acquaintance and Knowledge by Description' first appeared in *PAS*, 1910; it is reprinted with modifications in *Problems of Philosophy* and in *Mysticism and Logic*. See G. D. Hicks, G. E. Moore and others: 'Is there "Knowledge by Acquaintance"?' (*PASS*, 1919) and G. Hughes: 'Is There Knowledge by Acquaintance?' (*PASS*, 1949). See also Russell's articles 'On the Nature of Acquaintance' (*Monist*, 1914). Moore's distinction in *Some Main Problems of Philosophy* between 'direct' and 'indirect' apprehension is another form of the 'acquaintance' and 'description' contrast. But Moore's mature view, as expressed in a note added to that volume, is that 'knowledge by acquaintance' is neither 'knowledge' nor 'acquaintance'. 'There is,' he says, 'no common sense of "know" such that from the mere fact that I am seeing a person it follows that I am at that moment knowing him.'

26. S. Alexander's 'The Basis of Realism' (*PBA*, 1914); T. P. Nunn: 'Are Secondary Qualities Independent of Perception?' (*PAS*, 1909); E. B. Holt's 'The Place of Illusory Experience in a Realistic World' in *The New Realism* (ed. Marvin, 1912). See also Ch. 11 below.

27. On Russell's theory of sense-data, see G. D. Hicks 'The Nature of Sense-Data' (*Mind*, 1912) and Russell's reply (*Mind*, 1913); J. E. Turner: 'Mr Russell on Sense-Data and Knowledge' (*Mind*, 1914); H. A. Prichard: 'Mr Bertrand Russell on the Knowledge of the External World' (*Mind*, 1915); and 'Mr Bertrand Russell's *Outline of Philosophy*' (*Mind*, 1928); M. H. A. Newman: 'Mr Russell's Causal Theory of Perception' (*Mind*, 1928); C. A. Strong: 'Russell's Theory of the External World' (*Mind*, 1922); J. H. Woodger: 'Mr Russell's Theory of Perception' (*Monist*, 1930) as well as C. A. Fritz, *op. cit.* and various essays in P. A. Schilpp: *The Philosophy of Bertrand Russell*.

28. Compare John Laird: 'The Law of Parsimony' (*Monist*, 1919); John Wisdom: 'Logical Constructions' (*Mind*, 1931–3); L. S. Stebbing: 'Con-

structions' (*PAS*, 1933). Russell thought that the risk of error is diminished every time we get along without asserting, as distinct from positively denying, that an entity exists. 'You diminish the risk of error,' he wrote (*Monist*, 1919) 'with every diminution of entities and premises.' This is the mathematical logician speaking; in metaphysics as in logic he is looking for the bare minimum out of which a system can be constructed – the 'minimum vocabulary', which, conjoined with the 'syntax' laid down in *Principia Mathematica*, would constitute an ideal language.

29. See the articles with that title in *The Monist* (1918) and 'Logical Atomism' (*CPB* I). See also J. O. Urmson: *Philosophical Analysis*; D. F. Pears: 'Logical Atomism' (in *The Revolution in Philosophy*, 1956). Russell met Wittgenstein at Cambridge in 1912; he explains in the preface to his *Monist* articles that he had decided to publish them because he did not know even whether Wittgenstein was alive. But one should not overestimate his indebtedness to Wittgenstein: in many respects Russell, in these articles, is simply restating the pluralism he had learnt from Moore and from James – whom he described as 'the outstanding critic of monism'. See also what is said of W. E. Johnson in Ch. 6.

30. See Ch. 11; Russell was particularly influenced by Holt and Perry.

31. See E. P. Edwards: 'Are Percepts in the Brain?' (*AJP*, 1942); D. Cory: 'Are Sense-Data "in" the Brain?' (*JP*, 1948). See also Ch. 20.

32. See E. Götlind: *Bertrand Russell's Theories of Causation* (1952); A. C. Ewing, R. I. Aaron, D. G. C. MacNabb: 'The Causal Argument for Physical Objects' (*PASS*, 1945).

33. See especially his comments on M. Weitz's contributions to *The Philosophy of Bertrand Russell*.

34. W. Hay: 'Bertrand Russell on the Justification of Induction' (*PSC*, 1950); N. Malcolm: 'Russell's *Human Knowledge*' (*PR*, 1950); H. Reichenbach: 'A Conversation between Bertrand Russell and David Hume' (*JP*, 1949).

Notes

CHAPTER 10

1. See the memoir by A. S. L. Farquharson in *Statement and Inference*; memorial articles by H. A. Prichard (*Mind*, 1919) and H. W. B. Joseph (*PBA*, 1915); R. Robinson: *The Province of Logic: An Interpretation of Certain Parts of Cook Wilson's 'Statement and Inference'* (1931); the chapter on Cook Wilson in C. R. Morris: *Idealistic Logic* (1933); John Anderson: 'The Science of Logic' (*AJP*, 1933).

2. See E. J. Furlong: 'Cook Wilson and the Non-Euclideans' (*Mind*, 1941). For a later attempt to 'exemplify' knowledge, under Cook Wilson's influence, see R. I. Aaron: *The Nature of Knowing* (1930).

3. This is perhaps the most generally influential of all Cook Wilson's teachings. See, to mention the less obvious examples, G. F. Stout: 'Immediacy, Mediacy and Coherence' (*Mind*, 1908 and *Studies*); G. Ryle: 'Are

There Propositions?' (*PAS*, 1929); W. Kneale: *Probability and Induction* (1949). For criticism see D. R. Cousin: 'Some Doubts about Knowledge' (*PAS*, 1935) and John Laird: *Knowledge, Belief and Opinion* (1930).

4. See the symposium by W. Kneale and G. E. Moore: 'Is Existence a Predicate?' (*PASS*, 1936) which brings out the opposition between Moore and the Cook Wilsonians on 'attributes'.

5. Berkeley's theory of vision had been attacked by S. Bailey in his *A Review of Berkeley's Theory of Vision* (1842) and by T. K. Abbott in his *Sight and Touch* (1864). But it had lost none of its potency and was still the 'received view' among psychologists. There is a brief account of Bailey's and Abbott's criticism of Berkeley in a review by J. O. Wisdom in *BJPS*, 1953.

6. See E. F. Carritt: 'Professor H. A. Prichard: Personal Recollections' (*Mind*, 1948); H. H. Price's memorial notice in *PBA*, 1947.

7. It has often been said, I do not know with what justification, that Prichard was here the master and Cook Wilson the disciple. Certainly there is no hint of this in Prichard's own publications. See also Prichard's discussion of Descartes in *Knowledge and Perception*, which is a careful restatement of Cook Wilson's theory of knowledge.

8. See particularly his 'A Criticism of the Psychologist's Treatment of Knowledge' and Stout's reply 'Mr Prichard's Criticism of Psychology' (both in *Mind*, 1907). See also Prichard's attack on Ward in *Knowledge and Perception*.

9. See the obituary notice by H. A. Prichard in *Mind*, 1944.

10. *PBA*, 1929, reprinted in *Ancient and Modern Philosophy*, 1935. See also 'On Occupying Space' (*Mind*, 1919).

11. The finest flowers, on the scholarly side, of the Aristotelianism which Case and Cook Wilson revived are the Oxford Translations of Aristotle (1909-31) and the magnificent editions of major works by Aristotle prepared by W. D. Ross. Apart from his contributions to scholarship, Ross has been mainly interested in ethics: he, Prichard and Joseph are the main figures in Oxford moral theory. On the Aristotelian atmosphere of Oxford in the early years of the present century, see the remarks in E. Barker's autobiography: *Age and Youth*, 1953.

12. For a detailed account of this book, see the review by A. R. M. Murray (*Mind*, 1933). See also R. M. Yost: 'Price on Appearing and Appearances' (*JP*, 1964).

13. But see also his 'Some Considerations about Belief' (*PAS*, 1934) for Price's qualms on this subject.

14. See C. W. K. Mundle's discussion in *PQ* (1954) and R. J. Burgener: 'Price's Theory of the Concept' (*RM*, 1958).

Notes

CHAPTER 11

1. On Realism generally, see *RIP* (1938); R. B. Perry: *Present Philosophical Tendencies* (1912); R. P. Kremer: *La théorie de la connaissance chez 'es néo-réalistes anglais* (1928) and *Le néo-réalisme américaine* (1920); R. W. Sellars: 'Current Realism in Great Britain and the United States' (*Monist*, 1927); A. K. Rogers: *English and American Philosophy Since 1800* (1922); L. Boman: *Criticism and Construction in the Philosophy of the American New Realism* (1955); R. M. Chisholm: *Realism and the Background of Phenomenology* (1960, with bibliography).

2. *PAS*, 1909; Schiller is his fellow-symposiast. See also Nunn's book *The Aims and Achievements of Scientific Method* (1907).

3. 'Primary and Secondary Qualities' (1903) and 'Are Presentations Mental or Physical?' (1908), both in *PAS*.

4. Commonsense, to Peirce, must be our starting-point; so far Peirce and Moore would be of the one mind. But any *particular* commonsense doctrine, Peirce also says, may turn out to be false, even although commonsense as a whole can never be abandoned. See R. M. Chisholm on 'Fallibilism and Belief' in *Studies in the Philosophy of C. S. Peirce* (ed. P. P. Wiener and F. H. Young, 1952); J. Buchler: *Charles Peirce's Empiricism* (1939); W. B. Gallie: *Peirce and Pragmatism* (1952).

5. Montague in 'Professor Royce's Refutation of Realism' (*PR*, 1902) and Perry in 'Professor Royce's Refutation of Realism and Pluralism' (*Monist*, 1902). Compare James's attack on 'vicious intellectualism' (p. 108 above). See also Montague's 'Story of American Realism' (*Phil.*, 1937, reprinted in *Twentieth-Century Philosophy*, ed. D. D. Runes, 1943); R. B. Perry: 'W. P. Montague and the New Realists' (*JP*, 1954); obituaries of Perry by C. I. Lewis (*PPR*, 1957) and G. Deledalle (*Études Philosophiques*, 1957).

6. This was an age of manifestos, in philosophy, in literature, and in politics. There are interesting points of comparison between *The New Realism* and the *Imagist Anthology* (ed. Ezra Pound, 1914). Contrast G. Ryle: 'On Taking Sides' (*Phil.*, 1937).

7. Perry is the most devoted and scholarly of commentators on James; and he described Mach's *Analysis of Sensations* as 'among the classics of modern realism'. See Holt's *The Concept of Consciousness* (1914) and Perry's *Present Philosophical Tendencies*.

8. Woodbridge was invited, but refused, to join the New Realist group. They saw in his articles, particularly in 'The Concept of Consciousness' (*JP*, 1905), a post-Jamesian realism akin to their own. See his 'Confessions' in *Contemporary American Philosophy* (Vol. II). His influence was mainly exerted through his teaching and his occasional articles; his major book is *The Realm of Mind* (1926). For a brief account of his philosophy, see H. T.

Costello: 'The Naturalism of Frederick Woodbridge' (*Naturalism and the Human Spirit*, ed. Y. H. Krikorian, 1944).

9. Montague attempted to construct a synthesis of realism, subjectivism, and 'critical realism'. This is an ambition characteristic of much American philosophy, with its fondness for odd combinations of '-isms'. The contributions to *Contemporary American Philosophy* bear such titles as 'problematic realism', 'personal realism', 'empirical idealism', 'temperamental realism'. On the whole, the American philosopher has expected to find himself with a system on his hands, which he is quite happy to label as an '-ism', in sharp contrast with his contemporary British colleagues, who prefer to think of themselves as remote from the clamour of schools and are more than a little offended when their critics refuse to take this disclaimer at its face-value. The sociologist may find ground for reflection in this contrast. Montague's epistemology is summed up in *The Ways of Knowing* (1925). The dialogue at the end of that book, participated in by a new realist, a critical realist and an Idealist – with Montague as Hylonous the *true* realist, reconciling their differences – is a useful presentation of the principal points at issue in the epistemological controversies of the present century, even if Hylonous is insufferably superior. For Spaulding, see his *The New Rationalism* (1918), and for Marvin, *A First Book in Metaphysics* (1912).

10. One of a notable group of expatriates, of whom Gilbert Murray and Grafton Elliot Smith are perhaps the best known. Alexander likes to insist that his metaphysics is 'democratic' in spirit; it is not absurd to suggest that his Australian origins had a certain effect upon his revolt against Absolutism in metaphysics. It so happens that Alexander's work has been important in the development of Australian philosophy; the school centred on John Anderson in the University of Sydney owes much to the naturalistic and realistic tendencies in his argument. Many of those who have been in close contact with Anderson's work – not only his pupils and disciples – regard it as the most systematic presentation of a Realist philosophy. But he published only a few highly compressed articles brought together (with an introduction by J. A. Passmore) as *Studies in Empirical Philosophy* (1962). See in *AJP* Ryle: G. 'Logic and Professor Anderson' (1950) and J. L. Mackie's reply (1951), together with J. L. Mackie: 'The Philosophy of John Anderson' (1962). For Australian philosophy generally see J. A. Passmore: 'Philosophy' in *The Pattern of Australian Culture* (ed. A. L. McLeod, 1963). The writings of J. L. Mackie, P. H. Partridge, T. A. Rose, A. R. Walker, A. J. Baker, J. B. Thornton, G. F. McIntosh, D. M. Armstrong, J. A. Passmore, reveal in varying degrees Anderson's influence, which extends also into political philosophy, aesthetics and jurisprudence. For Alexander generally, see P. Devaux: *Le Système d'Alexander* (1929); J. M. McCarthy: *The Naturalism of Samuel Alexander* (1948); obituary notices by J. Laird (*PBA*, 1938), J. H. Muirhead (*Phil.*, 1939), G. F.Stout (*Mind*, 1940), A. Boyce Gibson (*AJP*, 1938); articles by G. F. Stout on 'The Philosophy of S. Alexander' (*Mind*, 1940); H. B. Loughnan on 'The Empiricism of Dr Alexander' (*AJP*, 1931) and 'Emergence and the Self' (*Monist*, 1936); John Laird's preface to Alexander's *Philosophical and Literary Pieces* (1939); A. P. Stiernotte: *God and Space-Time in the*

Philosophy of Alexander (1954); B. T. Brettschneider: *The Philosophy of Samuel Alexander* (1964).

11. See his 'Foundations and Sketch-Plan of a Conational Psychology' (*Br. Jnl. Psych.*, 1911). Alexander thought he had learnt his conational psychology from Stout. But Stout thought otherwise. See his 'A Criticism of Alexander's Theory of Mind and Knowledge' (*AJP*, 1944) and 'Professor Alexander's Theory of Sense-Perception' (*Mind*, 1922).

12. See John Anderson: 'The Non-Existence of Consciousness' (*AJP*, 1929); C. J. Ducasse: 'Introspection, Mental Acts, and Sensa' (*Mind*, 1936).

13. In, for example, his *Instinct and Experience* (1912). Although Lloyd Morgan and Alexander stood shoulder to shoulder on many issues, Lloyd Morgan was not a Realist. For a brief statement of his philosophical position see 'A Philosophy of Evolution' (*CBP*, I); his philosophical ideas are worked out at greater length in his Gifford Lectures, *Emergent Evolution* (1923) and *Life, Mind and Spirit* (1926).

14. A doctrine of this sort, which has its roots in Aristotle, had been maintained by that unorthodox novelist and publicist, Samuel Butler, in such works as *Life and Habit* (1877), composed at a time when the new orthodoxy was Darwinism. It was adapted for his own special purposes by Bernard Shaw in *Man and Superman* (1903) and *Back to Methuselah* (1921). The best known philosophical version of vitalism is Bergson's *Creative Evolution* (1907) in which the 'life force' appears as 'élan vital'. The theory of 'entelechies', as presented by the philosopher-biologist Hans Driesch in his *Science and Philosophy of the Organism* (1908), is another variety of the same mode of thought. See also the statesman J. C. Smuts: *Holism and Evolution* (1936).

15. At this point, Alexander stands very close to Dewey and to Marx – in the long run, that is, to Hegel. See P. H. Partridge: 'The Social Theory of Truth' (*AJP*, 1936).

16. A doctrine similar in certain respects had been maintained by physicists like Minkowski and Einstein. But Alexander's theory of Space-Time was arrived at, he says, by independent metaphysical speculation; he is glad to have the support of physics but makes no direct use of physical theory. Nor does he wholly accept the new physical conceptions. Indeed, one can easily detect two different approaches to Space-Time in Alexander, one relativist, the other not. See especially A. E. Murphy: 'Alexander's Metaphysics of Space-Time' (*Monist*, 1927); articles on *Space, Time and Deity* by C. D. Broad (*Mind*, 1921) with Alexander's reply 'Some Explanations'; G. Dawes Hicks (*Hibbert Jnl.*, 1921); R. B. Haldane (*Nature*, 1920); D. Emmet: 'Time is the Mind of Space' (*Phil.*, 1950).

17. See particularly Alexander's essay on 'The Historicity of Things' (in *Philosophy and History* ed. R. Klibansky and H. J. Paton, 1936). This is in many ways a very useful account of Alexander's metaphysics, less encumbered with complications than *Space, Time and Deity*.

18. There are, however, different threads in Alexander's theory of relations, which this brief account conceals. For something more satisfactory, see Murphy's *Monist* articles.

19. See Alexander's 'Natural Piety' (*Hibbert Jnl.*, 1922, reprinted in *Philosophical and Literary Pieces*, 1939).

20. For a presentation of this view, see particularly 'Some Explanations', and for criticism see Broad and Murphy (*op. cit.*). If we cut a cube into slices, Alexander argues, the slices do not 'add themselves together' to a cube; they are not, as separate slices, obviously slices of a cube. In contrast, if we move around a cube and take perspectives of it these perspectives overlap – 'one cries out for the next to complete it'. In the same way, spatio-temporal perspectives 'demand' Space-Time for their completion, as slices of simultaneous events would not.

21. See W. S. Urquhart's obituary in *PBA*, 1946.

22. Kemp Smith's first important contribution to scholarship, his *Studies in the Cartesian Philosophy* (1902), had already played a considerable part in the development of realism by drawing attention to weak points in the Cartesian dualism. See A. C. Ewing: 'N. K. Smith' (*PBA*, 1959).

23. See 'A Realist Philosophy of Life' in *CBP* II and, for a longer version, *Matter, Life, and Value* (1929).

Notes

CHAPTER 12

1. In Germany, a variety of 'Critical Realism' was maintained by A. Riehl as early as 1887. See the historical note in J. B. Pratt: *Personal Realism* (1937) and Ueberweg (Vol. 4) on 'Die realistische Richtung'. For Pratt himself see *Self, Religion and Metaphysics* (ed. G. E. Myers, 1961). See also in that volume R. W. Sellars: 'American Realism'.

2. His *Synthetica* (1906) was an intensely personal attempt to be an Idealist in metaphysics but a Realist in epistemology. See J. B. Baillie: 'Professor Laurie's Natural Realism' (*Mind*, 1908–9), and the writings of Laurie's French disciple G. Remacle, especially *La Philosophie de S. S. Laurie* (1909).

3. See Ch. 4 above. Pringle-Pattison's *Balfour Lectures on Realism* appeared in *The Philosophical Review* (1892–4) shortly after their delivery, but were not published in book form until 1933. See the accompanying memoir and John Laird's review in *Mind*, 1934.

4. See Sorley's introductory memoir; and articles on Adamson by H. Jones (*Mind*, 1902), G. Dawes Hicks (*Mind*, 1904), D. A. Rees (*PQ*, 1952). Like Seth, Adamson had come under Lotze's influence. Lotze's dictum: 'It is only inquiries conducted in the spirit of realism which will satisfy the aspirations of Idealism' could stand as the motto of Adamson's philosophical investigations. In the United States, G. S. Fullerton's *A System of Metaphysics* (1904) belongs to the same movement of ideas. See E. A. Singer on Fullerton in *JP* (1925).

5. See W. G. de Burgh's memorial notice in *PBA*, 1941.

6. See Dawes Hicks and Moore on 'Are the Materials of Sense Affections

of the Mind?' (*PAS*, 1916). On his theory of the cognitive act see the symposium in *PAS* (1920) with contributions by Laird, Moore, Broad and Dawes Hicks.

7. See the articles on Lovejoy in *JHI* (1948) and *PPR* (1963) together with A. J. Reck: 'The Philosophy of A. O. Lovejoy' (*RM*, 1963).

8. See Santayana on Strong in *The Philosophy of G. Santayana* (ed. P. Schilpp, 1940); W. P. Montague: 'Mr C. A. Strong's Creed for Sceptics' (*JP*, 1938).

9. See the account of Sellars by J. L. Blau: *Men and Movements in American Philosophy* (1952); Sellars: 'A Statement of Critical Realism' (*RIP*, 1938); and the symposium on the work of Sellars in *PPR* (1954), together with Sellars' reply (1955).

10. Thus Russell is the only British contributor to *The Philosophy of George Santayana* (ed. P. A. Schilpp, 1940). Santayana's reputation in Great Britain has mainly been at the level of 'Great Thoughts' or 'Gems from Santayana', to which his epigrammatic style admirably lends itself. A Sydney newspaper once referred to 'the Eastern Sage, Santayana'. See G. W. Howgate. *George Santayana* (1938); the Santayana number of *JP* (1954) and *RIP*, 1963; other articles in the former journal include S. P. Lamprecht: 'Santayana, Then and Now' (1928) and 'Naturalism and Agnosticism in Santayana' (1933); J. H. Randall: 'The Latent Idealism of a Materialist' (1931); see also M. R. Cohen in *Cambridge History of American Literature* (Vol. IV, 1917–21); D. L. Murray: 'A Modern Materialist' (*PAS*, 1911). Santayana's autobiographical volumes *Persons and Places* (1944–9) can also be consulted for both pleasure and profit.

11. See H. M. Kallen: 'America and the Life of Reason' (*JP*, 1921).

12. See that remarkable summary account of his philosophy, the *Apologia pro Mente Sua* appended to *The Philosophy of George Santayana*.

13. See his Herbert Spencer lecture on 'The Unknowable' (1923).

14. See *Freedom and Reason: Studies in Philosophy and Jewish Culture in Memory of Morris Raphael Cohen*, ed. S. W. Baron, E. Nagel, K. S. Pinson, 1951; Cohen's posthumously published autobiography: *A Dreamer's Journey*, 1949; L. D. Rosenfield: *Portrait of a Philosopher* (1962); E. Nagel's obituary in *JHI* (1957) and bibliographical supplement to *JHI* (1958).

15. For his views on Dewey's subordination of ontology to morals, see his 'Some Difficulties in Dewey's Anthropocentric Naturalism' (*PR*, 1940). His social interests lay particularly in the field of legal philosophy. See his *Law and the Social Order* (1933).

16. See D. J. Bronstein: 'The Principle of Polarity in Cohen's Philosophy' (in *Freedom and Reason*).

17. Best known for his contributions to *University of California Publications in Philosophy*, volumes of essays issued by the Department of Philosophy in the University of California since 1904, each volume centring on a single topic.

18. Brought together as *Sovereign Reason* (1954) and *Logic without Metaphysics* (1957). Nagel's *The Structure of Science* (1961) is restricted to more purely methodological topics. See Chapter 20.

19. See 'Towards a Naturalistic Conception of Logic' (*American Philosophy Today and Tomorrow*, ed. M. Kallen and S. Hook, 1935) as well as 'Logic Without Ontology' in *Naturalism and the Human Spirit*.

20. See his *Survey of Symbolic Logic* (1918), together with the amendments and corrections in Appendix II to C. I. Lewis and C. H. Langford: *Symbolic Logic* (1932). His system has paradoxes of its own – the 'paradoxes of strict implication'. If, for example, it is logically impossible for q to be false, then, clearly, it is logically impossible for p to be true and q to be false, i.e. any proposition whatsoever implies those propositions which are necessarily true. But these paradoxes, according to Lewis, do not conflict with our intuitive logical feelings. See also W. Kneale: 'Truths of Logic' (*PAS*, 1945).

21. See P. Devaux: 'Le pragmatisme conceptuel de C. I. Lewis' (*RMM*, 1934); J. B. Pratt: 'Logical Positivism and Professor Lewis' (*JP*, 1934).

22. See C. G. Hempel's review (*JSL*, 1947).

Notes

CHAPTER 13

1. See *Bernard Bosanquet and his Friends* (ed. J. H. Muirhead). Webb summarizes his views in 'Outlines of a Philosophy of Religion' (*CBP*, II).

2. See p. 114 above, and criticisms of *The Nature of Truth* by R. F. A. Hoernlé and B. Russell (*Mind*, 1906); G. E. Moore (*Mind*, 1907); G. Dawes Hicks (*Hibbert Jnl.*, 1907); L. A. Reid: 'Correspondence and Coherence' (*PR*, 1922).

3. See his 'Philosophy as the Development of the Notion and Reality of Self-Consciousness' (*CBP*, II).

4. See G. Marchesini: *La vita et il pensiero di R. Ardigo* (1907). Most of Spaventa's work was posthumously published (1901) by Gentile.

5. See G. de Ruggiero: *Modern Philosophy* (1912), trans. by A. H. Hannay and R. G. Collingwood (1921).

6. H. Wildon Carr: *The Philosophy of Benedetto Croce* (1917); R. Piccoli: *Benedetto Croce: An Introduction to his philosophy* (1922); C. Sprigge: *Benedetto Croce* (1952); the Croce number of *RIP* (1953). There are lengthy bibliographies in G. Castellano: *Benedetto Croce* (1936) and in *L'opera filosofica, storica e letteraria di Benedetto Croce* (1942). For a brief statement by Croce of his own philosophical position see 'My Philosophy', translated as part of a volume of essays with that title by E. F. Carritt (1949).

7. An enthusiastic ex-businessman who made his way through the Aristotelian Society to the Professorship in Philosophy at King's College, London, to which he was appointed at the age of sixty-one (1918); in 1925 he moved to the University of Southern California at Los Angeles. His own philosophy was an eclectic Idealism of a monadistic, Leibnizian, kind, so that he fitted happily into the 'personalist' atmosphere at Los Angeles. See his *A Theory of Monads* (1922) and *Cogitans Cogitata* (1930). But he is best

known for his work in introducing first Bergson and then Italian Idealism to a British audience.

8. The title Croce gave to a short work which was later revised and incorporated in *Saggio sullo Hegel* (1913). Croce habitually published his writings in a preliminary form, usually in the proceedings of a learned society, and then revised them for publication as a book. In both text and bibliography I have quoted the date of first publication in book-form, following the 'Cronologia delle opere del Croce' included in Volume 75 of *La Letteratura Italiana* (1951).

9. Italian philosopher of history, who greatly influenced the Italian Idealists, See Croce's *The Philosophy of G. B. Vico* (1911, trans. by R. G. Collingwood, 1913); and the translation of Vico's *Autobiography* by H. Fisch and G. Bergin (1944). The philosophical framework of Joyce's *Finnegan's Wake* derives from Vico.

10. Compare P. Romanell: *Croce versus Gentile* (1947), with bibliography. See also R. W. Holmes: *The Idealism of G. Gentile* (1937); C. Pellizi: 'The Problem of Religion for the Modern Italian Idealists' (*PAS*, 1923).

11. See E. W. F. Tomlin: *R. G. Collingwood* (1953); R. B. McCallum, T. M. Knox, I. A. Richmond in *PBA* (1943); T. M. Knox's preface to *The Idea of History* (1946); G. Ryle: 'Mr Collingwood and the Ontological Argument' (*Mind*, 1935); C. J. Ducasse: 'Mr Collingwood on Philosophical Method' (*JP*, 1936); A. D. Ritchie: 'The Logic of Question and Answer' (*Mind*, 1943); E. E. Harris: 'Collingwood on Eternal Problems' (*PQ*, 1951). This essay is included, in a revised form, in Harris's *Nature, Mind, and Modern Science* (1954) which is an attempt to show that modern developments in science presuppose a philosophy very like Collingwood's earlier theories, not at all the empiricism which most 'scientifically-minded' philosophers avow. See also G. R. Mure: 'Benedetto Croce and Oxford' (*PQ*, 1954).

12. For Collingwood's later thought see A. Donagan: *The Later Philosophy of R. G. Collingwood* (1962).

13. He translated two books by Croce, and two by Ruggiero. Compare what he says about Croce in *The Idea of History* (written 1936, although not published until 1946) with his own doctrine in the *Autobiography*. But Collingwood would have agreed with Croce that to talk of 'influence' is to treat the development of human thinking as if it were subject to mechanical pushes; one can be influenced only by that with which one already largely sympathizes. Croce, incidentally, criticized *Speculum Mentis* on the ground that it did not allow sufficient 'distinctness' to the activities of the human spirit.

14. See Ch. 8 above. See also John Wisdom: *Problems of Mind and Matter* (1934); C. D. Broad's review of *Mind and Matter* (*Mind*, 1932).

15. 'The Nature of Universals and Propositions' (*PBA*, 1921, reprinted in *Studies*) and 'Universals Again' (*PASS*, 1936). See also bibliographical note in *God and Nature* (footnote, p. 77). For criticism, see the symposium 'Are the Characters of Particular Things Universal or Particular?' with contributions by G. E. Moore, G. F. Stout, G. Dawes Hicks (*PASS*, 1923); N. K. Smith: 'The Nature of Universals' (*Mind*, 1927); H. Knight: 'Stout

on Universals' (*Mind*, 1936); R. I. Aaron: 'Two senses of the word "Universal"' (*Mind*, 1939); D. J. O'Connor: 'Stout's Theory of Universals' (*AJP*, 1949).

16. See N. K. Smith's articles on 'The Nature of Universals'; G. Ryle: 'Plato's *Parmenides*' (*Mind*, 1939).

17. His more recent *The Modern Predicament* (1955) is devoted to the philosophy of religion; the only ground for religious belief, he argues, is religious experience, in contradistinction from theological reasoning. But philosophy can at least, he thinks – in the manner of Kant's arguments for the 'thing-in-itself' – show that the world as science sees it does not really exhaust reality. See the critical review by A. B. Gibson in *RM*, 1956.

18. See C. D. Broad: 'Professor Hallett's *Aeternitas*' (*Mind*, 1933).

19. See, for example, C. A. Campbell: *Scepticism and Construction* (1931); A. D. Ritchie: *The Natural History of Mind* (1936); John MacMurray: *The Boundaries of Science* (1931) and contributions to *PAS* by D. M. MacKinnon. Most of these philosophers spent part of their philosophical career south of the border, but Scotland has provided them with a congenial atmosphere. The difference in tone between *Mind* and the (Scottish) *Philosophical Quarterly* (1950–) is unmistakable. At Cambridge, A. C. Ewing, better known as an ethical theorist, has maintained a variety of Idealism with some resemblance to Stout's. See his *Idealism: A Critical Survey* (1934).

20. The two volumes of *Contemporary American Idealism* (ed. G. P. Adams and W. P. Montague) contain a number of brief philosophical testaments, with bibliographies, by leading American Idealists, of whom G. P. Adams, that indomitable Absolutist M. W. Calkins, and G. Watts Cunningham are perhaps the best known. The dedication is to G. H. Palmer, a colleague at Harvard of James, Royce and Santayana, and a much-admired teacher. See also *Contemporary Idealism in America* (ed. C. Barrett, 1932). Of other contemporary American metaphysicians, outside the Idealist stream, one of the most discussed is C. J. Ducasse, whose *Nature, Mind and Death* (1951) sums up a long series of philosophical articles. He is particularly well-known as an ethical theorist and an aesthetician; the general thesis he sustained in his *Philosophy as a Science* (1941) – that philosophy concerns itself with the rational basis for appraisals – has not attracted many as a general definition of philosophy, but has aroused more interest as a description of ethics in particular. But Ducasse has also written freely about such topics as causality – where he defends the thesis that causal propositions are *necessary*, but not in the rationalist's sense of 'necessity' – and about the relation between mind and body. See particularly the symposium on his work in *PPR*, 1952.

21. See A. J. Reck: 'The Philosophy of Brand Blanshard' (*Tulane Studies*, 1964); E. Nagel: *Sovereign Reason* (1954); H. Khatchadourian: *The Coherence Theory of Truth* (1961). In *Reason and Analysis* (1962) Blanshard develops his metaphysical ideas in opposition to contemporary 'analytical philosophies'.

22. Blanshard excepts W. Mitchell's *Structure and Growth of the Mind*

(1907), which Bosanquet and Hoernlé had greeted enthusiastically on its first appearance. This is the only attempt to deal in detail with nineteenth-century psychology from a post-Bradleian point of view.

23. J. E. Smith: 'Beyond Realism and Idealism: An Appreciation of W. M. Urban' (*RM*, 1953).

24. This is an approach to metaphysics which has had a certain vogue in recent years, partly under neo-scholastic influence, as a way of defending metaphysics against its positivist critics. See for example, E. Bevan: *Symbolism and Belief* (1938); D. M. Emmet: *The Nature of Metaphysical Thinking* (1945) – the most substantial exposition of the analogical approach to metaphysics; A. N. Whitehead: *Symbolism: its Meaning and Effect* (1928), to which Emmet is much indebted. On the neo-scholastic theory, see M. Penido: *Le Rôle de l'analogie en théologie dogmatique* (1931); together with the works on Thomism mentioned below.

25. *The Philosophy of Ernst Cassirer* (ed. P. A. Schilpp, 1949); see also C. W. Hendel's preface to the English translation (1953) of *The Philosophy of Symbolic Forms* (1923). S. Langer's *Philosophy in a New Key* (1942) is a lively and independent working out of a 'philosophy of culture', largely based on Cassirer but drawing as well on other sources, especially Whitehead – and couched, on the whole, in less metaphysical terms.

26. See for example, the essays by I. K. Stephens and W. C. Swabey in *The Philosophy of Ernst Cassirer*.

27. Cassirer's work was taken over by E. A. Burtt in his influential *Metaphysical Foundations of Modern Physical Science* (1925).

28. Compare W. M. Solmitz: 'Cassirer on Galileo' in *The Philosophy of Ernst Cassirer*.

29. As might be expected, however, there are signs of a certain sympathy between some members of the post-Wittgenstein 'linguistic' movement and neo-scholasticism; the minute distinctions of scholastic analyses have come back into favour. Similarly, the revival of formal logic has brought with it an interest in the work of scholastic logicians. That interest was apparent in the writings of C. S. Peirce; more recently A. N. Prior has emphasized the resemblances between medieval and recent logic. See, for example, his *Formal Logic* (1955). For the attitude of English philosophers generally to neo-scholasticism, see J. S. Zybura: *Present-Day Thinkers and the New Scholasticism* (1926).

30. For bibliography, see P. Mandonnet and J. Destrez: *Bibliographie Thomiste* (1921) and V. J. Bourke: *Thomistic Bibliography, 1920–40* (1945). As an introduction to Thomism see A. G. Sertillanges: *Foundations of Thomistic Philosophy* (1928, English translation 1931); E. Gilson: *Le Thomisme* (1920), English translation as *The Philosophy of St Thomas Aquinas* (1924), and *The Spirit of Medieval Philosophy* (1932); G. van Riet: *Thomistic Epistemology* (1946; English translation 1965). For a brief account of the neo-scholastic revival, with references, see I. M. Bochenski: *Europaïsche Philosophie der Gegenwart* (1947; English translation 1956); for details on the first years of the revival, J. L. Pernier: *The Revival of Scholastic Philosophy in the Nineteenth Century* (1908). See also F. Aveling:' The Thomistic Outlook in Philosophy' (*PAS* 1923). Important neo-scholastic

journals include *The New Scholasticism, Dominican Studies* and the Journal of the *Institut supérieur de philosophie* at Louvain.

31. See C. A. Fecher: *The Philosophy of Jacques Maritain* (1953).

32. See the Brunschvicg number of *RIP* (1951) and of *RMM* (1945). On French Idealism generally see A. Etcheverry: *L'idéalisme français contemporain* (1934).

33. See O. Samuel: *A Foundation of Ontology, a Critical Analysis of Nicolai Hartmann,* (1954) and ed. R. Heimsoeth and R. Heiss: *Nicolai Hartmann, der Denker und sein Werk* (1952). It is still vigorous, too, in the United States especially in the work of Paul Weiss whose *Modes of Being* (1958) sets out to develop a metaphysics which shall incorporate, as partial illustrations, all that has been true in the metaphysical systems of the past. Stephen Pepper in his *World Hypotheses* (1942) is less optimistic about the possibility of developing an all-embracing metaphysics. He defends, rather, a 'reasonable eclecticism' which recognizes the need for keeping constantly before one's mind each of the main types of metaphysical theory in the course of trying to understand the world. For criticism see Manley Thompson: 'Metaphysics' in R. M. Chisholm *et al.: Humanistic Scholarship in America: Philosophy* (1964).

34. The three great philosophers of recent times, according to Bochenski, are Maritain, Hartmann and Whitehead. No remark could more aptly summarize the abyss between contemporary French-German-Latin and contemporary British philosophy, even if there are individual writers on both sides of the Channel who do not share the judgements of their countrymen. However, it is already apparent that Wittgenstein, with his sage-like manner, is far more assimilable to German taste than is, let us say, Ryle or Russell. He is studied in German universities which otherwise completely ignore British philosophy since Hume.

Notes

CHAPTER 14

1. For a comparison between Mach and Berkeley see K. R. Popper: 'A Note on Berkeley as Precursor of Mach', *BJPS* (1953).

2. Delivered 1870, posthumously published in *Lectures and Essays* (1879).

3. See the 1946 edition, with an introduction by J. R. Newman and a preface by Bertrand Russell.

4. Reprinted in *Mind* (1876, 1878) and in his *Popular Lectures on Scientific Subjects* (1865, English translation 1873). See on Helmholtz, V. F. Lenzen: 'Helmholtz's Theory of Knowledge' (in *Studies and Essays in Honour of George Sarton,* ed. M. A. Montagu, 1944).

5. See E. S. Pearson: 'K. Pearson, an Appreciation' (*Biometrika,* 1938).

6. At the same time, Pearson refers freely to Mach. To try to establish priorities as between Clifford, Pearson and Mach would be pointless.

7. See the discussion between J. Smart and P. Foulkes in *AJP* (1951-2).

8. See the Poincaré number of *RMM* (1913); T. Dantzig: *Henri Poincaré* (1954).

9. For example E. Le Roy. See his 'The Logic of Invention' (*RMM*, 1905). A species of conventionalism had been already applied to Chemistry by G. Milhaud in his *Le Rationnel* (1898). For French methodology generally – it is a branch of philosophy which is particularly active in France – see A. Lalande: 'Publications in the Philosophy of the Sciences brought out since 1900' in *Philosophical Thought in France and the United States* (ed. M. Farber, 1950). V. Lenzen in *The Nature of Physical Theory* (1931) and A. Pap in *The A Priori in Physical Theory* (1946) have tried to reconcile conventionalism with empiricism by arguing that 'extensively confirmed' hypotheses come to function as conventions; although subsequent experience, even then, *can* overthrow them. See also C. Lewy's review of Pap (*Mind*, 1947).

10. See Duhem's review of A. Rey, *La Théorie de la physique chez les physiciens contemporains* (1907), added as an appendix to the second edition (1914) of his most important work, *Physics: its Object, its Structure* (1906, English translation 1954).

11. See G. Boas: *A Critical Examination of the Philosophy of E. Meyerson* (1930); A. E. Blumberg: 'E. Meyerson's Critique of Positivism' (*Monist*, 1932); L. de Broglie's memorial essay in *Matter and Light* (1937, English translation 1939).

12. For details see A. Einstein and L. Infeld: *The Evolution of Physics* (1938); W. Wilson: *A Hundred Years of Physics* (1950).

13. A noteworthy exception is the experimentalist N. R. Campbell whose *Physics: the Elements* (1920) is particularly important for the account it offers of the relation between physical laws and physical theories. His chapter on 'The Structure of Theories' can be read in H. Feigl and M. Brodbeck: *Readings in the Philosophy of Science*. Campbell's work is not often referred to in recent methodological writings – a striking exception is R. B. Braithwaite's *Scientific Explanation* – but he is greatly admired and closely read by a considerable number of the younger British philosophers.

14. See the discussion in *Einstein: Philosopher-Scientist* (*Library of Living Philosophers*, ed. P. A. Schilpp, 1949).

15. As examples, see M. Planck: *Where is Science Going?* (1932, English translation 1933); W. Heisenberg: *Philosophic Problems of Nuclear Science* (1935, English translation 1952); M. Born: *Natural Philosophy of Cause and Chance* (1949); L. de Broglie: *Matter and Light* (1937, English translation 1939); H. Margenau: *The Nature of Physical Reality* (1950); H. Weyl: *The Philosophy of Mathematics and Natural Science* (augmented edition, 1949, of the 1926 German text).

16. As well as being an exceptionally distinguished statesman, Lord Haldane was the author of a long series of philosophical works, of which *The Pathway to Reality* (1903–4) is the most substantial. It is interesting to note that in *The Reign of Relativity* he urges upon British industry the importance of embarking upon an inquiry into the possibility of harnessing atomic energy; this sudden appearance of farsighted practicality within a

framework of Idealist metaphysics is typical of the man. See A. S. Pringle-Pattison's 'Obituary' in *PBA*, 1928.

17. See the Eddington memorial lectures by A. D. Ritchie (1948), E. Whittaker (1951), H. Dingle (1954); G. D. Hicks: 'Professor Eddington's "Philosophy of Nature"' (*PAS*, 1928); N. R. Campbell: 'The Errors of Sir Arthur Eddington' (*Phil.*, 1931); E. Whittaker: *From Euclid to Eddington* (1949); J. W. Yolton: *The Philosophy of Science of A. S. Eddington* (1960); J. Witt-Hansen: *Exposition and Critique of the Conceptions of Eddington* (1958).

18. See S. Stebbing: *Philosophy and the Physicists* (1937); P. Frank: *Interpretations and Misinterpretations of Modern Physics* (1938); the symposia on 'The New Physics and Metaphysical Materialism' (*PAS*, 1942) and 'Realism and Modern Physics' (*PASS*, 1929); E. Nagel: *Sovereign Reason* (1954).

19. See, for works based upon it, B. F. Skinner: *The Behaviour of Organisms* (1938); C. C. Pratt: *The Logic of Modern Psychology* (1939); the special number of the *Psychological Review* on 'Operationism in Psychology' (1945). The most thorough study is A. C. Benjamin: *Operationism* (1955). See also *The Validation of Scientific Theories* (ed. P. Frank, 1957). The Italian group of methodologists, publishers of the journal *Methodos* (1952), combine ideas derived from Bridgman with certain of the doctrines of the German ontological-methodologist Hugo Dingler.

20. Even so, anything shorter than V. Lowe: 'The Development of Whitehead's Philosophy' in *The Library of Living Philosophers: Alfred North Whitehead* (ed. P. A. Schilpp, 1941) is bound to be misleading. See also A. H. Johnson: *Whitehead's Theory of Reality* (1952, with a lengthy bibliography of critical articles); D. Emmet: *Whitehead's Philosophy of Organism* (1932), 'A. N. Whitehead' (*PBA*, 1947), 'A. N. Whitehead, the Last Phase' (*Mind*, 1948); W. W. Hammerschmidt: *Whitehead's Philosophy of Time* (1947); E. P. Shahan: *Whitehead's Theory of Experience* (1950); Miller, D. L. and Gentry. G.: *The Philosophy of A. N. Whitehead* (1938); V. Lowe, C. Hartshorne, A. H. Johnson: *Whitehead and the Modern World* (1950); I. Leclerc: *Whitehead's Metaphysics* (1958); W. A. Christian: *An Interpretation of Whitehead's Metaphysics* (1959); ed. I. Leclerc: *The Relevance of Whitehead* (1961); the Whitehead number of *RIP* (1961); V. Lowe: *Understanding Whitehead* (1962); W. E. Stokes: 'A Selected and Annotated Bibliography of A. N. Whitehead' (*Modern Schoolman* 1962).

21. See W. V. O. Quine: 'Whitehead and the Rise of Modern Logic' in Schilpp, *op. cit.*; C. I. Lewis: *Survey of Symbolic Logic*.

22. See Ch. 9 above. For an appreciation of Whitehead's share in *Principia Mathematica* see B. Russell: 'Whitehead and Principia Mathematica' (*Mind*, 1948). See also Whitehead's essay on 'The Organization of Thought' (1916), reprinted in the book with that title (1917) and in *The Aims of Education* (1929).

23. First published in *Philosophical Transactions of the Royal Society* (1906); reprinted in F. S. C. Northrop and M. W. Gross: *Alfred North Whitehead: An Anthology* (1953).

24. See the lectures of 1915–17 reprinted in *The Organisation of Thought*.

25. See also Whitehead's contribution to the symposium 'Time, Space and Material' (*PASS*, 1919). Broad's summary in his review (*Mind*, 1920) has been widely read as authoritative, although it unduly emphasizes what one might call, without disrespect, the 'Cambridge' side of Whitehead's philosophy of science.

26. The most important application in Whitehead's philosophy of the methods employed in *Principia Mathematica*. See for details *The Principles of Natural Knowledge* (Pt. III); *The Concept of Nature* (Ch. IV); *Process and Reality* (Pt. IV).

27. See L. S. Stebbing, R. B. Braithwaite, D. M. Wrinch: 'Is the "fallacy of simple location" a fallacy?' (*PASS*, 1927).

28. See W. E. Agar: *A Contribution to the Theory of the Living Organism* (1943) for a philosophy of biology worked out under Whitehead's influence. As we have already seen (Ch. 11) biologists, as well as physicists, have been driven into philosophy by difficulties arising out of their own scientific inquiries. See, for example, C. Sherrington: *Man on his Nature* (1940); J. S. Haldane: *The Philosophy of a Biologist* (1935); L. Hogben: *The Nature of Living Matter* (1930).

Notes

CHAPTER 15

1. Part I in 1921; Part II, with the sub-title *Demonstrative Inference: Deductive and Inductive*, in 1922; Part III, *The Logical Foundations of Science*, in 1924. Sections of the projected Part IV on Probability were posthumously published in *Mind*, 1932. See the note by 'A.D.' in *Mind*, 1932; C. D. Broad: 'W. E. Johnson' (*PBA*, 1931) and his critical review of Part II (*Mind*, 1922) and Part III (*Mind*, 1924); H. W. B. Joseph: 'What does Mr Johnson mean by a Proposition?' (*Mind*, 1927–8); A. N. Prior: 'Determinables, Determinates and Determinants' (*Mind*, 1949). Logic books which make use of Johnson's work include R. M. Eaton: *General Logic, an Introductory Survey* (1931); C. A. Mace: *The Principles of Logic* (1933); L. S. Stebbing: *A Modern Introduction to Logic* (1930).

2. See R. F. Harrod's *The Life of J. M. Keynes* (1951), not only for Keynes but for the atmosphere of the Moral Science Faculty at Cambridge.

3. See also the preface to H. Jeffreys: *Scientific Inference* (1931).

4. See *The Philosophy of C. D. Broad* (ed. P. A. Schilpp, 1959) and the review by R. Brown (*AJP*, 1962). In his *Sense-Perception and Matter* (1953), M. Lean has critically examined certain of Broad's statements about perception, a topic to which Broad has given great attention. See also, for discussions of Broad's theory of time, J. D. Mabbott: 'Our Direct Experience of Time' (*Mind*, 1951); C. W. K. Mundle's reply: 'How Specious is the Specious Present?' (*Mind*, 1954); R. M. Blake: 'Mr Broad's Theory of Time' (*Mind*, 1925).

5. See his contribution to *CBPI*, 'Critical and Speculative Philosophy'; *Scientific Thought* (1923); 'Some Methods of Speculative Philosophy' (*PAS*, 1947).

6. First published in *Philosophy* (1949), reprinted in *Religion, Philosophy and Psychical Research* (1953). See, in the same volume, 'Henry Sidgwick and Psychical Research' for the earlier history of psychical research at Cambridge. See, for example, A. G. N. Flew: *A New Approach to Psychical Research* (1953); H. H. Price: 'Some Philosophical Questions about Telepathy and Clairvoyance' (*Phil.*, 1940); M. Kneale, R. Robinson, C. W. K. Mundle: 'Is Psychical Research Relevant to Philosophy?' (*PASS*, 1950). See also Broad's *Lectures on Psychical Research* (1962) and H. H. Price's review (*Mind*, 1964).

7. The translation, one should add, is extraordinarily bad. It was re-translated by D. F. Pears and B. F. McGuiness in 1961.

8. Commentaries on the *Tractatus* include the commentary in G. C. M. Colombo's Italian translation and G. E. M. Anscombe: *Introduction to Wittgenstein's Tractatus* (1959); E. Stenius: *Wittgenstein's Tractatus* (1960); A. Maslow: *A Study in Wittgenstein's Tractatus* (1961); M. Black: *Companion and Critique of Wittgenstein's Tractatus* (the most detailed, 1964); D. Favrholdt: *Interpretation and Critique of Wittgenstein's Tractatus* (1964); J. P. Griffin: *Wittgenstein's Logical Atomism* (1964). Help can be derived from G. K. Plochmann and J. B. Lawson: *Terms in their Propositional Contexts in Wittgenstein's Tractatus; an Index* (1962) and the edition of Wittgenstein's *Note-books 1914–16* by G. E. M. Anscombe and H. G. von Wright (1961). See also D. A. T. Gasking: 'Anderson and the Tractatus Logico-Philosophicus: an Essay in Philosophical Translation' (*AJP*, 1949); J. R. Weinberg: *An Examination of Logical Positivism* (1936); M. Black: *Language and Philosophy* (1949); the critical notice by F. P. Ramsey in *Mind* (1923), reprinted in *Foundations of Mathematics* (1931); Russell's Introduction to the English edition of the *Tractatus*; G. Pitcher: *The Philosophy of Wittgenstein* (1964); J. Hartnack: *Wittgenstein and Modern Philosophy* (trans. M. Cranston 1965); J. O. Urmson: *Philosophical Analysis* (1956). On Wittgenstein generally, see the memorial notices by D. A. T. G[asking] and A. C. J[ackson] (*AJP*, 1951); G. Ryle (*Analysis*, 1951); J. Wisdom (*Mind*, 1952); B. Russell (*Mind*, 1951); K. Britton (*Cambridge Jnl.*, 1954); G. von Wright (*PR*, 1955); N. Malcolm, *Ludwig Wittgenstein: A Memoir* (1958).

9. It is a matter of controversy whether these objects are all of them particulars, or whether they include properties and relations. See I. M. Copi: 'Objects, Properties and Relations in the *Tractatus*', (*Mind*, 1958) and his review of Stenius's commentary (*PR*, 1963). G. E. M. Anscombe replies in *Mind* (1959). See also D. Keyt: 'Wittgenstein's Notion of an Object' (*PQ* 1963).

10. For discussion of this point, and as illustration of the difficulties which arise in interpreting Wittgenstein, see E. Daitz: 'The Picture Theory of Meaning' (*Mind*, 1953) and, in reply, E. Evans: 'Tractatus 3.1432' (*Mind*, 1955). See also D. Keyt: 'Wittgenstein's Picture Theory of Language' (*PR*, 1964).

11. Wittgenstein makes use of the work of an American logician, H. M. Sheffer, who, in 'A set of five independent postulates for Boolean Algebra' (*Trans. Am. Math. Soc.*, 1913) proved that all the truth-functions of a

proposition can be constructed out of simultaneous denial (*not-p and not-q*). Sheffer has published little, but has been an influential teacher. See *Structure, Method and Meaning: Essays in Honour of Henry M. Sheffer*, ed. P. Henle (1951). For a clear account of the truth-table method and Sheffer's 'stroke-notation' see P. F. Strawson: *Introduction to Logical Theory* (1952). Cf. p. 136 above on Johnson. Independently, E. L. Post and Lukasiewicz hit on 'truth-table' methods in 1920.

12. See W. H. Watson: *On Understanding Physics* (1938), for a theory of physics worked out under the influence of the *Tractatus*. S. Toulmin's *The Philosophy of Science* (1953) is a detailed application of Wittgenstein's point of view, worked out in a way which brings Toulmin close to Duhem; in particular, he sharply distinguishes between physical laws and empirical generalizations, between 'physics' and 'natural history'. See reviews by E. Nagel (*Mind*, 1954), and H. Dingle (*Phil.*, 1955).

13. Best known as a philosophical psychologist, who continues the work of Brentano and Stout, he has as well a lively awareness of contemporary philosophy. His *Principles of Logic* (1933) was one of the first text-books written along Cambridge lines, and he has written a number of articles on the relation between thought and language. For this period in the history of British philosophy, see J. O. Urmson: *Philosophical Analysis* (1956).

14. For specimens, apart from those mentioned in this chapter, see Ch. 9, footnote 12, p. 560.

15. Her *A Modern Introduction to Logic* (1930) did much to introduce modern logic, particularly as taught at Cambridge, to a wider audience. She wove together threads from Moore, Russell, Johnson, Whitehead and Broad. In her *Philosophy and the Physicists* (1937) she delivered a broadside, in the name of commonsense, against the speculations of Jeans and Eddington. See various references in *Philosophical Studies: Essays in Memory of L. Susan Stebbing* (1948); E. D. Bronstein: 'Miss Stebbing's Directional Analysis and Basic Facts' (*Analysis*, 1934).

16. See also, however, L. S. Stebbing: 'Logical Constructions and Know-ledge through Descriptions' (*Proc. of 7th Internat. Cong. of Phil.*, 1930). How much of what Stebbing and Wisdom wrote in these years derived from Moore's lectures I do not know: according to their own avowals, a great deal.

Notes

CHAPTER 16

1. For a full account of its formation and subsequent history see V. Kraft: *The Vienna Circle* (1950, English translation 1953) and O. Neurath: 'Le développement du Cercle de Vienne et l'avenir de l'empirisme logique' (*Actualités*, 1935). The phrase 'The Vienna Circle' dates back to 1928; the Circle's 'programme' was published in 1929 as 'Wissenschaftliche Weltauf-fassung der Wiener Kreis'; its main medium of publicity was the journal *Erkenntnis* (1930), renamed for 1939–40 *The Journal of Unified Science*.

The best-known members of the group were M. Schlick, R. Carnap, F. Waismann, O. Neurath, H. Feigl, B. von Juhos, F. Kaufmann, H. Hahn, K. Menger, K. Gödel. It worked in close association with the 'Society of Empirical Philosophy' at Berlin, which included as members H. Reichenbach – joint editor with Carnap of *Erkenntnis* – F. Kraus, W. Dubislav, K. Grelling. See also A. J. Ayer: *Logical Positivism* (1959) which includes a useful collection of essays by logical positivists and a lengthy bibliography; R. Carnap's intellectual autobiography in the *Philosophy of Rudolf Carnap* (ed. P. A. Schilpp, 1963); P. Frank: *Modern Science and its Philosophy* (1949).

2. What Wittgenstein may have told Schlick and Waismann can be gathered partly from his paper 'Some Remarks on Logical Form' (*PASS*, 1929), partly from the manuscripts brought together as *Philosophische Bemerkungen* (ed. R. Rhees, 1965) which date back to 1929–30.

3. But cf. John Anderson: 'Empiricism' (*AJP*, 1927).

4. The anti-metaphysical mathematician, H. Hahn, first drew the Circle's attention to the *Tractatus*. See his *Logique, mathématique, et connaissance de la réalité* (*Actualités*, 1935) and 'Die Bedeutung der wissenschaftlichen Weltauffassung' (*Erk.*, 1930). See P. Frank's obituary of Hahn (*Erk.*, 1934).

5. By Blumberg and Feigl: 'Logical Positivism' (*JP*, 1931). Schlick preferred the name 'consistent empiricism'. See also J. R. Weinberg: *An Examination of Logical Positivism* (1936); C. W. Morris: *Logical Positivism, Pragmatism and Scientific Empiricism* (*Actualités*, 1937); G. Bergmann: *The Metaphysics of Logical Positivism* (1954); R. von Mises: *Positivism* (1939, English translation, 1951); J. Jørgensen: 'The Development of Logical Empiricism' (*US*, 1951); L. S. Stebbing: 'Logical Positivism and Analysis' (*PBA*, 1933); E. Nagel: 'Analytic Philosophy in Europe' (*JP*, 1936); W. H. Werkmeister: 'Seven Theses of Logical Positivism Critically Examined' (*PR*, 1937); B. von Juhos: 'Principles of Logical Empiricism' (*Mind*, 1937); J. A. Passmore: 'Logical Positivism' (*AJP*, 1943, 1944, 1948); H. Feigl: 'Logical Empiricism' (*Twentieth-Century Philosophy*, ed. D. D. Runes, 1943); W. T. Stace: 'Positivism' (*Mind*, 1944); T. Storer: 'An Analysis of Logical Positivism' (*Methodos*, 1951).

6. By D. A. T. G[asking] and A. C. J[ackson], (*AJP*, 1951). But compare *Philosophische Bemerkungen* (1965), for his views in 1930.

7. Schlick's 'Positivismus und Realismus' (*Erk.*, 1932) is another early statement. See the commentary by D. Rynin attached to a French translation of this article in *Synthèse*, 1948. See, as well as general works on logical positivism, C. I. Lewis: 'Experience and Meaning' (*PR*, 1934); L. S. Stebbing, A. E. Heath, L. J. Russell: 'Communication and Verification' (*PASS*, 1934); M. Black: 'The Principle of Verifiability' (*Analysis*, 1934); E. Nagel: 'Verifiability, Truth and Verification' (*JP*, 1934); W. T. Stace: 'Metaphysics and Meaning' (*Mind*, 1935); C. J. Ducasse: 'Verification, Verifiability and Meaningfulness' (*JP*, 1936); G. Ryle: 'Unverifiability-by-Me' (*Analysis*, 1936); A. C. Ewing: 'Meaninglessness' (*Mind*, 1937); M. Lazerowitz: 'The Principle of Verifiability' (*Mind*, 1937) and 'Strong and Weak Verification' (*Mind*, 1939); J. Wisdom: 'Metaphysics and Verification' (*Mind*, 1938); I. Berlin: 'Verification' (*PAS*, 1938); D. MacKinnon, F. Waismann,

W. C. Kneale: 'Verifiability' (*PASS*, 1945); special numbers of *RIP* in 1950, 1951; C. G. Hempel: 'Conceptions of Cognitive Significance' in his *Aspects of Scientific Explanation* (1965).

8. See his 'L'école de Vienne et la philosophie traditionnelle' (*Actualités*, 1937). See also F. Waismann's preface to Schlick's *Gesammelte Aufsätze, 1926–36*, and obituary notices by H. Reichenbach (*Erk.*, 1936), P. Frank (*Erk.*, 1937) and H. Feigl (*Erk.*, 1939).

9. *Publications in Philosophy*, ed. The College of the Pacific (1932).

10. See the lectures on 'Form and Content' delivered in London in 1932, not published by Schlick himself, but printed in *Gesammelte Aufsätze*. In essentials, Schlick had already worked out his epistemology in his pre-Wittgenstein *Allgemeine Erkenntnislehre* (1918).

11. In America it inspired the work of Nelson Goodman whose *The Structure of Appearance* (1951) includes an illuminating critical account of Carnap's book. On Goodman's own attempt at a 'constructional' philosophy, see the critical notice by M. Dummett (*Mind*, 1955); G. Bergmann: 'Two types of Linguistic Philosophy' (*RM*, 1952, and *The Metaphysics of Logical Positivism*, 1954); V. Lowe and H. Wang on Goodman's conception of an individual, and C. G. Hempel's review (all in *PR*, 1953). See also N. Goodman: 'The Significance of *Der Logische Aufbau der Welt*' in *The Philosophy of Rudolf Carnap* (ed. P. A. Schilpp, 1963).

12. For the controversy between Schlick and Neurath, see *Actualités* (1935), which includes a French translation of Schlick's 'Über das Fundament der Erkenntnis' – the article which particularly aroused Neurath's hostility – 'Facts and Propositions', and Schlick's essay 'Sur les constatations'. See also Neurath's reply in 'Le développement du cercle de Vienne', C. G. Hempel's criticism of Schlick in 'The logical positivist's theory of truth' (*Analysis*, 1935), and B. von Juhos: 'Empiricism and Physicalism' (*ibid.*). This latter article illustrates the reaction of the more orthodox positivists to Neurath's innovations.

13. Note also the resemblance between what Neurath says and James's theory of reality (Chapter 5). Logical positivism acclimatized very easily in America; Schlick was invited to lecture there in the late twenties and a number of the leading positivists (Carnap, Bergmann, Feigl, Frank) settled in America when the persecutions began in Germany and Austria. C. W. Morris has especially devoted himself to acting as liaison-officer between pragmatism and positivism. See his 'Logical Positivism, Pragmatism and Scientific Empiricism' (*Actualités*, 1937).

14. The distinction between natural and spiritual sciences, as we have already seen (Chapter 4, Note 16), was widely accepted on the Continent of Europe, although it made little headway in England. A sociologist by training, Neurath was particularly concerned to combat the view that sociology is by its nature not an empirical inquiry. The 'thesis of the unity of science' stood very near to his heart. He organized congresses in its name – five of them, fully reported in *Erkenntnis*, in the years 1934–40 – and was editor-in-chief of the *Encyclopedia of Unified Science* (1938–). His philosophical position was never worked out in detail: agitation was his *forte*. See Vouillemin's introduction to Neurath's 'Le développement du Cercle de Vienne';

H. M. Kallen's obituary in *PPR* (1946); J. Laird on Neurath in *Chambers'
Encyclopedia* (1950). For physicalism generally see C. A. Mace: 'Physicalism'
(*PAS*, 1936) and Feigl's article in *The Philosophy of Rudolf Carnap*.

15. First published in *Erk.*, 1932 under the title 'Die physikalische Sprache
als Universalsprache der Wissenschaft'; translated into English as a *Psyche
Miniature* in 1934.

16. A Pap: 'Reduction Sentences and Disposition Concepts' in *The
Philosophy of R. Carnap*.

17. On this question, see also N. Malcolm: 'Certainty and Empirical
Statements' (*Mind*, 1942); P. Henle: 'On the Certainty of Empirical State-
ments', and W. T. Stace: 'Are all Empirical Statements Hypotheses?'
(*JP*, 1947).

18. On the whole, Ayer has been 'logical positivism' to conservative
British critics; C. E. M. Joad in his *Critique of Logical Positivism* (1950)
scarcely refers to anybody else. *Language, Truth and Logic* contains little
that is unfamiliar to readers of Continental positivism; but it created something of a sensation in England where such familiarity was by no means
widespread, and even the positivism of Clifford and Pearson seems to have
been forgotten. People heard with a sense of shock that metaphysical propositions are neither true nor false, but nonsense.

19. See L. Stebbing: *Logical Positivism and Analysis* and M. Black:
'Relations between Logical Positivism and the Cambridge School of
Analysis' (*Jnl. Unified Science*, 1939).

20. A similar view had already been adopted, under Wittgenstein's
influence, by G. A. Paul in his 'Is there a problem about sense-data?'
(*PASS*, 1936, reprinted in *LL* 1). This article has the status of a *locus
classicus* in recent epistemological discussion. Paul otherwise wrote little,
but was an influential teacher, both in England and in Australia, to which
country he introduced the teachings of Wittgenstein.

21. For subsequent controversy on this point see Ayer's 'The Terminology
of Sense-Data' in *Mind*, 1945 (reprinted in *Philosophical Essays*, 1954) and
the literature referred to therein.

22. See, for other contemporary discussions of this subject, articles on
phenomenalism in *PAS* by R. B. Braithwaite (1937), G. F. Stout (1938),
R. I. Aaron (1938), D. G. C. McNabb (1940), W. F. R. Hardie (1945), and
Ayer's second thoughts (1946). An elaborate phenomenalism is presented
by W. T. Stace in his *The Theory of Knowledge and Existence* (1932).

23. On basic propositions see also Ayer's essay in *Philosophical Analysis*,
ed. M. Black (1950), republished in *Philosophical Essays*.

24. See J. A. Passmore: *Hume's Intentions* (1952).

25. See for criticism A. Church in *JSL*, 1949.

26. See for the earlier view A. J. Ayer, C. H. Whiteley, M. Black: 'Truth
by Convention' (*Analysis*, 1936); see also N. Malcolm: 'Are Necessary
Propositions really Verbal?' (*Mind*, 1940); A. C. Ewing: 'The Linguistic
Theory of *a priori* Propositions' (*PAS*, 1939); W. C. Kneale, K. Britton, J.
O. Urmson: 'Are Necessary Truths True by Convention?' (*PASS*, 1947).

27. A. Pap: *Semantics and Necessary Truth* (1959).

28. For Ayer's defence of private languages see 'Can there be a private

language?' (*PASS*, 1954) and 'Privacy' (*PBA*, 1959), both reprinted in *The Concept of a Person* (1963).

29. See also Ayer's 'Basic Propositions' (*Philosophical Analysis*, ed. M. Black, 1950, reprinted in *Philosophical Essays*.)

30. See also 'Statements about the Past' (*PAS*, 1951) and 'Our Knowledge of Other Minds' (*Theoria*, 1953), both in *Philosophical Essays*. For Ayer's criticism of Carnap see 'Carnap's Treatment of the Problem of Other Minds' (*The Philosophy of Rudolf Carnap*, ed. P. A. Schilpp, 1963).

31. See A. P. Griffiths: 'Ayer on Perception' (*Mind*, 1960). In *The Problem of Knowledge*, Ayer defines sense-data more carefully and more narrowly than in his earlier writings.

32. H. Reichenbach: 'Logistic Empiricism in Germany' (*JP*, 1936).

Notes

CHAPTER 17

1. There are signs, however, that British philosophers are beginning to feel a new interest in symbolic logic; that is why I have included a brief guide for such philosophical explorers. I do not pretend that what I have written is an adequate account of a vast, diversified and difficult literature. For this consult the extensive reviews and bibliographies in *JSL*. See also R. Feys: 'Directions nouvelles de la logistique aux États-Unis' (*Revue néo-scholastique de philosophie*, 1946); M. Boll and J. Reinhart: 'Logic in France in the Twentieth Century' (in *Philosophical Thought in France and the United States*, ed. M. Farber, 1950); Hao Wang: *A Survey of Mathematical Logic* (1963); H. Mehlberg: 'The present Situation in the Philosophy of Mathematics' in *Logic and Language* (Synthèse Library, 1962); *Essays on the Foundations of Mathematics* (A. A. Fraenkel Festschrift, 1961). See also bibliography on p. 549 above.

2. See Chapter 9, p. 222 for the theory of types; that the Russellian axioms could be reduced to a single axiom was first shown by J. Nicod in 'A Reduction in the Number of the Primitive Propositions of Logic' (*Proceedings of the Cambridge Philosophical Society*, 1917).

3. For the points in dispute see M. Black: *The Nature of Mathematics* (1933); ed. F. Gonseth: *Philosophie Mathématique* (Actualités, 1939); the more technical discussion in S. C. Kleene: *Introduction to Metamathematics* (1952) and S. Körner: *The Philosophy of Mathematics* (1960).

4. See D. Hilbert: 'On the Foundations of Logic and Arithmetic' (*Monist*, 1905); D. Hilbert and P. Bernays: *Grundlagen der Mathematik* (1934, 1939); D. Hilbert and W. Ackermann: *Principles of Mathematical Logic* (1928; English translation of second edition with notes by R. F. Luce, 1950); H. B. Curry: *Outlines of a Formalist Philosophy of Mathematics* (1951). Attempts have also been made to formalize empirical sciences. See particularly the works of J. H. Woodger. His *The Technique of Theory Construction* (*US*, 1939) is a good introduction to the whole field. The formalist point of view is most fully worked out in his *Axiomatic Method*

in Biology (1937). His *Biology and Language* (1952) is somewhat less wedded to the axiomatic approach; it discusses a number of important problems in the methodology of experimental science. For a formalized psychology, see C. L. Hull: *Principles of Behaviour* (1943).

5. Gödel's essay 'Über formal unentscheidbare Sätze der *Principia Mathematica* und verwandter Systeme' appeared in *Monatshefte für Mathematik und Physik;* his argument is extended to other cases by A. Church in 'A Note on the Entscheidungsproblem' (*JSL*, 1936). See also B. Rosser: 'An Informal Exposition of proofs of Gödel's Theorems and Church's Theorem' (*JSL*, 1939); J. N. Findlay: 'Gödelian sentences; a non-numerical approach' (*Mind*, 1942); E. Nagel and J. R. Newman: *Gödel's Proof* (1959). For later discussions (with bibliography) see A. Tarski: *Undecidable Theories* (1953) and W. Ackermann: *Solvable Cases of the Decision Problem* (1954). The 'decision problem', or 'Entscheidungsproblem', is the problem of laying down the conditions under which a proposition is 'provable'.

6. For the philosophical background to intuitionism see L. E. J. Brouwer: 'Consciousness, Philosophy and Mathematics' (*Proceedings of the Tenth International Congress of Philosophy*, 1949). See also his 'Intuitionism and Formalism' (*Bulletin of the American Mathematical Society*, 1913). See also H. Weyl: *Philosophy of Mathematics and Natural Science* (1949); A. Dresden: 'Brouwer's Contributions to the Foundations of Mathematics' (*Bull. Am. Math. Soc.*, 1924); A. Ambrose: 'Finitism and the Limits of Empiricism' (*Mind*, 1937). Intuitional logic has been formalized by A. Heyting and A. Kolmogoroff. See A. Heyting: *Intuitionism* (1956).

7. Twardowski's emphasis, as a pupil of Meinong, on clear and exact distinctions opened the way in Poland for a revival of interest in logic. The most eminent of his pupils was Jan Lukasiewicz, to whom is due not only the special Polish symbolism, which greatly facilitated the formalization of complex logical relationships, but also very many of the fundamental ideas of the Polish logicians. Out of the same school – the Warsaw school – came Tarski, of whom more later, and S. Lesniewski – whose 'calculus of individuals' has recently attracted a good deal of attention (see, for example, N. Goodman's *The Structure of Appearance* and E. C. Luschei: *Logical Systems of Lesniewski*, 1962). The quite independent school of logicians at Cracow is best known through the work of L. Chwistek, the originator of 'the theory of constructive types' (1914–15). See his *The Limits of Science* (1935) and Chapter 9, Note 23. For details of the Polish school see Z. Jordan: *Philosophy and Ideology* (1963) which contains an extensive bibliography, A. N. Prior's *Formal Logic* (1955), which should be consulted generally for three-value and modal logics, and the same author's Review Article 'Lukasiewicz's Symbolic Logic' (*AJP*, 1952). See also I. Bochenski: *Précis de Logique Mathématique* (1948) which makes clear the relationship between the Polish and the Russellian symbolism. On post-war Polish logic see T. Kotarbinski: 'La Logique en Pologne, 1945–55' (*Les Études Philosophiques*, 1956).

8. His first book (in Polish) was on *The Principle of Contradiction in Aristotelian Logic* (1910). An interest in the relation between modern and ancient

(or medieval) logic has been characteristic of the Polish school and of those logicians who came under its influence. This is obvious in Prior's book, and in a number of the articles mentioned therein. See particularly I. Bochenski: *Ancient Formal Logic* (1951); P. Boehner: *Mediaeval Logic* (1952); J. Lukasiewicz: *Aristotle's Syllogistic* (1951); J. Hintikka: 'The Once and Future Seafight' (*PR*, 1964 with bibliography). For a formalized many-valued logic see J. B. Rosser and A. R. Turquette: *Many-Valued Logics* (1952). See also A. R. Anderson *et al.*: 'Modal and Many-valued logics' (*Boston Studies in the Philosophy of Science*, ed. M. V. Wartofsky 1963).

9. Modal functions had already played a prominent part in C. I. Lewis and C. H. Langford: *Symbolic Logic* (1932), with its emphasis on necessity. See also G. H. von Wright: *Logical Studies* (1957); R. Feys: *Modal Logics* (ed. J. Dopp, 1965).

10. For versions of an imperative logic see E. Mally: *Grundgesetze des Sollens* (1926); J. Jørgensen: 'Imperatives and Logic' (*Erk.*, 1938); A. Hofstadter and J. C. C. McKinsey: 'On the Logic of Imperatives' (*PSC*, 1939); A. Ross: 'Imperatives and Logic' (*PSC*, 1944); R. M. Hare: 'Imperative Sentences' (*Mind*, 1949); A. E. Duncan-Jones: 'Assertions and Commands' (*PAS*, 1951). On questions, see M. L. and A. N. Prior: 'Erotetic Logic' (*PR*, 1955). See G. H. von Wright: *Norm and Action* (1963), together with A. N. Prior: 'The Ethical Copula' (*AJP*, 1951) on 'deontic logic'.

11. See K. R. Popper, W. C. Kneale, A. J. Ayer: 'What can Logic do for Philosophy?' (*PASS*, 1948). On the general question whether there are 'alternative logics', or whether, as both Aristotle and Russell thought, there is a single, true, system of logic, see C. H. Langford: 'Concerning Logical Principles' (*Bull. Am. Math. Soc.*, 1928); P. Weiss: 'On Alternative Logics' (*PR*, 1933); F. Waismann: 'Are there Alternative Logics?' (*PAS*, 1945); C. I. Lewis pp. 294–5 above; E. Toms: 'The Law of Excluded Middle' (*PSC*, 1941); C. I. Lewis: 'Paul Weiss on Alternative Logics' (*PR*, 1934).

12. A good idea of the variety of 'semantics' in recent years can be gained from Max Black's *Language and Philosophy* (1949), which examines most of the semantic writings mentioned in this chapter. I have often had occasion to refer to Black's works in the present volume; written from the point of view of an unattached empiricist, they provide an excellent critical introduction to a great many of the leading problems in contemporary philosophy. The volume of essays collected together by L. Linsky as *Semantics and the Philosophy of Language* (1952) limits itself to more technical essays on such topics as synonymity, truth and meaning.

13. For a vigorous counter-attack see A. N. Prior: 'Entities' (*AJP*, 1954).

14. See Black, Stevenson and Richards: 'A Symposium on Emotive Meaning' (*PR*, 1948); for a criticism of the distinction between 'emotive' and 'descriptive' from an 'ordinary language' point of view, see S. E. Toulmin and K. Baier: 'On Describing' (*Mind*, 1952). There is a sober and substantial analysis of the forms of language in K. Britton: *Communication* (1939). Britton conjoins what he has learnt from Ogden and Richards with considerations derived from the study of Russell, Carnap and John Wisdom.

15. See, as well as Black, C. J. Ducasse: 'Some Comments on C. W.

Morris's *Foundations of the Theory of Signs*' (*PPR*, 1942) and the later controversy between Ducasse and John Wild (*PPR*, 1947). There is an extensive bibliography in Morris's *Signs, Language, and Behaviour* (1946).

16. As 'Der Wahrheitsbegriff in den formalisierten Sprachen' (1936). See also his 'The Semantic Conception of Truth' (*PPR*, 1944) reprinted in Linsky. For Kotarbinski, see R. Rand's article on his work in *Erk.*, 1938 (in German) or, for his metaphysics, 'The Fundamental Ideas of Pansomatism' (*Mind*, 1955), a translation of an article written in 1935. For Lesniewski see C. Lejewski: 'On Lesniewski's Ontology' (*Ratio*, 1958); W. Stegmüller: *Der Wahrheitsproblem und die Idee der Semantik* (1957).

17. See A. Stroll: 'Is Everyday Language Inconsistent?' (*Mind*, 1954) and the literature there referred to; and K. R. Popper: 'Self-Reference and Meaning in Ordinary Language' (*ibid.*).

18. See M. Black: 'The Semantic Definition of Truth' (*Analysis*, 1948) reprinted in *Language and Philosophy*, and 'Carnap on Semantics and Logic' (in *Problems of Analysis*, 1954); J. F. Thomson: 'A Note on Truth' (*Analysis*, 1949); P. F. Strawson: 'Truth' (*ibid.* and see also *PASS*, 1950). For developments of Carnap's semantics and pragmatics see R. M. Martin: *Truth and Denotation* (1958), *The Notion of Analytic Truth* (1959) and *Towards a Systematic Pragmatics* (1959). See articles on Carnap's semantics by R. Feys, J. Myhill, D. Davidson, R. M. Martin in *The Philosophy of Rudolph Carnap* (ed. P. A. Schilpp, 1963).

19. For Carnap's modifications to *The Logical Syntax of Language* see the appendix to *Introduction to Semantics* (1942). In many ways the clearest introduction to his new approach is his *The Foundations of Logic and Mathematics* (*US.*, 1939).

20. See Ryle's review in *Philosophy* (1949). 'My chief impression of this book,' he writes, 'is that it is an astonishing blend of technical sophistication with philosophical naïveté. Its theories belong to the age that waxed with Mill and began to wane soon after the *Principles of Mathematics*.' See also Nagel's review in *JP*, 1948, and Carnap's reply to Ryle and Nagel in 'Empiricism, Semantics and Ontology' (*RIP*, 1950, reprinted in Linsky).

21. First published in *American Mathematical Monthly* (1937); reprinted in a corrected version, with additional material, in *From a Logical Point of View* (1953). See also Chapter 9, Note 23.

22. See his 'Reference and Modality' in *From a Logical Point of View*, and the controversy with Carnap in *Meaning and Necessity*.

23. Both reprinted in *From a Logical Point of View*. See J. J. C. Smart's *Critical Notice* (*AJP*, 1955), and P. F. Strawson: 'A Logician's Landscape' (*Phil.*, 1955). For Quine's *Word and Object* see pp. 517–21 below.

24. See P. T. Geach, A. J. Ayer, W. V. O. Quine: 'On What There Is' (*PASS*, 1951); N. Goodman and W. V. O. Quine: 'Steps Towards a Constructive Nominalism' (*JSL*, 1947) with Quine's note on this paper in the bibliography to *On What There Is*; A. Church: 'The Need for Abstract Entities in Semantic Analysis' (*Proc. Am. Academy of Arts and Sciences*, 1951); R. Carnap: 'Empiricism, Semantics and Ontology' (*RIP*, 1950); G. J. Warnock: 'Metaphysics in Logic' (*PAS*, 1950); W. P. Alston: 'Onto-

logical Commitments' (*PS*, 1958); A. Church: 'Ontological Commitment' (*JP*, 1958).

25. See, in Linsky's *Semantics*, N. Goodman: 'On Likeness of Meaning' (revised version of a paper in *Analysis*, 1949); B. Mates: 'Synonymity' (*University of California Publications*, 1950); M. G. White: *Towards Reunion in Philosophy* (1956). In *Analysis* there are articles on synonymity by C. D. Rollins (1950), P. Wienpahl (1951), J. F. Thomson and L. Meckler (1953). See also H. P. Grice and P. F. Strawson: 'In Defense of a Dogma' (*PR*, 1956); A. Hofstadter: 'The Myth of the Whole' (*JP*, 1954); R. Carnap: 'Meaning and Synonymity in Natural Languages' (*PS*, 1955); D. W. Hamlyn: 'Analytic Truths' (*Mind*, 1956); A. Gewirth: 'The Distinction between Analytic and Synthetic Truths' (*JP*, 1953); P. F. Strawson: 'Propositions, Concepts and Logical Truths' (*PQ*, 1957); A. Pap: *Semantics and Necessary Truth* (1958); E. Pasch: *Experience and the Analytic* (1958); R. M. Martin: *The Notion of Analytic Truth* (1959); G. H. Bird: 'Analytic and Synthetic' (*PQ*, 1961); H. Putnam: 'The Analytic and the Synthetic' (*Minnesota Studies* III, 1962); W. V. Quine: 'Carnap and Logical Truth' in *The Philosophy of Rudolph Carnap*.

26. Cf. W. and M. Kneale: *Development of Logic* on 'natural deduction'.

27. See J. O. Wisdom: *Foundations of Inference in Natural Science* (1952); John Laird: *Recent Philosophy* (1936); V. Kraft: *The Vienna Circle* (1950); W. H. Werkmeister: 'Seven Theses of Logical Positivism Critically Examined' (*PR*, 1937); R. Carnap: 'Testability and Meaning' (*PSC*, 1936–7), and the works by Reichenbach, Carnap, Kneale and Braithwaite mentioned in this chapter. See also the Festschrift edited by M. Bunge: *The Critical Approach to Science and Philosophy* (1964) and discussions of the English version of *The Logic of Scientific Discovery* (1959) by G. J. Warnock (*Mind*, 1960); J. A. Passmore and J. C. Harsanyi (*Phil.* 1960); N. Rescher (*PPR*, 1961); H. Fain (*PSC*, 1961); Y. Bar-Hillel and S. Sambursky (*Isis*, 1960); D. C. Stove (*AJP*, 1960). For a view similar to Popper's which tries to answer what are commonly regarded as major objections to it see S. F. Barker: *Induction and Hypothesis* (1957). Popper's *The Poverty of Historicism* (1957) is an important contribution to the methodology of the social sciences – he is now Professor of Logic and Scientific Method at the London School of Economics – but, again, it would carry us too far from our main themes to survey it in detail.

28. As such, it influenced Carnap in his shift away from 'verifiability' to 'testability'. Neurath, on the other hand, was angrily critical. See his 'Pseudorationalismus der Falsifikation' (*Erk.*, 1935).

29. In a series of articles published in *BJPS* (1954, 1957, 1958), reprinted as Appendix IX to *The Logic of Scientific Discovery*. See also J. Agassi: 'The Role of Corroboration in Popper's Methodology' (*AJP*, 1961).

30. See A. Grünbaum: 'The Falsifiability of Theories: Total or Partial?' in *Boston Studies in the Philosophy of Science* (ed. M. W. Wartofsky, 1962).

31. For a more accurate, formalized, statement of this relationship see Addendum 2 to *Conjectures and Refutations* (1963). For criticisms of the idea of 'severity' see P. C. Gibbons: 'On the Severity of Tests' (*AJP*, 1962); G. Buchdahl: 'Convention, Falsification and Induction' (*PASS*, 1960);

R. H. Vincent: 'Popper on Qualitative Confirmation and Disconfirmation' (*AJP*, 1962).

32. In some sense of the word, he also thinks, such a theory will be the 'simpler' theory. On 'simplicity' see G. Schlesinger: *Method in the Physical Sciences* (1963); the discussion by N. Goodman and others in *PSC* (1961); J. G. Kemeny: 'The Use of Simplicity in Induction' (*PR*, 1953) and 'Two Measures of Complexity' (*JP*, 1955); R. Harré: 'Simplicity as a Criterion of Induction' (*Phil.*, 1959); J. Giedymin: 'Strength, Confirmation, Compatibility' in *The Critical Approach* (ed. M. Bunge, 1964); M. Bunge: *The Myth of Simplicity* (1963).

33. On this question see also J. J. C. Smart: 'The Reality of Theoretical Entities' (*AJP*, 1956); J. B. Thornton: 'Scientific Entities' (*AJP*, 1953); C. F. Presley: 'Laws and Theories in the Physical Sciences' (*AJP*, 1954). E. Nagel in *The Structure of Science* (1961) suggests that we can choose as we please between realist and instrumentalist interpretations of theories. That theoretical terms can always be eliminated was argued by F. P. Ramsey in *The Foundations of Mathematics* (1931) and by W. Craig in 'Replacement of Auxiliary Expressions' (*PR*, 1956). See H. Putnam: 'Craig's Theorem' (*JP*, 1965). For a general view of the controversy see G. Maxwell: 'The Ontological Status of Theoretical Entities' (*Minnesota Studies*, Vol. III, 1962) and other articles in the same volume. See also P. K. Feyerabend: 'Realism and Instrumentalism' in *The Critical Approach* (ed. M. Bunge, 1964) and 'The Meaning of Theoretical Terms' (*PR*, 1965); P. Achinstein: 'The Problem of Theoretical Terms' (*APQ*, 1965) and for a good general discussion, I. Scheffler: *The Anatomy of Inquiry* (1963).

34. Popper has sketched another approach to probability, a 'propensity' theory according to which probability statements are not *about* frequencies, even although they are tested by reference to frequencies, but about properties of the experimental conditions. See especially K. R. Popper: 'The propensity interpretation of the calculus of probabilities' in *Observation and Interpretation* (ed. S. Körner, 1957).

35. For a general account of recent works on probability see E. Nagel: *Principles of the Theory of Probability*, (*US*, 1939); M. G. Kendall: 'On the Reconciliation of Theories of Probability' (*Biometrika*, 1949 – an attempt by a leading statistician to reconcile Keynesian and frequency theories); 'Calcul des Probabilités' (*Actualités*, 1951); and the exceptionally wide-ranging and thorough symposium on probability in *PPR*, 1944–6 (G. Bergmann, R. Carnap, F. Kaufmann, E. Nagel, D. Williams).

36. 'Logische Analyse des Wahrscheinlichkeitsbegriffs'; the same number includes articles on probability by H. Reichenbach, R. von Mises, P. Hertz and H. Feigl.

37. English translation, 1939. See C. D. Broad's review in *Mind* (1937); R. L. Goodstein: 'On von Mises' Theory of Probability' (*Mind*, 1940); the discussions of von Mises in W. Kneale: *Probability and Induction;* criticisms by Waismann and Feigl in *Erk.* (1930). A different version of the frequency theory is worked out by the statistician A. Kolmogoroff in his *Foundations of the Theory of Probability* (1933, English translation 1950). See also the writings of the biologist-statistician R. A. Fisher, especially his

The Design of Experiments (1935) and *Statistical Methods and Scientific Inference* (1956).

38. See also A. H. Copeland: 'Predictions and Probabilities' (*Erk.*, 1936). Popper also worked out a formal definition of 'randomness'. On this theme see also G. B. Keene: 'Randomness' (*PASS*, 1957); N. Rescher: 'The Concept of Randomness' (*Theoria*, 1961); H. E. Kyburg: 'Probability and Randomness' (*Theoria*, 1963).

39. His *Theory of Probability* first appeared (in German) in 1935; the English translation (1949) includes additional material. See the criticisms by B. Russell in *Human Knowledge* (1948). On Russell's own views in that volume see H. Jeffreys: 'Bertrand Russell on Probability' (*Mind*, 1950). There is a more elementary account of Reichenbach's views on probability in his *Experience and Prediction* (1938). See also criticisms of Reichenbach in Popper's *Logic of Scientific Discovery* and by P. Hertz (*Erk.*, 1936); E. J. Nelson: 'Professor Reichenbach on Induction' (*JP*, 1936); E. Nagel's review of *The Theory of Probability* (*Mind*, 1936) and 'Probability and the Theory of Knowledge' (*PSC*, 1939); H. Geiringer: 'Über die Wahrscheinlichkeit von Hypothesen' (*Jnl. Unified Sc.*, 1939); I. P. Creed: 'The Justification of the Habit of Induction' (*JP*, 1940); A. W. Burks: 'Reichenbach's Theory of Probability and Induction' (*RM*, 1951). Replies by Reichenbach follow speedily in each case. On his epistemology see M. Capek: 'The Development of Reichenbach's Epistemology' (*RM*, 1957). See also the essays collected as H. Reichenbach: *The Philosophy of Science* (1959 – with complete bibliography).

40. See his *Logical Foundations of Probability* (1950) which is designed as the first of two volumes. The philosophically interesting parts of this book have been separately published as *The Nature and Application of Inductive Logic* (1951). See reviews and critical discussion by S. Toulmin (*Mind*, 1953); H. von Wright (*PR*, 1951); A. W. Burks (*JP*, 1951); J. G. Kemeny (*RM*, 1951). Kemeny has presented his modifications of Carnap in a relatively elementary form in *A Philosopher Looks at Science* (1959). See also G. Bergmann: 'Some Comments on Carnap's Logic of Induction' (*PSC*, 1946).

41. See *The Continuum of Inductive Methods* (1952) a monograph which is eventually to be absorbed into Volume II of *Probability and Induction*. See articles by J. G. Kemeny, A. W. Burks, H. Putnam and E. Nagel in *The Philosophy of Rudolf Carnap*. Nicod's *Logic of Induction* (1923), republished in *The Foundations of Geometry and Induction* (1930), is an interesting historical link between Keynes and confirmation-theory. Carnap makes considerable use of C. G. Hempel's 'Studies in the Logic of Confirmation' (*Mind*, 1945) and 'A Definition of Degree of Confirmation' (*PSC*, 1945, with P. Oppenheim). Hempel discusses in detail what counts as a 'confirmation' of a hypothesis. He rejects Nicod's view that a confirmation is always of the form 'this is both an *A* and a *B*', where the hypothesis is 'all *A* are *B*', on the ground that it provides neither a necessary nor a sufficient condition of confirmation. If a proposition confirms *p*, he argues, it must also confirm any proposition equivalent to *p*. But whereas 'this is a raven and black' confirms 'if anything is a raven, it is black' it does *not* confirm, on Nicod's

view, the equivalent proposition 'if anything is not black, it is not a raven'. But also, and paradoxically, 'this is not black and not a raven' confirms 'if anything is not black, it is not a raven' and, therefore 'if anything is a raven it is black'. So the existence of any non-black non-raven – e.g. a white swan – confirms the hypothesis that all ravens are black. Hempel tries so to define confirmation as to avoid both these extremes. Revised versions, with additional notes, of Hempel's essays are included in C. G. Hempel: *Aspects of Scientific Explanation* (1965). For criticism of confirmation theory see the controversy between Carnap and Goodman in *PPR*, 1947, and N. Goodman: *Fact, Fiction and Forecast* (1954). Goodman sketches a theory of 'projectibility' by which he hopes to avoid the paradoxes of confirmation theory. See also Popper's discussion of degrees of falsifiability in *The Logic of Scientific Investigation;* F. B. Fitch and A. W. Burks: 'Justification in Science' (ed. M. White: *Academic Freedom and Religion*, 1953); the controversy between Y. Bar-Hillel and Carnap in *BJPS* (1952); J. Hosiasson-Lindenbaum: 'On Confirmation' (*JSL*, 1940); I. J. Good: 'The Paradox of Confirmation' (*BJPS*, 1960–62); the discussion between Hempel and J. N. Watkins (*Phil.*, 1957–8); I. Scheffler: *The Anatomy of Inquiry* (1963); J. L. Mackie: 'The Paradox of Confirmation' (*BJPS*, 1963) which includes a general account of the whole controversy.

42. See also Williams: 'Probability, Induction and the Provident Man' in M. Farber: *Philosophic Thought in France and the United States*, in which Williams relates his position to Carnap's. The symposium on Probability in *PPR* (1944–6) is very largely devoted to criticisms of Williams's temerarious defence of the classical theory of probability. See also reviews by Nagel (*JP*, 1947), Kneale (*Phil.*, 1949), and Black (*JSL*, 1947), with Williams's reply 'On the Direct Probability of Inductions' (*Mind*, 1953).

43. Von Wright, a Finnish philosopher, was for a time Wittgenstein's successor in the Cambridge Chair, but has now returned to Finland. He studied under E. Kaila, who had participated in the discussions of the Vienna Circle. See C. D. Broad: 'Hr. von Wright on the Logic of Induction' (*Mind*, 1944); J. G. Kemeny: 'A Treatise on Induction and Probability' (*PR*, 1953) and the review by H. Jeffreys (*BJPS*, 1953). Wright's views on probability are briefly summarized in his article 'On Probability' in *Mind* (1940).

44. In particular, he restates Mill's methods as 'a logic of conditions'; here he has been influenced by C. D. Broad's 'The Principles of Demonstrative Induction' (*Mind*, 1930).

45. See Broad's review in *Mind* (1950); F. L. Will: 'Kneale's Theories of Probability and Induction' (*PR*, 1954); F. J. Anscombe: 'Mr Kneale on Probability and Induction' and Kneale's reply (*Mind*, 1951).

46. As Peirce had sometimes suggested. See also H. Feigl: 'The Logical Character of the Principle of Induction' (*PSC*, 1934), 'De Principiis non est disputandum' (*Philosophical Analysis*, ed. Black, 1950) and 'On the Vindication of Induction' (*PSC*, 1961). Feigl suggests that although inductive inference cannot be justified, it can be 'vindicated', by showing that it is at least *a* way of predicting the future. (Unlike Kneale he does not commit himself to saying that it is the *best* way.) Compare what was said of Reichen-

bach (p. 417 above). See W. Salmon: 'Vindication of Induction', in *Current Issues on the Philosophy of Science*, ed. H. Feigl and G. Maxwell (1961), together with S. Barker's criticism and Salmon's reply. In his *Problems of Analysis* (1954) Black criticizes the 'practical' defence of induction, in a number of its forms. Black argues that all these 'justifications' turn out to be tautologous; they assert that inductive policies are the only ways of achieving those particular objects the achievement of which distinguishes inductive from other policies. Black himself defends the view that induction can, without circularity, be inductively justified. So also his *Models and Metaphors* (1962) and the criticism by P. Achinstein in a series of articles in *Analysis* (1960, 1962, 1963). For the closely related 'ordinary language' approach to induction see pp. 458 below. For the relation between statistics and induction see also H. Leblanc: *Statistical and Inductive Probabilities* (1962). G. S. Brown in his *Probability and Scientific Inference* (1957) has raised some critical questions about probability theory, but has won few converts. So, from a different standpoint, has R. F. Harrod in *The Foundations of Inductive Logic* (1956) in the course of his defence of inductive reasoning. For recent work on 'subjective probability' and its relation to induction – an approach deriving in the long run from Ramsey – see H. Kyburg: *Probability and the Logic of Rational Belief* (1961) and H. Kyburg and H. Smokler (eds): *Readings in Subjective Probability* (1964).

47. See reviews of Braithwaite's book by L. J. Russell (*Phil.*, 1954) and R. J. Hirst (*PQ*, 1954); A. Shimony: 'Braithwaite on Scientific Method' (*RM*, 1954) and R. C. Coburn: 'Braithwaite's Inductive Justification of Induction'(*PSC*, 1961). Carnap had also paid some attention to the Neyman-Pearson School, but most probability-philosophers read no statisticians except R. A. Fisher. See, for example, J. Neyman and E. S. Pearson: 'The Testing of Statistical Hypotheses in relation to Probabilities *a priori*' (*Proc. Cambridge Phil. Soc.*, 1933) and the work of A. Wald, summed up in his *Statistical Decision Functions* (1950). For the theory of games see J. Neumann and O. Morgenstern: *Theory of Games and Economic Behaviour* (1944).

48. For inductive theory subsequent to Braithwaite see *Induction: Some Current Issues* (ed. H. E. Kyburg and E. Nagel, 1963) and H. E. Kyburg: 'Recent Work in Inductive Logic' (*APQ*, 1964), which includes a bibliography of the copious articles devoted to a working out and criticism of the theories discussed in this chapter. For an indication just how controversial the interpretation of probability still is, see the discussion in *Observation and Interpretation* (ed. S. Körner, 1957).

Notes

CHAPTER 18

1. Of what Wittgenstein taught at Cambridge between 1930, when he began to lecture there, and 1947, when he resigned from the Chair in which he had succeeded Moore, no full record has as yet been published. The 'Blue Book' and the 'Brown Book' first published in 1958 (ed. R. Rhees)

record lectures delivered by Wittgenstein at Cambridge in 1933–5. They circulated in various forms before the publication of *Philosophical Investigations* and were the means by which many of his contemporaries first came to be acquainted with Wittgenstein's later philosophy. So also ed. R. Rhees: *Philosophische Bemerkungen* (1965). These 'remarks' date back to 1930. Wittgenstein's *Philosophical Investigations* is in many respects a very puzzling and controversial work. All I have done is to pick out of that 'album '– as Wittgenstein himself describes it – one or two lines of thought which have exercised a general influence during the last three decades. See also the works on Wittgenstein referred to above (p. 578); G. E. Moore: 'Wittgenstein's Lectures in 1930–3' (*Mind*, 1954–5); J. N. Findlay: 'Some Reactions to Recent Cambridge Philosophy' (*AJP*, 1940–1), and 'Wittgenstein's Philosophical Investigations' (*RIP*, 1953); the reviews by N. Malcolm (*PR*, 1954), P. F. Strawson (*Mind*, 1954), J. N. Findlay (*Phil.*, 1955), P. Feyerabend (*PR*, 1955), P. L. Heath (*PQ*, 1956); G. A. Paul: 'Wittgenstein' in *The Revolution in Philosophy* (G. Ryle and others, 1956); David Pole: *The Later Philosophy of Wittgenstein* (1958); E. K. Specht: *Die Sprachphilosophischen und ontologischen Grundlagen im Spätwerk Ludwig Wittgenstein* (1963).

2. See H. Khatchadourian: 'Common Names and "Family Resemblances" ' (*PPR*, 1958); J. R. Bambrough: 'Universals and Family Resemblances' (*PAS*, 1961); H. Hervey: 'The Problem of the Model Language-Game' (*Phil.*, 1961); R. J. Richman: 'Something Common' (*JP*, 1962); M. Mandelbaum: 'Family Resemblances and Generalization Concerning the Arts' and K. Campbell: 'Family Resemblance Predicates' (*APQ*, 1965).

3. See B. A. Farrell: 'An Appraisal of Therapeutic Positivism' (*Mind*, 1946).

4. If I were asked to mention the two books, apart from the *Tractatus* (and the Frege-Russell tradition it incorporates), most suitable as background reading to the *Philosophical Investigations*, they would be Schlick's *Gesammelte Aufsätze* (especially his lectures on 'Form and Content') and William James's *Principles of Psychology*, supplemented by his *Pragmatism*. Wittgenstein several times refers to James – a rare distinction – but not, I think, quite so as to bring out the nature of his relationship to James. Wittgenstein also refers to the *Confessions* of St Augustine, which admirably illustrate, he thinks, the way in which philosophical problems actually arise. (I had written of James's influence on purely internal evidence. One of his former pupils, Mr A. C. Jackson, tells me that Wittgenstein very frequently referred to James in his lectures, even making on one occasion – to everybody's astonishment – a precise reference to a page-number! At one time, furthermore, James's *Principles* was the only philosophical work visible on his bookshelves.)

5. There has been a good deal of controversy on this point between followers of Carnap and 'ordinary language' philosophers. See, for example, Y. Bar-Hillel: 'Analysis of "Correct" Language' (*Mind*, 1946), and, on Wittgenstein's side, A. Ambrose: 'The Problem of Linguistic Inadequacy' (*Philosophical Analysis*, ed. M. Black, 1950). Reviewers in *JSL* often complain with some acerbity that the writings of British philosophers on logical topics are insufficiently formalized to be discussable. On the

building metaphor see R. Rhees: 'Wittgenstein's Builders' (*PAS*, 1960).

6. See A. J. Ayer and R. Rhees: 'Can there be a Private Language?' (*PASS*, 1954); A. J. Ayer: *The Concept of a Person* (1963); J. J. Thomson: 'Private Languages' (*APQ*, 1964); H. N. Castañeda *et al.*: 'The Private-Language Argument' in *Knowledge and Experience* (ed. C. D. Rollins, 1964); J. W. Cook: 'Wittgenstein on Privacy' (*PR*, 1965); C. S. Chihara and J. A. Fodor: 'Operationism and Ordinary Language' (*APQ*, 1965); W. C. K. Mundle: 'Private Language and Wittgenstein's Kind of Behaviourism' (*PQ*, 1965).

7. The contrast between 'first person' utterances such as 'I am in pain' and 'third-person' utterances such as 'he is in pain' was to be much employed in subsequent 'philosophical psychology'. In G. Ryle's *The Concept of Mind* (1949) such 'first-person' statements are described as 'avowals'. Ryle argues that in their 'primary employment' utterances like '*I* hate', '*I* intend' are not used to give the listener facts about the speaker. Nor are they based on some sort of self-observation by the speaker of his 'inner states'. Rather, they are part of the behaviour characteristic of being in that state. '*He* hates', '*he* intends', in contrast, are statements of the normal, information-giving kind. See also D. Gasking and M. Lean: 'Avowals' (*Analytical Philosophy*, ed. R. J. Butler, 1962); F. E. Sparshott: 'Avowals and their Uses' (*PAS*, 1962). For an alternative, but related, theory of pain see K. E. M. Baier: 'Pains' (*AJP*, 1962). See also J. L. Mackie: 'Are there any incorrigible empirical statements?' (*AJP*, 1963); R. D. Bradley: 'Avowals of Immediate Experience' (*Mind*, 1964). There is a general criticism of Wittgenstein's approach, with special reference to pain, in H. Putnam: 'Brains and Behaviour' (*Analytical Philosophy*, 2nd series, ed. R. J. Butler, 1965).

8. Ed. G. H. von Wright, R. Rhees, G. E. M. Anscombe, trans. G. E. M. Anscombe. It includes only manuscripts from the period 1937–44. Some earlier manuscripts are included in *Philosophische Bemerkungen* (1965).

9. In his *Philosophy of Wittgenstein*, Pitcher excuses himself, on the grounds of not being a specialist in the philosophy of mathematics, from saying anything about Wittgenstein's *Remarks*. For brief expositions and criticisms see: reviews by G. D. Duthie (*PQ*, 1957); R. L. Goodstein (*Mind*, 1957); P. Bernays (*Ratio*, 1959), together with A. Ambrose: 'Wittgenstein on Some Questions in Foundations of Mathematics' (*JP*, 1955); A. R. Anderson: 'Mathematics and the "Language-Game"' (*RM*, 1958); M. Dummett: 'Wittgenstein's Philosophy of Mathematics' (*PR*, 1959); C. F. Kielkopf: *Ludwig Wittgenstein's Remarks on the Foundations of Mathematics* (1965); A. B. Levison: 'Wittgenstein and Logical Laws' (*PQ*, 1964); C. S. Chihara: 'Wittgenstein and the Logical Compulsion' (*PAS*, 1961) and 'Mathematical Discovery and Concept Formation' (*PR*, 1963); J. L. Cowan: 'Wittgenstein's Philosophy of Logic' (*PR*, 1961); B. Stroud: 'Wittgenstein and Logical Necessity' (*PR*, 1965).

10. See also Ch. 15 above. He has written no books since *Problems of Mind and Matter* but has collected his articles together in *Other Minds* (1952), *Philosophy and Psycho-Analysis* (1953) and *Paradox and Discovery* (1965). His work is composed in an unusual style, which keeps close to the

rhythms of his speech, as distinct from the rhythms of written English; it is obscure, therefore, in a unique manner. See D. A. T. Gasking's discussion of Wisdom's philosophy in *AJP*, 1954, to which my own account owes a great deal. For other examples of post-Wittgenstein Cambridge philosophy see the writings of Norman Malcolm, C. Lewy, Alice Ambrose, G. E. M. Anscombe, G. Paul, D. A. T. Gasking. See the two volumes of *Logic and Language* (ed. A. G. N. Flew, 1951 and 1953) and M. Black's collection of essays *Philosophical Analysis* (1950).

11. Wisdom's version of the squirrel example used by James in his *Pragmatism* to make substantially the same point.

12. It strikes one as odd that a philosopher should be called 'Wisdom'; that two bearers of the name should be contemporary philosophers passes beyond the limits of the reasonable; that they should both be interested in psycho-analysis has produced in many minds the justifiable conviction that the two are one. But it must be none the less insisted that J. O. Wisdom of the London School of Economics, who in his *The Unconscious Origin of Berkeley's Philosophy* (1953) has tried to show in detail how it is possible to account in psycho-analytic terms for the peculiarities of Berkeley's philosophy, is not identical with his cousin Professor John Wisdom of the University of Cambridge.

13. For criticism see A. Flew and D. C. Williams in *Psychoanalysis Scientific Method and Philosophy* (ed. S. Hook, 1959) and B. Blanshard in *Metaphysics: Readings and Reappraisals* (ed. W. E. Kennick and M. Lazerowitz, 1966).

14. See M. Weitz: 'Oxford Philosophy' (*PR*, 1953); and for discussions of the precise nature of the appeal to ordinary language, K. Baier: 'The Ordinary Use of Words' (*PAS*, 1951); G. Ryle: 'Ordinary Language' (*PR*, 1953); A. G. N. Flew: 'Philosophy and Language' (*PQ*, 1955). Criticisms include J. A. Passmore: 'Reflections on Logic and Language' (*AJP*, 1952), and 'Professor Ryle's Use of "Use" and "Usage"' (*PR*, 1954); R. M. Chisholm: 'Philosophers and Ordinary Language' (*PR*, 1951) together with N. Malcom's reply 'Philosophy for Philosophers'; the essays in *Clarity is not Enough* (ed. H. D. Lewis, 1963); B. Mates: 'On the Verification of Statements about Ordinary Language' (*Inquiry*, 1958); J. J. Katz and J. A. Fodor: 'What's wrong with the philosophy of language?' (*Inquiry*, 1962). For the controversy between ordinary language philosophers and their critics see *Philosophy and Ordinary Language* (ed. C. E. Caton, 1963). *Ordinary Language* (ed. V. C. Chappell, 1964) is a useful collection. For a general discussion and a fuller bibliography see A. Quinton: 'Linguistic Analysis' in *Philosophy in the Mid-Century* (ed. R. Klibansky, 1958, Vol. II.) See also *La Philosophie Analytique*, Cahiers de Royaumont, IV (1962) for discussions between ordinary language and continental philosophers. The very great difference between Oxford ordinary language philosophy and logical positivism can be seen in G. J. Warnock's 'Verification and the Use of Language' (*RIP*, 1951) and in Ryle's review of Carnap's *Meaning and Necessity* (*Phil.*, 1949). See also the essays by P. F. Strawson and G. J. Warnock in *The Revolution in Philosophy* (1956). Recent Oxford philosophy is 'ordinary language' in two senses: first, in contrast with the formalized

writings of symbolic logicians, Oxford philosophers discuss logical issues in an informal way, without recourse to special invented languages, and secondly they believe that a consideration of 'What we ordinarily say' is at least a useful preliminary to the discussion of philosophical problems. But these points of agreement cover a great many disagreements about the precise importance of formalized logics, and the extent to which the detailed investigation of usages is *itself* of philosophical interest.

15. For criticism, see J. J. C. Smart: 'A Note on Categories' (*BJPS*, 1953), in which he argues that on Ryle's showing no two expressions would belong to the same category; A. J. Baker: 'Category Mistakes' (*AJP*, 1956); Manley Thompson: 'On Category Differences' (*PR*, 1957); R. C. Cross: 'Category Differences' (*PAS*, 1958); B. Harrison: 'Category Mistakes and Rules of Language' (*Mind*, 1965); J. A. Passmore: *Philosophical Reasoning* (1961).

16. Compare Russell's 'theory of types'.

17. See also Ryle's 'Heterologicality' (*Analysis*, 1950); J. L. Mackie and J. J. C. Smart: 'A Variant of the "Heterological" Paradox' (*ibid.* 1952).

18. See N. R. Hanson: 'Professor Ryle's "Mind"' (*PQ*, 1952).

19. See particularly S. Hampshire's review (*Mind*, 1950). Hampshire, one of the most versatile and unorthodox of recent Oxford philosophers, has devoted special attention to the philosophy of mind. See his 'On Referring and Intending' (*PR*, 1956), in which he tries to lay down a way of distinguishing between what is, and what is not, 'overt'. See also M. MacDonald: 'Professor Ryle on the Concept of Mind' (*PR*, 1951); John Wisdom: 'The Concept of Mind' (*PAS*, 1949); A. C. Garnett: 'Mind as Minding' (*Mind*, 1952); A. C. Ewing: 'Professor Ryle's Attack on Dualism' (*PAS*, 1952); L. Addis: 'Ryle's Ontology of Mind' in *Moore and Ryle* (Iowa Publications, 2, 1965). See also J. Holloway: *Language and Intelligence* (1951) which deals with connected topics in a similar manner. The Italian translation *Lo Spirito come Comportamento* (trans. F. Rossi-Landi) contains a very useful introductory essay by the translator.

20. It is a good idea to read C. D. Broad's *Mind and Its Place in Nature* alongside *The Concept of Mind*.

21. For criticism see D. Pears: 'The Logical Status of Supposition' (*PASS*, 1951); S. Hampshire: 'Dispositions' and A. R. White: 'Mr Hampshire and Prof. Ryle on Dispositions' (*Analysis*, 1953); G. H. Bird: 'Mr Hampshire on Dispositions' (*ibid*). See also the literature on the closely-related subject of 'counter-factual conditionals', i.e. hypothetical propositions such as 'if Caesar had not crossed the Rubicon, the Republic would not have fallen'. Recently, such propositions have been widely discussed because (1) they immediately arise within any phenomenalist or dispositionalist account of body or mind, (2) the difference between natural laws and bare regularities has often been supposed to consist in the fact (see Ch. 17 on Kneale) that laws do, whereas regularities do not, imply such conditionals, (3) they are distinctly awkward to interpret on a truth-functional logic. (On the material implication analysis of 'if . . ., then . . .', every counter-factual conditional is true in virtue of the bare fact that the antecedent is false; yet on the face of it some such propositions – for example, 'if the stone

had hit the glass it would have broken it' – are true, whereas others – 'if the feather had hit the glass, it would have broken it' – are false.) See R. M. Chisholm: 'The Contrary-to-Fact Conditional' (*Mind*, 1946); N. Goodman: 'The Problem of Counterfactual Conditionals' (*JP*, 1947), reprinted in *Fact, Fiction and Forecast* (1954) which is largely devoted to this theme; F. L. Will: 'The Contrary-to-Fact Conditional' (*Mind*, 1947); K. R. Popper: 'A Note on Natural Laws and So-called "Contrary to Fact" Conditionals' (*Mind*, 1949); D. Pears: 'Hypotheticals' and W. Kneale: 'Natural Laws and Contrary-to-Fact Conditionals' (*Analysis*, 1949); B. J. Diggs: 'Counterfactual Conditionals' (*Mind*, 1952); S. Hampshire: 'Subjunctive Conditionals' (*Analysis*, 1948); R. M. Chisholm: 'Law Statements and Counterfactual Inference' (*Analysis*, 1954); J. R. Weinberg: 'Contrary-to-Fact Conditionals' (*JP*, 1951); G. H. von Wright: *Logical Studies* (1957); E. Nagel: *The Structure of Science* (1961); J. L. Mackie: 'Counterfactuals and Causal Laws' (in *Analytical Philosophy*, ed. R. J. Butler, 1962).

22. See R. S. Peters: *The Concept of Motivation* (1958); A. R. White: 'The Language of Motives' (*Mind*, 1958); N. S. Sutherland: 'Motives as Explanations' (*Mind*, 1959); A. Kenny: *Action, Emotion and Will* (1963); D. S. Shwayder: *The Stratification of Behaviour* (1965).

23. See, apart from the reviews of *The Concept of Mind*, J. M. Shorter: 'Imagination' (*Mind*, 1952) with A. G. N. Flew's reply 'Facts and Imagination' (*Mind*, 1956). B. S. Benjamin on 'Remembering' (*ibid*.) discusses connected questions, as does W. Ginnane in 'Thoughts' (*Mind*, 1960). See also E. J. Furlong: *Imagination* (1961) and K. Lycos: 'Images and the Imaginary' (*AJP*, 1965).

24. P. Winch: 'Understanding a Primitive Society' (*APQ*, 1964) is an extreme instance of the sceptical interpretation of the 'language game' approach. See also J. J. C. Smart: 'The Existence of God' in *New Essays in Philosophical Theology* (1957) and, in reply, J. A. Passmore: 'Christianity and Positivism' (*AJP*, 1957). Smart, as we shall see, has now reacted strongly against the 'separatist' conception of philosophy. See also the concluding remarks in N. Malcolm's defence of an ontological argument (*PR*, 1960, reprinted in *Knowledge and Certainty*, 1963). Malcolm's essay is criticized by various writers in *PR*, 1961, and by J. Shaffer: 'Existence, Predication and the Ontological Argument' (*Mind*, 1962). For a criticism of what he calls 'the new scepticism' see S. Hampshire: 'Identification and Existence' (*CPB*, III).

25. Austin completed no books and made not a single contribution to a philosophical periodical. Of the ten papers brought together by J. O. Urmson and G. J. Warnock as *Philosophical Papers* (1961) four are contributions to symposia, one a radio talk, the other five were delivered to learned societies. Austin published only such of these as he was obliged to publish, as a condition of their being delivered. Warnock has skilfully reconstructed from Austin's (by no means full) lecture notes the course of lectures he was accustomed to offer to undergraduates on the theory of perception; this constitutes *Sense and Sensibilia* (1962). In 1955 Austin delivered at Harvard the William James lectures; these have been reconstructed by Urmson – again from notes – as *How to do things with Words* (1962). It is obvious that

Austin's criticisms did not spare himself. See the obituaries by S. Hampshire (*PAS*, 1960) and by G. J. Warnock (*PBA*, 1963). (In *Mind*, 1961, Warnock and J. O. Urmson comment critically on Hampshire's obituary.) Warnock exaggerates, I think, in denying that Wittgenstein had any influence whatever on Austin. But Austin strikingly exemplifies the continuity of the Oxford Aristotelian tradition, a continuity more explicable if one remembers that Oxford rarely appoints as teachers of philosophy men who have been trained anywhere else but at Oxford, and that most of them have been trained as classical scholars. See the critical studies of Austin by A. Ambrose, M. Black, W. F. R. Hardie, R. Harrod, M. Lazerowitz (*Phil.*, 1963) and R. Brown (*AJP*, 1962, 1963); M. Furberg: *Locutionary and Illocutionary Acts* (1963), which has a broader theme than its title suggests; the symposium on Austin by J. O. Urmson, N. Malcolm, W. V. Quine, S. Hampshire (*JP*, 1965); S. Cavell: 'Austin at Criticism' (*PR*, 1965). On Austin's *Philosophical Papers* see R. M. Chisholm (*Mind*, 1964) and A. Duncan-Jones: 'Performance and Promise' (*PQ*, 1964); on *Sense and Sensibilia*, R. Firth: 'Austin and the Argument from Illusion' (*PR*, 1964); the (very) critical study by R. J. Hirst (*PQ*, 1963). For a related criticism of sense-data see A. M. Quinton: 'The Problem of Perception' (*Mind*, 1955).

26. And *a fortiori* Nowell-Smith was mistaken in supposing that it *was* consistent. The classical modern exposition of this latter view is 'Freewill as involving Determinism and Inconceivable without it' (*Mind*, 1934), written by D. S. Miller under the pseudonym of R. E. Hobart. See also M. Schlick: *Problems of Ethics* (1939); for Moore, Nowell-Smith and Austin's criticisms see M. Warnock: *Ethics since 1900* (1960). See also P. Foot: 'Freewill as involving Determinism' (*PR*, 1957); R. Taylor: 'I can' (*PR*, 1960); V. J. Canfield: 'The Compatibility of Freewill and Determinism' (*PR*, 1962); A. M. Honoré: 'Can and Can't' (*Mind*, 1964).

27. See the discussion which followed his paper on 'Performative or Constative' (*Cahiers de Royaumont*, Philosophie No. IV, 1962, translated in *Philosophy and Ordinary Language*, ed. C. E. Caton, 1963).

28. On this point, see, for example, the critical articles by R. J. Hirst (*PQ*, 1963) and R. Brown (*AJP*, 1962); L. J. Goldstein: 'On Austin's Understanding of Philosophy' (*PPR*, 1964). See also S. Cavell: 'Austin at Criticism' (*PR*, 1965).

29. For a defence of sense-data against the ordinary language critics see H. H. Price: 'Appearing and Appearances' (*APQ*, 1964).

30. See, in contrast with Austin, D. M. Armstrong: *Perception and the Physical World* (1961) and, especially for the historical background, M. Mandelbaum: *Philosophy, Science and Sense-Perception* (1964). C. D. Broad: 'Some Elementary Reflexions on Sense-Perception' (*Phil.*, 1952) sums up the points at issue. This essay is reprinted in *Perceiving, Sensing and Knowing* (ed. R. J. Swartz, 1965), an unusually wide-ranging volume of readings in contemporary epistemology, with a lengthy bibliography.

31. Austin's work has been particularly interesting to moral and legal philosophers, who have suggested that it is a 'descriptive fallacy' to suppose that, for example, in calling something good we are describing it or that in

saying that somebody did something we are describing the person's bodily movements, as distinct from ascribing responsibility to him. See particularly the distinction between 'description' and 'ascription' in H. L. Hart: 'Th Ascription of Responsibility and Rights' (*PAS*, 1949, reprinted in *LL* 1) For criticism of Hart's approach see P. T. Geach: 'Ascriptivism' and G Pitcher: 'Hart on Action and Responsibility' (both in *PR*, 1960); J. L Mackie: 'Responsibility and Language' (*AJP*, 1955); J. Feinberg 'Action and Responsibility' in *Philosophy in America* (1965); fo similar views on ethics see J. R. Searle: 'Meaning and Speech Acts' (*PR* 1962).

32. Austin first used the word 'performative' in print in his symposium contribution on 'Truth' (*PASS*, 1950). For criticism see Jonathan Harrison 'Knowing and Promising' (*Mind*, 1962); W. H. F. Barnes: 'Knowing (*PR*, 1963); M. Wright: '"I Know" and Performative Utterances' (*AJP* 1965). For an attempt to develop a formalized theory of knowledge, see J Hintikka: *Knowledge and Belief* (1962).

33. Strawson was unconvinced by this reply, and Austin by his criticisms See the Austin-Strawson symposium (*PAS*, 1950), together with a defence o Austin by Warnock and a reply by Strawson in *Truth* (ed. G. Pitcher, 1964) Austin's 'Unfair to Facts' in *Philosophical Papers;* Strawson's 'Truth, reconsideration of Austin's Views' (*PQ*, 1965) and Warnock's 'Truth and Correspondence' in *Knowledge and Experience* (ed. C. D. Rollins, 1962) See also S. Cavell: 'Demonstrative and Descriptive Conventions' (*Phil* 1965).

34. See Warnock's description of Austin's plans for cooperative inquir into 'what we say' (Obituary, *PBA*, 1963) and J. O. Urmson's account o them based on an unpublished manuscript fragment, in *JP*, 1965. Hi method is sketched in 'A Plea for Excuses' and 'On Pretending' (both i *Philosophical Papers*). See, in criticism, B. Mates: 'On the Verification o Statements about "Ordinary Language"' (*Inquiry*, 1958); J. A. Fodor an J. J. Katz: 'The Availability of What We Say' (*PR*, 1963); L. J. Cohen *The Diversity of Meaning* (1962); in defence S. Cavell: 'Must We Mea What We Say?' (*Inquiry*, 1958) and R. G. Henson: 'What We Say' (*APQ* 1965). See also the introduction by J. A. Fodor and J. J. Katz to *Th Structure of Language* (1964), the essay by N. Chomsky in that volume o 'Current Issues in Linguistic Theory' and the discussion of linguistics b Chomsky and others in *Logic, Methodology and Philosophy of Scienc* (ed. E. Nagel *et al.*, 1962).

35. For developments of Austin's views see P. F. Strawson: 'Intention an Convention in Speech Acts' (*PR*, 1964) and D. S. Shwayder: *The Stratifica tion of Behaviour* (1965). See also W. P. Alston: 'Linguistic Acts' (*APQ* 1964).

36. See L. J. Cohen: 'Do Illocutionary Forces Exist?' (*PQ*, 1964).

37. As early as 'Are there *a priori* concepts?' (*PASS*, 1939) he had throw doubts on the analytic-synthetic contrast. At a great many points, he attack the habit of dichotomizing. On 'factual' and 'evaluative' see also (all in *PP* 1964) M. Black: 'The Gap between "is" and "should"'; J. R. Searl 'How to derive "Ought" from "Is"'; J. and J. Thomson: 'How not t

derive "Ought" from "Is"'; the discussion of 'ought' and 'is' in *Analysis*, 1964–5; R. Montague: ' "Ought" from "Is" ' (*AJP*, 1965); M. F. Cohen: ' "Is" and "Should" ': an unbridged gap' (*PR*, 1965); R. M. Hare: 'The Promising Game' (*RIP*, 1965).

38. See especially 'Pretending' (*PASS*, 1958).

39. Contrast L. J. Russell's contribution to the same symposium. 'Is a scientific theory of dynamics to be tested by its ability to explain and justify (or even explain without justifying) our usages of words like force, motion, cause and so on in the ordinary affairs of life? . . . If ordinary concepts are vague and inexact, they have to be replaced by more precise ones; and the scientist should have his eye on the development of his subject rather than on ordinary usages'. Toulmin's article, indeed, brings to a head the controversy between those who hold that probability theory ought to analyse our ordinary use of the word 'probability', and those who think it should concentrate its attention on the use of probability statements *in scientific inquiry*. Toulmin's own views are closely related to Ramsey's theory of probability – or, rather to Ramsey's various attempts to satisfy himself about probability – in *Foundations of Mathematics*. See also J. N. Findlay: 'Probability without Nonsense' (*PQ*, 1952) and J. King-Farlow: 'Toulmin's Analysis of Probability' (*Theoria*, 1963).

40. See also P. Edwards: 'Bertrand Russell's Doubts about Induction' (*LL* I); C. Lewy: 'On the "Justification" of Induction' (*Analysis*, 1939) and the discussion which followed (*Analysis*, 1940); A. Ambrose: 'The Problem of Justifying Inductive Inference' (*JP*, 1947); M. Black: *Problems of Analysis* (1954); N. R. Hanson: 'Good Inductive Reasons' (*PQ*, 1961). In his 'Some Questions concerning Validity' (*RIP*, 1953), J. O. Urmson, while accepting Strawson's general line of reasoning, argues that it is still possible and desirable to ask *why* we value inductive more highly than other kinds of reasoning.

41. See W. C. Salmon, S. F. Barker, H. E. Kyburg: 'Symposium on Inductive Evidence' (*APQ*, 1965).

42. [With P. Grice] 'In Defence of a Dogma' (*PR*, 1956). Grice, Strawson's tutor, has greatly influenced not only Strawson but other 'ordinary language' philosophers; a lively, critical teacher, he has written very little. On 'informal logic' see also Ryle's *Dilemmas*, and his 'If, So and Because' (*Philosophical Analysis*, ed. M. Black, 1950), in which he works out more fully the suggestion he made in *The Concept of Mind* that general statements are 'inference licences' – a view which has interesting relations to some of the things said about universal propositions by Mill and by Ramsey. See also H. G. Alexander: 'General Statements as Rules of Inference' (*Minnesota Studies*, Vol. II, 1958); H. N. Castañeda: 'Are Conditionals Principles of Inference?' (*Analysis*, 1958).

43. I have interpreted this article in the light of *Logical Theory*. See W. Sellars: 'Presupposing' and Strawson's reply (*PR*, 1954) in which he in some measure modifies his views; R. Clark: 'Presuppositions, Names and Descriptions' (*PQ*, 1956); B. Russell: 'Mr Strawson on Referring' (*Mind*, 1957); M. Black: *Models and Metaphors* (1962); G. Nehrlich: 'Presupposition and Entailment' (*APQ*, 1965); W. Wolterstorff: 'Referring and Exist-

ing' (*PQ*, 1961); P. F. Strawson: *Individuals* (1959). See also what has been said of Brentano (Ch. 8, n. 7) and F. C. S. Schiller, p. 170). A similar view had been suggested by J. L. Austin in 'The Meaning of a Word' – a paper delivered in 1940, first published in *Philosophical Papers* (1961). P. T. Geach: 'Russell's Theory of Descriptions' (*Analysis*, 1949) and H. L. Hart in 'A Logician's Fairy-Tale' (*PR*, 1951) make use of similar doctrines in a reconsideration of the traditional Aristotelian logic. Hart, who is now Professor of Jurisprudence at Oxford, is well-known for his application of 'ordinary language' techniques to problems in legal philosophy. P. T. Geach accuses Strawson of undue 'softness' towards traditional logic. See his 'Mr Strawson on Symbolic and Traditional Logic' (*Mind*, 1963). See also J. Jarvis: 'Notes on Strawson's Logic' (*Mind*, 1961)

44. For a formalist's reply see Quine's 'Mr Strawson on Logical Theory' (*Mind*, 1953). Strawson, he says, has conducted an 'able philological inquiry', but grossly underestimates the powers of a formalized logic. See also S. Toulmin: *The Uses of Argument* (1958) and J. C. Cooley: 'Toulmin's Revolution in Logic' (*JP*, 1959).

45. See S. Hampshire: 'Friedrich Waismann' (*PBA*, 1960). Waismann's *The Principles of Linguistic Philosophy*, designed as a text-book, was published in 1965, edited from a set of manuscripts by R. Harré.

46. An English translation appeared in 1951. Waismann tells us that he had read a number of Wittgenstein's manuscripts on mathematics. These were earlier in date than the manuscripts published as *Remarks on the Foundations of Mathematics*. Wittgenstein's earlier philosophy of mathematics was also introduced to philosophers outside Cambridge in such essays as A. Ambrose: 'Finitism and "The Limits of Empiricism"' (*Mind*, 1937) and 'Are there three consecutive Sevens in the Expansion of π?' (*Michigan Academy of Science, Arts and Letters*, 1936); D. A. T. Gasking: 'Mathematics and the World' (*LL* II).

47. These 'strata' are further characterized in 'Language Strata' (*LL* I). Different strata are distinguishable as having 'a different logic': 'true', 'meaningful', 'contradictory', 'verifiability' all have a different sense, he argues, when referring, say, to a mathematical proposition, a law of nature, a sensory observation. Waismann is reacting against the positivist insistence upon a single (scientific) order. On the application of Waismann's principles to the question whether there are alternative logics, see his paper in *PAS*, 1945, and R. J. Butler: 'Language Strata and Alternative Logics' (*AJP* 1955).

Notes

CHAPTER 19

1. On this contrast see R. M. Hare: 'A School for Philosophers' (*Ratio*, 1960). In the United States, however, existentialism and phenomenology are steadily growing in respectability, although they are often interpreted 'in the spirit of William James'. See J. M. Edie: 'Recent Work in Phenomeno-

logy' (*APQ*, 1964) and ed. J. M. Edie: *Invitation to Phenomenology* (1965). See also H. Spiegelberg: *The Phenomenological Movement* (1960); the Existentialism number of *RIP*, 1949; H. E. Barnes: *The Literature of Possibility* (1959); M. Natanson: *Literature, Philosophy and the Social Sciences* (1962); R. Jolivet: *Les doctrines existentialistes de Kierkegaard à Jean-Paul Sartre* (1948); J. Collins: *The Existentialists* (1952); K. F. Reinhardt: *The Existentialist Revolt* (1952); H. J. Blackham: *Six Existentialist Thinkers* (1952); F. H. Heinemann: *Existentialism and the Modern Predicament* (1953). Useful volumes of selections include: H. J. Blackham: *Reality, Man and Existence* (1965); W. Kaufmann: *Existentialism from Dostoevsky to Sartre* (1956). See also K. Douglas: *A Critical Bibliography of Existentialism* (1950); F. Copleston: *Contemporary Philosophy* (1956). For a characteristic critical attack see N. Bobbio: *The Philosophy of Decadentism* (1944, fuller English version in 1948); M. Grene: *Dreadful Freedom* (1948).

2. Most of his works have now been translated into English, and there is a considerable Kierkegaard literature. See *Søren Kierkegaard: International Bibliografi* (ed. J. Himmelstrup, 1962); W. Lowrie: *Kierkegaard* (1938); R. Jolivet: *Introduction to Kierkegaard* (1946, English translation 1950); M. Wyschogrod: *Kierkegaard and Heidegger* (1953); J. Wahl: *Études Kierkegaardiennes* (1938); J. Collins: *The Mind of Kierkegaard* (1953); P. Rohde: *Søren Kierkegaard* (1959, English translation 1963); J. Hohlenberg: *Søren Kierkegaard* (1940, English translation 1954); ed. H. A. Johnson: *A Kierkegaard Critique* (1962). Kierkegaard has also had a great influence on contemporary 'negative' theology and on literature, by way of Henrik Ibsen. See particularly Ibsen's *Brand* (1866).

3. See particularly, however, his preface to *The Concept of Dread* and *Philosophical Fragments* (both 1844), together with *Concluding Unscientific Postscript* (1846).

4. Contrast Alexander on the de-anthropomorphizing of philosophy. Note, on the other hand, the resemblance of existentialism to British 'personal idealism' (see especially Ch. 4 above, on Seth).

5. Contrast Santayana on the 'life of the spirit' (Ch. 12).

6. See also Ch. 5 above and, for Nietzsche's influence on Continental philosophy, G. Deleuze: *Nietzsche et la Philosophie* (1962).

7. The title of the English translation (1933); the German title is *Die geistige Situation der Zeit* (1931). I do not know why it has so often been thought necessary to rename Jaspers' works in the process of translating them. Jaspers' large-scale philosophical works – *Philosophie* (3 vols., 1932) and *Von der Wahrheit* (1947) – have not been translated into English. Segments of *Von der Wahrheit* have been translated as *Tragedy is not Enough* (1952) and *Truth and Symbol* (1959). Jaspers outlined his philosophical views in *Der Philosophische Glaube* (1948), translated as *The Perennial Scope of Philosophy* (1949) and in *Einführung in die Philosophie* (1950), translated as *The Way of Wisdom* (1951). See also the essay 'On my Philosophy' originally published in *Rechenschaft und Ausblick* (1951) and translated in *Existentialism* (ed. W. Kaufmann, 1957). For Jaspers' views on Nietzsche and Kierkegaard see *Nietzsche* (1936, English translation 1965)

and 'The Importance of Kierkegaard' (*Cross Currents*, 1952). For studies of Jaspers see, apart from general works on existentialism, E. Allen: *The Self and its Hazards: A Guide to the Thought of Karl Jaspers* (1951); A. Lichtigfeld: *Jaspers' Metaphysics* (1954), and *Aspects of Jaspers' Philosophy* (1963); J. Paumen: *Raison et existence chez Karl Jaspers* (1958); R. D. Knudsen: *The Idea of Transcendence in the Philosophy of Karl Jaspers* (1958); J. Wahl: *La Pensée de l'existence* (1951); ed. P. A. Schilpp: *The Philosophy of Karl Jaspers* (1957). Most of the contributors to that last volume, it is worth noting, are of French or German origin: none is English.

8. For Jaspers' critique of Descartes, see his essay in the Descartes supplement to *Revue Philosophique*, 1937, translated in *Leonardo, Descartes, Max Weber* (1965). Jaspers greatly admired Max Weber, both as a man and a politician. It is often said of Jaspers' *Psychopathology* (first published 1913; the English translation, 1962, is of the seventh edition, 1959) that he introduced Husserl's phenomenology into psychopathology. But the phenomenology of *Psychopathology* is 'descriptive psychology', not the 'science of essences', and Jaspers thinks of it only as one scientific procedure amongst others. Although Jaspers is the only existentialist to write in detail on psychopathology, 'existential psychiatry' derives from Heidegger, by way of Ludwig Binswanger, not from Jaspers. See *Psychoanalysis and Existential Philosophy* (ed. H. Ruitenbeek, 1962). Jaspers criticizes Binswanger's approach as being unduly dominated by a single theoretical idea, although he accepts some of his detailed analyses. In R. May *et al: Existence* (1958), Jaspers, Heidegger, and Freud are all extensively referred to. This volume includes translations of three essays by Binswanger.

9. See the discussion between Jaspers and Bultmann in *Die Frage der Entmythologisierung* (1954; English translation *Myth and Christianity*, 1958).

10. Compare Wittgenstein's *Tractatus* – 'the world is *my* world'. Jaspers would agree with Wittgenstein, too, that 'the subject does not belong to the world; rather, it is a limit of the world'. But only from a certain perspective.

11. *The Idea of a University* was published in two distinct versions in 1923 and 1946. The second version has been translated into English (1960). *The European Spirit* (English translation 1948) was first delivered as a lecture in Geneva (1946).

12. See especially H. Spiegelberg: *The Phenomenological Movement*, (1960), which incorporates one of the few accounts of Heidegger that is immediately intelligible to the British reader. Marjorie Grene's monograph: *Martin Heidegger* (1957) emphasizes the existentialist side of Heidegger's philosophy. See also T. Langan: *The Meaning of Heidegger* (1959) which tries to demonstrate the unity of Heidegger's thought; W. J. Richardson: *Heidegger: Through Phenomenology to Thought* (1963) – a substantial, difficult analysis by a scholastically-trained Jesuit with special emphasis on Heidegger's later thought and an elaborate bibliography and index; E. G. Ballard: 'A Brief Introduction to the Philosophy of Martin Heidegger' (*Tulane Studies*, 1963); M. King: *Heidegger's Philosophy* (1964); L. Versényi: *Heidegger, Being and Truth* (1965); the Heidegger number of *RIP* (1960) which includes a bibliography, and the discussion of Heidegger by J. Wild

and H. L. Dreyfus in *JP*, 1963. Important Continental commentaries include A. de Waelhens: *La Philosophie de Martin Heidegger* (1942, especially useful for *Being and Time*); K. Löwith: *Heidegger, Denker in dürftiger Zeit* (1953); and J. Kraft: *Von Husserl zu Heidegger* (1957). The more dithyrambic side of Heidegger is the centre of interest in V. Vycinas: *Earth and Gods* (1961).

13. Usually described as 'untranslatable, even into German' it has been put into a largely intelligible, if not always fully Heideggerian, English form in the translation by J. Macquarrie and E. Robinson (1962). See the discussion by J. Wild and others (*RM*, 1963 and 1964). *Being and Time* is summarized by W. Brock in *Existence and Being* (1949), which also includes a number of Heidegger's essays.

14. See also 'On the Essence of Truth' (1943), trans. in W. Brock: *Existence and Being* (1949); A. de Waelhens: *Phénoménologie et vérité* (1953); M. Farber: 'Heidegger on the Essence of Truth' (*PPR*, 1958); R. G. Turnbull: 'Heidegger on the Nature of Truth' (*JP*, 1957).

15. See Nietzsche: *The Twilight of the Gods* (1889). Heidegger's two-volume *Nietzsche* (1961) consists of a series of writings and lectures on Nietzsche, dating from the period 1936–46. It is interesting to observe that in the first set of lectures Heidegger places special stress on Nietzsche's *The Will to Power* (1885) and criticizes Jaspers' *Nietzsche* for not having done so. Heidegger's emphasis on 'will' and 'resoluteness' perhaps does something to explain his period of close association with the Nazi party, on which see G. Schneeberger: *Nachlese zu Heidegger* (1962), and the brief selection of documents in D. D. Runes: *German Existentialism* (1965). But Heidegger's Nazi period also illustrates the streak of intellectual irresponsibility, of 'primitivism', in Heidegger, which became more and more pronounced after *Being and Time*.

16. For Heidegger's views about non-European languages see the dialogue between a Japanese and an inquirer' under the title 'Aus einem Gespräch von der Sprache' in Heidegger's *Unterwegs zur Sprache* (1959).

17. In his *Kant and the Problem of Metaphysics* (1929, English translation 1962) Heidegger criticizes the view that 'anthropology' – the analysis of what it is to be a man – is the ultimate problem of philosophy, as distinct from its natural starting-point. He dedicates that book to Max Scheler, the most active of 'philosophical anthropologists'. See Scheler's *Man's Place in Nature* (1928, English translation 1961) or, for a Husserl-type analysis of a specific 'anthropological' phenomenon, *The Nature of Sympathy* (1913, English translation 1954). See also A. Schütz: 'Max Scheler's Epistemology and Ethics' (*RM*, 1958); M. Dupuy: *La Philosophie de Max Scheler* (1949).

18. Translated in W. Kaufmann: *Existentialism from Dostoevsky to Sartre* (1957).

19. Heidegger's essays on Hölderlin (1936) are translated in W. Brock: *Existence and Being*.

20. See G. J. Heidel: *Martin Heidegger and the Pre-Socratics* (1964).

21. For a full analysis of science (technology) and its importance in human life see Heidegger's 'Die Frage nach der Technik' in *Vorträge und Aufsätze* (1954) and, in an analysis which relates it to the traditional 'principle of sufficient reason', *Der Satz vom Grund* (1957).

22. Writing in reply to a set of questions from a French existentialist, Heidegger is in this letter busily dissociating himself from Sartre.

23. For the relations between existentialism and religion see R. Troisfontaines: *Existentialism and Christian Thought* (1950); *Christianity and the Existentialists* (ed. C. Michalson, 1956); D. E. Roberts: *Existentialism and Religious Belief* (1957); W. Earle *et al.*: *Christianity and Existentialism* (1963); J. Macquarrie: *An Existentialist Theology* (1955 – especially on Heidegger).

24. Recently Marcel, influenced perhaps by the papal condemnation of existentialism (1950), has denied that he is an existentialist; but he used proudly to proclaim that he had introduced existentialism into France. In 1947, indeed, E. Gilson and others published a volume entitled *Existentialisme chrétien: Gabriel Marcel*. Sartre's works are on the *Index*. Marcel's critical essay on Sartre (1946) is included as 'Existence and Human Freedom' in the set of essays published in England under the title *The Philosophy of Existence* (1948) and in the United States as *The Philosophy of Existentialism* (1956). For Marcel, see E. Sottiaux: *Gabriel Marcel: Philosophe et Dramaturge* (1956); K. T. Gallagher: *The Philosophy of Gabriel Marcel* (1962); S. Cain: *Gabriel Marcel* (1963). Marcel has summed up – so far as that phrase is applicable to such fluid thinking – his philosophical ideas in his William James lectures *The Existential Background of Human Dignity* (1963). His principal disciple is Paul Ricoeur. On contemporary French philosophy in general, see Colin Smith: *Contemporary French Philosophy* (1964); L. Lavelle: *La Philosophie française entre les deux guerres* (1942). Marcel is also a playwright, with special views about the relation between the drama and philosophy; for these see G. Fessard's prefatory essay to Marcel's *La Soif* (1938). See also the comparison between Marcel and Jaspers in P. Ricoeur: *Gabriel Marcel et Karl Jaspers: Philosophie du mystère et philosophie de paradoxe* (1947); W. E. Hocking: 'Marcel and the Ground Issues of Metaphysics' (*PPR*, 1954).

25. Particularly of the Anglo-Saxon sort. In *RMM* (1915–19) he wrote a lengthy essay on Royce, which has been published (1945) as a separate volume (English translation 1956). He also made a close study of Bradley whose influence is apparent even in his final philosophy. He worked towards a more 'personalist' philosophy as a result of the influence of Bergson and (especially) W. E. Hocking, to whom he jointly dedicated his *Metaphysical Journal*.

26. Published in 1950 under the general title of *The Mystery of Being* as *Reflection and Mystery* and *Faith and Reality*.

27. *RMM* (1925), republished as an appendix to the English translation (1952) of the *Metaphysical Journal*. This was probably the first public expression of an existentialist point of view in France.

28. This theme is further developed in *Being and Having* (1935) – a second metaphysical journal.

29. See particularly 'On the Ontological Mystery', originally published along with Marcel's play, *Le Monde Cassé* (1933); translated into English as the first essay in *The Philosophy of Existence* (1948).

30. See for example the essays collected as *The Decline of Wisdom* (1954)

and the essay on Sartre – 'Existence and Human Freedom' – in *The Philosophy of Existence*. For Marcel's politico-social views see especially his *Man against Humanity* (1951, English translation 1952), entitled in America *Man against Mass Society* (1952).

31. See R. Troisfontaines: *Le Choix de Jean-Paul Sartre* (1945); G. Varet: *L'Ontologie de Sartre* (1948); P. Dempsey: *The Psychology of Sartre* (1950) which covers a wider territory than its title suggests; I. Murdoch: *Sartre* (1953); A. J. Ayer: 'Novelist-Philosophers – Jean-Paul Sartre' (*Horizon*, 1945); W. Desan: *The Tragic Finale* (1954); F. Jeanson: *Sartre par lui-même* (1955); M. W. Cranston: *Sartre* (1962); M. Warnock: *The Philosophy of Sartre* (1965) – the best purely philosophical introduction; ed. R. D. Cumming: *The Philosophy of Jean-Paul Sartre* (1965); R. J. Champigny: *Stages on Sartre's Way 1938–52* (1959); ed. E. Kern: *Sartre: A Collection of Critical Essays* (1962). See also Sartre's autobiography *Words* (1964), which goes out of its way to underline the personal origins of his ontology in his own childhood experiences, and the autobiography of Simone de Beauvoir, especially *La Force de l'Age* (1960; English translation, *The Prime of Life*, 1962) and *La Force des Choses* (1963; English translation *Force of Circumstance*, 1965).

32. Hegel began to be influential in France, for the first time, only in the nineteen-thirties. The crucial Hegelian work, for his French admirers, is *The Phenomenology of Mind*. Jean Wahl in *Le malheur de la conscience dans la philosophie de Hegel* (1929) drew attention to the more humanistic early Hegel; Jean Hyppolite, a fellow-student of Sartre, translated and commented on the *Phenomenology* (1939) and in his *Études sur Marx et Hegel* (1955) interpreted Hegel as a philosopher of existence. It is ironical that a movement of ideas beginning in Kierkegaard should end in a revised Hegelianism. The difference between early and late Hegel and between early and late Marx is supposed to mitigate the irony. The Russian Marxist A. Kojève in his *Introduction à la lecture de Hegel* (1947) suggested a phenomenological interpretation of Hegel; Sartre had attended his lectures.

33. This has been translated into English (1956) by H. Barnes, who adds a lengthy introduction.

34. Translated as *The Diary of Antoine Roquentin* (1949); a more accurate translation appeared in 1965 with the title *Nausea*. The short story which gives its name to the collection *Le Mur* (1939) may also be read with profit, as may such plays as *Les Mouches* (1942) and *Huis-Clos* (1944). The novel-sequence *Les Chemins de la Liberté* (1945) brings out very clearly the ambiguous nature of Sartre's ethics. These literary works have all been translated into English. The peculiar character of Sartre's ethics comes out even more clearly in the work of his disciple S. de Beauvoir, particularly perhaps in her *Must We Burn de Sade?* (1953) and her *roman à clef, The Mandarins* (1954).

35. This short book has also been translated into English with the mis-leading title *Existentialism* (1947) and also as *Existentialism and Humanism* (1948). In it, Sartre tries to argue that he is not an individualist; that, somehow, when each of us chooses as an individual – chooses, say, rather to die than to surrender – he 'chooses for humanity'. Sartre's experience with the

French Resistance left him with a feeling of human solidarity quite absent from his earlier works, in which other people are most characteristically represented as Heidegger's 'They' – obstacles to our discovery of ourselves, nihilators of our possibilities. In his *Saint Genet* (1952, English translation 1964) the emphasis is still on existentialist analysis in opposition to deterministic sociology; in his incomplete and highly obscure *Critique de la Raison Dialectique* (1960) Sartre's Marxism swamps his existentialism, although he still criticizes modern Marxists, as distinct from Marx, for their 'abstractness', their lack of feeling for the concrete historical situation. The introduction to the *Critique* has been translated as *Problem of Method* (1964). See also *Marxisme et Existentialisme* (1962), a discussion between Sartre and other French philosophers; R. D. Laing and D. G. Cooper: *Reason and Violence* (1964); W. Desan: *The Marxism of Jean Paul Sartre* (1965).

36. Sartre has written a number of phenomenological analyses in a post-Husserlian style. See especially his *Sketch for a Theory of the Emotions* (1939, English translation 1962) and *L'Imaginaire* (1940, English translation as *The Psychology of Imagination*, 1949). Like the British philosophical psychologists (see Chapter 20) Sartre is critical of the attempt to formulate a naturalistic psychology. Any such psychology, he argues, flows out of 'bad faith' – the attempt to excuse ourselves by suggesting that our feelings, emotions, 'drives' are 'simply there' as something capable of overwhelming us, and thus as responsible for our actions. In fact, emotion is a 'debasement of consciousness', an attempt by consciousness to deal 'magically' rather than instrumentally with the world, e.g. by fainting in the face of danger rather than by confronting the danger. See especially J. P. Fell: *Emotion in the Thought of Sartre* (1965).

37. In his *Critique de la raison dialectique* this 'Being-in-itself' largely disappears as an unknowable; even in *Being and Nothingness* it plays a formal rather than a material role. Compare Bradley's 'Experience'.

38. It is characteristic of Sartre's disconcerting mixture of literary realism and abstract ontology – an ill-disposed critic has described *Being and Nothingness* as 'a mixture of French pornography and German metaphysics' – that Sartre takes as his prime instance of 'the gaze' a situation in which a man peering through a keyhole looks up and catches the eye of somebody who is watching him do so. See also A. Schütz: 'Sartre's Theory of the Alter Ego' (*PPR*, 1948, reprinted in *Collected Papers*, 1962).

39. See especially Sartre's introductory essay to his selections from Descartes (1946), translated as 'Cartesian Freedom' in *Literary and Philosophical Essays* (1957). Only in so far as there is a distinction between asserting the non-existence of consciousness and asserting that consciousness is Nothing can Sartre's epistemology be distinguished from neutral monism. Both Consciousness and Being have vanished into nonentity as his argument proceeds.

40. Sartre and Merleau-Ponty were closely associated, in the period 1945–52, as co-editors of *Les Temps modernes*. The official occasion for their break was political. Merleau-Ponty's criticisms of Sartre are most forcibly expressed in *Les Aventures de la Dialectique* (1955) and, in a more purely philosophical context, in *Le visible et l'invisible* (posthumously published,

NOTES

1963). S. de Beauvoir replied in 'Merleau-Ponty et le pseudo-Sartrisme' (*Les Temps modernes*, 1955, reprinted in *Privilèges*, 1955). The special number of *Les Temps modernes* (1961) devoted to Merleau-Ponty contains an appreciative commemorative essay by Sartre: 'Merleau-Ponty vivant'. See also A. de Waelhens' contribution to that number and his *Une Philosophie de l'Ambiguité* (1951); A. Robinet: *Merleau-Ponty* (1963); R. S. Kwant: *The Phenomenological Philosophy of Merleau-Ponty* (1963) which contains a lengthy bibliography; T. Langan: 'Maurice Merleau-Ponty: In Memoriam' (*RM*, 1963); R. Schmitt: 'Maurice Merleau-Ponty' (*RM*, 1966); D. Pejović: 'Maurice Merleau-Ponty' (*Praxis*, 1965) and the introductions to the English translations of *The Primacy of Perception* (a set of essays, trans. J. M. Edie, 1964); *The Structure of Behaviour* (1942, trans. 1963 by A. L. Fisher, with introductions by J. Wild and A. de Waelhens); *In Praise of Philosophy* (1953, trans. J. Wild and J. M. Edie, 1963); *Sense and non-Sense* (1948, trans. H. L. and P. A. Dreyfus, 1964); *Signs* (1960, trans. R. C. McCleary, 1964). For many years generally dismissed, outside France at least, as 'one of Sartre's academic disciples', Merleau-Ponty is now establishing a reputation in the English-speaking world for being the most 'sensible' of the existentialists.

41. First published in *RMM* (1962); translated in *The Primacy of Perception*.

42. He tells us that he is following up hints in Husserl's later manuscripts, now published in *Husserliana* VI (1954). The only leading French philosopher to defend Husserl's doctrine of the 'pure ego' is Gaston Berger: *Le Cogito dans la philosophie de Husserl* (1941). The peculiarity of French phenomenology lies in its running together of Heidegger, Husserl and Hegel. See also Merleau-Ponty's essay 'Phenomenology and the Sciences of Man' in *The Primacy of Perception* (1952). For a French interpretation of phenomenology see F. Jeanson: *La Phénoménologie* (1951). Jeanson is best known as an interpreter of Sartre.

43. See the very thorough study of phenomenological theories of the body in R. M. Zaner: *The Problem of Embodiment* (1964). There are obvious resemblances between Merleau-Ponty's doctrine of the body and Marcel's; Merleau-Ponty is oddly silent about this fact. See also M. R. Barral: *Merleau-Ponty: The Role of the Body-Subject* (1965).

44. See also Wittgenstein's discussion of the 'duck-rabbit' picture in *Philosophical Investigations*.

45. See also on this theme *Behaviourism and Phenomenology*, ed. T. W. Wann, 1964.

46. But, in an extensively documented work, without any mention at all of Locke, references to Hume only by way of quotations from Husserl and Scheler, comments on Berkeley only as the author of *The Theory of Vision* and without reference to any specific passages.

47. See the critical discussion by a number of French philosophers following Merleau-Ponty's 'The Primacy of Perception' (1947) in the book with that title.

48. For a phenomenological analysis of 'social reality', see especially the essays included in A. Schütz: *Collected Papers* (1962).

Notes

CHAPTER 20

1. See also P. F. Strawson: 'Analyse, Science et Métaphysique' in *La Philosophie Analytique* (Cahiers de Royaumont, No. IV, 1962) and his (anonymous) article on 'Philosophy in England' (*Times Literary Supplement*, 1961) in which he describes *Individuals* as 'a scaled-down Kantianism'. See also E. A. Burtt: 'Descriptive Metaphysics' (*Mind*, 1963) and, for a related contrast within psychology, see Kurt Lewin: 'The Conflict between Aristotelian and Galilean Modes of Thought in Contemporary Psychology' in *Dynamic Psychology* (1935).

2. See reviews by D. Pears (*PQ*, 1961); G. Bergmann (*JP*, 1960); J. O. Urmson (*Mind*, 1961); A. Plantinga (*RM*, 1961); A. J. Ayer: *The Concept of a Person* (1963).

3. On identification and metaphysics, see also S. Hampshire: 'Identification and Existence' (*CBP*, III); D. S. Shwayder: *Modes of Referring and the Problem of Universals* (1961); and Strawson's review of that book (*Mind*, 1962).

4. For criticism see J. Moravcsik: 'Strawson and Ontological Priority' (*Analytical Philosophy* II, ed. R. J. Butler, 1965). For a comparable argument see P. Zinkernagel: *Conditions for Description* (in Danish, 1957, English translation 1962). In order to establish his point Strawson considers the possibility of constructing an auditory universe, in which the basic particulars are sounds. See D. Locke: 'Strawson's Auditory Universe' (*PR*, 1961); S. Coval: 'Persons and Sounds' (*PQ*, 1963).

5. Similar questions are discussed, in a post-Wittgenstein spirit, in S. Shoemaker: *Self-Knowledge and Self-Identity* (1963).

6. For comment see A. J. Ayer: *The Concept of a Person* (1963); H. D. Lewis: 'Mind and Body' (*PAS*, 1963, reprinted in *Clarity is Not Enough*, ed. H. D. Lewis, 1963); C. D. Rollins: 'Personal Predicates' (*PQ*, 1960).

7. See reviews by M. Scriven (*Mind*, 1962); G. Weiler (*PQ*, 1961); D. J. O'Connor (*Philosophy*, 1961); J. J. Walsh: 'Remarks on Thought and Action' and Hampshire's reply (*JP*, 1963); and for Continental reactions, G. Viano (*Revista di Filosofia*, 1960) and (although he is English-based) H. J. Schüring in *Philosophischer Literaturanzeiger* (1961). In tone, it is worth observing, Hampshire's metaphysical writings resemble Continental rather than British philosophy. It is not only that he has made a close study of Spinoza and urges us to look to Leibniz rather than to Hume for inspiration. He is prepared to characterize philosophy as 'a search for a definition of man'; moral and political considerations lie at the heart of his thinking, not on its periphery; he takes art seriously as a critique of conventional morality; his philosophical style is ruminative, personal, aphoristic, rather than tightly structured or closely analytic.

8. See also the discussion between S. Hampshire, P. L. Gardiner, Iris Murdoch and D. F. Pears in *Freedom and the Will*, ed. D. F. Pears (1963).

9. For criticism, see M. Mandelbaum: 'Professor Ryle and Psychology' (*PR*, 1958). Austin, it is worth noting, took a different view of the matter and suggested that 'there is real danger in contempt for the "jargon" of psychology, at least when it sets out to supplement, and at least sometimes when it sets out to supplant the language of ordinary life' ('A Plea for Excuses', *PAS*, 1956, reprinted in *Philosophical Papers*, 1961).

10. cf. G. Bergmann: *Philosophy of Science* (1957): 'Psychology, at least in this country [U.S.A.] has found itself as a science.' See also E. H. Madden: *Philosophical Problems of Psychology* (1962).

11. Compare Sartre in his *Sketch of a Theory of the Emotions* (1939): 'Psychology will make great strides when it ceases to burden itself with ambiguous and contradictory experiments and starts bringing to light the essential structures constituting the subject of its investigations.'

12. On these monographs in general see W. Cerf: 'Studies in Philosophical Psychology' (*PPR*, 1962); on Geach in particular see reviews by A. Donagan (*PR*, 1958); A. C. Lloyd (*Phil.*, 1959); N. Cooper (*PQ*, 1959); J. J. C. Smart (*Mind*, 1958); C. Barrett: 'Concepts and Concept Formation' (*PAS*, 1963) See also the discussion of concept formation by S. Toulmin and others in *Dimensions of Mind* (ed. S. Hook, 1960).

13. As do many other 'philosophical psychologists', several of whom are Roman Catholics. 'Philosophical psychology', in abandoning the attempt to work out a 'science of man', takes the discussion of psychological concepts back to the point at which Aristotle and Aquinas had left it. It has acted as a bridge between neo-scholasticism and contemporary philosophy. In neo-scholastic circles the idea of a philosophical psychology never died out, although it was in many respects very different from what now goes under that name. See, for example, J. F. Donceel: *Philosophical Psychology* (1957).

14. But in 'A Theory of Practical Reason' (*PR*, 1965), R. Binkley suggests that logic is a 'special kind of psychology' for which some such name as 'rational psychology' ought to be invented. We are back, in short, at the old disputes about the difference between 'descriptive' and 'normative' psychology and the relation of these two psychologies to one another and to logic. It is by no means necessary to invent anew the phrase 'rational psychology'; it has had a long history.

15. R. Brown: 'Sound Sleep and Sound Scepticism' and Malcolm's reply (*AJP*, 1957); A. J. Ayer: 'Professor Malcolm on Dreams' (*JP*, 1960); V. J. Canfield: 'Judgments in Sleep' (*PR*, 1961); M. Kramer: 'Malcolm on Dreaming' and L. Linsky: 'Illusions and Dreams' (*Mind*, 1962); reviews by V. C. Chappell (*PQ*, 1963); D. F. Pears (*Mind*, 1961); C. Putnam: 'Dreaming and "Depth Grammar"' in *Analytical Philosophy* (ed. R. J. Butler, 1962); C. S. Chihara and J. A. Fodor: 'Operationalism and Ordinary Language' (*APQ*, 1965); R. L. Caldwell: 'Malcolm and the Criterion of Sleep' (*AJP*, 1965). See also, for comparable arguments, Malcolm's papers on remembering in *Knowledge and Certainty* (1963).

16. See especially the review by J. Jarvis (*JP*, 1959) and reviews by R. M. Chisholm (*PR*, 1959), K. W. Rankin (*Mind*, 1959), K. Baier (*AJP*, 1960), J. A. Passmore (*Indian Jnl. Phil.*, 1959); B. N. Fleming: 'On Intention'

(*PR*, 1964). For another work in the same *genre* see A. I. Melden: *Free Action* (1961).

17. The concept of 'knowledge without observation' derives from Wittgenstein's *Philosophical Investigations*. See also O. R. Jones: 'Things Known without Observation' (*PAS*, 1961); B. O'Shaughnessy: 'Observation and the Will' and K. S. Donnellan: 'Knowing What I am Doing' (*JP*, 1963); G. N. A. Vesey: 'Knowledge without Observation' (*PR*, 1963).

18. See J. Teichmann: 'Mental Cause and Effect' (*Mind*, 1961); D. F. Pears: 'Causes and Objects' (*Ratio*, 1962); J. Gosling: 'Mental Causes and Fear' (*Mind*, 1962).

19. See M. Mothersill: 'Anscombe's Account of the Practical Syllogism' (*PR*, 1962); J. Jarvis: 'Practical Reasoning' (*PQ*, 1962).

20. See, for example, the essays included in D. F. Gustafson: *Essays in Philosophical Psychology* (1964, with bibliography); R. S. Peters: *The Concept of Motivation* (1958); D. W. Hamlyn: *The Psychology of Perception* (1957) and, in a more sympathetic spirit, A. C. McIntyre: *The Unconscious* (1958).

21. Far too large to be fully describable. Most of the major topics are briefly discussed in A. Kenny: *Action, Emotion and Will* (1963), and at far greater length in D. S. Shwayder: *The Stratification of Behaviour* (1965).

22. In *Philosophy* (1953), reprinted in V. C. Chappell: *The Philosophy of Mind* (1962). See also, for a development of Hamlyn's views, P. C. Dodwell: 'Causes of Behaviour and Explanation in Psychology' (*Mind*, 1960). D. F. Gustafson replies in *Mind* (1964). See also D. Davidson, V. C. Chappell, W. D. Falk on 'Reasons' (*JP*, 1963). And note 36.

23. In general, 'philosophical psychologists' are more sympathetically inclined to Freud, in so far as he does no more than extend the use of everyday psychological concepts, than they are to any other contemporary psychologists. For the contrary view see some of the essays in *Psycho-analysis, Scientific Method and Philosophy* (ed. S. Hook, 1959) and H. J. Eysenck: *Uses and Abuses of Psychology* (1953). See also P. Alexander: 'Rational Behaviour and Psycho-Analytical Explanation' (*Mind*, 1962); S. Toulmin, H. Dingle, R. Peters, W. F. R. Hardie in *Analysis* (1948–50); B. Farrell and his critics in *Inquiry* (1964).

24. This is true, it is suggested, even of perception, understood as the successful completion of a task. For the opposite view see J. C. Taylor: *The Behavioural Basis of Perception* (1962) and B. A. Farrell's review (*Mind*, 1965). Farrell suggests that there is a shift within psychology in the use of visual concepts, so that the difficulties raised in, for example, H. Grice: 'Some Remarks about the Senses' (*Analytical Philosophy*, ed. R. J. Butler, 1962) about the behaviourist theory of perception may come to seem irrelevant. In other words the progress of psychology involves the revision of concepts.

25. In *The Stratification of Behaviour* Shwayder refers to his own approach as 'resolutely definitional'. It is so far characteristic of the new Aristotelianism, with its emphasis on definition rather than explanation. But Shwayder does not deny the possibility of constructing a causal-explanatory science of psychology.

26. See his 'Philosophy and the Scientific Image of Man' (*Frontiers of*

Science, ed. R. G. Colodny, 1962, reprinted in W. Sellars: *Science, Perception and Reality*, 1963).

27. Quine refers to *Individuals* only in footnotes since *Word and Object* was almost completed before that work appeared. But in such essays as 'Particular and General' (*PAS*, 1954) and 'Singular Terms, Ontology and Identity' (*Mind*, 1956) Strawson had already discussed some of the main topics of *Individuals*. For the most part *Word and Object* reiterates Quine's conclusions in his earlier articles (see pp. 403–5 above) but it approaches them in a different manner. It is a complex, often somewhat enigmatic, book which discusses a great range of logico-philosophical questions. See also the critical notice by C. F. Presley (*AJP*, 1961) and, on rather different issues, P. T. Geach (*Philosophical Books*, 1961).

28. For critical comments on Skinner see the review by N. Chomsky (*Language*, 1959); M. Scriven: 'A Study of Radical Behaviourism' (*Minnesota Studies*, I, 1956); N. Malcolm: 'Behaviourism as a Philosophy of Psychology', in *Behaviourism and Phenomenology*, ed. T. W. Wann (1964).

29. Similarly, J. J. C. Smart – at one time a disciple of Ryle – in his *Philosophy and Scientific Realism* (1963) defines philosophy as 'an attempt to think clearly and comprehensively about (*a*) the nature of the world and (*b*) the principles of conduct'. There has recently been, especially in America, a considerable revival of philosophical interest in problems of cosmology, as distinct from 'the logical structure of physical science'. See, for example, the essays included as Parts II, III and VI in *The Delaware Seminar on the Philosophy of Science* (Vol. 2, 1962–3); A. Grünbaum: *Philosophical Problems of Space and Time* (1963); articles by R. Harré and W. Davidson on 'Philosophical Aspects of Cosmology' (*PSC*, 1963). This philosophical interest in cosmology had persisted in the work of H. Reichenbach to whose *Philosophy of Space and Time* (1928, English translation 1958) Grünbaum is indebted but it had largely been left in the intervening years to professional cosmologists. See J. G. Whitrow: *The Natural Philosophy of Time* (1961). Note in a different area the emphasis on the importance of empirical investigations for the philosophy of language in the volume of readings edited by J. A. Fodor and J. J. Katz: *The Structure of Language* (1964), the growing body of references to the history of science in recent works on the philosophy of science and what is said, below, about the identity theory. The sharp contrast between the conceptual and the empirical is now widely questioned in the United States, if scarcely at all in Great Britain.

30. Compare p. 400 (above) on Charles Morris and see also B. L. Whorf: *Collected Papers on Metalinguistics* (1952). For a critical discussion of the Whorf-Quine view see L. J. Cohen: *The Diversity of Meaning* (1962).

31. On 'explication', see also R. Carnap: *Meaning and Necessity* (1947) from whom this approach derives. See also P. F. Strawson: 'Carnap's Views on Constructed Systems versus Natural Languages in Analytic Philosophy' (*The Philosophy of Rudolf Carnap*, ed. P. A. Schilpp, 1961) in which the points at issue are made very clear.

32. See the critical study by M. Scriven (*RM*, 1964) and review by M. Hesse (*Mind*, 1963). For the hypothetico-deductive model, see also K. R.

Popper: *The Logic of Scientific Discovery* (1934, English translation, 1959); I. Scheffler: *The Anatomy of Enquiry* (1963); A. Pap: *An Introduction to the Philosophy of Science* (1963); C. G. Hempel: *Aspects of Scientific Explanation* (1965). The hypothetico-deductive model was first fully developed by Hempel, whose book should be consulted for a fuller account of the model and the controversy it has aroused. See also the essays on explanation contained in *Minnesota Studies in the Philosophy of Science*, ed. H. Feigl and G. Maxwell, Vols. II (1958) and III (1962) and in *Philosophy of Science: The Delaware Seminar*, ed. B. Baumrin, Vol. I (1963) and II (1965). For my present purposes I have concentrated upon Nagel's theory of explanation. But *The Structure of Science* is largely devoted to another much controverted question: the relation between theories, models and empirical generalizations. Nagel presents a classical formulation of the view that these three can be sharply distinguished from one another. The entities mentioned in a theory – e.g. the 'points' and 'lines' of classical geometry or the molecules and 'energy' of the kinetic theory of gases – are to be understood, on his view, as *whatever will satisfy the postulates* of the theory. A model is an interpretation of a theory, e.g. the interpretation of the particles in the kinetic theory of gases as being like moving billiard balls: it is useful as suggesting extensions of the theory, and showing how it is related to possible experimental observations. 'Experimental laws', in contrast with theories, refer directly to observable kinds of entity. On this distinction see, in addition to the works cited above, the bibliography on 'theoretical entities' (Chapter 17, Note 33); N. R. Campbell: *Physics, the Elements* (1920); R. Braithwaite: *Scientific Explanation* (1953); R. Carnap: 'The Methodological Character of Theoretical Concepts' (*Minnesota Studies*, I, 1956); M. Hesse: *Models and Analogies in Science* (1963); the symposium on 'models' in *Logic, Methodology and Philosophy of Science* (ed. E. Nagel, P. Suppes, A. Tarski, 1962); A. Harré: 'Metaphor, Model and Mechanism' (*PAS*, 1960); ed. H. Freudentahl: *The Concept and the Role of the Model in Mathematics and Natural and Social Science* (1961); ed. H. Feigl and G. Maxwell: *Current Issues in the Philosophy of Science* (1961); M. Brodbeck: 'Models, Meanings and Theories' (*Symposium on Sociological Theory*, ed. L. Gross, 1959).

33. Compare Hilary Putnam on 'Minds and Machines' in *Minds and Machines* (ed. A. R. Anderson, 1964). The great weakness of commonsense psychology, he argues, is that it so often breaks down as an instrument for predicting. See also C. G. Hempel: *Aspects of Scientific Explanation* (1965) on 'reasons'.

34. See also J. G. Kemeny and P. Oppenheim: 'On Reduction' (*PS*, 1956); P. Oppenheim and H. Putnam: 'The Unity of Science as a Working Hypothesis' (*Minnesota Studies*, II, 1958).

35. On 'emergence' see also P. E. Meehl and Wilfrid Sellars: 'The Concept of Emergence' (*Minnesota Studies* I, 1956).

36. This has been forcibly argued by W. Dray in his *Laws and Explanation in History* (1956) who directs his fire especially against that version of the deductive theory of explanation – Dray calls it the 'covering law' theory – contained in C. G. Hempel: 'The Function of General Laws in History'

(*JP*, 1942, reprinted in *Aspects of Scientific Explanation*, 1965). Hempel replies to Dray in the essay giving its title to that volume, which contains an extensive bibliography. See also J. A. Passmore's critical notice of Dray (*Austn. Jnl. of Politics and History*, 1958) and his 'Explanation in Everyday Life, in Science and in History' (*History and Theory*, 1962, reprinted in *Studies in the Philosophy of History* ed. G. Nadel, 1965) together with Dray's reply to his critics in *Philosophy and History* (ed. S. Hook, 1963) and the critical defence of Dray by K. Nielsen in the same volume. See also J. L. Mackie: 'Causes and Conditions' (*APQ*, 1965). The possibility of constructing a natural-science type of social science is rejected by P. Winch: *The Idea of a Social Science* (1958). See also his 'Mr Louch's Idea of a Social Science' (*Inquiry*, 1964); A. Donagan: 'Are the Social Sciences really historical?' and (against Nagel on biology) B. Glass: 'The Relation of the Physical Sciences to Biology', both in *Philosophy of Science: The Delaware Seminar* I (1963). The most detailed critique of psychology is in C. Taylor: *The Explanation of Behaviour* (1964). It is, Taylor argues, an empirical question whether explanation in psychology must take a teleological form. He rejects the view, more characteristic of post-Wittgenstein teleologists, that our concept of human action is such as to rule out at once the possibility of a non-teleological account of it. We might, he argues, change our concept if we were forced to do so. But psychology, he tries to show, has completely failed to develop a non-teleological theory. (Taylor, it is interesting to observe, refers several times to Merleau-Ponty – one of the very few occasions on which an English-speaking critic of psychology makes any mention of the parallel French criticisms.) See also T. Mischel: 'Psychology and Explanations of Human Behaviour' (*PPR*, 1963). On the opposite side see R. Brown's review article on Taylor (*Phil.*, 1965) and his *Explanation in Social Science* (1963); A. J. Ayer: *Man as a Subject for Science* (1964); R. Brandt and J. Kim: 'Wants as Explanations of Actions' (*JP*, 1963); J. A. Fodor: 'Explanations in Psychology' in *Philosophy in America*, ed. M. Black (1965). See also the essays collected as *The Philosophy of the Social Sciences* (ed. M. Natanson, 1963), and H. L. Hart and A. M. Honoré: *Causation in the Law* (1959) which includes a substantial purely philosophical study of causality.

37. See especially 'Explanation, Reduction and Empiricism', in *Minnesota Studies*, Vol. 3 (1962). For an approach to the philosophy of science which, unlike Feyerabend, draws a sharp contrast between description and explanation see P. Alexander: *Sensationalism and Scientific Explanation* (1963).

38. For parallel views see S. Körner: *Conceptual Thinking* (1955) and W. Sellars' attack on 'the myth of the given' in 'Empiricism and the Philosophy of Mind' (*Minnesota Studies*, I, 1956, reprinted in *Science, Perception and Reality*, 1963). The doctrine of the 'given' is defended against Sellars by R. M. Chisholm in Chisholm *et al.*: *Humanistic Studies in America: Philosophy* (1964). In his *The Structure of Scientific Revolutions* (1962), T. S. Kuhn illustrates a thesis related to, but not identical with, Feyerabend's by reference to a number of episodes in the history of science. Whereas until about 1960, philosophy of science and history of science were

sharply sundered and most philosophers of science were content to illustrate their reflections on scientific methodology by, at most, one or two stock examples, the two have converged not only in Kuhn's book but in, for example, N. R. Hanson: *Patterns of Discovery* (1958) and *The Concept of the Positron* (1963), and in S. Toulmin: *Foresight and Understanding* (1961). See also the vigorous attack by a follower of Popper on the 'inductivist' conception of the history of science by J. Agassi: 'Towards a Historiography of Science' (*History and Theory*, Beiheft 2, 1963); and the essays contained in *Scientific Change*, ed. A. C. Crombie (1963). There are signs, too, that philosophy itself is moving out of a largely anti-historical period.

39. See also W. Sellars: 'The Language of Theories' in *Current Issues in the Philosophy of Science* (ed. H. Feigl and G. Maxwell, 1961). Sellars attacks the hypothetico-deductive model. For him, theories explain, not empirical laws themselves, but why objects obey such laws, in virtue of being configurations of theoretical entities. So the kinetic theory of gases explains why gases obey Boyle's law – because they are configurations of particles in motion. The 'theoretical framework' replaces the descriptive framework of everyday life. Room is found for the 'qualities' of everyday life – e.g. warmth – by supposing them to be neural processes.

40. *British Jnl. of Psychology* (1956), reprinted in V. C. Chappell: *The Philosophy of Mind* (1962). See also Place's reply to his critics in 'Materialism a Scientific Hypothesis' (*PR*, 1960). See also J. A. Shaffer: 'Recent Work on the Mind–Body Problem' (*APQ*, 1965, with an extensive bibliography); J. J. C. Smart: 'Sensations and Brain-Processes' (*PR*, 1959, reprinted in Chappell) and ensuing discussion in *PR*, 1960, 1961, 1963, *AJP* 1960, 1962, *JP*, 1961, 1963; W. Sellars: 'The Identity Approach to the Mind-Body Problem' (*RM*, 1965); W. Kneale: *On Having a Mind* (1962); T. Nagel: 'Physicalism' (*PR*, 1965). A connected issue is whether it is possible to construct machines of which it is proper to say that they have minds. On this see especially the essays collected by A. R. Anderson as *Mind and Machines* (1964, with bibliography). Essays on both sets of topics are included in *Dimensions of Mind* (ed. S. Hook, 1960). For physical detail see J. T. Culbertson: *The Minds of Robots* (1963). A major impulse behind the 'new materialism' is to get rid of obstacles to the total unification of science. See P. Oppenheim and H. Putnam: 'Unity of Science as a Working Hypothesis' (*Minnesota Studies*, II, 1958). 'That everything should be explicable in terms of physics except sensations', writes J. J. C. Smart in *Philosophy and Scientific Realism*, 'seems to be frankly unbelievable.'

41. For a more radical view of this matter see D. M. Armstrong's *Bodily Sensations* (1962) in which he suggests that we have a *bodily* sensation when 'it feels to us as if something were going on in our body'. In general, Armstrong's version of the identity-theory is, like Smart's, more 'physicalistic' than Feigl's. The main presentation of Feigl's views is 'The "Mental" and the "Physical"' (*Minnesota Studies*, II, 1958). See also 'Philosophical Embarrassments' (*Psychologische Beiträge*, 1962). The doctrine of 'raw feels' comes from E. C. Tolman: *Purposive Behaviour in Man and Animals* (1932). For the view that 'raw feels' are theoretical entities, see W. Sellars: 'Empiricism and the Philosophy of Mind' (*Minnesota Studies*, I, reprinted

in *Science, Perception and Reality*, 1963). On the 'analogy' theory of other minds, see also Feigl's 'Other Minds and the Egocentric Predicament' (*JP*, 1958) together with S. Hampshire: 'The Analogy of Feeling' (*Mind*, 1952). For criticisms see N. Malcolm: 'Knowledge of Other Minds' (*JP*, 1958); P. F. Strawson: *Individuals* (1959); B. Aune: 'The Problem of Other Minds' (*PR*, 1961).

42. For a criticism of the identity theory along these lines see J. Cornman: 'The Identity of Mind and Body' (*JP*, 1962), and in reply R. Rorty: 'Mind-Body Identity, Privacy and Categories' (*RM*, 1965).

43. See R. Grossmann: *The Structure of Mind* (1965); R. M. Chisholm: *Perceiving* (1957); the controversy between Chisholm and W. Sellars in *Minnesota Studies*, Vol. I (1956).

44. On the relations between identity-theory and physicalism see H. Feigl: 'Physicalism, the Unity of Science and the Foundations of Psychology' (*The Philosophy of R. Carnap*, ed. P. A. Schilpp, 1963).

45. Especially in 'Problems of Empiricism' in *Beyond the Edge of Certainty* (ed. R. G. Colodny, 1965) which contains a criticism of Feigl. See also, for very similar points, B. A. Farrell: 'Experience' (*Mind*, 1950).

46. See H. Feigl: 'The Mind-Body problem, not a pseudo-problem' in *Dimensions of Mind* (ed. S. Hook, 1960).

Further Reading

1. *For General Reference*

Encyclopedia of Philosophy, New York 1967. Contains lengthy articles on the major persons and tendencies of contemporary philosophy.

The Concise Encyclopaedia of Western Philosophy and Philosophers, ed. J. O. Urmson, London, 1960.
Contains (unsigned) articles by leading British philosophers.

A Critical History of Western Philosophy, ed. D. J. O'Connor, Glencoe, 1964.
The last half of this book contains important essays on philosophy since Mill, with extensive bibliographies.

La Philosophie au milieu du vingtième siècle, 4 vols., ed. R. Klibansky, Florence, 1958.
Essays in French and English on different aspects of contemporary philosophy with extensive bibliographies.

Die Philosophie im XX Jahrhundert, ed. F. Heinemann, Stuttgart, 1959.
An extensive survey (in German) of contemporary philosophy by a number of writers, all of them of German origin, but many of them now resident out of Germany.

Philosophic Thought in France and the United States. ed. M. Farber. Buffalo, 1950.
Essays by French and American philosophers on different aspects of the thought of their own countries.

Philosophy: Humanistic Studies in America, R. M. Chisholm, H. Feigl, W. K. Frankena, John Passmore, Manley Thompson, New Jersey, 1964.
Essays on contemporary American philosophy and philosophical scholarship.

2. *Short Histories*

I. M. Bochenski: *Contemporary European Philosophy*, 1947.
(English translation of second edition by D. Nicholl and K. Aschenbrenner, California, 1956).
A general account of twentieth-century philosophy by a Polish priest-logician, with extensive bibliographies, especially of French and German works.

F. Copleston: *Contemporary Philosophy*, London, 1956.
Also by a priest-philosopher. Concentrates especially on logical positivism and existentialism and their implications for theology.

W. Brock: *An Introduction to Contemporary German Philosophy*, Cambridge, 1935.

Geoffrey Warnock: *English Philosophy since* 1900, London, 1958.
Compact and clear but restricted to British philosophy of the analytic type.

J. O. Urmson: *Philosophical Analysis: its development between the two World Wars*, Oxford, 1956.

John Laird: *Recent Philosophy*, London, 1936.
  Covers both British and Continental philosophy.
A. J. Ayer *et al.*: *The Revolution in Philosophy*, London, 1956.
  Radio talks by distinguished contemporary British philosophers.

3. *Longer Histories*

R. Metz: *A Hundred Years of British Philosophy* (1935; English translation
  edited by J. H. Muirhead, London, 1938).
  A German scholar looks at philosophy in Great Britain. Especially
  good on nineteenth-century philosophy and on British Idealists.
Colin Smith: *Contemporary French Philosophy*, London, 1964.
  Emphasizes ethics, but covers a wide range of contemporary French
  thought.
H. Spiegelberg: *The Phenomenological Movement*, 2 vols., The Hague, 1960.
  This clearly-written and thorough work is an excellent introduction to
  such contemporary French and German philosophers as have been
  influenced by Brentano and Husserl.
W. H. Werkmeister: *A History of Philosophical Ideas in America*, New York,
  1949.
  Only very brief on philosophy subsequent to Dewey.
T. E. Hill: *Contemporary Theories of Knowledge*, New York, 1961.
  Detailed analyses, with full bibliographies. Restricts itself to Great
  Britain and the United States.

4. *Representative Essays – British*

ed. J. H. Muirhead: *Contemporary British Philosophy*, First and Second
  Series, London, 1924–5.
ed. H. D. Lewis: *Contemporary British Philosophy*, Third Series, London,
  1956.
ed. C. A. Mace: *British Philosophy in the Mid-Century*, London, 1957.
ed. A. G. N. Flew: *Logic and Language*, Oxford; First Series, 1951, Second
  Series, 1953.
ed. A. G. N. Flew: *Essays in Conceptual Analysis*, London, 1956.

5. *Representative Essays – American*

ed. G. P. Adams, W. P. Montague: *Contemporary American Philosophy*,
  vols. 1 and 2, London, 1930.
ed. S. Hook: *American Philosophers at Work*, New York, 1956.
ed. M. Black: *Philosophy in America*, London, 1965.
  For the younger American philosophers.

6. *Some important collections of readings*

Readings in the Philosophy of Science, ed. H. Feigl and M. Brodbeck, New
  York, 1953.
Readings in Philosophical Analysis, ed. H. Feigl and W. Sellars, New York,
  1949,
Philosophical Analysis. ed. M. Black, Ithaca, 1950.
Philosophy and Analysis, ed. M. Macdonald, Oxford, 1954.

Twentieth Century Philosophy: The Analytic Tradition, ed. M. Weitz, New York, 1965.

The Age of Analysis, ed. M. G. White, New York, 1955.

Logical Positivism, ed. A. J. Ayer, Glencoe (Ill.), 1959.

Realism and the Background of Phenomenology, ed. R. M. Chisholm, Glencoe (Ill.), 1960.

Perceiving, Sensing and Knowing, ed. R. J. Swartz, New York, 1965.

Essays in Philosophical Psychology, ed. D. G. Gustafson, New York, 1964.

Philosophy of Mind, ed. V. C. Chappell, New Jersey, 1962.

Ordinary Language, ed. V. C. Chappell, New Jersey, 1964.

Philosophy of Science, ed. A. Danto and S. Morgenbesser, New York, 1960.

The Validation of Scientific Theories, ed. P. G. Frank, Boston, 1956.

Philosophy of Mathematics, ed. P. Benacerraf and H. Putnam, New Jersey, 1964.

New Essays in Philosophical Theology, ed. A. G. N. Flew and A. MacIntyre, London, 1955.

The Age of Complexity, ed. H. Kohl, New York, 1965.

Existentialism from Dostoevsky to Sartre, ed. W. Kaufmann, New York, 1956.

Index of Names

Aaron, R. I., **563**, 572, 582
Abbott, T. K., 564
Abel, R., 548
Achinstein, P., 588, 591
Ackermann, W., 583, 584
Acton, H. B., 532, 535, 539, 556
Adams, G. P., 572
Adamson, R., **280–1**, 284, 536, 551, 553
Addis, L., 595
Agar, W. E., 577
Agassi, J., 614
Albritton, R., 426
Aldrich, H., 120
Alexander, H. G., 599
Alexander, P., 610, 613
Alexander, S., **265–9**, **270–7**, 281, 286, 311, 332, 340, 347, 517, 538, 562, 601
Aliotta, A., 536
Allen, E., 602
Alston, W. P., 586, 598
Ambrose, A., 584, 592, 593, 594, 597, 599, 600
Anderson, A. R., 585, 593, 612, 614
Anderson, J., 535, 563, **566**, 567, 578, 580
Anderson, P. R., 536
Andler, C., 544
Annan, N., 534
Anschutz, R. P., 20, 531, 532
Anscombe, F. J., 590
Anscombe, G. E. M., **513–15**, 553, 578, 593, 594
Anselm, 314
Antonelli, M. T., 538
Aquinas, St T., 314, 316–17, 512, 544
Ardigo, R., 299, 570
Aristotle, 121, 134, 166, 176, 216, 252, 307, 314, 397–8, 441, 442, 443, 476, 505, 515, 567, 609
Armstrong, D. M., 566, 597, 614
Augustine, St, 427, 592
Aune, B., 615
Austin, J. L., 390, 441, **450–8**, 479, 600, 609
Aveling, F., 573
Avenarius, R., **174**, 547
Ayer, A. J., 369, **386–93**, 452, 477, 532, 557, 560, 580, 585, 586, 593, 605, 608, 609, 613

Bacon, F., 124, 455
Baier, K., 585, 593, 594, 609
Bailey, S., 564
Baillie, J. D., 539, 568
Bain, A., 100, **531**, 535
Baker, A. J., 566, 595

Bakewell, C. M., 540, 543
Baldwin, J. M., 103, 117, 141, 202, 203, 207, 551, 554
Balfour, A. J. (Earl), 99–100, 538, 545
Ballard, E. G., 546, 602
Balsillie, D., 547
Bambrough, J. R., 592
Barbour, G. F., 539
Bar-Hillel, Y., 558, 562, 587, 590, 592
Barker, Sir E., 564
Barker, S. F., 587, 591, 599
Barnes, H., 605
Barnes, H. E., 601
Barnes, W. H. F., 598
Baron, S. W., 569
Barral, M. R., 607
Barrett, C., 572, 609
Baudelaire, C., 539
Baum, M., 547
Baumrin, B., 612
Baur, F. C., 538
Bayes, T., 550, 551
Baylis, C. A., 559
Baynes, T. S., 549
Beauvoir, S. de, 605, 607
Beck, L. J., 298
Bedoyère, M. de La, 539
Bell, E. T., 550, 552
Bell, J., 381
Benda, J., 546
Benjamin, A. C., 576
Benjamin, B. S., 596
Bentham, G., 550
Bentham, J., 13–16, 23, 550
Bentley, A. F., 549
Berg, J., 558
Berger, G., 607
Bergin, G., 571
Bergmann, G., **384**, 553, 580, 581, 588, 589, 608, 609
Bergson, H., **104–6**, 119, 174, **262**, 270, **271**, 278, 317, 326, 548, 567, 571, 604
Berkeley, Bishop, 13, 30–1, 46, 50, 52, 90, 96, 100, 196, 201, 210, 232, 247, 277, 283, 305, 321, 323, 331, 375, 387, 411, 466–7, 479, 495, 505, 506, 539, 544, 564, 574, 594, 607
Berlin, I., 580
Bernays, P., 583, 593
Bernstein, R. J., 546
Berry, G. D., 551
Bevan, E., 573
Bibby, C., 534
Binkley, R., 609
Binswanger, L., 602
Birjukov, B. V., 553

619

Index of Concepts

An asterisk indicates a bibliography

and propositions, 203–4, 444–5
open texture of, 464–5
relation to experience, 46, 105–6, 108–
10, 291, 301, 318, 331, 335, 338, 504–
29
conditionals, counter-factual, see also
hypothetical propositions, 595–6
confirmation, 386, 408, 419–20, 589–90*
connectives, see *constants, logical; disjunctives; hypotheticals*
connotation, see also *meaning*, 18–19,
138, 160, 242–3
conscience, 481
consciousness, see also *minds*, 30, 37,
39–40, 43, 57–60, 73, 96–7, 105–6,
192–3, 209, 262–3, 267–8, 274, 283,
496–7, 499–500, 547*, 565, 606
constants, logical, see also *copula; disjunctives; hypotheticals*, 136, 217–18,
355–6, 462
constructions, logical, 233, 255, 338, 365–
6, 374, 506, 562–3*, 579
content:
and mental act, 179–81, 195, 262, 267
and structure, 374, 382, 427
Continent, philosophy on the, 214, 319,
466–7, 475–6
contingents, problem of future, 397, 585*
contradiction, see also *paradoxes*
nature of, 46, 69–70, 172, 293–4, 357
principle of, 20n., 227
self-, 61, 63–6, 81, 310, 395, 436, 474
contrariety, 70, 171–2
conventionalism, 134, 325–8, 339, 379,
420, 643
copula, 123, 130–1, 139–40, 149, 152–4
correspondence, see *perception, representative; truth*
corrigibility, see *certainty; knowledge;
necessary truths*
corroboration, 408
counter-factual conditionals, see also
hypothetical propositions, 595–6

decision problem, 398, 584*
definitions, 344–5, 464–5
and axioms, 19, 326, 394
in mathematics, 19, 20, 394–5, 462–3
in philosophy, 304–5, 362, 364–5, 383
ostensive, 344, 370, 429
demonstratives, 237, 427–8
denotation, 18, 111–12, 226–8, 237, 243
descriptions, theory of, 226–9, 231, 353,
364, 387, 404, 443, 460, 562*
design, argument from, 33, 38–9, 111
determinables, 345
determining correspondence, principle
of 79–80, 541*
determinism, see *freewill*
dialectic, 45, 55, 60, 76, 299, 300–302,
501–2, 606

discourse, universe of, 126–7n.
disjunctives, interpretation of, 136, 166,
199, 356–7, 551
dispositional terms, 384, 447–8, 595–6*
dreams, 512–13

economics, 16, 360, 532, 550
egocentric particulars, 237, 461
emergence, 269–70, 274–5, 286, 349,
523–4
emotions, 606
empiricism, 15, 100, 120, 388
and logic, 20n., 120–1, 187–8, 293, 296,
372, 405
and mathematics, 19–20, 24, 145, 148,
321, 323, 367, 435
and probability, 414, 422
and science, 25, 28–9, 232–4, 291, 321,
325, 335, 383–4, 386, 404, 408
criticisms of, 25, 57–8, 60n., 70–1,
105, 115–16, 120, 188–9, 203, 238–9,
391–3, 453, 477–80, 489, 500–501,
506, 528
radical, 106–7
England, philosophy in, 13, 36, 49–50n.,
51–3, 56, 77, 82, 99, 100, 120, 194–5,
258, 281, 301, 302, 315, 317, 386,
394, 466–7, 536, 546
entailment, see also *implication*, 219
entropy, nightmare of, 111n.
epiphenomenalism, 39–40, 83
epistemology, 49, 90, 99, 219, 264–5,
318, 330, 344, 379, 387
error, 58, 70, 91–2, 95, 198–9, 263–4,
269, 281–2, 299
essences, see also *universals*, 188–9,
288–9, 291, 296, 411–12, 425–6, 431,
467, 469, 470, 488, 495
events, 275, 339
evolution, 38–9, 42–4, 56, 60, 103, 113,
471
emergent, 269–70, 274–5, 286, 349
excluded middle, principle of, 396, 405
existence:
proofs, 396
propositions asserting, 157, 179, 204,
484, 488–9
existential import, 134–5, 159–62, 179,
204, 242–3, 461
existentialism, 318, 466–503, 600–601*
experience, immediate, 27, 29–31, 57–8,
62–5, 66–8, 105–7, 116, 174, 177–8,
188–9, 196, 209–10, 230–3, 236,
251, 280, 283–5, 295–6, 303, 333,
373, 374–9, 479, 489, 501–3, 527–8
experimental methods, 24–8, 117–18,
132–3, 165, 420
explanation, see also *scientific law;
theories, science*, 16, 103–4, 143,
275, 320–1. 324, 328, 407, 411, 516,
521–6

633

and implications, 173, 217, 252, 294
from particulars to particulars, 22, 25, 27, 164–5
immediate, 21, 163
licences, 599
nature of, 20–1, 22, 139, 162–3, 168, 217, 359, 361, 405
instinct, and metaphysics, see *metaphysics, origins of*
instrumentalism, 97, 111, 116, 169, 411–12, 523, 524
intellect, as source of knowledge, 61–2, 85, 86, 95–6, 98–9, 101–2, 105–6, 470, 490
intellectualism, vicious, 108
intentionality, 178, 495, 528
intentions, 514–15
introjection, 174, 354
introspection, see *minds, our knowledge of our own*
intuitionism, see also *commonsense; belief, natural*, 14–15, 16, 30, 170, 190–1, 301
in mathematics, 394, 396, 435, 584*
Italy, philosophy in, 118–19, 147, 299–300, 317, 549, 571

judgement, see also *propositions*, 115, 117, 157–62, 179, 185, 241, 242–3, 250, 432, 495, 512, 513
ideas and, 157–8, 179, 202
objectives and, 183–5
propositions and, 136, 169–70, 343–4
statements and, 241

knowledge:
and goodness, 85
and perception, 206, 211, 230, 231–2, 239, 249–50, 253, 312
as comprescence, 267–9, 275
as conation, 261, 267, 341
as revelation, 484, 485
by acquaintance, 54n., 230–2
how and that, 446–7
nature of, 116–17, 241–2, 261–2, 268–9, 275, 305–6, 425–6, 454
objects of, 53, 58–9, 204, 210, 230, 245–6, 248–9
of God, 33, 40, 99, 101, 490
of other minds, 73, 175, 262–3, 373, 392, 433, 439, 447, 480–1, 527
of our own minds, 32, 100, 177–8, 231, 268, 280, 285–6, 300, 303, 318, 338–9, 372, 432–3, 496, 526–9
of the Absolute, 41, 52, 62, 66, 87
passivity of, 117–18, 305–6, 318, 326, 341
practical, 515
symbolic nature of, 303, 314–15, 333, 473
without observation, 514–15, 610*

language, see also *semantics; names; meaning*
alternative, 378–9, 388
as games, 426, 427, 429, 432
development of, 316, 520
hierarchy of, 382, 463–4, 600*
ideal, 154–5, 358, 377–80, 383–4, 404, 424–6, 427–8, 429, 464–5, 520, 562–3
misleading, 105, 138, 152–5, 159, 226, 229, 231, 244, 358, 379, 442
names and, 17, 226, 353, 356, 429
nature of, 377, 382–3, 427
ordinary, 54n., 205, 242–3, 383–4, 401, 425, 427, 430, 440–65, 504, 509, 526, 592–3*, 594*
private, 373, 377–8, 383, 391, 431, 593*
sense-datum, 388–9, 392
laws of nature, see *scientific law*
location, fallacy of simple, 339
logic:
and algebra, 121–2, 125–8, 130–1, 133–4, 137, 144–5, 336
and experience, 20, 144–5, 191, 291, 293–4, 362, 372–3, 405
and inquiry, 133, 157, 166, 168–9, 171, 294
and mathematics, 147, 149–50, 186–7, 216–18, 219–25, 240, 326, 358, 360–1, 381, 394–6, 403, 436, 462
and ontology, 163, 165, 234, 244–5, 291–2, 337, 404, 520
and ordinary language, 138, 140, 169–71, 242–3, 461, 520–1
and psychology, 157, 186, 512, 556–7*
the nature of, 17, 23, 122, 140–3, 156–8, 165–6, 169–73, 187–8, 190–1, 214–15, 240, 245, 256n., 291–2, 293–4, 344, 354, 356, 356–8, 361–2, 382, 394–7, 403, 405–6, 419, 461, 486, 510–12, 557–8, 587
utility of formal, 21, 120–1, 142–3, 146–7, 156–7, 162, 168–71, 186–7, 241, 397–8, 461
logic, systems of, see also *logistics*
alternative, 134, 294–7, 379, 397–8, 464, 585*, 600
equational, 121, 125–8, 130–1, 159
Idealist, 156–69, 172–3, 241, 252, 298–9, 343–4
many-valued, 397–8, 417
modal, 397–8, 403, 551, 585*
of imperatives, 397, 585*
of interrogatives, 397, 585*
of relations, 123, 137–8, 219, 336
Polish, 397–8, 584*, 585, 586
pure, 187, 189, 191
traditional, 21, 121, 130, 134, 146, 158–9, 161, 164, 172, 244, 252, 460
logical form, 121–2, 126–7, 130–1, 146, 215, 344–5, 424–5

logical powers, 445
logistics, 147, 149–50, 216–18, 219–25, 240, 326, 360–1, 382, 394–6, 403, 436, 462

Marxism, 44–7, 482, 605
material and formal mode, 376–7, 379–81, 444, 518
materialism, see also *physicalism*, 35–6, 38–40, 43–7, 55, 59, 71, 83, 88, 100, 110–11, 269, 274, 286, 289, 292–3, 310, 349, 526–9
mathematics, see also *formalism; intuitionism; logistics; psychologism*
  alternative, 146, 242, 381, 462
  as obedience to rules, 148, 322–3, 394–5, 434–5, 462
  as science of order, 145, 169
  as referring to concepts, 148–9, 153, 186
  consistency in, 146, 242, 323, 394–6, 436
  experience and, 19, 24, 144–6, 148, 238–9, 321, 323, 367–8, 396, 435
  logic and, 147, 149–50, 186–7, 216–18, 219–25, 240, 326, 358, 360–1, 381, 394–6, 403, 436, 462
  necessity of, 19, 24, 145, 148, 186, 367, 395, 434–5, 462
  proof in, 146, 323, 395, 396, 434–5
  tautology and, 357, 360–1, 380
  truth in, 146, 242, 323, 358
meaning, see also *analysis; denotation; language; names; operationalism; pragmatism; verifiability*
  of ideas and concepts, 93–4, 96, 109–10, 122, 158
  of propositions and sentences, 110–11, 151, 190, 226, 353–4, 356, 368–74, 378, 385–6, 389, 399–400, 406–7, 517–19
  of words and expressions, 17–18, 110, 142, 150–1, 226, 353–4, 370–1, 399–401, 402–3, 427–9, 431, 460–1, 517–19
  of world, 312, 372, 473
meaninglessness, 98, 109–10, 154, 191, 222–3, 358–9, 368, 371, 380, 386, 389, 391, 428, 436, 440, 460, 477, 551
mechanics, nature of, 320–1, 323–6, 360
mechanism, 36, 39, 44, 46–7, 48, 49–50, 53, 71, 83, 89, 269, 324
memory, 196, 263, 431, 609
mental acts, see also *judgement; memory; perception*, 181, 195
  nature of, 178–80, 209, 267, 283, 511
  rejection of, 236–7, 262, 447–50
mental processes, 430, 448
metalanguage, 382
metalogic, 398–9
metamathematics, 395, 399

metaphysics:
  a kind of poetry, 98, 324, 379, 486, 537
  and science, 98, 328, 383–4, 406
  as recommendation, 383, 440
  defined, 16, 17n., 49, 61n., 66, 265, 367–8, 485
  descriptive, 504–5, 508
  fulfils a need, 61n., 75–6, 98
  its method, 52–3, 77, 265–6, 340–1, 350, 504–5, 508
  its relation to religion, 48, 51, 75–6
  nonsensical, 97–8, 111, 358–9, 368, 370, 383, 387, 390, 477
  origins of, 61n., 97–8, 358–9, 426–7, 429–30, 437–40
  pragmatic criticism of, 109, 110–11
Mind, 531
minds and bodies, 37–40, 43, 58–9, 82–3, 88–9, 107, 274–5, 285–6, 310–11, 344, 348, 378, 392, 446, 489, 499–500, 501–2, 506–8, 508–9, 527–9
  and machines, 446, 614
minds, our knowledge of other, 73, 175, 262–3, 373, 392, 433, 439, 447, 480–1, 527
minds, our knowledge of our own, 32, 100, 177–8, 231, 268, 280, 285–6, 300, 303, 318, 338–9, 372, 432–3, 496, 526–9
mind-stuff, 535
miracles, 55
models, 611–12
monism, see also *Absolute; Idealism; materialism*, 43, 74, 84, 108, 207, 542
  neutral 236, 261–4, 606
motion, 45, 272
motives, 106, 448, 596*
mystery, 489–90

names, 17–18, 122, 154, 218, 226, 228–9, 237, 353, 355–6, 403–4, 428, 431, 458–9, 599–600
naturalism, see also *materialism*, 43, 51–2, 83, 100, 269, 286–94, 313
natural selection, 38, 42, 534*, 535
nature, uniformity of, 24, 100, 347
necessary connexion, 67, 163, 167–8, 172, 310, 313, 321, 359, 572
necessary truths, see also *axioms; tautologies*, 52, 163, 184, 186–7, 191, 193, 242, 313, 329, 334, 391, 402, 421, 457, 460, 462, 465
  and experience, 19–20, 24, 175, 294–7, 325–6, 360, 404–5, 427
  linguistic theory of, 19, 357, 360, 390, 464, 582*
negation, 45–6, 69, 140, 161, 355–6, 361, 477, 495–7
neo-Kantianism, 48–9, 57, 100, 280, 320–1, 333, 373, 477–8, 608

INDEX OF CONCEPTS

INDEX OF CONCEPTS